English Architecture to 1900: The Shropshire Experience

English Architecture to 1900:
The Shropshire Experience

by
Eric Mercer

Logaston Press

LOGASTON PRESS
Little Logaston, Logaston,
Woonton, Almeley, Herefordshire HR3 6QH

First published by Logaston Press 2003
Copyright © Eric Mercer 2003

ISBN 1 904396 08 9

Set in Times by Logaston Press
and printed in Great Britain by
Bell & Bain Ltd, Glasgow

Front cover illustration:
All Saints Church, Batchcott, Richard's Castle

Contents

		page
	Publisher's Acknowledgments	*vii*
	Foreword by Anne, Sarah & Helen Mercer	*ix*
	Preface by Eric Mercer	*xi*
	Introduction to Ecclesiastical Buildings	*xiii*
I	Anglo-Saxon Churches	1
II	Late 11th- to late 12th-Century Church Building	9
III	The 13th Century: Church Improvement and Extension	37
IV	The Decorated Period and Decline in Construction	57
V	The Perpendicular Period: Shropshire out of step	73
VI	Defensible Houses	91
VII	Lesser Stone Buildings	103
VIII	Late Medieval Timber Houses: Gentry and Peasantry	117
IX	Gestation of the Private House and the Gentleman's Residence 1550–1700	135
X	Houses of the Yeomanry 1550–1700	151
XI	Design, Style, and Ornament 1550–1700	157
XII	Modern Houses 1700–40	169
XIII	Secular Architecture 1740–1830	185
XIV	Public Buildings 1550–1800	221
XV	Domestic Architecture 1830–1900: The Classes and the Masses	225
XVI	Domestic Styles 1830–1900	251
XVII	Communal and Public Buildings: The 19th Century	261
XVIII	Ecclesiastical Architecture 1550–1800	279
XIX	Nonconformist Architecture	307
XX	Roman Catholic Churches	313
XXI	Anglican Architecture: The 19th Century	319
	References	337
	Index	369

Publisher's Acknowledgments

In bringing this book together over the past couple of years the greatest debt is owed to George Baugh for his attention to detail and dedication in seeing Eric Mercer's work to final publication. Virtually all the recent photographs used throughout the book and on its cover are © Crown copyright NMR / English Heritage (with the exceptions noted below) and I particularly wish to thank English Heritage in general for their help and co-operation, and Bob Skingle in particular. English Heritage are also acknowledged for allowing building plans to be copied and adapted from various guides and publications, notably those for Acton Burnell Castle and the abbeys at Buildwas, Haughmond and Lilleshall. Recent photographs for which acknowledgments are due other than to English Heritage are: Dr. Kathryn Baird for the illustration of the painting at Neenton on the rear cover; Sarah Zaluckyj for that on page 3; Douglas Grounds for that of Heath chapel on p.11, Logaston Press for those pages 2 and 93; and Madge Moran for those on pages 116, 124, 126 and 157. Many of the building plans have been drawn by Nicola Smith and Henry Hand, and Henry's speed and responsiveness in the closing stages of bringing the publication together, as well as quality of work, is much appreciated. Madge Moran has given permission for the use of the drawings on pages 108, 119, 120, 125, 126, 127 and 159. In addition I would like to thank Dennis B. Gallagher and Humphrey Woods for permission to use the drawing of Holy Trinity church in Much Wenlock on page 18; Peter Klein for the drawing of Ludford Church on page 62; the Society of Antiquaries of London for the use of W.H. St. John Hope's plan of Ludlow Castle on page 94; Peter Curnow for the drawing of Hopton Castle on page 102; Birmingham University Library for the drawing of Ænon Cottage from Joseph Dixon's journals on page 198; Shrewsbury and Atcham Borough Council for permission to make re-drawings of building control plans and Shropshire Records and Research Centre for use of and reproduction of material in their possession.

Andy Johnson
September 2003

Foreword

Eric Mercer was born on 31 May 1918 and died on 13 September 2001. He was educated at Battersea Grammar School and gained a Double First in History at Jesus College Cambridge in 1939. During the war he served in the Royal Signals and the Intelligence Corps, and from 1945-1946 he was attached to the Allied Control Commission for Germany. He joined the Royal Commission on Historical Monuments in 1948 and in the 1960s joined a small commission team recording buildings threatened with demolition. In 1976 he became head of the Commission's National Buildings Records and was made Deputy Secretary of the Commission in 1979. He retired in 1981 and was awarded the OBE.

Eric spent a very happy retirement writing this book, marred only by the delays to publication which he relates in the Preface. He often expressed the hope privately that the book might be the vehicle for the fuller expression of his views on the ways to understand developments in English architecture. But unfortunately there appears to be only an introductory fragment, which was originally written when the book was to be divided into sections, one of which covered ecclesiastical buildings. Perhaps his freedom from the shackles imposed by the VCH came too soon before the onset of the illness from which he eventually died, for him to distil these ideas for an introduction.

Eric's introduction to English Vernacular Houses laid out the principles on which he believed it was possible to relate 'regional developments to a national pattern'. Opposing the then current tendency to focus on geographical over historical themes in the study of architecture, he claimed that, using two basic principles—the accommodation provided by each type of house, what he here describes as its 'social function', and the concentration of each type at any one time 'it is possible to see a development common to the whole country, but beginning in each region at a different time, and perhaps reflecting regionally different social and economic developments'. This book perhaps stands as a template for regional studies based on such a theme.

Like Gordon Childe, whose work he greatly admired, Eric saw art and architecture as 'social products' and sought 'to trace the connection between men's social conditions and their aspirations, disappointments and accomplishments' in the buildings they produced. This viewpoint sprang from Eric's commitment to Marxism which had moulded his intellectual development since his youth. Moreover, he saw the study of architectural developments to be a means of providing solutions to historical problems where 'purely documentary sources are not, as yet, free from ambiguity'. Both sides of the relationship between the study of architecture and the study of broad historical developments are traced in this work.

Eric was imbued with a deep love of England's 'sights and sounds'. Throughout his life he strove for the wise conservation of our architectural heritage for all to enjoy and understand. These concerns permeate this book but in addition his method, which makes collective use of numerous specific instances of types of buildings to illuminate general social developments, is a strong argument for such conservation.

In so many other ways this is Eric's book: scattered with evidence of his encyclopaedic knowledge of literature, from Chaucer to Winnie the Pooh and with his thorough dissection of views with which he disagreed. He was a man of integrity, whose convictions and loves, once fixed, were not readily to be displaced: a rigorous intellectual adversary but a kindly mentor.

We would like to express our gratitude to Andy Johnson of Logaston Press and George Baugh for their part in ensuring this memory to his method and ideas saw the light of day.

Anne, Sarah and Helen Mercer
September 2003

Preface

In 1981, when I retired to Shropshire, the V.C.H. asked me to write a history of the county's architecture. It was to be a discursive work, setting that architecture within the national framework and relating it to broader themes within the county and the country. A full text of the work, then conceived as Volume V of the Shropshire *V.C.H.*, was presented in 1995, individual chapters having been presented throughout the period. However, as we got close to publication, I found that we had for a long time been at cross purposes. Early in 2001 I was told that every V.C.H. volume was a work of reference and was constructed to a fixed form. I could wish that I had been told that earlier, but there is no profit in crying over spilt ink, and I decided that the only solution to what seemed a hopeless impasse was a break with the V.C.H. I think that the new General Editor felt the same, but, as he never replied to the two letters I wrote to him, I cannot be sure.

A new publisher, however, was soon found, and I must thank Andrew Johnson and his colleague at Logaston Press for their ready interest in my work. I am also most grateful to John Cornforth and his fellow trustees of the Marc Fitch Fund, who greatly eased the problems of changing from one publisher to another by making a generous grant for the completion of the drawing work. At an earlier stage part of a grant to the Shropshire V.C.H. by Mr. T.S. Acton, of Acton Scott, had been used for some of the drawing, and for that too I record my gratitude to him.

It is a great pleasure to thank all those whose contributions have helped to bring about the present text and have ensured that it has some merit, and fewer errors than the original. Amongst them I owe an especial debt to Madge Moran, who has generously shared with me all her discoveries and her vast knowledge of the vernacular architecture of Shropshire; and to George Baugh who, as disappointed as I was at the V.C.H.'s behaviour, nobly offered, as a discharge of a debt of honour, to see the volume through to publication with my new publisher. I have benefited enormously from the comments of those who read individual chapters or sections: Kathryn Baird, Professor Peter Kidson, James Lawson, Sarah Pearson, Chris Wakeling, and Professor Andor Gomme, who in addition allowed me to see his text of *Smith of Warwick* before it was published. Janice Cox too very kindly lent me her study of Shrewsbury nonconformist chapels before that was printed. Bill Champion has kept me up-to-date with all his discoveries about the ownership of many Shrewsbury houses, and Andrew Arroll and Alan Snell have drawn my attention to several houses which they were working on. I am also indebted to Tony Carr, always a sure guide to the invaluable materials in his care at the Local Studies Library, Shrewsbury, now merged with the Shropshire Records and Research Centre; and to Paul Stamper for much practical advice and help.

How much my text is embellished by the illustrations will be apparent to the reader, and I am grateful to Nicola Smith and Henry Hand for their skilful drawings and to Bob Skingle for his splendid photographs. To my thanks to Bob Skingle should be added my further thanks to his then employer, the Royal Commission on the Historical Monuments of England (now merged with English Heritage), for making his time freely available to me during several highly enjoyable photographic campaigns. My thanks are also due to English Heritage for generous permission to reproduce photographs in copyright.

Eric Mercer
August 2001

Note on Asterisked Dates

Dates to which an asterisk (*) is prefixed are those which have been established by dendrochronology and systematically recorded from 1976 in *Vernacular Architecture*.

Introduction to Ecclesiastical Buildings

Medieval church architecture

English medieval architecture is commonly discussed within categories distinguished by decorative modes and constructional techniques related broadly to historical periods—as, for example, the Early English style reaching its climax in the 13th century. No one may now disregard that long established and indispensable convention, but in what follows the main temporal divisions are seen differently: as stages in which an adequate stock of churches was first provided throughout most of the county, and was then improved, and later embellished. Architectural elements cannot be confined within narrow time limits, but all the same no one would look for 13th-century fan vaulting or 15th-century stiff-leaf ornament; and it may be charged, in contrast, against the categories proposed here that some churches were added to the common stock in the 14th and 15th centuries and that some were improved and embellished in the 12th. Nevertheless within each proposed period the mass of building took the form stated above and in that way differentiated it from the others. The limits of the periods, too, cannot be closely drawn, but broadly the first comprises the late 11th century and much of the 12th century, the second the 13th century, and the third runs throughout the 14th and 15th centuries, and into the 16th.

To a large extent the proposed divisions correspond with well established stylistic phases: Anglo-Saxon and Norman, Transitional and Early English, and Decorated and Perpendicular. Nor is that correspondence wholly accidental. The conversion of the pagan English began as a conversion of kings and nobles, and the rich ornament and small size of many Anglo-Saxon churches suggest that throughout the period they were intended for select rather than popular congregations. The Norman newcomers, whose cause had been supported by the pope, wished to transform the English church in their image, and one way of doing that was to make it more prominent in day-to-day life. One of the problems which faced them, therefore, was to build a great number of stone churches, and to do so with limited resources, and in particular with an undeveloped building trade not yet capable of turning out a host of well trained and experienced masons. Elaborate fenestration, sophisticated vaulting, and rich decoration would have been worse than irrelevancies to most post-Conquest church builders; they would have been obstacles in the way. The Norman style, comparatively simple in technique and able to take decoration but not dependent upon it for aesthetic effect, was not developed in order to ease a church-building crisis in Shropshire, but it was well suited to that purpose; and it was at hand. And when that had been done carvers and masons, at what was then the 'cutting edge' of building technology, could develop their skills ever further and produce the artistic and structural triumphs of later years.

Of course limited resources affected parish churches and chapels far more than cathedrals and monasteries, but the latter were not wholly immune from them. The austerity of early Cistercian churches was an aspect of the reforming zeal of Cîteaux, but early Norman churches of the unreformed orders could be equally plain. The Benedictine foundation of Shrewsbury Abbey is a case in point, and, outside Shropshire, Benedictine St. Albans carried austerity, in the form of an absence of moulded ornament, to a level never reached by any Cistercian church. That is usually attributed to the hardness of the Roman brick which was re-used from *Verulamium*, but the builders' readiness to use it shows that carved or moulded ornament was not a major concern to them. Most 12th-century churches in the county, and all the monastic ones except Shrewsbury Abbey, Bromfield, and the first church at Haughmond, were built after 1150 when ornament had become commoner than before. Some of them had highly decorated individual features, but none approached the richness of ornament indulged in by the long established and wealthy Cluniac foundation at Much Wenlock, in the chapter house and on the west front of the dependent church of Holy Trinity. And none of the monasteries, again unlike Wenlock, attempted a large scale rebuilding in later years, but all were content to improve and embellish.

Modern church architecture

The apparently smooth sequence of medieval architectural events did not occur in wholly untroubled times, but until the end of the period the Church's role as the unique disseminator of Truth and its standing as the equal partner of the secular power were long unchallenged. By the late Middle Ages, however, the old and equal alliance between the church hierarchy and their kin among the great ruling families was beginning to break up under the stress of the increasing problems of feudal landlordship, and of the growing political weight of the gentry and the town patriciates, represented in a House of Commons which was often openly anti-clerical. The Reformation brought about both a massive expropriation of the Church in favour of secular landowners of all degrees, and secular control of its doctrine and organization. At the same time the intellectual changes of the Renaissance and the availability of printed books and tracts deprived the clergy of their near monopoly of the propagation of ideas, theological, social, and aesthetic.

The Church remained, nevertheless, a very important institution, and its fate was a major issue in the political and military struggles of the mid 17th century. Further, what could neither be appropriated nor wholly moulded by royal decree were the convictions of its dedicated members. Their piety often took a very different form from that of earlier ages—for example, the erection of almshouses rather than the endowment of chantries and the foundation of schools rather than the addition of aisles—but it ensured in many cases that church fabrics were maintained in a 'decent' condition.

One result of all these changes was that Government could use the Church to implement its policies, and Government was most tempted to do so in times of political and social stress: in Charles I's reign, when rigidity in Church and State was affronting the regime's critics and alienating many of its friends; and in the early 19th century, when the intellectual effects of the French Revolution and the social disturbances consequent upon a nascent industrial revolution were alarming all the propertied classes. In the hope of preserving as much of the Past as possible the defenders of the *status quo*—some from genuine feeling, some as a political tactic—sought to prolong, or to reintroduce, medieval practices and ideas. The influence upon architecture was necessarily indirect, but at both times it appeared—against the whole current of aesthetic development since the Middle Ages—as a revival of the Gothic forms of the past. Under Charles I it affected only a few churches, but nearly two hundred years later it changed the whole character of ecclesiastical architecture; and it affected secular architecture as well.

Between the Glorious Revolution and the outbreak of the French one there were a hundred years in which whatever was was right, and all seemed for the best in the best of all possible countries. This was a time of general social stability in which, as Namier showed, the resolution of political issues was governed by manoeuvres among aristocratic factions. Classical architecture, with its assured calm and its air of rationality and due proportion, was the best expression of such a confident society, and a church built in any other style was an eccentricity.

I   Anglo-Saxon Churches

The earliest surviving structure in Shropshire that is more than an earthwork is the 'Old Work',[1] the stretch of walling at Wroxeter, the Roman *Viroconium Cornoviorum*. Except as a quarry for later buildings, however, it has no relevance to the history of Shropshire architecture, which, like that of the county itself, begins in the Anglo-Saxon period.

It is a commonplace that the nature of English architecture did not change overnight in 1066, and the term 'Anglo-Saxon' is used here for buildings erected in a native style or manner up to the end of the 11th century and just beyond. They are rare in Shropshire. The churches of Atcham, Barrow, Diddlebury, Stanton Lacy, Stottesdon, and Wroxeter make up the whole of the generally accepted canon, though claims have been advanced for Quatt.[2] There is no complete structure. The most coherent survivals are the chancel at Barrow; the north wall of the nave and part of the north wall of the west tower at Diddlebury; and the north transept and the north and west walls of the nave at Stanton Lacy. There are side-alternate quoins at Atcham, Barrow, and Stanton Lacy, and plinths of square section at Atcham and, in three stages, at Barrow and Diddlebury. The north wall of the nave at Stanton Lacy has a doorway with pilaster-strip surrounds, and the north and west walls of the nave and the walls of the north transept are richly provided with pilaster strips. There is another on the south wall of the chancel at Barrow. At Barrow and Diddlebury there are double-splay windows and at Barrow the only surviving chancel arch, built of through-stones and originally with plain imposts.[3] In the north wall at Atcham there is a triangular-headed window, and Wroxeter has a square-section string course along part of the north wall. Walling in all of these is less than 3ft. thick and is generally well coursed; at

Barrow the chancel walls are only 2ft. 3in. thick. In addition the churches of Culmington, Rushbury, Sidbury, and Stanton upon Hine Heath have, together with Diddlebury, large stretches of herring-bone masonry, and there are small patches of it at Clee St. Margaret and Pitchford. They are discussed below.

It is not known when any pre-Conquest church was built. Domesday Book mentions churches or priests at Diddlebury, Stanton Lacy, Stottesdon, and Wroxeter,[4] and Ordericus Vitalis was baptized in a church at Atcham in 1075.[5] An early Saxon date has been claimed for Atcham and for Wroxeter because the walls of both have large stones probably taken from the ruins of *Viroconium*,[6] but there is no reason to think that *Viroconium* had ceased to be a convenient quarry by late Saxon times.[7] The chancel at Wroxeter was rebuilt in the 12th century, but the north wall of the nave is certainly Anglo-Saxon and its string course suggests it is late. Similarly at Atcham the square-section plinth, the use of large stones in the lower courses, and the mention by Orderic Vitalis are grounds for thinking that it too is of Anglo-Saxon origin but not for believing it to be early.[8] The herringbone masonry at Diddlebury places it in the late 11th century or just after. The chancel at Barrow, with a pilaster strip and a double-splay window, is perhaps of the mid 11th century, and Stanton Lacy may be *c*.1100.[9]

Little can be said about the plans of these churches because little has survived and less has been excavated, but it is reasonably clear that all of the survivors had aisleless naves: Atcham, Diddlebury, Stanton Lacy, and Wroxeter. Only one chancel is known for certain, at Barrow, and that is, and probably always was, square ended.[10] The apses found at Wenlock Priory church by the excavations of 1901 and 1962–3 are now considered to be post-

*The lintel over the doorway into the nave from the west tower
at Stottesdon church*

Conquest,[11] but at least the demolished Saxon church of St. Mary's, Shrewsbury, seems to have had an apsed chancel.[12] At Stanton Lacy the north and west walls, nave, and north transept of a cruciform church survive.[13]

Four churches need to be discussed at length because of their very individual character. The Anglo-Saxon date of Stottesdon is largely a deduction from the ornament on the west doorway of the nave, and that ornament is very odd indeed. Some writers seem to have accepted that the carved lintel above the doorway, the pilaster strips forming a curvilinear triangle above the tympanum, and the bearded human head at the apex of that triangle are all part of the original structure.[14] That may be doubted. The lintel is carved with figures of a seated cat, a lion passant gardant, and what may be a dog or a deer, and with a reticulated pattern perhaps meant as a net.[15] It is worked only on its present soffit; its top and ends are rough and have either never been worked or have been hacked about.[16] It is not integral with the tympanum above. The lion and the dog or deer are upside down, and if the stone were turned to set them right way up then the cat would be standing on its head. The iconography, if there is any, is so far unexplained. It is impossible to imagine any position in any building, which the stone with its present ornament would fit, and it was

probably intended as a coffin lid. The execution itself is lamentably poor, well below normal 11th- and 12th-century standards,[17] and the lintel was set in its present position long after the doorway was made. The pilaster strips above it are set asymmetrically and the curvilinear triangle they enclose is of unequal curvature. The human head is highly stylized and is more likely to be late 12th- than 11th-century work. The pilaster strips and the head, like the lintel, are bits and pieces inserted later.

All these odds and ends stand proud of the wall; when they are mentally stripped away there remain three tiers of saltire ornament above a plain doorway in a west wall that had an early 12th-century west tower and a late 12th-century nave added to it. The saltire ornament, made up of a number of small stones, is likewise not *in situ*. It is built into the head of a semicircular arch, without voussoirs, above a doorway which, before the insertion of the lintel, was of tall pre-Conquest proportions. The space behind the 'tympanum' above the lintel is filled in with rubble. The reused pilaster strips are the only early element in all the ornament, and in conjunction with the doorway they seem to show that part of the west wall of a pre-Conquest church of some pretensions still survives.

Diddlebury is notable for its plan, differing from all its compeers in the county in having evidence of a pre-Conquest structure west of the nave. It differs too from all but a few Anglo-Saxon churches in the kingdom, for the north wall of the west tower, if that is what it was, is in the same plane as that of the nave, and the three-stage plinth of the north wall of the nave continues along that of the west structure for a distance (including the thickness of the wall between the two) of 13ft. All else beyond is early Norman or later, and it may be that a Saxon west tower, square on plan and as wide as the nave—like that which may be inferred at Boarhunt (Hants.)[18] and another that was excavated at South Elmham St. Cross (Suff.)[19]—was rebuilt *c*.1100 more or less *in situ.* Nevertheless there is no evidence that the Saxon structure did continue west beyond the present westernmost limit of the plinth, and indeed the Saxon masonry above the plinth stops some 3ft. short of that point, a fact suggesting that the west wall returned there. Equally, therefore, it could be that only the west wall has been removed and that originally the west structure was similar to the earlier form postulated for Bywell St. Peter (Northumb.): as wide as the nave but only a few feet across (from east to west) and so more like a narthex than a porch or tower.[20] Indeed it may have been only a low forebuilding for no Saxon masonry survives higher than about 8ft. up from the plinth. Furthermore the original west opening of the present early Norman tower was a great archway, 14ft. high, 10ft. wide in the clear, and set within a wall only 17ft. long internally; it would pass for a chancel arch, were it not where it is. The lower part of the west wall thus had more void than solid, and the ground-floor compartment was open to the 'shock of all winds that blow'. That unique arrangement, in the nature of an unenclosed narthex, may perhaps be explained as the perpetuation of the form of an earlier forebuilding which had much the same function, and which may perhaps be compared with the later low forebuildings at Fountains and Byland. It is perhaps not surprising that in the late 12th century the arch was partly filled and a doorway of more usual dimensions provided.

Barrow has the only complete Anglo-Saxon chancel in the county.[21] It has been claimed as an 8th-century single-cell oratory, converted in the late Saxon period into the chancel of a two-cell church by the addition of a stone nave and the replacement of a former west doorway by the present chancel arch, the present nave being a rebuild (*c.*1100) of the late Saxon one.[22] There is little positive evidence for such an early date or for such an interpretation, which contradicted an earlier one that Barrow was a two-cell church of the 10th century with a stone chancel and with a timber nave replaced by the present one *c.*1100.[23] That interpretation itself was criticized on the ground that such a fine chancel arch was most unlikely to have been associated with a timber nave.[24] The objection has some weight if 'associated with' means 'built at the same time as'. It overlooks the possibility, however, that the existing church is the end product of a development

The chancel at Barrow

in which a two-cell timber church of unknown date was rebuilt in stages, the chancel before the Conquest and the nave *c.*1100. While there is general agreement about the date of the nave (*c.*1100), suggestions for the chancel have varied from the 8th to the early 11th century, and, on the whole, the more recent the judgement the later the proposed date.[25] The chancel was certainly, as far as there is any certainty in these matters, there by 1086, but to what period in the preceding hundred or more years it has to be assigned is quite uncertain.

Stanton Lacy is the least incomplete survival. Its nave and north transept are impressively tall and comparable in scale with such well known cruciform churches as Worth (Suss.) and St. Mary-in-Castro, Dover, and its early walls are richly covered with pilaster strips. It came as close to a fully transeptal form as any Anglo-Saxon church did, and it may have had a light crossing tower. Whether it was always cruciform may be doubted. On the north and west walls of the nave the pilaster strips stop half way up, while on the north transept they rise the full height of the walls. This may only mean that the upper parts of the nave walls were rebuilt at some time.[26] On the other hand it may mean that a late Saxon church was made cruciform by adding tall transepts and raising the walls of a former low nave not much earlier in date. The evidence is not

Plan of Stanton Lacy Church

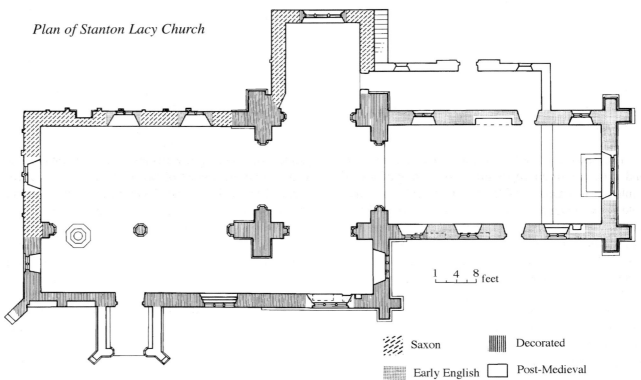

⫰⫰ Saxon	▦ Decorated
▦ Early English	☐ Post-Medieval

unequivocally in favour of either view, but, while both can explain the missing pilaster strips, the latter also explains why the masonry of the lower parts of the north and west walls of the nave is different from that of the transept and why the upper part of the north wall has the same masonry as the transept. Up to the tops of the pilaster strips the north and west walls of the nave are of large uncoursed stones. Above that level the west wall is in small uncoursed stones and appears to be a rough rebuild. The masonry of the north wall above the strips is (except for a few modern courses in small regular stones below eaves level) in large stones generally well coursed, and the same masonry is present in all the walls of the north transept.[27]

Besides the buildings discussed above there are others whose herringbone masonry suggests the late 11th or early 12th century: Clee St. Margaret, Culmington, Pitchford, Sidbury, and Stanton upon Hine Heath. Culmington is the most important, for it resembles Diddlebury and is unlike any other known church in England in having squared ashlar outside and herringbone masonry inside. Unlike Diddlebury, however, the external ashlar at Culmington is on the lower part of the north and south walls of the nave, up to *c*.8ft. above ground,

and there is herringbone masonry above; the herringbone inside is visible to *c*.8ft. above floor level and presumably—for the upper walls are heavily plastered—continues to the top. The nave has two early Norman windows, which do not appear to be replacements, and there is no sign of an Anglo-Saxon plinth. Diddlebury and Culmington are adjoining parishes and their churches are just over two miles apart. It is difficult to believe that the men who built the one in such an unparalleled technique did not also build the other; and yet, herringbone masonry apart, the one appears to be a pre-Conquest church and the other a post-Conquest one.

The dating of herringbone masonry has long been a matter of dispute.[28] There is nothing in the technique that can be clearly related to Anglo-Saxon practice, and for that reason it may well be post-1066. On the other hand it is very different from that 'new style of architecture' for which William of Malmesbury praised the Normans,[29] and it is accompanied at Diddlebury by such Anglo-Saxon elements as a double-splay window and three-stage plinth. At least some of its examples therefore may be attributed to Anglo-Saxon masons, but to Anglo-Saxon masons working in new conditions: for Norman lords who wanted larger churches and wanted them in a hurry. At Diddlebury one may see the two principles working together, with ashlar on the outer face of the walls and herringbone on the inner; while at Culmington it would appear that there was a similar intention at the beginning, but that before long the masons working in herringbone displaced the others. Diddlebury and Culmington, then, may be the earliest churches in the county with herringbone masonry.

The other churches have much less herringbone, and it occurs in an apparently more straightforward context. The chancel at Clee St. Margaret has no date-able early element except its masonry, and Pitchford has only a small window with a semicircular head cut from a single stone and set within a patch of herring-bone. The size of Stanton upon Hine Heath church and its early Norman windows date it clearly enough. At Sidbury, where the Victorian restoration was much less drastic than Pevsner suggests,[30] the herringbone courses in the west wall continue up over the head of the early Norman doorway, which must be presumed coeval with the fabric.

So little pre-12th-century work survives in the 60 Shropshire churches mentioned in Domesday Book,[31] or the five others whose probable existence in 1086 may be inferred,[32] that what may be said in general about Anglo-Saxon architecture in Shropshire is not very much. No building is demon-strably early, none has to be before the 11th century, and some may be of the early 12th. No church has wholly retained its former plan, but it is probable, to judge from surviving walls and the occasional exca-vation, that most were of two-cell nave-and-chancel form. Stanton Lacy may have had a light crossing tower, but there is no evidence of tower naves, nor, apart from Diddlebury, of west towers; and even at Diddlebury there may have been no more than a porch. No apsidal end has survived above ground level. The pre-Conquest St. Mary's, Shrewsbury, had one, but that is so much outside the known country-wide distribution range that it may have been unique, at least until the first post-Conquest church at Much Wenlock. Most of the diagnostic elements of Anglo-Saxon architecture are present—

Herringbone masonry at Diddlebury church

quoins, pilaster strips, double-splay windows, square-section plinths, thin walls—but never in abundance.

It is difficult to point to any distinctly local features, apart from the fabric at Diddlebury and Culmington, where squared ashlar is used as a facing to herringbone masonry. Presumably those two were not alone, but, apart from a shared parish boundary, there is no significant connection between them, and whether the practice ever spread beyond Corve Dale is uncertain. Some churches may have been low buildings; the walls of Barrow are 12ft. high internally, the possibility of an earlier structure at Stanton Lacy was mentioned above, and the change in the masonry of the upper parts of the walls at Culmington may be due to a decision to heighten in the course of building.

Whether or not Shropshire was retarded or impoverished in comparison with some parts of the country, or whether small churches were less open to wider influences than important ones, is difficult to determine; partly because so little of either category has survived and partly because the answer must depend upon the reliability of the suggested dates. Barrow was not a major church and its chancel arch has no composite piers, no jambs, no colonnettes, no orders, and has a very plain impost. If it is contemporary with the present nave of c.1100, it was not as up-to-date as some other churches. But it is more than possible that the present nave replaces an earlier one, and, if so, that arch could have been quite abreast of current practice when it was built. Similarly, if the important church at Stanton Lacy was built in the mid 11th century, then it was as advanced as anything at the time, and more advanced than most. But if, as has been implied, it could be of post-Conquest date, its ornament, but not its plan form, is retarded.[33] The combination of squared ashlar and herringbone masonry at Diddlebury and at Culmington shows that their builders were as technically expert as any in the country, no matter when they were working, and one may be sure that they could have handled orders and composite piers with little difficulty; but nothing remains to show that they did.

Little on the other hand has survived at such then-important sites as Wroxeter, with its four priests, nothing at Morville with its eight canons, nothing at Much Wenlock (the county's only pre-

Conquest monastic foundation), and nothing at any of those places (except Diddlebury and, to a much less degree, Stottesdon) that were royal manors and hundredal *capita*. Those were the communities most likely to be abreast of, and most able and most constrained to follow, innovations of form and ornament; and at Diddlebury the masons were clearly technically expert and aesthetically conscious. So much may have been done, so little survives, and dating is so uncertain that a not-proven verdict has to be returned to both questions raised in the preceding paragraph.

The pattern of survival

The survival of any building for a thousand years is the result of many accidents, but there can be a pattern to accidents. Human intervention in the form of rebuilding has been as great a menace to early buildings as natural decay. The early churches which have survived best are those which were important *c*.1100 but ceased to be soon after and so benefited from benign neglect in the form of make-do-and-mend. The best preserved early churches in the county are Diddlebury and Stanton Lacy, the former on a royal manor (Corfham) which was the *caput* of two hundreds in 1086, the latter on a vast manor held by the Lacy family and served by two priests endowed with 1½ hide. Corfham was replaced as a hundred *caput* perhaps as early as 1102,[34] and Ludlow soon replaced Stanton Lacy[35] as the *caput* of the Lacy honor and as the guardian of the route to their Herefordshire estates.

Domesday Book[36] records 30 manorial churches in present-day Shropshire.[37] None of them has Anglo-Saxon remains. Nevertheless there are two churches with Anglo-Saxon elements, Atcham and Barrow, and they have two other things in common; both are ignored by Domesday Book and both were on land belonging to, and easily accessible from, a minster or former minster: St. Alkmund's, Shrewsbury, and Wenlock Priory respectively. Domesday Book also records 28 'superior' churches in present-day Shropshire, *i.e.* either minsters (churches served by more than one priest),[38] or churches endowed with land, or else churches at the *caput* of a hundred or of a great manor. Some churches—Morville and Stanton Lacy, for example—qualified under more than one head.[39] Four of these superior churches—Diddlebury,

Stanton Lacy, Stottesdon, and Wroxeter—have retained Anglo-Saxon elements. If Atcham and Barrow are regarded as typical manorial churches, then the chances that the fabric of a manorial church will keep something from pre-Conquest times are 15:1 against; and, if the two are not so regarded, then the chances would appear to be negligible. The survival rate among superior churches is not high but is between five and six to one. All the survivals are of stone, and while that material did not guarantee longevity it was essential to it.

It is generally accepted that a church with two or more priests or endowed with land may be called superior, but it may be asked why one on a manor serving as the *caput* of a hundred is thereby 'superior'. 'Superior' is not insisted upon. It is merely one way of expressing a distinction. According to Domesday Book, and for whatever reason, 13 of the 14 manors which were—or, like Patton, had recently been—the *caput* of a hundred[40] had churches recorded in 1086; only one—Alberbury—had not.[41] Of the 376 manors which harboured neither the *caput* of a hundred nor a 'superior' church in the general meaning of the term, only 27 had a church. The chances of a manor at a hundred *caput* having a church were 13 to 1 on; the chances of any other manor having a church were 14 to 1 against. To put it another way, a church on a *caput* manor was a necessity, on other manors it was an optional extra. Of course, in the context of a weakly developed parochial system, churches with several priests serving a large area were also necessities. Perhaps the term 'superior', with its connotation of status, should be dropped in favour of 'necessary' or 'essential'. The question will then be asked 'Essential to whom?' In the absence of a parochial system, one answer will be 'Essential to the Church's mission'. Given the existence of a local administrative system based upon the hundred, another answer will be 'Essential to the secular rulers'.

The difference in size and complexity between northern and southern churches in the early 13th century[42] reinforces evidence that the South then had a more advanced economy than the North; and yet in 1086 the North had the more developed parochial system. That was not from any difference between the two areas in the number of minster churches, for numbers were much the same in all hundreds. There was, however, a great difference between North and South in the number of minster clergy: eight in the three northern hundreds[43] and 24 in the six southern ones.[44] And four of the northern eight were at Wroxeter, in the Deep South of the North. It would seem, therefore, that rich minsters with many clergy would appear in an economically advanced area and that the system might there reach such a level that its very success gave no encouragement to, and could militate against, the rapid development of a parochial system. Contrariwise the proliferation of manorial churches in the three northern hundreds, in concentrations on estates held by rich men and well endowed churches, was probably assisted by the less developed state of the minster system there.[45]

Even the church built shortly before the Conquest in what became Abbey Foregate, Shrewsbury, by Edward the Confessor's rich kinsman Siward,[46] endowed with land in two parishes[47] and with the tithes of Upton Magna,[48] was of timber;[49] and it is therefore likely that so were many manorial churches. If all or most or many Anglo-Saxon manorial churches were of timber, they would have disappeared of their own accord, for timber is less durable than stone. On the other hand some stone churches may have been largely swept away by the Normans, presumably because they were small and of little use to the conquerors who, for political reasons at least as much as from piety, wished to bring the message of the Church (which had blessed their Conquest)[50] to the masses and to show that they had the Church on their side. They had anticipated Milton: 'who overcomes / By force hath overcome but half his foe'.

While the wholesale physical disappearance of manorial churches recorded in Domesday Book is apparent throughout the county, their distribution was far from uniform. The minsters and 'essential' churches differed little in numbers from area to area. In general each hundred had either a minster and a church serving the *caput* or else a minster also serving the *caput*. The number of manorial churches, in contrast, varied enormously from area to area. In the three northern hundreds,[51] with 144 manors, there were 17 manorial churches and five 'essential' ones; in the six southern hundreds,[52] with 160 manors, the proportion was 9 to 8 and in the four western hundreds,[53] with 117 manors, it was 1 to 5. What Domesday Book gives us is a snapshot of the three parts of the present county, each caught at a different stage of ecclesiastical development. In the north the change to a parochial system was well under way, in the south it was gathering momentum, in the west it had hardly begun. The even distribution of 'essential' churches throughout every hundred had been brought about by an overriding authority, more than county-wide and with both ecclesiastical and secular aims, imposing a pattern upon a *tabula rasa*. In contrast, manorial churches, the product of the individual efforts of many lords, lack any pattern of distribution.

It is noticeable that, apart from Atcham and Barrow, the earliest parts of surviving parish churches are of herringbone masonry, and we saw above reasons for supposing that technique to belong to the 'Anglo-Saxon overlap'. Apart from Stanton upon Hine Heath, all such churches are in the south, and their appearance testifies not only to the newcomers' intentions, but as well perhaps, to an intensification of the developing parochial system there. Herringbone was dearer to build in than timber, and in 1086 all of these herringbone churches were on manors held by great men or by members of great families or by men holding a dozen or more manors. There had been great men in earlier times, and in 1066 a third of all the manors with churches recorded in 1086 were held by them. The failure of all those earlier churches to survive physically suggests that the rulers of Anglo-Saxon England spent less of their wealth on churches which served the population at large than did the Norman invaders.

II   Late 11th- to late 12th-Century Church Building

It is generally accepted that there were far more churches in late 11th-century England than Domesday Book records, and it is mistaken to visualize the Normans filling an empty countryside with them.[1] Nevertheless over a hundred Shropshire churches have Norman features, and it is undeniable that the newcomers carried out a large-scale building campaign. Few perhaps of their new churches were on virgin sites and many were probably rebuildings of earlier structures, often of timber.[2] The best explanations of the structural histories of Barrow,[3] Clee St. Margaret, and Stirchley[4] churches, for example, are that at Barrow a wooden church had its chancel rebuilt in stone shortly before the Conquest and its nave shortly after; and at Clee St. Margaret and Stirchley first the chancels and then the naves were rebuilt in stone, probably in two post-Conquest stages.

Not only did the newcomers often rebuild in stone, they built on a larger scale too. At Barrow the new nave was wider. In the 12th century the pre-Conquest church at Wroxeter was lengthened eastwards, and perhaps also westwards.[5] New work at Rushbury may have included an eastward extension of the nave, and another such extension happened at Diddlebury.[6] At Atcham, probably c.1200, a west tower was added, and at Stottesdon a west tower was added and then the nave was rebuilt. Thus at all the proved or reputed pre-Conquest survivals (except Stanton Lacy, which was new and big c.1100) Norman builders were turning small churches into larger ones. And it may be presumed that they were doing the same at many other places where no pre-Conquest work survives. Despite the marked concentration of survivals in the south, the overall achievement was impressive. In conjunction with the new monastic foundations and the string of fortifications in border areas, it must have transformed one aspect of the environment.

This was not a development peculiar to any one county and may perhaps be ascribed in general to the climatic amelioration of the age which, by making good land more productive and allowing more land to be brought into use, provided the resources for a large-scale building programme.[7] It seems to have resulted also from the character of the Anglo-Saxon church whose early policy had been to conciliate kings and nobles and to hope that the mass of the people would automatically embrace the faith of their betters. The paucity and smallness of Anglo-Saxon buildings in comparison with Norman ones suggest that that policy had never been wholly abandoned and that the alien Norman church, for whatever reasons, showed more concern, and certainly expended more resources, than ever the native church had done in spreading its message widely and persistently. William of Malmesbury's ambivalence towards the Normans did not stop him paying tribute to their revival of religious life and their widespread church building.[8] In Shropshire it would appear also to be a consequence of a concentration of local landownership among minor men. Many estates recorded as single manors in 1086 had been held as two, three, or four manors in 1066. Often the English co-owner had held a part or the whole of other manors elsewhere, and to that extent there was consolidation as well as concentration of ownership, but that too could increase a local landowner's ability to build a stone church on his estate.[9] Pitchford church may be a case in point. The parish was created, probably out of Cound, in the early 12th century and the building retains some herringbone masonry. At Domesday the manor belonged to Ralph of Pitchford who had ousted the three English landowners of 1066.[10]

Parish churches and chapels:
One- and two-cell buildings

Generally parish churches and chapels[11] that were built or rebuilt in the late 11th and the 12th century either have a nave with a structurally separate chancel or are single cells considerably longer than they are wide and accommodating both nave and chancel. All the survivors are square-ended. Apses have been found by excavation at St. Mary's, Shrewsbury (of Anglo-Saxon date), at Wenlock Priory church, at the round church in Ludlow Castle, on the north transept at Shifnal,[12] and at Shrewsbury Abbey.[13] A plan of 1885 of the old church at Felton (in Bromfield parish) shows a single-cell building, claimed to be of the 12th century, 28 x 20ft., with an apse of 5ft. 8in. radius.[14] It is not unlikely, therefore, that some single-cell churches of two builds have had an original apse replaced by a later eastward extension of the fabric.[15] It is generally accepted that single-cell churches were of less than parochial status and were a small proportion of the whole.[16] Both propositions have some validity when applied to Shropshire, but both, stated like that, conceal some of the truth.

It is possible to establish with some confidence the 12th-century form and status of 40 to 50 churches.[17] About a third were parish churches and all but a handful of them had structural chancels. Chapels with structural chancels were slightly commoner than those without. Thus a parish church was far more likely than a chapel to have a structural chancel, and a single-cell building was far more likely to be a chapel than a parish church. But the converse did not apply, for a chapel was more likely to have a structural chancel than not, and a chancel was at least as likely to belong to a chapel as to a parish church; indeed, while Bitterley parish church was a single cell, its dependent chapel of Hope Bagot had a nave and a structural chancel. Moreover, although structural chancels were commoner than single-cell buildings, it is an exaggeration to suggest that they were a large majority for the latter were a very substantial minority. How far Shropshire was exceptional in this respect is not easily ascertained. It was not different in kind from other counties for Worcestershire has seven or eight surviving one-cell structures, and they may have been known in south-east Wiltshire. On the other hand they are rare in the areas covered by volumes V and VI of the Royal Commission's Northamptonshire *Inventory* and seem to be unknown in neighbouring Staffordshire.[18] It would seem that, while Shropshire was not alone in having one-cell parish churches and chapels, it differs from other midland

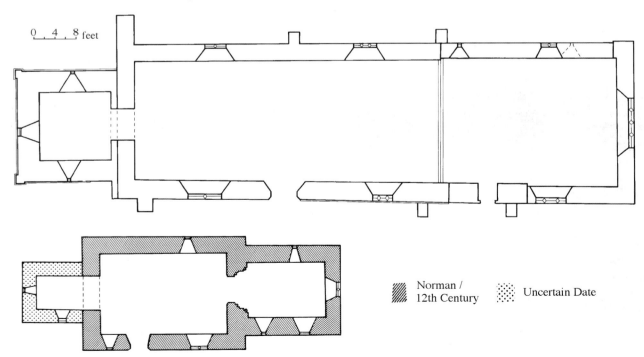

0 4 8 feet

Norman / 12th Century   Uncertain Date

Plans of Bitterley church (top) and Hope Bagot chapel to the same scale

10

Heath chapel—a 'perfect' example of the small Norman 'church'

The chancel arch at Morville

counties in having a very large number of them. The reasons for that are doubtless complex, and one partial explanation is discussed below.

Whatever ecclesiastical significance the distinction between parish churches and chapels might have had in this period, it had very little contemporary architectural consequence. Indeed Heath chapel, which has justly been described as a 'perfect' example of 'the small Norman church',[19] was in fact subject to Stoke St. Milborough parish church. Nor was the difference between parish church and chapel reflected in size. Some parish churches were very large by local standards: the nave at Holy Trinity, Much Wenlock, is 80 x 23ft., and Lydbury North, as completed in the late 12th century, is 110ft. long excluding the west tower. On the other hand the naves of Aston Botterell, Clunbury,[20] Eaton-under-Heywood, Kinlet, Morville, Onibury, and Sidbury parish churches are all 40ft. or less in length and vary in width from 15 to 21ft., and their chancels, where they survive, are of corresponding size. Some chapels were small indeed: the naves of Heath, Hope Bagot, and Upton Cressett are all under 30ft. long and none is wider

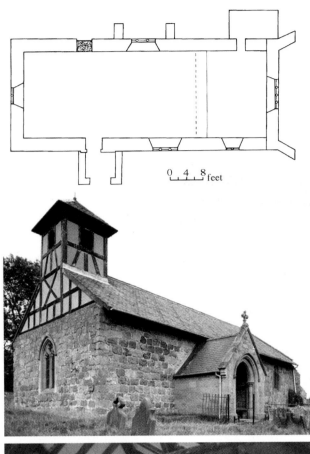

0 4 8 feet

Plan, exterior and interior of Hordley church

than 16ft. Against that, however, at Ruyton-XI-Towns, Barrow, Hopesay, and Moreton Say, which probably began as chapels,[21] the naves are all both longer and wider than those of the churches just mentioned.

Similarly there was no clear difference in size between one- and two-cell structures. Some single cells were very small: Lee Brockhurst's total length was 42ft.,[22] its width under 15ft. Small as Lee Brockhurst was, the two-cell Hope Bagot was smaller and Heath chapel no bigger, while the two-cell Clee St. Margaret, Milson, and Sidbury, though larger than Lee Brockhurst, were smaller than many other one-cell churches such as Ford, Hadnall, Halford, Hordley, Leebotwood, Lydham, and Little Ness. Moreover some single-cell structures were very large indeed: Moreton Say over 24ft. wide,[23] Stapleton 73ft. long, and Neen Savage 84ft. long.

Nevertheless there is one very important distinction to be made between single- and double-cell churches: the former hardly appear at all before the second half of the 12th century while all those churches which can be securely dated to the late 11th or early to mid 12th century had, where there is any certainty in the matter, structurally separate chancels. Of course, where a late 12th- or early 13th-century chancel has been added to an earlier structure to give a single-cell form, as at Culmington, there is no way of knowing, without excavation, whether a single cell has been lengthened or a structurally separate chancel has been demolished in favour of a wider one. One can say, however, that among standing structures the square-ended single-cell form, whether of one or two builds, has been brought about in the late 12th century or later, and that earlier single-cell structures, if they ever existed, have failed to survive in their original form in contrast with the many two-cell ones that have. That does not mean that the single cell superseded the double cell but that it seems to have been added to the local repertoire at that time.

The time lag in the appearance of the single cell makes it necessary to modify the earlier statement that single cells were a substantial minority of churches built between *c.*1066 and *c.*1200: until *c.*1150 they were insignificant in number while thereafter new structures were as likely to be single- as double-cell. Nor is that all for, apart from single-

Watercolour by Edw. Williams of St. Catherine's church, Tugford, showing the single-cell form after the lengthening of the chancel c.1200 (SRRC 6001/372/2.35)

cell churches of one build, many single-cell forms emerged from additions of the late 12th and early 13th century. Examples are Bitterley, Cardington, Culmington, Eaton-under-Heywood, Lilleshall, Pitchford, and Tugford, and to those may be added the mid to late 12th-century additions to the Anglo-Saxon churches of Diddlebury and Wroxeter.

One conclusion to be drawn from the above is that there is a simple reason for the less frequent occurrence of the single-cell form between the mid 11th and the early 13th century: it was being built over a shorter space of time than the other form. Furthermore the broad correlation between parish churches and structural chancels and between chapels and single cells is also a reflection of the later development of the single cell. By the late 12th century, when the single cell was appearing, the parochial system was becoming fixed, and the owners (in the process of turning into patrons) and incumbents of existing parish churches were generally able to ensure that new buildings for public worship should respect existing parochial rights and be content with chapel status.

Nevertheless there is more to it than that. Some pre-Conquest churches in England had been single-cell, but the form was virtually introduced or reintroduced into Shropshire in the late 12th and early 13th century. The revival calls for explanation. It accompanied the unprecedented amount of building of churches of all kinds at that period, which was itself a response to the pastoral problems resulting from the continuing increase in population and the colonization of new land that had been going on since before the Norman Conquest and was to continue into the early 14th century. These problems were aggravated by the tendency for post-Conquest monastic houses to replace a community of priests by a single priest (usually a vicar) in the churches they absorbed, and by the failure of the new orders of regular canons to assume, despite hopes to the contrary perhaps, some of the functions of the old minsters.[24] The single cell of this period may be seen as an attempt at a solution by building as simply as possible and avoiding the complications and expense of structural chancels and chancel arches or apsidal east ends. Indeed one can almost see mass production here, for the chapels of Hadnall, Hordley, and Little Ness, all within a few miles of one another, have almost identical dimensions; and, as far as can be told after its thorough restoration, so too had Clive chapel in the same area.

Thus the correlation between chapels and single cells is not due to any essentially chapel-like qualities in the single cell but arises because both, for different reasons, were proliferating at the same time. The common form and size of these churches probably reflects the similarity of the communities they served, but the very close correspondence in their measurements may be the result of the masons' employment of dimensions based on the 'golden section' and the square roots of 2, 3, and 5. That these are small rustic churches does not argue against the possible use of such sophisticated methods for there may well have been 'no clear-cut line of demarcation between the planning procedures of smart buildings and those lower down the social scale'.[25]

The coincidence between a late date and a single-cell form is clear among the surviving Norman churches in north Shropshire, where by Salopian standards Norman churches are rare; on the most generous reckoning they make up less than a fifth of the total number in the county. Only three of them—West Felton, Ruyton-XI-Towns, and Stanton upon Hine Heath—have any claim to be early, a proportion of early to late of something like 1:4. On the other hand, while none of those three is single-cell, two thirds of the later ones are, and over the whole period, in contrast with the county as a whole, single-cell buildings slightly outnumber double-cell churches. Because the moss-and-mere country was colonized late[26] and because the single cell is itself a late form, north Shropshire is less well endowed than the south with Norman churches of any form, has very few early ones, but is proportionately richer in late 12th-century single-cell structures, nearly all of them originally of chapel status.

In the ordinary 12th-century Shropshire parish church or chapel Romanesque concepts of 'articulation' and of 'repetitive units'[27] were irrelevant, and even variations of form were limited. Naves in two-cell churches were typically about twice as long as wide, and lengths of c.40ft. and widths of c.20ft.

were common. There are exceptions: the nave at Stanton upon Hine Heath is very long and three times as long as wide; at Upton Cressett the nave is very short, and the proportion of length to width is 5:3. So many chancels have been rebuilt or lengthened that generalization is not easy, but a proportion of length to width of c.3:2 was normal. Again there are exceptions: at Upton Magna the proportion is nearly 2:1 while at Milson, and originally at Ashford Carbonell, it was just over 1:1, and at Little Wenlock the chancel was a 12ft. square internally. Chancels were generally about half the length of the nave. As was suggested above, the dimensions of single-cell buildings varied enormously, but a length of c.50ft. was common and the proportions were usually about 5:2, exemplified, although on a larger scale than was normal, at Edstaston, 60 x 23ft. in its late 12th-century phase.[28]

Nearly all churches had a main doorway towards the west end of the south wall of the nave. North doorways were far less common; they are almost always opposite, but rarely exactly opposite, the south doorway. A notable exception is at Linley, where the south doorway is tight up against the west tower while the west jamb of the north doorway is about 10ft. east of it. The probable explanation, confirmed to some extent by disturbance in the masonry, is that the south doorway was moved west when the west tower was built. Occasionally the main doorway (as at Clive) or the only doorway (as at Middleton chapel) is on the north—for no obvious reason.[29] West doorways were rare, occurring generally in churches of collegiate origin or dependent upon a religious house.[30] An apparent exception is at Sidbury, where the west doorway is set within, and is clearly part of, the herringbone masonry of the west wall. There may have been objections to west doorways, for at Wistanstow an original one was blocked shortly after building, and conventional north and south openings were made, obliterating earlier windows.

In structural chancels south doorways were the general rule, except in small ones like Ashford Carbonell and Hope Bagot. In single-cell buildings, however, chancel doorways were not common, except in very long ones like Edstaston, Neen Savage, and Tugford. They do not seem to be related to ecclesiastical status, for they were present in some chapels and absent from some parish

The 12th-century south doorway of Shawbury church, set within a shallow projection

churches, and their presence seems to depend upon the size, and particularly the length, of a building, as though they were a dispensable luxury where space for openings in a lateral wall was limited.

Some churches have external doorways set within a shallow but wide projection. The clearest examples are on the south walls of the chancels at Edstaston and Morville, on the north wall of the nave at Church Stretton, and on north and south aisles at Shawbury. Such doorways in the south walls of some naves, for example Hordley (see plan on p.12), Lilleshall, and Onibury, are not easily recognized without measuring because later porches, wider than the projections and overlapping them, obscure their relationship with the main wall. The practice was known throughout the country[31] but seems to have been exceptionally popular in Shropshire, especially in the second half of the 12th century.[32]

The rarity of apses was commented on earlier. Equally rare is the relationship, noted elsewhere, in which the inner faces of the lateral walls of the nave

are in line with the outer faces of the chancel walls.[33] On the other hand chancel arches were not as rare as one would expect from Cranage's statement that, as far as he could tell, fewer than half of the county's churches had one.[34] What he says is formally correct but somewhat misleading, for he includes single-cell structures which almost by definition[35] will be without a chancel arch. If they are excluded, the proportion of churches without a chancel arch falls sharply, and the overwhelming majority—more than three-quarters—had one. The earlier the church the more likely it is to have a chancel arch, but that again is mainly a reflection of the late appearance of single-cell buildings.

The lack of architectural difference between parish churches and chapels appears again when we turn from plans and forms to ornament. The nature of ornament will be discussed later; here it is sufficient to note that most of the examples of non-monastic decoration that are usually singled out for mention are on or within former chapels: the outstanding tympanum at Aston Eyre, the richly worked doorways at Edstaston and Little Ness, the south chancel window at Monkhopton,[36] the chancel arches at Stirchley and Upton Cressett, the tripartite chancel arch at Caynham, and the tympana at Barrow, Billingsley, Linley, and Uppington. There is of course equally rich work in parish churches: Holdgate, Neen Savage, Quatford, Shifnal, and St. Mary's, Shrewsbury, to name a few. Nevertheless a parish church was no likelier than a chapel to be richly decorated. To some extent, however, the richness of decoration upon chapels is another aspect of their late appearance, for ornament became more lavish as the 12th century wore on.

In 12th-century Shropshire differences between churches in architectural treatment, form, and ornament less often reflected ecclesiastical status than the religious feelings, the resources, and often the proximity of the manorial lords on whose estates new places of worship were erected. A landowner might build as lavishly as he pleased, but he had less and less power to gain parochial status for his new church,[37] however much that lack might have been to his tenants' spiritual detriment.

At the end of the 12th century the usual local church in Shropshire was a very simple building. Many were single-celled, and plan forms more elaborate than a structurally separate nave and chancel

The north nave arcade at Shawbury church, looking south-east

The north nave arcade at Kinlet church, looking south-east

were extremely rare; and they had generally come about by additions rather than by conscious design. The only one, other than Stanton Lacy, which can be shown to have had transepts before the mid century was St. Mary's, Shrewsbury, where they were intended from the start. The north transept at Condover is late 12th-century, and the cruciform

The arch from the nave into the west tower at Linley church

plans of Shifnal, Church Stretton, Wistanstow, and Wrockwardine are *c.*1200.[38] Claverley and West Felton have aisles which are probably coeval with the early 12th-century naves there, but those at Clun, Kinlet, Knockin, Morville, and Shawbury are *c.*1200; except at Knockin they are later than the naves. The commonest elaboration upon the basic plan was a west tower. Generally—as at Linley, Lydbury North, Morville, St. Mary's Shrewsbury, and Holy Trinity Much Wenlock—it was a late 12th-century addition to an early 12th-century nave; at Stottesdon it was an early 12th-century addition to an earlier nave (see overleaf). Sometimes, for example at Albrighton, the tower is the earliest surviving structure and may well have been added in the 12th century to a very much earlier nave. Occasionally, as at Barrow, Munslow, and Neen Savage, it may be supposed, in the absence of evidence to the contrary, to be coeval with the nave. The importance attached to a west tower in the late 12th century is shown starkly at Holy Trinity, Much Wenlock, where it defaced a carefully composed and richly ornamented west front of the early 12th century (see overleaf).

These churches were as simple in appearance as in plan, with walls 2ft. 9in. to 3ft. thick and with large areas of stonework (usually rubble) pierced (apart from the doorway) by no more than occasional small narrow windows set, with one or two possible exceptions discussed below, in no coherent pattern. Buttresses were almost wholly absent, and do not appear even in the long stretches of walling at Culmington or at Neen Savage. The most notable exception is Heath chapel, where they are in company with a string course. At Silvington there is a buttress centrally in the wall of the nave, and the

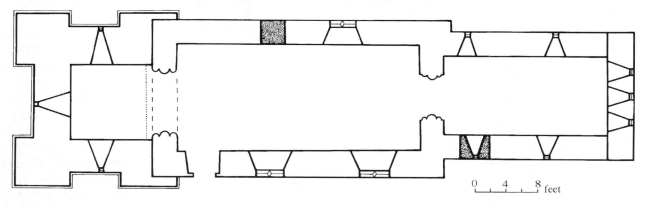

0   4   8 feet

Plan of Linley church

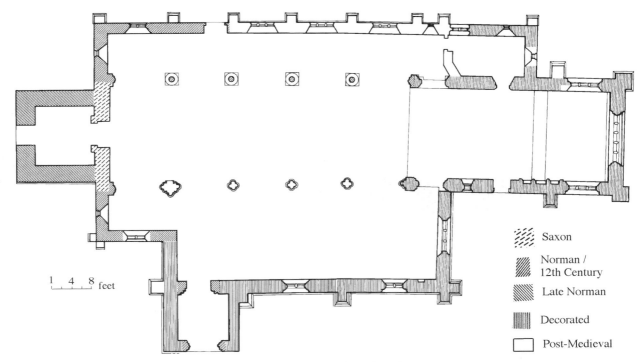

Saxon

Norman /
12th Century

Late Norman

Decorated

Post-Medieval

1 4 8 feet

Plan of Stottesdon church

0   5   10 m

*The west front of Holy Trinity, Much Wenlock,
which was obscured by the addition
of a west tower*

chancel of the now demolished church at Mainstone may have had several.[39] The flatness of the elevations is relieved, to some extent, at Edstaston by an enriched corbel table, and in the chancel at Ruyton-XI-Towns by a string course running above, and linking, the door head with the window heads. The setting of the doorway in a shallow projection[40] helps to give depth to the elevation, and some doorways of that type in Worcestershire have an attic enriched with blank arcading above, but those in Shropshire are invariably plain. An apparent exception is at Morville where there is foliage in a kind of tympanum and a band of proto-dog-tooth ornament above the door head, all beneath a straight pediment formed by strips of roll moulding. A plaque (1685) below the pediment, however, warns of later alterations: the band of ornament has been cut on either side of the 'tympanum' and the doorway has a flat head and plain jambs. While the projection itself may be regarded as late 12th-century all the rest is, like the tympanum at Stottesdon, a later make-up of pieces from destroyed original elements.

Only exeptionally—for nearly all have been altered by the later insertion of large and usually traceried windows—can one feel the effect of these elevations of almost blank walls. Good examples

*Mainstone church (rebuilt 1887) c.1790 as painted by Edw. Williams (SRRC 6001/372/3.23),
suggesting buttresses to the chancel*

are the chancels of Milson, of Upton Cressett with a tiny window in the centre of the lateral wall, and best of all, despite the buttresses and string courses,

*The interior of the crossing at Shifnal church,
looking east*

of Heath chapel. It would be timidly apprehensive to call them forbidding, but all the same they exude an air of reticence, indeed of deep mystery. It may be on that account that they have survived mostly in chancels: as Donne put it, 'Churches are best for Prayer, that have least light'. By the end of the century windows were becoming larger, and the effect, whether intended or not, was to illuminate such internal decoration as wall paintings and the occasional richly decorated arch to chancel or tower.

Larger churches

A few parish churches stood out by their very size. At Holy Trinity, Much Wenlock, the nave was slightly over 80ft. long, at Shifnal it was slightly under 80ft., and at Stottesdon nearly 70ft.; at Lydbury North the combined length of nave and chancel was 110ft.; by the mid 12th century St. Mary's, Shrewsbury, had a 70ft.-long nave and transepts too; Clun and Baschurch were over 80 ft. long. All of these were of far more than local seignorial importance in the late 11th and early 12th centuries. Holy Trinity at Much Wenlock was built by the priory there;[41] Shifnal may have been the mother church of a large parish;[42] Stottesdon was at the *caput* of the post-Conquest hundred of the same name;[43] Lydbury North was at the centre of a large episcopal manor;[44] St. Mary's, Shrewsbury, was a collegiate church in royal patronage;[45] Clun was

*Plan of
St. Mary's church,
Shrewsbury*

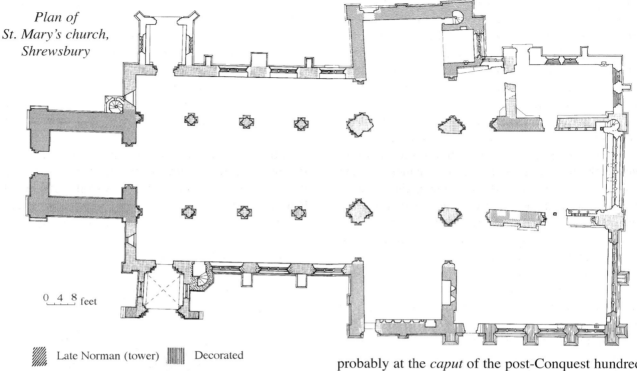

0 4 8 feet

▨	Late Norman (tower)	▥	Decorated
▧	Norman / 12th Century	▦	Perpendicular (vice)
▦	Early English	▢	Post-Medieval

The nave, St. Mary's church, Shrewsbury

probably at the *caput* of the post-Conquest hundred of Purslow;[46] and Baschurch was at the *caput* of the pre-Conquest hundred of the same name.[47]

Among these Holy Trinity was distinguished not merely by its size but also by the splendour of its early 12th-century west front, equal to anything of comparable age in the country (see p.18). That front was a symmetrical composition with a central doorway and a west window above flanked by shallow clasping buttresses rising to gable height. The gable, into the lower level of which the head of the window rises, has three diminishing tiers of round-headed blind arcading. The openings and the arcading are lavishly ornamented with chevron and zigzag motifs, and the west window has a form of egg-and-dart. In richness the front[48] is comparable with the nearly contemporary decoration upon the neighbouring chapter house at Wenlock Priory; and that is the explanation of its exceptional nature, for while it was a parish church in function, it was in ecclesiastical law and in its location a part of that wealthy Cluniac foundation. It is a manifestation of the contemporary liking for, and the ability to create, the highly ornamented west fronts seen most obviously in the 'screen façades' of some major churches.[49] The concomitant of that preference is the rarity of west towers—so common later[50]— before the latter half of the 12th century. That rarity was responsible for, or at least allowed, the presence of a round-headed window set within the central buttress of the west wall in two churches in Corve Dale, Holdgate and Tugford, and their near-neighbour, the upland Heath chapel. At Uffington the east and west walls had each a central buttress and a long lancet set within it.[51]

The most outstanding of all surviving parish churches of the period is St. Mary's, Shrewsbury. By *c*.1175 it was an impressive church on a cruciform plan with full transepts, a two-bay chancel, a long nave, and a west tower. It was perhaps the grandest parish church in the county at the time, for Holy Trinity, Much Wenlock, despite its west front, had no more than a nave and chancel, and building had barely begun at Ludlow and Shifnal. It is, however, possible that St. Mary's was challenged by its neighbours, St. Alkmund's and St. Chad's, which at the end of the Middle Ages were not far behind in size and splendour[52] and may have been so at the end of the 12th century, for they too incorporated Norman work when they were demolished in the 18th century. It is possible therefore that St. Mary's grandeur was due less to any special position that it held within the town than to the town's general importance.

Monastic foundations

By the mid 12th century the monastic foundations were into their stride and building in a manner which eclipsed almost any parish church, even though none of the county's greater churches, with the exception of Shrewsbury Abbey, was in the front rank of 12th-century buildings. The abbey, now Holy Cross parish church, was founded by Earl Roger, ever generous in endowing the Church with stolen property.[53] It was Norman policy to establish spiritual garrisons of monks throughout the land; Wulfstan, an English bishop who made his peace with the conquerors, increased the establishment at Worcester from just over 12 monks to around 50.[54] Roger seems also to have intended his abbey of St. Peter and St. Paul to reflect his quasi-palatine pre-eminence locally.

Little of the original building survives,[55] but it is clear that his church was built on a grand scale, with a nave of 120ft., with presbytery, transepts, aisles, and with triforia and clerestorys, a combination which no other medieval Shropshire church ever achieved. Begun at the end of the 11th century, it

lacks the ornament of later Norman churches and is content with simple scallop capitals and roll mouldings. The aisles were probably groin-vaulted. The piers of the arcade are round and stocky, the arches heavy and plain; superimposed upon them, equally heavy and plain, are the short piers and arches of the former triforium, originally without intermediate colonnettes.[56] The nave is without vaulting shafts or other bay divisions, and even in its present truncated state the arcade produces that impression of massive strength striding with measured tread into the distance that is the most awesome effect of Romanesque architecture. The arcade has been compared with the tall, powerful, and severely plain giant piers of the somewhat later nave at Tewkesbury (Glos.). The resemblance may not be

Drawing by E.P. Owen of Shrewsbury Abbey church, showing a pre-Victorian nave bay (SRRC 6001/198, f.451)

accidental for Roger's daughter Sybil was an important patron of Séez and both foundations were staffed by monks from that abbey.[57] The church was far from complete when Roger was buried there in 1094,[58] but it was to be an apt translation into stone of what had been his overwhelming power within the county.

The only Shropshire church to approach Shrewsbury Abbey in size was that at Buildwas, founded in 1135 as a Savigniac house by Roger de Clinton, bishop of Chester, and becoming Cistercian when the two orders merged in 1147.[59] Construction in stone probably did not begin for several years after that,[60] and when it did it was conformist rather than innovative, following the common Cistercian plan of a generation earlier.[61] There was a fully

aisled nave, transepts with square-ended eastern chapels, a square-ended vaulted presbytery, and a low tower scarcely rising above the roof levels of the limbs, similar to that at Kirkstall (Yorks. W.R.), and perhaps conceived as a structural expedient, providing a convenient abutment for the roofs of nave, chancel, and transepts, rather than as a bell tower.[62] The transept chapels had ribbed vaults in an up-to-date style but were backward in form by comparison with those at Byland (Yorks. N.R.) and Roche (Yorks. W.R.), retaining solid dividing walls between them. In contrast with many Cistercian churches, building was prolonged and it is likely that the nave was not completed much before the end of the century. It has no triforium and, with a nave broader in relation to the aisles than in most

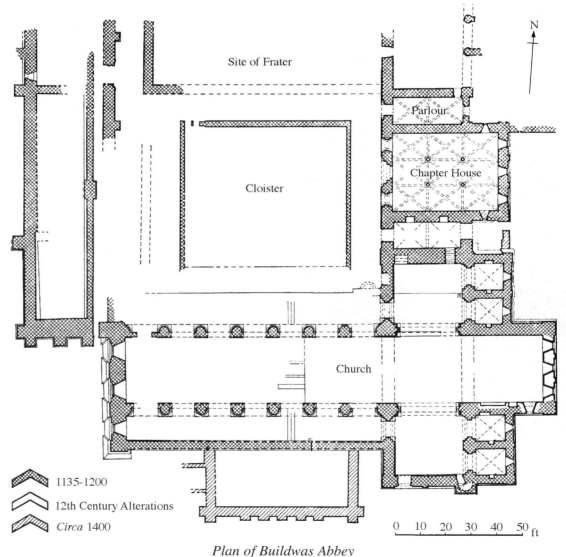

Site of Frater

Parlour

Chapter House

Cloister

Church

N

1135-1200

12th Century Alterations

Circa 1400

0 10 20 30 40 50 ft

Plan of Buildwas Abbey

large churches of the time, is of low proportions.[63] An apt contrast has been made between its 'intimacy' and the 'calculated authority' of the northern Cistercian churches.[64] The nave is noticeably less austere than anything to the east; the clerestory openings have floriated nook shafts, the piers have water-holding bases and angle spurs, and the exterior of the west wall has decoration of rosettes and a form of geometrical interlace. Two very long large windows there were flanked by smaller ones in the aisles and must have made a very impressive west front. The exterior of the chapter house is plain, with the usual tripartite arrangement, but the interior is well on the way to Gothic: four slender piers, alternately round and octagonal, with capitals ornamented in a very flat style and carrying ribbed vaulting, create a light and airy effect. The date is probably very late in the 12th century.

The very much earlier dating proposed by Fergusson[65] seems to be based on misunderstandings. The claim that either the shafts of the crossing piers are later additions or (for the wording is ambiguous) that the piers have been wholly rebuilt

is untenable either way. First, some of the shafts are cut from the same stones that form the faces of the north and south walls of the presbytery; and, secondly, there is no sign of any change in, or disturbance of, the masonry of those walls. Furthermore it is not true that the chapter-house vault webs are 'cut ashlar rather than rubble fill'; they are rubble. Again the implication that angle spurs and water-holding bases occur in only the two easternmost bays of the nave is untrue; they occur in nearly all the nave bays. The evidence for a raising of the presbytery walls by 8 to 10 courses is tenuous; and there is no evidence for a former barrel vault there, apart from what may or may not be deduced from the thickness of the north and south walls. In addition, the highly individual doorways that occur at both Buildwas and Lilleshall[66] must make any attempt to date the one without considering the other very dubious.

Smaller and less ambitious than Buildwas were the late 12th-century churches of Augustinian canons at Haughmond and Lilleshall. The community at Haughmond existed by c.1130,[67] but its first church was built to a very small scale and was wholly rebuilt in the late 12th century.[68] Its second church and that at Lilleshall were very similar: each

The chapter house at Buildwas Abbey,
looking north-east

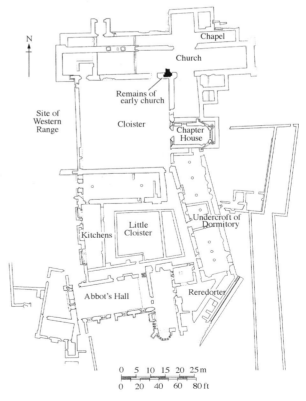

Plan of Haughmond Abbey

with a long narrow aisleless nave, a square-ended presbytery, square-ended eastern chapels in echelon to the transepts, and perhaps a low central tower. Both have early and late Cistercian elements in their plans: an aisleless nave on the one hand, as at the first church at Tintern (Mon.) and at Waverley (Surrey), and full transepts and eastern chapels on the other, as at Byland (Yorks. N.R.) and Roche (Yorks. W.R.). That was, of course, less a deliberate intent than a practical and temporary convenience, for Haughmond's nave acquired a north aisle in the 13th century, and the arch at the east end of the nave at Lilleshall suggests that an intention to build an aisle was abandoned. Apart from the ornate doorway to the cloister at the west end of the nave very little of the church at Haughmond remains above ground. The grandest survival there from the 12th century is the façade of the chapter house.[69]

Lilleshall Abbey church, which was begun some time after 1148,[70] is the only Shropshire church which may have had a vaulted nave by c.1200. The presbytery was meant from the start to be vaulted, but apparently at a low level, for the placing of the springers is incompatible with the present upper tier of windows, and those windows are out of register with the lower tier and on the exterior they have different surrounds. The present height of the presbytery, therefore, belongs to a secondary phase and was perhaps a consequence of the later decision to vault the nave at a higher level. The east front originally had two superimposed tiers of round-headed windows and the east chapels of the transepts were rib-vaulted.

In the easternmost bay of the south wall of the nave there is, as at Haughmond, a processional doorway from the cloister, richly decorated with

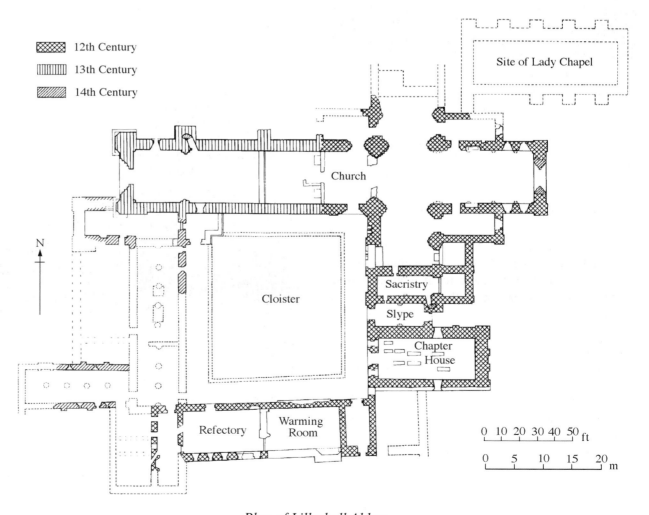

Plan of Lilleshall Abbey

The richly decorated processional doorway from the cloister to the nave of the abbey church at Lilleshall

believe if there were any evidence elsewhere in the nave of such deliberate archaism, but there is not; and Romanesque elements occur only in the westernmost bay and, to anticipate the 13th-century story, in the form of a semicircular arch to the doorway of the west front: in positions, that is, where they could play the smallest possible role in wedding the new work to work at the east. And the west doorway is within a wholly Gothic context of Gothic mouldings to the orders of the arch, of stiff-leaf capitals, of stiff-leaf ornament to the hood mould, and of now vanished hood-mould stops in the form of outward-leaning human demi-figures. Furthermore above the level of the doorway the flanking projections of the west front have arcades of pointed cusped arches which originally flanked a great west window with shafted lancets. The builder of a 13th-century west front did not usually disfigure his design for the sake of a far away and almost invisible eastern end, and in the circum-

Lilleshall Abbey church, showing Transitional vaulting shafts in the north wall of the nave

motifs that are unlikely to be earlier than the last quarter of the 12th century.[71] Breaks in the masonry show that there was a pause in construction after the building of that bay, and the nave did not receive its present west front until well into the 13th century. The surviving clerestory opening in the easternmost bay of the north wall has multiple shafts and moulded caps and is of clear 13th-century origin, but it does not date the nave for it is an insertion, partly within an earlier 12th-century arch. The intention from the beginning was presumably to vault the nave, for the vaulting shafts appear to be part of the original masonry, and those in the westernmost bay have odd trumpet-like capitals of Transitional character at the latest.[72] Twelfth-century vaulted naves, however, are rare in England and to be found in only the grandest churches, and it is the accepted view that the whole of the nave, apart from the easternmost bay, is of early to mid 13th-century date and was purposely given something of a Romanesque air in order to marry it with the earlier easternmost bay of the nave and with the presbytery and transepts. That might be easier to stances it is worth asking whether there may not be a more plausible explanation of the incongruity of that doorway. Whether the nave was in fact vaulted before *c.*1200, or not until the time of the present opening in the easternmost bay, the height of any vault had already been determined by the vaulting shafts of the earlier builders who thus unwittingly created a dilemma for their successors. The latter apparently wanted both a tall and wide west doorway and a tall west window in the prevailing style, and not having the necessary vertical space within the limits imposed upon them to achieve both, had to compromise by reviving an old-fashioned form in order to get the apex of their magnificent west doorway low enough to allow their equally grand west window sufficient height.[73]

In its use of Romanesque arches within a Gothic context Lilleshall was not unique in Shropshire, for in St. Mary's, Shrewsbury, semicircular arches appeared, when aisles were added in the early 13th century within a similar context of slender arcade piers and stiff-leaf foliage; and in St. Mary's there can be no question of attempting to preserve a Romanesque aura, for the late 12th-century west tower there had been given a tall two-centred opening to the nave a generation earlier. But St. Mary's had a problem similar to Lilleshall's for, as the masonry shows, the north and south walls of the nave were, until their raising to accommodate the early 13th-century reconstruction of the crossing, very low and quite unable to accommodate an arcade with two-centred arches of reasonable proportions. It may be suggested that at Lilleshall and St. Mary's similar problems produced similar solutions; and the more readily because it is clear that the masons who worked at Lilleshall in the late 12th century worked at St. Mary's too.[74] Perhaps it is not fanciful to suppose that, whether or not the canons of Lilleshall had achieved a vaulted nave by the end of the 12th century, they had seriously intended one. In that they may have been influenced by the example of Worcester: the nave vault there was begun *c.*1180, and the cathedral had a great influence upon the architecture of western England in the late 12th century.[75]

The other 12th-century monastic churches were small: the priories of Bromfield and White Ladies and the original church at Haughmond. Each is, or was, cruciform, with an aisleless nave of moderate length and a square-ended chancel, and with north and south arms which lack eastern chapels and are in fact more like porticuses than transepts.[76] Bromfield was built in the early 12th century, the earlier church at Haughmond was completed in the mid century,[77] and White Ladies church probably not much before 1200.[78]

To these must be added the chapter house at Wenlock Priory, perhaps of *c.*1150.[79] Wenlock was the only monastic foundation with a long history behind it, and the church was probably almost wholly rebuilt in the years after the Conquest, when what had been a Saxon minster was transformed into a Cluniac priory. Of that rebuilding only the chapter house survives: as richly decorated externally as the one at Haughmond and equally richly internally.

Despite their different origins there is something of a family likeness among the mid to late 12th-century monastic churches in the county. Of course much of this consists of elements common to many churches in many parts of the country, such as the decoration lavished upon doorways at Haughmond and Lilleshall, the plans of the east ends at those two and Buildwas, and the superimposed tiers of windows in the east ends of Lilleshall and Buildwas. But there are other features which are not so widespread and are found at Cistercian Buildwas, at Augustinian Lilleshall, and at Benedictine Bromfield. One of these is a predilection for low buildings, seen in the original low vault of the presbytery at Lilleshall, in the absence of a triforium storey at Buildwas and Lilleshall, and in the absence of both triforium and clerestory at Bromfield. There is no record of the height of Haughmond or of White Ladies, but their small size makes it unlikely that they were tall. All these were built by men of lesser standing than Roger of Montgomery and without the resources which financed his munificence at Shrewsbury, but it was these which were typical of the greater churches in Shropshire. And they marked the path for the future, for Shrewsbury Abbey was an aberration in the history of architecture in the county, a church as magnificent as almost anything else in the country at the time. In the absence of a bishop's seat, or of a shrine with a wide repute, and with no magnate ever again approaching the power and wealth of Earl Roger, no other building, with the possible exception of the 13th-century Wenlock Priory church, was of national importance, or at any rate has been recognized as such.

At Buildwas and Lilleshall, built at very much the same time, there is a highly individual type of doorway in which the normal straight lintel is replaced by a lintel formed as a shallow segmental arch, within the main semicircular arch. The most striking example is the processional doorway from cloister to nave at Lilleshall, with enriched orders above the opening;[80] but the form occurs with a plain tympanum above the lintel on several claustral doorways there. It also occurs at Buildwas: on the doorway from the north transept to the slype, on the doorway from the cloister to the room or passage that runs under the north end of the north transept, and on the doorways to the two rooms to the north of the chapter house. It is found too on the west doorway of the west tower that was added to St. Mary's, Shrewsbury, probably in the third quarter of the century, and on the south doorways of nave and chancel at Ruyton-XI-Towns, founded within the lee of a castle of the Stranges.[81]

Some general conclusions may be drawn from all this, and they will be discussed later. A particular conclusion may be mentioned here: it is that the very late date of the processional doorway at Lilleshall (no earlier than the last quarter of the 12th century) must throw doubt upon any attempt to put into the 1150s or 1160s those parts of Buildwas that are later than the north transept or slype. That probably applies to the nave and must apply to the chapter house.

Wholly different from every church discussed so far is St. Mary Magdalen's chapel in the inner bailey of Ludlow Castle, built in the mid 12th century with a round nave and a chancel (demolished in the later 16th century) with a semi-octagonal apse.[82] The nave is without the aisles found in many round churches and was originally lit only by three tall round-headed windows in the upper part of the wall. There is nothing to show that the building originally had an upper floor and, since it is likely that there was a private chapel elsewhere within the enceinte, it seems that this was not a *Doppelkappelle* in the manner (for example) of that of Aachen or, nearer in

The blind arcading in the nave of the round chapel in the bailey of Ludlow Castle, with one of the original three windows above

space and time, Bishop Losinga's chapel at Hereford.[83] The Ludlow chapel is richly decorated with billet and zigzag ornament above the openings, with scallop capitals to the nook shafts, and with blind arcading internally on the ground floor. It probably served as the castle's garrison church. On the other hand it has all the wealth of ornament of a great monastic church. In form it resembled neither type. Round churches of the 12th century, modelled on the church of the Holy Sepulchre in Jerusalem, were a product of the military adventure of the Crusades. They were much favoured by the Knights of the Temple, and it may have been felt that this was the proper form for a free-standing church within a military complex.

Architectural ornament

Although they lagged behind many of their compatriots in size, the major churches of mid and late 12th-century Shropshire were equal to those anywhere in the richness of ornament on selected pieces. After the church the chapter house was the most highly regarded part of a monastery, and, since Cluniac houses had no bias to austerity and Wenlock was the county's richest foundation[84] and had rebuilt its church just before or just after the Conquest,[85] it is not surprising that the mid or late 12th-century chapter house there and the west front of Holy Trinity are the supreme examples of Norman decoration in Shropshire. The north and

The three-tiered intersecting arcading in the chapter house at Wenlock Priory

south walls of the chapter house are covered with three tiers of intersecting arcading, the lowest set on shafts with enriched capitals and having an inner order with zigzag and lozenge motifs.[86] The late 12th-century lavatorium in a different style, unparalleled elsewhere in the county, has well modelled biblical scenes in high relief beneath a frieze of naturalistic foliage. At Haughmond too the chapter-house entrance is ornate, with three stepped round-headed arches, each with three orders with plain shafts and enriched capitals.[87] Haughmond also has a processional doorway with three orders, the shafts with enriched capitals and a hood mould with deeply undercut ornament.[88] At Lilleshall another processional doorway has shafts covered with barley-sugar, lozenge, and zigzag ornament.[89] At Buildwas, as befitted a Cistercian house, there is little applied decoration. In the crossing and chapter house there are capitals with leaf ornament and the nook shafts of the windows in the nave clerestory have moulded bases and floriated capitals.[90] The slender piers that carry the chapter-house vaulting, however, have a highly decorative effect.

Differences between the decoration on smaller and greater churches are mostly, but not wholly, of degree. Both of course use the common motifs of the time, such as beakhead, chevron, and lozenge ornament and billet and reel mouldings; and in both there are examples of heavily concentrated ornament. Nevertheless, while the monastic churches are not more richly ornamented in proportion to their size than parish churches, their individual examples are grander. Apart from those at Edstaston none of the lavish doorways or chancel arches in small churches can compete in splendour with the triple-arched entrance to Haughmond chapter house or with the elaboration of the processional doorway at Lilleshall. While several small churches, of which Linley is perhaps the best example, have tympana ornamented with a diaper pattern, Wenlock chapter house has the walls covered with the far more elaborate intersecting arcading, a motif which also appears on Ludlow Castle chapel, a small building but one erected for the occupants of a major fortification and not for a parish congregation or a local lord. As was seen earlier, the one parish church in the county which surpassed any monastic foundation in the glory of its west front was Holy Trinity, Much Wenlock, and that, like Ludlow Castle chapel,

The late 12th-century lavatorium at Wenlock Priory
with biblical scenes set below a frieze of naturalistic foliage

The triple-arched entrance to the chapter house at Haughmond Abbey

was not the product of local parochial wealth. The first was the creation of a prestigious monastic institution, the second of an important secular power.[91]

It will be noticed that the very distinctive doorways mentioned earlier are confined to the monastic houses of Buildwas and Lilleshall, to an urban collegiate church which was also a royal free chapel (St. Mary's, Shrewsbury), and to a church (Ruyton-XI-Towns) built at the seat of a family—the Stranges—second in importance only to the FitzAlans and the Corbets. None of the examples is closely dated and it is impossible to say which is the earliest. There is also a very distinctive motif which Pevsner has aptly described as 'a chain of crocus-like blossoms'.[92] It is found above the south doorway of Halford chapel, dependent upon Bromfield Priory (which itself belonged to Gloucester Abbey from 1155);[93] above the doorway of the chapter house at Haughmond; above the tower arch of Munslow church at the new hundred *caput*; above the south doorway of the chancel at Neen Savage, which was given to Wigmore Abbey c.1179 by Hugh de Mortimer;[94] upon the most elaborate doorways of any parish church in Shropshire at Edstaston, where it is in conjunction with dog-tooth ornament;[95] and upon the inner doorway of the south porch at St. Mary's, Shrewsbury. Again there is little solid reason for picking upon any one as the earliest, although it is probable that that at St. Mary's, which cannot be earlier than the south aisle there, is the latest. Again the motif is confined to important churches or to churches associated with important men or institutions.[96] Of course there were many such churches in Shropshire, and there was a good chance that any element which appeared only a few times would do so exclusively upon them; nevertheless the bias is clear.

What appears odd is that these 'local' motifs are restricted to churches which are not only important or well connected but also have far-flung aesthetic associations. Buildwas, for example, belonged to an international order, was built to an internationally standard plan, had elements in common with faraway churches in Yorkshire and Ireland, and details have been variously described as 'Anglo-Norman', 'Burgundian', and 'French'; at the same time it shared localized elements with other churches in the county, both parish churches and those belonging to another order.[97] The same was

true of Lilleshall and Haughmond, and there were among the greater churches local likenesses within the wider architectural context. In contrast the ornament in local churches had no 'local' character and was restricted to the run-of-the-mill motifs of the age. This is probably less the result of differences of taste among different levels of the church-building classes than of the greater ability of rich men and institutions to employ the best craftsmen; and the best craftsmen were those most likely to have ideas of their own to express.

Sculpture

Among those other bearers of ornament, fonts, the difference between greater and lesser churches is not so clear, partly because the greatest churches do not come into the reckoning and partly because a font was a fitting rather than a part of the structure and an expensive one might well be provided by a local benefactor of no great wealth. Nevertheless, although the important church of Morville and the local chapel of Linley had very similar fonts, it was in an important church like Stottesdon that the most

The font at Linley church

The font at Sidbury church

and various linear patterns below. Upton Cressett's has arcading with plain piers with exaggerated caps and bases and with the space above filled with incised lines radiating from the tops of the piers. The upper part of the bowl at Sidbury was covered with thick tendrils with occasional knots and foliage; the lower had intersecting arcading with the two orders of the arches decorated with pellets and giving a double-ribbon appearance.

The best known Norman font in Shropshire is that at Stottesdon, which has long been recognized as a work of the 'Herefordshire' school.[99] It has many of the motifs of that school as described by Professor Zarnecki, and its most prominent element, a chain of medallions enclosing figures, is almost identical with the left side of the outermost order of the south doorway at Kilpeck (Herefs.). There is, however, a difference. At both churches the medallions are joined by links. At Kilpeck the links are perhaps best described as a pair of scissors or shears, points upward and with very prominent 'handles' at the base, the whole flanked by what look like wire bands around the rims of the medallions. At Stottesdon the motif has been simplified, coarsened, and turned upside down so that the

accomplished appeared. Many fonts were plain bowls, or often with no more than a cable mould at top or bottom, but others were decorated in a variety of ways. On the fonts at Linley and Morville rosettes formed by bands of pellet ornament enclose foliage and geometrical designs. Edgmond's font has a profusion of billet and zigzag ornament. Holdgate's has interlace, rosettes, thick tendrils, and foliage; it has a short stem with chevron ornament and stands on a spur base. At Claverley, at St. Michael's, Lilleshall, at Upton Cressett, and formerly at Sidbury the fonts have blind arcading[98] but of very different kinds. On the Claverley font the piers of the arcading are ornamented with chevrons and look like attenuated arches, and the spandrels are filled with thin foliage. The font at Lilleshall has a deep band of fluting at the top, a band of arcading and other ornament in the middle,

The font at Stottesdon church

'handles' look like large eyes and prominent eyebrows and the stem like a long nose. At Morville, with similar medallions, the links have become square plaques, with the Stottesdon motif turned into a stylized human face; at Linley the faces have become less stylized. These are interesting, along with Anglo-Saxon coins and the later works of the Burton alabasterers, as examples of the 'degeneration' of an oft-copied motif, but what is significant is that it is the 'upside down' motif of Stottesdon, and not the original one at Kilpeck, that has been copied at Morville and rendered more naturalistic at Linley. The Kilpeck artist also may have intended a stylized human face but, absent-mindedly, carved it the wrong way round, so that when fitted into place it was upside down. But all the other faces, human or animal, on the south door at Kilpeck and on the corbel table there, and those at Morville and Stottesdon, have eyes with large pupils, while the 'handles' of the 'scissors' at Kilpeck are left plain. In view of the sheila-na-gig on the corbel table there and what may be a green man on the jamb of the south doorway it is possible that this is another fertility symbol, a phallus.[100] If so, the inversion at Morville and Stottesdon may be an early Bowdlerization.[101]

Figure sculpture was rare and ranged from the naive to the sophisticated. The former may be dealt with first, for it allows less room for argument about which far distant sources it was derived from. The lintel over the west doorway at Stottesdon was mentioned earlier.[102] Its ability is negligible and its iconography, if any, unexplained. Slightly less naive are the human faces on the font at Berrington, accompanied by an ungainly quadruped with thick legs, probably a heffalump. At a not much higher level are most of the faces on the fonts at Linley and Morville. The figure in the tympanum of the north doorway at Linley, perhaps a green man, reveals no great skill in delineating the human form, but its lively combination of an enormous child's head, wide eyes, and large ears with a very resolute frontal stance was clearly capable of keeping any evil influence at bay. None of these is easily dateable, but the tympanum at Linley may be presumed to be coeval with the church itself, and probably of the early 12th century.

The earliest survivals of more sophisticated work are the tympanum above the north doorway at

The font at Berrington church

Uppington and the inserted lintel above the later doorway in the south wall of the chapter house at Wenlock. Uppington has a dragon in a flat *Ringerike*-derived style biting a long and elaborately twisted tail; it is probably late Saxon work.[103] The lintel at Wenlock is in a more plastic manner. It has two addorsed beasts with pellet ornament along their flanks and, centrally, a realistic lion or leopard head. Since the piece has no integral connection with the decoration on the chapter house, nor even necessarily with the priory, it cannot be dated from

Tympanum with zigzag marking over the south door at Linley church

Possible green man in the tympanum over the blocked door on north side of Linley church

its location.[104] The head in the centre has some affinity with two heads on the fonts at Linley and Morville—very different from the stylized ones

Soldier or forester figure of the Herefordshire school of Romanesque sculpture at the Old Bell House, Alveley

mentioned earlier—and the whole may be another local derivative of the 'Herefordshire' school, perhaps of the mid 12th century.

More certain works of that school are the pieces of sculpture, dated by Professor Zarnecki to *c*.1130–60,[105] now built into the walls of the Old Bell House at Alveley but doubtless originally in a nearby church[106] or chapel.[107] They are of a high standard and include such 'Herefordshire' motifs as a trousered figure amidst tendrils, Samson bestriding the Lion, probably St. Michael and the Serpent,[108] small figures set beneath round-headed arches, dragons strangled by their own tails, and interlace. There is also an engaged colonnette and capital. These are clearly fragments of what was a very large and complex scheme and, as the most important known 'Herefordshire' work in the county, doubtless came from a generously patron-ized church[109] or chapel.[110] The sculptors must have spent a long time in the area and their *oeuvre* may have included many works that have not survived. It may be therefore that the figures at Alveley and the fonts at Stottesdon, Morville, and Linley came from a workshop active in south-east Shropshire in the

The tympanum over the south door of Aston Eyre church

mid 12th century, its craftsmen becoming in time less and less like their Kilpeck progenitors. Further examples of their work, or of the influence of their work upon other men, may be the fonts at Holdgate and Sidbury with their Kilpeck-derived motifs, and perhaps that at Upton Cressett, linked in one way to Morville by its overall background of incised lines.

The best known of 12th-century sculptures in Shropshire are the tympanum at Aston Eyre and the figures on the lavatorium at Wenlock Priory. The first has been claimed as a work of the 'Herefordshire' school, but it is not.[111] The subject is Christ's entry into Jerusalem, and in contrast with the energy and aggression of the 'Herefordshire' figures this has an air of unhurried calm, from Christ raising his hand in blessing to the disciple spreading branches on the ground and to the ass planted four-square and clearly intending to move only when he chooses. The figures are stocky, the faces broad, and

the execution is realistic and competent in a bold and simple manner which is yet far from unsophisticated. The church is probably late 12th-century,[112] but that need not date the sculpture, for there are some reasons for thinking that it is not *in situ*. In contrast with nearly every other piece of sculpture of the time it has no accompanying ornament at all, not even the surround, with cable mould at the base, of Stretton Sugwas (Herefs.). The slab does not fit the space, and at the top and on the right side gaps have been filled with cement. Pevsner noted that the capitals of the columns flanking the doorway appear to be later insertions of modern date; if so they were perhaps introduced when the upper stonework had been dismantled in order to manoeuvre the slab into its present position.[113]

The figures on the lavatorium at Wenlock — Christ walking on the water and a standing and a seated apostle beneath blind arcading (see p.29) —

are squat and have very large heads. They have been dated *c*.1190 and related, presumably for their architectural setting, to faraway early fonts at Southrop (Glos.) and Stanton Fitzwarren (Wilts.).[114] The foliage on them is different from that of those two and has some affinity with the palm leaves at Aston Eyre,[115] and the motifs in the frieze above the 'walking on the water' scene have a distant affinity with the 'scissors' and 'wire bands' of the south doorway at Kilpeck. The stance of the figures differs from that of any of the examples discussed above, and in place of the energy of the 'Herefordshire' scenes and the fulfilled calm of Aston Eyre they have a solid self-assurance, the Church Militant and that 'great Church victorious' of the earlier pieces becoming 'the Church at rest'.

Twelfth-century sculpture in Shropshire was extremely heterogeneous, and in several ways. Sophisticated and naive work existed side by side, for example the figure on the north doorway at Linley and the rosettes on the font there. Work of varying skill and style may be found upon the same piece as on the font at Morville, where the difference between the rosettes and the links between them is astounding. Different styles were current at much the same time upon the same building; the fragment of a figure recently excavated at Much Wenlock and dated *c*.1130, is wholly different in style from the contemporary chapter house and has been compared with sculpture in the chapter house at Durham and with the drawings in the St. Alban's psalter.[116] The county is not peculiar in this. Three different styles, or at any rate three craftsmen with very different methods, have been identified at Kilpeck itself,[117] and in the Evesham neighbourhood the difference between the tympana at Beckford (Glos.) and Rous Lench (Worcs.) is greater than any contrast in Shropshire. Nevertheless the differences occur in more ways here and often in close proximity.

Amid all the diversity two strands may be picked out. There was a group of sculptors working in a 'Herefordshire' style in the south-east of the county—as far as survivals show—and upon important churches. There was also a number of less skilled, presumably home-bred, craftsmen working mainly in minor churches and on less ambitious projects. They were able to absorb indirectly from Alveley or Stottesdon some of the 'Herefordshire'

motifs and were occasionally employed—so we must infer from the Linley and Morville fonts—upon work that 'Herefordshire' men had left unfinished. Their creations may be seen in the figures above the north doorways at Linley and Church Stretton, on the 'Tree of Life' at High Ercall,[118] on the font at Berrington, on the pieces linking the rosettes at Linley and Morville, and upon such fonts as those at Sidbury and Upton Cressett. It is possible, too, that the tympanum at Aston Eyre is a local work, in style more homely and in skill less assured than the 'Herefordshire' and Much Wenlock figures. Admittedly there is nothing else in the county to compare it with, but then there is nothing similar in any neighbouring county; and the only claims that have ever been made for an alien origin are based upon a misreading of Professor Zarnecki.

The character of Shropshire churches

The Norman period, or at least the mid to late 12th century, saw a great amount of ecclesiastical building in Shropshire, but nearly all of it of secondary importance individually: from monastic structures generally without aisles or, if aisled, without triforia or galleries, to parish churches and chapels, nearly all of them small and very many built as simple boxes. But that was not a necessary aspect of the architecture of the county, for up to about the mid 12th century it was, as far as surviving remains can tell us, the equal of most of its fellows in the quality of its churches. Stanton Lacy, even at the end of the 11th century, was larger than most parish churches in England; Wenlock Priory church of the mid 11th century onwards was, to judge by its foundations, a major building by contemporary standards; and so too was Shrewsbury Abbey of the late 11th and early 12th centuries, 'one of the great churches of the Benedictine supremacy'.[119] In the late 12th century, however, not a church was built that was in the first rank. At a lower level of monastic building Bromfield was built in the early 12th century to a form that was both sufficient and modern; in the middle years that form at the first Haughmond was not hopelessly retarded; at the end of the century at White Ladies church it was all that a poor nunnery could afford.

That one small house should build an out-of-date church is not of any great moment in itself, but it draws attention to the most important shortcoming of 12th-century architecture in Shropshire: it did not fail to develop, nor yet to follow current modes, but it did fail to keep up with the scale of changes elsewhere. It is tempting to ascribe this phenomenon to remoteness and backwardness, but that cannot be the whole answer for many of the churches were built by, or for, churchmen who were not even insular, still less provincial, in their outlook. It is probable that the greatest role was played by that slower pace of economic development in the north and west as compared with the south and east that characterized English history from about the Conquest to at least the end of the 17th century. But there were other more local and more particular forces at work too. Once Earl Roger's heirs had

gone there was no dominant family with power and possessions in the county equal to his to endow a favourite foundation. The FitzAlans and their vassals the Stranges to some extent stepped into his shoes, and the former made Haughmond almost their family monastery, but even the FitzAlans never came near to Roger's overwhelming, almost 'palatine', importance. Furthermore there was no richly endowed cathedral or minster ready to take part in the architectural competition between sees that was beginning in the late 12th century. And, although there was land for monastic institutions to exploit in 12th-century Shropshire, there were no opportunities equal to those presented to the Cistercians in the recently devastated North.

III The 13th Century: Church Improvement and Extension

Monastic churches

Between *c*.1050 and *c*.1200 all five of what were to be the major monasteries in the county had their churches built or rebuilt, or both built and rebuilt; and so too had those minor houses of which anything is known. The amount of monastic church building in the 13th century was much less, and at Much Wenlock alone was a major rebuilding carried out.

The only new foundations of any importance,[1] with much surviving above ground, were the priories of Alberbury and Chirbury. Alberbury, founded by Fulk Fitz Warin (III) as an Arrouaisian priory subject to Lilleshall, was soon transferred to the Grandmontine order. The burial of Fulk's first wife in the priory in 1226 confirms that at least part of the church had been built by then. Work probably began between 1221 and 1226,[2] and excavations in 1925 revealed a simple rectangular church with an aisleless nave, a square-ended chancel, and overall dimensions of approximately 109 x 22ft. Grandmontine houses ran very strictly to pattern and the deviations at Alberbury—the square-ended chancel and unvaulted nave—suggest that the church was built before the transfer to Grandmont.[3] The south doorway from the church to the cloister, part of an unvaulted nave, and three vaulted bays of a chapel to the north are the only standing remains, mostly hidden within the modern farmhouse known as White Abbey. The stiff-leaf capitals of the shafts flanking the doorway and the broad ribs of the vaulting, with heavy bosses at the intersections, confirm the date which the documents propose.

At Chirbury the only remains are the nave of the church and the base of a column which was probably in the chapter house. The column is early 13th-century, richly moulded with multiple shafts, and its character suggests that the chapter house at least was of some splendour. The nave too is probably

13th-century, and, even if the body is not, the aisles certainly are (see overleaf). Since the nave was parochial[4] it will be discussed among the parish churches.

At Haughmond the bases of the jambs of the north porch and of three piers of the arcade of the north aisle remain from the 13th century. They are quatrelobe in plan, with broad fillets and water-holding bases, and of the early years of the century. The aisle was probably added at the same time as the cloister, almost immediately after the late 12th-century rebuilding of the church.[5] Of much more importance is the work at Lilleshall, but that, as the belated completion of the original church and the response to a problem bequeathed by the 12th-century builders, was discussed in the previous chapter.[6]

The builders of Wenlock Priory church had no such problem, for they were not completing an older structure but ruthlessly sweeping away all earlier work to produce the largest and grandest church in the county, with an imposing west front, a long aisled and vaulted nave of three stages, a crossing with a central tower, aisled transepts, a long aisled choir, and (probably slightly later) a Lady chapel. A length of 350ft. was half as long again as Shrewsbury and Lilleshall, twice as long as Buildwas and Haughmond, and three times as long as little Alberbury. By comparison with such West Country predecessors or contemporaries as Abbey Dore (Herefs.), Glastonbury (Som.), Pershore (Worcs.), Worcester, and Wells (Som.), Wenlock is plain for it is without the enriched arch mouldings, elaborate triforia, and profusion and variety of foliage ornament on the capitals that are found together or singly at those churches. The bay design is still slightly Romanesque in feeling: the piers are sturdy, less height is allotted to the clerestory and

Chirbury church as painted by Edw. Williams (SRRC 6001/372/3.60)

more to the triforium than had become the advanced practice by the second quarter of the 13th century, there is more solid and less void in the clerestory, and little of the light and height of the choirs of Worcester and Pershore of the 1220s. Nevertheless it is clear that building progressed from east to west and that changes occurred in the course of it. In the north transept (and in the north-ernmost bay of the south transept) the clerestory has more prominence than in the earlier south transept, and the westernmost bays of the nave are fully developed with two large lights in the clerestory. A conversion, or at any rate a nod, to Gothic methods of construction may be seen in the contrast between the shallow clasping buttresses of the earlier north transept and the deep projection of those in the south wall of the nave.

The priory church has two very unusual features. In the three westernmost bays of the south aisle of the nave a vaulted chamber with two-light windows with plate tracery was contrived within the triforium space. It was probably intended as a chapel of St. Michael,[7] perhaps for the prior's use, since it had no access from the church but was reached by a doorway from the first floor of the west range. As a consequence of the rebuilding of the south transept the library (or sacristy) was displaced from the usual site between the south wall of the south transept and the chapter house and instead, since the retention of the older chapter house left no room for it else-where, was set parallel with the transept and between it and the east walk of the cloister so that there that walk shares no part of its wall with a transept—an arrangement almost without parallel elsewhere.[8]

By the second half of the 13th century Wenlock outclassed all other monastic churches in the county. It was new; it was much the biggest; it was the only church with aisled transepts; apart from Shrewsbury Abbey it was the only church known to have had a three-stage nave; and apart from Lilleshall Abbey, again as far as is known, it was the only church with a vaulted nave. Anything that any of the others had it had too, and much more besides.

There was general agreement that the work at Wenlock was probably begun *c*.1200 and completed about 50 years later,[9] but recently a starting date in the 1220s has been proposed.[10] That is not impossible stylistically, but it implies, of course, that the church was considerably out-of-date when it was begun, even if it caught up with the fashions later. The view is based less upon the building than upon documents, and in particular upon the appropriation *c.*1230 of Clun Rectory to the priory fabric fund, which until then had had no endowment. In 1291 the rectory was worth £36 13s. 4d. a year. That was a large sum, but it was hardly sufficient to influence such a major decision as that to rebuild the church; and it is equally arguable that it was the decision to rebuild, and the subsequent costs, which later moved the monks to seek the appropriation. Furthermore the priory's enjoyment of the rectory was long postponed: the prior was unable to establish his title as late as 1249, and the rector then beneficed, apparently unconnected with Wenlock, did not resign until 1271, when the priory finally secured the rectory.[11] Further, it has recently been shown that the appropriation should be dated to 1230–4;[12] and that, in view of the style of the structure, makes a connection between the decision to rebuild and the appropriation much less plausible. It is thus reasonable to take the fabric evidence at its face value and to conclude that Wenlock was neither noticeably *avant garde* nor yet retarded throughout a building period that occupied all of the first half of the 13th century.

Shropshire was not peculiar in seeing a decline in the amount of monastic church building in the 13th century, but the fall there was steeper than in the country at large, where about half of all the major houses that had built or rebuilt their churches between *c.*1050 and *c.*1200 rebuilt them again, or extensively remodelled them, in the next hundred years.[13] Wenlock alone in the 13th century resembled its contemporaries elsewhere. Fashionable and impressive churches now took far more building than their predecessors had done, and in Shropshire no other foundation was, or felt, able to indulge in extensive modernization.[14] As a result the 12th-century Shropshire pattern of five great churches of comparable standing and prestige was replaced by another of one super-church pre-eminent architecturally among four others of moderate size and old-fashioned form.

To some extent the picture is distorted by the loss of some of its detail, for the six friaries founded in the 13th century[15] have almost wholly disap-

peared.[16] Some of the houses, for example Bridgnorth and Woodhouse, are known to have been small, but excavations at the Austin Friars of Ludlow have revealed a very large complex, comparable with any other in the country, having an aisled church with approximate dimensions of 100 x 50ft. for the nave and 75 x 30ft. for the chancel, together with conventual buildings on a large scale.[17] Not all of this was of 13th-century origin and the church was probably not completed before the early 14th century, but by then it was an impressive structure. Nothing survives of the Dominican friary at Shrewsbury, but documents suggest that it was on a comparable scale.[18] On the other hand the small friary at Bridgnorth, excavated in 1989,[19] was probably complete by the end of the 13th century, with only 'cosmetic' changes thereafter.[20]

Parish churches: Transepts

By the end of the 12th century a massive building and rebuilding of parish churches had been carried through, generally to a simple one- or two-cell form. Some grand and elaborate churches had appeared, but they were few and atypical. In the next century the amount of building was probably as great as in the previous one, but it was directed mainly into enlarging, extending, and improving earlier fabrics. Admittedly it is not always possible to decide whether a church has been wholly or only partly rebuilt at a particular time. The likeliest 'new' churches of the years around 1200 are Berrington, Ditton Priors, Knockin, Leebotwood, Lydham, Neen Savage, Church Preen, Stapleton, Wistanstow, and Woolstaston. Most of the effort went into the provision of transepts, aisles, long chancels, and west towers, and many simple early plans were modified into more complex forms. Neither those forms nor their constituent elements were new in the years around 1200, but it was then that they became common, and it is their relative and absolute numbers which distinguish the earlier from the later period.

St. Mary's, Shrewsbury, probably had transepts by the mid 12th century, but in that, as in much else, it seems to have been exceptional among surviving Shropshire parish churches. All the other transepts in parish churches built between the Conquest and *c.*1300 are of the years around 1200.[21] None of them was certainly built as a whole to that form.

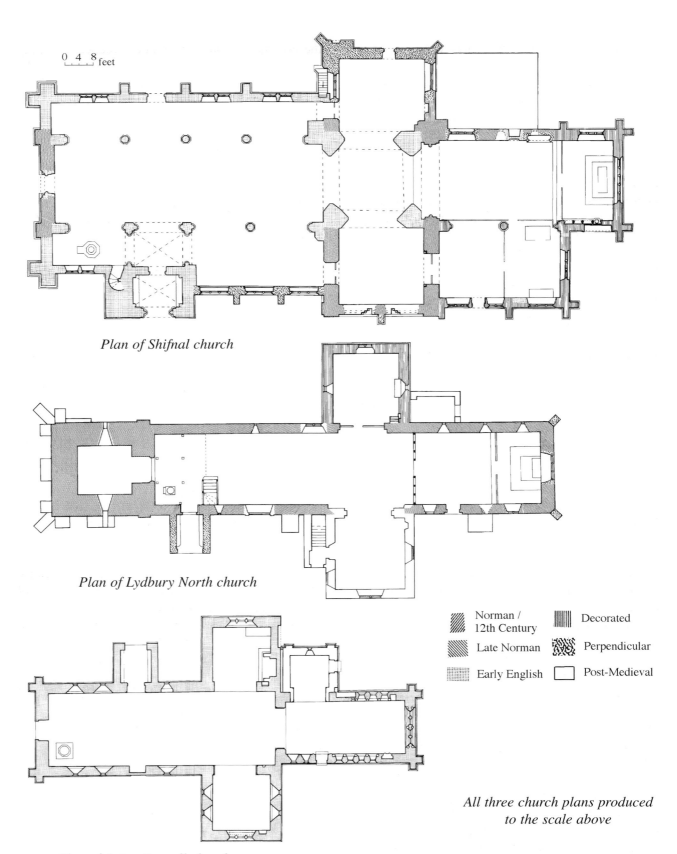

0 4 8 feet

Plan of Shifnal church

Plan of Lydbury North church

Norman /
12th Century

Late Norman

Early English

Decorated

Perpendicular

Post-Medieval

*All three church plans produced
to the scale above*

Plan of Acton Burnell church

Wistanstow has the best claim to be of one build, but even there the north transept has windows of an earlier form than the rest, has a roof of *1200-21,[22] and is wider than the nave, and it may be an addition to an earlier church, later incorporated into a general rebuild. Condover's late 12th-century north transept is all that remains of the early church, and its relationship to the rest of the structure is now indeterminable. At Shifnal the transepts are probably parts of a total rebuilding of the east end of an earlier church, and at Church Stretton and Wrockwardine they are certainly additions to earlier buildings. Much of the evidence at Ellesmere was swept away by Scott in 1849, but Cranage thought that the transepts were later than the nave,[23] and a drawing of 1788 appears to confirm his surmise for it shows that the north transept had been intruded into the easternmost of the five bays of the nave.[24] At Lydbury North the transepts seem to have been added in the 13th century, and not necessarily at the same time. At all, except perhaps the last, the cruciform plan has, nevertheless, been brought about, in the later stages of building at least, by deliberate design.

Rural churches with transepts stood out prominently from the crowd in 12th- and 13th-century Shropshire. Their architectural distinction reflected their ecclesiastical or secular importance, for all of them were of collegiate status[25] or recorded in Domesday Book as having a priest or a church[26] or as being at the *caput* of a hundred.[27] Such attributes were of course far commoner than cruciform churches, but no cruciform church has survived, or as far as is known ever appeared, where they were absent.[28]

An apparent exception is Acton Burnell, but there the cruciform character appears to be an afterthought. There is no crossing, and the transepts open out of the nave through arches off-centre to them—with returns of more than 5ft. from the openings to the east walls of the transepts but of only a few inches to the west walls. Externally, at the east end of the south wall of the nave (the north wall is obscured at that end by a modern addition), there appears to be the start of a corbel table, partly obliterated by the east wall of the transept. It seems clear that the church was originally designed, and partly built, as nave and structural chancel and that transepts were decided upon in the course of building the nave. The original design perpetuated the not uncommon 12th-century practice of setting the outer face of the chancel wall in line with the inner face of the nave wall. The church was built, or refurbished with added transepts, by Robert Burnell, bishop of Bath and Wells and chancellor of England, and its form, along with the lavish ornament of the chancel, reflects his importance.

Parish churches: Aisles

Aisles, by contrast, were provided in many churches in the late 12th and early 13th centuries, but few non-monastic churches can confidently be shown to have had them before then. At Claverley, as at West Felton, the north aisle is probably part of an early 12th-century build.[29] At Ellesmere the one surviving pier of the former north arcade[30] has a very plain capital and abacus and, since a drawing of 1788 shows the arcade to have been intruded upon by the north transept of *c*.1200, it is likely that there too the aisle was part of an early 12th-century church. They were appearing more often in the later 12th century and by the early 13th were becoming common, giving the carvers opportunities to show their skills with motifs ranging from the scallops and the flat foliage upon the capitals at Stottesdon to the stiff leaf at St. Mary's, Shrewsbury. By *c*.1200 aisles had been added at Alveley, Clun, Kinlet, Morville, Shawbury, and probably at Chelmarsh.[31] Within the next generation they also appeared at Aston Botterell, Cleobury Mortimer (see plan overleaf), Diddlebury, Child's Ercall, Munslow, Great Ness,[32] Pontesbury,[33] St Mary's Shrewsbury, Holy Trinity Much Wenlock, and Westbury. At Clun and Morville north and south aisles were contemporaneous; and at Edgmond the piers of the Perpendicular north and south arcades stand on 13th-century bases, which, if not coeval, are very close in date. At Alveley, Child's Ercall, Kinlet (see plan overleaf), and St. Mary's, Shrewsbury, second aisles were added soon after the first.

All those aisles which may be dated before *c*.1150, all of which were probably coeval with the nave, were on the north.[34] Whatever significance that may have had, however, disappeared early for from *c*.1200 north and south aisles, whether added to a nave or coeval with it, were equally common. Where two aisles appeared at slightly different dates there was no marked preference for north or south:

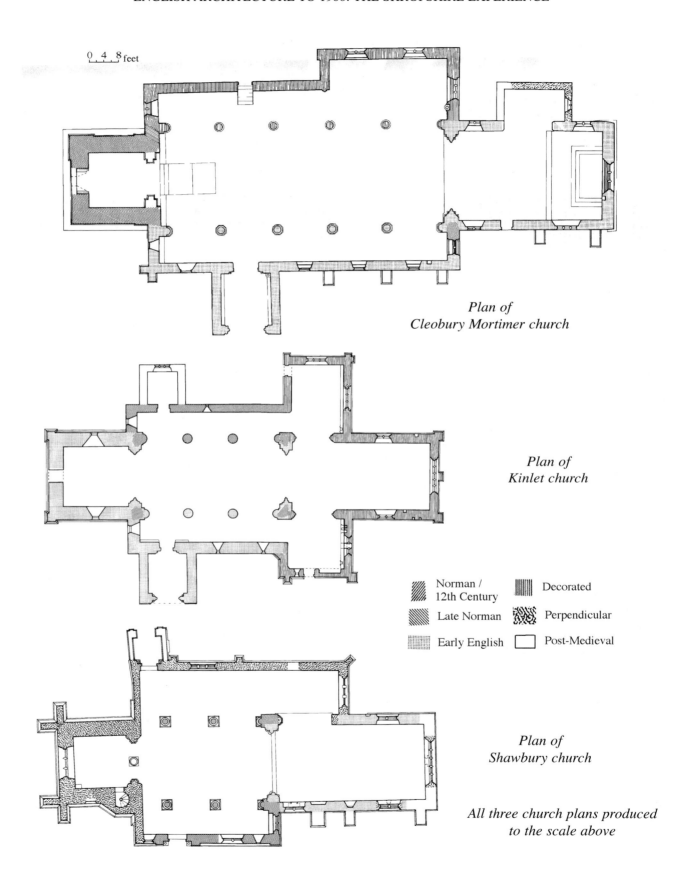

*Plan of
Cleobury Mortimer church*

*Plan of
Kinlet church*

	Norman / 12th Century		Decorated
	Late Norman		Perpendicular
	Early English		Post-Medieval

*Plan of
Shawbury church*

*All three church plans produced
to the scale above*

South aisle at Berrington church, looking south-east

while the north aisle was the earlier at Alveley and Kinlet, the south was built first at Child's Ercall and St. Mary's, Shrewsbury. Many early aisles have been rebuilt, and only the arcade remains to date them, but where the original outside wall remains or can be traced, as for example at Alveley, Berrington, Clun, Childs Ercall, and Shawbury, they are generally narrow, ranging from a width of 6ft. at Shawbury to just over 7ft. at Berrington and 9ft. in the south aisle at Alveley and the north aisle at Child's Ercall. The tendency for later aisles to be wider is illustrated at Kinlet, where neither aisle is very wide, but the earlier north aisle is just under 6ft. and the later south aisle just over 7ft. wide.

Occasionally a more ambitious but yet economical course was perhaps followed. At Cound the 12th-century-type window in the wall of the south aisle, together with the 3ft. thickness of the south and west walls of that aisle in comparison with the 2ft. 6in. of the arcade wall, suggests that a new nave was built in the early 13th century and that part of the former nave became the south aisle. Such economy in an ambitious building programme was certainly displayed at St. Lawrence's, Ludlow, where the nave of the 12th-century church was incorporated into the south aisle of the large structure that was begun in the 13th century.[35]

At all the churches mentioned above it is reasonably clear that aisles were added in the late 12th and early 13th century to pre-existing naves. Building an aisled nave *de novo* was far less common. Two aisles were intended from the start at Stottesdon in the very late 12th century, at High Ercall and Shawbury c.1200, and at Shifnal in the 13th century. These churches varied in size—three bays to the nave at High Ercall and Shawbury, four at Shifnal and Stottesdon. All four served very large parishes and, as their architectural qualities would suggest, were buildings of more ecclesiastical importance than most parish churches.[36]

Another church that may have been built with two aisles is Worthen. It has an early 13th-century north tower and south doorway, an 18th-century chancel, and a chancel arch of indeterminate date. The now aisleless nave, 76ft. long, has a 17th-century roof spanning 33ft. Such a span is unparalleled in Shropshire in the 13th century or earlier[37] and is unsurpassed, and very rarely equalled, by any unaisled building anywhere in the country before c.1300. It is difficult to explain in a remote parish church, and it is possible that there was originally at Worthen (as there was much later at Dudleston, Harley, and Llanfair Waterdine)[38] a timber arcade or arcades, forming an aisle or aisles within a stone shell, which were swept away in modern times, perhaps when the present roof was erected. And there must be some doubt about a 13th-century date for Worthen's nave, for the only positive evidence is the south doorway, which could be reset, and the north tower, which may be earlier than the present nave. The nave's enormous size, together with the Perpendicular window in the west wall, drawn in 1790,[39] and a donation in 1429 to 'the making of the church and of the steeple of Worthen'[40] could suggest a 15th-century date, but still, presumably, originally aisled.

It should be stressed that any predilection for two aisles was a late development, for earlier churches built with aisles *de novo* had only one: Claverley, West Felton, and probably Ellesmere.[41] Nor must it be supposed that no later nave was ever built *de novo* with a single aisle. At Ditton Priors the nave and south aisle appear to be a single early 13th-century build.[42] At Berrington the thickness (2ft. 3in.) of the wall above the arcade compared with that (2ft. 11in.) of the aisle wall, together with the 13th-century window in the north wall of the nave and the 13th-century piscina and south doorway in the south aisle, suggest that there too aisle and nave are contemporary.

With one exception, at Knockin, no surviving chapel was provided with an aisle in the 12th and 13th centuries. In earlier years, as was seen, the architectural distinction between parish churches and chapels was far from absolute, but now the architecture was reflecting a very clear difference in standing, and an aisle was an almost certain sign of parochial status. Most mother churches served communities which were generally on more economically favourable sites than those of the communities served by their daughter churches, and so were more able to afford to add an aisle if it were wanted. It might be wanted for two reasons: to accommodate a growing population and to keep up with developing liturgical and devotional practices.[43] And here too the mother church had an advantage. The medieval clergy were not all of one class; the 'povre ... persoun of a toun' was less likely than the rector of a wealthy benefice or the portioner of a former minster to be well informed of the latest changes in the liturgy and the need for an aisle to practise them in. And, even if he were aware of them, he was likely to have greater difficulty in persuading his parishioners to bear any cost since his own contribution would have to be small.

Sometimes an aisle, or part of an aisle, accommodated a chapel for the patron and his family. Occasionally too an added aisle was shorter than the nave and may have been intended as a chapel, as at Alberbury at a later date the Loton chapel was built for the Corbets. It is possible too that the now demolished short aisle (c.1300) at Great Ness was a chapel, as was the later, also demolished, south aisle at Stanton upon Hine Heath.

Knockin chapel, with nave, chancel, and at least one aisle, possibly two, was exceptional.[44] The 'new chapel of Knockin' stood in the shadow of Knockin Castle, centre of the wide estates of the Stranges, and was given by Ralph le Strange to Haughmond Abbey c.1190-1195.[45] It probably had much the same function as St. Mary Magdalen's chapel in the inner bailey of Ludlow Castle,[46] intended for the servants and retainers of the family that built it, and its architectural distinction was a mark of the Strange's exceptional power and wealth.

Parish churches: Enlargement of chancels

As common as the addition of aisles was the enlargement of chancels. That happened in various ways, but the addition of a structural chancel to a previously single-cell church was rare, or at least is rarely demonstrable. The chancels at Baschurch and Munslow may have been added to buildings that were originally, like Moreton Say, large single cells accommodating both nave and chancel. It is more likely than not that a structural chancel was also

*Looking east through the chancel arch
at Cleobury Mortimer*

added at Holdgate. The present 12th-century nave there is 54 x 17ft., dimensions that could have been those of a single cell containing nave and chancel. The chancel itself has no feature earlier than the 13th century, its walls are 4 to 5in. thinner than those of the nave, and there is no evidence of an original chancel arch. The evidence does not wholly preclude a rebuild in the 13th century but gives less support to that than to the likelihood that it was added.[47] Again at Cleobury Mortimer and Shawbury the early 13th-century chancels may be rebuilds of smaller earlier ones or additions to the original structure. Of course at all of these it is possible, but in the absence of excavation indeterminable, that a shallow eastern apse has been swept away. In contrast, at the cruciform church of Stanton Lacy the chancel, with 2-light cusped openings beneath plate tracery and probably of the late 13th century, is almost certainly a total rebuild of its Anglo-Saxon predecessor.[48]

A more usual, or anyhow more easily recognizable, practice was to extend an existing structurally separate chancel. At St. Mary's, Shrewsbury, the early Norman chancel was not only lengthened in

*Edw. Williams's painting of Stanton Lacy church:
the chancel was probably a total rebuild of the late 13th century (SRRC 6001/372/2.55)*

Lithograph by Radclyffe of the formerly vaulted chancel, St. Mary's church, Shrewsbury: Early English chancel arch (centre) and arches to the north transept and St. Catherine's chapel

the early 13th century but was also heightened and vaulted. At Ashford Carbonell, Morville, Great Ness, Quatt, and Shifnal the evidence for the extension of the chancel is clear from the fabric itself. At Onibury there is no direct fabric evidence, and the Early English windows in the chancel in association with a 12th-century chancel arch need imply no more than a refenestration. Nevertheless the chancel's dimensions (33 x 13ft.) are very different from those of the earlier period, and at the same time the short nave (40ft.) appears to rule out the possibility of a chancel's having been added to a single-cell church. So here again it seems likely that an early chancel was lengthened in the 13th century.

Although a structural chancel was rarely added to a single-cell church, it would appear that the liturgical chancel of many a single cell was lengthened. Of course in the absence of excavation it is rarely possible to be certain that an original narrow chancel has not been replaced by a larger one as wide as the nave, or that an apsidal east end has not been removed. Nevertheless there is little structural

evidence for that, and no instance has been found of a structural chancel being turned (one might say demoted) into a liturgical one. The extension of a liturgical chancel in the late 12th or early 13th century is deducible from the fabric of such 11th- and early 12th-century churches as Bitterley, Culmington, Diddlebury, Eaton-under-Heywood, Lilleshall,[49] Pitchford, Rushbury, and Tugford; and it may be inferred from the length of Cardington's chancel.

These long chancels were of varying sizes, but nearly all were well over 30ft. long, however small the church they were in. Extreme examples are Ashford Carbonell (mentioned above) and Church Preen, which has a chancel nearly 35ft. long in a single-cell building 13ft. wide and with a total length of 70ft. They contrast with lengths of perhaps 20ft. and 16ft. respectively at the important early 12th-century churches of Morville and Holy Trinity, Much Wenlock, and with lengths of 15 to 18ft. at such earlier smaller churches as Clee St. Margaret, Heath, Hope Bagot, and Upton Cressett. Naturally in all such extensions the chancel's width was unaltered and so their proportions changed considerably. A former mean length to width ratio of 3:2 or even 3:2-plus, changed to *c.*2:1; at Hopesay and Holdgate, both 28 x 14ft., the ratio was exactly 2:1; at Ashford Carbonell (34ft. x 12ft. 6in.) and Onibury (33 x 13ft.) it was nearly 3:1. But of course the wider the original structure the less the proportions changed, and at Bitterley the extended liturgical chancel, although, at 33ft., as long as almost any, still had a width of 25ft. and a length to width ratio of under 3:2.

Since the nave itself was generally left unaltered the ratio between the nave and chancel lengths changed too. A former very common ratio of *c.*2:1 was often reduced to *c.*3:2 and sometimes to *c.*1:1. At Onibury the ratio between nave and extended chancel is *c.*4:3; at Rushbury the two are (or were) almost exactly equal.[50] At Culmington the nave was only very slightly longer than the extended chancel; at Stanton Lacy the 13th-century chancel and pre-Conquest nave are the same length; at Morville the nave is very slightly the shorter; at Shawbury it is 3ft. shorter. At Wroxeter the late 12th-century chancel was considerably longer and slightly wider than the Anglo-Saxon nave to which it was added; at Tugford the nave is only three-quarters of the original length of the extended chancel. The increase in

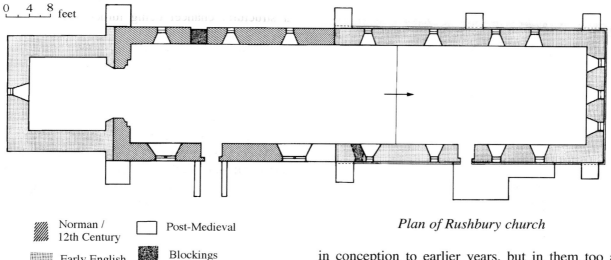

Plan of Rushbury church

Norman / 12th Century

Post-Medieval

Early English

Blockings

the relative and absolute size of the chancel is evident also at some of the cruciform churches mentioned earlier: at Church Stretton and Lydbury North the ratio of nave to chancel is *c*.4:3 and Wistanstow's nave and chancel are almost exactly the same length and width. Nevertheless there were exceptions. At the immensely long church of Neen Savage, built *de novo c*.1200, the relative lengths of nave and chancel are nearly 2:1; at Ford, of much the same date, there was, before the lengthening of the chancel in the late 13th century, a similar relationship between nave and chancel, and the latter was nearly as wide as it was long.

Perhaps not surprisingly, extended chancels, like aisles, were something of a mark of parochial status, and in the late 12th and early 13th century extensions appeared as often at single-cell as at double-cell parish churches. Nevertheless at least two chapels, Ashford Carbonell and Tugford, had their chancels lengthened at that time, and at each the new chancel was very long indeed, 34ft. at the one and 39ft. at the other. Both chapels were subject to great ecclesiastical foundations, the first to Hereford cathedral[51] and the second to Shrewsbury Abbey.[52] The upkeep of the chancels of those chapels was thus the responsibility of two great corporate churches, and it may be supposed that it was their recognition of that duty, together with the extent of their resources, which provided Ashford Carbonell and Tugford with their spacious east ends.

Two other churches, of a broad single-cell form, built *de novo* in the early 13th century, belong partly in conception to earlier years, but in them too an increase in the size of the chancel relative to the nave is very apparent. At Lydham and Leebotwood[53] the ratios of the lengths of nave to chancel are respectively 12:11 and 7:6. But because, like Bitterley, these two had wide naves the ratio of chancel length to chancel width tended, in contrast with the general development, to revert to the more or less square dimensions of earlier chancels, being again respectively 4:3 and 1:1. These may be compared and contrasted with Moreton Say, a large single-cell church of the late 12th century, where also the chancel is very broad, but although broader it is only half the length and therefore half the size of the nave, while at Lydham and Leebotwood the chancels had almost the same floor space as the naves. The aggrandisement of the chancel at this time, therefore, was not merely, and not always, a matter of turning it into a long compartment; that was but the commonest aspect of a general tendency to increase its size relative to the nave, irrespective of what form that increase might take. The tendency then was not solely the result of developments in ritual or in relations between the priest and his congregation; at a deeper level it expressed the wealth, the independence, and that attainment of equality with the secular power for which the Church had been fighting over many centuries. That aggrandisement was not reflected in parish churches alone. The splendid rebuilding of St. Hugh's choir at Lincoln from 1192 was intended to demonstrate the 'superiority of clergy over laity in the spiritual hierarchy'.[54]

Another aspect of that assertion of the Church's status revealed by the enlarged chancels is the distribution of such chancels under 'ecclesiastical' and under 'lay' patronage. By the 13th century about half of the parish churches and chapels in the county were 'ecclesiastical' in the sense that they were in the patronage of, or had been appropriated to, a religious house or because the church was still, even if vestigially, collegiate. The distribution of large chancels was very different: two thirds of those that were more than half as long as the nave were 'ecclesiastical'. That the comparison is of some significance is shown when the distribution of aisles between 'lay' and 'ecclesiastical' churches is considered. If those aisles that were built before a lay church became 'ecclesiastical' are counted as lay, the numbers are more or less equal; and even if they are counted as 'ecclesiastical' the ratio is still only 4:3 in their favour.[55] The 'lay' or 'ecclesiastical' character of the patron or appropriator thus made little difference to the presence or absence of

an aisle but a very great difference to the probability of a large chancel.

Parish churches: Towers

By the end of the period west towers were as common as aisles and long chancels, and they could perhaps claim what aisles and long chancels could not, a pre-Conquest precursor in the west forebuilding at Diddlebury. Nevertheless only three surviving west towers can be dated before *c.*1170 with much confidence: those at Barrow, St. Mary's Shrewsbury, and Stottesdon. All three were added to earlier naves. In addition the reconstruction of the west forebuilding at Diddlebury is probably early 12th-century, for it has a late 12th-century doorway set within the blocking of an earlier post-Conquest arch. Most west towers are later than that, and they are not common before *c.*1200. Most too were added to earlier naves, as at Linley.[56] At Atcham,

Edw. Williams's painting of Neen Savage church,
where chancel, nave and tower all seem to have been built as one (SRRC 6001/372/3.45)

Cardington, and Clunbury they are probably coeval with a westward lengthening of the nave. At Bitterley, Morville, Rushbury, Tugford, and Wroxeter the added west tower is more or less coeval with the lengthening of the chancel, as though congregation and incumbent were happily working as one to improve their church. A few west towers were built at the same time as the body of the church: at Alveley, Cleobury Mortimer, and Munslow the tower and the nave were part of one campaign; at Caynham, Neen Savage, and Great Ness[57] chancel, nave, and tower appear all to have been built as one.

The importance attached c.1200 to a west tower is shown starkly at Holy Trinity, Much Wenlock, where, with ruthless vandalism, it was allowed to obliterate an earlier west front whose splendour was unequalled anywhere in the county.[58] In the light of that it is not surprising that west towers, like aisles and long chancels, were something of a mark of parochial status, being four times as likely to be attached to a church as to a chapel. On the other hand the presence or absence of west towers, like aisles and unlike that of chancels, was little affected by the lay or ecclesiastical character of patrons or appropriators. In contrast, however, there was a very marked bias in topographical distribution. Only three early west towers survive in north Shropshire —at Baschurch, Great Ness, and Stanton upon Hine Heath—and probably none of them is before 1200. Doubtless there were once more, but unless north Shropshire was subject to destructive forces that were absent from, or less intense in, the south it must be supposed that the ratio between survivors reflects, more or less accurately, an original disparity of numbers. That disparity parallels another, noted earlier, between the typical single-cell church of the north and the generally earlier double-cell church of the south. The absence of west towers, therefore, is but another aspect of the long-standing differences in development between north and south Shropshire.

In addition to the towers conventionally sited at the west and above transeptal crossings, several towers were placed north or south of naves. All of them belonged to parish churches, but apart from that they are a very mixed bag, and there seems to be no general reason for their unconventional siting. It may have been to avoid blocking light from a west window, but late 12th-century west windows were

Edw. Williams's painting of Caynham church,
where, likewise, chancel, nave and tower all seem to have been built as one (SRRC 6001/372/3.35)

Eaton-under-Heywood church with its tower to the south; and plan below

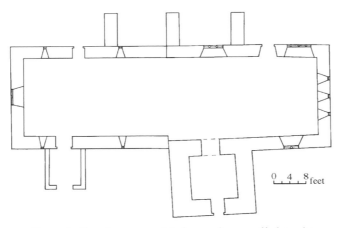

has been claimed that the more westerly towers were used as places of refuge,[62] presumably from Welsh raiders, and indeed there is in the south-west of the county a group of four churches—Bishop's Castle, Clun, Hopesay, and More—with very squat defensive-looking west towers.[63] Apart from the tower at Oswestry, however, a massive giant among the others and structurally free standing, no tower had much greater defensive capabilities than any other contemporary stone building with thick walls and narrow openings. And, like some of the lesser castles, though they might have seen off a raid, they could never have withstood a serious attack.[64]

The Early English style

The first phase of ecclesiastical provision coincided roughly with the stylistic periods known as Anglo-Saxon and Norman, and the second in the main with the advent of the Gothic mode and the Early English style. The emergence of that style was of course far more than a matter of ornament, but ornament was an important element in it. The exuberant and undisciplined Norman carving on capitals, doorway surrounds, tympana, corbel tables, etc., was replaced either by plain mouldings or by foliage developing into elaborately carved naturalistic stiff-leaf forms, seen best in the north arcade of St. Mary's, Shrewsbury. The new style's only abstract item was the dog-tooth motif, commoner in early rather than late years. The paucity of carving was compensated in part by the depth and variety of mouldings around openings, often in association with detached shafts. An early example is the west doorway at Atcham. The style is seen in its maturity in the chancel arches at Cleobury Mortimer and Kinlet, the former with banded and filleted shafts and stiff-leaf capitals and the latter with attached shafts, fillets, water-holding bases, and plain capitals. The new ornament came into existence partly in response to, and was wholly dependent upon, developments in building skills. The use of the

small and the loss would have been slight. At Claverley, Eaton-under-Heywood, Oswestry, and Worfield the tower is to the south, at Bromfield[59] and Worthen, and formerly at Pontesbury,[60] to the north. At Bromfield, Oswestry, and Worfield it is at the west end, and at Claverley, Eaton-under-Heywood, and formerly at Pontesbury at the east end, of the nave. At Worthen the north tower stands halfway along the nave and at Madeley[61] it was at the east end of the nave. At Bromfield, Eaton-under-Heywood, and Worthen the lower stage served, or could have served, as a porch, and it may have done so at Pontesbury; at Claverley, Oswestry, and Worfield there is nothing to show that it ever did. It pointed arch in conjunction with walling that served less for load bearing than as a curtain against the weather brought about alterations in the proportions of buildings and in the size of windows, more easily glazed than previously: the ultimate results included the transformation of Romanesque strength into Gothic grace and the replacement of low, dimly lit interiors (where ornament had to be bold to be seen) by high, well lit spaces in which the worshipper could appreciate delicate forms and the light-and-shade effects of deeply cut mouldings. The effect of the structural changes was at first most apparent in monastic establishments: the total rebuilding of Wenlock Priory church on a large and lofty scale; the west front, the nave vaulting, and (as claimed earlier) the chancel revaulting at Lilleshall Abbey;[65] the delicate vaults of the Buildwas chapter house; the vaults of the surviving parts of Alberbury Priory; and the high arcades of the Chirbury nave.

The effect on parish churches was very much less consistent. The arch of the west tower at St. Mary's, Shrewsbury, was given a pointed form probably in the third quarter of the 12th century, but more than a generation later the arcades of the aisles were still built with semicircular arches. It was argued earlier that that was probably an economy measure to avoid raising the north and south walls,[66] but the fact that such an economy was thinkable suggests that the new building methods were still far from d*e rigeur* even at a late date and in such an important church as St. Mary's. At Clun and High Ercall the arcades were given pointed arches accompanied with chevron ornament and rams' heads; at Alveley an arcade of round arches has stiff-leaf capitals to the east and west responds; at Clee St. Margaret the pointed chancel arch is unmoulded and has very plain imposts; at Atcham the early 13th-century west doorway, much restored but with many original

elements still discernible, has a round-headed arch above five orders of shafts with water-holding bases, and was similar to the south doorway at St. Mary's which had, in addition, stiff-leaf capitals; and at Ditton Priors the south arcade, all of one build, has two round-headed and two pointed arches.[68]

In contrast therefore with the practice in greater churches, where advances in building methods were essential to the total effect, the use of the new technique in smaller ones was at first arbitrary, and the commonest advance towards it was the provision of larger windows, either as insertions or *de novo*, within walling still of considerable thickness. That development, seen earlier among greater churches, appears first at parish level among churches of some importance, for example the windows in the transepts at Condover and Shifnal. At Wistanstow the original north and south windows at the west end of the nave, later blocked to allow for north and south doorways, are long, broad, and round-headed; at Hope Bagot a round-headed window in the north wall of the chancel has diaper ornament at head and sill but is of considerable width; and at the small late 12th-century church of Milson the original openings in nave and chancel are short but broad and with slightly pointed heads. At Morville the arches of the arcades are semicircular, but the windows in the

Edw. Williams's painting of Milson church, showing original window openings (SRRC 6001/372/3.54)

aisles are long and narrow with two-centred heads.[69] The change is seen very clearly in the south wall at Pitchford, where the round-headed window of c.1100 in the masonry above the stretch of herring-bone walling is short and narrow in contrast with its neighbour in the added or rebuilt walling of about a hundred years later. It is seen in another way in the late 12th-century east wall of the chancel at Ashford Carbonell, with two narrow windows set beneath a simple vesica,[70] and in the now vanished east window at Milson with two long round-headed lights side by side beneath an overall semicircular arch with unpierced spandrel.[71] In a larger church it was seen in the difference between the three round-headed windows in the north wall of the north transept at St. Alkmund's Shrewsbury, and in the much longer pointed lancets in the corresponding wall of the south transept there.[72]

The typical Early English lancet, very long in relation to its width and with a two-centred head, had appeared by the early years of the 13th century, although most examples in the county are probably of the middle and later years.[73] Among the earliest are those in the south aisles at Cleobury Mortimer, Clun, and Ditton Priors, in the side walls of the transepts of St. Mary's, Shrewsbury, and (formerly) in the chancel at Baschurch.[74] Most call for little comment, but some are extremely long, running almost from plinth level to wall top and reminiscent, in their modest way, of the almost continuous vertical fenestration of the greater churches of the 13th century, the east transepts at Worcester Cathedral being the nearest and among the earliest. The best examples are in the north aisle at Bromfield and perhaps those formerly in the south wall of the nave at Caynham (see illustration p.49).[75] The increasing size of lancets was accompanied by a tendency to have more of them than formerly and generally—in

the east walls and the north and south walls of transepts—and to group them in a pattern of three and with the central lancet rising above its fellows.[76] There are, or were, such windows at Cound, Ditton Priors, Greete, Rushbury, Stapleton, Sutton Maddock, and Woolstaston and, in an unstepped form, at Church Preen.[77] By the mid 13th century refenestration, or rebuilding in the new manner, had transformed much of the external appearances of the three greater churches of Shrewsbury. St. Alkmund's has been mentioned, and St. Mary's, the only survivor, is discussed below. At old St. Chad's both transepts had long lancets in the east and west walls, three close-set lancets in the north and south walls, and a long range of lancets in the nave clerestory.[78]

The grouping of lancets on east ends and on north and south walls of transepts was, in part at least, an attempt to solve the problems caused by accommodating several large openings with wide splays within a limited space; but it was done elsewhere as well, either for practical reasons or, more probably, for the effect. Groups of three lancets

The nave and chancel at Bromfield church, showing the tall lancets in the north wall of the aisle

Edw. Williams's painting of Longnor church, showing grouped lancet windows (SRRC 6001/372/1.82), with plan below

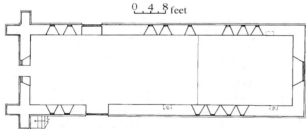

occur on the south walls of the chancels of Ditton Priors and Wistanstow, on the north wall of the nave at Wroxeter, and, stepped, on the north wall of the chancel there and on the south aisle at Morville.[79] The north chancel chapel at Cheswardine has three separate groups of three lancets. In the last quarter of the century they were used, almost certainly for effect alone and in a curiously mannered way, at Acton Burnell and nearby Longnor, the first erected by Bishop Burnell and the other by the Sprenchoses, vassals of the Stranges. At Acton Burnell the north wall of the chancel has an unstepped group of three cusped lancets with contiguous hood moulds and four orders of shallow concave mouldings; the south wall has a similar group of four at the east end and two separate lancets at the west. At Longnor the south wall of the chancel has four grouped, but not contiguous, uncusped lancets beneath a linking hood mould; the north wall has a group of three

similar lancets beneath a linking hood mould which runs on to encompass a single lancet at the west end of the chancel and two associated lancets at the east end of the nave. At the west end of the nave both north and south walls have two grouped lancets. Pevsner has rightly commented on the differences in size and ornament between a church put up for a great man at the centre of affairs and one for a gentry family.[80] Equally, however, the similarities call for comment. First, the groupings of three and

The chancel at Acton Burnell showing grouped lancet windows

four lights are confined at both churches to the chancel, and secondly the windows at both are disposed in an undisciplined way without regard for the relationship of one to the other, except for the formal connection provided by the linking hood moulds.

Design in minor churches

The frequent references in general surveys to Acton Burnell would suggest that it was the outstanding 13th-century parish church in Shropshire. In one way it was, but yet in its unorganized manner of dealing with long façades it contrasts, and not necessarily favourably, with a handful of minor 13th-century churches which reveal an attempt at a coherent design rather than a stunning effect. On the north wall of the north chancel chapel at Cheswardine lancets are grouped together as at Acton Burnell and Longnor, but each group is related to the other two in a very regular composition. On the south wall of the chancel at Alveley three tall cusped lancets under a continuous hood mould and with a doorway set between two of them are similar to, but yet more regularly spaced than those at Acton Burnell and Longnor.[81] Far more striking is the design of the south wall of Pontesbury chancel, probably *c*.1300, where a central doorway with a short window above is flanked by two symmetrically spaced larger windows.[82] The composition had been anticipated on the south walls of the chancels of Chetton and Nash.[83] On the south wall of Hopesay chancel the shorter lancet above the central doorway proves, or goes far towards proving, that the later-style larger window west of the doorway is a replacement not an insertion.[84] And with that in mind we may be reasonably certain that the later-style easternmost window in the south wall of the chancel of St. Michael's, Lilleshall, is equally a replacement.[85] To these may perhaps be added the south wall of the nave at Caynham as it was in 1791, with a central doorway flanked symmetrically by two very long lancets.[86] In the studied relationships between doorways and windows these examples are approaching the rigorous symmetry of the former 18th-century chancel at Westbury[87] and the surviving south chancel chapel at Wroxeter.[88] Such symmetry on a long façade is extremely rare before the Renaissance, and its appearance in Shropshire at this time calls for explanation.

These churches had much in common. Hopesay had been founded as a free chapel by the FitzAlans,[89] overlords of the Stranges who owned the manors of Alveley and Cheswardine[90] and were themselves overlords of the Sprenchoses of Longnor. Pontesbury Manor was held under the Corbet lords of Caus until *c*.1307 when it passed to the Charltons who thereafter held it in chief.[91] Lilleshall church had been appropriated to Lilleshall Abbey, which numbered the FitzAlans and the Stranges among its benefactors.[92] Nash was a portion of the minster church of Burford at the *caput* of the Fitz Osberns' barony and of Overs hundred.[93] What is clear is that most of these churches were connected either with important ecclesiastical foundations or with Shropshire's greatest feudatories the FitzAlans, or with their most powerful vassals the Stranges, or with an important family such as the Corbets of Caus or (for Pontesbury chancel may well be early 14th-century) the Charltons, trusted royal servants. Such combinations of wealth and rank were the first essential, for those were the qualities most able to fund, or to assist in funding, the large-scale building campaign that alone could do more than make piecemeal alterations and could complete an overall design.

That in itself, however, was not sufficient, for many large-scale building operations had been, and were to be, carried out in the county without any such designs emerging. These attempts at symmetry, however, occurred a time when chancels were peculiarly liable to be built or rebuilt and when the lateral walls of chancels, free from any functional or liturgical restraints upon the siting of doors and windows, were particularly susceptible of such treatment. Moreover this was also a time when building skills and materials were developing rapidly but had not yet reached the level of coping with the enormous windows of later years, and builders did not therefore need to provide ranges of buttresses breaking up the elevation with a rhythm of their own. At Pontesbury, the latest of the three, the design is partly vitiated by the buttress in the middle of the wall.

Nevertheless to explain adequately why symmetrical façades appeared at all at that time it is also necessary to explain why they were so few. That was in part because , whilst chancels were the main focus of attention, not all that many were built or rebuilt, in part because the original fenestration of a 13th-century building can rarely be identified with much confidence, but also because contemporary builders were somewhat mesmerized by their own skill in massing ornament to create a rich effect, as they did so successfully at Acton Burnell. By contrast, at Hopesay, Lilleshall, and Pontesbury the openings are plain, and they add to what was said above—that for designs like these to appear a fourth condition was necessary: not only that money should be available but that there should not be too much of it lavished on any one building.

That Gothic construction was commoner at an early date among greater than among lesser churches will surprise nobody, but perhaps it is not always sufficiently recognized that it was so because it was upon the greater churches, with their aisles, crossings, lofty chancel arches, and vaults, that builders had most opportunity to display their acquaintance with the new elements. It is more for that reason than for any demonstrable lack of appreciation among their patrons, incumbents, or congregations that the smaller churches appear as a whole to lag behind. Indeed, as some of the examples quoted above may reveal and as far as any precedence at all can be established in the absence of firm dates, the builders of some small churches were as quick as those of the greater to emulate the new methods of construction, or at least some of the elements associated with it. At St. Mary's, Shrewsbury, the masons adding the nave aisles had no intention of vaulting, but they decorated their piers with vaulting shafts similar to those in the westernmost bays of Worcester Cathedral.[94] When the builders of some very minor churches had the opportunity to use the new motifs and the new style of ornament, they appear to have done so as soon as anyone; and it would be difficult to produce any stiff-leaf or near-stiff-leaf ornament in the county earlier than that on the doorways of Edstaston, Moreton Say, and Tugford. And again, at another level of comparison, the mouldings of the chancel arches at Cleobury Mortimer and Kinlet are as developed as anything at the more-or-less contemporary Wenlock Priory and Lilleshall Abbey. Furthermore, if the recently suggested starting date of the 1230s for Wenlock Priory church were confirmed, then Cleobury Mortimer and Kinlet

would probably turn out to have anticipated the most important early 13th-century church in the county; and the hood-mould stops in the form of human busts on the north window of the chancel at St. Mary's, Shrewsbury, are probably earlier than those which once flanked the west doorway at Lilleshall abbey.[95] Finally, symmetrical designs for lateral façades were produced by builders of small churches without any encouragement from colleagues working upon large ones; the latter had few comparable opportunities and also more alluring alternatives. It is not a matter therefore of lesser churches being influenced by the greater in favour of this mode or that. Where the opportunity to exploit any mode existed it might be as readily embraced by the builders of small churches as of great ones; and for the very good reason that (as was seen above in discussion of the Buildwas and Lilleshall doorways and the crocus-leaf ornament) some masons worked at both, and in any particular case it was a matter of chance where they worked first.

Similar considerations apply when one attempts to set local progress within a national context. Masons working at the frontiers of technology and art were most likely to be employed on the structural and aesthetic problems of very large churches, and there was only one of those in the county at the time: Wenlock Priory church. That church was built, or at least begun, in a surprisingly austere style and, while the newly proposed starting date of c.1230 need not be accepted, it is still probable that most innovations reached the county from elsewhere and at second hand; but that does not mean that no early 13th-century work in Shropshire was in the van. The piers of the arcades at St. Mary's, Shrewsbury, with clusters of attached shafts, are in the western manner usually associated with Abbey Dore and Wells, and they may well be just as early. The piers of the arcades and the north doorway have been cited as examples of the influence of Worcester Cathedral, rebuilt from c.1180.[96] On the other hand the view has been expressed that the masons working originally at St. Mary's went on to Wells and introduced some of their practices and ideas there.[97]

Few building campaigns of the period are well documented, and none in Shropshire is. Thus arguments about precedence usually have to proceed without benefit of dates. It is, however, clear that the chancel at Acton Burnell is not of local origin. Its most remarkable features are the four-light and three-light windows in the south and north walls respectively. They are not multi-light mullioned windows at all but are trefoiled and heavily moulded lancets massed together so that the length of walling between each light is as great as the light itself. They are exaggerated forms of the bulky piers of the upper arcade of the choir at Chester Cathedral. It is reasonable to suppose that the dying mouldings of the east window are from the same source and are of the 1270s or even slightly later. Jean Bony considered Chester and Acton Burnell to be the work of the same masons, or at any rate the same workshop, and he seems, by implication, to date Chester to 1277 and later. He nowhere suggested that Chester precedes Acton Burnell,[98] but that seems the likelier sequence and would suggest that Acton Burnell could well be of the early 1280s. Nevertheless Virginia Jansen dates Acton Burnell *c.*1275 and Chester 1278-85. She may be right but gives no reason for the Acton Burnell date;[99] the only one deducible from her text is that, as dying mouldings spread from southern England, they would have reached Acton Burnell before Chester. The main thread of the argument here about Acton Burnell is unaffected, whatever the sequence was. It is possible too that one or more of the masons at Acton Burnell worked also at Longnor just over a couple of miles away. There too, although in a different way, lancets are massed together on the south and north walls of the chancel, and the east window, with its three uncusped stepped lancets surmounted by three uncusped stepped circles, is identical with the original north and south windows of the transepts at Acton Burnell.[100] But, despite Acton Burnell's outstanding quality, its influence on Longnor was all the impact it had upon local architecture; and, while it is the most widely known of 13th-century parish churches in Shropshire, it is wholly untypical. Of course one could argue that it would not have had much impact on the parish churches of any county, for the well-lit spaces called for by changes in ecclesiastical practices and made possible by advances in the techniques and skills of masons and glaziers demanded multi-light windows with thin mullions. In Shropshire, however, where few church builders could indulge in the rich ornament that Bishop Burnell could afford, and where there was, if anything, a tendency to relate openings to one another rather than to mass them together, the impact was even less than it might have been elsewhere.[101]

IV   The Decorated Period and Decline in Construction

The great campaign of new-building, enlarging, and improving the churches of Shropshire, which had gone on since the Conquest and in the 13th century had displayed the power and prestige of the Church, continued beyond 1300 but on a much narrower front. The combined output of the next two and a half centuries was less than that of either of the preceding two, and, although the first half of the 14th century was its more prolific half, it was less productive than any equal period since 1100. Monastic church building was negligible, and in parish churches few chancels were rebuilt or enlarged. The Franciscans in Shrewsbury and the Austin friars in Ludlow were still active in one way or another, and from 1350 onwards the Carmelites of Ludlow were building a large church, probably aisled, which Leland later called 'fair and costly'.[1] The total disappearance of all their work has made the scene look darker than it was but has not wholly distorted it. The decline in ecclesiastical construction, and particularly in the rebuilding of chancels throughout most of the 14th century, was to some extent offset by the provision of aisles, transepts, towers, and chapels, but that was in itself a portent of the future domination of church building and refurbishing for lay concerns and with lay resources.

Dating problems

The accelerating pace of national stylistic development in this period makes a close dating of Shropshire churches more desirable than ever, and it is unfortunate that this greater need should arise in the 14th century when the almost total cessation of monastic church building was reducing the amount of documentary evidence available. In consequence assertions about dates are largely based on the assumption that then, as in the 13th century, local stylistic developments were not hopelessly out of line with national trends. To a limited extent that assumption is confirmed by one likely date, that of the north aisle at St. Lawrence's, Ludlow, where three north windows have early heraldic glass with the arms of Theobald de Verdun (d.1316) and his wives Maud de Mortimer (d.1312) and Elizabeth de Clare.[2] Verdun married Elizabeth in 1316 and died the same year; Elizabeth remarried and was widowed for the last time in 1322.[3] If it was she who ordered the glass, she was most likely to have done so in or soon after 1316 and before she remarried. But she may have had little incentive to remember her husband, for he had abducted her,[4] and no more to commemorate her predecessor. The person with the strongest reason to erect a monument to Verdun and both his wives was Verdun himself, parading his highly distinguished connections; and so it may well be that the glass is of c.1316 and well compatible in date with the windows, which have circles enclosing cinquefoils in the heads, and with the profuse ballflower ornament of the west window of the aisle.

Further evidence comes from Chelmarsh church, which had almost certainly been rebuilt by 1345,[5] when Sir Hugh de Mortimer endowed a chantry there (see plan and illustrations overleaf). The present north arcade, which replaces an earlier one, has some ballflower ornament upon it. The south and east walls are total rebuilds, the one with tall slender two-light windows with quatrefoils in the heads, the other with an east window with intersecting cusped tracery and a sexfoil in the head. It is possible that the north arcade and the two walls are all of one build and, on the basis of the ballflower ornament, can all be assigned to the first quarter of the century.[6] Nevertheless the south wall is taller than the wall above the north arcade, and it seems

Plan of Chelmarsh church

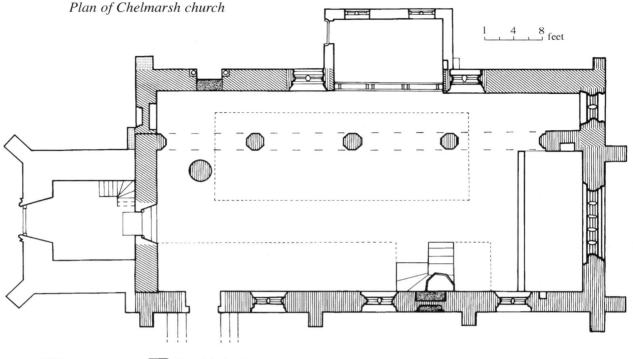

1 4 8 feet

Late Norman   Post-Medieval

Early English   Blockings

Decorated

The north arcade to the nave, Chelmarsh church

more likely that the south and east walls are later than the arcade and therefore that the east window's intersecting tracery is probably of the second quarter. Nevertheless similar tracery had appeared elsewhere in the country by *c.*1300 and as far apart as Merton College chapel, Exeter Cathedral Lady chapel, and the domestic chapels in the bishop's palace at Wells and the bishop of Ely's London house (St. Etheldreda's, Ely Place).[7] It is therefore more than possible that other Shropshire examples—Kinlet, Pontesbury, and Stottesdon—are as much as 30 to 40 years earlier than Chelmarsh; and that all that one can say of that type of tracery in Shropshire is that it is of the first half of the 14th century.

Much the same is true of that form of reticulated tracery in which cusped arches stand in diminishing tiers upon the apexes of those below. It ranges from Lichfield to Wells and Exeter and is found in Shropshire at Claverley, Munslow, Shifnal, and Holy Trinity Much Wenlock, and was formerly present at Clungunford.[8] Extant examples are commonly dated to the early 14th century,[9] but since the tracery in the choir aisle at Lichfield is probably between 1321 and 1337[10] and that in Wells Lady chapel is perhaps after 1323,[11] some of the Shropshire examples may be later than supposed, and again the motif can probably occur at any time

Chelmarsh church from the south-east

Rebuilding of earlier work

Six churches were wholly or largely rebuilt in, or just before, the first half of the 14th century: Chelmarsh, Clungunford, Loppington, Nash, Neen Sollars, and Prees; another, Hughley, was rebuilt in the mid century. Nevertheless the record may not be quite as impressive as that, for on architectural evidence Nash and Neen Sollars are as likely to be before 1300 as after;[17] and at Neen Sollars, where the chancel was rebuilt in 1859,[18] the walls are over 3ft. thick, and the work of *c*.1300 may have amounted to no more than a refenestration, a reconstruction of the crossing, and the addition of a central tower. Similarly at Prees the south wall of the nave may survive from an earlier structure, as the north aisle at Chelmarsh certainly does. Pevsner thought that at Clungunford both nave and chancel were of *c*.1300,[19] but it is probable, as Cranage suggested, that they are of two builds;[20] the differences between the plinths and the masonry of the two parts are clear, and, together with the asymmetrical siting of the chancel arch in relation to both nave and chancel, they suggest that the former nave and north chancel chapel were present when the chancel was rebuilt. The chancel formerly had an east window with tracery of the Wells Lady chapel type;[21] the east window of the north chapel and the west window of the nave have triple lancets, and there may have been as much as 20 or 30 years between the two building campaigns. At Hughley most, if not all, of the north wall survives from an earlier church.[22] At Loppington alone the argument for a wholly new church of the first half of the 14th century—a date based on the sunk chamfer of the north doorway and the reticulated tracery of the east window—appears beyond cavil. But when all those reservations have been made it is still reasonable to regard these six churches as essentially of this period while at the same time contrasting the uncertainties about the amount of the work then carried out with the number of indisputably new churches erected in earlier periods of comparable length.

in the first half of the century. Broader limits may be allowed to the plainer forms of reticulation, so common in two-light windows and which appear, in association with Perpendicular forms, in the west window at Ludlow, of the late 14th century at the earliest and perhaps as late as the great rebuilding of 1433 onwards. Battlefield church (1406-9)[12] has Decorated windows rubbing shoulders with Perpendicular ones.[13]

Similarly, flowing or curvilinear tracery has to be given a wide time span, not because there are early or late dated examples but because there are no well dated ones at all. It was proliferating in some parts of the country in the 1320s,[14] but it is unlikely to have appeared in Shropshire much before the middle of the century[15] and may have continued well beyond its end.

Of course there are other indications of date besides tracery, and the mouldings at Battlefield are far more easily reconciled with an early 15th- than with an early to mid 14th-century date; but mouldings are little more susceptible of close dating than tracery itself. If Battlefield were as ill documented as many others, the temptation to date it to 30 or 40 years earlier than it is known to be would be irresistible, did one not remember that in the Decorated period 'designs were added to the repertoire, but ... few or none were discarded'.[16]

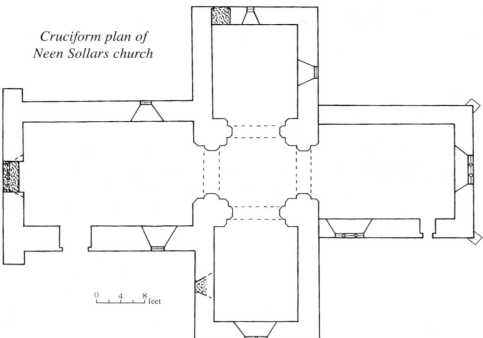

Cruciform plan of Neen Sollars church

0   4   8 feet

Priory by the local family of Lee, who also held the manor of the priory.[28]

In their plans the seven are a mixed bag. Hughley, Nash, and Loppington were built as unaisled rectangles with naves and chancels in one and without chancel arches, Chelmarsh and Prees as aisled rectangles,[29] again in one campaign and without chancel arches; Clungunford has a structurally separate chancel, and Neen Sollars is cruciform. What is noticeable is the absence from five of the seven of any structural division between nave and chancel, and where such a division does appear it may result from the two phases of building at Clungunford and from the cruciform plan at Neen Sollars which, as suggested above, may have been determined by an earlier build. Of course the absence of a structural division between nave and chancel was nothing new in Shropshire in the early 14th century, and it was claimed earlier that the feature was both commoner and of a higher status there than has generally been allowed;[30] but, as far as a small sample can suggest, it would appear by this period to have become the accepted norm when a fresh start was being made and there were accordingly no countervailing restraints.

Where there were such restraints, where a chancel was rebuilt against the east wall of the nave, an imposing chancel arch was almost invariable. The exception is the early 14th-century chancel at Stottesdon; and that would seem not to have been a result of free choice. When the chancel was rebuilt the north aisle of the nave was extended eastwards to overlap the chancel by one bay, and the south aisle was widened and similarly extended. The east window of the south aisle has flowing tracery while the windows of the chancel have reticulated and cusped intersecting tracery,[31] and it is likely that the extended aisles are slightly later than the rebuilt chancel. Whatever the date of the extension, the

There is little certainty about the circumstances in which these churches were built, but at three of them it is possible that a local landowner, wealthy or pious or both, was a begetter, even if not the only one. Sir Hugh de Mortimer's endowment of a chantry at Chelmarsh may have been part of a larger benefaction towards the fabric there. The grant in 1330 of 5 marks a year to a chaplain at Nash,[23] then subject to Burford, may have a similar implication, and so too may the acquisition, before 1287, of the advowson of Neen Sollars by the Mortimers of Wigmore.[24] And the north aisle at Ludlow, it may be recalled, was probably built by or for a man connected by marriage with two very illustrious families. At Clungunford, Loppington, Hughley, and Prees, although there is nothing definite to connect the building activity to any known event, three of the churches were connected with religious houses or the diocesan bishop and a fourth, Clungunford, was in the patronage of the FitzAlans, earls of Arundel.[25] Loppington had been appropriated to Wombridge Priory in 1232;[26] at Prees most of the rectory had been appropriated soon after 1235 to a prebend in Lichfield Cathedral but the vicarage remained in the bishop's patronage;[27] and at Hughley the advowson of what was then a chapel in the parish of Holy Trinity, Much Wenlock, was, on payment of an annual pension, held of Wenlock

The chancel south wall at Albrighton church

removal of the former east walls of the aisles robbed any tall and wide chancel arch which may have been there of its necessary abutments and presented the builders with the choice of supporting it with buttresses protruding into the aisles[32] or with flying

buttresses restricting the possible width of the aisles, or else of taking it down altogether. There are therefore reasons for thinking that the absence of a chancel arch at Stottesdon is no more than another instance of aesthetic preferences having to submit to practical structural considerations. Nevertheless it will be argued later that things were not so simple, and that the practical dilemma was itself created by other and conflicting aesthetic pressures.

New chancels were not much commoner than new churches. Stottesdon has already been mentioned, and others were Beckbury, Donington, Edgmond, Pontesbury, and Worfield, all probably well before the mid century, and Albrighton and Claverley perhaps somewhat later. Pontesbury has uncusped intersecting tracery in the east window, and it and Donington are probably the earliest of these and perhaps to be dated *c*.1300. Donington has uncusped, and Beckbury has cusped, tracery in the east window. At Edgmond the east window which preceded the present one appears to have been of five lights with reticulated tracery.[33] The present south windows at Worfield are 19th-century inven-

The long, finely proportioned chancel at Pontesbury church

61

tions[34] and so too is the east window,[35] and the dating of the chancel depends mainly on the ball-flower on the chancel arch, confirmed, or at least not contradicted, by the nature of the buttresses.[36] At Albrighton and Claverley the east windows are of five lights; at both the centre light stops short at the top to allow a large quatrefoil in the head at Claverley and a spherical quatrefoil enclosing four conjoined quatrefoils at Albrighton. The east window at Albrighton is very wide and tall with transoms to cusped lower lights just below half-height; at Claverley the north and south chancel windows are eccentric in design, more easily illustrated than described.[37] A drawing of 1821 confirms the authenticity of the east window at Claverley and can be interpreted as doing the same for the south window of the chancel.[38] At Albrighton, however, another early 19th-century drawing confirms that there was then a large tall window with a transom, but with what seems to be reticulated tracery in the head.[39] Nevertheless a date around the mid century appears likely for both chancels.

Ludford chancel has also been attributed to the early 14th century because of the double chamfer and pyramid stops of the chancel arch. But doubts have to be expressed about that for the chancel is almost square on plan, the walls are nearly 3ft. thick, and drawings of 1805 or later[40] and of 1827[41] show that there were no buttresses originally and that the present east window is a 19th-century replacement with no resemblance to its predecessor. That very odd earlier window may well have been

The five-light east window with, at the top, a spherical quatrefoil enclosing four conjoined quatrefoils at Albrighton church

Ludford church showing the chancel in the early 1800s with no buttresses and probable early 14th-century east window

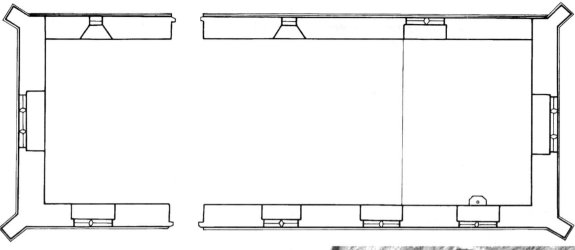

0 — 4 — 8 feet

Hughley church: plan (above)
and east window with flowing tracery (right)

of the early 14th century and will be discussed later; on balance, however, it is most likely that the chancel at Ludford is *c*.1200, refurbished about a hundred years later.

With or without a chancel arch 14th-century chancels continued to be large. Even in a small church with a short nave such as Beckbury it was over 20ft. long, and others—Albrighton, Donington, and Loppington—have chancels of up to 30ft. long. The length of the chancel at Nash was 38ft., and in some larger churches—Claverley, Edgmond, Ponntesbury, Prees,[42] and Worfield—chancels were up to 50ft. long and 22ft. wide. Hughley, which is probably later than most of those mentioned above and whose east and west windows have flowing tracery, is exceptional.[43] There, in a church of 59ft. from east to west, the chancel is only 16ft. long and considerably broader, at 23ft., than its length. That may be the original disposition, but it is worth noting that the upper part of the medieval screen cuts across the top of the easternmost south window of the present nave, and it is possible that in modern times the nave has encroached on the chancel and that the screen has been moved eastwards by as much as 12ft.[44] In building long chancels the early 14th century was doing no more than the 13th century had done, but since, like its predecessors, it built to a larger scale, its productions surpassed theirs. Pontesbury and Worfield were less important churches than St. Mary's and St. Chad's at

Kinlet church from the south-east, showing the southern 'transept'

Shrewsbury, but their Decorated chancels were considerably longer than the mainly Early English chancels of those two impressive foundations.[45]

At Ruyton-XI-Towns the chancel was lengthened, probably in the mid century. It has been claimed that the chancel of St. Michael's, Lilleshall, was lengthened in the 14th century, but the evidence is not convincing.[46] Two other enlargements may be cited, but neither is the usual straightforward lengthening. At Great Ness the chancel arch and reticulated tracery of the east window are of the early 14th century, as is the masonry of the south and east walls; but the north wall is in the 12th-century masonry of the nave. In combination with the off-centre siting of the chancel arch this would appear to reflect a widening of the chancel southwards by about 3ft. rather than a total rebuild. At Kinlet the chancel has an east window with cusped interlacing and north and south windows of two cusped lights with a quatrefoil in the head. The so-called transepts, placed very oddly to the east of the 13th-century chancel arch, have windows with cusped interlacing, and the south limb has a south doorway with ballflower ornament. It is clear that the transepts and the fenestration of the chancel are of

very similar date, and Cranage and Pevsner think that the transepts were newly built and the chancel rebuilt at the same time.[47] However it is likely that the chancel was not rebuilt but lengthened and that the transepts antedate any work on the chancel. The transepts are odd not only because of their position but also because the arches opening into them rise by an incongruous foot or two above the tops of the north and south walls of the chancel. Of course it is possible that, having built a fine new chancel, the masons then proceeded to spoil their creation with the present botched arrangement; or that, having got their transepts, they then rebuilt the chancel with its walls of the same height as before and leaving the same incongruity. What is more likely is that they punched their openings through the walls of the 13th-century chancel. Further, that view would explain why the string course of the south transept abuts the south wall of the chancel—as the masonry also appears to do—instead of returning along it.[48] The 'transepts' themselves are more in the nature of chapels than transepts and are discussed below.

The rebuilding of a whole church was, as we saw, more likely to occur where there was a lay patron rather than an ecclesiastical patron or appro-

Hodnet church from the south, c.1790, as painted by Edw. Williams, see p.331 (SRRC 6001/372/11.62)

priator. The reverse is true of chancels. Only at Beckbury and Pontesbury was the patronage exercised by local lords, and at Beckbury the advowson belonged formally to the prior of Wenlock.[49] Shrewsbury Abbey, the appropriator of Stottesdon, was also the patron of Donington and Edgmond; Worfield was appropriated to the dean and chapter of Lichfield; Alberbury was appropriated to Alberbury Priory;[50] and Claverley belonged to the royal free chapel of St. Mary Magdalen in Bridgnorth Castle.[51] Eyton was often provoked into inveighing against the unworthy motives of monastic appropriators, and with very good reason, but it must be allowed that not all appropriators and ecclesiastical patrons wholly neglected their responsibilities in the early 14th century.

Accommodation of the laity

In contrast with the decline in the attention paid to chancels the amount of building for lay use in the first half of the 14th century in the form of aisles, family chapels,

and monuments, was not much less than it had been before. North aisles were added at Cleobury Mortimer (see overleaf), Hodnet,[52] Lilleshall, Ludlow, and Munslow, a south aisle at Stanton Lacy, and north and south aisles at Worfield. At Stottesdon the south aisle was widened, and at Ruyton-XI-Towns a 13th-century north aisle was lengthened and probably widened. The new north aisle at Hodnet was as wide as the original nave, and at Worfield the two aisles together were half as wide

Hodnet church from the north-east: original nave and chancel on the south, present nave and chancel added to the north in the 14th century (see p.72); tower also Decorated; the north chapel was added in 1870; the east windows are revived Decorated

Cleobury Mortimer church: Decorated north arcade, north aisle, and St. Nicholas's chapel

again as the nave. About 1820 Pontesbury church still had its south aisle of four bays with pointed arches and reticulated window tracery.[53] Aisles and transepts were added at Kinlet at this time and the south transept was added at Ludlow.

One of the new, or newly prominent, features of the period was the provision of family chapels, and the south transept at Kinlet, with a piscina, two aumbries, a wall tomb, and an altar in the east wall with an image bracket above, is a richly furnished example. At Alveley the addition at the east end of the south aisle of the nave, with ballflower ornament on the opening into the aisle and originally with uncusped intersecting tracery in the windows,[54] was probably a chapel of the Strange family. And at Cleobury Mortimer St. Nicholas's chapel was founded, probably *c*.1350, by Roger de Mortimer.[55] The west wall of the south aisle at Moreton Corbet

has a convex-sided triangular window (see illustration p.78), and so too has the west wall of the south aisle at Alberbury, the Loton chapel; their arcades suggest that both aisles are of the early 14th century.

Chancel aisles were rare in Shropshire before 1300, and when they appeared they were likely to be in monastic or collegiate churches. Probably the earliest were, as might be expected, in the grand early 13th-century creation at Wenlock Priory. There is a 13th-century south aisle in Holy Trinity, Much Wenlock, and there was probably a 13th-century south aisle to the choir of St. Julian's, Shrewsbury.[56] The south aisles of the chancels at Ludlow[57] and Upton Cressett[58] and the north aisle of that at Clungunford[59] have been claimed as 13th-century parochial examples, but the only one about which there can be no dispute is the north aisle of the chancel at Cheswardine, mentioned earlier as a

*The Loton Chapel in Alberbury church,
looking west*

very deliberate design of the mid to late 13th century and built for the mighty Stranges of Knockin.[60] By the early to mid 14th century chancel aisles were not uncommon in parish churches. A clear and striking example is the north aisle at Hodnet mentioned above. The almost wholly rebuilt church at Prees had a north aisle which stopped only a few feet short of the east end, and at Chelmarsh (after the rebuilding) the north aisle flanked both nave and chancel. At Quatt the north aisle was probably added when the chancel was lengthened in the early 14th century. At Ellesmere the piers of the westernmost bays of the north arcade survive from an early 14th-century aisle, and piers of possibly similar date in the south arcade of the chancel at St. Mary's, Shrewsbury, may suggest an aisle of there then.[61] On a smaller scale

part-aisles to the chancel were contrived at Stottesdon, where both aisles of the nave were extended east to flank the west end of the chancel, and a similar one-bay south aisle to the chancel was created at Holy Trinity, Much Wenlock. It is also likely that both aisles flanking the west end of the chancel at Market Drayton are also of this period.

To the worshipper the most important distinction between nave and chancel was spiritual. Because the priest celebrated mass in the latter it was the most sacred part of a sacred building.[62] There was another distinction as well: while the parishioners were responsible for the fabric of the nave, the rector had to maintain the chancel, which was thus doubly and peculiarly the domain of the clergy. During the services, however, a few others—patrons, benefactors, local notabilities—would have sat close to the chancel. Parallel with an increase in family chapels, there was an increase in elaborate monuments, generally in the fashionable form of a tomb chest recessed into the wall and with an effigy on it. Apart from one in the north wall of the chancel at Shifnal,[63] nearly all such tombs in the county are of the early 14th century, most of them datable by their ballflower ornament. A great family had not then reached the level where Richard Corbet would complain that a monument 'Above the Host and Altar reared is', but the few who in life sat near the

*Tomb recesses on the north wall of the chancel of Tugford church,
possibly of late 13th-century date*

Berrington church south aisle:
wooden effigy in tomb recess

chancel throughout the service expected a place
there after death to

> lie through centuries
> And hear the blessed mutter of the mass.

For that reason many such tombs were put in a
chancel, as at Bitterley, Burford, Culmington,
Diddlebury (two), Eaton-under-Heywood, Shifnal,
St. Giles Shrewsbury and Stanton Long. But
perhaps not all men received their deserts: at Acton
Burnell there is one such tomb in the south transept,
and there are others in the south aisle of the nave as
at Baschurch (three), Berrington and Shrewsbury
Abbey. The recesses mentioned so far were indoors,
but there were some outside. External recessed
tombs are rare in the country as a whole, but in
Shropshire, besides one at Shifnal (south wall of the
chancel) and another at Clun (towards the east end
of the north aisle), there is a remarkable concentration in Corve Dale at Stanton Lacy and Tugford. Six
of the eight there are on the north or south walls of
the chancels,[64] but two at Stanton Lacy are on the
wall of the south aisle of the nave. The four at
Tugford may be late 13th-century, but those at
Stanton Lacy are early 14th-century.

Tower at Hodnet church

Fertility of local design

The great period of building, rebuilding, and heightening of west towers and of providing porches was yet to come, but a crossing tower was introduced or reconstructed at Stanton Lacy and another was raised at Shifnal; a west tower with a stone broach spire (never completed) was built at Culmington, and a very imposing west tower at Market Drayton. Pevsner has commented on the number of timber broach spires in the Cleobury Mortimer area,[65] and while their dates are uncertain it is possible that the stone spire at Culmington set an early 14th-century local fashion for them. The most remarkable tower of all, at the west end of the added north aisle at Hodnet, is on an octagonal plan throughout, with buttresses rising to belfry stage at each angle. As impressive as the exterior is the arch opening from the aisle with six recessed orders of alternating wave moulds and sunk chamfers. The fondness for playing with shapes exhibited by that structure is shown again in the hexagonal south porch at Ludlow. Pevsner thought it might antedate the porch of similar plan at St. Mary Redcliffe, Bristol, while Bony took it for granted that Ludlow was a copy of Bristol.[66] Priorities of that sort in an ill-documented age are not easily established and rarely convince anyone but their propounders, but stylistically the porch at Ludlow is no later, and could be earlier, than the north aisle there and so might well be before the date of c.1320-1330 usually assigned to the Bristol porch. Moreover, plan apart, the porch at St. Lawrence's, Ludlow, bears little resemblance to that at St. Mary Redcliffe, either in decoration, in vaulting pattern, or in possible function.[67]

There are only three such porches in England,[68] and only a handful of towers on an octagonal plan from top to bottom. The presence of one of each of such rarities in the county suggests that designers there in the early 14th century were apt to be, according to one's point of view, provincial, or eccentric, or highly original. That is true not only of the plans of porches and towers but of their fenestration as well. There are, as has been seen, many Shropshire examples of windows and window tracery within the national stream of development, but there are also some in side channels. A fondness for uncommon forms appears in the south window of the Loton chapel at Alberbury, where the lights are stopped short to allow for a large pattern of four radiating trefoils in the head; at Claverley, where an almost horizontal effect is created by the tracery in the south window of the chancel; and at Worfield, where the windows of the north aisle have Kentish tracery.[69] The windows at Chelmarsh, Kinlet, Pontesbury, and Stottesdon, where the intersecting tracery is broken at the top by a sexfoil in the head, are similar in approach but less strikingly bizarre.

One very notable predilection was for windows in the form of convex-sided triangles. They were nothing new in the early 14th century. They had

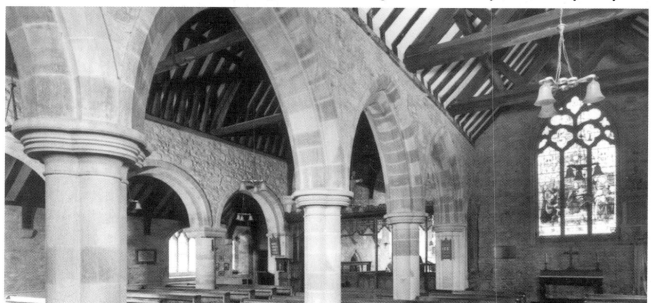

Stottesdon church south aisle: flowing tracery and 'Gothic' arcade of 1868; the north arcade is Norman

appeared in the nave triforium at Westminster Abbey by *c.*1250 and twenty or thirty years later, with the same tracery of three conjoined triangles, in the clerestory of the nave at Lichfield Cathedral. By *c.*1300 their use had spread to parish churches, as in the clerestorys of Barton Seagrave and Cranford St. Andrew (Northants.).[70] The windows in the nave triforium at Westminster, with straight bases, have the look of ordinary window heads arbitrarily cut off from their lower parts, but those at Lichfield, given a curved base, are complete entities elegantly filling an awkward space and in sympathy with those in the lower registers. In contrast the Shropshire examples are the only openings in an east or west wall, prominently and centrally sited within a space with ample room for a conventionally shaped window: in no way were they used to

solve a difficult problem of design but rather were employed for their own sakes.

At Alberbury and Moreton Corbet two such windows fill much of the west walls of the ambitious aisles there. They are identical twins, each enclosing a cusped concave-sided triangle within a complex design more easily illustrated than succinctly described.[71] That the aisles themselves and their arcades are of the first half of the 14th century will be generally allowed, but doubts have been cast on the authenticity of the windows, suspected to be inventions of 19th-century ecclesiologists.[72] Both manors belonged to a branch of the Corbet family,[73] and it is not unreasonable to suppose that that accounts for the similarity of the windows and of the arcades; moreover, since that connection between Moreton Corbet and Alberbury ceased after 1382,[74] it is equally reasonable to believe that the windows are of medieval origin and so presumably of the early 14th century. It is, however, the size, the siting, and the tracery of those windows which raise most doubts about their medieval origins, and since there are no early drawings of them,[75] it is perhaps necessary to establish that such windows existed elsewhere in Shropshire before any learned restorers had got to work. The former east window of the chancel at Ludford, as shown in drawings of 1805 or later and of 1827, was also a convex-sided triangle, similar in size to the others and filling much of the east wall. The two drawings are not wholly in agreement about the pattern of the tracery,[76] but both show the window as a large convex-sided triangle sited prominently and by itself in the east wall; and Archdeacon Plymley's reference in 1793 to 'a singular window' in the chancel there[77] would seem to put its pre-19th-century origin beyond doubt. If the window is

Alberbury church: nave roof; south arcade, with Loton chapel beyond

earlier than the 19th century, then there is no more plausible period to ascribe it to than the early 14th century—the period that the arcades and the tenurial evidence suggest for Alberbury and Moreton Corbet. In itself each of these may be no more remarkable than the circular window enclosing three small spherical triangles that fills much of the west wall of the south chapel at Boyton (Wilts.); taken together they can perhaps be seen as fruits of a very individual local taste, perhaps of a patron, or of a family,[78] but, in view of the work at Ludford, more probably of a mason or workshop.

There is another window of the same form in the east wall of the raised upper part of St. Catherine's chapel in St. Mary's, Shrewsbury, and there is yet another[79] in that church, high in the gable above the east window of Trinity chapel.[80] The one in St. Catherine's chapel has sexfoil cusping and a surround with what appears to be a sunk chamfer. Its relation to the other three is uncertain, but there is no reason to suppose that it is later than they are[81] and its tracery relates it most closely to the west window of the Berkeley chapel (1309-21) in St. Augustine's Abbey, Bristol.[82] Of a similar form to these was the now vanished east window of Sidbury chancel, the only opening in the east wall. Cranage's description of it and a not very clear representation of 1791 show that it was triangular, with a broad convexly curved and trefoiled base and with the other two sides forming an ogee arch.[83] Its siting in a gable again recalls the Berkeley chapel window.

The liking for odd or unusual forms was accompanied by a lack of the more extravagant ornament of the time. There is none of the exuberant tracery to be found elsewhere, and the tomb recesses, so often the objects of rich ornament, are, for the period, generally plain with a limited amount of crocketting and ballflower ornament; one of the richest is that on the external south wall of Shifnal chancel. Except in the west window of the north aisle at Ludlow, ballflower, in contrast with some churches just over the Herefordshire boundary, is used sparingly.[84] Sometimes, as upon the capitals of the crossing piers at Stanton Lacy, there is no more than an odd flower or two. No church has the richly carved capitals associated with the best known work of the period. Hodnet's tower arch, with six orders of alternating wave mould and sunk chamfer, is a

splendid creation, but it gains its effect in the older manner, from the interplay of mouldings and not from any decoration; even so nothing else in the county approaches it. And, although there are many arches, jambs, and mullions with typical Decorated mouldings, there are many others with nothing more than a fillet or a plain chamfer, and in the north aisle at Munslow and in the east window of the south aisle at Worfield the mullions are finished with a half-round. The only vaulting is in the porch at Ludlow, and that had plain chamfered ribs to a central boss; the contrast in ornament with its suggested model at St. Mary Redcliffe is immense. A rare exception, and it is not in a parish church, is the addition of brackets, with nodding ogees above, to the earlier cloister doorway at Haughmond Abbey.

Of course Shropshire had not been notable for excessive ornament at any earlier period, but then neither had most other counties for the Decorated period is so called for good reason. That the comparative plainness at this time is not to be seen as an eternal local phenomenon is shown by the earlier richness of Acton Burnell and the later splendours of Battlefield, Ludlow, Tong, and the west front of Shrewsbury Abbey. The plainness, however, went hand in hand with a habit of using long-known elements in a new way: spherical triangles as the prominent and only windows in a wall, echoes of rayonnant tracery at Ludford and in the south window at Alberbury. At the same time there was a fondness for the more out-of-the-way forms of up to date motifs: reticulated tracery with arches on the apexes of those below, intersecting tracery with a sexfoil in the head, the Kentish tracery at Worfield, and the intricate patterns of windows at Alberbury and Moreton Corbet. It has been claimed that the south porch at Ludlow was imitated from that at St. Mary Redcliffe[85] and that the west windows at Alberbury and Moreton Corbet were influenced by that in the Berkeley chapel in the abbey at Bristol;[86] and it is possible that the south windows at Alberbury and Claverley are reminiscences of the east window of the choir and the south windows of the Lady chapel there. If so, then the individual character of Shropshire architecture of the time may well be the product of Bristol-trained or Bristol-influenced masons working for patrons less affluent and with fewer fixed aesthetic predilections than the purse-proud burgesses or the prestigious Augustinian abbey of that self-confident city. On the other hand, if Shropshire masons or patrons needed a model for their spherical windows, they had a nearer and better one in the imposing array in the nave clerestory of Lichfield Cathedral. But then again at Worfield, which was appropriated to the Lichfield chapter, the only unusual ornament is the Kentish tracery in the north aisle; and there is no sign of that at Lichfield. Furthermore the tracery of the spherical windows at Alberbury and Moreton Corbet is, and that at Ludford was, wholly different from that at Bristol, Lichfield, or (to go farther afield) Westminster. Perhaps all that one can say, with any hope of avoiding instant rebuttal, is that, because of Shropshire's geographical position, on the northern edge of the West of England school of English Gothic, masons and patrons had a wide choice of forms and motifs and, because of the absence from the county of any prestigious building work at the time able to impress a style on local craftsmen, some of them seized the opportunity to indulge their fancy.

The copying or adaptation at local level of fashionable forms and motifs can be reasonably well demonstrated. Only at the risk of comic incongruity, however, can broader theories of aesthetic intent, derived from the study of larger buildings, be applied to humbler ones in remote places. Nevertheless at Prees and Hodnet, where very wide naves and almost equally wide aisles separated by long arcades run uninterruptedly together for almost the full length of the building, a very clear effect is achieved of multiple spaces merging to form an integrated whole. It may be argued that that is no more than the fortuitous result of a practical need to emulate the preaching spaces of the friars' churches, and such considerations may well have been present,[87] but they were not present alone. At Hodnet the builders, who added what is now the undivided nave and chancel to the former nave and narrower chancel (now the south aisle), went to considerable trouble, for no great practical advantage, to pull down the north wall of the former

chancel and extend its east wall several feet to the north in order to achieve the long vista of the seven-bay arcade.[88] At Ludlow at a later date what were in effect giant flying buttresses were used to support the north-east and north-west piers of the crossing tower and to allow an uninterrupted view from the north aisle of the nave throughout the transept and into the chancel aisle, a contrast with the 'practical' approach to the same problem at Stanton Lacy, where the buttress of the south-west pier of the crossing intrudes into the south aisle and separates it visually from the south transept or chapel. At Stottesdon a chancel arch was forgone so that the nave aisles might run on into the chancel chapels; and at Holy Trinity, Much Wenlock, a similar effect was contrived for the south aisle.[89] Aesthetic concepts of this sort were not peculiar to any architectural province but were a nationwide phenomenon and one in which, when opportunity arose, Shropshire men shared as far as they were able. Their contribution was small, not because local designers were in an aesthetic backwater but rather because small-scale works presented but small opportunity.

The sum total of Shropshire architecture in the early to mid 14th century was not great; few examples gain a mention in national surveys, and when they do—as for instance the west tower at Hodnet— it is often for their oddity rather than their architectural merits. The timber spires of the Cleobury Mortimer area look like the poor relations of the stone ones of the limestone belt; and it is perhaps symbolic that the only attempt to rival the outsiders, at Culmington, was never completed. The county has an air not of poverty, but of limited means. The monasteries were more or less content with the fabric of their churches, and in any case many benefactions which might earlier have come to them were going to the friars;[90] revenues from agriculture, on which most benefactions still depended, were generally falling sharply;[91] and the urban communities were only at the beginning of their later role of enlarging and aggrandizing their parish churches.

V   The Perpendicular Period—Shropshire out of step

The Perpendicular, covering roughly the last two centuries of English Gothic architecture, is generally seen as the most native of styles and as the most widespread of medieval ones. In the words of two authorities: 'There is no period in which money was lavished so freely on English parish churches as in the 15th century' and 'Our country is dominated by its parish churches and they in their turn by the imprint of the Perpendicular style'.[1] Few would quarrel seriously with those nationwide generalizations, but they do not apply to Shropshire, where the years from the end of the 14th century to the Reformation produced less church building than any of the shorter periods discussed above. Further, little work on any scale was carried out in an ordinary parish church. The first important Shropshire work in the new style was the rebuilding of the west end of Shrewsbury Abbey with its great west window. It was followed by the wholly new collegiate church at Battlefield and the new collegiate foundation at Tong. Comparable with, indeed surpassing, those works is the remodelling of the nave, chancel, and central tower of St. Lawrence's, Ludlow. Those four works apart, the only others of any magnitude were the new nave and north aisle at Ightfield, but they were built at two different times within the long period of the Perpendicular style.[2] Minor works are the north and south chancel chapels and nave clerestory at Claverley, the north and south aisles at Edgmond, the north chancel chapel at Ellesmere and the raising, or part-rebuilding, of the tower there, the south aisle at Loppington, the north arcade at Quatt, the north aisle at St. Martin's, the north chapel at Shawbury, and the reconstruction of the Trinity chapel and the provision of a nave clerestory at St. Mary's, Shrewsbury. There are also south porches at Claverley and Ightfield, new or rebuilt west towers at about 30 churches,[3] refenestration of varying extent at about a score of others, and the addition of spires at St. Alkmund's and St. Mary's in Shrewsbury.

It may be objected that such a list of survivals must seriously underestimate the amount of Perpendicular work carried out. It is notorious that mid 19th-century restorers, under the influence of the Ecclesiological Society[4] and its journal *The Ecclesiologist*, often destroyed original Perpendicular creations in order to replace them with something more to their taste, generally in the Early English style. Comparison of present structures with late 18th- and early 19th-century drawings, however, produces no more than four certain examples of that process: the replacement of windows at Clive, Great Ness, and Rushbury, and the removal of crenellations at Edgmond (see illustrations overleaf). In contrast with the wholesale sweeping away of plain rectangular windows of late 16th- and 17th-century date the amount of Perpendicular work lost to that cause is negligible; indeed at Neen Savage just such a plain window was replaced by one in a Perpendicular style. More serious losses were occasioned by the 18th-century destruction of four important town churches: St. Alkmund's, Whitchurch, in 1711, All Saints', Wellington, in 1787, and St. Chad's and St. Alkmund's at Shrewsbury in 1788 and 1794 respectively.[5] All had some Perpendicular work and, while most of it may have been no more than refenestration, the possibility that aisles, for example, had been completely rebuilt cannot be ruled out. Cranage thought that a bequest of 1477 to the 'new building' at St. Mary's, Shrewsbury, referred to the additions of the spire and the nave clerestory, and a 1472 reference to the *novam fabricam* at St. Alkmund's, Shrewsbury, may also refer to the tower, but another of 1499 to the 'new chapel' there suggests that some of the Perpendicular windows visible in 1789 were part of an addition or rebuilding rather than inserted.[6] But, although the list of losses given above is probably far from exhaustive, for not all churches have the necessary documentation, we can nevertheless be reasonably confident that Perpendicular architecture in

Shropshire, much of which was itself a replacement, has suffered at the very least no worse than earlier styles from improvers and restorers.

Major works: out-county and urban financing
With only four works amounting to more than minor additions or alterations there is little to be said about

Edgmond church, as painted by Edw. Williams (SRRC 6001/372/I.38) with a full complement of crenellations, and as it is today

Looking up the nave to the chancel in Tong church

the general form of churches founded or partly rebuilt in the period. Battlefield college, intended for a master and five chaplains, is the only one that was built *de novo*.[7] The church is a large rectangle 96 x 30ft.; the chancel, one bay longer than the nave, is now distinguished from it by a lower roof[8] and was always distinguished architecturally by its taller windows with their internal hood moulds and by windows with reticulated tracery (see overleaf). Tong also was collegiate, but with a large lay element, for its five priests and two clerks were joined by, and responsible for, 13 almspeople. In addition it was founded within the existing parish church.[9] The nave incorporates a 13th-century south arcade and the present form of a double-aisled nave perpetuates, in part at least, the layout of the earlier church. The nave aisles are prolonged eastwards as transepts to a central crossing with a tower, square at base and octagonal above, and the chancel is twice as long as broad.

There are precise dates for both were new foundations. Licence to acquire a site for Battlefield was obtained in 1406 and lead for the roof was being supplied in 1409.[10] Isabel de Pembridge was permitted to buy the advowson of Tong and to convert the church to a collegiate foundation in 1410,[11] and the building was perhaps completed within the next 20 years. As befitted collegiate churches both had very long chancels and the choir at Tong, which extended beyond the crossing, was, as at Battlefield, longer than the nave. There, however, the similarities end. Despite its earlier date Battlefield is a far more advanced church than Tong. The criticism of the latter—that its architectural qualities are destroyed by the multitude of its monuments—is true, though perhaps ungrateful, for no one would wish such a splendid collection away. Even without the monuments, however, Tong's low ceilings and the break-up of its area into small compartments give it an out-of-date, gloomy, and confined appearance by contrast with the clarity and lightness and airiness of Battlefield's great open space.[12] Battlefield's more developed character is seen again in its architectural ornament which, apart from the extraordinary reticulated windows, is in a fully formed and austere Perpendicular fashion, while Tong still has more than a hint of the earlier style. It is possible, since the king was the main

Battlefield church: contemporaneous reticulated and Perpendicular tracery

benefactor, that Battlefield owes its ornament, or much of it, to tracery drawings supplied by the king's works at Westminster,[13] but the differences in form between the two churches are the consequences of Battlefield's having been built on a virgin site and solely as a memorial chapel and Tong's being a constitutional and structural adaptation of a parish church.

Limitations imposed by an earlier building on the same site were not insurmountable when, as apparently at St. Lawrence's, Ludlow, there was no lack of funds, of civic pride, or of guild piety. As was seen earlier, St. Lawrence's was greatly enlarged in the 14th century, and in the next—mainly between 1433 and 1471—it was almost completely reconstructed.[14] The chancel was lengthened and raised in height, a north chapel was added, the north and south transepts were heightened, the nave arcades were rebuilt and a clerestory added, and a central tower was erected, surpassing

anything in the county and rivalling the greatest in the land. The interior was divided up as much as Tong's, and St. Lawrence's innumerable chapels with their screens and altars, served by the numerous chaplains of the Palmers' Guild, occupied as much of the floor space as the tombs still do at Tong, perhaps even more; nevertheless the great height of the reconstructed nave, the slenderness of the arcade pillars, with the wave moulds between the shafts running uninterruptedly to the apex of the arch, and the many large windows give St. Lawrence's the same light and airy feeling as Battlefield church, but on a grander scale.

The rebuilding of Shrewsbury Abbey's two westernmost bays at the end of the 14th century and the insertion of the great west window there had been in the same vein. It is the earliest developed Perpendicular work in the county, preceding Ludlow by perhaps as much as two generations, and markedly different from the general plainness of many later productions. The very tall seven-light window has a plethora of quatrefoils and daggers in the tracery; a multitude of super-transoms, all, like the main transoms, with miniature battlementing; shafts enriched with caps; a surround of moulded cinquefoil panelling; and over all a steep crocketted ogee hood mould. No later individual piece in Shropshire ever approached the splendour of that window. Even if the parishioners of Holy Cross may be surmised to have made a contribution, it may be regarded as the last fling of monastic church architecture in the county.

Minor works

Not everyone could build on the scale of those churches, but the trend towards 'height and light', noticeable since the 13th century, now accelerated. Large windows had been inserted in churches in the early to mid 14th century—for example the curvilinear east window at Berrington and the reticulated west window at Bromfield—but not in great numbers. The insertion of large Perpendicular windows may be instanced at Ditton Priors, Edstaston, Llanyblodwel, Loppington, Shifnal, St. Alkmund's, St. Chad's and St. Mary's in Shrewsbury, Holy Trinity Much Wenlock, Wrockwardine, and Wroxeter. Typical examples are at the simple 12th-century church at Woodcote with a large three-light east window; at the equally simple one at Little Ness, with three Perpendicular windows of two different forms, probably inserted at two different times; and in the south wall at Prees with windows of three differing forms.[15] Before those insertions all three churches must have been very dark inside. The most determined search for height and light is to be seen in the clerestorys added to the naves at Alveley, Claverley, Kinlet (see illustrations pp.64 and 87), and St. Mary's, Shrewsbury; in the clerestory effect achieved at Highley by replacing the original fenestration with two large early 16th-century windows set at the top of the south wall; and in the remodelling of the westernmost bays of Shrewsbury Abbey.

Nearly as many aisles and chapels were added as in the early and mid 14th century, but of course over a far longer time. Chapels were added to the north of the chancel at Claverley, Ellesmere, Ludlow, and Shawbury, to the south at Claverley, and at the south-east end of the nave at Tong; and earlier chapels were enlarged and refurbished at Ellesmere and Ludlow. The greatest of these, and probably the earliest, was the Palmers' Guild chapel at Ludlow. It is probable, too, that one of the chapels at Claverley was a guild chapel: the imposing timber-framed building abutting the churchyard there (now miscalled the Old Vicarage) has all the features of a guildhall, and the guild that could erect such a hall would probably have had its own chapel in the church. The guild may not, however, have built it, for chapels of earlier date were sometimes appropriated, as the Shrewsbury Drapers appropriated the Trinity chapel in St. Mary's.[16] The roof of the south chapel at Ellesmere has a boss with the 'Legs of Man', a badge of the Stanleys,[17] who owned the manor c.1480–1600[18] and probably paid for, or subscribed to, the refurbishing of the building; and the Golden chapel at Tong was built by the Vernons.[19] On the other hand the addition of north aisles to the naves at Ightfield and St. Martin's and of south aisles at Edgmond and Loppington, and the rebuilding of Edgmond's north aisle were probably parochial affairs, even when, as perhaps at Ightfield, a large contribution was made by the local family.[20] The north chancel chapel at Shawbury, one bay long, was built as a continuation of the widening of the north aisle there and was probably part of a parochial initiative. Much of this work seems to be late, and some of it is 'Tudor' rather than Perpendicular in form, for example the low depressed arches of the north aisle at St. Martin's.

West towers are a conspicuous feature of the period, and in its fondness for them Shropshire was most in line with national trends. One firmly dated pre-Elizabethan one is at Moreton Corbet (see illustration overleaf), and that was still building in 1539[21] and was to have its upper stage rebuilt or added in the 18th century. Another is that at Cheswardine of c.1470.[22] The west tower bearing the date 1579 at Sutton Maddock provides some negative evidence for dating the others, for its belfry openings—with three uncusped lights with four-centred heads, all beneath a flat label—are wholly unlike anything else and may be thought to provide a *terminus ad quem*, even if a very far distant one. With some reservations, and remembering that the west tower at Myddle of c.1634[23] has a very Perpendicular look, one may identify just over 20 towers that were built during this period and as

The pre-Elizabethan tower at Moreton Corbet church. Note too the Decorated convex triangular window in the south aisle

many that had an upper stage added or reconstructed, presumably for bell frames.[24] In form they are very similar: of three stages, with multi-stage buttresses, with a west window in the lower stage and a traceried belfry window at the top, battlemented, and with a low pyramidal roof. All have diagonal buttresses, except three with angle-buttresses. About half of the belfry openings are of two cusped lights with a quatrefoil in the head; slightly fewer than half are of three lights with Perpendicular tracery; at St. Martin's the opening has uncusped **Y** tracery. There is no obvious pattern or significance in these variations, although the uncusped **Y** tracery at St. Martin's, similar to that at Myddle, may indicate a late date, at least for the upper stage. Again there is no pattern in the almost equal division between those with, and those without, a west doorway, but there may be a significance in that equal division itself, for west doorways in early west towers in parish churches were rare and these later ones may perhaps be the first signs of the 17th- and 18th-century tendency to put the main, or even the only, doorway at the west.[25]

By contrast with those in many counties, and not only those for which Somerset is famous, most

St. Lawrence's church, Ludlow, as depicted in the Gentleman's Magazine *in 1812, its tower the most impressive piece of Perpendicular work in the county*

Shropshire towers are very plain. More than half have no external ornament, and in those that have any at all it is usually confined to a narrow frieze below the battlementing, generally of quatrefoils of various designs. At Cheswardine there is also a quatrefoil above the west doorway; at Moreton Corbet the spandrels of the west doorway are carved with foliage and a shield of the royal arms with the lioncels facing the wrong way; and at old St. Alkmund's, Shrewsbury, the merlons of the battlements were ornamented with cusping. The greatest amount of decoration is on the central tower of St. Lawrence's, Ludlow, but that is in a class by itself. Its lower stage has a three-light traceried window and its upper has a four-light window with similar tracery, set above a range of blank traceried panelling and beneath richly ornamented battlementing. Both stages are very tall and the tower is the most impressive single piece of Perpendicular work in the county, visible from many miles around and confidently challenging Shrewsbury's high gleaming vanes.

Little of this ornament is closely datable, and some of it may be very late. At Ightfield the aisle and the upper stage of the west tower, built of a green stone, are later than the nave and the lower stage of the tower, which bond together; in 1791 the tower had a west window similar to that in the south wall of the nave,[26] called 'peculiar and unusual' by Cranage and 'odd' by Pevsner.[27] That south window has, and had in 1791, a couched lion and another couched beast, carved in a bold coarse style, as label stops; and a couched lion and a couched wyvern carved in the same style are on the lowest offsets of the east buttresses of the west tower at Cheswardine, which is probably c.1470.[28] If the nave and the lower stage of the tower at Ightfield are about that date as well, then the tower's upper stage, with its quatrefoil frieze, and so the north aisle with its three-light, nearly triangular-headed, windows, might be c.1500. Some of the other west towers with similar friezes might also be c.1500,[29] but not all examples are late, for that at Ellesmere is of 1439–49.[30]

In their lack of decoration west towers are typical of the architecture as a whole. Generally external ornament amounted to little more than crenellation, often with crockets, and almost universal on west towers, except of course those with broach spires.

Crenellation was not uncommon on other parts of the church. That it became common in the 15th century is shown by the frequent contrast in one building between a crenellated Perpendicular limb and an uncrenellated earlier one. It may well have been favoured for its undoubted social cachet,[31] but equally it may have been intended also to reinforce the vertical effect of Perpendicular window tracery. Earlier those buildings which had anything more than overhanging eaves usually had a plain parapet such as, in Shrewsbury, crowned the Perpendicular additions and improvements at old St. Alkmund's and at St. Mary's. In contrast the south aisle added at Edgmond, the south chancel chapel and rebuilt south aisle at Claverley, and the nave at Ightfield were all crenellated. No particular pattern is discernible. The quite humble south aisle at Loppington and the prestigious church at Battlefield had no more than overhanging eaves, while the equally prestigious Tong was crenellated throughout.[32] It seems likely that crenellation, like a parapet, was provided when the means ran to it. The fondness for crenellation is clear at Edgmond, where the south wall of the Decorated chancel was raised to the height of the new Perpendicular south aisle and crenellated to match the new work, while at the same time the east gable of the chancel, at a lower pitch than before, was also crenellated (see illustration p.74).[33] Similarly at the little 12th-century church of Woodcote the east gable was probably crenellated when the large Perpendicular east window was inserted.[34]

Individual motifs upon Perpendicular buildings in Shropshire have sometimes been attributed to influences from forerunners near and not so near. The west window in Shrewsbury Abbey has had most attention and been compared with work at Beverley and Holy Trinity, Hull, at Nantwich, and at Ely and Winchester cathedrals.[35] When, however, one considers that 27 separate tracery patterns, each sufficiently different from the rest to be given its own name, have been distinguished within a single county[36] it becomes doubtful whether such comparisons are of much significance. The Perpendicular style, by contrast with the Decorated, often has a very uniform appearance in Shropshire, where it is mostly run-of-the-mill and where much of it seems to be late. The great west window of Shrewsbury Abbey, and to a lesser extent the windows of Tong, retain something of a Decorated air, and at Battlefield windows with reticulated tracery were used side by side with Perpendicular ones, but by the time of Ludlow chancel, completed by 1447,[37] the new style was in full control. The impressive and highly decorative ogee hood mould of the Shrewsbury Abbey west window had no successor, and windows were generally plain and even austere. In the large openings of such a church as St. Lawrence's, Ludlow, with the elaborate pattern of the mullions, transoms, and super-mullions, and with cusped heads of many lights, the effect is still rich. More typical, however, are the east windows of the chancel and north chapel at Shawbury, lacking a multitude of transoms and with plain and uncompromisingly vertical tracery. Occasionally a more fanciful look was attempted, the most notable examples being the windows of St. John's chapel in the north chancel aisle at Ellesmere, with triangular heads and triangular-headed multi-cusped lights. Captious critics might call them eccentric and apply that word also to the south window at Ightfield. That window, mentioned earlier, and the west window of the lower stage of the west tower,[38] were of three lights and had a tier of large quatrefoils interposed between the lower openings and the super-mullions above; and a very similar window was in the south wall of old St. Alkmund's, Shrewsbury.[39] It is perhaps not surprising that the same pattern also appears at Claverley in the south window of the chancel, a favoured habitat of eccentricity (it may be remembered) in the Decorated period.[40] Most of

these oddities are probably late. Another, a window with a triangular or nearly triangular head, appeared in the south clerestory of the nave at Worcester in the early 14th century.[41] The form was taken up in architecturally advanced circles in the early to mid 15th century, and perhaps the windows at Ellesmere are of that time for similar windows in the prior's lodging at Much Wenlock have been dated to *1425. That dating means that other similar windows—in the north aisle at Edgmond, in the clerestory of St. Mary's, Shrewsbury, and in the east wall at Wroxeter—could be as early, though Cranage puts them later, and those in the north aisle at Ightfield are presumed to be late 15th-century.

For the Ellesmere windows a much earlier date has been proposed: the 1380s.[42] The argument is elaborate, and it attempts to show that Ellesmere church received a new chancel, a north chapel, and a west window at that time. The evidence comes

The north chapel and chancel at Ellesmere church

80

partly from the east window of the chancel, which has significant similarities to the west window of Shrewsbury Abbey, and partly from the resemblance of the former west window at Ellesmere (removed in 1848) to the windows in the north chapel. The present east window, of 1887, may well be (as claimed) an authentic copy of the window that it then replaced, but that window was not of the 1380s or any other medieval decade but of 1822, when the east wall was raised by three courses and the new window inserted.[43] It is possible that the 1822 window was a copy of an original window of the 1380s, but it is equally possible that it was not for, apart from the present east window itself, there is no compelling reason to date the chancel to the late 14th century. Indeed it can equally well be argued that it was the 1822 window that was a free paraphrase of the one in Shrewsbury Abbey, somewhat as the present east window (1858) at St. Mary's, Shrewsbury, was based upon the east window of Carlisle Cathedral. Nor was the west window at Ellesmere (which resembled the windows in St. John's chapel and was replaced in 1848) of the 1380s, for it had been inserted shortly before 1840.[44] Again it is possible that that window copied an earlier one which it replaced, but again it is possible that it did not. These objections do not disprove a date in the 1380s for the windows at Ellesmere, but, in conjunction with the use of red sandstone in the north chapel and a date of *1425 for similar windows in the prior's lodging at Much Wenlock, they make it less compelling.

Compared with the problems of dating, and the lack of apparent significance in the variations in ornament and design, the pattern of the distribution of the major works is clear. Apart from the rebuilding of St. Lawrence's at Ludlow—and that was perhaps as much a national as a local effort—there is little to be seen in south Shropshire,[45] and the great bulk of the work is in the north. That is the reverse of earlier centuries, when the south was the scene of most activity.

The distinction between north and south is now perhaps least obvious in the nature and prevalence of church towers. Even today churches without a tower are commoner than those with one, and in the north, in contrast with the south, towers were rare before the 15th century. Early towers were covered with low pyramidal roofs, as may still be seen at, for example, Barrow and Linley and were formerly present at many others, such as Moreton Corbet before 1769 and Ludford in 1805.[46] It is likely that tall pyramidal roofs, as those at Hope Bowdler and formerly at Wrockwardine,[47] the unfinished stone spire at Culmington, and the group of timber spires around Cleobury Mortimer were among the earliest attempts at emphasizing the height and importance of a tower,[48] and these were mostly in the south.

By the 15th century, however, the lust for crenellation, not merely for its value as punctuation and ornament, but also for its aristocratic aura, was transforming towers throughout the county. In the south many towers were given a crenellated parapet or had an upper stage added or rebuilt with one: Bromfield, Diddlebury, Lydbury North, and Worthen, to mention a few. The transformation happened in the north as well, at Ellesmere, at St. Alkmund's and St. Julians's, Shrewsbury, at Stanton upon Hine Heath, and at old St. Alkmund's, Whitchurch.[49] But in the north early towers were few and more commonly new towers were built: Battlefield, Cheswardine, Edgmond, Ightfield, Loppington, Ruyton-XI-Towns, and Upton Magna. That these works went on throughout the 15th and early 16th centuries seems clear, and by the Reformation the difference between north and south Shropshire in the prevalence and nature of church towers had been almost eliminated.

To some extent, of course, the preponderance of northern work in the later period does no more than reflect the earlier preponderance of the south and perhaps demonstrates the north's need to make good its deficiencies and the south's temptation to be content with what it had. Nevertheless the change in the pattern of building activity parallels the change that had come over the county since Domesday Book. In 1086 the highest land values were around Shrewsbury and in, or near, the Severn valley downstream from Shrewsbury, and there too were all the great ecclesiastical foundations. That central area apart, south Shropshire was then economically and ecclesiastically more developed than the north; and yet by the time of the 1327 lay subsidy the uplands of the south and south-west were the poor areas.[50] There was therefore not merely a greater need to build in the north; there were as well greater resources to do so; and it was not smug self-satisfaction alone that inhibited the south but also (as we shall see) comparatively fewer resources to finance extensions and improvements at a time when conditions in the county generally were inimical to church building.

Nevertheless, while greater prosperity may explain why church building in the north caught up with the south in the very late Middle Ages, it cannot account for one difference between northern and southern church towers which appeared at that time. At Ellesmere, at St. Julian's, Shrewsbury, at old St. Alkmund's, Whitchurch,[51] and at all but two of the new towers listed above there was an element almost wholly absent from southern builds or rebuilds: a band of panelled ornament, generally of quatrefoils or saltires, immediately below the parapet. Only Donington and Wroxeter among southern towers have that ornament, and they are not far south. They were, like their northern compeers, in the diocese of Lichfield, and so too are a number of towers in western Staffordshire with similar ornament: there is a cluster of examples from Stafford to the Shropshire boundary, with an outlier as far away as Leek.[52] It might be thought that the contrasting absence of such ornament from south Shropshire towers, mostly in Hereford diocese, was the result of differing diocesan policies or practices. It seems more likely, however, that it was due to practical problems which limited the activities of a workshop sited near the Shropshire–Staffordshire border to an area 25 miles around. Unlike some other motifs this one had, within the west midlands, a very local habitation.

Lack of new work

That Shropshire was out of step with much of the rest of the country is clear. The reason is not known, but perhaps a tentative explanation may be advanced. By the mid 14th century the county's economy had been declining for some time. The lay subsidies of 1327 and 1340 show that in nearly half of the vills surveyed land had gone out of use since 1291, and in well over half the returns were less than in earlier surveys.[53] Much of the fall was reported from the uplands of the south and south-west, but then upland farming is often a barometer of tomorrow's agrarian conditions, and throughout the early 15th century the revenues of the Talbots' estate at Whitchurch, in the north Shropshire plain,

fell steadily to about three-quarters of their earlier level, despite up-to-date and aggressive management.[54] It is noticeable that none of the three major 15th-century works was financed by local rural wealth. Battlefield college was founded by the rector of Albright Hussey, but the bulk of its endowment came from Henry IV,[55] presumably partly in gratitude for his victory at Shrewsbury in 1403 and partly in recognition of its human cost. Sir Fulk de Pembridge, whose widow founded the college at Tong, had been knight of the shire for Shropshire in 1397 but was most notable for his connection with the Vernons and his friendship with the Beauforts; and, apart from the rectory of Tong, virtually all the college's property was in other counties.[56] The virtual rebuilding of St. Lawrence's, Ludlow, throughout the late 14th and 15th centuries was a reflection partly of municipal wealth and pride and partly of the prestige of the Palmers' Guild there, nearly as much a national as a local institution.[57] The largest single contribution of local wealth was the rebuilding at Ightfield, where 'good' William Mainwaring (d.1498), member of a notable Cheshire family,[58] acquired the manor c.1439[59] and was a 'special benefactor' to the church,[60] in which he founded, or helped to found, a family chantry.[61]

By themselves, however, the agrarian and seignorial crises of the time do not suffice to explain the peculiar character of Shropshire architecture, for the county was not alone in suffering such troubles; nor is there anything to suggest that Shropshire was more gravely afflicted than other counties. The north and west, from Oswestry and Whitchurch south through Church Pulverbatch to Down (between Lydbury North and Clun) bore much of the brunt of the warfare consequent on Glyn Dwr's bid for Welsh independence, but it largely recovered within the next 20 to 30 years.[62] Moreover it is in the north that most Perpendicular work is found. Remembering what was said earlier about the relative decline in Shropshire architecture from c.1200 onwards, we might perhaps be more surprised if the situation were different, if the county were as rich in Perpendicular as it is in Norman and Transitional work. The great diminution in monastic church building that marked the 13th century continued throughout the 14th and 15th centuries and, since there was no episcopal see in Shropshire, it was not offset, as in some other counties, by a great amount of cathedral work. And that long-standing negative factor was reinforced by a new and developing one. The county's landholding structure was dominated by six great monastic estates and as many lay ones, the most important of which belonged to the FitzAlan earls of Arundel.[63] FitzAlan policy was to invest the profits of their Shropshire properties outside the county,[64] and indeed by the end of the 14th century great lay lords 'rarely visited the county except to hunt'.[65] Shropshire suffered therefore from having some of the features of a 'colonial' economy: much of the wealth that might have developed its own infrastructure, including churches, went elsewhere. As well as great lords there were of course many local ones with no reason to spend any surplus they might have outside the county; but, although the economy was stabilizing or even improving by the mid 15th century, landlords' fortunes were not, for the disintegration of the 'structure of seignorial privilege and monopoly' was affecting them adversely.[66] No doubt that was to the corresponding advantage of their tenants, but landlords with something to spare would have been more likely to find the resources necessary for church building than were their tenants, engaged in primitive accumulation in an active peasant land market. Furthermore economic conditions in Shropshire, 'though more favourable to tenants than to lords, were not so conducive to rapid peasant enrichment as in other regions'.[67] There were, it is true, other means of accumulating resources less

directly tied to the land, and in 1326 Shrewsbury became the staple for the Welsh wool trade.[68] That trade, however, was never on the scale of that carried on in the Cotswolds, in Yorkshire, or in East Anglia. It may have helped to rebuild St. Lawrence's at Ludlow and parts of the formerly impressive church of St. Oswald at Oswestry—for by the mid 15th century those towns, much closer to the Welsh wool producers, were filching Shrewsbury's trade[69]—but its effect was limited.

Increasing internal ornament

The paucity of new building and its concentration in the north contrasts with the common and widespread embellishment of interiors. Most conspicuous was probably the provision of elaborately decorated timber chancel screens. Chancel screens were nothing new, and the long-ruinous Malinslee chapel has the remains of a 12th-century stone one. Early timber screens have not survived, but that, it may be suggested, has less to do with their fragility than with the advance in woodworking techniques from the early 14th century onwards, which allowed a delicacy of structure and intricacy of detail largely unknown before. The change occurred in furniture[70] and, as we shall see, occurred in roofs, and its effect on screens and similar structures was to render much earlier work hopelessly out of keeping with contemporary taste. Moreover, since the erection of a timber screen was, by comparison with the building of a church or the addition of an aisle, a

Edw. Williams's painting of Bettws-y-crwyn church in 1791—a surprising venue for a screen with delicate perpendicular tracery (SRRC 6001/372/3.24)

very moderate expense, such screens proliferated at the time and, despite much later and wanton destruction,[71] as many as 20 survive wholly or in part. Perhaps among the earliest in style is the one at Hughley, mingling Decorated and Perpendicular elements.[72] One of the latest was that at Munslow, which, to judge from the depressed head of the doorway to the rood stair, was probably c.1500. At the collegiate church of Tong, probably completed by 1430, an elaborate screen and stalls survive, and by the mid 15th century St. Lawrence's, Ludlow, had an equally impressive chancel screen, and no fewer than four other screens—to the transepts and the north and south chancel chapels. It also has choir stalls and misericords unsurpassed anywhere in the country. Some of the work dates from the 1420s and some from 1447, and the subjects of the misericords range from the badges of royal and noble houses to illustrations of fables and scenes of common life.[73] Even a remote little church like Bettws-y-crwyn, looking more like a barn than a church before its Victorian transformation,[74] had a screen, happily preserved, with delicate Perpendicular tracery in the openings and the members covered with quatrefoils, rosettes, and other motifs. Many of the later screens probably had a rood above,[75] though none has survived. Even the absence of any sign of a former superstructure upon the existing screen is not to be taken as evidence that there never was one, for the rood stair at Culmington proves beyond doubt that the screen there carried a loft, although there is now nothing else to indicate it. That many rood lofts were later than the building they were in is shown by the *ad hoc* practice of providing access to them by a staircase contrived partly within the external lateral wall and partly within a projection from it. Culmington is an example, as also are Claverley, Highley, Munslow, and the former church at Hope Bowdler.[76]

The change that came over screens affected roofs too. More roofs than screens survive from the period, but it is not to be supposed that more were constructed. A new roof is a far more serious and expensive matter than a new screen and far more difficult for iconoclasts or restorers to destroy. Surviving screens therefore are probably only a fraction of the number that were erected, while surviving Perpendicular roofs are almost certainly a sizeable proportion of the whole. Early church roofs in Shropshire—to judge from such rarities as those over the north transept (*1192–1226) at Wistanstow and the chancel at Pontesbury (probably c.1300)— had closely spaced coupled-rafter or scissor-rafter trusses and were, with the possible exception of the cornice, extremely plain.[77] By 1400 a characteristic and wholly different type of roof had appeared in which the main trusses had arch braces rising to a collar, above which heavily cusped raking queen struts in conjunction with cusped principals formed a bold pattern of quatrefoils and trefoils; and the richness thus created was enhanced by several tiers of similarly cusped wind braces forming large quatrefoil patterns. An early example, with the trusses still closely spaced, is above the aisled hall of Ludlow's guildhall of *1411; and a very similar roof was erected at Halston in *1437. Inserted ceilings have obscured the Ludlow roof, and the grandest roofs to be seen are over the nave at Alberbury, with five tiers of cusped wind braces, and above the north aisle at Clun, with shield-bearing angels on the cornice. Almost equally impressive is the nave roof at Hopesay with three tiers of braces, followed by others with two tiers at West Felton,

The screen at Bettws-y-crwyn church

The chancel roof at Pontesbury church, comprised of closely-spaced plain scissor-rafter trusses

indigenous products not of Shropshire alone but of a region embracing both sides of the Welsh border. The other notable roof type of the period is national—in the sense that it may be paralleled in many far distant parts of the country. The type is low-pitched, sometimes with a short king post to the ridge. The large areas delimited by principals, purlins, and ridge are divided by richly moulded intermediate members into many small panels, with the junctions of the timbers emphasized or masked by ornamental bosses. Bosses are generally carved with foliage or an abstract pattern, but above the chancel at Ludlow the badges of Lancastrian and Yorkist families appear and at the junctions of the main beams are angels' heads; above the nave long rectangular panels with trefoiled heads emphasize the pitch of the roof. Cornices are usually highly decorated: at Eaton-under-Heywood each section between the principals has its own motif of a trefoiled panel, or a Decorated 'dagger' swirling within a circle, or sunken-facetted lozenges. The character of the

Great Ness, Ruyton-XI-Towns, and St. Martin's, and there are others with a single tier at Cleobury Mortimer and Kenley. In all those roofs the main trusses are more widely spaced than in Ludlow's guildhall, and all are probably late 15th- or early 16th-century. The Alberbury roof, with an integral hammer-beam truss at the west end and multiple half-round mouldings in the timbers, may be much later for, as will be seen,[78] hammer beams are very much an Elizabethan and Stuart element in Shropshire churches. At Church Stretton the south transept roof is probably Jacobean, representing the tail end of the tradition. Whatever doubts one may have about their dates, the distribution of these roofs in the county is very clear: they are concentrated in the west and there is a tendency for them to have fewer tiers of wind braces, and probably to be later, the farther east they are.

The roofs discussed above, common to churches and houses, may be thought of as

The chancel roof at Eaton-under-Heywood church

The nave roof in Highley church

ornament is thus wholly different from the bold forms of the other roof type and is similar in its intricacy and richness to that of the screens. The difference occurs because these creations, contemporary with other low-pitched roofs, are conceived as ceilings. At Ellesmere, Ludlow, St. Mary's, Shrewsbury,[79] and Tong they are part of the building or rebuilding campaign and are set at a considerable height, but in the chancels at Eaton-under-Heywood and Highley they appear to be inserted beneath an earlier steeply pitched roof and their ceiling nature is apparent when compared with the roofs of the naves. Unlike the 'western' roofs these national ones have no western bias but are scattered throughout the county, often in the larger and grander town churches then being improved but also in the well endowed and well connected church at Tong and in the two smaller parish churches of Eaton-under-Heywood and Highley, both on great estates that may have given them good connections.

Wenlock Priory owned the manor and the church at Eaton; the church at Highley belonged to Wigmore Abbey, the manor to the earldom of March.[80] In contrast with other roof types they have a short date range, perhaps of less than a hundred years. The Tong roof is presumably more or less coeval with the fabric itself and was probably there by *c.*1430; and the Ludlow roofs, again presumably more or less contemporary with the remodelling of the nave and chancel, are mid 15th-century. The nave roof at St. Mary's, Shrewsbury, integral with the added clerestory, has running vine leaf ornament and grotesque masks on the cornice and may be dated to *c.*1500. The roofs at Eaton-under-Heywood and Highley could, from their mouldings, be as late as the early to mid 16th century.

The intricate and finely carved detail on these low-pitched, panelled, ceiling-like roofs was more expensive yard for yard, and not less fashionable on that account, than the bold quatrefoils and trefoils on the traditional arch-braced roofs. For that reason they are largely confined to churches supported by wealthy townsmen or favoured by noble, and perhaps monastic, patrons. Screens on the other hand, very much smaller and within the means of rural communities, occur in great and small churches throughout the county, and they are in the same style and created with the same skill. It is unlikely, however, that the carpenters in the west, still producing their traditional arch-braced roofs, were the same men as those who created the delicate ornament of the screens and of the low-pitched ceilings, and there was clearly a division of labour within the county. That, however, should not be seen as a simple distinction between old fashioned 'natives' and new-fangled 'foreigners', even if it began that way, but as one between an old craft supplying a long-standing and continuing need and a new craft emerging from within it to develop the

expensive skills needed to create sophisticated products that only the rich could afford. In much the same way as, many years later in the furniture trade, the cabinet makers separated from the joiners.[81]

The open arch-braced roof and the new 'ceiling' roof both went out of production about the middle of the 16th century. Unlike roofs meant to be seen at a distance, the ceiling roof was something of an aberration, for its aesthetic effect was the work of carvers rather than carpenters. The iconoclasm of the Reformation, however, was as destructive of the skills of carvers as it was of those of painters and sculptors.[82] Some idea of the opportunities lost to carvers by the ending of the Old Faith appears from a contract of 1524–5 for a reredos in the chapel of the Palmers' Guild in St. Lawrence's, Ludlow. The work was to have three tiers of ornament with figures of the Virgin, of other saints, and of doctors of the church, and scenes of the palmers' encounters

The nave and roof with its sharply angled crucks and timber clerestory in Kinlet church, looking east

87

with St. John the Evangelist and St. Edward the Confessor.[83] With the market for screens and images gone, the carvers' craft could not keep going on the chance of an occasional roof. In contrast the Reformation had little effect upon the carpenters who built the open roofs, for that was only a part of their trade. They could find employment in many other directions, retaining and developing their skills, and taking the opportunity, when it came, of constructing a simple workaday roof or an impressive newly fashionable hammer-beam one.

Two very individual roofs, eccentric but informative, need to be mentioned. In the 15th century the nave at Kinlet was given a clerestory which, for whatever reason, was built of timber not stone. Its roof was carried by crucks, functioning as arch braces, rising from the top of the stone wall of the nave to a collar, with two tiers of purlins and curved wind braces (see illustration on previous page). The clerestory survived long enough to be carefully

The fan vault in the Golden chapel at Tong

restored in the late 19th century.[84] In one way it may be said to demonstrate that cruck construction, for all its domestic associations, was not wholly alien from church architecture. On the other hand (it may be asked) what better solution could there be to the problem of putting a timber clerestory above a stone wall than sharply angled crucks?

Very different was the roof over the chantry chapel that Sir Henry Vernon founded at Tong in 1515. Now known as the Golden chapel, it has the only fan vault in Shropshire, indeed the only vault of any kind there from the period. That it should stand alone is not surprising, for fan vaults in out of the way places are associated only with men connected with London or the Court;[85] and Sir Henry was just such a man, married into the nationally important Talbot family and formerly governor and treasurer to Prince Arthur.[86] The chapel is as much a grateful compliment to the Talbots as anything else, for in his will Sir John ordered it to be 'better and more honourable' because of his wife's Talbot blood.[87]

The chapels of rich companies and guilds, as in St. Mary's, Shrewsbury, and St. Lawrence's, Ludlow, were as impressive as, and larger than, the Golden chapel, but no other family in the county had anything to match it, and the Golden chapel was only a part of the unequalled assemblage of splendid altar tombs by the fashionable Nottingham alabasterers with which the Vernons filled the east

An effigy to a member of the Cornewall family c.1426 set in an earlier recess in Burford church

88

end of the nave at Tong. Whatever Isabel de Pembridge's intentions may have been, her Vernon successors exercised their right as patrons to turn the church into a family mausoleum, almost another Fontévrault. But then the Vernons were not a typical Shropshire family, indeed hardly a Shropshire family at all. Their main seat was at Haddon (Derb.), their wealth came from varied sources outside the county, and they were in a class well above the native gentry.[88] The Cornewalls may seem typical, and their monuments in Burford church are a brass of c.1370, an effigy of c.1426 set within an earlier recess, an altar tomb of 1508, and the well known painted triptych of 1588 signed by Melchior Salaboss. The Cornewalls too were a cut above most of their fellows. They claimed royal descent,[89] and their kinsman Sir John Cornewall, of Ampthill (Beds.), married a daughter of John of Gaunt in 1400 and later did very well in the French wars. When his wife died in 1425 her body was brought for burial at the Cornewalls' seat,[90] and hers is the effigy of c.1426.

It is probable that today we exaggerate the contribution of tombs, however splendid, to the impression given by a late medieval church interior, in which mural paintings and stained glass created a much greater effect, or at least a more immediately striking one. Very few murals survive, but it is clear from the scattered remains that they were once ubiquitous. At Edstaston chapel, dedicated to St. Mary, there were murals depicting, *inter alia*, the founder presenting his church to the saint, another of him kneeling before her, figures of a bishop and a high official, a scene of unknown import, and other pictures of the Blessed Virgin, all probably of c.1500; there were also other paintings, presumably earlier, of figures beneath a round-headed arcade.[91] At Morville in 1859 there were murals of several dates, difficult to interpret, but two perhaps of Adam and Eve and of the Prodigal Son.[92]

The painted tryptych of 1588 in Burford church

Despite its fragility, and probably because of its value and prestige, rather more stained glass has survived than mural painting. The earliest pieces—the Jesse window at the east end of St. Mary's, Shrewsbury,[93] and that in the Lady chapel at St. Lawrence's, Ludlow, and the heraldic glass in St. Lawrence's north aisle—are all of probably much the same date, c.1330–50; and the Jesse windows have a family likeness to nearly a dozen others of the same age in the Marches.[94] Important landowners commissioned St. Mary's Jesse window[95] and St. Lawrence's north-aisle glass,[96] and records of the now lost heraldic schemes in the south aisle at Ludlow,[97] in the west window of Shrewsbury Abbey,[98] and in Battlefield[99] and Tong[100] collegiate churches suggest that such men remained the most important patrons for a long time. The glass in the side aisle at Ludlow is probably the same age as that in the north aisle, the Shrewsbury Abbey glass is of Richard II's time, and that at Battlefield of 1434–45. It was probably not until the early decades of the 15th century that the wealth and piety of townspeople began to play a major role in encouraging the production of glass and determining the bias of its subject matter. The outstanding example is the glass at Ludlow, and its earliest manifestation is probably the window in the north aisle of the chancel, paid for by the Shearmen's Guild in 1425[101] and probably adapted to its present position when the chancel was rebuilt from 1433 onwards. The south window there is of 1445,[102] the Annunciation window in the chapel of St. John the Evangelist probably of c.1449,[103] and the rest of the glass is of much the same age.[104] It has a highly didactic purpose: in the chancel east window is the story of St. Lawrence, and in the east window of the Palmers' Guild chapel the subject is the palmers' association with St. John the Evangelist and St. Edward the Confessor. Other windows illustrate the Decalogue, the Creed, and the Catechism. Despite much restoration the collection is of a splendour unsurpassed in any other parish church in the country. In conjunction with the rebuilding of much of the fabric in the 15th century, with the other sumptuous furnishings, and with the close association between the guild and the town council[105] it may be seen as a part of the town's bid, in the face of Shrewsbury's declining fortunes at the time, to present itself as *primus inter pares* in the county—or even further afield.

VI   Defensible Houses

The earliest remains of domestic architecture are Norman, and, because the Normans needed to protect themselves against those whom they had conquered, they are fortified dwellings. The oldest survivors are those originally built in stone. In them defensive considerations were paramount, and they are strongly built with thick walls that have resisted time at least as successfully as they ever resisted an enemy. Such great structures as the White Tower and Colchester Castle were more or less self-sufficient, but early fortifications in Shropshire were generally on a smaller scale and the accommodation was complemented by other buildings within the enceinte. These were often of timber, and, as standards of comfort rose among the upper classes, they were likely to be swept away and replaced by stone. In consequence the earliest Shropshire secular buildings about which much can be said are towers, of such varying character as those at Alberbury, Clun, Hopton Castle, Ludlow, Moreton Corbet, Stokesay, and Wattlesborough. That so many should have survived is not wholly fortuitous. They are sited along the Welsh border, where towers were an even greater comfort—and for a longer time—than elsewhere, and thereby they had perhaps slightly more chance of survival;[1] and equally, in the circumstances of the Marches, there were more of them to survive.

In discussing medieval domestic architecture it is necessary to distinguish at first between the dwellings of the magnates and those of the lesser nobility. The surviving 12th- and 13th-century buildings mentioned above may all be classified as 'towers', but by itself that obscures important differences between them. The great tower at Ludlow of c.1100 is the earliest such structure in the county. Its present square keep-like profile is the result of later truncation at the north and of additions at east and west. Originally it was a rectangle nearly twice as long as wide and with two slight projections, to east and west at the south, giving it a **T** plan.[2] Like the similar, and similarly sited, structure at Richmond (Yorks. N.R.), which also projects forward of the more or less contemporary curtain wall, it was built as a gatehouse—and one of some splendour, with the inner entry lined with blank arcading with scalloped capitals and with a unique wall passage allowing pedestrian communication with the exterior when the great gate was shut. As far as is known there was nothing like it in the county until the erection of the 'keep' at Bridgnorth in the later 12th century,[3] and there are only a dozen surviving structures of that date and scale in the country. Apart from those built by the Conqueror in the important towns of London and Colchester and within the Roman fort at Pevensey (Sussex), early stone castles were on rocky sites where earthworks were difficult to construct and where a stone building, assuming that the masons were available, was, if not the cheapest product, then at least the 'best buy'. Ludlow on its promontory was just such a site.

The Lacys held extensive lands in chief in south Shropshire and Herefordshire.[4] 'Castles ... were built to hold territory',[5] and Ludlow was situated at the south-western extremity of their huge and valuable manor of Stanton Lacy and was on the road to their Herefordshire lands. Moreover, despite the lack of a Domesday reference, it is possible that the family already had a castle somewhere within their manor of Stanton, where Domesday lists three sub-tenants with Norman names, each holding $1\frac{1}{2}$ hide, and three riding men, 'suggestive if not of a castle at least of the residence of a great lord'.[6] The Lacys had both the incentive and the resources for such a building as Ludlow's great tower, and it may have been there before 1100.[7]

Most castles built in Shropshire before 1200 were either ring works or motte-and-baileys with timber towers and earthwork defences, and most of them never progressed beyond that stage.[8] Throughout most of the later 12th century that had perhaps not mattered very much, for warfare had not greatly changed and Henry II had achieved some stability along the border by bribing and conciliating the Welsh princelings there.[9] By the early years of the next century, after the absentee rule of Richard I and with the troubles of John's reign being succeeded by those of Henry III's, such powerful Welsh rulers as the lords of southern Powys and of Gwynedd saw an opportunity to recover Welsh lands that had been lost, and great marcher families like the Corbets, FitzAlans, and Mortimers and lesser ones like the Fitz Warins and the Stranges saw an equal chance to seize land, either from the Welsh or from their neighbours. When Fulk Fitz Warin (III) was licensed to refortify Whittington in 1221 it was stipulated that he should do only so much as was necessary to make it safe against the Welsh.[10] That caveat probably arose from well founded doubts of his loyalty, but it suggests that the Welsh lacked the skills or the resources for siegecraft and that fortresses which they could take were not of the greatest strength. And yet at the end of the 12th century and in the beginning of the 13th they captured, sometimes in association with English allies, such presumably important strongholds as Caus, Clun, Kinnerley, Oswestry, Shrawardine, Shrewsbury, and Whittington.[11] The implication would seem to be that at least some of those had been neglected or had not been brought up to date to face the challenges of improved means of assault.[12] Throughout the country in the early 13th century, many castles were being built or rebuilt in stone, but along the Welsh border there appears to have been a concentrated effort at refortification which resulted in a chain of new or rebuilt defences from Whittington in the north through Knockin, Shrawardine, Shrewsbury, Caus, Montgomery, and Bryn Amlwg to Clun in the south.[13] The Crown was responsible for Shrewsbury and Montgomery[14] and subsidized the building of at least one of the private ones, Caus,[15] but the result of all the work was less the effect of strategic planning than that of every lord siting his castle where it would best defend his own lands;[16] and ten of the more important in the county were built by the two major families of the Shropshire border, the Corbets and the FitzAlans.[17]

Among those, Whittington, despite the Crown's attempt to impose limitations, must have been one of the most formidable. The present ruins include a moat, two outer baileys, a main gatehouse with flanking towers, a motte revetted in masonry, with its own gatehouse set between two round towers, and with three other towers at the angles, and a 'keep', now destroyed down to ground level, of 31 by 20ft. internally, with masonry about 7–8ft. thick[18] and probably of three or four storeys originally. Caus Castle, of which little more than the earthworks are now visible, was equally strong, with a shell-keep upon a motte, inner and outer baileys, each with a gatehouse, and curtain walls with towers.[19] The great tower at Clun was accompanied, quite apart from whatever other towers there may have been, by a barbican which in 1440 housed a chapel and two 'great chambers' and must have been as imposing a structure[20] as that which survives at Whittington. Despite the notorious conservatism of military practice, it is as likely to have been put up in the 13th century, when it was needed, as in the 14th and 15th centuries when it was not. All of these seem to testify to a serious military intent at a time when Welsh power was still formidable.

Castle accommodation

A castle was not only a fortress but a dwelling as well, and it had to provide shelter and the comforts consonant with the standards of the time and of the status of the family which, with its retinue, permanently resided in it or regularly visited. Whatever accommodation may have been provided in the early gatehouse at Ludlow would have been inadequate for all the occupants of the castle, and there must have been other buildings within the enceinte, such as a hall, chambers, and offices. Most of them were probably of timber, but the presence of 12th-century masonry in the east wall of the 14th-century hall suggests that one building at least, perhaps itself the earlier hall, was of stone. If so, it was in the same position vis-à-vis the gatehouse as Scolland's Hall at Richmond, and it may have been as grand. The blocking of the entry of the gatehouse in the late 12th century was a consequence of the smaller need for it after the outer bailey had been added, but the ending or diminution of its military function allowed its use for domestic purposes, attested by the reorganization of the upper floor and by the additions built against the west wall.

Every early structure at Ludlow, apart from the gatehouse and the round nave of St. Mary Magdalen's chapel,[21] has gone or been greatly altered. So have whatever early structures there may have been elsewhere in the county, and there is little local evidence of the nature or amount of accommodation provided, even in the houses of the very great, before the 13th century. One may, however, suppose that the rich ornament in the former gatehouse and upon the chapel at Ludlow, whether or not the family used it or had their own private chapel elsewhere, suggests an equally high standard of domestic comfort. How soon Fulk FitzWarin began his rebuilding at Whittington is uncertain, but surviving masonry shows that by the end of the 13th century the twin towers of the main gatehouse and those of the gatehouse to the inner bailey, together with three other towers around the bailey walls and the large tower on the top of it, provided a great amount of accommodation, although more scattered than had become usual by that time. A building to the east of the great tower, apparently of later date, may have been a hall, or the undercroft of a hall, but if so a very 'private' one, for the bailey, on a restricted site and with its own gatehouse, was probably reserved for the lord and his equals, and a great hall was more probably sited in the north-west bailey. The present great tower at Clun was an advance on Whittington in concentrating several chambers in one large block. It had three floors and a part-basement, with internal measurements on the upper floors of 56 by 30ft. Many of its elements are now lost, but it had three habitable floors, each with a wall fireplace, and there was perhaps a kitchen in the basement capable of serving the occupants of the rooms above. Its form, with heated chamber above heated chamber in a part of the complex distinguished from the rest, anticipates such a later integrated residence as Bolton Castle in Wensleydale and suggests that it was more probably intended for the lord and his family than for guests. Its siting on the side of the motte shows that an earlier, and presumably less commodious, building on the top had become out of date with the rising standards of accommodation of the magnate class.

The date of the tower at Clun is a matter of some interest. A thorough survey of the standing remains has argued for a late 13th-century date on the grounds that the tower was neither very defensible in itself nor in a very defensible position; and the undeniably 'early' features are explained as deliberate archaism. An inquisition post mortem of 1272 spoke of a 'little castle' at Clun and recommended that the top of a tower there should be covered with lead, and both of those remarks would support the view that the present great tower was not then built. That the tower was set into the side of the motte suggests that it was more probably erected in the late years of the 13th century, when Welsh power was declining, than in the early ones when it was still formidable.[22] The arguments are cogent, but there are counter arguments. It is clear from other references in the 1272 survey—'outside the castle is a bailey', 'the castle bridge'—that 'castle' is there used to mean the motte and not any particular building upon it; and the motte itself might well be called 'little'. Further, the survey speaks of a gateway and a wall to the bailey having been begun, of which 200ft. had already been built. Five years after that, in 1277, the town of Clun obtained a grant of murage, and in 1302 'great outlays' of £20 a year were being spent upon the castle.[23] And, since there is no mention of it in the 1272 survey, the barbican

The great tower at Clun

93

referred to in 1440 (see above) might equally well be *c*.1300. It could be claimed, therefore, that the authorities at Clun were as concerned about defence in 1272 and later as they had been 50 or 60 years before; and, if the siting of the great tower is to be attributed to an indifference to defence,[24] then it should be ascribed not to the late 13th century but to the early 14th, or later. Such a tower then would have been archaism beyond all cavil.

One is, of course, reluctant to accept archaism as a solution of problems in 13th-century architecture. In the first place it automatically bedevils any system of dating, and, if it throws light upon one small part of the subject, it does so by further darkening the obscurity of all the rest. Secondly, as will be discussed later in relation to Acton Burnell, it is not at all certain that building in a 'fortified' style in the late 13th century was archaism at all. It may be claimed that archaism was not unknown in the 13th and 14th centuries, and at Lichfield Cathedral in the late 13th century and at St. Albans Abbey after 1323 arcades were built with the triforia given more prominence than was then usual in order to harmonize with earlier work which they adjoined.[25] These, however, were wholly different operations from erecting a new building—detached from, and serving a different purpose from, everything else on the site—in an out-of-date form. Further, the archaizers (if such they were) at Clun, working for the grand FitzAlans, introduced Gothic windows into their would-be archaic elevations and were less determinedly archaic than those working for minor gentry at Wattlesborough—where archaism and imitation of Clun and other castles has also been suspected.[26] The latter, less elevated but apparently more thoroughgoing artists, single-mindedly pursued the Romanesque. In the absence of an equivalent to dendrochronology for stone the date of the tower at Clun, and the dates of very many other structures, must remain uncertain, but an early to mid 13th-century origin is, at the least, as compatible with the documents and the standing remains as one in the late 13th century; and it does not need to invoke archaism.

The new standards are seen at their highest at Shrewsbury, a royal castle, and at Ludlow, from 1308 belonging to the Mortimers of Wigmore. There probably never was a stone 'keep' in Shrewsbury Castle, and whatever earlier buildings there may have been within the enceinte were either drastically altered or wholly swept away in later improvements.[27] The most important survival is the large first-floor hall, entered from a lobby at the head of a flight of external stairs, and with a range of lancet windows opening onto the bailey on the one side and onto the outside world on the other. At Ludlow a sumptuous suite had come into being by the early 14th century,

Plan of Ludlow Castle (from St. John Hope)

comprising a first-floor great hall, with large two-light windows to the bailey and single-light windows to the outside, set between two three-storeyed blocks of chambers placed one above the other, and with the east block furnished with its own garderobe tower. The effect was one of calculated magnificence, and the building was the most imposing residence in the county, indeed throughout the Marches, and unsurpassed at the time anywhere: a fitting monument to the Mortimers, then at the height of their power and pretensions.

Such a creation was not achieved in one building campaign. The work was probably begun in the late 13th century by the Geneville family and completed in a grander form after 1308, when Geoffrey de Geneville granted the property to Roger Mortimer, his granddaughter's new husband.[28] It is clear that there were major changes at Ludlow in the years around 1300.[29] That the west block has been raised by a storey is shown by the change in masonry between the lower storeys and the present second storey and by the chases in the east and west walls, incompatible with the fenestration of the second storey and best interpreted as housings for the wall posts of the roof of a two-storey building. Further, there is toothing at the east end of the south wall on the second storey but not on the storeys below. That argues that a three-storey structure, now demolished, was built against the south end part of the east wall of the west block, to which, at the same time, a third storey was added. The new structure could only have been a two-storey porch to the hall with a chamber above, a chamber which was entered from the second floor of the west block by the doorway still visible in the south-east corner. The porch may have been an addition to an earlier hall, but it is noticeable that the floor-level of the chamber in the west block is about a foot below that of the hall, and it is unlikely, if the two were built at the same time, or if the hall was given its present form at the same time, that they would not have been made to correspond. It is probable therefore that the date of the vanished porch is that of the present hall, that the Genevilles built a two-storey solar block and either took over, or built for themselves, a hall of a different form from the present. That hall may have been a ground-floor one, wherein no question of communication between hall and first-floor chamber would arise and where there would not

have been—what there is now—the very odd feature of a chamber of some elaboration stepped down into from something like a screens passage. The east (the present great-chamber) block has all the structural elements of the west block and may also have been built by the Genevilles and raised by the Mortimers, and it was perhaps the original service end.

Solar towers

There were limits to the resources of even the greatest men which often compelled them to build in stages, and men of lesser, but still gentle, status were yet more restricted. Not for them a vast structure with curtain walls, gatehouses, keep, and splendid domestic accommodation. Instead they seem to have had, when they could afford to build in stone at all, what may be called a solar tower, free-standing, and probably accompanied by a timber hall and ancillary buildings, and perhaps enclosed by an earthwork. Three 13th-century Shropshire towers are well enough preserved for something to

Solar tower at Wattlesborough Hall

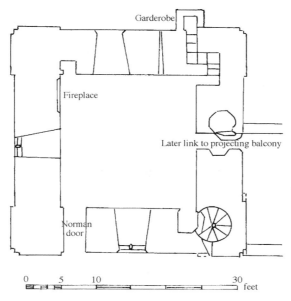

First floor plan of the solar tower at Wattlesborough Hall

be gleaned about their internal arrangements. Wattlesborough Hall is the smallest and, it will be argued, the oldest of them, erected by a minor branch of the Corbets.[30] Internally it is about 20ft. square on the first floor and was originally of two storeys, with the walls carried up above the apex of the steeply pitched roof, both to protect it and to provide a wall walk reached by a vice from the first floor. It was free-standing and the doorway was on the first floor at the south end of the east wall; entry to the ground floor, lit by nothing more than ventilation slits, was presumably by a ladder from above. The first floor consisted of a single large room, provided with a garderobe and slop drain, with three, and perhaps originally four, large round-headed two-light windows in deep embrasures which may once have accommodated window seats. Despite the absence of any clear evidence of a fireplace the room was a solar, reached as at Stokesay by an outside staircase, but here from a detached hall. The tower is clearly a compromise between the needs of defence, which necessitated a dark and not very useful ground floor, and those of accommodation, which sacrificed strength to the comfort of large double-light windows at no very great height above ground level. Doubtless it was the best that a man of moderate means could hope for: a large and, by contemporary standards, well appointed room within a tower that would never

laugh a siege to scorn,[31] but could hold off a band of freebooters.[32]

Two recent accounts of Wattlesborough ascribe it to the late 13th century,[33] but a date in the mid century is perhaps more easily justified. Three features are adduced in favour of a later date: the late 13th- or early 14th-century form of the ground-floor doorway, the shouldered arches of the doorways from the staircase, and the enlargement of the window mullions at mid height to take draw bars. If the ground-floor doorway were original, then the argument for a late date for the tower would be incontestable, but the evidence is against that. The doorway presents a fair face to the room and has a rebate to the exterior; it was clearly not meant to lead into the room but from it into an adjoining building. The tower, however, was built free standing. Anything that adjoined it must therefore be later, and so must a doorway leading into it. The shouldered arches of the doorways off the staircase are not to the purpose, for they lead into a room and a space created only when a second floor was inserted, probably in the early 14th century. The thickening of the mullions at half height for a draw-bar hole, common in the late 13th century and later, is a stronger argument, but it has to be set against the Romanesque windows and the contrast of those with the Gothic form of the openings in Clun Castle not so far away.

Whatever its date, Wattlesborough is in no sense a keep; it is a solar tower. So too, probably, were the free-standing structures, of smaller superficial area, at Alberbury[34] and Moreton Corbet. The latter is the better preserved, with a fireplace of early 13th-century form on the first floor, which was probably the solar, and perhaps another chamber above. Both differ markedly from Wattlesborough in having the comfort of stone curtain walls around the complexes that they were in, but the curtain at Moreton Corbet, built up against the tower, is clearly later and is probably no more than was hoped for at Wattlesborough. The so called keep at Bridgnorth, rebuilt by Henry II,[35] has what G.T. Clark long ago referred to as the 'very unworthy' dimensions of 20ft. square internally, no bigger than Wattlesborough.[36] It too, despite its royal origins, is to be seen as a solar tower, at first perhaps the only, or the most prestigious, stone building within the enceinte. At times even kings might be short of resources.

What may be thought of as a purpose-built variation upon the solar-tower theme is the so called Forester's Lodge at Upper Millichope (in Eaton-under-Heywood), identified by Eyton as the dwelling of the royal official responsible for enforcing the forest law in the Long forest,[37] and of the mid to late 13th century.[38] The walls are 6ft. thick and the ground floor was lit only by ventilation slits. The defensive quality was lessened not only by the large first-floor windows at no great height above ground but also by the highly unusual stone stairway from ground to first floor. That the stair was not intended purely as a convenience is shown by the draw-bar tunnel in the doorway at its head, placed to bar entry from below.[39] Foresters were not popular with most of their neighbours, and forest prisons were never absent from the medieval scene.[40] The first floor at Millichope was intended as a comfortable solar; the ground floor was probably used both for storage and as a lock-up for suspects waiting to be taken to Bridgnorth or Shrewsbury for trial.[41] The draw bar was meant to stop them from breaking out through the solar, and the thick walls were intended as much to keep malefactors in as to keep desperadoes out.

Among these houses of lower standing than the great castles Stokesay Castle is unique in the extent and variety of its surviving accommodation, and that is probably due to its ownership by the wool merchant Lawrence of Ludlow, one of the richest men in the country in the late 13th century.[42] Unlike many other owners of one house, and unlike many rich owners of several houses, Lawrence could afford to lavish large sums upon a single building over a short period; and he was the better able to do so because he had not the usual feudal calls on his wealth in the form of followers and clients. His descendants owned Stokesay for three hundred years after his death,[43] and it never came into the hands of anyone interested enough to rebuild it or indifferent enough to allow it to decay. It is now very much as it was when built: surrounded by a moat, with a north tower of three storeys, a great hall, a two-storey solar block, and a south tower of three storeys and a basement, each storey with a luxurious multi-windowed heated chamber.

At first glance Stokesay seems very different from the solar towers discussed above, but it is within that context that it is best understood. The multi-angular north tower has generally been dated, on the evidence of the stonework, to the 12th or earlier 13th century, and the rest of the complex to the last two decades of the 13th century. It is now

Forester's Lodge, Upper Millichope   *Interior of the Hall looking north, Stokesay Castle*

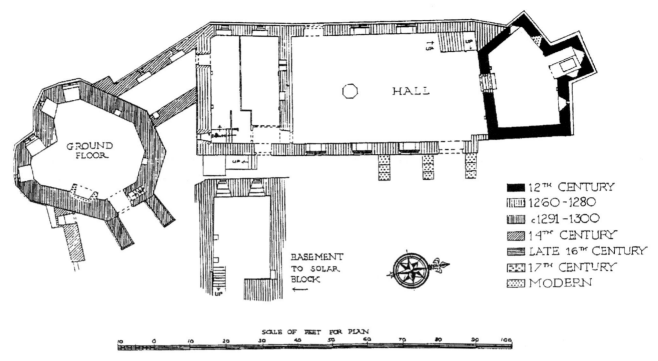

■	12TH CENTURY
	1260 -1280
	c1291 -1300
	14TH CENTURY
	LATE 16TH CENTURY
	17TH CENTURY
	MODERN

SCALE OF FEET FOR PLAN

Plan of Stokesay Castle

clear, however, that the whole was roofed in one campaign at the *end of the 13th century. Nevertheless it seems most likely that the north tower was then only repaired, reroofed, and rebuilt at its junction with the east wall of the present hall, having previously stood free, but presumably accompanied by an earlier timber hall on the site of the present one. The string course of the west wall of the hall is not present upon the north tower; and the doorway at the north end of the hall, leading

Fireplace in the north tower, Stokesay Castle

awkwardly into the lowest stage of the tower several feet below the ground level of the hall, would seem to have been inserted when the present hall replaced an earlier detached timber one at a lower level. The original entry into the tower was probably at first-floor level, as one would expect in a tower, perhaps in the position of the doorway now at the head of the first flight of the wooden stairway. On the other hand, there is no clear break in the walling where the east wall of the hall meets the tower, and there was probably some rebuilding there.

The emphasis that is often put on Stokesay as the earliest fortified manor house is not misplaced, but it tends to obscure its origin as another solar tower with a detached timber hall, like Wattlesborough and others, but with a different later history. Although Lawrence of Ludlow built a highly sophisticated up-to-date dwelling, he was still in some ways under the influence of earlier concepts, as the arrangements at the south (dais) end of the hall reveal. There was no direct internal access from that end to the chamber, but, instead, the lord and his suite had to go out into the open air and up an external stairway to reach the upper floor of the solar, exactly as the occupants of solar towers had had to do.

By *c.*1300 the free standing solar tower had lost much of its purpose. The south tower at Stokesay[44] and the surviving block at Clun Castle are free standing, but each was intended as a suite of chambers and not as a solar tower. The contrast with Stokesay is to be seen at Aston Eyre, probably of the 1320s,[45] where an elegant stone block with no defensive quality was built up against an aisled timber hall. The end wall of the hall became the partition wall between it and the new block, and there would then have been direct access from the ground floor of the hall to that of the solar block and thence to its upper storey. The hall was later rebuilt in stone in what would appear to be a curiously retrograde fashion,[46] but which may be seen as an architectural illustration of the late medieval distancing of the lord and his family from the rest of the community.

Compact residences

If Stokesay and the others may be called fortified manor houses, then perhaps Acton Burnell Castle (see illustrations overleaf), and to some extent its near contemporary Hopton Castle, may be called unfortified castles. 'Unfortified' because, with large windows and doorways on the ground floor, Acton Burnell has, despite its crenellations and corner towers, very little defensive capability in itself, and there is no sign of defensive earthworks around it; and 'castle' because it began as more than a solar tower and contained an almost complete dwelling from the start. It was built in the 1280s, on land that had belonged to the Burnells since the end of the 12th century,[47] by the most successful member of the family, Robert, chancellor of England 1274–92 and bishop of Bath and Wells 1275–92. The house was a 'retreat' or 'pleasaunce'. Its keep-like form, serving a wholly domestic purpose, called for some ingenuity in design. It was accompanied by now vanished ancillary buildings, of which the ruined so called 'Parliament barn' is the sole survivor. The ground floor of the main block—68ft. by 48ft. internally, excluding angle turrets and garderobe towers—was divided for three quarters of its length into two compartments by a central wall. That on the north, lit by lancets, may have been for storage and that on the south, with large two-light windows with evidence of cusping, was perhaps a hall for the steward. Beyond, at the west end, were service

rooms on the north and a smaller, well lit, room, which may have been the steward's chamber.[48]

The first floor, entered through a finely vaulted lobby in the north-east turret reached from a now destroyed external staircase,[49] must have led into what, without prejudice to later discussion of first floors, may be called a hall. Since it was then beyond the capability of carpenters to roof a span of 48ft., two parallel spans had to be built—their roof lines of shallow pitch may be seen on the east wall—and that demanded on the first floor an arcade, or a wall, standing upon the spine wall below. If, as has recently been supposed, there was an arcade, then the hall had very odd, almost square, proportions, and with a central arcade the siting of the dais must have been a problem. More importantly it is difficult to see how the room could have been heated. There were no fireplaces in the side walls and, since the floor below was not vaulted, the only site for an open hearth was either above the arches of the arcade below, as at Ludlow, or upon a free standing stone pillar rising from the ground, as at Much Wenlock.[50] Although all the walls or foundations are *in situ*, there is no sign of the latter, and a fire lit, if that were possible, beneath one of the arches of the arcade would have provided little heat and much smoke. If, however, as earlier writers thought, the first floor, like the ground floor, was divided into two by a solid wall then the north compartment, the hall, would have had reasonable proportions of about two to one, there would be no problem in siting the dais, and heating could have been provided by a fireplace in the spine wall. Further, the great chamber, instead of being sited, as previously supposed, in the poorly lit compartment at the west end, with a staircase and three garderobes opening out of it, could have been in a well lit south room, heated, again, by a fireplace in the spine wall. The three serving hatches in the east wall were reached by an external staircase, probably of wood: two are sited to north and south of the central division and one up against it, and it must be supposed that both hall and chamber were screened off at the east end to form a serving lobby, lit by the two-light windows in the east wall, and that at its east end the spine wall terminated in an arch which allowed access between the north and south parts of the lobby. Above the first floor at the west end was another part-floor, reached from a staircase in the

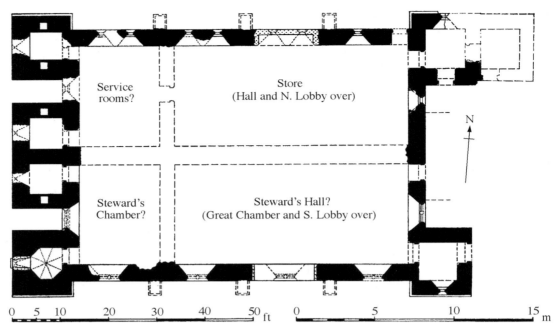

Service rooms?

Store
(Hall and N. Lobby over)

N

Steward's Chamber?

Steward's Hall?
(Great Chamber and S. Lobby over)

0 5 10   20   30   40   50 ft   0   5   10   15 m

Plan of Acton Burnell Castle

Watercolour of Acton Burnell Castle by Edw. Williams in the 1790s

south-west tower and probably serving as a private suite for the owner. In effect, what Burnell built was a detached block, more advanced than that at Clun: paradoxically a reversion in form to such northern keeps as Middleham (Yorks. N.R.) and Norham (Northumb.) in their later phases, a forerunner of the reserved private accommodation incorporated within the main structure of later more elaborate castles.

Much of the present crenellation at Acton Burnell is modern, but the licence to crenellate, the Buck engraving of 1731, a drawing of 1786, and the doorways from the corner towers to the wall walks show that crenellation, or something like it, was always intended.[51] With his house well away from the Border, Burnell had little need to keep up his guard so long as he kept up appearances. The battlements and towers of his house, like the mural towers of such later houses as Broncroft, Myddle, and (if it is later) Holdgate, were a statement of social position rather than of military intent. However, the keep-like form of Burnell's house has been seen, like Clun and Wattlesborough, as deliberate archaism.[52] 'Archaism' is perhaps an odd attitude to ascribe to a man who was erecting a building of long-established form but of innovative character and adorning it with traceried ornament of the latest fashion. If archaism it was, then it was so only in the sense that stone towers had a long history behind them, and their function—sheltering those at the top of society—automatically gave them a social cachet. And if crenellation was archaic in the late 13th century, then it had a long career ahead of it in that role, for it continued in use for almost another three hundred years—partly with serious intent upon fortifications, partly as a way of emphasizing an eaves level or a roof line, and partly as a status symbol—upon innumerable domestic and ecclesiastical buildings of all kinds.[53] Crenellation, like towers, was an attribute of the homes of the very great—it was used ornamentally by Henry III at Woodstock and Havering in 1249 and 1251[54]—and was copied by other men for that reason. 'Archaism' in a 13th-century dwelling, if that is what it is, is not easily distinguishable from social assertion or social climbing. The epithet 'archaic' arises, like that of 'old fashioned' for the Lady chapel at Glastonbury,[55] from isolating one or two elements within a structure and considering them out of their context. It is a very different matter from the archaism of, say, Strawberry Hill Gothic, and it is misleading to call it by the same name. That later fashion was practised by aristocrats, not to advertise their social standing architecturally, for their Renaissance mansions already did that, but to set themselves apart as men of taste, as an aesthetic élite within their own class.

Hopton Castle, with internal dimensions of 28 by 30ft. (see also reconstruction drawing overleaf) and

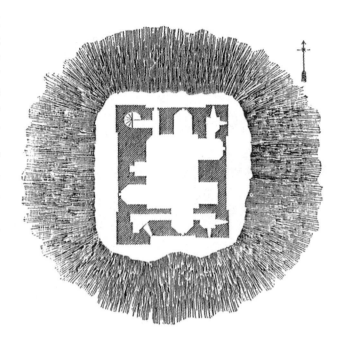

Plan of Hopton Castle

built to much the same form as Acton Burnell, has details which suggest a date of *c*.1300. Although furnished with surrounding earthworks or curtain walls, it differs from the solar towers in having a ground-floor entry, and it shows little concern with defence and much with comfort and convenience. It also makes some attempt at display, for the entrance doorway was 'clearly designed as a frontispiece to impress the visitor'. The main accommodation was on the first floor, entered as at Acton Burnell through a lobby at the head of the stairs, but the ground floor was probably residential too, well lit and provided with a fireplace. On a mezzanine second floor a small room was probably the owner's inner chamber, an amenity again anticipated at Acton Burnell. The castle was probably built by Walter of Hopton, not a tenant-in-chief but holding land of three tenants-in-chief and a justice in several counties. Like Burnell, but on a much lower level, he was a man of royal affairs and may have felt that he needed to look the part. The connection between, and the significance of, his house and Burnell's has been noted before and succinctly stated: both of them 'looked backward to the keep and forward to the ingenious planning of the fourteenth century',[56] to the form of the earlier dwelling and to the content of the later one.

Reconstruction drawing of Hopton Castle (P. Curnow)

VII   Lesser Stone Buildings

The nature of the hall

It will have been noticed that so far the hall, whether of stone or timber, on the ground or the first floor, has been discussed without much consideration of its function or significance. It was built by all men of any substance and was the most important room in the house and the most important building in a complex. For a thousand years it carried with it an aura of being something more than a room, of being the 'soul' of the house. In a moving passage of his *History*, written almost 13 centuries ago, Bede saw it, with its warmth and light shining out upon the cold and dark of a winter's eve, as a symbol of life itself.[1] A recent account has stressed its early function as a banqueting room for an élite, for a tribal leader or noble, or a king and his comrades in arms and boon companions.[2] William of Malmesbury, obliquely criticizing prelates who built ostentatiously, used 'hall' and 'banqueting chamber' almost as synonyms when praising Bishop Wulfstan of Worcester for never having built one on any of his manors.[3] That perhaps was an ascetic's view; over two hundred years later Chaucer said of the Franklin, in no very critical tone

> His table dormant in his halle alway
> Stood redy covered al the longe day.

The hall had another function as well, perhaps embryonic in early Anglo-Saxon times:[4] as the manorial system developed, the lord's dwelling, the manor house, became ever more important as the centre of a basic, but complex, unit of production, as the seat of whatever local government there was, and of a court—the hall moot[5]—which adjudicated upon nearly all the matters which touched the lives of the manor's population. The manorial hall, as the place where the lord and his connections dined and his household lived and where the local community gathered for most secular purposes, was the architectural expression of the manorial economy and the accompanying legal and social relationships at the base of feudal society.

As a room which contained the only fire which many of the occupants ever saw, where multifarious activities were carried on, often at the same time, and where many people mingled, the hall needed to be lofty. That was not because the smoke from an open fire could be dealt with only in that way. Northern halls often solved that problem with a fire hood and many later great halls with a side fireplace, but all were still open to a high roof. Many people bustling around in a limited and low space might well have created a stink which a high roof could alleviate, but it is doubtful if practical considerations were the most important. It seems more likely that a lofty, often highly ornamented, roof provided some of the grandeur appropriate to a building that was the focus of the community which used it. And similar, and stronger, demands for grandeur operated in some of the halls of great men, where manorial business, if transacted there at all, was less important than the entertainment of the lord's peers.

Whatever effect the manor as an economic institution may have had in fostering a local sense of community was strengthened by the prevailing feudal stress upon the mutuality of 'good lordship' and 'service', of the natural bond between lord and man. That ethic masked a very unequal relationship and was often breached, but that it was a powerful ideology is shown by its longevity[6] and by the general peasant desire, except at such a critical time as 1381, for the reform of lordship rather than its destruction.

The ethic was common to all, and those much above the level of a manorial lord yet lived within the same economy and with the same ideology. They too needed a hall for their vassals and retainers, but also perhaps one where they mingled with their social equals, present either as guests or as men of affairs. And equally, when men well below manorial level, wealthy peasants, came to build, they built in the unquestioned form: not mainly, if at all, because they were aping their betters or hoping to join them, but because they too saw their houses as serving an economic and social unit, however small in comparison with a manor.

First-floor halls

Any discussion of first-floor halls is probably best approached with that concept of the hall in mind. In all the large houses mentioned so far, except for Stokesay, the hall was claimed to be on an upper floor, not only in tower-like structures such as Acton Burnell and Hopton castles but also where it was part of a large complex, as in Ludlow and Shrewsbury castles. Currently, however, the concept of the first-floor hall is under attack, or else the hall is seen as the product of a fortified site.[7] It is almost certainly right to refuse to recognize the first-floor hall at normal manorial level and to reinterpret many accepted instances as solar blocks formerly accompanying now vanished timber halls. Several two-storey stone blocks in Shropshire may be cited in support. At Wenlock Priory such a building of the 13th century has two adjacent ground-floor doorways in the long wall and, at a higher level, two corbels so spaced along the wall that there can be little doubt that the doorways led into a hall and that the corbels mark the position of the arcades of an aisled hall. There is no sign on the wall of any disturbance of the masonry, and the vanished hall must have been of timber. Similar doorways and a corbel survive at Chelmarsh Hall, the 13th-century home of a cadet branch of the Mortimers of Wigmore.[8] A similar stone block at Aston Botterell, probably of 13th-century date,[9] is without the evidence of doorways and corbels but is accompanied by a timber hall range of c.1500, probably the successor of an earlier timber hall.[10] Similar vanished timber halls may be surmised at Aston Eyre and at the Provost's House (former rectory), Edgmond.[11] In addition to these individual examples Alexander Neckham's account (c.1200) of the aisled hall may be read to imply that that was the normal, indeed almost the universal, hall form.[12]

Nevertheless to unmask some frauds is not to convict every pretender of being an impostor,[13] and it is not yet necessary to believe that there was no such thing as a first-floor hall, or that, if there was, it was forced upon its occupants by the necessities of defence. That might be argued of Ludlow or Shrewsbury, where putting a ground-floor hall, with its great windows, against an external wall might well have been foolhardy. It is not relevant at Acton Burnell, which has large windows in both long ground-floor walls, nor at Wenlock Priory or Lilleshall Abbey which were both unfortified, nor even at Hopton Castle where the entrance was on the ground floor. Nor yet can it be said that halls were put on the first floor because space was limited, for at Acton Burnell and at Much Wenlock there was ample room for a ground-floor hall. Further, it is difficult to argue that the claimed halls in those houses were, in fact, not halls at all but great chambers. The arrangement at Acton Burnell was discussed above.[14] At Hopton Castle the first-floor room was entered from a lobby, like that at Acton Burnell, and in Alexander Neckham's view a

The Provost's House, Edgmond, showing the three service doorways on the right

lobby or porch[15] was the mark of a hall. At Much Wenlock the main room on the first floor of the prior's lodging has a splendid open roof with a louvre, and formerly, like the halls at Acton Burnell and Ludlow, it had an open hearth;[16] and a solar or chamber with an open hearth is a great rarity.

Perhaps the significance of Neckham's account of the aisled hall is different from what has been supposed. It is noticeable that, although he was building in nothing more expensive than parchment, his hall had only a single chamber, which may not have been on an upper floor and may have been of timber. In contrast the bishop of Winchester's early 12th-century house at Wolvesey (Hants), the late 12th-century former royal manor house at Grove (Beds.), and Luddesdown Court (Kent), a 13th-century house of the enormously rich nobleman Warin de Munchensy (d.1255),[17] all had two or more chambers in a two-storey stone block.[18] Neckham's house would appear to have been the home of a landowner of lesser status than the owners of those houses. Its hall component was perpetuating an age-old form which was first known in the homes of the very great and which in Neckham's time was still in use in their houses both to shelter the retainers and others needed to keep up their magnate status, and to accommodate all the communal, judicial, and administrative functions which their role necessitated.

Great men, however, had other needs or desires as well. While all halls had a public function distinct from the private function of the bower or solar or chamber, it was not in every hall that an undifferentiated public was being received. Men at the top of society might want a general hall—for retainers or for local public business or for men on minor errands—and an élite hall where they welcomed their equals or near equals, whether on personal visits or on affairs of state. There were many ecclesiastical and secular complexes with two halls: there were probably second halls at Ludlow, Clun, and Hopton, and one may survive at Acton Burnell, the so called Parliament barn there.[19] In function élite first-floor halls differed not at all from élite ground-floor ones, but with their grand staircases, porches, and lobbies, as at Acton Burnell, Ludlow, and Shrewsbury, they were perhaps more imposing.

The frequent presence of a first-floor hall upon a defensible site or within a compound was not there-fore primarily a matter of defensibility or of cramped space but of the way of life of men of importance. Whatever practical constraints there were upon their building were happily accepted because there was a long tradition of first-floor living brought about by the tower keeps of earlier years. It has been noted as a 'curious fact' that the 'integrated' house of the later Middle Ages with screens, through passage, and easy communication between the hall and service rooms occurs earliest among lesser men[20] and at ground level. Ground level was not a sufficient condition for its emergence, but—except perhaps in such a vast residence as Bolton Castle in Wensleydale—it was a necessary one; and among the great the first-floor tradition stood in its way.

It has recently been suggested that not all first-floor halls are what they seem to be, and a distinction has been drawn between a 'true' first-floor hall above another hall, as at Acton Burnell, and a hall above an undercroft or similar space of menial function, as at Ludlow: the latter (it is argued) is not to be seen as a first-floor hall but as an 'elaborate' ground-floor hall.[21] It is not clear in what way such a 'ground-floor' hall is 'elaborate', except that it is not on the ground floor. But the distinction seems to be edging towards the one made here: that halls should not be classified primarily by their height above ground; that what distinguishes one type of hall from another is its function; and that floor levels are only a subdivision within the more significant categories of 'public' and 'private' or, perhaps better, 'common' and 'reserved'. That suggestion is not without difficulties, for the difference between 'ground-floor' and 'first-floor' halls is more easily recognized than that between 'common' and 'reserved' ones or between 'reserved hall' and 'solar' or 'chamber'; but it is better than the ambiguity of calling a room raised several feet above ground level a 'ground-floor' hall. It has also the advantage of removing the present embarrassment of calling a room above a tradesman's shop or premises by the same term as the accommodation at Acton Burnell and Ludlow.

Urban first-floor halls

First-floor halls, to use the established terminology, may have been common in Shropshire towns. Some were built above stone undercrofts, generally by the

Vaughan's Mansion, Shrewsbury, drawn in 1780

wealthier townsmen, and the north side of Pride Hill, Shrewsbury, seems to have had a concentration of them.[22] It is not always possible to establish the function of a particular room. At the best known, Bennett's Hall of *c.*1250, the room with a richly decorated fireplace and, formerly, a doorway is not certainly a hall; but neither is it certainly anything else.[23] Rather more has been preserved of the larger stone houses in the town. Vaughan's Mansion, now part of the Music Hall, and drastically altered several times, appears from an early 19th-century account and drawing to have had a first-floor hall of mid 14th-century date, entered through a lobby at the stair head.[24] Bellstone Hall was partly rebuilt in the late 16th century; an early 19th-century drawing shows it with an entry at first-floor level, and a description suggests that it still encapsulated a late medieval first-floor hall.[25] Lord Charlton of Powis,[26] chamberlain of the king's household 1310–18, was licensed to crenellate his mansion in Shrewsbury in 1325.[27] Buckler shows a grand ground-floor hall there, and there may have been a first-floor hall as well.[28] Medieval urban remains are tantalizingly fragmentary and difficult to interpret, but it seems clear, despite the difficulties of distinguishing between a solar and a hall on an upper floor, that stone first-floor halls were an urban house-type in Shrewsbury in the 13th and 14th centuries, although probably built for, or occupied by, important gentry and exceptionally wealthy merchant families.[29] They may have been well known in less important Shropshire towns, but little evidence is available as yet. In Ludlow, survivals and documents suggest that timber-framed halls were common, at least in the larger properties. The evidence is not conclusive, but some of them may have been first-floor halls. It is noticeable, however, that there are several references to 'shop and solar' or 'shop and chamber', and in such multi-occupied buildings as the Corner Shop (Bodenhams) in Broad Street, Ludlow, it is doubtful whether any room could fittingly be called a hall.[30]

Early monastic building

To the distinction made earlier between the dwellings of magnates and of lesser nobles must be added one between lay and clerical builders. In contrast with some counties—Kent for example[31]—Shropshire had only one great episcopal manor: Lydbury North belonging to the bishop of Hereford. None of its buildings has survived, and in practice ecclesiastical domestic building in the county is that of monastic institutions and of their heads. In a land where, for many centuries, any conceivable armed force—native or foreign, rebellious or loyal—would see monasteries as protected buildings there was no need of anything more defensible than a precinct wall and a gatehouse to keep the occasional miscreant out, and perhaps some of the occupants in. In consequence, although some of the surviving buildings are older than most of the secular ones discussed earlier, only one, at Much Wenlock, is built as a tower.[32]

A further contrast between secular and ecclesiastical domestic architecture is that the great monastic institutions had to provide permanent shelter for many people in a way that peripatetic magnates and small landowners did not. Consequently many of their buildings with a communal function—refectories, dormitories, infirmaries—were among the most impressive of 12th- and 13th-century creations. In comparison with the churches that they served they were, at first, workaday structures with little of the ornate decoration or elegant vaulting of the chapter houses at Buildwas, Haughmond, and Wenlock.[33] The cloisters themselves, with their openings to the garth, probably always had some architectural ornament, and—if one can trust such scanty remains as the *lavatorium* at Wenlock,[34] the processional doorway at Lilleshall, and the arcade discovered at Haughmond (see illustrations pp.25 and 29)[35]—they may well have had very rich overall decoration. In general, however, domestic construction was plain but massive, achieving a monumental effect with long ranges of late Romanesque windows, as in the so called infirmary at Wenlock[36] and the refectory at Lilleshall, or, as in the *cellarium* at Haughmond, by sheer size. Even when some decoration was present, such as the blind arcading and columns with carved capitals at the west end of the refectory at Haughmond, it was limited in extent.

In another way monastic and secular occasions and buildings were not dissimilar. The stone tower was a blessing imported from Normandy for secular lords, but a home-grown and enduring comfort was the timber aisled hall. Some of pre- and immediately post-Conquest date have been recovered by excavation in other parts of the country, and they continued to be built until the end of the Middle Ages in counties as widely separated as Kent and Yorkshire.[37] In Shropshire 13th-century ecclesiastical examples

may be claimed at Haughmond Abbey and Wenlock Priory. At the first the building has been identified by excavation,[38] and the other has been discussed above. Since stone was an expensive material it is not surprising that early timber aisled halls can be demonstrated from surviving evidence only in the residences or complexes of the wealthy: of a priory at Much Wenlock and of a cadet branch of the Mortimers at Chelmarsh Hall.[39] It is possible that they were well known in the county, but, since among minor men they would have been accompanied, if accompanied at all, by an equally vulnerable timber solar, the evidence which might reveal one particular relationship between secular and ecclesiastical building has disappeared.

The unaisled ground-floor hall in Shropshire

It is ironic in view of the current scepticism about first-floor halls—all of stone—that the earliest known stone structures in the county which may have been ground-floor halls, Madeley Court and Great Oxenbold, are not earlier than the mid 13th century. The same lack is evident elsewhere: in Kent, for example, there is no survivor earlier than 1303;[40] and throughout the country not many stone ground-floor halls earlier than the mid 13th century have survived, or can be surmised. That is perhaps explicable. Magnates, who alone could afford a stone hall, were often building within an enceinte and utilizing space to the best advantage with first-floor halls. They built ground-floor halls in stone as well, but not as many as they might have done without the constraint of space, and since their resources were not unlimited they often built in timber as well. Stone halls were beyond the means of other men, but some of them might afford a timber hall and a commodious solar block rather than a solar tower.

The ambiguity of early survivals

Madeley Court and Great Oxenbold (the earliest Shropshire domestic buildings to survive outside an enceinte) are ambiguous in the sense that it is difficult to tell whether they are undeveloped ground-floor halls or would-be first-floor halls, or not halls at all. The timbers of the joists of the undercroft ceiling at Great Oxenbold were felled in *1242. Both houses belonged to Wenlock Priory[41] and are so similar in form and detail that it is almost certain that they are close contemporaries, built in Prior Humbert's time (1221–60). Both were built on sites sloping downwards from south to north and each had an upper and a lower room. Seen from the north, Madeley Court has the appearance of a hall above an undercroft. At Great Oxenbold entry was by a doorway at the end of the north wall, reached by an external stairway which proclaimed an undercroft and implied a first-floor hall. In each house a stairway was contrived in the thickness of the masonry at the junction of a side and end wall, and each upper room had two long high-transomed two-light windows with blank heads in an end wall and similar windows in the side walls. At Madeley the lower room runs the whole length of the building and has a fireplace and two windows and a doorway in the north wall. At Great Oxenbold, where the ground slopes down from east to west as well as from north to south, the undercroft in the eastern section of the house is limited in length and width and is now reached by an external flight of steps down from ground level; it can never have been intended for anything but storage.[42] At Madeley the upper room has a fireplace in the north wall. At Great Oxenbold the only possible place for a fire was under a canopy at the west end of the south wall.

Neither of these upper rooms has any clear 'hall' quality other than its loftiness. Both are without a through passage at one end, although at Great Oxenbold a doorway at the east end of the south wall, opposite that in the north wall, would have presented no constructional difficulties. They are without a screens passage, without doorways into a lower end, and without an open hearth. If they are ground-floor halls they are primitive ones, not merely in the obvious sense that they are separated phys-ically from services and chambers, but also in the sense that, while not subject to the restraints of a hall in a tower block (where the through passage, the doorways to services and chambers, and the open hearth were physically impossible), they eschew all but one of the elements of ground-floor halls and—again as though they were in a tower block—communicate internally only by a staircase. If they were intended as halls, they were designed by men thinking in terms of first-floor halls; and that might lead one to suspect that among the 12th- and 13th-century élite the first-floor hall was seen, if not as the norm, then at least as the ideal, as was suggested above.[43]

It may be that these two buildings were not intended as halls; nor yet as solars, for it is difficult to see how such large lofty rooms communicating with, and only with, a basement could have been used in either way. Perhaps they were the product of peculiar local circumstances. Both are less than six miles from

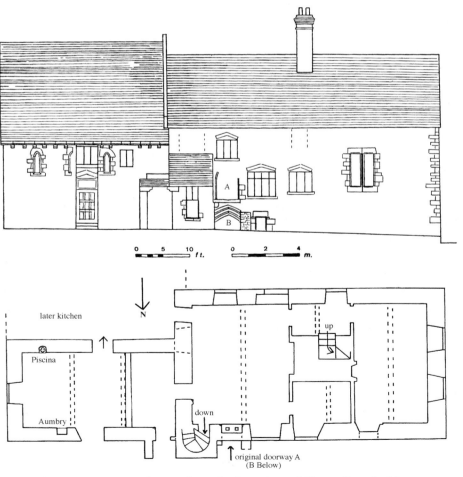

Ground floor plan and north elevation of Great Oxenbold

Much Wenlock as the crow flies, and even over medieval roads, and with a ferry crossing of the Severn for Madeley, not much more than an hour's ride away. Both had a park. In 1251 Prior Humbert paid the enormous sum of £200 to inclose Oxenbold Park, stock it with game, and keep the houses built there. At the same time he paid £100 to have houses at Madeley, where the king had caused some to be 'thrown down' because they were in the royal forest; that may indicate the beginning, or planning, of a park at Madeley, eventually licensed in 1283.[44] All this suggests that, like Chaucer's monk, Prior Humbert was 'A manly man to been an abbot able' and 'loved venerie'. His buildings, then, may be difficult to see as either halls or solars because they were not for normal use but for hunting: functioning much as a Palladian villa like Chiswick House, to which the owner, and his friends or suite, could ride out for a day and where they could gather for refreshment before or after the entertainment.

The argument applies more strongly to Great Oxenbold than to Madeley Court, and perhaps the latter was, as first suggested, a primitive ground-floor hall of stone based upon first-floor exemplars which happily did equally well for a hunting 'villa'. Although the 'hall' at Madeley was built free standing, it was not the earliest building on that site but was preceded by another of perhaps earlier 13th-century date, and of uncertain size and purpose.[45] It is possible that the length of blank walling at the west end of the south wall at Great Oxenbold may show that there was an earlier structure to the south. Certainly other buildings were erected or rebuilt soon afterwards: at Great Oxenbold an attached block to the east, which served at one time as a chapel, and at Madeley a whole series of attached and nearby structures.[46] Despite Chaucer's sly jibe, not every abbot or prior was a hunting man, and it is probable that Humbert's building at Madeley served as nothing but a hunting rendezvous for only a short time and was used by his successors as a normal residence. What happened at Great Oxenbold is much less clear, but the presence of a chapel suggests that in later years at least the site had taken on a different function or additional ones.[47]

The ambiguity in these two houses is not to be ascribed to any shortage of funds. That Prior Humbert, like the heads of some other religious communities, was not niggardly about his comforts and pleasures is shown not only by his houses, but as well by the evident lavish expenditure upon Great Oxenbold which once had a costly lead roof.[48] At the top of the building are six moulded joists—1ft. square in section, without tenons or mortices or any other sign of ever having been connected to other timbers, and, very unusually for joists, with a slight camber on the top—here interpreted as required for the necessary slight slope of a lead roof. They rested originally upon the tops of the stone walls, and now—except for the one trapped *in situ* when the present axial chimney stack was inserted—they rest upon added brick courses. At the west end of the house is part of a similar joist with a *fleur de lys* worked upon it. Except for the one at the west they are smoke blackened, but so lightly that nothing more than a leak from a chimney is at issue. They have no function now, but in the past they would have carried a boarded ceiling, and the one trapped by the inserted stack has the remains of a board upon it. Happily, these joists too can be dated and come from trees felled in *1246–7.[49]

The classic ground-floor hall

It was claimed earlier that, if Madeley Court and Great Oxenbold were indeed ground-floor halls, then they were primitive ones. The classic ground-floor hall that was almost universal in England in the later Middle Ages, whether of stone or of timber, utilized space more efficiently than those two houses would have done. Typically it consisted of a large lofty hall, open to the roof and with a hearth in or near the middle.[50] It was entered at one end from a transverse passage, divided from the hall by a timber screen and acting as a corridor through the width of the building. At the lower (passage) end, and entered from it, was a two-storey service block with a pantry and buttery on the ground floor and a chamber on the first. Generally sited near that end was the kitchen, often a flimsy structure which would be no great loss if, as many did, it burned down. At the upper (dais) end was the two-storey solar block with private accommodation for the owner and his family. That basic form served many social levels from the highest to all but the lowest, and variations upon it, over and above differences of size, were numerous: a hall between ends of two or one-and-a-half storeys or even one storey; between ends in the same plane as the hall or projecting one or both sides at one or both ends; or else with one end only that served as both solar and service. In the larger houses very elaborate accommodation might be provided. The rebuilding of the hall range at Ludlow in the late 13th and early 14th centuries saw a proliferation of chambers. At Clun there were, apart from others elsewhere, two 'great chambers' in the barbican, and at Caus, illustrating the very formal relations between most upper-class married couples, 'the chamber of the lord' and 'the chamber of the lady'.[51] And since great men spent only a small part of their time at any one residence a chamber, or even a suite, would be provided for whoever was looking after things in their absence, the constable, or the steward, or the auditor. It will be found, however, that ground-floor halls in Shropshire, with one or two possible exceptions, survive from dwellings of less magnificence and complexity than those just mentioned.

Royal service and stone building

Whether or not Stokesay is the earliest surviving fortified manor house, it has good claim, in its form of *c*.1300 and despite its atypical north and south towers, to be the earliest surviving example in the county of the ground-floor-hall house.[52] It was followed in the early 14th century by other houses with stone halls: Apley Castle, Edgmond rectory, Myddle Castle, Charlton Hall, Shrewsbury, Silvington Manor House, and Whitton Court.[53] That none of them had much defensive character was probably a consequence of their greater distance from the Welsh border and of the confidence of their owners that the Welsh, for the time being at least, had been pacified: a confidence not wholly misplaced, for it was nearly a hundred years before Glyn Dwr and his followers shook their confidence and devastated some of their lands. No example is as well preserved as Stokesay, but despite alterations and rebuildings some evidence of their nature remains. At Apley Castle it is reasonable to infer[54] an early 14th-century open hall between storeyed ends. At Edgmond old rectory the survival of a service block with the classical arrangement of three service doorways in the through passage (see illustration p.104) supposes an open hall. At Whitton Court 14th-century windows on two storeys and the doorway of a through passage beyond allow a similar inference. The surviving stair turret at

Myddle evidently abutted a ground-floor hall,[55] and the halls at Charlton Hall, Shrewsbury, have already been discussed.[56] At Silvington the 14th-century two-storeyed solar end is clearly identifiable, separated by a timber partition from the hall, at the far end of which are the remains of a doorway to the through passage. At Aston Eyre at a later date a stone-built open hall replaced a timber-framed one.[57]

In contrast with the grand builders of known aisled halls and of first-floor halls, the men who erected these houses were generally of lesser social standing, though making their way in the world by talent or good connections. Stokesay is of course the classic *nouveau riche* house. The issue of a licence to crenellate to the Shrewsbury wool merchant Lawrence of Ludlow, a man of no social distinction, emphasizes his utility to the Crown, and to several magnates. He seems to have been instrumental in persuading his fellow merchants to accept the unpopular tax on wool, the maletot, levied by the Crown in 1294.[58] John the Moneyer, of Ludlow, who bought Whitton in the mid 13th century, was of similar background.[59] The descendants of both were well ensconced among the local landed families by the middle of the next century.[60] Either Walter de Beysin (d.1309) or his son Thomas (d.1319)[61] may have built Silvington Manor House. The Beysins were minor tenants in chief, serjeants enfeoffed by Henry I;[62] *c*.1243 a share of the estates of the Broseley family,[63] Fitz Warin[64] cadets, fell to them, and their manors and estates in eastern Shropshire and western Staffordshire[65] brought them increased prosperity and regular contact with the great.[66] They began to make a mark on their times. Walter made a good marriage[67] and in the 1290s and 1300s was an assessor and collector of taxes and a commissioner of array; he received military summonses and sat as a knight of the shire for Shropshire in the parliament of 1302.[68] He was also under-sheriff and a commissioner of oyer and terminer. In 1303, in unusual circumstances, the Exchequer appointed him sheriff of Staffordshire and Shropshire; consequent involvement in Shrewsbury faction-fighting brought him a spell in gaol and a fine,[69] but such things did not irremediably mar a career[70] or necessarily halt the social[71] and economic[72] advance of a knightly family. Another, Sir Alan Charlton, licensed to crenellate the mansions of Apley and Great Wytheford in 1327,[73] was only a younger son—but his elder brothers were Lord Charlton of Powis and Thomas, bishop of Hereford, two important men in the royal administration in the early 14th century;[74] moreover he married very well, to Lord Zouche's widowed co-heir, whose Devon estates he continued to enjoy during the many years he survived her.[75] He was the royal custodian of the castles of Wigmore and Montgomery in the early 1330s and was responsible for raising levies for the king in four border counties.[76] The rectory of Edgmond was among the richest livings in Shropshire;[77] in the early 14th century its well connected rectors enjoyed study leave, and in the 1320s one was absent in the service of Lord Charlton of Powis, head of a family long and intimately connected with the interests of his patron, the abbot and convent of Shrewsbury.[78] In 1308 Lord Strange of Knockin was licensed to crenellate his house at Myddle.[79] Next year, however, he died, and the house may have been built—was certainly occupied—by a John le Strange who was his kinsman (but not his heir)[80] and evidently a courtier, for in 1328–9 he was 'the king's beloved yeoman'.[81]

Some ground-floor stone halls in Shropshire may have been erected by men at the top of society: that at Myddle, for example, if it was Lord Strange's work rather than his kinsman's. At Whittington castle a 14th-century structure of five bays in the inner bailey may be interpreted as the remains of a ground-floor hall[82] for the Fitz Warins.[83] A monastic example is the early 14th-century building at Haughmond Abbey generally known as the Infirmary but more likely to have been the abbot's hall,[84] for at the upper end it connects directly through two doorways to what is generally recognized as the abbot's lodging. It is a structure of some splendour, with a great west window of six trefoiled lights beneath now destroyed tracery and with windows of two transomed and trefoiled lights beneath a cusped head in the side walls. While there must be some doubt about all of these, it is not to be supposed that every stone ground-floor hall in Shropshire at this time was the home of a minor man. Nevertheless, if the few survivals are typical, then they were in general the homes of knightly families, but not of 'mere' knights drawing on

nothing more than the revenues from their lands.[85] Instead they were built by men of knightly origin fashioning careers for themselves in the king's service, either as *buzones*—men busy about county affairs[86]—or at court. Such careers had become possible because the expansion of royal administration, the development of legal processes, and the proliferation of written records had created opportunities for able men of that class.[87]

Nor are stone blocks with timber halls readily attributable to 'mere' knights. Those at Wenlock Priory and Chelmarsh Hall[88] were the creations respectively of a great institution and of the cadet branch of a great family. That at Aston Eyre has usually been ascribed to the FitzAers, who held Aston as a knight's fee from the FitzAlans. From the 1260s Sir John FitzAer (d.1293) served many local offices, including that of keeper of the peace, and his frequent attestation of private deeds suggests that he was highly regarded by his contemporaries; he was returned as a knight of the shire for the parliament of 1290.[89] His son Hugh inherited his father's coronership and was one of the six knightly jurors to perambulate the royal forests in 1298.[90] The solar block, however, is most probably of the 1320s, and it is not at all clear that it was built by the FitAers' resources. Their heiress Margery (b. 1314) was betrothed, and later married, to Sir Alan Charlton's son Alan (*c.*1318–1349), bringing with her Aston Eyre and Great Wytheford. The younger Alan then leased these estates to his father for £20 a year.[91] As has been seen, in 1327 Sir Alan was licensed to crenellate 'his houses' at Apley and Wytheford.[92] If he was treating Wytheford as 'his', he was perhaps doing the same at Aston Eyre, and he is the likeliest builder of the solar block there.

The 13th-century stone block at Aston Botterell has the best claim to have been built by a 'mere' knight: like the FitzAers, the Botterells held their manor, for which they obtained a market and fair in 1263, as a knight's fee from the FitzAlans, and they were patrons of Aston Botterell church. Nevertheless Sir Thomas Botterell was at one time constable of Clun Castle, and in 1281 he was one of four knights commissioned to report on the king's castle at Bridgnorth. His family cannot be said to have been in the royal service in the sense in which Sir Alan Charlton and the others were, but they apparently ranked above the usual knightly family.[93]

Private chapels

The distinction between secular and religious buildings is not one that can always be maintained, and many large, and not so large, houses had their own chapel. In the mid 14th century the Charltons had one in Charlton Castle, as did the Fitz Warins in Whittington Castle and the Corbets in Hadley manor house.[94] The Talbots had one in 1401 in their house at Blakemere.[95] At Caus in 1399–1400 there was a chapel with a prison below, and at Clun in 1440 there was one in the barbican with a chamber below.[96] Men of lesser standing in less impressive houses might have similar comforts, and in 1370 Edward de Acton, a man of some local importance, six times knight of the shire, had an oratory in his, presumably timber, house at Longnor.[97] It has been suggested that domestic chapels became commoner in the later Middle Ages as religion became more 'private'.[98] Certainly there are far more documentary references to domestic chapels in the 14th and 15th centuries than there are earlier—at least among men of merely local importance[99]—but then there are far more documents from later years. In fact few early chapels can be identified with certainty on the ground; examples are at Ludlow Castle and Great Oxenbold, respectively of the 12th and 13th centuries, and at Apley Castle of the 14th century. But then again, the first was perhaps more of a garrison church than a private chapel, and it may be assumed that there would, sooner or later, have been a chapel in every house which the prior of Wenlock regularly visited.[100] How far that 'keeping one's distance' attitude, which led to the lord and his family ceasing to dine in the hall, also affected worship is not wholly clear. What may, however, be seen is that the early practice of building a church in the immediate vicinity of a big house, as at Acton Burnell, Holdgate, Knockin, Longnor, Ludlow, Meole Brace,[101] and Ruyton-XI-Towns, perhaps declined in later years. That is partly an aspect of the decline in church building, partly an aspect of the tendency to accommodate many functions within the house rather than have the expense and inconvenience of building a separate structure, and partly a result of the decline in building of any kind in Shropshire by the very great. A desire for more 'private' worship would not have conflicted with any of these aspects.

Architectural display

Despite their ruinous and incomplete state these late 13th- and early 14th-century houses retain much of their original effect, an effect which may be presumed to have been at least partly intended. At Stokesay and at Ludlow the hall with its range of graceful windows is flanked by towers or by tall solar ends; at Acton Burnell the lavish and delicate ornament of the fenestration alleviates the solidity of the four-square block with its corner turrets; at Edgmond the doorways in the passage are richly moulded and decorated; and even at Aston Eyre, Silvington, and Whitton Court enough remains to suggest their original qualities. That Shropshire dwellings attain more architectural character, or at any rate contain more architectural elements, as they shed much of their defensive role is clear, but the one was an accompaniment and not the result of the other. Early fortresses had not been wholly utilitarian. The gatehouse at Ludlow, with its richly carved blind arcade and its first-floor windows with nook shafts and cushion capitals, had betrayed much consciousness of the value of architectural ornament, and had, indeed, far more of it than many churches built at that time. Moreover the late 12th-century north gate of Bridgnorth Castle was as highly ornamented[102] as any surviving doorway in the county, outside Lilleshall Abbey. When the opportunity was present castle builders were as ready as church builders to indulge in artistry; a notable element of early towers is the slight thickening of the wall at the angles, similar to the pilaster buttresses of Norman churches, and providing, like them, not so much structural support as architectural punctuation.

That later houses, and later halls and chambers within fortifications, have more obvious architectural intent than earlier towers and castles is not because less attention is paid to defence, and only partly because more is paid to residential needs; it is mainly because, with the development of masonry techniques, the size of openings and the mode of fenestration had changed and windows in castles, as in churches, were larger and more intensely exploited as a means of architectural expression than they had been. Defensive worries could sometimes inhibit the use of the most up-to-date forms, as in the hall at Ludlow, where the windows to the courtyard are of two lights while those to the exterior are of one. Even those single lights, however, were given tracery and transoms, and such inhibitions were by no means typical for at Stokesay Castle, as at Shrewsbury Castle earlier, the windows to the exterior and to the courtyard were the same.

Furthermore there is nothing to show that, at a time when most houses carried some element of fortification, their architectural ornament was meagre or retarded in comparison with churches. At Stokesay the tracery of the hall windows, with cuspless circles above trefoiled lights, is in advance of that originally in the east and west windows of Longnor church and in the north and south windows of the transepts at Acton Burnell church, which originally had no cusping at all.[103] The tracery of the windows in Acton Burnell Castle is even more advanced: curved triangles with sexfoil cusping above cinquefoil lights. In fact the castle—even in its present state, stripped of its buttresses and with two great barn doorways driven through its north and south walls—is an impressively deliberate composition. The two houses may be as much as a generation later than the two churches, and, while they do not show that secular architecture was in advance of ecclesiastical, they do show that it did not lag behind. The architectural contrasts to be seen in buildings of that time are not those between defended and undefended or secular and ecclesiastical structures, or (very much) between the work of one generation and the next. The contrasts arise from the varied resources and opportunities available to builders. Whether he was commissioning a church or a house, Burnell had more resources than Roger Sprenchose of Longnor,[104] and was probably in closer contact with advanced architectural ideas than Lawrence of Ludlow. It is for that reason that Acton Burnell church surpasses Longnor church and that Acton Burnell Castle is more of the latest fashion than Stokesay Castle.

It was in the 14th and 15th centuries when, as in parish churches, activity was mainly restricted to 'improvements' that more ornament appeared, noticeably in refectories. The Grey Friars' 'refectory' at Shrewsbury had a window with intersecting tracery inserted at its east end in place of the plain lancets of the rest of the elevation.[105] In the refectory at Haughmond the original round-headed windows of the west end were replaced in the 14th century with a large transomed traceried window. Shrewsbury Abbey's refectory had an elaborate 14th-century pulpit, corbelled out from the wall on three sides, with tall cusped lancets for its openings having traceried panels in their lower halves, and with head stops to the mouldings.[106] Even in the sad state which they were in by the early 19th century, the west and south ranges of the cloister at Shrewsbury were still an imposing pile of buildings.[107]

Late-medieval monastic splendour

Two of the most impressive pieces of domestic architecture were produced towards the end of the period by religious communities. Unlike so much Shropshire building of the later Middle Ages they were typical of their time, attesting the current practice among such institutions of spending large sums on luxurious accommodation, especially for their heads.[108] Such expenditure reveals the wordliness with which, in an age of rising anti-clericalism, reformers were always reproaching the late medieval church.

The lesser of the two examples is the abbot's lodging at Haughmond, refurbished in the years around 1500 and provided with a splendid five-sided bay window with large cinquefoil lights under four-centred heads. Far more important is the prior's lodging at Wenlock (see illustration overleaf), one of the outstanding domestic buildings of the age. It is a reconstruction of an earlier range running north–south and includes at its north end a chapel that may have served the infirmary and a heated room which perhaps provided accommodation for the infirmarer.[109] The main part has a great hall and solar on the first floor, and kitchen and service rooms below; on each floor the rooms are entered from a multi-windowed two-storeyed gallery; the roof over the upper gallery forms the lower part of the roof pitched over the whole building. The hall roof has arch braces springing from moulded wall posts and one narrow tier of cusped wind braces, or perhaps, more accurately, of cusped ornament. Provision is made for a louvre to take away the smoke from a central open hearth and the beams beneath the hall floor have had timbers spliced into them to allow them to continue to carry the floor after the removal of the great stone column that had supported the former open hearth.[110] Two flues in the very thick transverse wall at the lower end of the hall serve fireplaces in the room below the hall and in the 'infirmarer's' room. Within the same wall are two ingenious interlocking spiral staircases, one from the 'infirmarer's' room to the room above, and one from the room below the hall up to the hall itself;[111] this staircase is continued within the wall from the hall to a second-storey room above the 'infirmarer's' accommodation. The whole is a remarkably sophisticated self-sufficient suite of living and service rooms.

The elevations are equally carefully designed. The gallery along the west front is a symmetrical composition of seven main bays punctuated by deeply projecting buttresses. Each bay is divided by lesser buttresses into two smaller bays, each with two two-light windows. The elaborate effect is enhanced by the vast plain catslide roof of grey and brown Harnage slates brooding above. The east elevation, from its south end to the north end of the 'infirmarer's' rooms, is, despite the garderobe in the solar, an organized balanced composition with groups of two-light windows on both floors spaced to emphasize the centre and the ends. A complete symmetry is displayed in the south gable wall, and everywhere the effect is heightened by lavish use of a green- and red-veined sandstone, brought from an as yet unidentified quarry. The windows have two cusped lights beneath heads of nearly triangular form, and the upper ones have blank panels at the base.

The south wall and the east wall, except at its north end, are contemporary with the fenestration and with the west gallery, but the west wall, now hidden behind the gallery, is probably a survival from the earlier 12th-century range and retains two early doorways opening into a hall and chamber reached from the gallery.[112] The roof of the hall, and the roofs to north and south of it, have been dated to *1425 and, whether or not they were erected then or a year or two later, they now turn out to be two to three generations earlier than was previously supposed. It is not impossible to match elements of the roof and of the east and west elevations with those of early 15th-century structures elsewhere, and the angularity of the fenestration compares with that of the windows in the north chancel chapel of Ellesmere church.[113] The west gallery too could be written off as no more than seven identical symmetrical bays, but the form of the rebuilt east elevation, from the south end to the north wall of the so called infirmarer's chamber, is a very different affair: a deliberate composition with windows sited where a balancing symmetry demands, with internal arrangements in the hall accommodated to the external design (and that moreover in a range lit from one side only), and marred only by the intrusive garderobe projection. And, since the original west wall, if exposed to view, would be a very irreg-

The east façade of the Prior's House at Much Wenlock

ular composition, the gallery itself, also with a date of *1425 for the roof, must be seen as an attempt to mask an unsightly elevation by clapping a false front onto it: and then using the space so created to provide access to separate rooms within a suite, a convenience that was not to become common within a private house for at least another two hundred years.[114] Despite the problems which a date of the late 1420s or early 1430s raises, the structure must be supposed to be a full decade earlier than the better known but far less developed designs of such houses as Hurstmonceux (Sussex) and South Wingfield (Derb.). Whether it was a wholly local creation, or whether master masons from elsewhere were called in is unknown and probably unknowable; but whoever the master mason was he first showed his hand, as far as surviving evidence goes, at Much Wenlock.

The evidence from dendrochronology for the date of the roofs is presumably beyond challenge, but of course it can be argued that that dates no more

The south gable of the
Prior's House at Much Wenlock

than the roofs themselves; that at some time between their erection and the mid 16th century they were underpinned along most of the east elevation and a new wall inserted beneath; or that they were dismantled while a new wall was built and were then re-erected; or that the east wall has been refronted internally and externally. The best, indeed the only, structural evidence in favour of such a claim is that in the north-west angle of the hall the corbel of the wall post is partly obscured by the swelling of the cross wall there, occasioned by the need to accommodate the staircase from the hall to the second floor of the part of the building to the north of it. Since the cross wall appears to bond with the east wall[115] that could suggest that both cross wall and east wall are later than the roof. Nevertheless the cross wall's encroachment on the truss is slight and need be no more than the result of a small miscalculation, common enough in building, which got the cross wall to the south of where the builders wanted it. Furthermore it should be noted that, swelling apart, the cross wall perfectly fits the truss at both ends, and the likeliest explanation is that the decision to take one part of the intertwining staircase up from the hall to the second-floor room to the north of the hall was a late one and necessitated the enlargement of the cross wall in the north-west corner of the hall. It may also be noted that the roof trusses in the hall (despite being irregularly spaced with a louvre bay towards the north) are sited to fit the elevations and not *vice versa*, and that suggests that the trusses were made for the present elevations. And the form of the staircase, at least up to the first floor, was well and widely known by the early 14th century.[116] Until structural evidence to the contrary emerges the date of *1425 for the remodelling of the earlier range has to be accepted.

The abandonment of stone

All the surviving buildings discussed so far, whether ecclesiastical or secular, were constructed of stone: not because no other materials were used, but because nothing else has endured from the two hundred years following the Conquest. On the other hand, hundreds of timber buildings survive from the next two hundred years and, while their presence then calls as much for explanation as their absence earlier, the fact itself will surprise no-one. What is surprising is the almost total absence of secular stone buildings from the later period. From the mid 14th century to the early 16th, outside towns and conventual precincts, the only stone structures in the county that have left either remains or records are the hall and service block added in different stone to the chamber block at Aston Eyre;[117] Broncroft Castle, described somewhat ambiguously by Leland as 'a very goodly place like a castle';[118] whatever was done at Tong in 1381 and at Cheney Longville in 1394, when licences to crenellate were granted;[119] the 15th-century work incorporated into the 16th-century Plaish Hall; and the building, or rebuilding, in *1452 of Hall Farm, Stottesdon as a four-bay hall.[120] It is possible, too, that the 'new chamber' at Clun, which was 'whitewashed' in 1386–7, and the 'newly built great house' referred to in 1440[121] were of stone. By contrast no fewer than a dozen stone houses survive in whole or in part from the late 13th and early 14th centuries,[122] and another four are recorded.[123]

There is little to be said about the medieval architecture of the first four mentioned above and nothing about the rest. The most substantial remains are at what is probably the earliest of the four, Aston Eyre, where the shell of the hall and service block still stand. As has been seen, they were probably

built in the 1320s by the Charltons,[124] who long retained the manor (still holding it in the early 19th century)[125] but had a second seat elsewhere[126]—facts which probably helped to preserve the building.[127] Broncroft Castle was thoroughly rebuilt in the 19th century, and little more than the base of a tower remains from an early period. Originally there was a walled courtyard with a great hall along the south wall, flanked by towers at the south-east and south-west angles—somewhat reminiscent of the final plan of Stokesay. John Burley, who was six times knight of the shire between 1399 and 1411, and William Burley, who succeeded him, both trusted officers of the FitzAlans and Talbots, were 'of Broncroft',[128] but the castle was probably built before their time.

Tong was almost wholly obliterated by the brick house put up by the Vernons in the early 16th century. Cheney Longville has retained its medieval form of a courtyard with four ranges enclosed within a moat, but it has been much rebuilt. In the south wall are two 14th-century doorways, side by side, with no space for a wall between and thus clearly reset. On the first floor of the west range a transverse wall has a doorway with a Caernarvon arch, but that too may be reset. The licences to crenellate at Tong and at Cheney Longville went, respectively, to Sir Fulk de Pembridge, who by 1397 was a friend of the Beauforts and a supporter of the king,[129] and to Sir Hugh Cheyne, who was in the king's service.[130]

The infrequent use of stone from the mid 14th to the mid 16th century has to be seen in conjunction with the later nearly universal use of timber in secular structures and is discussed at the end of the next chapter.

The hall and chamber at Aston Eyre

VIII   Late Medieval Timber Houses: Gentry and Peasantry

Dating sources

The significance of the almost total suspension of building in stone will be discussed later. For the moment it may be noted that all the houses mentioned so far belonged to men, families, or institutions that figure in official records or the records of magnates; many of the houses can be related to a known person and may be dated and considered in that light. For timber-framed houses the position is different: very few of them can be so identified, and even when they can be associated with a family they can rarely be attributed to an individual.[1] Those that can be linked in any way are generally the homes of gentry or near-gentry. Nevertheless, where the records of an area have been systematically studied, as for example in the hundreds of Condover and Ford, the borough of Wenlock, and parts of Bradford and Munslow hundreds,[2] it is occasionally possible to associate a surviving small building with a less exalted family or (more often) with a type of tenancy.[3] Even more rarely a document will allow something to be gleaned about the form and date of construction of a named tenant's house.[4]

Records are of less use in establishing a sequence of securely dated buildings as a guide to the general development, but happily dendrochronology is now providing reasonably reliable dates, often very different from those previously accepted.[5] As many houses were cruck-built and the difficulty of dating crucks is notorious, the technique is invaluable, but even with its aid the dates of many buildings not sampled by it must be regarded as provisional.

Aisled and base-cruck halls

Compared with the nearly 300 cruck houses, all other surviving medieval timber framed-houses in Shropshire are negligible in numbers, but they will be dealt with first. The timber-framed aisled hall is typologically early, and in some counties early ones survive.[6] Aisled halls of 13th-century date in Shropshire, all belonging to institutions or men of high standing, were mentioned in chapter VII,[7] but the only surviving hall is the Guildhall in Mill Street, Ludlow, of *1411 (see illustrations overleaf). It was built by the wealthy Palmers' Guild, largely responsible for the magnificent rebuilding of St. Lawrence's church, and it may owe its form and its late date to its institutional origin.

In early years the aisled hall was built by kings and nobles and bishops and abbots, but in the course of the 13th century it fell from favour among them, while persisting among lesser men in some counties throughout the Middle Ages.[8] It is the prevailing view that the base-cruck hall was developed by the owners of aisled halls, irked at the inconvenience of arcade posts and enabled by advances in carpentry to dispense with them.[9] That idea is based partly upon the rough coincidence in date between the first appearance of the one and the disappearance of the other; partly upon the assumption that the aisled hall was normal, almost universal, in 12th-century houses; partly upon the presence in some base-cruck halls of a spere truss and an upper-end wall with the main posts disposed in an aisled pattern;[10] and partly upon the substitution in 1297, at Harwell (Berks.), of a base-cruck for a rotted aisle truss.[11]

All of those propositions, apart from the coincidence of dates, may be questioned. There is nothing to show that arcade posts were thought inconvenient by the 13th century. When, *c.*1200, Alexander Neckham wrote his account of the aisled hall he singled out the arcade posts not as necessary evils but for approving comment.[12] The change among the great from aisled to unaisled halls may have been brought about by aesthetic considerations, by a

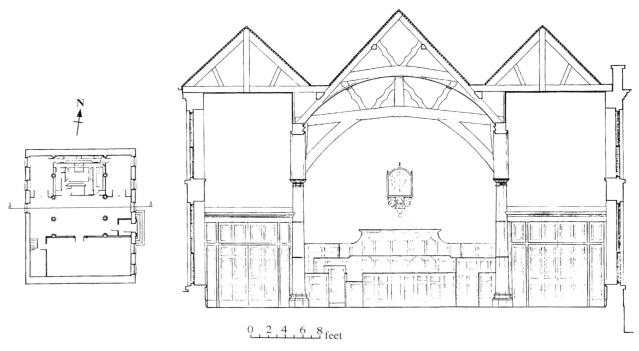

0 2 4 6 8 feet

Plan (not to scale) and section of the Guildhall, Ludlow, showing the surviving medieval nave roof and aisles raised and re-roofed

desire to transform their houses into the lofty, well lit buildings of the Gothic style, and to that end both exploiting and encouraging the increasing skills of

View of six pairs of V-shaped cusped struts in the roof space of the Guildhall, Ludlow

carpenters. As was argued above, Neckham may not have been thinking of all builders but of men somewhat below magnate level, or members of a cadet branch, perhaps the equivalent in their own county of the Corbets of Wattlesborough, with their timber hall and single chamber.[13]

Moreover, the significance of the spere truss, wherever it may first have appeared, must be considered not in isolation but in relation to its function. It has to be remembered that in the late 13th century—a time when aisled, unaisled, base-cruck, and cruck halls were all present—the hall was developing into its mature form, with a through passage at the lower end and, as a necessary adjunct, a screen to divide the passage from the hall proper. It seems to be generally accepted, although as a 'curious fact', that the through passage appeared first in the houses of men of moderate standing;[14] and so too, then, did its necessary accompaniment, the timber screen, of which the spere truss was only one form among several, and probably not the earliest. That great men later covered it with splendid ornament, and that lesser men aspired to do so, is not evidence for the derivation of base-cruck halls from aisled ones. Nor is it certain that spere trusses appeared first in aisled halls, for the base-cruck hall of West Bromwich Manor House (Staffs.), of *1273–93, has a spere truss,[15] and there are remains of one at Plowden Hall (in Lydbury North), of *1273–1302; and as yet there are no known spere trusses of earlier date in aisled halls. Further, the relationship between spere trusses and aisled halls does not suggest a necessary connection between them. Many years ago Margaret Wood—although believing in such a connection—felt constrained to remark on their 'strange' distribution: spere trusses are common in the north-west and rare in the south-east, while the distribution of aisled halls is the reverse.[16] Nothing in all that disproves the aisled-

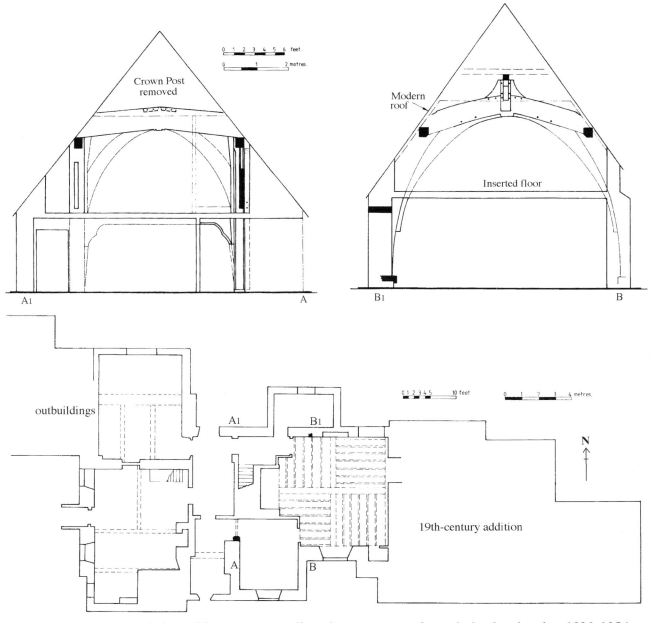

Ground floor plan of The Bold, Aston Botterell, and sections as indicated, dendro-dated to 1320-1354

hall origin of spere trusses, but equally there is nothing to support it. And, finally, the substitution of a base-cruck truss for an aisled one at Harwell has no bearing on the issue of precedence, for it occurred at least six years after West Bromwich Manor House had been built.

In Shropshire the argument for the descent of the base-cruck hall from the aisled hall is the weaker because the men who built base-cruck halls were, as will be shown later, of the gentry and of lesser standing than the grand builders of aisled halls. While all the identifiable aisled halls sooner or later had stone solar blocks, base-cruck halls invariably had timber ends, and the most exalted builders in the county in the 14th and 15th centuries were building unaisled halls. As its form would suggest, the base-cruck hall is most reasonably seen as an improvement upon the cruck hall.[17]

The earliest dates established by dendrochronology for base-cruck halls in the country at large are of the last quarter of the 13th century, but the great majority are of the first three quarters of the next. That is based upon no more than a handful of examples and, as more dates are known, the pattern may change. The dated Shropshire examples are Plowden Hall (*1302), 23 Barrow Street (*1327–30), Much Wenlock, the Bold (*1320–54), Aston Botterell, High Grosvenor (*1375–77), Claverley, and 15 High Street (*1408), Much Wenlock. In addition Cottage Farm, Easthope, and Upton Cressett Hall (*1430 and *1431 respectively) are more probably base-cruck halls than aisled halls. While base crucks therefore appear in the county at much the same time as in the country they, or something very like them, were still appearing in the 15th century. Wolverton Hall (*1475), Eaton-under-Heywood, has the same form, dimensions, and scantling as the earlier examples and differs only in the base cruck's terminating not at the collar but slightly above it, whence a secondary cruck couple rises to the apex.[18] Wolverton could be called a 'two tiered' cruck rather than a base cruck, but one may agree with Dr. Brunskill that the distinction is of little moment,[19] except perhaps to provide an approximate date for such related structures as Cleeton Court, Cleeton St. Mary, and Tir-y-coed, Kinnerley.[20] That may not be a Salopian idiosyn-

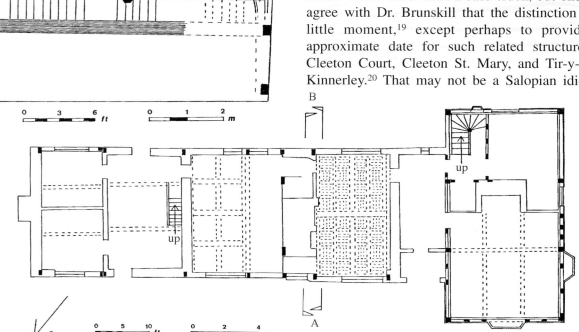

Ground-floor plan of Wolverton Hall, Eaton-under-Heywood, and section A-B, dendro-dated to 1475

Cusped spere trusses at Brookgate Farm, Plealey, Pontesbury

Reconstructed barn to the south-west of the farm-house, Brookgate Farm, Plealey, Pontesbury

crasy, for it would seem that in neighbouring Herefordshire too base crucks went well into the 15th century, and it is possible that in Kent, where they first appeared *c*.1300, they were being built as late as 1440–80.[21]

The typical base-cruck hall in Shropshire has a spere truss and crown posts. All the crown posts are short, plain, and with downward-swinging braces. Plowden Hall, the Bold, and High Grosvenor have no decoration upon the timbers; at 23 Barrow Street, Much Wenlock, the arch braces have a double roll-and-fillet mould; Easthope Cottage has some slight cusping; 15 High Street, Much Wenlock, and Upton Cressett Hall have very rich cusping. At Wolverton Hall and at Cleeton Court there is a richly cusped **V** strut above the tie. Oldfields Farm, Moreton Say, has no crown post, no evidence for any timbers above the tie, no spere truss (although both end-trusses remain), and no ornament. Unhappily, it failed to produce a reliable dendrochronology date. The original roof has gone, but presumably it was of coupled-rafter type, and that and the absence of cusping might suggest a very early date; on the

other hand its character might be due to limited resources at any date.

Base-cruck halls often give an impression, internally, of massive solidity, which few aisled or box-framed halls attain. But very few of their solar- or service-ends have survived in the county. No hall now has two original ends, and several have none. At Upton Cressett there is a four-bay two-storey upper end contemporary with the hall. At the Cottage, Easthope, a two-storey lower end was built 20 years after the hall and presumably replaced an earlier structure.[22] The only evidence for a parlour end is at 23 Barrow Street, Much Wenlock, where the surviving bay of the hall has no spere truss to prove a lower end and is flanked by a jettied wing. It may be, as has been suggested for Kent, that the vanished ends were often 'low built' and not adaptable to later needs.[23] There are, indeed, several cruck halls in Shropshire with later box-frame ends which have replaced earlier cruck ends: Brookgate Farm, Plealey, for example (see illustrations this page and overleaf). But all the base-cruck hall ends that have survived are box-framed, even at the lower

121

end, and it is unlikely that any at the upper end were not. Some halls may, like the Cottage, Easthope, have been built up against an existing 'low built' structure which, unlike the one there, did duty for a long time before being superseded. But it may also be that the classic two-ended hall of the later Middle Ages was not standard among these houses, many of which may have had a combined service–solar end alone. That may well be true of Upton Cressett, where there is an exceptionally large four-bay wing at one end of the hall, beyond a spere truss, and where the fall of the ground makes it difficult to suppose a second end beyond the now truncated hall.

Something may be said about the occupiers of base-cruck halls. In the mid 13th century Plowden was held of the bishop of Hereford for 40 days' castle guard at Bishop's Castle in time of war, and in 1272 Philip of Plowden was listed fifth among the Purslow hundred jurors at the eyre.[24]

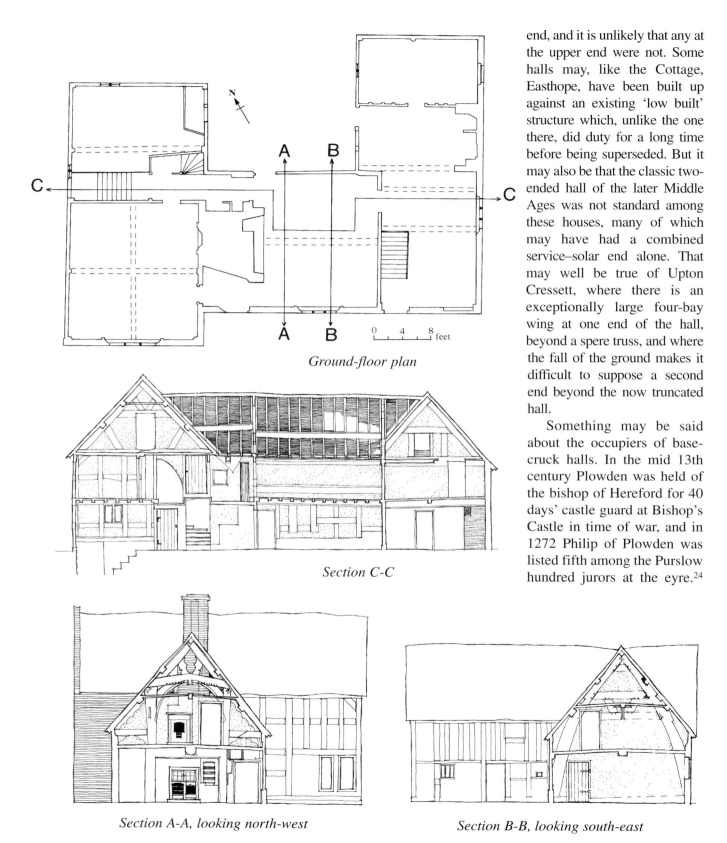

Ground-floor plan

Section C-C

Section A-A, looking north-west

Section B-B, looking south-east

Brookgate Farm, Plealey, Pontesbury, all drawings to scale shown

In the late 13th century the Bold was held as a knight's fee, and in 1274 Adam of Bold was a juror in Stottesdon hundred.[25] In 1306 the manor of Easthope was held by service of a man and a horse at Oswestry for 40 days.[26] William, Richard, and Thomas of Oldfields served on juries between 1284 and 1314.[27] Under a 14th-century settlement Upton, 1/2 knight's fee held of the FitzAlans, passed from the Uptons to the Cressetts, and Hugh, apparently the first Cressett to live at Upton, built the *1431 house. His Upton ancestors had held minor office in the forest and county—agister, verderer and coroner; but Hugh was sheriff 1434–5,[28] and his house, with its very rich cusped timbers, reflects the Cressetts' transition from minor gentry to a more substantial place in county society. The Jenks family of Wolverton were of sufficient standing by the 15th century for one of them to marry a daughter of the knightly family of Bowdler of Hope Bowdler.[29] Two of the base-cruck halls are in Much Wenlock, perhaps the homes of lay officers of the priory, and it may be supposed that in Shropshire base-cruck halls were occupied in the main by minor gentry, as has been suggested for Herefordshire,[30] by men holding minor office under the Crown, and perhaps by officials of other magnates and institutions. The contrast in distribution between base crucks in Shropshire and in Wales may be illuminating here. In the former base crucks are widespread; the Welsh examples, seven in all so far known, are strung out along the Border, in the middle and northern marches, from Radnorshire to Flintshire. None has a crown post; nearly all have highly decorated **V** strut roofs or, like Bryndraenog near Beguildy, even more ornamentation; they have been called 'aristocratic'.[31] The most important officials of the marcher lordships were largely recruited from the minor English gentry of the Border counties,[32] and it is tempting to see such men as the source of 'English' houses in present-day Wales,[33] and to see these 'aristocratic' houses as some confirmation of the status of the Shropshire ones, allowing for the different shades of meaning of that word east and west of the Border. On the other hand it appears that in Kent base crucks were the homes of 'substantial peasant freeholders', the 'forerunners of the later class of prosperous yeomen',[34] a striking illustration, if the attributions in both counties are correct, of the relative precocity of the Southeast or the backwardness of the West.

Box-framed halls

It was suggested in the previous section that the storeyed ends of most base-cruck halls were of box-frame rather than of cruck construction, and certainly the oldest box-frame structures are as old as any base cruck in Shropshire. They include the storeyed ends at the Buck's Head (*1281–1321), Church Stretton; at the Rectory (*1313–28), College Street, Ludlow; at 29–30 Woolstaston (*1398–9); and in such urban buildings as 3–4 Broad Street (*1358), Ludlow. The dais beam in the Palmers' Guild College (*1393), Ludlow, may have come from an unaisled box-framed hall, but the earliest such hall so far known in the county is the quite small one at Great Binnal (*1459), Astley Abbots. The now demolished example (provable from the timbers of the surviving spere truss) in the yard of the Nag's Head, Wyle Cop, Shrewsbury, has a date of *1420. The Moat House, Longnor, is of the *1460s, and the early part of the Guildhall at Newport of *1487. The cusping of the roof at Walleybourne Farm (Church Pulverbatch) and the mouldings of the central trusses at Padmore (Onibury)[35] and at Colemere Farm (Astley Abbots) suggest dates in the 15th century. The Barracks at Cardington, where the central and end trusses have crown posts with downward braces, may be earlier, but it would seem that box-framed halls were not common in Shropshire before the 15th century.

They varied considerably in size and in amount of ornament, and the one did not necessarily match the other. At Coats Farm, Rushbury, the hall was 27ft. wide; at Lower Harcourt Cottages, Stottesdon, less than 20ft. The Moat House, Longnor, has a main truss carrying a roof with cusped struts above, some of the side walling is in close studding with a deep crenellated cornice; the posts have carved capitals with enormously exaggerated jowels, carrying a double row of crenellations. The Moat House is very much *sui generis*, the grandest timber building in the county, and surpassed by few in the country. At the Nag's Head the spere truss has a crown post with cusped braces, cusped brackets to the framing, and ogee heads to the doorways. Newport Guildhall has a cusped arch-braced truss and cusped wind braces in a quatrefoil pattern. Walleybourne, Padmore, and Colemere were also decorated. In contrast at Coats Farm the very large hall had a spere truss and a central truss wholly without ornament.

There were also some urban box-framed halls: the open hall behind the Nag's Head, Shrewsbury, and others at 53 Broad Street and 112 Corve Street, Ludlow.[36] At the King's Head, Mardol, Shrewsbury, a floor cuts across a chimney, with a painting upon it which belongs stylistically to *c*.1500; the chimney served a hall of *1403–4 open to the roof.[37] Time has dealt harshly with medieval urban dwellings, and it is possible that such 15th-century storeyed buildings as Mytton's Mansion, Wyle Cop, and the Abbot's House (*1456), Butcher Row, Shrewsbury, had open halls within the curtilage. The box-framed range (*c*.*1426) on the east side of Barrack Passage, however, was jettied on two floors throughout and never had an open hall; it was probably a largely industrial range[38] built by the brewer Nicholas Clement, who also built Henry Tudor House (*1430) immediately to the north, on Wyle Cop, after buying the whole site in 1429.[39]

Box framing was widely used in late medieval towns, very often in dwellings which had no open ground-floor hall, such as Bodenham's (*1403–4) on the corner of King and Broad streets, Ludlow, which had a number of chambers above ground-floor shops;[40] and the building on the corner of Mardol and Roushill, Shrewsbury, built—as the main post jowelled two ways shows—as two parallel ranges.[41] These houses mark a change in urban building not only in their lack of open halls but also in their continuous street frontages: they contrast with the open-courtyard effect of many earlier dwellings, an effect still visible in Dogpole, Shrewsbury, at nos. 14–15 and 20 (the Old House).[42]

The Moat House, Longnor, dendro-dated to 1466

The grandest box-framed hall, the Moat House, Longnor, was erected for a family which had been building up a freehold estate in the parish since the early 14th century. Edward de Acton, six times knight of the shire, had a licence for an oratory at Longnor in 1370,[43] but the builder of the present house (*1466) was his descendant Thomas Acton, a highly trusted officer and adviser of the Talbots, succeeding in the late 1450s, along with his brother-in-law, Thomas Horde, to that dominant position among Shropshire gentry formerly held by William Burley of Broncroft.[44] Coats Farm belonged to a branch of the Leighton family, and the John Leighton who owned it in the late 15th century was the nephew and namesake of a leading man in the county.[45] Walleybourne was largest of the freehold estates created in Church Pulverbatch in the early 13th century. The family also held lands in Pontesbury, and by the mid 15th century these had come by descent to Thomas Jennings, who held another freehold estate in Westbury parish.[46] In 1435 Padmore was held of the Ludlows of Stokesay by a free tenant at a rent of 20s. a year;[47] earlier John of Padmore, as one of Onibury's more substantial men, had paid 1s. to the subsidy of 1327.[48] Colemere was an 'important place' in the 14th century,[49] and Lower Harcourt Cottages may be the successor of Harcourt Manor Farm.[50]

The unaisled box-framed hall clearly had a wide social distribution in Shropshire, and the same is true of the spere truss. By its very presence a spere truss added to the architectural effect of an open hall and was as well a useful vehicle for the display of rich ornament. Spere trusses are found in nearly all of those base-cruck halls which retain a lower end; they appear also in box-framed halls, for example, Walleybourne Farm, the Nag's Head, Shrewsbury, and Coats Farm, Rushbury; they occur occasionally in cruck halls, and nowhere more magnificently than in the one-bay hall at Brookgate Farm (*1490), Plealey.

While it is possible that the connection of earlier years between social groups and house forms was less rigid than the scanty evidence would suggest, the new and wider distribution of the box-framed hall may be seen as a result of a new cohesion among the 'middling sort'. The demise of the stone hall—described above and discussed below—removed one distinction between the houses of the great and the not-so-great, and the aspirations of prospering freeholders and free tenants to gentle status was beginning to remove another. All these were set to embrace the greater convenience of the box-framed hall and the splendour of the spere truss. The distinction between 'gentle' and 'non gentle' was in danger of becoming blurred, and it was at this time that it became necessary to institute heraldic visitations as a means of recognizing worth and rebuking presumption.[51]

Cruck halls

All other surviving medieval timber framed houses in Shropshire are negligible in numbers compared with the 250 and more cruck houses there. The evidence from dendrochronology and from documentary references of 1284 and 1372[52] shows that they range in date from the later 13th to the mid 16th century but are overwhelmingly of the mid to late 15th century.[53] The late medieval plan of a two-bay hall between ends or wings and with a through passage at the service end was as common among them as among other forms. One-bay halls were not unknown, and three dated examples are St. Owen's Well House (*1415), Much Wenlock, 19–21 Drayton Road (*1467), Hodnet, and Brookgate Farm (*1490), Plealey.

The commonest surviving cruck halls are of two bays and have central trusses with arch-braced collars carrying **V** struts. Often the **V** struts are cusped, as at the Old School House, Condover; and sometimes, as at Catherton Cottage (*1485), Hopton Wafers, the blades above collar level and the upper face of the collar are also cusped, to form a very rich pattern.[54] At Llwyn-y-Go, Kinnerley, where, unusually, a king post replaces **V** struts, the post and the blades are cusped.[55] Often, however, the **V** struts and all the upper timbers are left plain; examples are Wheathall (Condover), Condover Court (*1445), and nos. 38–9 Woolstaston (*1398-9).[56] In some cruck halls the collar of the central truss carried, as far as one can tell, nothing at all, and collar and blades enclosed an empty space: one may cite no. 25 Kempton;[57] Tyr-y-Coed, Melverley;[58] Old House Farm, Loppington;[59] and Condover Court.[60]

In general the more lavish the cusping the grander the house, and Catherton Cottage is larger than, and superior to, Old House Farm. But excep-

tions are many. The halls of nos. 38–9 Woolstaston and of Wheathall, with plain **V** struts, and of Condover Court, with nothing at all above the collar, are respectively larger and as large as that at Catherton Cottage, but, while Catherton Cottage seems originally to have had cruck ends, the other two have box-framed solar wings. The cruck hall of Bedstone Manor (*1448) (see illustrations this page and overleaf) is one of the grandest in the county, but the central truss carries no cusping at all and the ornament is provided—in the manner of box-framed halls like the Moat House, Longnor, and Padmore—by the mouldings, richer towards the upper end, on the main timbers and on the intermediate trusses in the roof.[61] Shootrough (Cardington) and Wheathall are similar but without the intermediate trusses. Cruck houses with lavish cusping resemble those with spere trusses in box-framed houses: their presence is the sign of an owner with some pretensions among his peers, but their absence does not necessarily reveal the opposite.

In all these houses, even where the main truss has little or no ornament, the crucks themselves are of heavy scantling and well formed. There are, however, some crucks that are not. The couples at 3 Upton Magna which are later than that of *1269 and those at 19–20 Drayton Road (*1467), Hodnet, have blades cut from separate small trees, instead of from a large one split into twin blades, and at Holly Cottage, Loppington, and Cross End Cottages,[62] Prees, the crucks are of poor scantling.

Although the standard late medieval plan was as dominant in cruck houses as in others, there were more variations on the theme, for cruck halls could

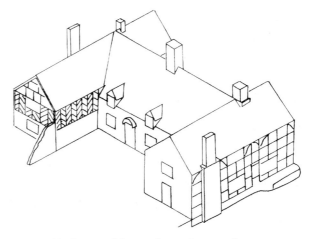

Bedstone Manor from the south-east

Bedstone Manor from the north-east

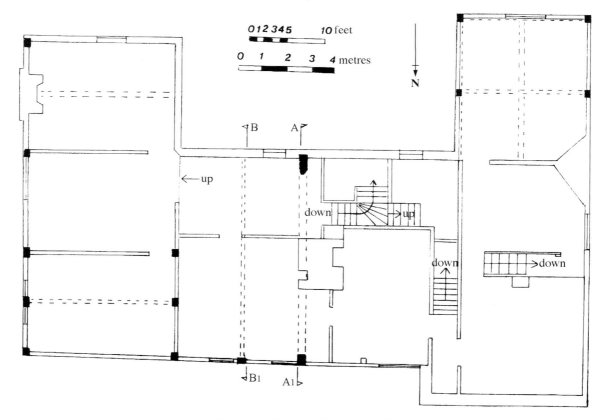

Bedstone Manor first-floor plan

have either cruck or box-framed ends or wings. It is almost certain that the majority had cruck ends, as for example at Sibberscott, Pontesbury; at Binweston Farm, Worthen; Tyr-y-Coed; Llwyn-y-Go; Birch Row, Pontesbury;[63] and, at a higher level, Brookgate Farm, Plealey, and the lower ends of Condover Court and Manor Farm, Stoney Stretton.[64] Furthermore there are nearly 40 known cruck-built halls with later box-framed wings that probably replace cruck ones.[65] That a box-framed end or wing is a replacement rather than an addition is not always demonstrable, but that is clear enough at Brookgate Farm, where the original purlins of the lower end run on several feet beyond the through passage and are there truncated to accommodate the new wing with a date of *1612. A few cruck halls retain an original cruck-built wing rather than end: the White Horse Inn, Castle Pulverbatch; Crowther's House, Easthope; Lower Spoad Farm, Newcastle; and Clun Farm.

Cruck cross wings, as distinct from ends, are almost always to be seen as a 'superior' feature[66] and so too are box-framed ends and wings. There

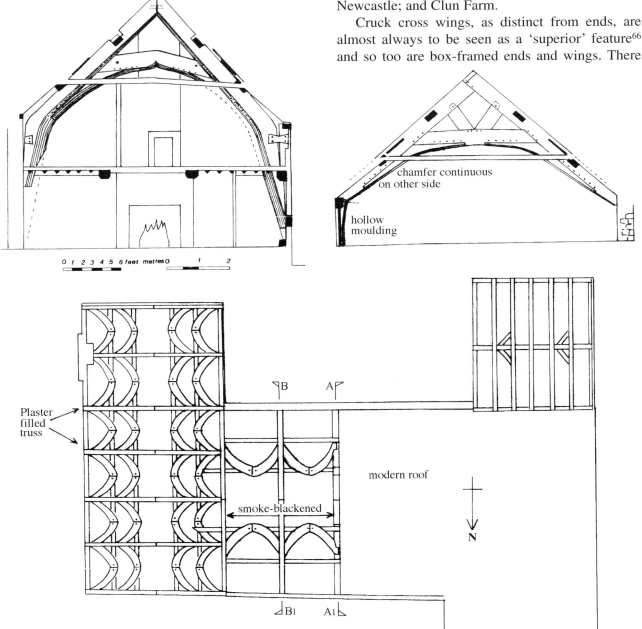

Bedstone Manor roof plan, and sections A-A₁ (left) and B-B₁ (right)

are a dozen known cruck halls with apparently original box-framed solar wings. At nos. 38–9 Woolstaston the box-framed cross wing of *1398–9 and the cruck hall are of equal date. At Condover Court and at Stoney Stretton Manor Farm the wings are accompanied by cruck lower ends. At Bedstone Manor and at Wheathall the lower end has been rebuilt in stone or brick; at the Old School House, Condover, the lower end has gone. At Bedstone and at Wheathall the rebuilding of the lower end suggests that, in contrast with the upper, it was of cruck rather than box-framed construction, and there is no surviving example of an original box-framed lower end. Nevertheless they may have existed. At Catherton Cottage the upper end has gone, but the lower has a box-framed truss, and that suggests not only that that end was box-framed, but that the upper end also was, for the lower end was unlikely to get better treatment than the upper.

There was a tendency in the later Middle Ages in southern and midland England to cut down the size of the hall, either by building it with a single bay or by flooring over one bay of a two-bay hall.[67] Brookgate Farm may be seen as part of that development, but its spere truss, one of the most lavishly decorated in the county, seems to suggest that, while the domestic function of the open hall was declining, its status remained as high as ever. That theme is pursued further below,[68] when the disappearance of the open hall in the course of the 16th century is discussed.

A through passage was as universal in these small houses, as in great ones. It might be within the lower bay of the hall, or in a bay beyond the hall, or it might be no more than opposed doorways at the lower end of the hall. The part beyond the passage was used for service and storage, but whether it ever served as a byre, in long-house fashion, is uncertain. Without such positive evidence as a drainage channel or a feeding walk or tethering posts the former presence of cattle is very difficult to establish. Nevertheless it has been claimed that at Padmore the framing of the farther truss of the through passage is more consistent with a byre beyond than with a mere service room or rooms.[69] A similar possibility has been raised for the very much grander Ty-Mawr, Castel Caereinion, across the border in Montgomeryshire.[70] There are grave difficulties about such interpretations, and it cannot be

said at the moment that the long house is a proven medieval form in Shropshire.

In the absence of documents and of radiocarbon or dendrochronology dates it is difficult to assign any one cruck house to a narrow period. A cruck truss at Upton Magna has a date of *1269, and in a lease of 1372 a tenant undertook to build a house of 'five couples of forks'.[71] There is nothing in that phrase to prove a two-bay hall and storeyed ends, but the likeliest interpretation is that at least a four-bay cruck house was intended; and presumably such houses were well known by then. But, apart from the one at Upton Magna, cruck houses in Shropshire have been dated *1398–9, *1415, *1445, *1448, *1467, *1485, *1490, and *1550.

The builders of these cruck houses were no more homogeneous than those of more important ones. Some of the builders were town or suburb dwellers, as shown by the surviving cruck truss at 92 Frankwell, Shrewsbury, and by a reference in 1297 to a cruck hall in Corve Street, Ludlow.[72] Some were probably owners or farmers of manors. Bedstone Manor probably deserves its appellation, and Church House, Condover, which retains a cruck wing, was probably the manor house until the 1590s.[73] The richness of the spere truss at Brookgate Farm suggests that the builder was a man of some standing, or at least of some wealth. But none of these attributions is certain, and any family that can definitely be associated with a cruck house turns out to be one of less than manorial standing. The five-bay domus in Sutton Maddock parish, 20ft. wide and with 14-ft. bays, to be completed by Easter day 1284, was to be built by the miller of Brockton.[74] Condover Court belonged to the Gosnell family, known in the parish from the 13th century, owners of a mill and a fulling mill and holding in 1528 the largest copyhold estate in the parish and some freehold land too.[75] Wheathall, in the same parish, belonged to the Campions, who had leased the fishery of Bomere in 1255 and in 1545 held the largest amount of assarted land in the area.[76] Manor Farm, Stoney Stretton, and Upper Lake Farm, Westbury, both with cruck halls, were medieval freeholds.[77] Nos. 38–9 Woolstaston was the home of the Bowdlers, who had held the largest freehold in the parish since 1310.[78] William Cobin, the tenant who in 1372 undertook to build a cruck house, was leasing a messuage and a virgate from the manor of Arnegrove in Wistanstow parish.[79]

If such men were of less than manorial status, that does not mean that they were not distinguished in other ways from their fellows. Shropshire peasant society had become highly differentiated by the end of the 13th century when, in the county as a whole, 35 per cent of holdings were ¼ virgate or less, 50 per cent were between ¼ and ½ virgate, and 15 per cent about a virgate or more.[80] Of course the figures varied enormously from parish to parish and from manor to manor, but in 1363 56 out of 90 tenants in Condover held less than ½ virgate and only two tenants held a virgate or more of 'old hold' land; many held assarts as well, but that did not even up the score very much.[81] Peasant society in the 14th-century March has been described as 'not so much a pyramid in terms of wealth, but rather a broad plateau above which rose a few peaks'.[82] Shropshire may have been somewhere between the two, but it is reasonably clear that William Cobin of 1372, with his virgate and with his heriot guaranteed by his father, belonged to a family very much at the top of, or even just above, peasant society. It does not stretch matters to say the same of the miller of Brockton, of the Bowdlers, the Campions, the Gosnells, and the freeholders of Manor Farm at Stoney Stretton and Upper Lake Farm, Westbury. The evidence is meagre, but at the moment it is all there is, and it seems to show—despite Bedstone Manor and Brookgate Farm—that most cruck halls in Shropshire, or at least in those parts that have been thoroughly investigated documentarily, were peasant homes, though far from being the homes of all the peasantry. There is, perhaps, a parallel here with Long Crendon (Bucks.), a village with an exceptionally large number of surviving cruck houses. The occupiers of 11 of these can be traced back to medieval and early modern times, i.e. before the Civil War. With two exceptions they are all virgaters or tradesmen; of the exceptions, perhaps of gentle status, one held 4½ virgates and one held nearly four. 'Such a large number of cruck buildings in one village demands explanation and it is to be found in the fact that the standard peasant holding (in Long Crendon) was a whole virgate'.[83]

It might perhaps be claimed that the absence of surviving houses documented as belonging to men below the level of those just singled out reflects a lack of documents rather than of houses. There is no lack of surviving deeds: parcels of land as small as half an acre were being conveyed by charter to many peasants as early as the late 13th century, and hundreds of conveyances of small pieces of land in Brockton and Larden (both in Shipton parish) illustrate the vigorous peasant land market in 14th-century Shropshire. It can, however, be conceded that correlations between documents and buildings (described in documents or surviving) cannot easily be accumulated. Further, a conveyance does not of course record the parties' unconveyed land (from which an impression of their relative wealth might be formed), and phrases usefully descriptive of buildings are scarce. Medieval surveys and extents, potentially more informative, are rarer and often inconclusive, as at Brockton. There in 1403–4 the lord's house and most of his demesne was let to the lord of Nether Larden, and there were 5 ½-virgaters and one virgater for the 6 messuages that were doubtless the main farmhouses. Non-residents held most of the assarts, but a ½-virgater held the biggest one and may thus have been as substantial a man as the virgater. Besides the farmhouses, a mill, and two cottages Brockton then had some 14 tofts or house places that were mostly vacant, and several of which were held by a resident freeholder. The extent may reflect the disappearance of houses made redundant by sales of their occupants' land, poorer peasants having been bought out by richer ones; but there is no structural evidence concerning peasant houses in Brockton, where no medieval house survives.[84]

Thus the only plausible counter to the conclusion that the houses of the more substantial medieval peasants have survived because they were better built is to argue that the houses of all the peasants in a particular area were built to the same standard in the late Middle Ages, but that subsequent economic developments so adversely affected the mass of the peasantry (while not so affecting—perhaps even favouring—an upper stratum) that they became incapable of maintaining their equally good houses as well as their more prosperous neighbours did; and that consequently their dwellings have vanished, thereby distorting the architectural record. It is difficult to imagine what facts could be adduced in support of that argument. Moreover there is some evidence, again from Long Crendon, which casts doubt on its validity. Between 1437 and 1547 42 tenants there were presented for having their houses out of repair; only two of them were virgaters, although virgaters made up two thirds of the land-holders in the village. As far back as the mid 15th century, therefore, men below virgater standing were almost 40 times as likely as virgaters to have their houses in disrepair. So the difference between virgater and non-virgater housing was apparent from the mid 15th century at the latest. And that is important, for dendrochronology shows that no surviving cruck house in Long Crendon is earlier than that, and many are much later.[85] It seems reasonable, then, to conclude that the surviving cruck houses of Long Crendon were built by a class of men whose presentments for disrepair over a period of a hundred years were negligible, rather than by those who were constantly in trouble for not being able to keep even what houses they had in repair.

One may perhaps labour this point, for it is widely assumed that all peasant houses were of the same constructional standard and differed from one another, within a region, only in size. It has been reckoned that in the early 15th century a peasant house of three bays cost between £2 and £3,[86] and indeed in 1472–3 the farmer of the demesne at Hughley was allowed 46s. 8d. to build a new hall and chamber.[87] Earlier, however, when houses in the hamlet of Bicton, in the lordship of Clun, were built, the facts seem less clear cut. In 1411 the lord helped three peasants there to build four houses: one man had half of his rent rebated for two years to build a 'good' house; another had half of his rent rebated for one year to build two 'new' houses; and the third had no rent rebate for the 'new' house that he was to build, but the lord's officers were to provide him with the necessary timber.[88] We may suggest, for the sake of argument, that the peasants with rent rebates may have been paying as much as 10s. a year each for a virgate;[89] the suggestion concedes much to the £2–£3 reckoning,[90] but, on this assumption, one man was being allowed 10s. to build a 'good' house (presumably for himself, for it was on land that had been his father's) and the other was getting 5s. to build two 'new' ones (possibly for under-tenants, for they were on land which had belonged to another family). Even if these were one-bay houses, the peasants ought to have been allowed, on the basis of the reckoning cited above, a sum closer to £1 than to 10s., and, since they were allowed less than that, it might seem that they were building to lower, and more varied, constructional standards than the cited figure of £2 to £3 implies.[91]

However, it is not necessary to suppose that the Bicton peasants were building one-bay houses, for it seems that it was at one time possible to build cruck houses for as little as 10s., if one were content with something less than the splendid timbers which have survived. In 1581–2 the Worfield churchwar-dens built a house for Goodwife Garbot. For its 'making'—for the thatching, the carriage of the thatch, the digging, carriage and application of the clay daubing, the 'poles' for the roof, the crucks, the wall plate, the door post and boards for the door—the wardens paid 6s.[92] The house was probably of one bay only, but, if a poor one-bay house could be built for 6s., then a three-bay cruck house could have been built for something less than 18s. And, if a three-bay cruck house of sorts could be built for that sum in 1581–2, after the enormous price rise of the 16th century,[93] then houses of that standard could have been built for 10s. in the early 15th century; and the 1411 reference seems to show that they were being built, at any rate around Clun. And no one need be surprised at that, for such '10s. houses' were common in the 13th century, probably for smallholders,[94] and smallholders did not go out of existence in the course of the next two centuries.

There is perhaps a hint of this 'double standard' in peasant housing in the leases granted by Haughmond Abbey throughout the 14th and 15th centuries. They were generally granted on condition that the tenant built a house on the holding, but, while nearly all the leases of 6s. a year and more specified that the abbey would provide 'big timbers', none of those for less than that sum did so:[95] as if 'big timbers' were irrelevant in such cases. Of course it can be argued that the references of 1411, 1472–4, and 1581–2, and the Haughmond leases are scattered and do not amount to much, but then that can be said of nearly all documentary references to medieval peasant buildings.

That does not mean that every surviving cruck house was built by a virgater. In Condover no fewer than eight cruck houses survive, and some of them might be the homes of less wealthy peasants. In 1363 there were only two tenants out of the 90 in the manor who held a virgate or more and, while a few of them may have risen to that level in the next 150 years, it must not be supposed that a cruck house and a virgate necessarily went together, but the tendency was that way. Even in Condover three of the eight survivors were the homes of men who can be shown to have been well above their fellows— Church House, Condover Court, and Wheathall; and a fourth, the Old School House, shows by its box-framed wing its owner's standing or ambitions.

While there appears to be a marked social variation in peasant housing in the 15th century it is far from certain that it was present earlier, for until the advent of dendrochronology the dating of timber-framed buildings was something of a guessing game. Now that there is a corpus of reliable dates from that technique a clear and surprising pattern emerges in Shropshire: a solitary cruck truss of *1269 (incorporated into a later house), no other cruck survivors before 1399, and many from the 15th and 16th centuries. A similar pattern occurs in other cruck counties and also in counties where box-framed houses were normal, for example Kent.[96]

The current orthodoxy on the nature of medieval timber-framed houses is that all, or very nearly all, peasant houses were built to the structural standards of those which have survived.[97] It follows that, if there are no surviving peasant houses from before c.1400, that must be because they have all gone. But their disappearance cannot be due to their great age, for many other 14th-century houses built to the same standards have survived. The reason must lie not with natural causes but with human activities, and in particular with peasant dissatisfaction in the years after c.1400 with houses which were well built but with low halls and one-storey ends. In consequence most peasant houses were pulled down and replaced by others with lofty halls and two-storeyed ends. All the rest had a storey added and had the hall raised or rebuilt higher, thereby disguising their 14th-century origin. The peasant's taste for a loftier hall was perhaps the equivalent of the 'symbolic' entrance halls which wealthy merchants were including in their city houses, an advertisement of one's standing in the late medieval and early modern world.[98]

The practice of raising the height of a house is not in doubt, for there are innumerable instances, but not even one example has yet been shown by dendrochronology to have been carried out on any 14th-century house which has any claim to have been the house of a peasant. And in fact there is at least one surviving well built but one-storeyed house, Ashby Cottage, Westbere (Kent). Oddly enough, however, it is not of the 14th century but of c.1500.[99] How it ever got built in that form and at that time is a problem; unless perhaps it alone survives because it was well built while its 14th-century predecessors were not. Moreover Ashby Cottage is neither a unique survival nor yet is it the youngest, for one-storeyed houses were being built as late as the 17th century, and some of them were still inhabited in the 20th. It is difficult to believe that in an age of limited resources thrifty peasants, however much displeased with their accommodation, would have chosen to pull down a well built house and put up a taller one rather than keep the old for non-domestic uses and erect a new one nearby. That too was a common practice, for a farmhouse accompanied by a nearby house surviving from an earlier date but now converted into a barn or byre is a common element in the countryside. Moreover peasants were not the only people improving their housing conditions in the 15th and early 16th centuries: the gentry were too. A gentleman had far more resources than a peasant and was more able and more likely to have a cavalier attitude towards out-of-date buildings, and yet in cruck counties the number of base-cruck halls surviving from the late 13th and 14th centuries is greater than the number of peasant houses claimed to have survived that long, even when the latter are given the benefit of doubts about their status. The same comparative rarity of peasant houses appears to be true in non-cruck counties. It is very odd when we remember that the peasantry were many many times more numerous than the gentry and so too, presumably, were their houses, built, we are told, to the same standards.

Another explanation—which does not attempt to argue away the evidence from dendrochronology— is that in the late 13th century rich peasants were able to build houses which have survived to this day, but that in the feudal crisis of the 14th century their general standards, and therefore their housing standards, fell catastrophically. Although they went on building cruck houses (for we have documentary evidence of that), they built less well, and so none of their houses has survived. There is, however, no reason to think that surviving 13th-century cruck houses were peasant houses. Of the handful of buildings throughout the country with crucks of *13th-century date, one is Stokesay Castle, two were manorial barns, one was a rectory, one was the home of a freeholder on a holding of 40 acres, another was probably the home of a freeholder, and one was on a holding of 40 acres or more on the estates of the bishop of Winchester. It may be objected that freeholders were also peasants, for some at least paid dues to a lord, but those dues were little more than chief rents and were a minor burden in comparison with those falling upon unfree men. Similar doubts must be expressed about attempts to associate early box-framed houses, for example Lime Tree House, Harwell (Berks.), with peasants.[100]

There is a third explanation which accepts the evidence from dendrochronology at its face value and does not suppose that, because 15th-century cruck houses were built almost wholly by peasants, then 13th- and 14th-century cruck houses were therefore peasant buildings.[101] Of cruck buildings dated by dendrochronology to the *14th century, six are houses whose status is unknown, and one or two of them may have been peasant houses, but if so they were the homes of highly exceptional individuals rather than typical of a social group. All the others were built by gentry families and by such men as freeholders and wealthy local clergy. At that time, however, the gentry were also building base-cruck halls, and their two types of building may reflect an economic differentiation within the class, but it is more likely that the difference was between those building in the old way and those favouring the new. It is noticeable that, while base-cruck halls continue into the 15th century, surviving cruck halls become fewer as the 14th century progresses. In the years around 1300 leading gentry families were becoming increasingly prominent, and it may be that the cruck hall, which had been normal amongst them, was then being superseded by the superior base-cruck hall.

A hundred years later the manorial system was losing some of its effectiveness as a means of exploiting the peasantry, and the feudal classes, having got over the shock of the Peasants' Revolt of 1381 and perhaps having learnt lessons from it, were both less anxious and less able to perpetuate

the conditions of serfdom. Instead, by abandoning or alleviating those conditions, they were, wittingly or not, accelerating the growth of a class of rich peasants with an interest in maintaining the new economy. Rich peasants were nothing new then, but serfdom, with its numerous and often arbitrary requisitions upon peasant wealth, had never created that sense of security in their property which would make heavy expenditure upon buildings a far-sighted rather than a doubtful investment. With this new-found security there was, from *c*.1400 onwards, a vast amount of building by peasants of houses of a structural standard which had previously been confined to their betters. Their houses varied in form, and to some extent in date, from region to region, but the development was countrywide.

Medieval Shropshire houses within the national picture

In many ways the story of domestic architecture in medieval Shropshire is no more than an illustration of the national theme. The earliest houses to survive are those of the Crown or of great magnates, lay or ecclesiastical, and are generally fortresses. Progressively they become more residential, and at the same time the dwellings of other men come into the standing record. Eventually the homes of an upper stratum among the peasantry appear, although the nature of the separate stages does not always resemble those in other areas. The open hall and its storeyed ends was as universal in Shropshire as elsewhere: present in the houses of many men from peers to peasants for at least 300 years, and probably for much longer. Moreover, while not all the country shared the Salopian predilection for crucks, some of the neighbouring shires did, and the vast amount of timber building of later years was paralleled in most of the South and the midlands.

In two respects, however, Shropshire's story is different from that of the country as a whole. In the 12th century the Great Tower at Ludlow was surpassed only by such royal works as the White Tower and Colchester Castle, and stone towers, at least in the western part of the county, were commoner than in most parts of England in the 13th century. In the late 13th and early 14th centuries such houses as Acton Burnell Castle, Aston Eyre, and Stokesay Castle were as advanced as any others anywhere and were as thick on the ground, or thicker. In the early 14th century the palatial accommodation of the Mortimers in Ludlow castle was second to none. In contrast, from the late 14th century to the mid 16th, nothing of any high standard has survived, apart from the prior's lodging at Much Wenlock and the Moat House at Longnor.

Thus for nearly 300 years domestic architecture in Shropshire was more or less on a level with the country as a whole, but by the end of the Middle Ages it had become not so much 'provincial' as—if the expression may be used in the context—'middle class'. To say that is, in part, to restate in more general terms what was noted earlier: the paucity of stone building in the two hundred years from c.1350 to c.1550 by comparison with the previous hundred years. That phenomenon is not confined to Shropshire, for it has been noticed in neighbouring Herefordshire and in far away Kent,[102] and, between the two, in the Vale of the White Horse (Berks.).[103] To some extent, therefore, it is to be explained by developments common to much of the country. Perhaps, however, there were causes peculiar to Shropshire, where 'the estates of the great aristocratic landowning dynasties, largely absentee, ... dominated [the county] in the late Middle Ages'. Among them the FitzAlans, earls of Arundel, and later the Talbots, earls of Shrewsbury, were preeminent, rarely visiting the county and interested in it mainly for the studs which they maintained there and for the rents they could take out of it.[104] Whatever houses they already had were enough for them, and it is symbolic that when, in 1459, the 2nd earl of Shrewsbury wanted a great house he did not build anything in Shropshire but instead bought the double-courtyard mansion of South Wingfield in Derbyshire.[105] Furthermore, the three bishops whose dioceses covered the county were not large-scale Shropshire landowners and had no need for large houses to accommodate them or their officials. The only known episcopal residence of any quality in the county was at Bishop's Castle,[106] in contrast with a dozen in the neighbouring counties of Herefordshire, Staffordshire, and Worcestershire.[107]

That, however, cannot be the whole story, for the stone houses—as distinct from fortresses—of the late 13th and early 14th centuries were not, in the main, erected by great magnates but by men of lesser standing. As was seen earlier, nearly all of them were built by those who, like Lawrence of Ludlow, had financial dealings with the Crown or those, generally of gentry origin, who were royal servants, carrying out royal policies and rewarded well enough to allow them to build the houses that distinguished them from their fellows. After Edward II's defeat by the marcher lords the Crown's power and interest in the county waned and the FitzAlans, and later the Talbots, took over.[108] Many of the leading figures in the county—knights of the shire, magistrates, and even some sheriffs—were more their men than the king's.[109] These great lords were not ungenerous to their higher officials, whose fees increased during the 15th century,[110] but they did not have as many gifts at their disposal as the Crown had had. More importantly, however, they had less reason to be lavish. They had come to power when the conquest of Wales and effective control of the Marches had been achieved. The political importance of the Border counties consequently declined as the region became peripheral to the main concerns of the rulers of England. Neither the Crown nor the great lords needed any longer to maintain a huge following and a high presence there; rather they had to concentrate their resources in the more important political arenas to the east. Shrewsbury's purchase of South Wingfield was doubly symbolic, for he was buying more than a big house; he was buying the seat and centre of power of his dead political friend Ralph, Lord Cromwell, treasurer of England 1433–43 and a major figure in mid 15th-century affairs.[111]

The decline in domestic stone building and in the scale of individual houses is paralleled, it will be remembered, by an equal decline in the volume of ecclesiastical building in the county in the last two centuries of the Middle Ages. The paucity there of 15th-century stone houses and of Perpendicular churches are two sides of the same coin: the siphoning away of much of the wealth of the county by 'the Great and the Good' in order to further their interests elsewhere. However, this eastward move of political power was only made possible by the 'pacification' of Wales, disrupted but once—by Glyn Dwr's War of Independence—in more than two hundred years. In contrast, along the Scottish Border, where the Scots gave as good as they got, gentry in the Northern Marches, presumably no wealthier as a class than gentry in Shropshire, were investing from 1350 onwards in a great number of small stone towers.[112] And in the late 16th and early 17th centuries very ordinary men there, holding by 'Border Right' tenancy, which they had manipulated in their favour, were building innumerable stone houses, defensible against bands of moss-troopers.[113]

IX Gestation of the Private House and the Gentleman's Residence 1550–1700

Abandonment of the open hall

It is almost tautology to say that the end of the open hall marked the end of the Middle Ages for its presence or absence is what distinguishes medieval from modern houses. Its demise, like the 'waning of the Middle Ages', was a lengthy process, but signs of it were there from at least the middle of the 14th century in the denunciation by moralists of the increasing preference of the lord and his family for dining in the solar rather than in the hall.[1] In later years and at moderate social levels the decline is seen more clearly in the appearance of halls of only one bay or a bay and a half. Brookgate Farm, Plealey, was built in *1490 with a magnificent spere truss in a hall of but a single bay.[2] In 1555 Habberley Hall was built as a timber-framed block, jettied on all sides and floored overall except for a small rectangular space in the centre, marked as a fireplace by the form of the chamfers on the main and subsidiary beams enclosing it.[3] The disposition of the joists at New Hall, Eaton-under-Heywood, suggests that there too, and at about the same time, the open hall had been cut down to a small fire-space from which the smoke escaped by a large plaster flue. An early sequence of inserted chimney and later inserted floor may be seen in Shrewsbury at the King's Head inn, Mardol, where the floor cuts across a late-medieval-style painting on the face of the chimney flue.[4] The process went on widely in later years. Between 1566 and 1610 the two-bay base-cruck hall at High Grosvenor, Claverley, had one bay floored over and the 'hall' reduced to a single bay.[5] By the mid 16th century a house without an open hall was nothing new to many men. Even if, as sometimes claimed, the average 15th-century peasant lived in a house similar to those which have survived from then, it is clear that many

townsmen did not. To the diverse occupants of the upper storey of Bodenham's in Ludlow the 'hall' could have been no more than a general-purpose room.[6] And that was often true elsewhere; in Bury St. Edmunds in the late 15th century two-storeyed houses were being built which were floored throughout.[7] The two-storey hall, which perpetuated the form, but not the function, of the medieval open hall, never wholly disappeared. It survived, fossilized, in a few of the greatest houses of the

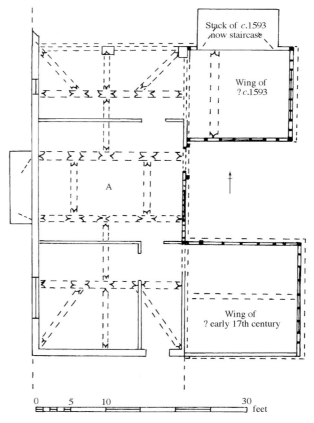

Floor plan of Habberley Hall showing the central fireplace area (A)

early 17th century, was present as an imposing entrance hall in many of those of the late 17th and early 18th centuries,[8] and was revived, romanticized, in some Victorian country mansions.

It is a commonplace that the change in the nature of the hall was an aspect of an early stage in the development from a feudal to a capitalist society, but what still needs to be explained is why that development affected house forms in a particular way at a particular time. One long-standing explanation on the practical level is that a new desire for privacy robbed the open hall of its function and rendered it unnecessary and inconvenient. But privacy was nothing new at the end of the Middle Ages. Long before then the south tower at Stokesay had provided a suite of luxurious private rooms, the so called 'keep' at Clun had done the same, and at Caus castle the lord and lady each had a private chamber, although they seem to have had to share a garderobe.[9] And privacy was not a Salopian eccentricity: in far away Wensleydale the Scropes enjoyed it on even grander scale in Bolton Castle. In any case, the medieval hall had many more functions than that of a dining room.

Recently a serious attempt at a deeper explanation has emphasized the effect on social behaviour and domestic organization of the stress laid on the 'Self' by the secular and religious individualism of the Renaissance and Reformation, the consequent decline in 'community feeling', and a rise, or at any rate a change, in the status of women.[10] Undoubtedly these were important elements in the transformation of the medieval into the modern world, but they do not in themselves account for the decline of the hall; nor yet do they explain why it lingered so long. More important was the changing relationship between those who worked upon the land and those who exercised property rights over it. The change was defined by Maitland[11] as one from 'status' to 'contract' and by Carlyle and Marx, two more openly partisan observers, as the result of 'cash-payment—the one nexus of man to man' dissolving the 'motley feudal ties which bound man to his "natural superiors"'. Of course cash payment had been there long before the 16th century: it is possible to trace a market economy back to Anglo-Saxon times,[12] money rents had probably been as common as rents in kind or labour dues for several centuries, and wage labour and long leases were far

from unknown.[13] But as these became ever commoner, and as lords withdrew more and more from direct exploitation of their demesnes, the manor, the institution which organized agricultural procedures, enforced seignorial control over the vill, accounted for tax to the Crown's representative, and settled local disputes in its own court, lost more and more of its *raison d'être*. The manor house ceased to be the centre of communal activities; a body of magistrates administered local government and justice; and the cash nexus, instead of being one relationship among many between lord and tenant, slowly became the only, or at any rate the dominant, one. A gentleman was less and less likely to see his house as sheltering dependants as well as close relatives and as an all-purpose gathering place for all those associated with him or his estate.[14] Consequently the manorial hall, whose size and loftiness accommodated a throng of servants and suitors and whose splendour emphasized the lord's dominance among them, was becoming an anachronism; and at the same time there was ever less incentive, practical or ideological, for other men, with holdings too large to be worked solely by family labour, to build in the old way.

That the change was accelerating rapidly in the late 16th century, at least in the South and the midlands, may be partly explained by the forcing process of the 'mid-Tudor crisis'. One of its important causes was a system of taxation which fell more heavily upon moneyed than upon landed men.[15] Moreover, after a generation of unprecedented inflation, the Crown further undermined the value of money: more or less simultaneously the immense landed estates it had acquired at the Dissolution were offered, relatively cheaply, for sale, and—'the single greatest fraud deliberately carried out by any English government on its own people'—the Great Debasement of the coinage in the 1540s gave a further impetus to inflation.[16] Thus moneyed men's long-standing inclination to invest in land was strongly encouraged; and the background of such men fitted them more easily into the role of 'farmer' than of manorial lord.[17]

The resulting change in the prevailing concept of a house is symbolized in general by the disappearance of the through passage, used by everybody, and its replacement by a reception hall for the quality and a side door or back door for all the rest. In

Shropshire it is seen clearly at Attingham, built for Lord Berwick in the late 18th century, where an imposing entrance hall reached by a flight of steps is flanked,[18] at semi-basement level, by a servants' hall and a tenants' parlour, each with its own external entry.

Changes in social relationships in the country-side were one aspect of the decay of feudalism; another was the advent of the absolutist Tudor state. It has become fashionable recently to play down the absolutism of Tudor government and the differences between the Tudors and the Lancastrian and Yorkist kings, and to emphasize the limitations on Tudor power.[19] Undoubtedly those who thought that Absolutism came into the world out of Nothingness and that the Tudor or any other absolute state could do whatever its least whim moved it to have been justly rebuked—if they ever existed. It may well be that Tudor power was not unbreakable, but it was never broken. Contemporaries, with a few exceptions who soon regretted their eccentricity, came to regard it with awe; and, although the unprincipled aristocratic factions that had squabbled over the control of government machinery in the 15th century were not destroyed by the Tudors, they were disciplined—and for their own good. Great men might still manipulate the state for their own ends, or those of their peers, but only by serving, or seeming to serve, it. Their houses might still be bases of local power but no longer as centres for retainers and dependants upon their lands. Bishop Goodman noted of Burghley's great house at Theobalds that it had 'neither lordship nor tenants',[20] and in Bacon's advice to would-be builders on choosing a site 'lordship' and 'tenants' were almost the only matters not taken into account.[21] What was more important for the men whom he was addressing, and for others with ambitions, was a house big enough to entertain the sovereign and impress the county, or a house which, although smaller, was in the same mould. They wanted grand rooms, including entrance halls, but had no need for their predecessors' generalized meeting places, open to half the world.

Thus old constraints on the nature and form of dwellings had been more or less thrown off, but new ones were imposed. The advent in England of Renaissance modes of thought, of which the Tudor state was both a broker and a beneficiary, was accompanied by Renaissance notions of architectural design and, in particular, the canon of symmetrical composition. Symmetry had been a desirable quality in many medieval minds, and the garden front of the prior's lodging at Wenlock, it will be remembered, was a very sophisticated production; nevertheless symmetry had nearly always been subordinate to other considerations. From now on it was to be the major one.

Renaissance art and social tradition

That, however, was only one side of the coin. Society changed, but it changed very slowly and so too did men's understanding that it was changing; and the age-old concepts of good lordship and of the bond between master and man went very deep. They may be seen surviving in the countryside, though as little more than a wistful sentiment, in the mid 19th century: in *Under the Greenwood Tree* a labourer refused an invitation to attend the wedding of his former master's daughter saying simply 'Don't work for the family now'.[22] And in the 20th century uncertain times could revive tenants' anxiety for their landlord's protection.[23]

The major builders of Tudor times had been brought up in houses of late medieval form, and, in an age in which lineage was becoming an obsession, the old form in a new house offered a guarantee that the owner was not an upstart, or, if he was, did something to hide the fact. There was, however, more to it than that. The classic late medieval plan and usage served very well the needs of a house in which the owner and his family were distinct from the other occupants, but yet part of the community which lived there. The house in its physical form was sharply divided between an upper and a lower end; but its occupants were not. The highest was far above the lowest, and the community was intensely hierarchic; but there were many grades and distinctions and nowhere a sharp break between the bottom and the top or anything like the 'upstairs–downstairs' division of later years. So long, therefore, as elements of late medieval social relations still prevailed, the late medieval house, with its focal hall and its upper and lower ends was well fitted to survive.

At the top of society the idea of the hall as the hospitable heart of the house, as the room around which all the others were grouped, perpetuated the siting of service rooms near to it. They were still separated from it only by the screens passage which served as the entry into the house for all comers and gave access to the lower end of the hall. The hall and the service rooms were publicly linked, and even a man of such advanced aesthetic views as Sir Henry Wotton, a spokesman for the Virtuosi, deplored the continental practice of putting the service rooms at the rear or in a basement because 'by the natural hospitality of England the buttery must be more visible'.[24] For men of considerable means it was no great problem to continue, and to emphasize, the entry into a passage at the lower end of the hall and yet to set it centrally and symmetrically within a very long main range. That amount of building, however, was beyond the resources of most men, and the tension between lingering medieval ideals and burgeoning Renaissance aesthetics, between 'use' and 'uniformity' as Bacon tersely put it, delayed for a long time the widespread appearance of a plan form more suited to the developing social relationships and more amenable to Renaissance notions of design.

Some of the Great continued for a long time to build magnificent open halls, as Salisbury and Suffolk did at Hatfield and Audley End, but these, like their richly ornamented screens, had display as their only function. There was no-one of the standing of those two in Shropshire, but neverthe-

less old traditions died hard, and just how hard may be seen at Plaish. The present form of the house, which incorporated parts of an earlier one, is of the 1570s or 1580s.[25] In its use of brick and with its tall identical wings of two and a half storeys, Plaish was in advance of many of its contemporaries. Nevertheless it was still built under the influence of earlier habits: it had a great hall rising through two storeys, a pretended hammer-beam roof, an entry at one end of the hall range into a through passage separating the hall from the service end, and a spiral staircase at each end of the hall to serve each of the wings. It may be considered as the last medieval and the first modern house to be built in the county.[26]

An advance on Plaish, but still with a vestige of the lofty open hall, was Wilderhope, built c. 1590 by Francis Smalman.[27] Wilderhope has a one-storey hall with an important room above, but the hall is distinguished by being higher than the ground-floor room of the service wing to the east. In consequence the floor of the room over the hall is at a higher level than the first floor of that wing, and Wilderhope, like Plaish, had to have two separate stairways because there was originally no first-floor communication between the two parts of the house:[28] the last fling of an old tradition.

It would, however, be mistaken to exaggerate the speed and amount of change in Shropshire. Men of the highest rank, best able to combine comfort and

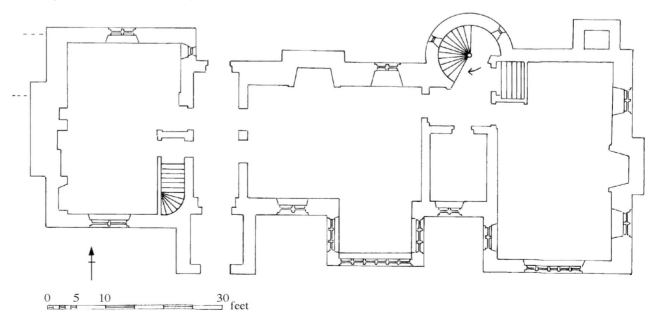

Ground-floor plan of Wilderhope Manor

The south front of Wilderhope Manor

luxury with architectural effect, were not building there in the late 16th century, and it is perhaps symbolic that Moreton Corbet, built by a diplomat and courtier in a style which contemporaries called 'Italian'[29] and on a scale intended to rival the greatest houses in the land, was left unfinished at his death and was never completed to his designs. Most builders in the county were men of lesser pretensions building on a smaller scale and adapting the new ideas to their own needs and resources. Furthermore, many of the builders of the time were unable or unwilling to build *de novo* and were often restricted not merely by limited means but also by the exigencies of an old site and the buildings already on it. Much new construction, therefore, took the form of adapting or adding to earlier buildings, or cladding a timber building in stone or brick, as for example at Chatwall Farm, Cardington, and Little Stretton Manor. Change could happen in one or more stages, and with divergent results. At High Grosvenor, Claverley, as at Larden Hall and Beslow (both now gone), timber-framed parlour blocks, jettied on all sides, were added to earlier main ranges.[30] At the first nothing else was done and the parlour block dominates the scene today; at the second the main range was replaced in 1607 by a tall stone building, and the former parlour block became a subordinate part of the complex;[31] at the

third a hall range and service wing were added in the early 17th century, in a slightly out-of-date style of timber framing, to give a grand symmetrical and uniform front to the house.[32] Tinkering was commonest where money was tightest, but even important families often practised it. In the late 16th century the Ottleys[33] extended Pitchford in at least two phases;[34] and the Leightons adapted an older house at Plaish, while at Habberley they added what is now the core of the Hall to an older building. Early in the next century the Harveys and Charltons altered and enlarged Whitton Court,[35] the Corbets added a vast hall with a great chamber above to Stanwardine in the Wood,[36] the Charltons incorporated their medieval house at Apley Castle into a grand Jacobean mansion,[37] and the Actons rebuilt part of their courtyard house at Aldenham.[38] All of these, and others, were attempts at adapting to new purposes houses which had become too small or too inconvenient for contemporary ways of living.

Most men who were erecting houses were still tied to the old form with a single-pile main range set between single-pile cross wings. In big houses it was possible to have a symmetrical main range in which a large one-storey hall, entered traditionally from a screens passage at the lower end, was balanced on the other side of the emphasized entry by a room or rooms of similar length. Condover is the most notable survivor in Shropshire, but it was not alone, and Pitchford, Millichope, and Park Hall, Whittington, did much the same, albeit in timber. In smaller houses (and they were the great majority), where the hall, or the hall and a small room, occupied the whole of the main range, such symmetry was eschewed and at Dunval, Plaish, Steventon Manor, Bostock Hall, Whixall, and in the rebuilt brick front of Whitton Court, the entry was placed asymmetrically at one end of the range. At a few others, the refashioned Apley Castle, Shipton Hall,[39] Benthall Hall, and Ludstone Hall, symmetry, or at any rate balance, was achieved, but at the price of abandoning the emphasis upon the entry and placing

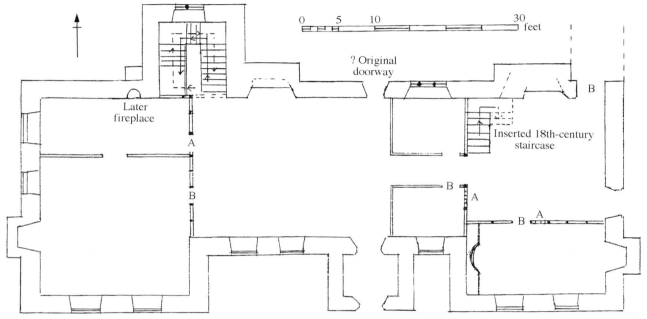

A indicates the position of original doorways, B those of later doorways.
The arrows in the stair turret show the original direction of the ascent, now reversed

Plan and south elevation of Steventon Manor

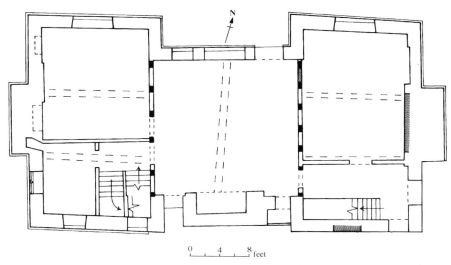

0 4 8 feet

Plan of Bostock Hall, Whixall

Precocity in smaller houses

By the mid 17th century lesser men were solving the aesthetic problem that followed from building on a **U** or **H** plan with a hall range of only one room. They were demoting the hall still further, transforming its character from a general entrance for all comers into a reception room for persons of quality. To do that they eliminated the through passage and thereby the need for an entry at one end of the hall. They could now place the entrance doorway centrally in the front wall of the hall and symmetrically in the elevation as a whole. That such an apparently simple solution of a problem took so long to achieve is a measure of how formidably the persistence of old ways of living and old modes of thought, developed originally within a wholly different social and architectural milieu, could hamper the full expression of Renaissance ideas; and that, as we shall see, despite the presence of exemplars within their own county.

it inconspicuously in a side wall of one or other of the symmetrically sited projections at the end of the range. The effect at Apley and Ludstone, and to a lesser extent at Shipton and Benthall, where one of the projections was clearly an entrance porch, was to give the entrance elevation an inhospitable air. All these houses were, as their other qualities show, built with fashionable intent, but they were all ready to sacrifice one or other of the elements of an up-to-date house in order to perpetuate a main feature of the medieval hall, the entry at the lower end.

Steps towards the new concept of the hall were taken at the now demolished Bostock Hall, Whixall, and at Stirchley Hall. At Bostock the strapwork on the parlour ceiling, the decor on the newel of the stair, and the nature of the brickwork perhaps suggest a date of *c*.1640. The entry was still at the end of the hall and asymmetrically sited in the elevation, but the through passage had disappeared and the presence of an independent external entry to the service wing demonstrated a reception hall rather than a common entrance hall.[40] Two near contemporaries, each with a stone front range added to an earlier timber-framed wing, are Aston Munslow Hall and Chatwall Hall, Cardington, the latter probably of 1659.[41] Each has the fireplace in the hall sited very oddly in a corner. At Stirchley in the stone range added in

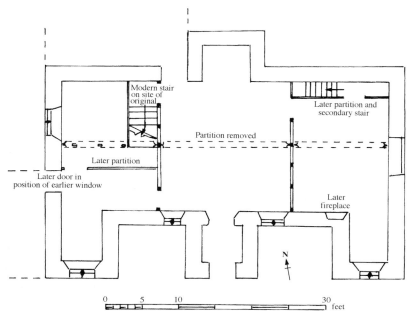

Modern stair on site of original

Later partition and secondary stair

Partition removed

Later partition

Later door in position of earlier window

Later fireplace

N

0 5 10 30 feet

Plan of Holt Farm, Cardington

1653 to a now almost completely vanished timber range a further advance was made.[42] The hall is only 15ft. long and with no through passage; its reception character is clear. It is still entered at one end, but because the parlour on one side is nearly as long as the hall and the staircase cell on the other is not much wider than the main entrance door, that door can come almost centrally in the elevation, centrally enough to give at first glance an air of complete symmetry.

The date of the first fully developed 'reception hall' is far from certain, but it is likely that Holt Farm, Cardington, is one of the earliest examples. The beam sections in hall and parlour, the timber lintels, and the absence of wind braces from the roof above the hall range perhaps suggest that it is c.1630. It is a very small house without a through passage, in which the hall may have served as the kitchen as well, and the parlour was originally unheated. The aesthetic predilections of the age are epitomized in its complete symmetry with a tall central porch and tall wings crowned by steep gables. Seen from across the valley it is highly impressive, and only on a close approach does its lack of size become apparent.[43] The virtuosity of its design suggests that it was more than a farmhouse, and yet it was certainly well below normal gentry levels of accommodation. It is likely that it was built purely as a residence by someone of modest means, free of the cares of either agriculture or of office, and free as well from sub-medieval notions of the functions of a hall. Since Holt Preen manor was owned by the Leightons of nearby Plaish from the mid 16th century to 1655 or later,[44] it was perhaps meant for a minor, or superannuated, member of that family.

More closely datable, and more of the size with which we have been dealing, is Preston Brockhurst Hall, built by 'a Mr. Wingfield, of Shrewsbury', on land which Sir Vincent Corbet had had to sell to pay his delinquency fine.[45] Internally the house has been considerably altered, but the main east front has been preserved and is the paragon of the mature small **H** or **U** plan house with identical wings crowned by large gables flanking a symmetrical hall range with central doorway and a two-storeyed porch set centrally in the elevation and crowned with a large gable. From Preston Brockhurst onwards there are a number of houses with the main entrance in the centre of the elevation and of the hall. At Moreton Hall, Weston Rhyn, where a brick range was added to an earlier timber-framed house, the deep overhanging eaves with scrolled brackets indicate that the house is c.1660. Braggington, now demolished, had a date of 1675 over the doorway. Its relevance has been disputed, but it looks reasonable enough and in any case provided a *terminus ad quem*. Great Lyth, happily now restored, was built on land conveyed to the Gibbons family of Shrewsbury in 1664 and is probably of the years around that date.[46] Two timber-framed mid-century examples are the Nook, Loppington, and Colehurst Manor, Sutton upon Tern. Later examples are Micklewood Farm, Longnor, and the Red House, Lydbury North. The formula lingered into the next century, in a slightly different architectural dress, when timber-framed houses were given a brick or stone cladding. Two examples are Whitton Hall, Westbury, and Eaton Mascott Hall, the latter with a date stone of 1734.

Within these small **U** or **H** plan houses there was an almost standard disposition of rooms in which the entrance hall, from which the through passage had been eliminated, generally occupied the whole of the main range, had a fireplace in the rear wall, and was entered by a doorway placed

Ground-floor plan of Moreton Hall, Weston Rhyn

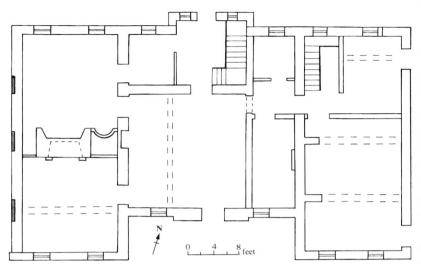

Ground-floor plan of Whitton Court, Westbury

centrally in the elevation and in the hall itself. On one side the hall was flanked by the kitchen at the front of one of the wings and with its service room at the rear, the latter with its own external entry; on the other side it was flanked by the parlour at the front of the wing and by an imposing main staircase at the rear. Typical examples are Great Lyth, Bostock Hall, Preston Brockhurst Hall, Micklewood Farm, and Braggington Hall.[47] There were of course variations upon the basic theme as it was adapted to circumstances: to the small size of Holt Farm, Plaish; to the **L** plan of Charlton Hill House; to the earlier timber-framed rear wings at Aston Hall, Munslow, and at Moreton Hall, Weston Rhyn.

These advances in the design and planning of the houses of the minor gentry, and of wealthy townsmen moving into the country, occurred very rapidly in the third quarter of the 17th century, and by c.1675–80 a standard form of their house was widespread. From then on, however, and for a considerable time, the minor gentry built little. In contrast the major gentry began building on a large scale, and in a way the two groups played Box and Cox in the mid to late 17th century.

Great chamber and grand staircase

The decline of the open hall was accompanied by the proliferation of other rooms. In a new house, or in an old house brought up to date, there would now be a great chamber, one or more parlours, a dining room, and whatever else might be thought desirable.

These might be accommodated, as at Pitchford, in added or extended wings, or, as at Shipton and Lutwyche, in the wings of a new **U** plan or **H** plan house. Sometimes the hall range itself (which in a late medieval **H** or **T** plan house never contained more than the hall and through passage) had other rooms within it. That occurred on the largest scale at Condover which of all surviving Shropshire houses approached closest to the typical Jacobean 'prodigy' house. It occurred also at Benthall Hall, Wilderhope, Steventon Manor, the hall block added at Stanwardine, the now demolished Birch Farm,[48] Kinlet, and Wolverley Hall, Wem.

Of all the new rooms the great chamber, which had taken on some of the public functions of the hall as the room where honoured guests were entertained, was the most splendid and was generally at least as imposing as the hall itself. Its prestige demanded that, like the hall, it should occupy the most important position in the house. At first glance this might appear to have been an insoluble problem, but with the hall reduced to one storey in height the contradiction between the claims of the two rooms could be happily resolved by siting the great chamber in the centre of the main range but on the first floor in what had been the upper part of the hall, symbolically appropriating some of its space as well as some of its functions. By the late 16th century a standard house was appearing in which the centre was divided horizontally between hall below and great chamber above. This relationship was common not only in new houses, but as well in older ones brought up to date, like Whitton Court, and in the reception blocks added to older houses, as at Stanwardine.

Such an impressive room, as the great chamber was meant to be, needed an impressive way up to it and certainly something more convenient and more imposing than the vice-staircase of earlier years, as fossilized at Plaish. What were needed were broad stairways with easy ascents and straight flights, but that requirement faced the builders of the time with a dilemma. In most houses, with a single-pile hall range set between single-pile cross wings, a large and stately staircase put pressure upon the available space. In houses as big as Condover it was possible to accommodate the staircase within a long hall range or more or less centrally within a long cross wing. When, however, the hall range contained no more than the hall, and perhaps a small room beside it, and when the cross wings were of no great length, it was impractical to sacrifice space in that way; instead the stair still had to be put, in a medieval fashion, in a projection at the rear of the hall. This, however, could no longer be of vice-like form but had to house either a well-staircase or a dog-legged one with broad and shallow treads.

The change did not come all at once; and again Wilderhope catches the development in mid flight, for there the main stair, though still a winder (see also plan on p.138), is broad in comparison with

Detail of spiral stair at Wilderhope Manor

what had gone before, and is of easy ascent and not without dignity. At Greete Court too, which is probably slightly earlier than Wilderhope, the stair turret is rectangular on plan though still with a winder. The earliest closely dated example of the fully developed form is the turret at the rear of the wing, comprising a hall with chamber above, which was added to Larden Hall in 1607. Other examples of near date in which a stair turret still survives are Steventon Manor, Stanwardine Hall, and Stoke House at Greete; and of a later date in the 1650s or 1660s, is Charlton Hill House, Wroxeter; and probably even later the Red House at Lydbury North. Similar turrets with convenient stairs were also provided in older houses which were being refurbished in the years around 1600, as at Upton Cressett, and at Belswardine. At Treflack Hall the character of the original turret has been disguised, with the stair removed and a floor inserted, and at Lutwyche and Shipton the original stair was probably in one of the rear projections.[49] All these were houses of some standing, but the stair turret appeared as well in less pretentious houses and in timber-framed ones, as at Petsey, at Berrington Manor, and at Birch Farm, Earnwood, where the turret opened from the rear wall of the hall. In all these the stair led directly into the great chamber which took on, at first-floor level and not very conveniently, some of the crossroads character that the hall had once had.

In houses built to the traditional hall-and-cross-wings plan and of limited size, the stair turret remained in use for a long time, for it was a convenient way of dealing with a broad stair where space was limited. Nevertheless, superior as it was to the old vice and imposing as it could be in such an example as Stanwardine, it was yet less imposing, and less susceptible of fashionable decoration, than the free-standing stair in the body of the house. At first it was only in large houses or in very small ones where magnificence was not a consideration, that the stair turret was eschewed; but later, coinciding with and partly conditioned by, the efflorescence of the exuberant Jacobean and Carolean joinery, the free-standing stair with all its opportunities for elaboration began to dominate. The main staircase at Ludstone, sited at the upper end of the hall in the centre of a wing, is a splendid example. The more or less contemporary rebuilding and resiting of the

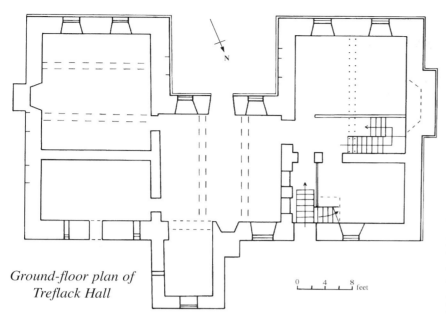

Ground-floor plan of Treflack Hall

0   4   8 feet

staircases at Benthall Hall and at Reaside Manor of *c*.1620–30 illustrate the same trend. Even small houses might have richly carved stairways, like those dated 1667 and 1668 at Whitley Grange and Pentre Morgan respectively and that of similar form in 15 St. Mary's Street, Shrewsbury. By the mid century many houses built on a **U** or **H** plan— whether on a fairly large scale like Preston Brockhurst, or medium sized like Aston Munslow Hall, or as small as Holt Farm—had a staircase within one or other of the wings. In some **U** and **H** plan houses, for example Ludstone Hall, a staircase in each wing allowed all first-floor rooms to be reached from the ground floor without violating the privacy of the great chamber. By the later years of the century the stair turret had been wholly abandoned.

In all that has been said so far the houses of the gentry in the years from *c*.1550 to the Restoration have been treated as the buildings of a more or less homogeneous social group. It is perhaps useful, however, to distinguish, as far as one can, between major and minor figures: between men of merely local standing and men who carried weight throughout the county or large parts of it, and even beyond. The distinction of course will not always be clear; but that problem besets every attempt at historical analysis and, despite all the uncertainties, it is possible to distinguish some families who were indisputably at the apex of county society in the late

16th and early 17th century and whose houses date in whole or in part from that time: the Ottleys of Pitchford, the Corbets of Moreton Corbet and Acton Reynald, the Newports of High Ercall and of Eyton on Severn, the Owens of Condover. There were other men, then of equal importance, whose building activities were minor or are unknown to us: the Cressetts who were content to improve rather than rebuild their very large house at Upton Cressett; the Leightons of Loton whose house of that time, whatever its form, was almost wholly obliterated by later rebuilding;[50] the Talbots of Longford and the Actons of Aldenham of whose houses little is known beyond that they were of courtyard form and probably of various dates; the Kynastons of Oteley, whose vast timber-framed house there on a courtyard plan was pulled down without much of a record.[51] It is perhaps later destruction as much as the remoteness of Shropshire from the sphere of royal peregrinations that has made Condover the only known house in the county with that hallmark of the 'courtier' house, the Long Gallery.[52]

The larger houses of the years from *c*.1550 to *c*.1630 which can be discussed in detail are few, but those which survive, and those of whose nature something is known, are all different from the run of gentry houses which were discussed above. Either, like Pitchford and Condover, they were on a **U** or **H** plan but with a very long main range allowing both a symmetrically placed entry and a screens passage; or, like Acton Reynald, Aldenham, Longford, and Oteley, they were built around a courtyard; or like Upton Cressett they consisted of several ranges of timber buildings with additions and improvements in brick or stone. The Newports' great house at High Ercall, now on an irregular **L** plan, was built either around a courtyard or on a very large **U** plan; it had a now demolished range with a loggia, a fashionable element known elsewhere in the county only at Condover and at the demolished Berwick Maviston.[53] The total evidence is not great but enough to show that there was a difference both in size and form between the houses of major and of minor gentry.

There is very little in the years between *c*.1630 and *c*.1670 that can be attributed to major gentry. A possible exception is Soulton Hall, built by a member of the Hill family, but of a minor branch.[54] Generally, however, it would seem that there was a hiatus in building by the leading families at that time. It is likely that some of them, the Corbets and Newports for example, had over-built, but that cannot be the whole story, for many of them had done very little building in the preceding 50 years. Nearly all the major gentry were Royalists in the Civil War, while the minor gentry were roughly equally divided between the parties. Delinquency fines after the war, and perhaps fears about the future before it, may well have affected the former's lust of building.

The early double-pile house

By the Restoration gentry houses in Shropshire had been freed from much of the evidence of their medieval origins. The open hall, the screens passage with its end-entry into the hall, and the staircase set in a turret had been replaced by the reception hall entered directly from the exterior, with a great chamber above and a staircase of some splendour in a wing. Nevertheless, they still retained that medieval form of a main range set between upper- and lower-end cross wings, a form which was the accompaniment of the conception of the house as the shelter for a community. Before the end of the century the last vestiges of the Middle Ages had been eliminated by the advent of the double-pile house: a square or rectangular block, two rooms thick, with a symmetrical main façade in one plane, sometimes with slight projections to punctuate the ends; with a hall, entered directly from outside through a central doorway and reserved for the 'quality'; and with the service rooms out of sight and with their own separate and unseen entrances.[55] In these houses the divorce between the family and its dependants which had begun with the elimination of the open hall had been made absolute and they might be seen as the end product of a long and logical process in which each generation adopted and adapted the innovations of the one before and which came to fruition by a 'broadening down from precedent to precedent'. That, however, would be to overlook a simple fact, that the double-pile house, which solved all the problems of post-medieval planning and aesthetics, had been known in all its essentials for a hundred years before it became common in Shropshire, or anywhere else in England. The first known survivor of the type anywhere in the country is Whitehall, in what is now a suburb of Shrewsbury.[56] It was built from 1579 onwards by Richard Prince, the son of a Shrewsbury shoemaker, who made a fortune practising law before the Council in the Marches, made friends in high places, married a daughter of Leighton of Plaish, and took out a grant of arms in 1584.[57] Lest it should be claimed that it was during his stay in London studying law that he picked up from cultural circles there the idea of the double-pile house it must be pointed out that he was in his 30s when he was admitted to the Inner Temple in 1554. He was permanently back in Shrewsbury by 1560 and there is no evidence that the concept of the double-pile house had entered anyone's head in London at that time. And, if he was in touch with advanced architectural thought, then he was singu-

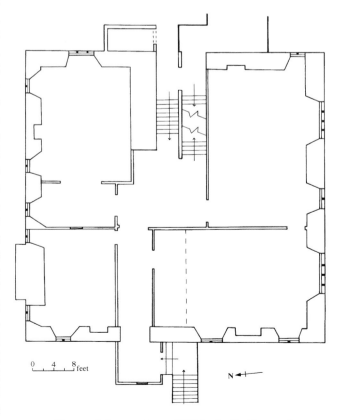

Ground-floor plan of Whitehall, Shrewsbury

146

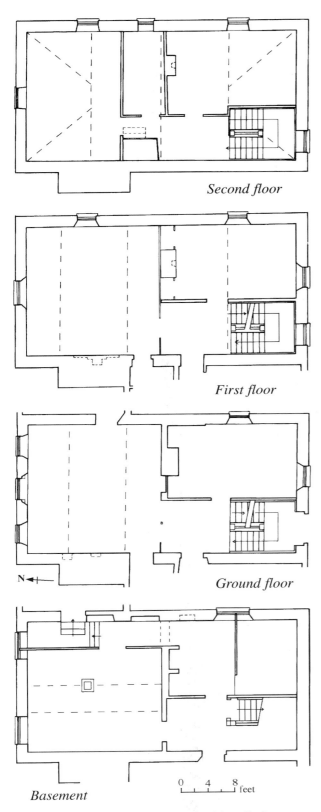

Second floor

First floor

N

Ground floor

0   4   8 feet

Basement

*Plans of Whitley Grange, a double-pile house
in an informal style*

larly unreceptive, for in style Whitehall is wholly in a local traditional idiom. He may have been adapting to another use the concept of lodges and 'pleasaunces'—informal, 'leisure activity' buildings—of which Frodesley Lodge, Penkridge Hall, and Whitley Grange are local examples. These have the basement services which were an important innovatory element of the double-pile house, but none is built to that plan and none is known to be earlier than Whitehall.[58] That house arose not out of London fashions nor out of aristocratic pleasures, but out of the circumstances of its builder: a man, despite his social advancement, outside of the general milieu of landed society, and residing as close to his occupation as he could.

Whitehall was followed in about 20 years by Acton Scott (see plans overleaf) and, later, by Soulton Hall, probably of *c*.1640.[59] These all had a wholly symmetrical front with an emphasized entrance central to the elevation and to the room which it led into; and that had been achieved elsewhere before the end of James I's reign only at the very greatest houses, at Condover and perhaps at the now demolished Millichope and on the east front of the much restored Acton Reynald. Moreover, in these early double-pile houses the service rooms were generally huddled away from polite eyes and placed partly at the rear and partly in the basement. They had, too, their own entrances and the quality had the entry into the hall to themselves. These houses had as well the great advantage that the stairs, either sited centrally or accompanied by corridors, were easily reached from all parts of the house and gave easy access to all the first-floor rooms. They thereby avoided the inconvenience, present even in such a **U** or **H** plan house as Ludstone with its two staircases, of having to go through the great chamber to get from one wing to another on the first floor. That that was more than a minor irritation is shown by the common later practice of adding a block at the rear of the main range to provide independent communication on the first floor. Examples may be seen at Ludstone itself, at Shipton, at Aston Munslow Hall, and at Hampton Hall. The absence of long wings or of a long main range made a 'long gallery' of any length a near impossibility, but these houses were built by men with no ambition to entertain the Court or the Great, nor even to pretend that they could.

147

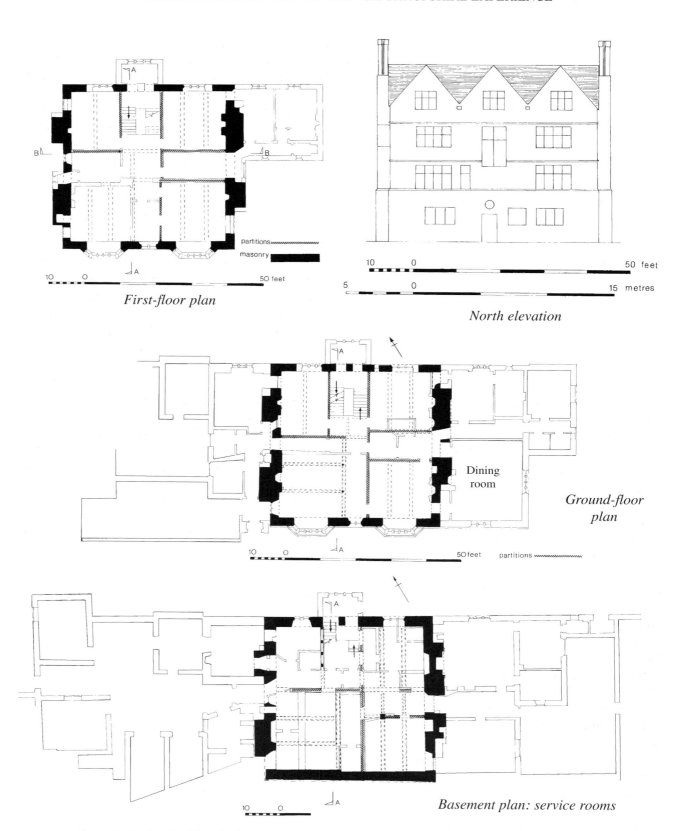

First-floor plan

North elevation

Ground-floor plan

Dining room

Basement plan: service rooms

Acton Scott Hall, the double-pile house in black. Much altered from the early 19th century, its central entrance in the main, south, front (see ground-floor plan) became a window, an entrance porch was made to the west, a dining room added to the east, and stairs were altered

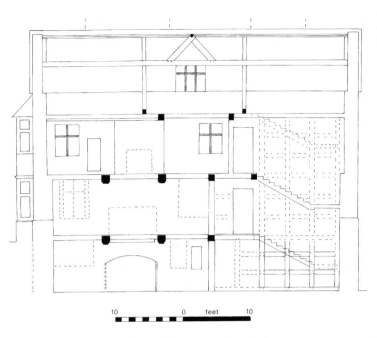

Acton Scott, section A-A

If the presence of exemplars to copy had been the only factors in the history of architecture in the 16th and 17th centuries, then double-pile houses would have been common long before Pratt commended their 'great spare of walling' or Fuller cautioned against the folly of building for 'an extraordinary occasion'.[60] But other forces were there and it is noticeable that when the arbiters of Taste at the Court and in the Metropolis caught up with Salopian, or at any rate provincial, practice they did so, until after the Civil War, mainly in urban or suburban contexts, where old ideas of lordship least applied. Only when the Crown had been stripped of its powers and patronage, when entertaining an omnipotent Sovereign was no longer a means of obtaining, or keeping, favours from the State, did the large double-pile house, of the type of Coleshill (Berks.) and Thorpe Hall (Northants.), appear under the Commonwealth and proliferate under the restored, but chastened, monarchy.

By the end of the 17th century many of those greater families who had been building earlier, and others who had but recently risen, were erecting houses on a grand scale: the Corbetts at Longnor, one

branch of the Hills at Court of Hill and another at Hawkstone, the Myttons at Halston, the Wolryches at Dudmaston, and the Leightons at Loton. Apart from them, the Needhams, elevated to the peerage, were building an enormous house at Shavington, and some up-and-coming families like the Powells at Hampton Hall, Worthen, and the Popes at Woolstaston were indulging in houses considerably bigger than those of the minor gentry.

In contrast with the later assured near-unaminity of style, the earlier houses of the period are varied in form—although the double pile is generally present—and seem often to be experimental. Two of the most important, Longnor Hall on a double-pile plan and Hampton Hall on an **H** plan, are, or were, remarkable for the length of the hall; described recently at the first as 'a remarkably big room filling five out of the seven bays of the house',[61] and at the second in 1889 as 'filling the whole space between the wings'.[62] In neither is it possible to suggest a conventional siting for the grand staircase and it seems likely that at both the stairway was sited within the hall itself and to one side of the entrance,[63] as it is at the more or less contemporary Hanbury Hall (Worcs.), and was at Fetcham Park (Surr.).[64] At Shavington Hall, commensurate with the splendour of the Needhams as Viscounts Kilmorey, the hall rose in the old manner, but with a new intent, through two storeys.[65] In some houses, too, the grandest room was sited on the first floor, as

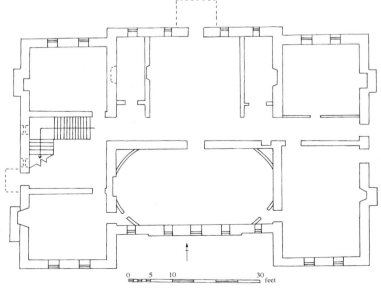

Plan of Halston Hall

at the reconstructed Court of Hill, at Aldenham Park, and originally, as one must suppose from the absence of any grand room on the ground floor, at Longnor itself. In all of these a magnificent doorway is sited on the first floor near to the head of the stairs.

That the age of experiment was over by the 1690s is shown by the uniform plans of Loton Park, Dudmaston, and Halston Hall (see previous page), all probably erected then, built as double piles with end pavilions, with a hall in the centre of the main front, a saloon beyond, lesser rooms flanking both, and a staircase in the middle of one of the sides. Loton has been much rebuilt,[66] and the other two have lost their original staircases,[67] but at all three the original disposition is clear. In these houses, too, there was probably an important reception room on the first floor, but there is evidence at Dudmaston, at least, that the corridor on that floor, despite the later decor, is original and that the entry to any room there was not as dramatic as at Court of Hill and at Aldenham.

By c.1700, then, the major gentry had evolved, or were evolving, a standard plan form, as the minor gentry had done about 30 or so years before. In retrospect we can see that in the years from c.1630 onwards it was the minor gentry who were setting the pace in introducing the central-entry reception hall and abandoning the through passage and its consequent plan. That was partly because greater men were more attached than the lesser men to the old plan type and partly because they were, for whatever reasons, indulging in little building at the time. By contrast, in the last quarter of the century it was the major gentry, and not their immediate social inferiors, who were fully exploiting the double-pile plan. Again that was not because the latter had found the ultimate solution to their housing problems but because they were then building very few houses. It was suggested earlier that the main reason for the hiatus in major gentry building in the mid century was their foreboding about, and their financial losses after, the Civil War. And it is likely that the interruption in building by lesser men in the last years of the century was not wholly or even partly because, as a class, they had over-built themselves, but rather because the general depression in gentry fortunes at the time, to which Professor Mingay has drawn attention, was affecting them, or at any rate most of them in Shropshire, more severely than it was affecting greater men.[68]

X   Houses of the Yeomanry 1550–1700

From all that has been said so far it might seem that most 'new' houses of the period were wholly new, and indeed at the top of society many were. At lower levels, however, the new form, eliminating the open hall and the through passage, was often brought about by modifying and partly rebuilding a medieval house. Indeed it has been said by the two writers who may claim to know most about Shropshire farmhouses that surprisingly few were wholly new built in the 16th and 17th centuries.[1] At that level—and well above it, at the level of men occupying the large cruck and base-cruck halls of earlier years—modernizing was often piecemeal, and long delayed: for example, the insertion of a smoke hood into the hall at Wolverton[2] between *1557 and 1589; the addition of a storeyed wing to an open hall at Baxter's House, Eaton Constantine; the insertion of a floor and chimney into the hall, and the building of a parlour block on the site of the former service end, at Brookgate Farm,[3] Plealey, in *1612; and similar alterations and additions at High Grosvenor,[4] Claverley, in the *late 16th or early 17th century. Other instances are the addition of a hall range and parlour block to a pre-existing range at Berrington Manor in 1658; the insertion of a floor at Church Farm, Loppington, in 1664; and as late as 1721, at Wheathall, Condover, the erection of a parlour range replacing the service end of a cruck hall.[5]

Long after great men had stopped building open halls they went on providing their houses with what was in effect a through passage, at least in Shropshire.[6] Lesser men there abandoned both elements in new houses and eliminated them by alterations from old ones.[7] The commonest result was the appearance of the 'lobby entrance' house, entered via a space (lobby) opposite an axial chimney and leading into a room to left or right, or

rooms to left and right. The classic form, though not the commonest in Shropshire, was a two-storey, three-cell timber-framed range with a parlour to one side of the lobby, a hall and a service room beyond on the other side, and a staircase beside the stack in the space opposite the lobby. A poorer type of one and a half storey was common, and there were superior ones of two and a half storeys. Any choice of examples[8] is somewhat arbitrary, but among the first variant are Old Farm, Clunton, and no. 39 Preston Brockhurst; among the second Middle Farm, Westley, nos. 26–7 Kempton, and 22 Drayton Road, Hodnet; and among the third Eye Farm, Leighton. There were as well smaller houses of two cells only (the 'baffle entry' house) with the entry against a stack at the end of the hall and with a service room beyond the hall, and generally of one and a half storey. Examples are common, and one may cite 1 Shrewsbury Road, Hodnet, no. 8 Upton Magna, no. 1 Leebotwood, and the Lea Gates, Hungry Hatton, Child's Ercall.

A variation on the theme is Arleston Manor (formerly Arleston House), Wellington, with a two-cell front range, a lobby entrance, and a shorter parallel rear range comprising a small service room, a staircase, and a kitchen with its fireplace in the side of the stack in the front range. If the dates on the front and rear ranges, of 1614 and 1630, are reliable, the building may be a two-cell lobby-entrance house with a later addition, or a two-cell parlour addition to an earlier house replaced by the present rear range.

There is thus a happy symmetry in the history of the through passage. It seems that men of minor standing were the first to introduce it into English houses[9] and the first to eliminate it from them; and in both instances they were belatedly copied by the Great.

Many of these houses have been rebuilt in brick or stone or have been altered and are not always immediately recognizable: 2 Shrewsbury Street, Prees, nos. 3–4 Aston, Claverley, and Hatchett's Farm, Loppington. Some, such as 22 Drayton Road, Hodnet, no. 1 Leebotwood, and Gandersbank, Whixall, have had the doorway removed to a central position, and at no. 8 Upton Magna it has been moved to the gable wall. Some, like no. 3 Harley, and several in Westbury parish, have had additions[10] or, like Steps Cottage, Shrawardine, have had an end rebuilt. At Middle Farm, Westley, the present plan form may be the result of a modification of an earlier one. At no. 25 Kempton the baffle-entry form has been brought about by inserting a stack into the remaining bay of a two-bay cruck house, and the same is probably true of the Thatched Cottage at Shipton. Despite problems of identification it seems reasonably clear that the lobby-entrance and baffle-entry house forms were dominant at vernacular level in post-medieval Shropshire and that, as in neighbouring Montgomeryshire, the second was commoner than the first; but neither was as common in the county as across the Border.[11]

Poorer than all of these are a few timber-framed houses of one room. They are perhaps better described as 'open to the roof' rather than as 'open halls', although they are tall enough to have had a very low upper storey, or at any rate a crogloft, inserted later. In these too the entry was at the end of a lateral wall and against a stack or a fire hood. Examples include the now demolished Donkey House at Berrington, the Old Shop at Somerwood, Upton Magna, and Fulway Cottage in Cound parish. The Donkey House, built on a high stone plinth and with small timber panels, was probably of c.1600.[12] A late 16th-century date has been suggested for the Old Shop.[13] Fulway Cottage, which has its own oddities, is discussed below.

The house with the entry against a chimney stack was common among men of very varied means, but it was not the only type. There were some other houses in which the entry was into the lower end of the main room and away from the stack at the other end. Laburnum Cottage, Loppington, is a somewhat lone example in north Shropshire, but there are several in Westbury parish, originally probably of timber but now clad in stone. It is, of course, often very difficult to say whether a building has always

been of stone or whether the stone covers or replaces original timber framing. Mapps Cottage, Kenley, is a case in point. It is now wholly of stone, but until 1967 the lower end was of timber.[14] And it is very doubtful whether the upper end was always of stone, for the beams, joists, and trusses of the same late 17th-century date as the enormous external stack do not fit the present walls. The entry is now into the lower end of the main room, but it is impossible to tell whether that is its original position. Brooke Cottage, Westbury, is of stone and has a massive external stack, but all the present openings are of 19th-century character and may or may not be the original ones. Also in Westbury parish Brook Farm, Yockleton, and Lower Wigmore, Marsh, are 17th-century timber-framed houses later clad in brick, and again the site of the original entries is uncertain. Instances were cited earlier of houses that have had the entry moved to a central position, and what does seem certain is that that plan form became common in the area in the 18th and 19th centuries. It was probably then, rather than in the 17th century, that—as at Pontesbury[15]—many of the stone cottages in Kenley and on the Clee Hills were built. That there were stone built one-cell cottages in Coalbrookdale in the 16th century seems equally uncertain, and a claimed example, 58–9 Hodgebower, seems to be a late conversion to two dwellings of an earlier building.

Equally uncertain is the presence of post-medieval long houses in Shropshire. There are examples of house and byre in one range: the addition to the Old Shop at Somerwood and the use, until 1967, of the unceiled lower end of Mapps Cottage as a byre. These are not long houses in the accepted use of the term, but claims have been made for the occurrence of the classic long house in Westbury and the uplands to the south.[16] There are several houses there with a third room that may have been added, or rebuilt, as a byre. In no case, however, has anything been adduced to suggest a drain, or a feeding walk, or tethering posts, or entry from a through passage into both house and byre. Evidence of that sort may eventually come to light, but at the moment the post-medieval, like the medieval, long house remains unproven in Shropshire.

There are very few certain, or probable, dates for any of these houses. No. 1 Shrewsbury Road,

Hodnet, has a date, which appears to be genuine, of 1585 above the doorway. Dates of 1614 and 1630 were mentioned earlier for Arleston House. Nos. 2–3 Muckleton, Shawbury, is a lobby-entrance house with an older wing attached; the parlour has a hewn jetty and there is a date of 1620 above the doorway. Berrington Manor has a date plaque, with initials which relate to the known owner, of 1658, and the early part of Golding Hall, Cound, is dated *1660. Fulway Cottage, also in Cound parish, is a very unusual structure, originally of one storey with close-studded walls,[17] and perhaps built as a 'pleasaunce' or a forester's lodge. It has a date of *1603 for the fabric and one of *1639 for the inserted floor. The latter is probably the date of the fire hood as well and of the conversion to a 'one up, one down' cottage with a baffle entry.[18] Where there has been no benefit from inscriptions or from dendrochronology, recorders have tended, on stylistic evidence, to put these axial-chimney houses into the early to mid 17th century, and it seems likely that they were not becoming common until then. That gets some confirmation from the date of *1550 for Ashwood, in Whitchurch, a cruck-built house with crucks of reasonable scantling and apparently an open hall.[19] It would seem probable that the demise of the open hall was a slow one, that some were being built well into the late 16th century. Many were tolerated for long after that, for at Church Farm, Loppington, the floor was not inserted until 1664.[20]

Many of the bigger houses differ also from their smaller neighbours in being built to a **T** plan with a hall, or kitchen, on the ground floor of the upright of the **T** and a parlour and another room in the cross stroke. Most two-and-a-half-storey houses were on a **T** plan and most **T** plan houses were of two and a half storeys.[21] Some of these, and especially those on the north Shropshire plain, where by the 1660s dairy farming had increased enormously, may be thought to reflect a very local prosperity.[22] Some, like Well House, Drawwell Lane, Wem, incorporated a dairy in the parlour wing, and so too did Wytheford Grange,[23] Shawbury. At the last there is now no sign of that arrangement, and it is likely that dairies have been eliminated from other houses on this plan. They were certainly common at what may have been poorer houses. One was added to the parlour block at Old House Farm, Loppington, shortly after that had itself been added to an earlier range, and at Ashwood the lower end of the hall was converted to that purpose.

Not all large **T** plan houses incorporated a dairy into the parlour block. There is no evidence for that at Berrington Manor or at Golding Hall, and at Cross House, Longden, the evidence is against it (see drawings overleaf). The second room there, of the same size as the parlour and with similar stops on the beams, could have been reached originally only from the parlour. Most of these new or altered houses were the homes of working farmers, some employing wage labour in part or at times, some relying on family labour.[24] They belonged to a transitional period of petty commodity production, and, while their owners had abandoned the open hall of feudal agriculture, they had not embraced the later classical farmhouse, its genteel front emphasizing the social distinction between capitalist farmers,

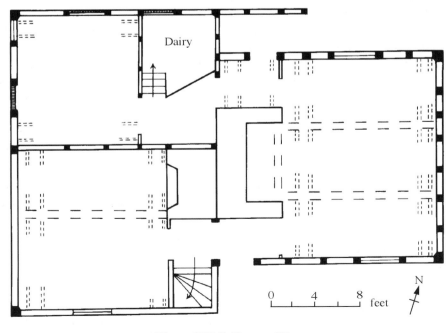

Plan of Well House, Wem

Dairy

0   4   8 feet

N

whether tenants or freeholders, and landless labourers.[25] They were substantial men. The Blakeways of Berrington had contributed 20s. to the royal benevolence of 1491, and in the mid 16th and early 17th centuries they owned, apart from land, lime kilns and forges.[26] George Langley was a tenant of part of Golding in 1598, but in 1606 he bought it outright.[27] The Cross family had held a copyhold estate and a small freehold in Pontesbury since the early 15th century.[28]

Their houses may be seen as a step—at a level just below the gentry—towards increased private accommodation for the family and its separation from other occupants. The form of these houses had perhaps been anticipated among the minor gentry at such houses as Cherrington Manor of 1635[29] and Marrington Hall. These appear to be two-cell timber framed, lobby-entrance houses, but at both that form was a later contrivance. At both, the present 'lobby entrance' block began as a parlour block with an axial chimney, added to and entered from a pre-existing range, at what is now the rear, which contained whatever stairway there was to the upper floor of the new addition. The early range has been replaced by a later one at Cherrington and by a corridor at Marrington, and at both a central doorway has been made in the new block and a passage driven through the stack to give access to the rear. The advantages of the original plan, before later fashion demanded a symmetrical entrance front, were twofold. Something more than the cramped lobby entrance and its equally cramped staircase could be provided in the rear block and, since the hall in the existing range had its own heating, the axial chimney in the new block could heat both parlours, an improvement on the 'vernacular' **T** plan

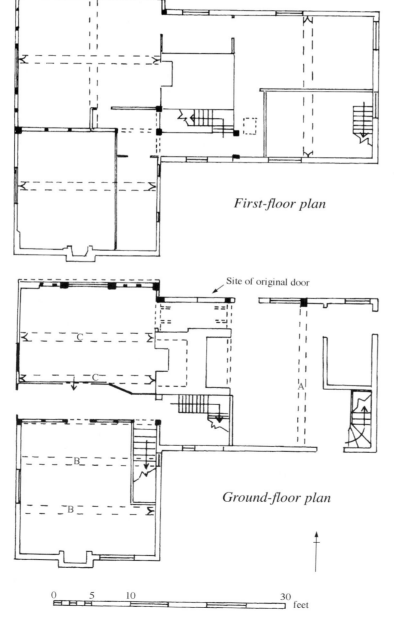

First-floor plan

Site of original door

Ground-floor plan

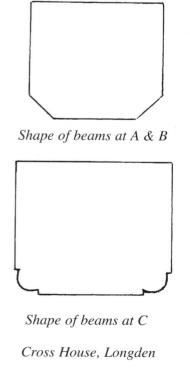

Shape of beams at A & B

Shape of beams at C

Cross House, Longden

0 5 10 30 feet

of, for example, Cross House, Longden, where the stack could heat only one parlour.

The details of what happened in the earlier ranges at Cherrington and Marrington are unknown, but from the Restoration onwards men at, or aspiring towards, the minor gentry level developed a more commodious **T** plan house. This had a brick parlour wing, with an axial chimney heating two parlours in the cross stroke of the **T**, a spacious staircase-and-entry hall in the upper part of the upright, and the services in a refashioned earlier wing in the lower part. Preeshenlle Old Hall (near Gobowen), the probably pre-1698 Old Vicarage at High Ercall,[30] and Sambrook Manor (Chetwynd), with a date plaque on the new wing of 1702, are examples. In all of these the second parlour was also heated and—as at Cross House, Longden, and in the probably mid 17th-century parlour wing at Glebe Farm, Diddlebury—could not be reached directly from the entrance hall but only through the first parlour.[31] In all of them the stairs were broad and convenient; at Preeshenlle, probably the earliest, they retain pierced raking balusters in a Jacobean style and an ornamental string, and at Sambrook early 18th-century balusters.

There is a clear progression in comfort, convenience, and, one might say, elegance from the lobby-entrance house in one range to the lobby-entrance house on a **T** plan and thence to the **T** plan house with a stairway entrance hall and a parlour wing with two heated rooms.

A further step, foreshadowing later developments, although in an eccentric way, was taken at Brickhouse Farm, Greete. It is built on a rectangular plan with a symmetrical elevation and with a central passage enlarged at the rear to take the staircase. Each of the four ground-floor rooms has a corner fireplace sited between the two outside walls and one of the front rooms seems originally to have been open to the passage, functioning perhaps as a hall. The staircase is in a provincial Jacobean style with flat raking balusters and stocky newel posts, but the house may be as late as *c.*1700.[32]

It is unlikely that the builders of these houses were very different from those who had built the **T** plan houses of about a generation before, but their aspirations were rising. Little is known about Preeshenlle Old Hall, and that in itself suggests that it was of no very high standing. The Old Vicarage at High Ercall, when compared for example with Cardeston Rectory of two generations earlier, is a symptom of the rising status of the parish clergy. Sambrook Manor was built by a man climbing into gentility and marrying a coheir of the long estab-

Brickhouse Farm, Greete

The staircase at Brickhouse Farm, Greete

lished Sambrooks.[33] Presumably these men did the best they could with limited means.

In contrast, where wealth had become available, the transformation of a vernacular into a gentry house could be sudden and dramatic. The Langleys of Golding built their new timber-framed **T** plan house with a lobby entrance in *1660. A few years later, between *1666 and 1668, they added a brick parlour wing with a main room, a smaller room and a spacious staircase hall, creating an **H** plan.[34] Soon afterwards they clad the older house in brick and moved the entrance away from the stack to the centre of the hall elevation. They then had, in appearance at least, an up-to-date gentry house of the type of Great Lyth, Micklewood Farm, Hampton Hall, and Braggington Hall. Golding's was a spectacular transformation; it was soon to be endlessly repeated on a smaller scale in the change from the vernacular farmhouse of the past into the farmhouse, posing as a modest gentleman's residence, of the 18th and 19th centuries.

XI   Design, Style, and Ornament 1550–1700

Stone and brick

Social custom, convenience, Renaissance canons, and political pressures were not the only forces affecting the architecture of the time. By the end of the Middle Ages men of moderate standing had developed an open hall accompanied by one or by two large cross wings whose bulk beneath a broad gable played some part in the elevation, along with such other projections as porch and oriel. Well known examples, of course, are Great Chalfield and South Wraxall (both Wilts.). Cross wings were highly admired at the time, and were regarded as a mark of status, and many attempts were made to create the impression without having to provide the substance. The most striking examples are the 'Wealden Houses', so common in south-east England, which by an ingenious trick of carpentry give to a plain rectangle the look of a house with two jettied cross wings. Later instances occur in

Shropshire as well. At Ivy Farm in Little Dawley a functionless gable has been added at one end of a rectangular building and at right angles to the roof to give a hall-and-cross-wing form. At Shadeoak a gable was added along the front when the house was brought up to date in the mid 17th century. Even at Whitehall, an early stone-built double-pile house (discussed earlier, pp.146-7), the façades were crowned by a series of small gables.

The visual result, in the late 16th century, of the prevalence of the **U** or **H** plan within an aesthetic context in which sub-medieval and Renaissance inclinations jostled for place is a number of houses in which the design is dominated by the gabled wings and other projections from the main range of the building. In a large house like Condover the dominance is less marked, for gabled wings and an emphasized entrance could there be happily integrated into a symmetrical composition. In smaller

Condover Court showing a mixture of gables and pronounced entrance

houses the end-entry into the hall dictated a main entrance at one end of the main range, and builders tended to use bay windows or oriels at the other end of the range to give balance to an asymmetrical elevation. To say that is not to decry them, for they have an individuality which Condover with its up-to-date fashion rather misses. Indeed it is possible to find other Condovers elsewhere in the country, but not so easy to parallel Wilderhope, Shipton, and Benthall Hall, early examples of the undeveloped **U** or **H** plan, all built at much the same time and of a local stone. At Wilderhope and at Benthall porches and oriels still play an important part in the effect, and at Shipton too, as we saw above,[1] there was originally a two-storey bay window at the upper end of the hall to balance the tower at its lower end. Such **U** and **H** plan houses were mostly of stone or brick, but some were of timber and with main ranges big enough to have included respectable halls. The best known ones are Pitchford Hall and Park Hall, Whittington. Others are Beslow Farm (formerly Hall), pulled down in 1985,[2] Wolverley Hall, Wem, and a house, now demolished, at Earnwood, Kinlet, which also had a stair turret at the rear.

These houses, however, were somewhat old fashioned in their design even as they were built, for other contemporaries in brick or timber, such as Plaish, Lea Hall, and Dunval, had abandoned projections of any consequence along the main range and had two symmetrical wings flanking a main range in one plane and with an off-centre entry into the hall. By the early 17th century the form had become more or less standard, sometimes with a porch as the one projection from the main range, as at Steventon Manor, Meeson Hall, Stoke House at Greete, and in the brick refronting of Whitton Court. In these houses it is the wings which hold attention and not the main range or the entrance into the house. Indeed it is ironical that the desire to maintain the old end-entry in conjunction with the old emphasis on the wings was leading, within the context of developing Renaissance canons, to a point where all architectural reference to the entry was progressively suppressed. The development culminated at Ludstone Hall, where a projecting bay is sited symmetrically in the centre of the main range and in the manner of a porch, but actually serves as a bay window while the entrance is inconspicuous in the side of a wing.[3]

Because architectural effect in these **U** and **H** plan houses was sought in the balance and contrast of masses rather than in a rhythm of individual elements they are on the whole devoid of much applied ornament. The great exception is the south front at Moreton Corbet built by Robert Corbet, 'carried away with the affectionate delight of architecture ... after the Italian model'.[4] The suggestion has been made that it is based on designs by Palladio[5] and, if so, it illustrates again how florid his work was in comparison with the austerity of most Elizabethan and Jacobean houses in Shropshire.

That exoticism apart, the amount of decoration on Shropshire houses of this period is small, at least on those of brick or stone. Applied ornament generally took a classical form of pilasters or pediments or a sub-medieval one of heraldic badges and achievements of arms; often both forms appeared together on the same building, as at Moreton Corbet and Preston Brockhurst.[6] Nevertheless the use of brick had in the end a widespread aesthetic effect.

Example of the rich ornamentation on the south front of Moreton Corbet

Plaish—the earliest Shropshire house built in brick to retain anything like its original form

Brick was being used in Shropshire from the early 15th century but, with perhaps one exception, apparently for chimneys or, as at Caus in the 1550s, as paving to a 'walke'.[7] The Talbots' great brick house at Tong has gone, and that at Longford has been very effectively disguised, and Shropshire's earliest brick house surviving in anything like its original form is Plaish, probably of the 1570s or 1580s.[8] The most noticeable effect of the new material was produced not by any ornament but by the 'studies in red and white' afforded by the contrast between the red brick of the fabric and the white or cream of the freestone used for the surrounds to openings, for window mullions, string courses, gable copings and the occasional balustrade. Chimney stacks were highly decorated sometimes with elaborately twisted shafts and almost universally with a moulded capping. The most striking variation upon the general pattern occurs upon the mid 17th-century timber wing at Abcott, Clungunford, where a pair of tall shafts, richly orna-mented with ribbed rectangular designs, are linked by lozenge-patterned cross pieces.[9] Yet in general it was only the prestigious rooms in a house which were served by an ornate chimney stack. At White Abbey, Alberbury, the former priory, the main range had a stack with twin shafts linked by decora-tive cross pieces, while an apparently contemporary stack serving a minor wing had a shaft with a simple rib up each side.[10]

Diaper patterning upon brickwork occurs most noticeably at Plaish Hall, at Upton Cressett, and at Albrighton Hall and, in conjunction with a zigzag pattern, at Alkington Hall, but it is not very common and is conspicuously absent from such important houses as Lee Hall and Stanwardine Hall. At Brickhouse Farm, Greete, the window heads have alternating headers picked out in a darker colour.

The use of moulded brick is also rare. Outstanding is Crowleasows Farm (Bitterley), of the mid 17th century. The doorway is flanked by

Crowleasows Farm, Bitterley, which uses moulded brick pilasters, banding and ornamental brickwork in the gables

rusticated brick pilasters, the massive external chimney stack has bands of moulding upon it, and the gables have ornamental brickwork. The nearby and now demolished Park Hall Farm, with crow-stepped gables, was apparently in the same vein.[11] The porch opening and window surrounds of Charlton Hill House (Wroxeter) were similarly treated,[12] and the gables of the wings at Pentre Farm, Trefonen, near Oswestry, with a date stone of 1695, have alternate courses of brick standing proud of the wall. The usage, as might be expected, is commoner in the towns, especially in Shrewsbury and to a lesser extent in Bridgnorth, and is generally of the mid 17th century and in an 'Artisan Mannerist' style. Surviving Shrewsbury examples are 24 Claremont Hill, 1 Church Street (1665), and 37–8 Abbey Foregate.[13] In Bridgnorth 7–8 St. John's Street and the much altered 1–3 Mill Street are similar. What is surprising is the rarity of the Anglo-Flemish and the typically Jacobean ornament upon brick buildings. Ludstone Hall, with curvilinear gables and with strap work above the window heads, is unusual, and so too was the now demolished addition to Chelmarsh Hall.[14]

In most other houses of the time there is little of that ornament. Despite the popular myth to the contrary, English architecture of the period is on the whole plain and even austere, but nevertheless Shropshire architecture gives a greater impression of plainness than that of many other English counties. One reason for that is the rarity of any houses comparable with the great Elizabethan and Jacobean 'prodigy houses'. Neither Moreton Corbet nor Sir Francis Newport's great house at High Ercall was completed, and even at Condover, where the great porch could have provided the opportunity for an ornate frontispiece, the decoration is sparse. Yet it was upon houses of that standing, and especially upon their frontispieces, that so much of the ornament of the time was concentrated, and it is therefore less the ornament itself that is missing than the houses to receive it. Yet the ornament itself may not have been so readily available. Lord Herbert of Chirbury, building his brick house just across the border at Montgomery, had to import skilled workers from Essex and Hertfordshire in the 1620s.[15]

There is, however, perhaps more to it than that, for as well as the absence of prodigy houses there is, from c.1620 at the latest, a very marked diminution

in the amount of building by major gentry families and no sign of an upturn until after the Restoration.[16] That diminution occurred just at the time when Jacobean and Carolean ornament was at its most exuberant, and the lack of building then by those most able to indulge in ornament, even though on a smaller scale than the builders of very large houses, helped to intensify the undecorated character of the architecture in brick and stone within the county at the time.

By 1660 the architectural climate was very different from that of c.1600. The influence of Inigo Jones and the Virtuosi had initiated a sort of modified astylar Palladianism, which eschewed bold projections and broken skylines for elevations more or less in one plane: achieving effect by mass, by the nature of the ornament, and by the clearly expressed proportions of storey to storey and voids to solids, it was integrated by a single dominating overall roof line. There is nothing to suggest that it was introduced for any other reason than aesthetic dogma, but it was a style well suited to a double-pile house and less suited to a **U** or **H** plan house.

It began as a Court style and it appeared belatedly in Shropshire and in a local form dictated by the almost universal use of brick rather than stone. In some ways, despite foreign elements within it, it is the successor of the plain 'red and white' style of many earlier houses. It is indeed the style not merely of the greater men but of all the Shropshire gentry in the period and is found indeed earlier in the smaller houses than in the large. Its most prominent elements are the use of red brick with freestone dressings, the lack of extraneous ornament apart from a cartouche of arms above the doorway and occasionally, in an old fashioned way, columns flanking it. Windows are of sash proportions but with out-of-date transoms, as originally at Longnor and still *in situ* at the rear of Court of Hill; storeys are marked externally by a plain plat band and with a carved cornice to underline the overall roof. At Court of Hill (1683)[17] the roof itself is punctuated by dormers; at Longnor (c.1670) a huge curvilinear gable dominated the elevation;[18] at Halston Hall (perhaps of the 1690s) the entrance front has a slightly projecting centrepiece crowned by a pediment.[19] Other houses share the same style: from the enormous Shavington to a small **H** plan house like Micklewood Farm and a large one like Hampton Hall.

The uniformity of style is emphatic in itself, and is further emphasized by the almost complete absence from rural houses of the other styles of the time: Artisan Mannerism and the manner of Sir Roger Pratt and his successors. The former style was of course old fashioned in the 1670s but it was, or had been, well enough known, at least in Shrewsbury. Yet there is little sign of it in the countryside. The other style, with its contrasting preference for stone and for openings surmounted by straight and curved pediments, found no favour in Shropshire, not even among the Needhams in their new splendour as Viscounts Kilmorey. It was, however, not so much stone and profuse ornament that local men were eschewing as the fine ashlar masonry and the careful and precise carving that were features of the very great houses of the time. Only at Aldenham was stone used in such a house at this time, perhaps because there it was necessary to blend with earlier stone. Indeed it may well be that by the late 17th century the shortage of skilled brickworkers that had earlier inhibited local builders had given way to a shortage not of masons, but of masons skilled enough to produce the kind of work that the style of Pratt and Talman required.[20]

Timber framing

Until the end of the 17th century nearly all smaller houses were of timber, and it was upon timber that the most profuse decoration appeared. In early timber framing the function of the braces between vertical and horizontal timbers was to strengthen the structure, and any pattern which resulted was a happy by-product. Towards the end of the Middle Ages decoration was becoming a desired effect. At Pitchford Hall, of *c*.1550, the structural panels were filled with a pattern of lozenges within lozenges, a design repeated later at Beslow Hall and at many others.[21] Where space was limited and a lozenge was not possible a herringbone pattern was used. And many combinations were possible. Gibbon's Mansion, Wyle Cop, Shrewsbury, probably of the last quarter of the 16th century, had large plain panels on the end elevations and close studding on all three storeys of the front.[22] The decorative use of bold structural timbers was accompanied by that of delicate small-scale carving upon the timbers themselves: sunk quatrefoils almost anywhere, the twisted shafts known as 'barley-sugar columns' upon uprights, and vine scroll upon gables and prominent cross members. The most striking example in the county, indeed perhaps in the country, is Pitchford Hall, where large lozenges dominate the picture and are offset at close quarters by the small-scale decoration.

In time this bizarre combination of bold geometric patterning and delicate carved ornament gave way to a florid but unemphasized mode in which the elevation was covered with a profusion of small panels containing curvilinear lozenges enriched with cusping to form what may be called degenerate quatrefoils. The earlier carved ornament was supplanted by blank arcading and balustrading. Park Hall, Whittington, probably of the early 17th

Pitchford Hall: the most striking use of bold timber patterns in the county,
and which also has small-scale decoration

161

century, was one of the few later timber houses comparable in size with Pitchford; and it made a complete contrast.[23]

The story was, of course, far more complex than that juxtaposition would suggest, and the two manners existed side by side for a very long time. The bold patterns of Pitchford were repeated, for instance, at Lee Old Hall in 1594,[24] at Habberley Hall, at Larden Hall on the pre-1607 jettied parlour block, at Beslow Hall probably in the 1630s,[25] and at Cherrington Manor as late as 1635.[26] Vertical panelling was used at the very large and now demolished Millichope Hall[27] and on the parlour wing at Abcott Manor, Clungunford, which has internal plaster decoration of late-Jacobean or Carolean date. A common, almost standard, formula was to use vertical panels on the ground floor and bold lozenges above: some examples are Thonglands, All Stretton Manor, Langley Gatehouse, and Downton Farm at Upton Magna. On the much altered jettied ranges at Beslow lozenges were used on the first floor of the front elevation and on the side elevations towards the front, while close studding with a middle rail appeared elsewhere. In Shrewsbury barley-sugar columns are in conjunction with sunk quatrefoils at Drapers' Hall and Owen's Mansion and, together with vertical panelling, at Ireland's Mansion. Often, whatever might be below, degenerate quatrefoils were set at the tops of the gables.

Town houses were the most lavishly ornamented of all timber buildings, not because their owners, either individually or as a whole, were wealthier than the upper classes in the countryside, but because they were not. Most of the gentry were building in brick or stone, and prosperous townsmen therefore had the field of timber building pretty well to themselves. Although not rich enough to use the most expensive materials, they could afford opulent decoration in timber upon the short street elevations that their generally restricted sites produced. It is not by chance, therefore, that the most ornate surviving timber house in the county is the Feathers Inn, formerly a private house, at Ludlow. Lozenges of various forms, barley-sugar columns, and round-headed arcading, together with the floreated brackets that were a feature of Ludlow carpentry, appear in conjunction and in profusion upon its street front.[28] It once had equals, such as 46 Pride Hill (demolished in the 1880s), Shrewsbury,

The well-known Feathers at Ludlow,
with its profusion of decoration

with close studding, barley-sugar columns, and blind arcading, and in addition carved floral ornament upon the fascia of its pentice.[29] At a higher social level, using ornament as profusely but more modishly, is the Gatehouse to the Shrewsbury seat of the Council in the Marches. It is dated 1620 and its elevations are covered with degenerate quatrefoils in association with blind arcading, with a pediment and with classical columns upon enriched podia.

Urban and rural builders differed as well in their choice of motifs. Thus large-scale patterning continued in some favour in the countryside up to the Civil War, but was little used and soon abandoned in the towns. There, in contrast, barley-sugar columns were still popular in the early 17th century and there the rich Jacobean forms were widely used. It is likely that large-scale patterns were more viable in the country, where they could be seen from a distance, than in the town, where, generally, they could not. In town streets rich ornament, seen at close quarters, could be better appreciated.

To say when the old manner declined and the new became dominant is difficult, partly because of a lack of reliable dates, especially between 1590 and 1610. One may accept 1590 at Penkridge Hall and 1592 at Owen's Mansion,[30] but many other claims have to be dismissed: those of Habberley Hall

(1593),[31] Marrington Hall (1595),[32] Hall Farm (1601),[33] Deuxhill, Llwyd Mansion (1604),[34] Oswestry, and Marshe Manor (1604)[35] for instance. Further, patterning in timber framing can be altered with ease, and has been altered at Albright Hussey,[36] at Berrington Manor,[37] and at Dunval.[38] It is often impossible to spot such changes without the help of earlier illustrations, and caution is even more necessary here than elsewhere. Perhaps all that one can say is that the new modes came into prominence, and the differences between town and country became more apparent, in the early part of James I's reign.

By itself, however, the above account may give a distorted picture of the nature of timber framing in the period. Most timber buildings had no ornament on them at all, apart from the occasional curvilinear lozenge at the top of a gable. Whatever decorative effect there might be was adventitiously produced by the pattern of the wholly utilitarian framing, generally small panels about two and a half to three feet square. After the Restoration all the rich turned to stone or brick. Timber became poor men's material,[39] so there was very little applied ornament; moreover increasingly economical use of thinner timbers in larger panels eliminated the last trace of the earlier patterned appearance.

Interior decoration

Interior decoration was less dependent than external ornament upon the forms of houses or upon their materials, and it may be discussed as a whole. In general in Shropshire it was neither distinctive nor distinguished but was occasionally peculiar to a small area. Most of the more ostentatious ornament was upon fireplaces, staircases, ceilings, and friezes, but there was much wainscot as well. The wainscot, formerly in the hall and now in a bedroom, at Shipton is elaborately patterned with raised central panels and with an ornamental frieze above. In general, however, and throughout the period it was very plain: at first in small panels, sometimes mitred, sometimes butted, sometimes with a ribbed moulding, and later in large bolection-moulded panels. Occasionally the fashionable elaboration of Knole or Tissington was attempted: at Belswardine the wainscot of the parlour was divided into sections by giant fluted pilasters, and at Ludstone by pilasters enriched with newel and carrot-drop orna-

Fireplace in the entrance hall of the Old House, 11 Dogpole, Shrewsbury

Fireplace in the drawing room of the Old House, 11 Dogpole, Shrewsbury, with its panel raised to reveal the mural behind

*Fireplace dated 1553 in the billiards room of
the Old House, 11 Dogpole, Shrewsbury*

ment. In the 17th century the chamfers of door jambs were often given decorative stops near ground level; plain examples survive at Plaish and at Steventon Manor. At Whitton Court there is an elaborate stop with a whorl above a bobbin motif.

Fireplace in the hall of Wilderhope Manor

For about a generation after the mid 16th century a correct classicism was sometimes attempted upon fireplaces. Examples in timber with decoration upon them are the overmantels in the Old House (1553), Dogpole, Shrewsbury, and Lea Hall (1584), Preston Gubbals, with fluted Ionic pilasters and colonnettes. At Stanwardine the stone fireplace in the hall was flanked by giant Doric pilasters. Classical feeling declined later in favour of such vernacular motifs as the billet mould and leaf ornament at Wilderhope, the enriched arcading, stumpy fluted pilasters, and geometrical ornament of Moat Farm, Stapleton, the herms and strapwork of Anglo-Flemish fashion in the solar at Stokesay, and biblical stories such as Joseph and Potiphar's Wife at Ludstone. Some indecision about which style to prefer may be seen at Moat Hall, Little Hanwood. Two fireplaces there have typical round-headed arcading on the overmantel, but one has the opening flanked by fluted pilasters and the other by lanky naked figures presumably meant for herms. By the 1620s grandiose creations were in favour: the fireplace at Condover, with its standing figures under arcades, and the overmantels at Park Hall, lavishly covered with herms, columns, and enriched arcading. In the mid 17th century a chaster style developed, seen at Lee Old Hall (1657), Ellesmere, at Shadeoak (1659), Cockshutt, and at Charlton Hill House, Wroxeter, with plain arcading and sparse and elegant carrot-drop ornament. By the end of the century decoration upon overmantels was often little more than panelling, and the commonest fireplace surround was a bolection mould or an eared architrave. Perhaps the most decorative piece is that in the hall at Whitton Court, of 1682, with its painting of a stag hunt.[40] Standing apart from all these is the fireplace bressummer at Green Farm, Winnington, which has fellows across the border in Montgomeryshire at Llwynmelyn and Gwernfyrda.[41] These are carved in low relief with interlacing, a bleeding heart, an amphisbaena, and human and animal figures. On a bressummer at Lower Spoad Farm, Clun, a hunting scene is carved in the same stylized low relief. These last are in houses socially beneath those discussed above and reveal a local folk style and iconography.

No imposing 16th-century staircase has survived, and there were probably very few, for most houses then favoured the enclosed stair turret.

What there were probably resembled the secondary stair at Ludstone with a turned newel post and heavy symmetrically turned balusters. By the early 17th century the main staircase in an important house was of some splendour, as at Ludstone itself and at Jones's Mansion, St. Mary's Street, Shrewsbury, with square set and highly ornamented newels and open raking balusters with caps and bases. The fashion continued for a long time. The staircases of the same character at Whitley Grange, near Hookagate, and at Pentre Morgan, Dudleston, have dates upon them of 1667 and 1668 respectively. A staircase of that type was removed early in the 20th century from Braggington Hall of 1675, and one at Plas-y-Court, Wollaston, may be of *c.*1678—the date on a fireback removed, like the staircase, from the old house to the present one.[42] Plainer stairs with the same elements were commoner, still set at Charlton Hill House of *c.*1650–60 within a stair turret. Before then, however, at Benthall Hall the panelled balustrading of the mid century had already appeared, and by the 1670s at Longnor Hall the staircase had plain newels, a heavy handrail, and

symmetrical plump balusters. A decade or so later at Shavington the elegant turned balusters typical of the next century were already present.

In most houses before the end of the 17th century the beams and joists of the ceiling were exposed to view and enriched, in the important rooms, with chamfers and stops. In the late 16th century there was a fashion for dividing ceilings into large panels and setting the joists in each panel at right angles to those in neighbouring panels. An example is the ceiling inserted into the open hall at High Grosvenor, Claverley, between 1566 and 1610. The earliest dated plaster ceiling in the county, that of 1576 at Aston Botterell, has thin ribs in a curvilinear pattern, enclosing the Botterell arms, and accompanied by a frieze with natural floral ornament. There are similar ceilings at Windsor House, off Castle Street, Shrewsbury, perhaps of *c.*1581, and at Moat Hall, Little Hanwood. Ceilings of that type continued for a long time and were the background against which most of the local 'Wilderhope' motifs appeared: Tudor roses, portcullises, fleurs-de-lis, the word 'Jesu' and an Old French motto meaning in

The staircase at Benthall Hall showing the panelled balustrading common to the mid 17th century

The staircase at Longnor Hall showing plain newel posts, a heavy handrail and symmetrical plump balusters

essence 'Hands Off!' Their form is identical at Wilderhope, Morville, the 'Abbot's Lodging' at Buildwas abbey, Hughley Old Hall, Easthope Manor, Belswardine Hall, and the gatehouse at Upton Cressett. These must all be from the same moulds and it is impossible to say how often or to what extent they are affirmations of the old faith and how far the chance results of a ready acceptance of a local plasterer's stock-in-trade. Moulds were also re-used in later years: at Benthall Hall and at

Plaster ceiling of the hall at Wilderhope Manor

Plaster ceiling of the drawing room at Benthall Hall

Reaside Manor the friezes have identical patterns of medallions bearing various motifs and set within a strapwork surround. The geometric patterning in broad flat ribs that was so typically Jacobean is not common in the county, although it appears in an exaggerated form in the parlour at Belswardine and contrasts there with the older style of the ceiling of the room above. It is in conjunction with strapwork and trabeated ceiling beams at Abcott and was formerly at Park Hall, Whittington, where the figure of Neptune in the central panel of the dining room ceiling was of the highest standard and almost certainly not of local origin. At the end of the century at Longnor, Ludford, Shavington, and Whitton Court the more baroque style of heavy compartments formed by enriched members was in control.

Painted decoration, which was all that many men could afford, was the commonest,[43] but has been the most vulnerable, of all ornament. Fragments of it appear in many houses, generally having been found beneath later decoration, whitewash, or panelling. It appears to have been most popular in the late 16th and early 17th centuries, when it covered the entire surface of a room's wall and sometimes the ceiling as well. Typically it comprised a frieze, a main panel, and a dado with ornament bands separating those elements. An eclectic mix of motifs was used, some medieval or even classical and some of Renaissance inspiration. The black and white 'antique' work at Petsey, Stoke upon Tern, is an overpainting of an earlier scheme, as is the floral decoration at Sutton Court, Little Sutton (in Diddlebury), where imitation panelling, a common form of decoration, shows through the later scheme. Imitation textile hanging was another popular theme, often including exotic motifs (such as the pomegranate) in imitation of expensive imported cut velvets. Shootrough Farm, Cardington, has the remains of a painted paned textile hanging in the hall, with imitation

Plasterwork in the drawing room at Benthall Hall

panelling, complete with fluted border, in the parlour. The surviving evidence suggests that, if a house was of sufficient standing to have painted decoration, then more than one room would be painted. Where a more lavish effect was intended the wainscot was painted, as in the so called Oak

The more baroque style of ceiling preferred at the end of the 17th century, as here in the drawing room at Longnor Hall

Room at Plaish, where it is enriched with gold stars, and at Madeley Court.

In other counties where wall paintings have been recorded similarities between some schemes have been noted, but none has such a distinctive design as the scroll pattern, of which 15[44] instances have been found in Shropshire; only one other is known, just over the Herefordshire border. The most complete example is at Church Farm, Neenton: it consists of four foliate scrolls diametrically opposed forming a square, with stylized flowers in the interstices—a full flower in the centre, half flowers at the side, and quarter flowers in the corners; each square is separated by a band of running motif, usually a guilloche, and the frieze has a different motif, often a zigzag with a stylized flower or imitation fluted panelling.

Figures and figured scenes, surviving occasionally in houses, provide an insight into the significance of some of this painted decoration. Hunting scenes dating from the late 17th century survive at Whitton Court, and others, probably at least 100 years earlier, at New Hall (Eaton-under-Heywood), where the scene has a more Germanic feel, suggesting that it may have been copied from some imported hanging. Of greater interest at New Hall are the three surviving panels in the parlour depicting figures in Elizabethan dress, one holding symbolic flowers and others holding musical instruments; also featured are a demon-like figure, an eagle, and a hare. The Nine Worthies at Great Binnal, Astley Abbots, (see illustrations overleaf) are very well preserved, though a similar set in Wenlock Abbey (the former prior's lodging) is known only from a drawing.[45] Significantly both of these are found at the dais end of the hall, where they would be intended to reflect and reinforce the worthiness of the owner of the house. Also to be included in figured schemes is the painting in a chamber at Cotton's House (57 Shropshire Street), Market Drayton: fanciful animals based upon an ostrich, deer, rabbit, and dog inhabit a woodland landscape; the typical form of frieze and main panels divided by ornament borders is well preserved, suggesting a date in the first quarter of the 17th century (see illustrations overleaf).

The role of painted cloths in interior decoration remains something of a mystery as so few survive. Evidence from probate inventories makes it clear

Left: The Nine Worthies at Great Binnal with details of Hector and Alexander the Great (centre) and King David and Judas Maccabeus (bottom)

that they were widespread and cheap in the mid to late 16th century, predating or contemporary with wall painting. References to them largely die out during the 17th century, either because they were too commonplace to be worth mentioning or because they ceased to be used. The character of those which hung until recently in a late 17th-century wing of Munslow Farm[46] is different from the typical wall paintings of the late 16th century: the Munslow cloths depict rural scenes with occasional buildings, and they have a distinctive style not found in earlier wall painting.

Detail of the wall painting of a stag and hounds at 57 Shropshire Street, Market Drayton

XII   Modern Houses 1700–40

Plain living

Until Queen Anne's accession polite architecture in Shropshire was homogeneous in style, and it was only in size, and to some extent in plan, that the houses of the greater and lesser gentry differed. At that time, however, the uniformity was starting to dissolve as a style derived from that of late 17th-century Court architects was adopted for the greater houses while the established local style was developed further for the smaller ones. Since the latter is the background against which the changes within the greater houses can be seen, it may be dealt with first.

The differences between the two styles must not, however, be overstressed, for this was the heyday of the master builder or craftsman-architect, very different from the earlier gentleman-architect—Pratt, Wren, Vanbrugh—designing houses for other gentlemen, and from the later professional architect—Robert Adam—anxious to dissociate himself from 'reptile artizans'.[1] These were tradesmen—masons, bricklayers, carpenters—competent at their trade and well enough educated or highly enough talented, or both, to design or erect buildings for other men. At the same time they were conscious of their social standing and were ready to build without demur to the designs or orders of their clients, or of their clients' agents. Those clients were overwhelmingly members of gentry families with similar backgrounds and similar needs, and their new houses were soon common in the southern and midland counties. It has been said of Francis Smith, in a list that includes Acton Round Hall, Ash Hall (Whitchurch), Downton Hall, Dudmaston Hall, and Mawley Hall, that 'almost any of these smaller houses might be [his design]'.[2] Doubtless much the same could be said of other master builders of the age, for it was their clients, not they, who were the arbiters of provincial taste.

By c.1700 timber-framing had been wholly eliminated from houses of any architectural pretension, generally in favour of brick. In areas where good building stone was readily available some stone houses were built: the present vicarage at Clun, Stonehouse Farm at Rushbury, what is now the Castle Hotel at Bishop's Castle, and Lower Farm (1738),[3] Willstone, near Cardington. But examples are few, and none of them is of the highest social standing. Nevertheless, though brick was the dominant material, it was far from giving a standardized look to the buildings of the time. Bricklayers had achieved high levels of skill, but their work was still not uniform and even in the matter of bonds there was much variation. At Sambrook Manor (1702),[4] Chetwynd, and in the additions to Stoke Court (of much the same date), Greete, the bond is irregular; at Madeley (Old) Vicarage, perhaps of the second decade of the 18th century, the bond is still irregular but tends to be Flemish; at Brickhouse Farm (c.1700), Greete, the front elevation is in Flemish bond and the others are in an irregular bond; at Pool Hall (probably 1700),[5] Alveley, the bond is Flemish throughout while at the splendid Dower House, Quatt, English bond predominates. Ultimately of course Flemish bond was to become standard, but at that time it was the brick itself that was *de rigeur* and the bond, and therefore the texture of the structure when seen close up, was less important. That may have been due partly to the generally dark red colour of the local brick and the thickness of the jointing, a background against which the patterning of the bond mattered less; but not all bricklayers may have been convinced of the structural superiority of Flemish bond, nor had they yet managed to educate the cognoscenti in the subtleties of brickwork.

The intensification of earlier developments is also seen in the uncompromising symmetry of all the polite houses of the period, despite the difficulties it caused in the smaller ones. A case in point is Madeley Vicarage where an 18th-century house was erected unconformably (to borrow the geologists' term) on the intractable foundations of an earlier one. The result is a symmetrical front, of five bays on the ground floor and of four above, which wholly belies the disposition of the rooms behind it. Further examples, occasioned this time by the use of an outmoded plan form, are Pool Hall, Alveley, and Brickhouse Farm, Greete, where main elevations conceal large entrance halls entered at one end.[6] Somewhat later, at Broseley Hall, where planning conventions compelled the entrance in the garden front to be placed slightly off centre, the doorway there was given a false companion at its side, achieving symmetry at the expense of sense. Usually, even when exigencies of site or resources required a new block to be placed cheek by jowl with an old one, the new was itself made symmetrical,[7] as at Burford House in 1728, when a parlour block (now the main building) was set next to a timber-framed house (since demolished).

The overall hipped roof and the eaves-cornice of the double-pile houses of the previous century were also perpetuated. Idsall House (1699), Shifnal, and Nevin's House (about the same date), Claverley, are in that regard as typical as Ford House and Upper Berwick, both of which are perhaps as much as a quarter of a century later. When single-pile ranges were added to earlier houses, as at Sambrook Manor, or when earlier buildings were refronted, as at Stoke House, Greete, or when small buildings like Cardington school were erected, overhanging eaves were still the normal form. Among small houses Pool Hall, Alveley, and Madeley Vicarage with their parapets are quite exceptional for their date. Or rather they were exceptional, for in many cases, as for example at 2 Church Street, Cleobury Mortimer, it can be seen that an original eaves has been replaced by a parapet. At Clun Vicarage a parapet added in the early 19th century along what is now the garden front has been recently removed and the overhanging eaves restored.

In all these matters small Shropshire houses of the early 18th century did no more than continue the practices of their immediate predecessors, but they broke with the past in abandoning the balanced masses that had dominated country house designs for over a century. Projecting wings, porches, and recessed centres were eschewed and instead elevations in one plane, or with only the slightest projection, became almost universal. Houses with a rear elevation recessed in the centre, like Ash Hall and Withington Hall, might seem to refute the last statement, but in fact they serve to show the shifts that some men might be put to in keeping up with the mode.[8] The fashionable overall roof, hipped at all four angles, was, in comparison with a gabled roof, difficult to construct, and some builders, conscious of that, and of the rainwater problems presented by parallel roofs, and yet desirous of more space than a strictly double-pile house of modest length could provide, obtained a handsome main elevation more easily by hipping at the front only and having slightly projecting gabled wings at the rear. In larger houses, for example Kinlet and Mawley, the form is probably the result of having three compartments flanking the hall and saloon.[9] Willstone Lower Farm (1738), smaller and of less standing than Ash Hall or Madeley Vicarage but on a rectangular plan, attempted to solve the problem with a gabled roof parallel to the axis at the front and three gables at right angles to it at the rear.[10]

The elevations of these houses were generally divided horizontally along the whole front by plat bands above ground-floor window level and were punctuated at the ends by quoins, sometimes of brick as at Sambrook Manor but more often of brick rendered to look like stone. Considerable skill was necessary in their creation and sometimes the bricklayers were not up to their task; at Madeley Vicarage, for example, and at Newport House (the Guildhall from c.1920), Shrewsbury, they either failed to marry in the plat band with the quoins or else they added it in the course of building. Doorways were always centrally placed in the elevation and were generally emphasized, usually with a surround or with a shell hood. At first, and in the older manner, a more elaborate emphasis of the entrance was occasionally attempted, such as the apparently contemporary porch at Pool Hall and the columns flanking the doorways of the Dower House, Quatt. The transomed windows of the later 17th century appear on a few houses: at Sambrook Manor, at Nevin's House, Claverley, on the unaltered side elevations of Newnham (1723), Pontesbury, and on the rear elevation of Pool Hall.

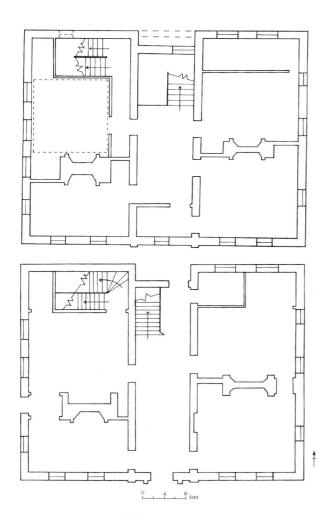

Ash Hall
The south front
with, centre, the ground-floor plan
and, top, first-floor plan

However, tall narrow sashed windows were normal on a main elevation, and they were usually very plain, without surround or architrave or apron but increasingly, as time went on, with a rubbed-brick head and a keystone. The ogee curve to the window heads at Upper Berwick, though paralleled at Withington Hall and at the larger Peplow Hall of 1725, is rare. What ornament there was, was largely confined to plat bands, quoins, and cornices, intended to emphasize the form of the structure and not to mark any individual feature.

The general effect of these houses is of down-to-earth common sense. Devoid of much extraneous ornament, they are simple, reticent, and yet placed four-square in their surroundings and modestly conscious of their worth. They are, of course, the forerunners of the style that was to be perpetuated among smaller town and country houses for many years, and there is little that is particularly Salopian about them. Any one example might have been found anywhere in the midlands and the south of England in the first decades of the 18th century, though they can perhaps be distinguished from their contemporaries in the south-east by the deeper colour of their brick and their sparser ornament.

Gentlemen's houses

Whatever the house's plan it was now *de rigeur* to have the main doorway placed centrally in a symmetrical elevation, no matter what difficulties might follow. Examples are common: Upper Berwick on a double-pile plan; Dinthill (1734) and Felhampton Court on an **L** plan;[11] Withington Hall, Ash Hall, and Garmston House[12] with centrally recessed rear elevations. It was fashionable as well, but at first not wholly essential, to contrive that the doorway came centrally not merely within the elevation, but within the hall itself. It was there, however, that limitations of size caused problems. A century earlier the builders of middling houses had found it very difficult to integrate the traditional entry at the upper end of the hall into a symmetrical façade; and often they had forgone symmetry. That was no longer possible. Where old ways persisted, where a large heated reception hall was still wanted, the problem could be solved, as it had been at those early double-pile houses mentioned earlier with an entrance doorway central in the elevation but at one end of the hall; and it was the desire for a heated hall that much later gave Pool Hall, Alveley, and Brickhouse Farm, Greete, their retarded plan form.

To most men of limited means, however, a large asymmetrical hall was both old fashioned and a vain expense. All they needed was an entry hall, but they wanted that to impress; and there they were in a dilemma. To be impressive a hall needed to be two bays wide, and along a front of limited length it could be so only at the expense of one or more of the reception rooms. In a six-bay elevation it was possible, as at Upper Berwick, Dinthill, Felhampton Court, and Withington Hall, to combine a two-bay entrance hall with two two-bay reception rooms by placing the doorway centrally and flanking it with narrow windows that simultaneously lit the hall and preserved both external and internal symmetry; a trick widely used in urban terrace houses, for example in St. John's Hill, Shrewsbury. But where a two-bay hall was insisted upon in a five-bay elevation, as at Ford House, the price was the reduction of one of the reception rooms to a single bay, and even then without getting the doorway set symmetrically within the hall itself.[13]

It was not long before it was realized that an unheated hall,[14] in which no one was expected to linger, did not have to be either large or impressive and that it was worth restricting its width to one bay in favour of larger reception rooms.[15] A step in that direction was indeed taken at Upper Berwick, where the fenestration of six bays does not strictly reflect the interior arrangement; the hall is somewhat less than two bays wide and the reception rooms correspondingly more. At Wheathall, Condover, the one-room-thick reception block, which was added in 1721 to a cruck-built hall-house, has a one-bay entrance hall giving access to reception rooms left and right and accommodating an elegant staircase; probably the earliest examples of purpose-built one-bay halls are at Ash Hall, at Garmston House,[16] and at Willstone Lower Farm (1738). In all three the staircase was sited at the rear of what was an entrance passage,[17] in the manner of many contemporary and later town houses. By the third quarter of the century the form was not uncommon in houses of some pretension and occurs, for example, at Ashford Bowdler Hall.[18] At Pentre Morgan, Dudleston, the main elevation, which is considerably later than the magnificent staircase of 1668, has a one-bay recessed centre between two two-bay

ends and appears to be publicly proclaiming a one-bay hall within.

In all these small double-pile houses, whether the front range was divided into three sections (hall between two rooms) or two (hall with a room on one side), the rear was always in three, generally with a central stairway. Even at Brickhouse Farm, where the stairway is not separated by a partition from the main rear room, it forms in effect a separate central section. At Ford Mansion it is placed centrally in two bays and within what is an imposing staircase hall, while at Upper Berwick and at Madeley Vicarage it is set, as at Ash Hall and Garmston House, in what is the continuation of the front entrance passage. In all these there is, at the side of the stairway, a rear doorway so that a passage runs through the house from front to back, a feature that probably occurred at Whitehall, Shrewsbury, over a century earlier, certainly occurred c.1680 at Rossall[19] near Shrewsbury, and was to be standard in small houses for many years to come. In **L** plan houses, such as Dinthill and Felhampton Court, the stairway was sited strategically in the wing and at its junction with the main range. In all cases it was intended to rise to a landing or lobby more or less central within the house and giving direct access, as far as possible, to all the first-floor rooms without the wasted space of a corridor or the inconvenience of passage rooms.

Secondary stairways in these smaller houses are uncommon, but at Ford House there seems to have been one from the beginning, sited between the kitchen and a reception room and arriving on the first floor at the side of the landing of the grand stair. At Willstone Lower Farm, where the kitchen occupies half of the front range, the secondary staircase rises out of the room at the rear of it. At Ash Hall an original secondary stair is in one of the rear projections and gives access on the first floor to a corridor leading to the landing reached by the main stair.[20] When a reception block was added to an earlier house and was given its own stair, as at Wheathall in 1721, then, of course, the original stair in the older part might assume the functions of a service stair. Generally, however, it is the absence of a service stair, like the presence of a hall of no more than two bays, that is one of the marks of a small, rather than of a grand or would-be grand, house. Nevertheless the early 18th-century Badger Hall (later incorporated into Wyatt's building of 1779–83) was of seven bays with a large hall, a saloon, two parlours, and a drawing room but had only a single staircase, miserably sited in a passage adjoining the kitchen.[21]

The purposes of individual rooms are not always very clear, except that, again in contrast with the greater houses, there is little to suggest that there were reception rooms on the first floor, and on that floor there is little sign of the bedroom and dressing room suites known in the larger houses. A possible example occurs at Ash Hall, in many ways a house of betwixt-and-between status, where a first-floor front room has original communication with a small room over the entrance hall. Such small heated ground-floor rooms as may be seen at Ford House and at Brickhouse Farm may have been 'studies' or 'offices' or had some special function, but on the whole it is difficult to say whether a room was a parlour or a dining room or a morning room or had anything but a general purpose. It might be thought that at least the kitchen would be easily identifiable either from its form or its siting, but that is not invariably so, and at Ford House one has to suppose, however reluctantly, that it has always been the large front room flanking the hall. That this was not wholly an eccentricity appears from a similar siting of the kitchen at Willstone Lower Farm, and later examples occur at Broseley Hall and at Chatford House (1776), Condover.[22]

These houses have been referred to as 'small' rather than as the homes of the minor gentry, as earlier houses were labelled. Some of them were certainly built by established gentry families: Pool Hall, Upper Berwick, and Dinthill Hall for example.[23] Substantial copyholders, however, and yeomen boasting no exalted ancestry also built some, including Sambrook Manor, Wheathall, Ford House, Willstone Lower Farm, and Newnham.[24] Yet others were built for parish clergy, whose housing standards were beginning to rise: Stockton Rectory and Madeley Vicarage are among them. In other cases the builders were industrialists from outside the county: Burford House, for example, was built by the proprietor of the Vauxhall Glassworks. Of course heterogeneity of a sort had been true of the builders of 'gentry' houses in earlier years, for on the one hand many had been lawyers or merchants or office-holders turning themselves into gentry and on the other hand many such men had come from

gentry families and many gentry families had been founded by such men in former times. What seem to be new in early 18th-century Shropshire are houses above farmhouse status in appearance and yet smaller than the older houses of minor gentry: houses whose owners are perhaps best thought of as 'gentlemen' rather than as 'gentry'. Some of the increase in small 'gentlemen's residences' is the outcome of that rise in the status of the parish clergy referred to earlier.[25] Some of it may be attributed to that impassable division between barristers and solicitors which had been established by the end of the 16th century.[26] Solicitors were by then firmly excluded from pleading in the superior royal courts, but in the end they were compensated by a virtual monopoly of local legal business and between c.1660 and 1750 took over all conveyancing from the Bar.[27] The result was that, in place of the large fortune made by such a successful local lawyer as Prince of Whitehall, more modest fortunes were made by several practitioners.[28]

The 'Cound' style of the major gentry

It has been claimed that a section of the gentry was becoming a depressed class ('depressed' that is by their standards) in the early 18th century[29] and, to the extent that minor rather than major gentry are at issue, the smaller houses of the county may be thought to bear out the claim. There, is, however, no lack of large and impressive houses, at least from c.1720 onwards. Their builders, unlike the builders of the smaller houses, seem to have been a socially homogeneous group, mostly members of rich and long established landed families. Sometimes that wealth was supplemented from other sources: the building of Acton Round was probably made possible by the fortunate marriage of the Whitmore heir with the heiress of a London merchant,[30] and Davenport House appears to have risen on the foundation of a nabob fortune made by a younger son of that important family.[31] But such were the exceptions. More typical were the building of Berwick House by Thomas Powys, of Brogyntyn by the Owens, of Buntingsdale by the Mackworths, of Cound by the Cressetts, of Kinlet by the Childes, of Mawley by the Blounts,[32] of Hardwick by the Kynastons,[33] of Coton Hall by the Lees of Alveley,[34] of Moor Park by the Salweys,[35] the grand refurbishing of Eaton Mascott by the husband of an

Owen heiress,[36] the building of Henley Hall by a branch of the Powys family,[37] of Hawkstone by the Hills,[38] of Loton Park by the Leightons,[39] and perhaps (for their status is more doubtful) of Brand Hall by the Davisons.[40]

In discussing the 'greater' houses of Shropshire at this time it must be remembered, however, that they were 'great' only by local reckoning. In comparison with Castle Howard or Blenheim, Wanstead or Houghton they were no more than middling. Indeed it was not until the end of the century that large Shropshire houses were as big as the largest of their contemporaries elsewhere—and then only because by that time no-one was building very large houses anywhere. It must also be remembered when the differences between greater and smaller houses are discussed that they had much in common: the ubiquity of brick, the overall roof, the absence of projecting masses or heavily emphasized entrances, the plain openings, the deliberate colour contrast between the brickwork of the fabric and the genuine or simulated stone of the dressings.

Greater houses differed from lesser ones in size, and especially in the size of the hall, and in their almost invariable use of a double-pile plan with a hall and saloon both flanked by a room on each side.

They were also distinguished by their ornament and by their use of it. Their style at the beginning of the 18th century was based on the practices then current among fashionable Court architects, and it is possible to attribute this contrast between greater and smaller Shropshire houses to the ingrained provincialism of minor men and to their deeper ignorance of, or indifference to, the aesthetic fancies of the very great. Such attitudes probably played a part, but it also seems likely that lesser men ignored the Court style because they could not afford its expensive ornament, and that that ornament was not so well suited to the shorter façades of their smaller houses. In the 1720s and 1730s, when a strict Palladianism was the fashion among the cognoscenti, the larger builders in the county demonstrated a marked kinship with their lesser fellows in revealing a common lack of interest in the canons of that movement.

The essential elements of the style favoured by the greater families probably first appeared in the county at Cound Hall, designed by John Prince, a London surveyor and architect, in 1703–4.[41] Cound is a large, tall rectangular building with its main elevations more or less in one plane. It is of nine bays and three full storeys above a low basement,

The south and west fronts of Cound Hall, built in nine bays and three stories

surmounted by a parapet, and with a central pediment. The doorway is only slightly emphasized and the windows, apart from those in the centre of the entrance front, have no ornament other than keystones. The main elevations are dominated and punctuated by giant fluted Corinthian pilasters rising from ground level and dividing the whole into three equal parts. Despite the handling of the pilasters, which fail to integrate with the storey division as expressed by the windows,[42] the effect is rich and stately.

The Cound formula was repeated at most of the large houses in the county over the next 30 years: on the north front at Loton Park (c.1709), at Acton Round (1713), at Buntingsdale (c.1719–23 and by Cound's architect, John Prince),[43] at Davenport (1726), at Kinlet (1727), at Hardwick and Mawley (both probably c.1730), at Berwick House (1731), perhaps at Brongyntyn from 1734,[44] and to some extent in the proposals of 1720 for alterations at Hawkstone.[45] Naturally there were variations on the theme. At Acton Round, at Kinlet, and on the entrance front, but not the garden front, of Hardwick there are only seven bays. Acton Round is of two storeys only, with dormers, and most of the others are of two storeys and an attic rather than the three storeys of Cound. With the exception of Loton Park and to a less extent of Acton Round, the elevations are in one plane or have only a very slightly recessed or projecting centrepiece, although at Kinlet and Mawley the rear elevation is deeply recessed in the manner referred to earlier. The giant fluted pilasters of Cound appear again on the front proposed for Hawkstone in 1721, at Buntingsdale, at Berwick House and, in an unfluted form, at Hardwick and Mawley, and alternately fluted and unfluted at Buntingsdale. At Acton Round, Hardwick, Davenport, Loton, and Kinlet, and at the now demolished Badger Hall,[46] something of the effect of a giant order was produced by the employment of boldly rusticated French quoins from ground level to parapet, either at the ends of the elevation or, alternatively or additionally, at the ends of the slightly projecting or recessed blocks. The windows generally have no decoration other than a keystone or a rubbed-brick head, but occasionally there is something more: the carved stone surrounds of those in the central section of the entrance front at Cound, the surround of the window above the doorway and the moulded stone aprons at Mawley, and the brackets at Davenport. The doorways are equally reticent, generally flanked by slight pilasters or engaged columns and surmounted by a low pediment, as at Loton at the beginning of the period and Buntingsdale in the middle of it. Pediments above the centre of the main elevation are also not uncommon and occur at Cound, Moor Park, and Mawley. Apart from the great curved pediment at Hardwick, however, recalling that at Longnor of 60 years or so before, they are unobtrusive and do not brood above the elevation. Most of these houses stand isolated from any other building, but at Davenport, Hardwick, and Kinlet the main block is linked by screen walls to lower detached pavilions which served as offices and at the same time provided a framework within which to appreciate the proportions of the whole.

Not every house of comparable size erected or refurbished in the first 40 years of the century conformed to the pattern sketched above. Priorslee Hall did not, nor did Moor Park, nor the remodelled west front of Hawkstone (1725),[47] Peplow Hall

The south and west fronts of Peplow Hall

175

*Exterior of a window at Peplow Hall
with a shaped brick head*

(1725),[48] or Tunstall Hall (probably of the 1730s). Priorslee is a retarded example of a late 17th-century house and Peplow is a *mélange* of the plain repetitive fenestration of later years, of the pilasters of the Cound style, and of mannerisms of its own, in particular the plat band breaking upwards above the ground-floor windows gives the impression that the first-floor windows have aprons. Moor Park resembled the first reconstruction of Hawkstone, which is discussed below, and Tunstall Hall, with its emphasized distinction between the ground floor and the first and attic floors and its regularly spaced pedimented windows, is an exercise in Palladian motifs.

These apart, the dominance of the Cound Hall type of house over these years is remarkable. It is not merely that there are more examples of the type than in other midland counties, many of which are architecturally richer, but that in Shropshire the type had a near monopoly in large houses. And since the Smiths of Warwick (William and his more famous younger brother Francis) are known to have been the architects of some of these and may have been responsible for many, it is tempting to attribute the uniformity to them. In a way that is true. The resemblance of Coton Hall, Alveley, to William Smith's Umberslade (Warws.) is clear,[49] and by the 1720s the firm had acquired, or was acquiring, a reputation for honesty and reliability, and its patrons could be confident that they would get what they wanted at a cost in money and anxiety which they could afford. Within half a century of Francis Smith's death his houses, and especially his plans, were being criticized for their sameness,[50] but to early 18th-century gentry builders, not eager to set themselves apart from their neighbours, that was probably a recommendation. Nevertheless, that is only part of the story. The Smiths are not known to have had connections with Cound, nor with such early examples of the style as Acton Round and the north front of Loton Park; and it now appears that their activities at Buntingsdale were either under John Prince's direction or were limited to taking over when the house was nearly completed.[51] Further, the discovery that Buntingsdale, where there seemed to be good documentary evidence for their authorship, was not designed by them must make other attributions less compelling than they have been. It may be noted, too, that outside Shropshire the Smiths were by no means limited to a formula, but produced houses on a large scale and in a different manner. There, however, they were often working for grand and wealthy patrons, while in Shropshire they were employed by gentry. Summerson has noted that something like a building boom began in the 1720s,[52] and it was at that moment that Francis Smith was on the spot with a reputation for the virtues that most owners would look for first in an architect, and offering a type of house that forerunners had made familiar to local gentlemen.

In their plans these greater houses continued the form, common throughout the country, which had been developed at Dudmaston and Halston.

Typically they had a large entrance hall, never occupying less than a third of the main front or less than half the depth of the house. A saloon as long as the hall but not as deep occupied the centre of the garden front and a grand stairway was sited in a compartment somewhere along the side of the building. Communication on the ground floor was generally provided by a passage running centrally along the length of the building and opening into the rear of the hall; at Kinlet the rear space was marked off from the rest of the hall by a colonnade. A 1761 plan of Badger Hall shows the corridor (with an exterior doorway in a side wall) running only two thirds of the length of the house and terminating at its far end at a doorway into the 'Best Parlour'.[53] Often, as at Davenport, Hardwick, and Kinlet, the kitchen and other offices were placed in detached pavilions linked by screen walls to the main block; in most other houses they were in the lofty basement. The other rooms on the ground floor were reception rooms of various kinds, generally indistinguishable architecturally from one another. Often one of them functioned, sometimes with a larger dressing room beside it, as the owner's bedroom. Variations on this basic theme occur. At Hardwick the saloon is longer than the hall[54] and to accommo-

date it aesthetically the garden front is divided into nine bays instead of the seven bays of the entrance front. At Mawley there is, where one would normally expect to find the saloon, a magnificent staircase.

Whatever variation there might be, however, the hall was never anything but a very large and imposing room, and it is at this point perhaps that one should remark that the size of the hall is the clearest criterion for distinguishing, where there may otherwise be a doubt, between the greater and lesser houses of the county and between the latter and farmhouses. There is a graduation from the last with its entry into a lobby entrance or into a generalized room serving as kitchen-cum-working room, through the minor polite house, with its small hall which might be little more than a passageway, to the great house, with the entrance doorway placed centrally in a large and often lofty reception hall. Indeed it is on that basis that one may best estimate the pretensions, if not the true worth, of those who at the time refurbished older houses rather than built anew. In the alterations at Stoke Court, Greete, at Eaton Mascott, and somewhat later at Cruckton Hall a large and imposing entrance hall was contrived; at Stoke, and probably at Cruckton, it has since been

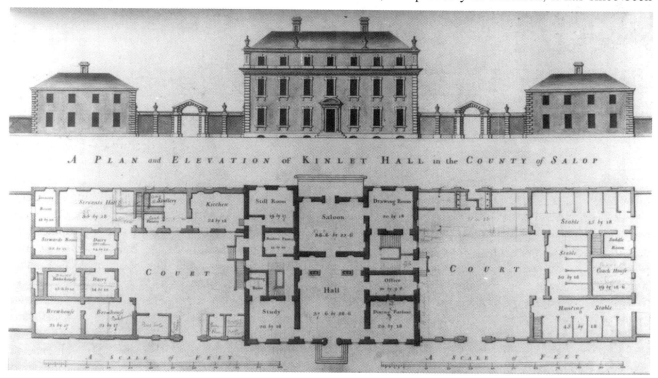

Plan and elevation of Kinlet Hall

reduced in size. At Shipton there was no need to enlarge the hall when it was given its elaborate plasterwork in the mid century, but the doorway was moved from one end of the front wall to the middle.[55] At Treflack Hall, too, the '1704' above the doorway probably dates its removal to its present site in the centre of the elevation. Further, the imposing block added at Brand Hall, Norton in Hales, in the early years of the century[56] originally had a large entrance hall more in keeping than the present hall with the grandeur of the engaged pilasters and armorial pediment of the façade.[57]

Despite the general unanimity in the planning of the ground floor, these houses fall into two classes in their first-floor disposition: those with a long axial corridor and those without. The first-floor corridor in a double-pile house of some size avoided the inconvenience,[58] so plain at Ludstone for example, of having to use a main reception room on that floor as a passage way. Its advent marks the

final stage in a long process which brought about the modern sharp distinction between a bedroom and a reception room. Medieval potentates, and medieval ladies, often received formal, and informal, visitors sitting upon a bed; and beds were prominent in Renaissance great chambers and in the salons of such leaders of 17th-century French society as Mme. de Rambouillet.[59] As the concept not only of 'public' and 'private', but also of 'family' and 'personal' rooms became stronger, different kinds of room were put on different floors, with 'open' rooms on the ground, or main, floor and with the others above. But when there was no great 'open' room on an upper floor there was no need for a magnificent entry into it, and a corridor, served by a staircase at the side of the house, was as good a means of access to other rooms as anything else. One may almost see the process at work at Hawkstone Hall. A plan of 1718 shows that it was built as a double-pile house with short wings

The entrance hall at Davenport House looking through to the stairs hall

*Detail of balusters to the principal staircase at
Davenport House*

making a formal **H** plan and having a grand stair-case-hall centrally at the rear of the entrance hall.[60] The reception rooms on the ground floor were no more than a 'drawing room' and a 'parlour' and it is probable that the staircase led to a saloon above the entrance hall. After the reconstruction of 1719 onwards there was a magnificent saloon where the staircase had been, and the staircase had been removed to a side position.[61]

It was suggested above that such a corridor was probably planned from the start at Dudmaston and at Halston, and it would appear to have been present originally at Cound, where a central projection from one of the side elevations partly accommodated a secondary staircase placed at the opposite end of the house from the grand staircase. A few years later at Acton Round, where it is beyond cavil that there was such a corridor from the start, similar side projections were used to accommodate the half-landings of the main staircase at the west end and of the secondary staircase at the east end. Acton Round, a comparatively small house, is the best example of the locally conceived first-floor

corridor, where the corridor and the opposing stairs which served it are architecturally expressed, in a manner similar to, but more sophisticated than, the architectural expression in earlier houses of the staircase in a projecting turret. Perhaps because of the added complications in construction, perhaps because such projections offended against the fashion for elevations (even side ones) in a single plane, Acton Round's formula was not copied, and when Hardwick and Kinlet were built more than a decade later with first-floor corridors they eschewed the side projections.

A corridor, however, relegated the grand stair-case to a position where its magnificence was not so easily expressed, and many men still adhered to the traditions of a great chamber on the first floor. From the start the greater double-pile houses had avoided the corridor; they had put the staircase either centrally at the front or rear of the house, as at Coleshill (Berks.), or else in the centre of the flank of the building but giving onto a gallery across the upper part of a great entrance hall that rose through two storeys, as at the Grange, Northington (Hants). That many options were still open, however, in the third and fourth decades of the century is shown by a consideration of those of Francis Smith's Shropshire houses—authenticated or reasonably attributed—whose original plans are still recoverable. Despite the accusations of monotony of plan form which have been brought against him, Smith was very willing to experiment, at least in ways of reaching and treating the first floor. At Kinlet, as we have seen, he built a first-floor corridor house. At Davenport he placed the grand staircase at the front of the house and next to the hall, and by treating it decoratively in much the same way as he had treated the hall, created a very imposing access to the grand room over the hall; but he did so at the cost of a very awkward disposition of the rest of that floor. At Mawley he fell back on an older solution: with a staircase hall at the rear of the entrance hall.

Magnificence at less cost

In their own way most of these houses stand as four-square and upright as their smaller fellows. There were, however, a few—with which Smith's name has never been convincingly connected—which seem to be pretending to be more than they are. It was a pretence for which we may now be grateful, not only

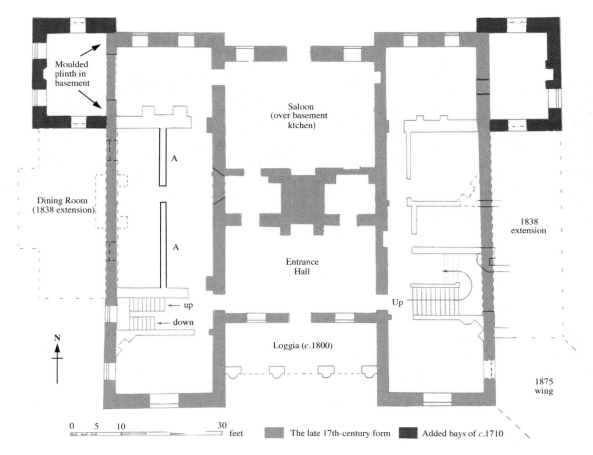

Ground-floor plan of Loton Park.
The south-western stair may be the original secondary stair, the south-eastern is probably of 1838.
The wall A - A was built in 1838 across the old dining room which was extended west

for the aesthetic pleasure provided, but for what it tells us: that some Shropshire owners appreciated that the longer the façade the more aesthetically effective the Cound style could be, and the more their own standing in society could be emphasized without committing them to vast building expense.

The deception took the form of building a façade two bays longer than the house behind it. At Loton Park the original house was rebuilt some time before 1690 on a typical late 17th-century **U** plan, and with a main elevation of seven bays. It was decided *c.*1710 to have a new and grander north front, and so a bay was added at each end of the late 17th-century elevation[62] which was refronted in the Cound style. The added bays, however, were only one room deep so that before the additions of 1838 they projected a bay's length from the north ends of the east and west elevations. In that way the Leightons achieved a magnificent nine-bay front

without having to build an enormous nine-bay house. There were similar flanking bays with slight forward projections at Moor Park (not long before 1722).[63] At Berwick House a grand front was designed, but the original imposing nine-bay front was for a third of its length only one room thick. At Coton Hall the tall centre block had nothing but a corridor and staircases behind the front rooms. At Hardwick, which unlike the other three is a true double-pile, the main front is of seven bays, but the garden front of nine. The extra, but of course shorter, bays there are a solution to the problems raised by making the saloon, very unusually, longer than the hall; but the effect is to make the house look bigger, with a superior nine-bay front. At a later date Ashford Bowdler Hall, probably of the 1760s, was given a seven-bay front, but the two end bays were only one room thick—as happened somewhat later at Linley Hall near Broseley.

Hawkstone Hall

The events at Loton and elsewhere are reasonably clear and not all that difficult to disentangle, but it will probably be less readily agreed that something similar happened at Hawkstone. John Russell's late 18th-century drawing of the south façade before Lewis Wyatt's alterations and the plan of 1718 mentioned above, make it clear that Hawkstone was once a rectangular house with projecting bays at its four corners. Comparisons have been made with such Elizabethan or Jacobean houses as Lulworth Castle (Dors.) or Ruperra (Glam.) and with a late 17th-century house like Ragley (Warws.). When looked at more closely, however, the comparison breaks down. At those, and at other known examples, the towers or extensions project equally from side and front elevations or else they project far more boldly from the front than from the side. Hawkstone differs from them all, and from such later designs as Houghton, Holkham, and Ditchley, for Hawkstone's towers or bays project very slightly from the front but very boldly indeed from the side. It cannot therefore be regarded as merely one more instance of a well known type, for its projections are wholly eccentric; and how eccentric they are is emphasized by the ill-proportioned and incorrect porticoes, unknown elsewhere, which linked them along the north and south elevations.[64] Nevertheless it is not unique, for the same disposition of slight forward projections and very bold side ones was exactly paralleled, as has been noted, on the north front at Loton. Had Loton been a rectangular house and had its south front been treated as the north front was *c.*1710, then Loton and Hawkstone would, in respect of their projec-

tions, have been identical twins. Hawkstone, in brief, would appear to be a 'double Loton', and indeed in its originally intended form the extensions there, as at Loton, were merely bays, not towers. Even after they had been transformed into towers they still had the effect of making the house look bigger than it was. The builders of Loton and of Hawkstone were among the most important or richest men in the county, and the economy with which they attempted to realize their aspirations emphasizes what was said earlier: that even the greatest of Shropshire landowners were not great by the standards of some other counties.

Refurbished houses

So far the architecture of the first 30 or 40 years of the century has been treated as though there were only two kinds of house, differing in size and manner of ornament. There were, however, houses which may be regarded as of middling status, and in one of two ways: either as houses somewhat smaller and less prestigious than the greater houses, or else as houses of some age and status refurbished in one way or another. Examples of the first, or at any rate clearly datable ones, are uncommon. One is Peplow Hall, Hodnet, of 1725: a double-pile house of seven bays but only two and a half storeys. It has been much altered but retains its original east façade and much of the south façade, both of which eschew the elaboration of the great houses in favour of simple but effective brickwork ornament, plain pilasters, curved rubbed-brick heads to the windows of the south front and the integration of window heads, sills, and plat band along the east front. Ash Hall is another, especially in the contrast between its modest entrance hall one bay wide and its grand pedimented frontispiece flanked by giant pilasters. Commoner, however, than new-built examples like Peplow and Ash Hall are up-dated houses of the period. At Brand Hall the parlour block was added in front of an earlier timber-framed house itself originally of some size and magnificence; at Eaton Mascott and at Whitton Court an earlier **U** plan timber-framed house was refronted and up-dated; at Stoke Court a timber-framed house was refronted in brick and curved gables introduced on the wings; at Belswardine at about the same date a many-gabled timber front was clad in brick; and at Henley Hall, Bitterley, a front with projecting wings and a central porch was refaced and built up between the wings to give an elevation in more or less one plane.

At none of these refurbished houses was the Cound style employed. That, it may be thought, was because the style was not so well suited to parlour blocks of no great size in themselves and often not standing alone but placed cheek by jowl with highly incongruous earlier ranges. Nor yet did it blend happily with short elevations in several planes. For such reasons, as well as from economy, nearly all these houses were without much ornament, indulging at the most in no more than keystones to the openings, in plat bands, plain parapets, and quoins; and sometimes in marking the centre of the elevation with a low pediment, as at Henley, Whitton Court, and Eaton Mascott. Only at the last, with its Venetian windows flanking the doorway, and at Brand Hall, with its giant pilasters and pediment above, is anything grander attempted.

Although these refurbished houses differ from greater ones in their make-do-and-mend attitude and in the nature of their ornament, they nevertheless aspired to be counted among the great. That is apparent from the size of their entrance halls. In all those whose early 18th-century dimensions can be established—Peplow Hall, Stoke Court, Eaton Mascott, Whitton Court, and Brand Hall—the entrance hall is or was of three bays, contrasting with the two bays or less of the smaller houses and comparable with the halls of the greater ones.

There is another and final difference, somewhat paradoxical perhaps, between the smaller and greater houses of the county in the early 18th century. The owners of the former, continuing and intensifying the practices of earlier years, were in line with their peers throughout much of the country, content to develop what had soon after 1700 become a traditional, almost a 'vernacular', small-house architecture. The latter, by contrast, though well abreast of the most advanced taste in the early years of the century, had by the end of the third decade failed to keep pace with the fashions of the very great and were then becoming noticeably out of date by national standards, though still the leaders of local style. This onset of retardation, by contrast with earlier awareness of advanced thought, needs to be explained. It was not that Shropshire men had lapsed again into a natural backwardness but rather that up to about the mid century the stricter Palladianism fashionable in London was still associated with Whig noblemen. Most men in Shropshire had no contact with their enormous houses and their villas along the Thames, and in any event could not have afforded to build them and for which they would have had little use.

Interior decoration

The difference in façades and in form that distinguished large from small houses in this period were less apparent inside. A general interior style prevailed, common to all houses of any pretension and varying from one to another mainly in the amount of ornament that could be afforded. In Shropshire that style is perhaps best characterized as the Cound manner carried out on the smaller scale that interiors necessarily imposed. Its most obvious and most impressive elements are the giant fluted pilasters, so common on the fronts of the greater houses, employed not, as there, to punctuate a length of walling but to flank and emphasize such features as chimney pieces and doorways. Examples are numerous; one may cite among greater houses Mawley and Davenport; among smaller ones Burford House and the Lawns, Broseley; among refurbished houses Whitton Court, Westbury, and Lutwyche Hall. At Buntingsdale attenuated pilasters, with something of a neo-classical look, flanked the window openings of a first-floor room, and at Mawley and Davenport engaged three-quarter columns are used. Perhaps their most impressive use is in the saloon at Berwick House, where they flank and frame what must be among the most richly carved over-doors in the whole country.

Where it could be afforded plain wainscot covered the walls in important rooms, generally large heavy bolection-moulded panels in earlier houses like Cound and Acton Round, but with the usually smaller and far less heavily moulded fielded panels becoming common as time went on; an early example is in the parlour block added at Wheathall in 1721. The notable exceptions to that generalization are Mawley and Davenport. At Mawley, one of the most richly decorated houses in England, the small drawing room has a parquetry floor in a radiating pattern and wainscot and flanking pilasters with marquetry ornament. Marquetry appears too upon the pilasters and overmantel of the chimney piece in the saloon at Davenport. Plaster decoration was rare in contrast, not only on wall surfaces but on ceilings as well, and usually ran to no more than an elaborate cornice in the better rooms. Again the exceptions are Mawley and Davenport. At Mawley, where the plasterwork is extraordinarily profuse— 'Nowhere else in England has plasterwork taken over to this degree'[65]—and may well be later than 1740, the staircase hall has its walls covered with rococo decoration in plaster panels containing busts and human figures; the ceilings of the staircase-hall and of the hall have swirling rococo ornament around recessed central panels; that of the small drawing room has birds and flowers with a figure of Aurora, and in the room over it the ceiling has a central panel with an eared surround and figures of amorini and centaurs. At Davenport the plasterwork in the hall and staircase is also remarkable, not only for its technical virtuosity but as an attempt to create

Detail of fireplace in morning room on the first floor of Davenport House

an architectural illusion of wide-jointed ashlar walling.

In general the greatest amount of ornament was, as in earlier years, concentrated on the chimney piece. The splendid trophy of arms on the hall piece at Mawley is again exceptional in its virtuosity, but typical in its intent. Whether or not chimney pieces were flanked by giant pilasters they were at first nearly always distinguished by the richer treatment of the overmantel and that treatment was nearly always architectural.[66] Typically, above a fireplace opening with an eared surround and a heavily moulded mantel, was set a large rectangular panel, often both eared and hipped, flanked by tall narrow panels and surmounted by a heavy broken pediment. At Kinlet, where two such pieces face each other in the saloon, the effect in combination with the wainscot and the curved pediments above the doorways is impressive indeed. Joinery of such magnificence, however, was expensive, and smaller houses were usually more restrained. In the saloon added to Preston Brockhurst in the early 18th century the central panel and its flanking fellows were much plainer and so too was the overmantel in the saloon at Burford House.

Nevertheless not all restraint was necessarily due to lack of means. The first signs of a change of taste are also apparent. In the hall and staircase hall at Davenport, where money seems to have been plentiful, the walls are neither panelled nor elaborately plastered but are treated as though they were exterior walls faced with wide-jointed ashlar and the openings in them are heavily rusticated; the apparent intention being to produce the effect of an Italian *cortile*. This proto-Palladianism, or Palladianism at several removes, is evidenced as well in some other houses where lugged panels and bold curved pediments and swags give way to more severe motifs. An example is the chimney piece in a room at Morville Hall that was probably redecorated in the 1730s and 1740s. It is flanked by the giant pilasters of earlier taste but has a low straight pediment immediately above the opening surmounted by plain-shaped fielded panels. A chimney piece of *c*.1722 at the Lawns, Broseley, has similar pilasters flanking plain fielded panels on the overmantel. At Davenport itself the chimney piece in the hall, again flanked by pilasters, has an overmantel which merely continues the simulated ashlar

The staircase at Peplow Hall

of walls, and in the study the overmantel is similar to that at Morville.

The other major recipient of decoration was the staircase, which—ornament apart—was often impressive in its own right, set in its own spacious and well lit compartment. Here again the outstanding example in a house of the period is at Mawley Hall, where the hand rail has been given a sinuous rippling form like an undulating snake and the face of the string is carved with sea creatures, fish nets, and musical instruments. In their general form staircases in Shropshire are in the national vein: the best of them generally with a cut string, three elegantly turned or twisted balusters to a tread, a heavily moulded handrail, and ornament on the cheeks of the risers. At Hardwick the latter are enriched with carving and at Peplow with richly carved terminal brackets; at Kinlet they are decorated with an heraldic crest within an arabesque pattern. In other houses, however, the risers have nothing but a plain scroll marking their end. Balusters were universally ornamented, either twisted, turned, or fluted. In some of the larger houses—Buntingsdale, Hardwick, Hawkstone— four turned balusters grouped together take the place of a newel post. At some houses, including such minor ones as Ford House, Whitton Court, and (formerly) Burford House,[67] all three types are repeated upon each tread, while at Peplow each tread has two twisted balusters and a turned one. Sometimes, as at Preston Montford and on the stair inserted at Whitton Court in the early years of the century, there are only two balusters to a tread, and those tend to be heavier than those that come in threes. Coarser balusters tend to occur as well on those stairs which retain straight strings, for example in the added block at Wheathall of 1721, at Upper Berwick, the Old Hall, Withington, and in the stair turret added at Belswardine. They occur also on servants' stairs and there they generally contrast strongly with the main stair, as at Kinlet and at Whitton Court. Nevertheless these stairs, coarser as they are, are in the same style as the finer ones and in comparison with anything else would be considered elegant. They help to confirm what was said earlier: that in their internal decoration Shropshire builders from the greatest to all but the very humble shared a common taste.

XIII   Secular Architecture 1740–1830

In the second quarter of the 18th century domestic architecture in Shropshire developed in several ways: by a very limited display of the Palladianism of Burlington and his followers; by the cessation of traditional vernacular building and the use in nearly all houses of the plain manner of minor men of the previous generation; by the wide employment of London architects and the almost simultaneous emergence of home-grown ones; and by the appearance of a variety of superficially different but basically similar styles. At the end of the century Shropshire buildings had a more homogeneous look than they had ever had before, and the county's architecture was closer than in any earlier period to an overall national pattern.

Palladianism

Palladianism played so large a part in the national story that it becomes *de rigeur* to discuss it in a local context. The history of Shropshire architecture at this time could be written without much reference to Lord Burlington's views or Colen Campbell's publications, and it is best, therefore, to clear the subject out of the way at the start.

The county was not blessed with the main residences of any of the men who were, originally, the patrons of that style: the immensely rich Whig noblemen who ruled England in the names of the first two Georges and controlled much of national and local politics from their magnificent palaces in the countryside. The only markedly Palladian house in the county, Linley Hall (in More), was built by Robert More, of an old Whig family, M.P. for Bishop's Castle and later for Shrewsbury; a man with scientific interests and very well travelled, and not merely along the conventional grand tour routes.[1] Because of his politics and his connections with up-to-date cultural circles he built in a Palladian style, but because he was of moderate means he built a house that was closer to the

Linley Hall

informal villas of the Thames valley, the retreats of the great in their off-duty moments, than to the huge mansions where the Whig peers lived in state.

Linley was built 1743–6, to the designs of Henry Joynes, then clerk of works at Kensington Palace and formerly so at Blenheim, a protégé of Sir John Vanbrugh. The house is less than purely Palladian and has prominent keystones to some of the windows, obtrusive chimney stacks, and a multiplicity of planes in the manner of Vanbrugh. Nevertheless many of the strict Palladian elements are there: a rusticated basement, a main storey with attic storey above, pediments above the windows, pedimented end pavilions, and a Venetian window immediately above the main entrance and lighting the grand staircase. Furthermore it is built of stone instead of the almost universal brick of Shropshire houses of the period.

Linley's Palladianism, like the 'Italianism' of Moreton Corbet nearly two centuries earlier, was too rarefied to receive a general welcome in the county. After Linley the house with the clearest Palladian elements is Hawkstone as it was completed in the 1740s (see illustration p.181). The saloon, which Professor Gomme has, with some reservations, ascribed to Henry Flitcroft,[2] is a wholly Palladian piece of internal design; Palladian too is the pedimented and rusticated frontispiece of the east elevation with its main openings surmounted by blind attic windows with scrolled keystones. On the west front, too, there is an engaged portico of giant columns, and there are corner pavilions in the common manner of the English version of the style. Nevertheless, Hawkstone is far from being a Palladian design. It has no *piano nobile* and nothing more than an apology for a rusticated basement storey. The proportions are those of a late 17th-century house and the whole is in the prevailing red brick of the time. Other houses have no more than scattered Palladian elements, such as the engaged portico and columns at Brand Hall and the alternating straight and curved pediments above the windows at the nearby Tunstall Hall. It is probable too that the tripartite windows at such houses as Eaton Mascott Hall, Leighton Hall, Hungerford Farm, Munslow, and Richard's Castle Rectory are of Palladian inspiration, for Palladianism was often a slogan rather than a way of architecture and some Shropshire men

39 Broad Street, Ludlow,
an un-Palladian profusion of Venetian windows

were probably as proud as those in other counties to catch cold at a Venetian opening. Nevertheless, as Professor Downes has pointed out, Venetian windows in England antedate the Palladian movement,[3] and it is noticeable that where they are used most strikingly in Shropshire—on the front of 39 Broad Street, Ludlow—they are in profusion and set side by side in a most un-Palladian manner. Moreover they are used in the most impressively correct manner not on any early house but at Rudge Hall, a neo-Georgian creation of *c.*1930.

There are many other houses in the county besides Linley and Hawkstone which have been called Palladian, but generally with no more precise a meaning than that they have symmetrical main elevations and are free, inside and out, of baroque, rococo, or Gothick ornament. In this connection it is instructive to compare the two houses which Clive of India built for himself in Shropshire in the 1760s with the one he built in Surrey in the 1770s. Walcot Hall, near Bishop's Castle, and Styche Hall, at the opposite end of the county near Market Drayton, are both of brick, have no more ornamental emphasis on their elevations than is provided by plat bands and quoins, and make little differentiation between storeys.[4] The Surrey house, Claremont near Esher, is built of stone, has a *piano nobile*, attic windows to the first storey, alternate straight and curved pediments above the openings, and a tetrastyle portico. The first two, designed by William Chambers, have few specifically Palladian elements, while the third, by Capability Brown perhaps with the aid of Henry Holland, is replete with them. If Brown and Holland had been among the staunchest defenders of the faith and Chambers a notorious backslider, it would be possible to attribute the differences to the architects themselves. But Chambers, while not a blind worshipper of Palladio, was a more faithful disciple than the other two. Or again, had Palladianism been an up-and-coming creed in the late 18th century, it might well be that ideas that had arrived in Surrey by 1770 had failed to reach Shropshire ten years earlier. In fact, however, the Palladian tide was flowing more strongly in the 1760s than in the 1770s, and when Walcot was being reconstructed Linley Hall, hardly five miles away, was already 20 years old. The conclusion seems inescapable that in Surrey Clive was labouring to impress the political and aesthetic big-wigs of the capital, while in Shropshire, to further his political ambitions there, he built his houses in a style that would be familiar and reassuring to the local gentry whom he was entertaining in them.

Clive acted as he did because the absence from Shropshire of great Whig magnates had ensured that the local gentry would continue to be the arbiters of architectural fashion in the county. Few of them, whether Whig or Tory, could afford to build to a Palladian scale; indeed 'A middle-class Palladian architecture is a contradiction in terms'.[5] And so that style exercised whatever influence it may have had mainly in a negative way: by helping to discredit the older Cound manner among the major gentry. But if Cound was out of fashion among men with any claim to educated taste, and if Palladio was out of touch for political reasons or out of reach for financial ones, then the builders of larger houses had little choice but to fall back on the plainness and simplicity which their lesser brethren had been practising for some time past. As a result there was throughout the county in the mid 18th century a style—perhaps best thought of as a vernacular classicism—common to the houses of all men who could afford to build.

Nevertheless there was one building—Millington's Hospital, Shrewsbury—for which a design was prepared so Palladian in intent that it might be seen as a provincial attempt at a small-scale adaptation of Kent's Horse Guards, if it didn't antedate that prestigious structure by several years. The original design of 1747 by Edward Massey, a carpenter, and Richard Scoltock, a bricklayer, both of Shrewsbury, has a main block and two flanking pavilions, all with plain pediments, connected by

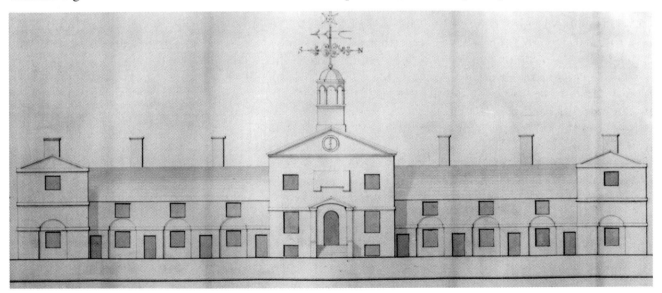

Millington's Hospital, Frankwell, Shrewsbury (SRRC 2133/125)

two ranges of dwellings with a low attic storey above the ground floor and beneath overhanging eaves. The ground-floor windows of the ranges, with heavy keystones, are set within round-headed recesses and give the impression of arcaded linking blocks. The building was of brick, but the architects' drawing suggests that, to give a Palladian air and to heighten the effect of an arcade, the brickwork of all the main fronts was either rendered or whitewashed while that of the recesses was left in its natural darker colour.[6] Because of later alterations it is unclear whether or not the design was modified in the building,[7] but despite its solecisms, it shows that, if not a 'middle-class Palladianism', then at least a small-scale Palladianism was achieved by two Salopian tradesmen. It was a public rather than a private building, but that is not an explanation of it for no other public building of the time in the county was in the same vein.[8]

An architecture common to all Men of Property: the elimination of vernacular architecture

The 'vernacular classicism' just referred to was brought about not only by a change in the taste of those at the top of local society but also by a change in the fortunes of those below. In earlier years yeomen's houses had been more or less distinct, in size or form or ornament, from those of the men above them. Those men had occupied a very different economic niche from the gentry, and their homes had necessarily expressed the difference, for the buildings proper to a small farm were not appropriate to a large landed estate. In the 18th century, however, small farms began to disappear from the Shropshire scene. The basis of rural society in the 17th century had been prosperous peasant families with between 10 and 50 acres and extensive rights of common. On Richard Hill's Hawkstone estate it was policy in the 1720s to consolidate farms whenever possible,[9] and throughout Shropshire by the end of the 18th century most holdings had been converted into tenancies at will and many small farms engrossed into larger ones of up to 200 acres or more. The unique pattern of the modern English countryside was emerging: a society eventually polarized between landless labourers and large capitalist farmers. The latter, increasingly sundered economically and ideologically from the mass of the rural population,[10] identified themselves in thought

with the other landed interests and lived in houses which, while still farmhouses, were intended to look like genteel residences, for example, Welbatch (c.1800), near Shrewsbury. The reverse side of the picture—the gulf between farmers and labourers—is well shown by the buildings put up by the Leveson-Gowers on their estate in east Shropshire. Honnington Grange, Lilleshall, built as a farmhouse 1817–19, had, besides a 'kitchen and house-place' and several service rooms, a parlour, a 'family room', a 'master's room', and seven bedrooms.[11] Cottages on the same estate were built on a 'two up and two down' plan and, while providing reasonable accommodation by the standards of the time, could never, unlike the houses of earlier smallholders, function as, or be mistaken for, farmhouses.[12]

The rise in the status of the clergy and the expansion of the professions were mentioned earlier.[13] The latter process had of course been going on from time immemorial, from Lawrence of Ludlow at Stokesay in the late 13th century to William Owen at Whitley Grange and Edward Gibbon at Great Lyth in the late 17th century. As the 18th century wore on it became so common that architectural designs were published for 'Persons of Moderate Income and for Comfortable Retirement'.[14] At the same time the improvement in the housing standards of the parish clergy was very widely reflected in the enlargement and rebuilding of rectories and vicarages throughout the century and beyond. It is not often that one can make a direct comparison in a parish between the parson's house in the 17th century and in the early 19th, but one may do so for Cardeston Rectory, for a drawing of the old house may be compared with the house which replaced it. The old rectory was a 17th-century house of three bays and 1½ storey, with a lobby entrance:[15] vernacular in every way, and not at the top of the vernacular tree either.[16] It was replaced by Francis Leighton[17] in 1833 in a Tudor Gothic style with, on the ground floor, a drawing room, dining room, study, kitchen, butler's pantry, housekeeper's room and a servants' stair: a complete gentleman's residence.[18] Its character is such that, having come into lay ownership, it has been renamed, without any incongruity, Cardeston Manor. The present Berrington Hall, built by Joseph Bromfield in 1805 as a rectory for the wealthy Richard Noel Hill, and at an estimated cost of £2,300, replaced a timber

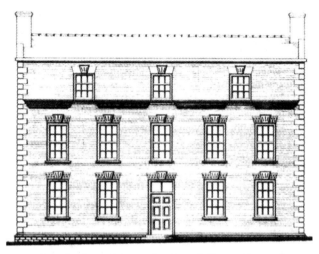

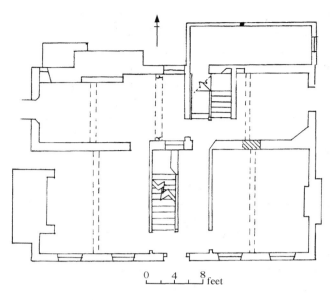

*South elevation and ground-floor plan of
Lower House Farm, Church Pulverbatch*

0 4 8 feet

framed house of four bays.[19] The rectory at Woolstaston was a three-bay brick house of 2½ storeys built before 1716; the new rector in 1855 called it a 'mere cottage' and enlarged and remodelled it.[20] Similar, though less spectacular, improve-

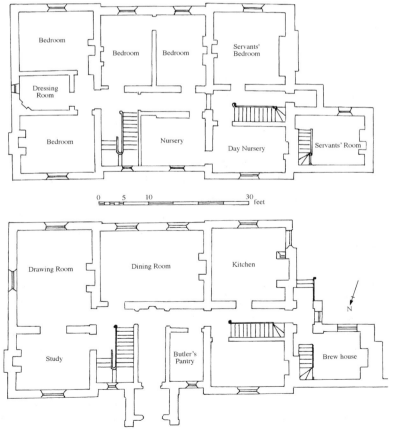

Ground- and first-floor plans of Cardeston Rectory

ments occurred at, for example, Lilleshall, Madeley, Preston upon the Weald Moors, and Shifnal.[21]

The most obvious result of these changes in the second half of the century was a uniformity in the style and the form of nearly all new houses, irrespective of their size and contrasting with the diversity of earlier years. The phenomenon, of course, was not peculiar to Shropshire, but because of the lack of great Palladian mansions there it was more noticeable than in some other counties, and the dominance of what Horace Walpole called the 'smug' houses of 'middle people' was more complete.

Typical of the new small houses of the middle years of the century are Lower House Farm, Church Pulverbatch, and Grange Farm, Eardington. The first, dated 1757, was built for the Jaundrell family, who had been freeholders in the parish since the 15th century;[22] and the second is of much the same date. Both houses have strictly symmetrical façades with end-chimneys, quoins at the angles, keystones to the window heads, and heavy eaves-cornices, much in the manner of earlier houses of higher standing. Grange Farm also has a projecting centrepiece with a pediment above. Both have been added to and have been altered internally, but it is clear that the former was built to a strict **L** plan and the latter to the same plan, but with an earlier one-storey range in the re-entrant angle. They were not identical in their make-up, for at Grange Farm the staircase was sited in the entrance passage, as it had been in the parlour block added to Wheathall in 1721, while at Lower House Farm the staircase, now in the same position as at Grange Farm, was formerly in the rear wing, as at Felhampton Court. Even when they were on the same plan, therefore, houses of this size might vary; not every one of them was a working farmhouse, but in their determined symmetry and their mode of ornament they are all uniform with the houses of the men above them in the social scale.

Nevertheless symmetry had, of course, been a highly desirable quality for nearly two centuries,

Red Abbey, Alberbury.
Above: living room at the front;
below: stair turret at the rear

and its adoption by men of very limited means was not so much because ideas took all that time to penetrate their heads, as because they were now less constrained by the functions their houses had formerly had to serve. Some small men were not building farmhouses and could therefore erect pure residences; others could afford to build farmhouses big enough to be both functional and symmetrical. Nevertheless, yet others still had to build with very limited means indeed, and one may see how all-pervasive the cult of symmetry had become by considering houses in which practical convenience, and the advances made in domestic planning over the previous 150 years, had to give way before it. Lower House Farm, Church Pulverbatch, provides an illustration. Originally the entrance in the fashionable symmetrical front led directly into a large hall-kitchen with a huge fireplace and opposed doorways: a very odd revival of a sub-medieval plan which had been abandoned in most Shropshire farmhouses since the late 16th century. Much the same disposition occurred originally at the much plainer farmhouse of *c*.1800 known as the Red Abbey, Alberbury.[23] In both houses the far doorway led not into the open air but into a kind of vestibule which gave access to a service room, to a small unheated room, and to the stairway, placed at the Red Abbey in a beautifully proportioned brick stair turret which rivals Frodesley in its elegance. The strange combination at both houses of an up-to-date symmetrical elevation and a sophisticated disposition at the rear with an old-fashioned plan arose from an attempt to get the large hall-kitchen of a farmhouse into the limited front of a small purely residential house.[24]

An architecture common to all Men of Property: plan development

Above the vernacular level such an obvious conflict of priorities did not arise, and houses of very different sizes were built more or less to the same pattern: on a double-pile plan with a strictly symmetrical front composed of a central compartment flanked by reception rooms of approximately equal dimensions and with the service rooms at the rear. The differences, apart from size, were mainly in the function and the form of the central compartment and, broadly, these reflected the differences between small, middling, and large houses.

In smaller houses, and especially those built on an **L** plan, the central compartment was of shallow depth, running through only one range of building, and it contained both the unheated entrance passage and the main staircase; and service rooms were sited in the rear wing. An early example is Grange Farm, Eardington, and another of about 60 or 70 years later, was Holly Grove outside Market Drayton. In the 19th century, as men of ever lower status began to build or occupy new and substantially built houses, the **L** plan with an unheated staircase-cum-entrance passage became very common, and has persisted in one form or another into our own times. In the 18th century, however, the narrow staircase-cum-entrance passage was less commonly found in new houses than in the symmetrical reception ranges that were often added in front of earlier dwellings. A precocious example, already cited in a different context, is at Wheathall and is dated 1721; later ones are, or were, at Chatford House, Condover, of 1776, at Ford Mansion of 1779,[25] and at Besford Grange and the Cottage, Ruyton-XI-Towns, both *c*.1800.

Where more space was available, that is in houses built to much the same scale but on a full double-pile plan, the narrow central entrance hall might still be present, but it was free of the main staircase, which was relegated to the rear range and generally sited centrally there. Ash Hall was mentioned earlier, an example as precocious in its way as Wheathall, and later ones are Broseley Hall, built some time before 1747,[26] and Ashford Bowdler Hall, which appears to date from the 1760s.

The difference in form between double-pile and **L** plan houses lay also in the presence or absence of a secondary staircase. Small houses of the early years of the century were often without such a convenience; by the middle years double-pile houses almost invariably had one. There are exceptions, or seeming exceptions. The Elms, Ash Parva, was built in the late 18th century with a five-bay elevation, four ground-floor rooms, a central entrance hall, but only one staircase, sited in the rear of the central compartment. The house was, however, quite small, 41ft. by 25ft. externally, and not a true double pile for the rear rooms were only two-thirds as deep as the front ones.[27] Nevertheless it was not only size and plan form which could determine the presence or absence of a secondary

stair. Eardington Grange and Felhampton Court were built as **L** plan houses, but each had a secondary stair, presumably to assert its social standing. By the next century farmhouses were following suit. Bretchell Farm on the Loton estate was built in 1833 with a secondary stair,[28] and Welbatch, near Hookagate, a double-pile farmhouse of *c*.1800, and Cross House, Longden, a 17th-century timber-framed building,[29] had each a secondary stair contrived later. The purpose of these stairs was to give access to a servants' bedroom otherwise inaccessible.

At the top levels of local society, however, a mere entrance passage, with or without a staircase, would not do. That top section, and those who wished to be thought part of it, was far from socially homogeneous and included rich gentry like Plowden Slaney at Hatton Grange,[30] nabobs like Clive at Styche and Walcot, rich Shrewsbury businessmen like Joshua Blakeway at Lythwood Hall, and new peers like Lord Berwick at Attingham. Despite such social diversity it was still obligatory among them to have a large and imposing entrance hall, and nearly always a heated one. Throughout the last half of the century the old-style entrance hall, unchanged in form from those of the builders of the first half of the century, was perpetuated at, *inter alia*, Delbury Hall (*c*.1753–4),[31] Walcot Hall (*c*.1764), Hatton Grange (1764–8), the remodelled Cruckton Hall (*c*.1770), Lythwood Hall (*c*.1782), Attingham, as remodelled from the older Tern Hall in 1784–5, and in the proposals for a rebuilding at Moreton Corbet in 1796.[32] Those houses are not alike in every respect—Cruckton Hall had the entry at the end of the hall, Attingham is a vast house with long wings, and Walcot and Delbury have peculiarities of their own that will be discussed later—but they all distinguish themselves from the ruck of the 'middling sort', with which they share a plan form, by their large entrance halls.

At the end of the century the use of a country mansion for political ends was declining and the cult of the Picturesque was growing, and that movement's integration of the house within its landscape tended to demote the entrance front to one among others.[33] In consequence, some large houses were built with the smaller halls that lesser men had been favouring for a long time,[34] and that had been foreshadowed by the designer of Linley Hall, to whom

Longford Hall (SRRC uncatalogued)

the hall was 'a Room to pass thro' '.[35] The earliest one known is the now demolished Tong Castle, built *c*.1765 for George Durant, a young man who had amassed a fortune as paymaster to the 1762 expedition against Havana.[36] It was a very large house, the grounds laid out by Capability Brown,[37] with a hall no bigger than either of the drawing rooms, smaller than the dining room and less than half the size of the saloon.[38] Another is Longford Hall, remodelled between 1789 and 1794 by Joseph Bonomi for Ralph Leeke, a returning nabob, but a full generation later than Clive and without political ambition. Almost exactly contemporary was Aston Hall, Oswestry, remodelled by James Wyatt for a local landowner J.R. Lloyd, rector of Whittington and Selattyn. Each of these houses retains a recognizable entrance hall communicating directly with the most important rooms on the principal floor, but of such dimensions—about 20ft. by 15—that it is absolutely smaller than the halls of many earlier smaller houses and is not the largest room, nor even among the largest rooms, in the house.[39] Later houses took the development further still and eliminated the traditional hall in favour of a vestibule, an entry into the house which communicated not with all the other important rooms on the principal floor, but only with another and larger space beyond.[40] In a design of 1724 for a merchant's house in Bristol the 'vestibule' was a small space immediately inside the front door and screened off from the rooms

beyond. The quality presumably passed through it since it was meant for 'the convenience of common people' waiting to be attended to. In later grander houses, where 'common people' went to a side or back door, it had a different purpose.[41] Early and notable grand examples are Willey Hall (1812–20) by Lewis Wyatt, C.R. Cockerell's Oakly Park of 1819 onwards, and Sir John Soane's Pell Wall (1822 onwards), Market Drayton. It will have been noticed that these houses were designed by London architects of wide repute. It is, however, a mark of the times, and of the integration of local architects into the national framework, that an equally early house with a vestibule, the now demolished Onslow Hall near Shrewsbury, was designed in 1815 by Edward Haycock, pupil of Jeffry Wyatt and son of John Hiram Haycock, whose local practice he inherited. Moreover Edward himself had been anticipated by his father, who in 1810 had produced a design for Roveries House, Lydham, with an entrance vestibule, 16ft. long by 6ft. wide, leading into the 'Best Staircase' hall.[42]

It is probable that the earliest vestibule in Shropshire was at the medium sized Hopton Court, remodelled some time after 1806 and, according to the nephew of the then owner, by John Nash.[43] The vestibule there, like those at Oakly and Onslow and like the small halls at Aston and Longford, led into a top-lit staircase hall of some splendour, but not overwhelmingly so. And at Pell Wall it led presum-

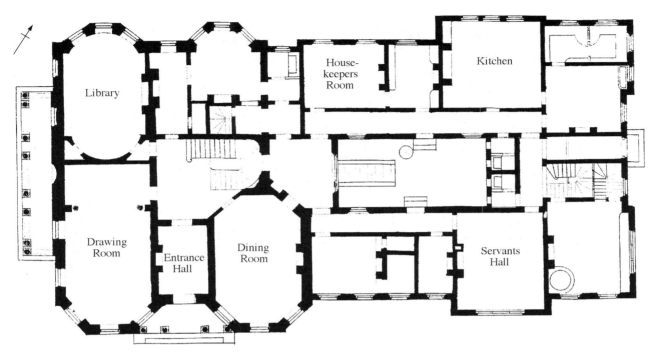

Plan of the ground floor of Hopton Court

ably, for there have been alterations, into a series of domed compartments in Soanean style. But at Leaton Knolls[44] it led, and at Willey it leads, into a magnificent top-lit arcaded central hall with galleries on the first floor in the manner of, if not imitating, Belsay (Northumb.). Similarly at Millichope, by Edward Haycock and of the later 1830s, a galleried central hall was reached by a

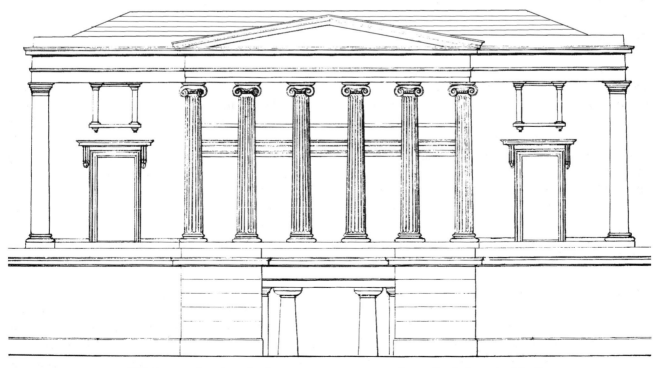

Millichope, showing the basement entrance to the galleried central hall

stairway coming up from a basement entrance.[45] The purpose of the vestibule in large houses, with its 'one way only' circulation, was to bring the visitor inexorably from a confined area into the spaciousness of the central hall.[46] The shift therefore from an imposing entrance hall to a small vestibule is not to be regarded as a renunciation of grandeur by the great but as a change in their manner of creating an impression upon their guests, and in the nature of the guests whom they wished to impress. They no longer wanted to make a stately procession for a *grand seigneur* from one magnificent room to another but instead to create a sudden and dramatic effect upon men and women of romantic sensibility. All the houses referred to here, apart from Tong Castle, are in a neo-classic or a Greek Revival style, but, despite their differences in decor, these vestibules and central halls are akin to the vaulted porches and great halls of the later Gothic Revival.

Though by modern standards manners were still extremely formal, they were nevertheless relaxed compared with those of earlier years when great landlords, little kings in their own countryside, kept up as much of the ceremony of a Court as they could and were imitated as far as possible by lesser men. An architectural expression of the new attitude, evident by the mid century, was a laxity among architects and pattern-book makers in the naming of rooms.[47] Indeed Robert Morris did not trouble to name rooms in his designs, declaring that a room the architect meant for one use could equally well be put to another.[48] Before the end of the century, as the concept of the country house changed, names often indicated rooms designed for the cultured and leisured recreations that country-house life was then providing: music room, picture gallery, billiards room. Very large-scale alterations to Attingham in 1806 provided a picture gallery, and in his proposals for refurbishing Moreton Corbet Castle in 1796 J.H. Haycock, perhaps unsure of his client's proclivities, suggested fitting up the ground floor of a long wing as either picture gallery or billiards room.[49]

A plain style

Large and small houses shared in the later years of the century not merely a common attitude towards planning, but a common ornament as well. It was claimed earlier that in the first half of the century the smaller houses were plainer than the large ones. In the second half most houses, great or small, were plainer than ever, and many of them may fairly be called severe or even stark. The plainness was partly brought about by an aversion from the decorative idiom of the previous generations and, at first, a failure or a disinclination to invent any other. Indeed the new style is best described negatively, by specifying what it lacks rather than what it has. The most striking element of decoration in the earlier larger houses, the engaged highly ornamented giant pilasters of Cound and Buntingsdale, disappeared entirely. The carved modillioned cornices were displaced by parapets, sometimes with balustrading as at Walcot, sometimes broken by a pediment with an achievement of arms, as at Swan Hill Court, Shrewsbury, but usually with plain expanses of brick or stonework. Plat bands were not wholly discarded but were much less freely used than before and were often confined to the ground floor as at Delbury Hall. In his rejected designs for Onslow Hall George Steuart had a plat band above the ground and first floors,[50] but when he carried the same design into execution at Lythwood the upper one was eliminated.[51] The bold quoins that punctuated earlier fronts so clearly were still occasionally used, but were absent from most houses. Windows tended to become plain openings with no other decoration than a finely rubbed brick head, and any that were still given surrounds or keystones, as at Hatton Grange and Ford Mansion, were generally concentrated upon a projecting centrepiece.[52] It was in fact in some smaller houses that keystones lingered, as at Chatford House (Condover) and Holly Grove (Market Drayton).[53] The main entrance had not been over-prominent in earlier houses, but now it was given very little emphasis at all, having at best, as at Delbury and Morville Hall, no more than slight engaged columns with a low pediment over. A typical late example is Orleton Hall, Wrockwardine, as refronted in stucco in 1830: a tall elevation of three storeys, with a parapet broken by a pediment above a projecting centrepiece, the windows devoid of any ornament, the façade without plat band or quoins, and the doorway little more than an opening.

This plainness was not solely the result of developments within Shropshire. From the mid century professional architects were playing a part, and their role needs some discussion. They were not a wholly new phenomenon in the county, where the Smiths of Warwick had been active for at least a generation and Cound (1704), Buntingsdale (*c*.1719–23),[54] and Linley (1742) had been designed by professionals from London. Nevertheless the Smiths had been pretty well on their own, and neither John Prince (Cound and Buntingsdale) nor Henry Joynes (Linley) had been anywhere near the top of their profession. It is instructive to note that in Colen Campbell's three volumes of *Vitruvius Britannicus* (1717–25) and Woolfe and Gandon's two volumes of continuation (1767–71) not a single Shropshire house appears.[55] To some extent, given Campbell's bias, this is merely stating what was said earlier: that there are no great Palladian mansions in the county. Woolfe and Gandon's silence, however, cannot be attributed to that cause: it reflects not merely an absence of Palladian buildings but an absence of buildings designed by leading architects. Matters altered in the 1760s. From then until the end of the century Shropshire houses were designed by such London-based architects as William Chambers (Styche and Walcot), James Wyatt (Badger Hall and Aston Hall, Oswestry), George Steuart (Attingham and Lythwood Hall), Joseph Bonomi (Longford), and perhaps Robert Mylne.[56] Attingham (1783–5) and Longford (1789–94) were reproduced in George Richardson's *New Vitruvius Britannicus* (1802–8).

Meanwhile several local architects were emerging. They were 'local' not merely as the Smiths had been and as William Baker of Audlem and the Hiorns of Warwick were: midlands architects with some practice in Shropshire. Rather they were Shropshire men born and bred, or at any rate based, in the county: such were Joseph Bromfield, the elder John Carline, J.H. Haycock, T.F. Pritchard, the Scoltocks of Shrewsbury, and the Smiths of Shifnal.[57] Most of them were still building-tradesmen acting occasionally as architects, and there are more of them known than there had been earlier, partly because the second half of the 18th century is better documented than the first. Nevertheless they represent a new phase in the history of architecture in the county. Among them Pritchard has the largest corpus of known work and was presumably highly regarded in Shropshire and neighbouring counties. He did not escape criticism, however. Bitter words were said about what he did

in Wyle Cop, Shrewsbury, and he was dismissed as unsatisfactory by the Batemans of Shobdon Court (Herefs.) and blamed by Noel Hill at Tern Hall in 1768.[58] Nevertheless a full account of his work at many houses is inclined to discount the significance of these criticisms.[59]

It was not local men, however, who had the best chance to set the pace but men from elsewhere with established reputations; for, despite Pritchard's commissions at Hatton Grange and Swan Hill Court and the Hiorns' at Delbury, until the beginning of the next century the local men were more often employed on additions to, or refurbishings of, older houses than on important new works. It is noticeable that, while Thomas Hill was happy to employ Pritchard at the modest Tern Hall in 1759 and his son Noel tried him there again in 1768, in 1783 Noel, about to be ennobled as Lord Berwick, went to an established architect from outside for his vast new house of Attingham.[60] But most such architects who got commissions in Shropshire in the late 18th century were either latter-day Palladians like Chambers, with an insistence on 'manly ornament', or else exponents to a greater or lesser degree of the new style much influenced by French models that has come to be called neo-classical: men like Wyatt, Steuart, and Bonomi. Consequently outsiders reinforced whatever native predilections there may already have been for austere exteriors. By the end of the century, after many decades of architectural publications, there were Shropshire men who felt themselves to be, or felt that they ought to be, in the forefront of taste. They were far more open to whatever architectural winds might be blowing than their fathers had been, and some were ready to applaud not only accepted canons of the time but many other styles that architects, amateur or professional, were developing. As a result, within the uniformity mentioned above there was also a wide diversity of decorative motifs. In contrast, however, with the preceding 200 years architectural styles no longer reflected social differences but differences between the preferences of those individuals—from all social classes—who had the resources to build houses of their own. The presence or absence of great magnates, or regional variations in the building needs of yeoman farmers, were no longer determining elements in the architecture of the county.

The architecture of Enlightenment—
the Picturesque

The near contemporaneity of the end of vernacular architecture in the county and of Palladianism in the country allowed Shropshire to respond more closely to national developments at a time when a number of styles, superficially diverse but closely related, existed simultaneously or followed one another in quick succession. All were aspects of that late 18th-century movement of intellectual, emotional, and aesthetic liberation which avidly plundered past ages and distant climes and explored fresh aspects of the physical world in order to express its new and essentially home-grown sensibility.

It coincided in Britain with the eclipse of the great Whig oligarchs,[61] the greater independence of country gentlemen, and a vast increase in the wealth of the country, or, more specifically, with an increase in the number of wealthy merchants, bankers, and manufacturers, and, as noted earlier, in a professional 'middle class'. To call the new aesthetics 'bourgeois' as opposed to 'aristocratic' would be a gross simplification, partly because the categories are not mutually exclusive and partly because the new attitudes appealed to, and were created by, aristocrats as much as commoners. Nevertheless they were taken up by men from a far wider section of the population than had previously patronized architects, a section which was attaining some measure of power and influence and was already setting its stamp upon the morality and the literature of the age.

Such men had less predilection, and less occasion, for ceremony and solemnity in their houses and rather favoured a genteel elegance. The light-hearted chinoiserie and rococo ornament of the mid century were architectural forerunners of the new taste, in the limited sense that they relieved the heavy formality of the prevailing modes. They had, however, neither the emotional content that thrilled to the 'sublimity' of Gothic and to the archaic 'simplicity' of Greek, nor the intellectual content which demanded 'rationality' in architecture. By contrast the new sensibility would, in Walpole's words, 'Soften the terms, and mellow the uncouth horror' of earlier ages,[62] and at the same time it would produce a knowledgeable neo-classicism which felt under no obligation to be classically correct,[63] or even strictly symmetrical.[64] All of these

trends may be subsumed under 'the Picturesque', a broad church which could happily embrace many creeds. One of its leading exponents, Richard Payne Knight, of a dynasty of ironmasters, built at Downton (Herefs.) the first massive and asymmetrical Gothic castle; and he fitted out the interior in a classical style.[65]

Despite all the architectural theorizing of the time the aspect of the Picturesque which affected country-house architecture most lastingly was not architectural at all. Rather it was that growing control over Nature which Science and Industry were achieving, coupled with the declining influence of the Whig oligarchy with its stiff grandeur: these changes allowed an appreciation of other landscapes than the smug orderliness of the Thames valley and of other prospects than the formal gardens of Versailles. Instead of sheltering men from the terrors of Nature the country house was now to introduce them to her charms. The attitude is well illustrated in Walpole's slighting remark about Thornbury Castle (Glos.), Buckingham's up-to-date early 16th-century house: 'all the windows of the great apartment look into the inner court. The prospect was left to the servants'.[66]

The work of such gardeners as Capability Brown and Humphry Repton affected not merely the grounds of a great house, but also the relationship between house and grounds, both in the siting of a new house and in the disposition of the rooms in a new or refurbished one. Previously the entrance front had been of prime importance, not merely because of the impact it was meant to have on visitors, but also because the formal vista from the rooms ranged along it was also meant to impress. As taste turned towards carefully designed 'natural' landscapes the entrance front could become a problem, especially in a remodelled house on a site determined by earlier considerations, for it might be very difficult to obtain a 'natural' view from it. Local architects were as conscious of the problems as London men were, and in the early 1770s T.F. Pritchard was critical of the failure at Powis Castle to exploit the view across the Severn.[67] As a consequence the entrance front often ceased to be the most important elevation or to accommodate the most important rooms.

At first it was the effect upon the disposition of rooms that was most noticeable, and early occurrences of it may be suspected at Ford House, Broseley Hall, and Delbury Hall. At the first two the exigencies of the site give the rooms along the entrance front, but not at the rear, a very restricted view and, contrary to all normal planning conventions, the kitchens in both these houses are at the front, leaving the rear free for reception rooms. It is not necessary to suppose that their owners wanted the kind of prospect that Brown or Repton would have given them, but they did want to see something more than an entrance courtyard. At Delbury the south front, which faces up a slope, is the entrance front and the north front has an open view. There, and that again is most unusual, the main staircase is sited in the entrance hall itself, leaving the north front, the one with a view, free for reception rooms.

As houses were integrated more with their surroundings there was a tendency to use much, or even all, of the entrance front for smaller and less important rooms, and to put the more constantly used rooms—library, drawing room, breakfast room—at the side or rear and where the best view was. When Thomas Jones of Chester rebuilt Oteley Park for Charles Mainwaring c.1830 he gave the entrance a splendid Tudor-style *porte cochère* but placed all the reception rooms at the side and rear of the main block, overlooking the Mere;[68] and the present oddity of Longnor Hall's plan is the result of alterations in the earlier 19th century, which put the sitting rooms at the former rear of the house, where they provided Panton Corbett's family with a romantic view to the south.[69] The decline in size and splendour of the entrance hall, and its transformation into a mere vestibule (see above), was but one aspect of the process and often resulted in the side elevations being more impressive than the front. At Walcot, which encapsulates a late 16th-century house, the entrance front, even with Joseph Bromfield's portico of the 1780s, is subdued by comparison with the side elevation, the former front of the earlier house, which looks up the valley and whence at one time Clive's tree planting to spell out the boast of PLASSEY must have been visible. At Willey the great colonnaded bow window of the library makes the side elevation at least as impressive as the front. At Hopton Court, as it was refurbished some time after 1806, the entrance front of what had been a more or less square house was left short, while the side elevation was extended by over

half as much again of its original length and was provided with a long portico of Ionic columns. At Evelith Manor, too, the front was shorter and less impressive than the side elevation, while at Cronkhill there can hardly be said to be an entrance front, the main doorway being almost hidden away in a very minor elevation. Sometimes at this date, and later, a new entrance was made at the side to allow of a long garden front, as at Church Stretton (Old) Rectory.

Cronkhill, of course, was an asymmetrical house, and in such houses even the concept of an entrance front becomes nebulous as the main entry is frankly set in a side of the house which has no claim to be a front of any sort. Much the same, however, could happen at a symmetrical house. At Millichope, which has been described as 'a singularly perfect combination of a classical house overlooking a Picturesque landscape',[70] there was a highly picturesque classical entrance and elsewhere a portico of a type that conventionally stood before the main entrance; but there was no entrance front at all. The external beauties of the edifice could never be more than glimpsed in the approach to the house, nor viewed properly until the visitor had been conducted through the house and into the gardens, which could themselves be seen as a wholly picturesque landscape untainted by a modern carriage drive. Millichope is the epitome of the Picturesque; it combines the dramatic effects of neo-classicism, the forms of the Greek Revival, and the 'naturalism' of English landscape gardening with a libertarian disregard of the stately formal approach to a great mansion which classicist theory had maintained without challenge since the Renaissance.

Millichope's site is also of interest as an early Shropshire example of the erection of small buildings—temples, grottoes, etc.—to adorn the grounds of a mansion and often to enliven the prospect from the house. While the old timber-framed hall at Millichope was still occupied, indeed 60 years before Haycock was active there, George Steuart in almost his first known work designed an Ionic temple in the grounds that was probably meant to be seen from the house. In the mid to late 18th century Acton Burnell park was embellished with a number of curiosities: an entrance lodge was remodelled in the Gothic style and the 'Shell House' was built as a grotto on an octagonal plan and 'Sham Castle' (1779–80) as a tower on a triangular plan.[71] And it may have been soon afterwards that the crenellations along the south front of Acton Burnell Castle were added.[72] Some time before 1760 Arthur Weaver planted two rows of elms in front of Morville Hall to lead the eye to a pyramidal obelisk, or rather to a board painted to look like one.[73] A picture at Longner Hall, perhaps of the 1790s, shows a 'castle' in the grounds with battlements, one pointed window, and several Georgian ones. The two Citadels at Hawkstone, those of *c*.1785 and 1824–5, were both intended not merely to house their occupants but also to embellish the estate. When the county was building Tern bridge in 1778–81 the owner of Tern Hall—predecessor of Attingham—contributed the cost of the 'decoration' because he wanted a 'view' from his house.[74] It is not unlikely that the unusual north-east orientation of the main front at Cronkhill, the residence of Lord Berwick's steward,[75] was to allow its picturesque outlines to be seen across the river from the great house at Attingham[76] in a manner similar to Repton's (thwarted) intention to add a spire to Wroxeter church in order to improve the view from the same house.[77]

Not every owner had the resources to set his house within its own tailor-made landscape, and many had to content themselves with taking what opportunities there were to bring house and grounds together. One easy way in a small dwelling was to have a veranda. The veranda was a borrowing from the East and in its way was as aptly romantic as the Jacobean loggia had been aptly Italianate. But while the latter was conceived as a stately exterior gallery bringing the out-of-doors into the room, the former was an out-of-doors room for informal use;

Two views of Ænon Cottage, Shrewsbury. Above: as seen from the river in Joseph Dixon's journals; below: north-east view by T. Saunders (SRRC uncatalogued)

although at Cronkhill it might still have the stone or brick arcade of a loggia, it wasn't long before cast-iron columns, and often a glass roof, became typical. Outstanding examples are those at Shelbrook Hill and at the Lyth, Ellesmere, where anthemion cresting runs around three sides. The *cottage ornée* which Robert Pemberton built in Abbey Foregate, Shrewsbury, *c*.1810, had a veranda beneath a thatched roof and with the supports hidden beneath climbing foliage.[78] Lock House, on the former Ellesmere Canal at Grindley Brook, has a timber veranda in association with a massive bow window and with slight pilasters upon the façade: a blending of the rustic with the neo-classic in a building of the developing industrial age.

The blend is seen as well in those small houses, copied from the idealized landscapes of Claude Lorrain and Poussin, which combine 'the vernacular of the Italian campagna, a style which had no architectural credentials whatever',[79] with the small-scale charm of an English cottage. Here again Cronkhill is the pioneer, and a follower is Oxon Hall near Shrewsbury. Oxon takes over from Cronkhill the pyramidal tower roof, the overhanging eaves, and the low attic storey immediately beneath them, but it eschews Cronkhill's roundels in the attic and round-headed windows elsewhere for three-light flat-headed windows with shallow sunken panels in the dividing uprights.

An example of another aspect of the Picturesque, the vogue for the 'simple life', seen on a smaller scale, was the *cottage ornée*. One of those, Ænon Cottage at Shrewsbury, with its thatched roof, eyebrow dormers, and gardens running down to the river, was locally famous. It was built by John Palmer, the minister of the Baptist chapel, was eulogized in a pamphlet of 1808, and was celebrated in verse:

> Near Salop's Castle's antiquated pile
> A lonely cottage stands in humble style,

a couplet which manages to include most of the qualities of Picturesqueness.[80]

Cronkhill and Oxon, eminently practical in early 19th-century conditions, nevertheless illustrate as well as any building of the Greek or Gothic Revival the make-believe nature of the Picturesque. Despite what they purport to be they are far larger than villas and are accompanied by more or less hidden ranges of living and service rooms. Reality, historical or contemporary, was not what the practitioners of the Picturesque wished to deal in, and that helps to account for the strict limits to their sensibilities. Timber-framing, which later generations were to see as the acme of Picturesqueness, and which was even more conspicuous in Shropshire then than now, was almost wholly ignored there.[81] Unlike Greek temples, Gothic castles, and villas in the Campagna, timber-framed farmhouses and cottages were occupied by living local people, who might be objects of fear or of compassion but not of romantic interest to their betters, many of whom, often from very worthy motives, were busy pulling down timber-framed houses or replacing them with modern ones.

The architecture of Enlightenment: the Gothick

The Gothick of the mid-to-late 18th century was the clearest and the most widespread expression in domestic architecture of the Picturesque. Of all the Gothic revivals it was aesthetically the 'purest', neither tainted by the sectarian propaganda intent of those of the 17th and 19th centuries nor fettered by the increasingly onerous demands of a deepening scholarship.[82] Horace Walpole was not its progenitor, but he was its most typical, or at any rate its most prominent, exponent. 'Serious business was a trifle to him and trifles were his serious business',[83] and it may be argued that at first the Revival was no more than an aspect of the frivolous eclecticism of the mid 18th century; but that itself was in part a reaction against what a contemporary, probably John Gwynn, called the 'dull sameness' that Palladianism was bringing about.[84] Its earliest large scale manifestation in Shropshire was Tong Castle (see illustrations overleaf), *c*.1765 for George Durant.[85] Tong was a modern symmetrically designed mansion dressed up in Gothic ornament, and in other ornament as well. Its crenellations, loopholed towers, ogee-headed openings, and windows with hood moulds were accompanied by an overriding baroque dome, by Jacobean cupolas, by wholly contemporary bay windows, and by battlemented pediments along the main front. A later local comment, that it was as much Moorish as Gothic,[86] is formally incorrect but gives a fair idea of the eclectic nature of the house.[87]

Tong was not the first example of this early revival. In the 1750s the wall of the garden front at Sibdon Carwood was raised and crenellated at the centre and ends to give the effect of a medieval castle. Woodhouse Farm, Stoke upon Tern, begun in 1754, was designed by William Baker with the centre of the wall on each front similarly raised and crenellated. It is a small double-pile house, and this castellated effect necessitated a large chimney stack in the middle of the building, formidably inconvenient to the present farmer and presumably not less so to his predecessors. Woodhouse Farm was erected for a tenant and is the largest of those Gothic dwellings erected neither by the prospective occupant nor with much thought for his comfort, but to please the man of sensibility passing by; and condemned by Archdeacon Plymley as 'deceit', and unsuccessful deceit at that.[88] Now that Tong has gone they are, apart from churches, the most easily visible aspect of this early revival, generally recognizable by the ogee heads or the two-centred heads to the openings or by crockets or crenellations. A dated one is the Toll House at Minsterley of *c*.1768; probably of much the same time are 3 and 5 St.

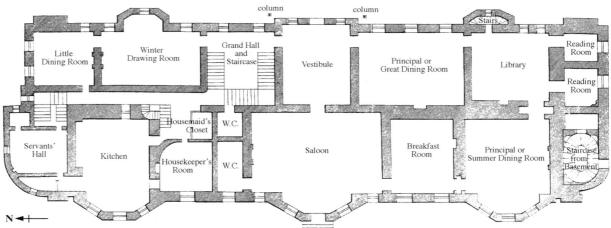

Ground-floor plan and east front of Tong Castle (SRRC 6001/3167)

Woodhouse Farm, Stoke upon Tern, a small double-pile house designed by William Baker

Mary's Lane, Much Wenlock, and the Lodge at Stanton Lacy, which resemble one another in the broad surrounds to the openings. The so-called 'Smithy' at Beambridge had until 1957, a very high false castellated front in the manner of Woodhouse and Sibdon Carwood. Thin uncusped tracery with a **Y** pattern set in windows with two-centred heads occurred as well upon the less prominent elevation of some large houses, as at Shipton Hall, and on the service buildings of others, as the stable block at Caughley Hall.[89]

A more delicate aspect of that early revival is seen in the style of T.F. Pritchard, although the most famous example of it is in Herefordshire, at Croft Castle. In 1761 Pritchard submitted proposals for work at Ludford House[90] (then also in Herefs.), and it must have been then that he executed the very pretty first-floor windows there, with two-centred trefoiled heads to the lights and with triple-clustered colonnettes as mullions. In 1774–6 he was repairing and refitting Ludlow Guildhall, and, while he transformed the interior in contemporary style and hid the magnificent medieval roof behind a plaster ceiling, he gave the street doorway a steep ogee head and flanked it with his favourite triple colonnettes. These are so much a mark of Pritchard that

they may be regarded as *prima facie* evidence of his responsibility for any building within the county on which they appear, for example 7 The Square, Shrewsbury, and the wooden summer house or temple at Broseley Hall, where he is known to have supplied chimney pieces. Though it is perhaps fair to say that his Gothic is of the Batty Langley type,[91] it is nevertheless far and away the best of the period in the area; and, whatever the truth about his contribution to the structure of the Iron Bridge near Coalbrookdale, he made his mark in the history of the Industrial Revolution as the man who, at the very least, designed the abutments and the Gothic ornament of the ironwork.[92]

In all of the above, and in Telford's Laura's Tower in Shrewsbury Castle, the Gothic element was little more than applied decoration, pretty or amusing, and paralleled indoors by the fashion for rococo ornament, as at Shipton and Lutwyche, or for chinoiserie as at Delbury Hall. By *c.*1800, however, the mood had changed and, while Tong had had no compeers, many large houses were then being erected wholly in the Gothic style, not yet built to the scholarly standards established by the time of Victoria's accession, but nevertheless intended as serious re-creations of medieval architecture.

Old habits, however, did not change all that quickly, and for a long time many houses were given, at least on the main elevation, as strict a symmetry as Tong or any neo-Palladian building. Among large Gothic, or early Tudor, houses are Sundorne Castle (before 1816),[93] and the additions to Stanley Hall (1816); among smaller houses are Hodnet Rectory (1812), Hardwick Grange (1820), and Cardeston Rectory (1833). Similarly, some of the preferences of the early revival were carried on, and in particular the fancy for a castle-like air, revealed clearly in such names as the Citadel at Hawkstone, Quatford Castle, Sundorne Castle, and Rowton Castle. The latter two encapsulate run-of-the-mill 18th-century houses, and Quatford was built for himself by the successful local builder and architect, John Smalman. In a small house like Earlsdale (probably soon after 1811), Pontesford, and at Broadward House, Clungunford, the castle-like effect amounted to little more than a show of the crenellations of earlier years, and at Apley Park the battlemented pediments of Tong were repeated.

Nevertheless change did come. At Apley Park the effect is not wholly symmetrical, and by 1805 John Nash was building a deliberately asymmetrical house at Longner, which was followed by Rowton Castle (by George Wyatt, probably 1810–12), Lilleshall House (later Hall, by Sir Jeffry Wyatville 1826–30), and Oteley Park (by Thomas Jones of Chester, 1826–30, demolished 1960).[94] At Hawkstone and Rowton the thin and wholly unconvincing corner towers of Tong were transformed into massive formidable bastions, at Sundorne a reasonably accurate pastiche of a 15th-century house like Herstmonceux (Suss.) or Kirby Muxloe (Leics.) was achieved, and at Lilleshall and Oteley fashionable *portes cochères* were effectively disguised as late medieval porches. But the most important change was the abandonment of openings with two-centred heads and **Y** tracery and the general adoption of the more domestic late Perpendicular or early Tudor style, the result largely of a desire by the wealthy to use Gothic in their own houses rather than in eye-catchers occupied by their dependants.[95] The new manner first appeared at Longner where Nash used cusped Perpendicular tracery in the windows of the reception rooms and of the stairway hall, and humdrum Tudor Gothic in the offices.[96] A similar use, and contrast, was apparent as well at Apley Park. Smaller houses, however, like Hodnet Rectory, Hardwick Grange, and Cardeston Rectory, were wholly in the Tudor style, and so too were the fashionable loggias incorporated into new houses or added to older ones, as, for example, at the earlier Rudge Hall which preceded the large scale reconstruction of *c*.1930. In later years Perpendicular tracery was reserved for emphasis, as at Oteley where it was employed on the entrance tower that was also a *porte cochère*.

In the early 19th century the Gothic Revival was more conspicuous in domestic buildings in Shropshire than the Greek Revival, both in the number of houses and in its readier acceptance in the first 20 years. To some extent, however, the latter, like Palladianism earlier, was not well adapted, except as applied ornament, to smaller houses, and, if they are left out of the reckoning, the difference in numbers in domestic architecture between the two styles disappears. By the second quarter of the century the builders of large houses showed no great preference for the one over the other. Nor yet, though perhaps because very few great houses were built at that time by the *nouveaux riches*, was either style more favoured by rich newcomers than by old-established families.

The difference in the fortunes of the two styles is more curious than that. In contrast with Edward Haycock's near monopoly in the Greek Revival not one of the large Gothic houses is known to be by him. Only one, the additions to Stanley Hall, is even by a Shropshire man, John Smalman, while five are by outsiders: Nash's Longner, Apley Park by John Webb of Armitage (Staffs.), George Wyatt's Rowton, Wyatville's Lilleshall House, and Thomas Jones's Oteley Park. Haycock did get two minor commissions—Hodnet Rectory for Reginald Heber and the Headmaster's House in School Gardens, Shrewsbury, both in Tudor Gothic—but when a large Gothic house was in question he seems to have been consistently overlooked.[97] The Gothic churches which he designed are extremely ordinary and it is possible that he had little liking for that style and that Shropshire patrons were perspicacious enough to recognize both his fluency in Greek and his lack of it in Gothic. It is in this connection that one may refer to the stress that has been laid upon the role played by amateurs in the architecture of the early 19th century. However large nationally the contribution of individual amateurs to aesthetic theory, and however their predilections affected their choice of architects and, thereby, the architectural scene, there is very little evidence, despite the occasional reference to an owner's being 'his own architect', that they had any but the most insignificant part in designing buildings of importance in Shropshire.[98]

The architecture of Enlightenment: Neo-classical
Ever since there has been an architectural profession its more articulate members, and their admirers, have produced aesthetic theories intended to validate their predilections and practical activities: each theory more elaborate than the last, and as ephemeral. 'Neo-classical' architects—who would have repudiated that mid-19th century coinage—were intent on creating a 'rational' architecture without 'superfluities'. Nevertheless, neo-classicism was as romantic and backward-looking as neo-Gothic: 'Romantic elements ... breaking through the classic crust of the antique'.[99] In effect its 'rationality' meant

dispensing with the excesses of the baroque and the rococo and returning to a more austere manner which was still in the classical tradition but based itself upon Greek, and especially 'simple' early Greek, models rather than on Roman ones.

In practice this showed itself most commonly in a clarity of form and a stark contrast of line, a 'precision of contour' as Winkelmann called it.[100] The expression of purely architectural qualities, unobscured by ornament, was a very broad plank in the neo-classical platform and was present in various ways in the larger houses of the last quarter of the century and beyond. At Woodhouse and at Bonomi's Longford Hall (1789–94) it was achieved with a heavy cornice, plain openings, and slight pilasters, Ionic and Doric respectively, at the angles. At Attingham, George Steuart left the corners of the main block severely plain and accentuated the outline with the return of the heavy cornice and with plat bands, and not long after, at Aston Hall, Oswestry, James Wyatt gave his outlines almost a cutting edge with shallow niches at the corners. At Willey Hall (1812–20) Lewis Wyatt used similar niches to a similar purpose on the garden front and originally would have dispensed with the present giant order along the main front.[101] In smaller houses too the same effect was often striven for: at Steuart's Lythwood Hall with a plat band above the ground floor; at Glenyrafon (c.1790),[102] Llanyblodwel, with a double plat band at first-floor

level that boldly delineates the form of the house. Similar effects were achieved, to mention a few, at the Priory, Wellington (built as the vicarage c.1807,[103] demolished c.1962),[104] Eardington Manor, Sheinton Manor, Clungunford Hall, Aston Hall at Aston-on-Clun, and Evelith Manor, Shifnal. To some extent, and especially in such starkly plain houses as Welbatch and Ackleton House, Worfield, which dispense even with plat bands, this was probably due as much to that small-house plainness mentioned earlier as to neo-classical aesthetics, but is clear that the two forces could work happily to one end.[105] And nowhere more than at 121-4 Abbey Foregate, Shrewsbury (see illustration p.220), where slight variations in the size and siting of the openings have transformed a terrace of four houses into a strikingly elegant composition in that neo-classical manner that has been called 'compensated symmetry'.[106]

They worked together as well to produce the flat almost two-dimensional façades of the period in which the windows have no element that projects beyond the face of the wall other than a sill. What exceptions there are have only slight decoration: at Longford and at Acton Burnell Hall as refronted in 1814 the windows have slight plain surrounds; at Attingham, and on the design for Lythwood Hall, but not on the actual building, the ground-floor windows, and those only, are given projecting lintels.[107] All those were of stone, but on brick build-

Copthorne House (recently called Mytton Villa), Copthorne Road, Shrewsbury. General view from the south-west and details of the tympana over the ground-floor windows in the two wings

ings, of course, the window heads are often ornamental in themselves without any projection from the plane of the wall. Quite often stucco was used, in very slight relief, to simulate stone voussoirs or keystones. At 91 High Street, Wem, the lintels have paterae upon them. The round-headed windows at 25 Castle Street, Shrewsbury, have fan-like decoration in the tympana, and Copthorne House has similar windows with much effaced human figures (see illustrations previous page). In general, however, and whether in conscious designs or in farmhouses and cottages erected by local builders, the window surrounds are rarely allowed to stand proud of the wall surface.

The further step of recessing the window surrounds in one or more planes within the thickness of the wall, and thereby doing something to convince the observer that the wall had thickness, was solely due to neo-classical feeling. It too was found at most levels: on important houses like Aston Hall, Oswestry, and Pell Wall and on small ones like the Priory, Wellington, Sheinton Manor, and Allatt's School, Shrewsbury. Associated with it was the practice of recessing the entry. In its simplest form, as at Malinslee Hall, the doorway was merely set within the same sort of recess as the windows. At its grandest—at Woodhouse, and on a lesser scale at Decker Hill, at Chetton Grange, and at Brockton House, Sutton Maddock—the doorway is set behind columns *in antis*. Urban examples are Robert

Smirke's Shirehall (1834–7) and the early 19th-century refurbishing of College Hill House, Shrewsbury. Perhaps the most ingenious use is at the Old Rectory at Church Stretton, where the entrance is now set between two earlier projecting chimney stacks sited symmetrically near the centre of the elevation. The doorway is flanked by columns which are, in fact, proud of the wall, but which give the effect, in relation to the stacks, of being *in antis*. Most striking of all are Shellbrook Hill, Dudleston, where the doorway is set back within a very deep recess outlined by a bold semicircular arch rising well into the first floor, and Aston Hall, Church Aston, where the recess is framed by a segmental-headed arch that rises to eaves level, a design paralleled on a smaller scale in a house at Hinstock. Something of the same effect, but by the use of a forebuilding, was achieved by Nash at Cronkhill in 1804. The dates of Shellbrook Hill and of Aston Hall are not known but it is unlikely, in view of their more advanced form, that either was influenced by Cronkhill, and indeed Aston Hall, with its tall segmental arch and slight pilasters with incised ornament, has more than a hint of Soane.

It was not, however, possible to leave façades wholly unpunctuated and, if openings were not to be used for that purpose, then one alternative was to use pilasters along a front, as they had been used earlier at Cound and elsewhere, but of a very different kind and in a very different manner. Then

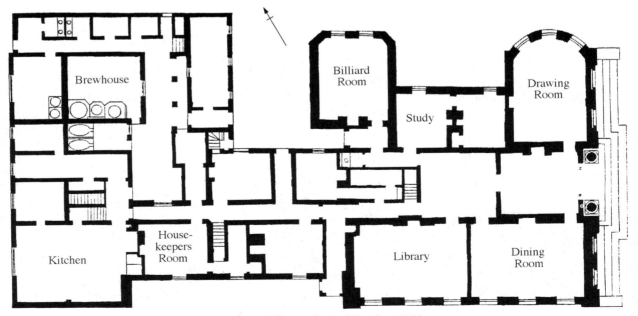

Ground-floor plan of Decker Hill

the pilasters or engaged columns were bold and obtrusive, intended to decorate as well as to punctuate; now they were plain, with caps and bases of ever more debased form and of such slight projection that they became in effect little more than linear markings on the face of the building. In the earlier houses of the time, such as Longford, the pilasters were more in the earlier style and, while plainer than before, were still intended to adorn as well as to punctuate; and at Attingham the attenuated twin pilasters in the centre of the side elevations, unrelated to any horizontal levels, were probably intended to amuse, or to shock in a mild way, as well. At Sweeney Hall near Oswestry, built by J.H. Haycock in 1805, a very plain front was punctuated, and the angles emphasized, by giant Tuscan pilasters. Elsewhere the pilasters were often reduced to little more than raised strips dividing the front into large panels. Examples are numerous, and one may cite medium sized houses such as Hope Court and Totterton Hall, farmhouses like Home Farm, Munslow, suburban villas like Trent House, Chetwynd End, Newport, and buildings of the transport revolution like the octagonal toll house at Montford, where each wall forms a recessed panel between pilaster strips. Most of these are after the turn of the century and, given the ease with which a pilaster strip can be formed in that material, it is not

surprising that most are of brick, sometimes rendered and sometimes not; but one or two are in stone, for example Lower Farm, Cardeston, built of the local breccia which c.1820 in that neighbourhood was coming conspicuously into use for small houses. At Admaston Spa in 1843[108] pilaster strips were chamfered and stopped in the neo-Jacobean manner that was beginning to find favour.

On earlier symmetrical elevations in Shropshire the entrance had usually been emphasized not by any profuse ornament of its own but by its position in an accentuated centrepiece. Given the flat façades of the late 18th century, that device was not much favoured, but when it was, as for instance at Glenyrafon and at Wombridge Farm, no portico or porch was included in the design; nor yet at Aston Hall, Oswestry, where the entrance was flanked by giant fluted pilasters and engaged columns. In most larger houses, however, emphasis was now obtained with imposing boldly projecting temple-like porticoes. They occur in a succession of grand houses, from Woodhouse, where a portico was ingeniously combined with columns *in antis*, through Attingham, where Steuart's attenuated columns gave a Mannerist elegance, to Longford with Tuscan columns, Acton Burnell and Apley Castle with Ionic, Onslow Hall with Greek Doric, and Willey Hall with Corinthian ones. Locally a portico

Trent House, Chetwynd End, Newport, showing use of pilasters

was becoming almost a mark of social standing. Porticoes were added in the late 1780s to Walcot Hall and to Styche Hall 1796–8, and at Millichope Park an impressive hexastyle one was provided for status rather than for use, for it had nothing whatever to do with the entrance, which was in the basement storey. Indeed there seems to have been something of an architectural hierarchy, not as previously in plan form or in type of ornament, but in the way of marking the entry. In contrast with the houses just mentioned, medium sized ones were generally content with a one-storeyed porch, carried of course on classical columns: Corinthian at Lythwood, Tuscan at the Priory, Wellington, Greek Doric at Evelith Manor and at Aston Hall, Aston-on-Clun. Smaller houses generally had not even a porch, or at least not until later years when porches, or if necessary porticoes, became almost obligatory and were added, often insensitively, to houses such as Pell Wall and Aston Hall, Oswestry, that were better off without them.

Temple-like porticoes were nothing new in the country at large in the late 18th century, however unknown in Shropshire until then. Nor yet were bay windows that rose the full height of the elevation through two or three storeys: they had occurred at Linley Hall (1742) and at Pritchard's Tern Hill (1759 onwards). In semicircular form, and as the central and only emphasis along a front, they occurred at Buntingsdale (c.1719–23) and Woodhouse (1773–4);[109] and they are, or were, enriched at Willey Hall with engaged columns, at Pell Wall with Soane's incised ornament, and at Leaton Knolls with a low semicircular colonnade. Such a use was very much a mark of grandeur, however, and more usually there were two set near the ends of a long garden elevation, as at Adderley, or flanking the doorway of a short entrance elevation as at Ashford Carbonell and as contrived at Betton House, Norton-in-Hales. They were also employed, and in both ways, on very small houses, as for example the Old Rectory, Ightfield; but in that context they are perhaps better thought of as picturesque rather than neo-classical.

The architecture of Enlightenment: Greek Revival

It was said earlier that aesthetic trends in this period were complex and intermingled, and some of the examples discussed above could have been viewed from a different angle and, in particular, seen as aspects of the Greek Revival. Decker Hill, for example, and Aston Hall, Church Aston, have the incised ornament of Soane's idiosyncratic version of Greek and could be seen as neo-classical; Longford Hall, on the other hand, with its Tuscan columns to the portico and its figured frieze in the hall has Grecian qualities over and above neo-classical. There were also eccentricities: Astley House has a late 18th-century block that was later given a Doric porch and giant Corinthian columns on the upper storeys and was linked by a screen to pavilions in the form of Greek temples with Doric columns *in antis*. And the commonest manifestations of the movement in Shropshire were the Greek columns and entablatures ornamenting innumerable doorways and porches in town streets: in Shrewsbury, Crescent Place (16-20 Town Walls) and 1-8 Claremont Bank are good instances.

Since most of the buildings that architects were then erecting were country houses designed for social and climatic conditions far removed from those of classical Greece, and since neo-classicism had already brought about an austerity of style, the Revival was generally little more than a matter of clapping Greek elements on to a native structure, even of red brick as at Oakly Park. It was best suited to monuments and to public buildings rather than to private houses, and the first important occasion of its use in the county was in 1814 at Shrewsbury, when an enormous Doric column on a high podium was set up to commemorate Lord Hill's military achievements in the Peninsula. It had been the subject of a national competition, won in the end by Edward Haycock, then only 24 years old. Haycock had to submit to the guidance of Thomas Harrison of Chester in the construction of the Column, presumably to reprimand him for his impudence in winning such a prize at such an age, but it must have made his reputation locally, and perhaps more widely.[110]

It is indeed Haycock himself who is the most striking aspect of the Revival in Shropshire. For the first time since the appearance of the architectural profession most of the examples of a fashionable style in the countryside, and many in the county town, were the work of a Shropshire man. Haycock had the luck to come at exactly the right moment.

1-8 Claremont Bank, Shrewsbury, showing the use of Greek columns and entablatures

Earlier men—Pritchard, Bromfield, Carline, and Haycock's own father—had laid the basis for, if they had not quite established, an architectural profession in Shrewsbury; the level of general and aesthetic education in the county was high enough for the works of the leading London architects to be known and appreciated; and the railways had not yet made it possible for those architects to exercise that minute supervision of building operations on the client's behalf which was now beginning to distinguish the professional architect from the tradesman-builder.[111] There is a very clear illustration of the last point at Aston Hall, Oswestry. James Wyatt's involvement there came to very little more than providing elevations and plans and having a couple of discussions at Aston and in London with the owner and his representative. All the other functions that were coming to be demanded of the architect, even to the extent of radical modifications of Wyatt's original plan, had to be decided on and carried through by a man on the spot.[112] When Edward Haycock appeared with a local base and connections provided by his father, with a London training under Jeffry Wyatt, and with a considerable

talent which he had an early opportunity to demonstrate, he quickly became the leading exponent in the county of the new style. Between 1814 and 1840 he was responsible for three of the four major Greek Revival houses in the county whose architect is known and for four of the six major public buildings in the county town in like case. In contrast, between 1714 and 1814 three out of every four major commissions obtained by known architects had gone to men from outside the county, and between Pritchard's death in 1777 and Haycock's national success in 1814 four out of every five went to London men. To some extent these figures are subjective, for opinions about 'importance' may differ and, if one includes 'minor' works, then the proportion of local successes goes up; but not all that much and not in a way that can alter the significance of Edward Haycock's part in the Greek Revival within his own county.

Despite the publicity which accompanied the erection of the Column at Shrewsbury the Revival in Shropshire got off to a slow start. Haycock began the remodelling of Onslow Hall in 1815 and C.R. Cockerell that of Oakly Park in 1819, but it was not until the mid 1820s that the movement got fully under way with Leaton Knolls,[113] the Salop Infirmary in Shrewsbury of 1827–30,[114] Millichope Park of 1835–40,[115] and the Music Hall in Shrewsbury of 1839,[116] all by Haycock, together with the Butter Market built in 1835 at the Shrewsbury Canal's Howard Street terminus and designed by Fallows & Hart of Birmingham. Of the four country houses listed above, Onslow and Oakly Park are known to be remodellings of late 18th-century houses and Leaton Knolls had all the looks of one, and it is probably for that reason that at all three the Greek element is (or was) little more externally than a display of Greek Doric columns: at Onslow fluted columns in a two-storey tetrastyle portico; at Oakly Park, where Cockerell was demonstrating his learning, plain ones copied from the temple of Apollo at Delos and arranged in two one-storey porticoes; and at Leaton Knolls fluted again in a one-storey hexastyle portico along the entrance front and in a low colonnade around a two-storey semicircular bay window on the garden front.

At Millichope, however, where the old timber-framed house was completely swept away and where the Ionic temple of 1770 by George Steuart suggests that some landscaping had already been carried out, Haycock produced a highly original design. The conventional hexastyle portico of the principal floor had no function except to deceive, and to play its part in integrating the house with the landscape. The entrance, approached through an artificial gorge, was in the basement storey and was flanked by cyclopean Tuscan columns *in antis* intended to be of overpowering effect—a composition that one would expect to see in a visionary's portfolio rather than on solid earth (see illustration on p.193).[117] That basement storey has now been suppressed, and one has to rely on other men's judgements of its success or failure; but it shows that Haycock was well aware of the essentially romantic nature of the Greek Revival. At the same time the interiors of all these houses combine Grecian elements with the dramatic spatial effects of neo-classicism, having top-lit halls, with impressive first-floor galleries and classical arcading, reached unexpectedly either from a smaller lower entrance room or vestibule or, as at Millichope, by a stairway from the entrance in the basement—a device paralleled in Shropshire (hunting lodges

apart) only at Linley Hall. At the same time there is considerable variation among them, for their interpretations of Greek differ: Doric at Leaton Knolls; Ionic at Millichope; Ionic again at Oakly Park, but again of recondite derivation; and at Onslow an almost Soanean composition with the capitals of the arcading reduced to vestigial imposts.

From the early 19th century public buildings, both official and unofficial, began to proliferate. What was perhaps the most important of them, Sir Robert Smirke's Shirehall at Shrewsbury, had very little of the Revival about it. Other important buildings in the town, however, the Salop Infirmary and the Music Hall, were both Greek in character, the former with a two-storey Doric portico and giant Doric pilasters and the latter with a giant attached Ionic portico. Outside Shrewsbury perhaps only Ellesmere town hall needs to be considered. Apart from its windows there is little specifically Greek about it, but the great overhanging pediment of the

The Doric portico entrance to the Butter Market, Howard Street, Shrewsbury

façade and the overhanging eaves above the side walls give it an air of the Revival. The most significant of all the public buildings in the style, however, is the Butter Market at the canal terminus in Howard Street, Shrewsbury. Its great Doric portico, though notable in itself, is even more so for being only a façade to a vast aisled hall standing above a vaulted basement storey and with its roof carried on tall cast-iron columns: a forerunner of many other buildings of the Transport Revolution and a commentary on the admiration for an earlier, and supposedly stable, society by the leaders of one that was being hurried into an unknown future.

Interior decoration

The architectural historian, unless he knows himself to be infallible, must always be haunted by the fear that, in the absence of documentation, he may mistake for a period piece what is an innocent copy or a deliberate forgery by a later age; or that he may make the opposite error. That danger is greatest when discussing 18th-century interior decoration, both because interiors are very susceptible to modernizing or archaizing fashions, which may leave no trace of what was there before,[118] and because later craftsmen have found that century the most satisfying to imitate. Earlier centuries, in contrast, have less often been successfully plagiarized and the apparently early 16th-century ceiling at Plaish, for example, with its monogram of Henry VIII, must arouse the suspicions of any reasonably well informed observer who has the opportunity to examine it carefully; and there was no published reference to it before the 20th century.[119] Again, the saloon at Halston, alleged to be by Robert Mylne, is such a surprisingly pre-Adam piece of Adamesque that it must make any student uneasy; and with good cause, for documents show it to be a product of the 1920s. But few would suspect, in the absence of documents, that the staircase at Halston and the panelling in the dining room there, which fit their positions perfectly and appear to be splendid examples of their period, are also of the 1920s.[120] These are intimations of potential error which need always to be borne in mind, and nowhere more than in the discussion which follows.

The change discussed above—from highly ornamented exteriors with bold decorative elements to plain or only slightly ornamented façades relying for their effects on architectural form—was paralleled in interiors. Very few of the early-to-mid century are as profusely and as heavily decorated as the saloon at Hawkstone, but that may perhaps be taken as the standard that the rest aspired to. That room, of c.1740 and variously attributed to Kent and Flitcroft, has a coved and painted ceiling with stucco relief in the centre, a modillioned cornice and a frieze with acanthus ornament and medallions, large panels with heavy eared surrounds on the walls, and doorways with eared architraves, deep cornices, scrolled brackets, and pediments. The chimney piece has cherubs' heads on the jambs of the fireplace opening, an overmantel flanked by terms, a broken pediment enclosing a bust, and, in the frieze above the whole, medallions, musical instruments, and bunches of fruit; all is embellished with much gold leaf. The effect is rich; indeed, if it had been carried out for men of lesser rank than the Hills of Hawkstone, it would probably have been thought vulgarly pretentious. At any rate later houses were to show more restraint.

The first step in that direction is seen in the plasterwork at Shipton and Lutwyche, considered earlier to be perhaps of the 1740s. Ornament there is still profuse and widely spread over walls and ceilings, but it is thin in comparison with Hawkstone's and allows much space to remain blank. At Shipton the ceiling has a central sunburst within a thinly outlined panel, and above the fireplace there is an achievement of arms with mantling (see illustration overleaf). At Lutwyche the exuberant decoration on the overmantel and above the doorways is light and has a hint of chinoiserie about it.[121] In the 1760s at Walcot, where the drawing-room ceiling was divided into panels by the beams of the earlier 16th-century building, each panel had a plain central roundel with quarter roundels in the corners. Almost simultaneously, at Hatton Grange the dining room was given elaborate plaster work but lightly carried out and with a *mélange* of Gothick and rococo elements. As the centrepiece of the main wall a trophy, not of arms but of 'Tools with the comely names', symbolized the agriculture that ultimately paid for it. In the dining room of c.1780 at Oakly Park, untouched by Cockerell,[122] there was no other plasterwork than a central spray upon the ceiling and a thin wreath of foliage around it. Even at Attingham, built to be the most impressive house in the county, although there is a great amount of plasterwork, it is lightly, even fancifully, carried out, whether in important rooms like the hall and dining room or in small informal ones like the Round room or the Octagon room. In J.H. Haycock's refurbishing of Acton Reynald c.1800 the plaster ornament is both light and sparse. Instances may be multiplied at all social levels, and one may compare Mylne's elegant central roundel in the dining room at Woodhouse[123] with the very similar, nearly contemporary, but slightly provincial one in the staircase hall at Ford Mansion.

Other media underwent similar changes. Heavy fluted pilasters flanking doorways or chimney pieces lingered beyond the mid century, as in a first-floor room at Morville Hall and in the hall at Sibdon Carwood. Generally, however, woodwork became very plain. Columns and pilasters might still be used to integrate a wall surface, as at Attingham, but they were light and graceful. Wall panelling did not disappear but was generally limited to a dado which, as time went on, became ever shallower. Moreover, technical advances developed new coverings, or cheaper ways of producing old ones like wallpaper, which could be more easily changed or discarded to keep up with the whims of fashion. Doorways lost their pedimented heads and elaborate architraves, and door surrounds were given the simple and easily repeated reed moulding of Sweeney Hall, the plain sunk panels of Aston Hall, Oswestry, or the sunk panels with a Greek fret of Haycock's work at Acton Reynald.

Nowhere was the new manner more clearly apparent than on chimney pieces. For two centuries the fireplace, and especially the overmantel, had been the most important object of decoration in any room. In the saloon which Pritchard added to Shipton Hall in the mid century the overmantel is still highly ornamented and two probably contemporary overmantels at Broseley Hall and another at

Reception room from the east at Shipton Hall, showing the use of plasterwork

Sibdon Carwood are still given considerable emphasis. Nevertheless it is arguable that as early as the hall at Lutwyche, and in the dining room at Hatton Grange where the overmantel is only one centre of interest among others, there are clear signs of the coming change. By the end of the third quarter of the century it was there beyond doubt. It is always possible that what appears to be an early specimen because it is in an early house has in fact replaced an original and wholly different predecessor, but it seems very likely that the fireplaces on the first floor at Hatton Grange can be safely considered coeval with the building. By the 1780s, even at Attingham, a piece which retained considerable decoration around the fireplace opening would have nothing above it but a plain surround to frame a picture. And by the 1790s even the decoration around the opening had become plain, and often severe. A chimney piece at Longford has urns with the Leeke family crest flanking the opening; at Aston Hall, Oswestry, openings are flanked by slender Ionic columns in thin vertical strips of black and white marble; and coloured marble was used in a restrained manner on the fireplaces in the remodelled Styche Hall of 1796–8.[124] At Hopton Court plain Doric columns flanking the opening are the only decoration of any kind on some fireplaces. So much was restraint and plainness the rule that the fireplace with sunk panels in the surrounds that was formerly in the boardroom at the starkly plain and functional Morda workhouse of 1791–2 would not have looked out of place in the drawing room of a contemporary country house.

Like overmantels, staircases had been bearers of prodigious ornament since the 16th century, and like them they succumbed to the new taste, most obviously in the elimination from most great houses of ornately carved or turned wooden balusters in favour of iron ones. No doubt that was facilitated by the advances of the Industrial Revolution, but only in the sense that craftsmen now had the techniques, the skill, and the material to produce in metal at an acceptable cost more delicate and elegant forms than timber of the same strength was susceptible of. Wooden balusters were from the mid century onwards relegated on the whole to minor houses or, as at Hopton Court, to servants' quarters, and were plain with Tuscan column newels and with plain or only slightly ornamented cheeks to the risers. The

iron balustrading assumed a number of forms, sometimes with wholly plain balusters, or crocketted at the top as at Cronkhill, or more elaborately decorated as at Berrington Hall and Onslow, but always with a slim outline and an air of lightness. At Cound c.1800 a wholly free-standing staircase of iron, rising through three storeys, was inserted into the hall. Its main members are hidden by timber cladding in the form of classical columns and it stands in a restricted space, but it gives a delicate, insubstantial, almost cobweb effect, that no stone or timber stairway could begin to match. It was never copied in any other great house,[125] probably because its qualities were too advanced for contemporary taste, which wanted the reassurance that beneath all its Greek and Gothic fantasies and neo-classic elegance there were solid foundations both material and social.

Of the craftsmen who carried out all this work little is known for certain. Roger Eykyn, a Staffordshire man, may have carved the doors at Chambers's Styche Hall (1760–4), and Sefferin Alken was employed as a carver at Chambers's other Shropshire house, Walcot. The plasterers Thomas Collins and his teacher William Wilton were also at Walcot, and in the same year (1765) they were also at Linley Hall, More. The plasterwork at Hatton Grange may perhaps be attributed to the Italian, Francesco Vassali, on the ground of its likeness to that at Hagley (Worcs.), and the medallions at Mawley Hall are identical with those known to be by him at Towneley Hall,[126] Burnley (Lancs.). Architects often used the same (satisfactory) craftsmen at many houses, as Chambers used Thomas Collins; and the certain connection between Francis Smith and Vassali at Sutton Scarsdale (Derb.) and the probable connection at Mawley Hall make it not unlikely that Vassali worked at several Shropshire houses—not all by Smith: Professor Gomme gives reasons for attributing some of the decoration in the saloon at Hawkstone Hall to Vassali and his compatriots, Giuseppe Artari and Francesco Serena.[127] The identification of a craftsman at a building may occasionally be a clue to the identification of the architect. The fact that Thomas Collins, who worked widely for Chambers and was later one of his trustees and executors, was at Walcot and at nearby Linley Hall at the time when his employer was remodelling the former makes it not implausible that the ornament of the saloon and the balustrading of the main staircase at the latter are from designs by Chambers.

The variety in decorative styles throughout the period was perhaps more obvious than significant. At Attingham Steuart followed French fashions and also used paint lavishly; at Longford Bonomi set a figured frieze around the hall, probably inspired by that on the Parthenon, and decorated the staircase with painted roundels of the Seasons; at Longner Nash put up an elaborate fan vault; and at Oakly Cockerell copied the frieze of the Battle with the Amazons from the temple of Apollo at Bassae. Often elements of different styles rubbed shoulders in the same house or in the same room. Pritchard's Gothic and classic ornament side by side at Hatton Grange may perhaps be regarded as merely another instance of the mid century's half-serious flirtation with the Gothic, but at Sundorne Castle in the 1820s a typical mid 18th-century staircase with turned

balusters was allowed to remain in a would-be Gothic great hall. At Oteley Park at much the same time cusping and crenellated newel posts ornamented an imperial staircase. The detail itself mattered less than the architectural forms to which it was applied and the spatial tricks that could be played.

A favourite device was a classical arcade to create an illusion of length and open a vista. A notable instance is at Woodhouse, where an Ionic arcade between the entrance and staircase hall half screens and wholly reveals the imposing imperial staircase. A similar effect was intended in J.H. Haycock's plans for refurbishing Moreton Corbet Castle. At Longford, where the hall has a figured Greek frieze, an arcade between hall and staircase hall is crowned by a pediment as though it were the entrance to a temple. The picture gallery of 1806 at Attingham has its cast-iron glass roof terminated at one end upon an arcade, beyond which a darker

Entrance hall from the south-east, Longford Hall

The staircase at Longford Hall

oval,[128] and the same form is repeated in the vestibule and in the staircase hall. Swan Hill House, Shrewsbury, has a similar oval room with doorways fitting the curve of the walls. Again the bastions of the Citadel at Hawkstone and the engaged round tower at Cronkhill created curved spaces in the rooms within. Before Cockerell began work at Oakly in 1818, a precursor had already introduced a circular vestibule and probably apses to the study and library. At Hopton Court the library anticipated on a smaller scale the arrangement at Willey, and the dining room, drawing room, staircase hall, and study there all managed to avoid being rectangular, the vestibule alone defeating the architect's ingenuity.

This sense of movement is particularly noticeable on staircases. The progression of a typical early or mid 18th-century stair, proceeding in easy flights in right angle turns, was largely abandoned for stairs, often cantilevered out from the wall, which swept in an elegant unbroken curve up to the next floor. In the restricted halls of lesser men, as at Glanyrafon, Cronkhill, and the Priory, Wellington, such staircases saved valuable space, but they occurred in large houses as well and nowhere more magnificently than at Willey Hall, which has a double staircase with the flights uniting on the first floor; or more dramatically (one may suppose) than at the now demolished Apley Castle newly designed by Joseph Bromfield in 1792–4,[129] with its top-lit oval staircase. Even on staircases where the treads turned at right angles, as at Aston Hall, Oswestry, and Onslow Hall, or where they were canted, as at Oakly, the iron balustrading, dispensing with newels, and the handrail, sweeping in a continuous curve around the angles, produced a similar effect.

The same liking for flowing curves is seen again in the use of segmental arches for ceilings and above alcove recesses. On exteriors this fashion generally appeared in the form of the so called 'Wyatt window', tripartite like a Palladian one and as wide, but with an overall segmental head instead of a semicircular head above the middle light. In Shropshire it generally occurs in small houses like the Priory, Wellington, and Chorley Hall, Stottesdon. Internally, on the other hand, the usage was largely confined to the great, and the finest examples are the ceilings in the library at Willey, the music room at Millichope, and the vestibule at

solid-roofed space gives further and not wholly fathomed length to the room. At Hopton Court the dining room was divided from a buffet area in the same way: a fashion common in the country as a whole but not much seen in Shropshire. That usage culminated in those top-lit halls referred to earlier, at Willey and at Oakly for example, in the conversion (probably by Edward Haycock) of the former courtyard at Aldenham into just such a hall, and above all at Haycock's Millichope, where vistas were created in three dimensions.

At the same time, in place of the almost invariably rectangular spaces of earlier houses, with each wall at right angles to its neighbour, curves were introduced to give variety to rooms and to create an impression of movement. The great bow windows which punctuated such neo-classical fronts as those of Woodhouse and Longford served also to enliven the interiors. In the library at Willey the arc of the bow window is reflected at the opposite end of the room, producing a straight-sided

Oakly. The segmental arch also occurs above recesses, as in the library at Aldenham. The staircase at Cound has such an arch in the soffit of the landing and incorporated in the iron tracery of the framework. In the stair hall at Longford it helps, in conjunction with the pendentives of the lantern and the painted roundels on the walls, to produce a starkly neo-classical effect (see illustrations on previous pages).

At Belswardine Hall, near Cressage, there are coloured French panoramic wallpapers from a set of 32 published probably in 1814 or earlier and entitled '*Les Français en Egypte*'. They commemorate the French victory at Heliopolis in 1800 and consist mainly of realistic battle scenes. Very few wallpapers survive from an early period and these, apart from two panels in the Castle Museum at York, are probably the only ones of this set in the country.[130]

Shropshire architecture and the early Industrial Revolution

It is acknowledged everywhere, except of course in Cornwall, that Shropshire was the cradle of the Industrial Revolution, and it is therefore necessary to discuss the effect of that pre-eminence on the architecture of the county. What is at issue is not the effect of industrialization in general, but of that aspect that is primarily associated with Coalbrookdale and the Severn Gorge. Its most immediately striking aspect was the use of iron as a building material, symbolized, in its earliest and most breathtaking manifestation, by the Iron Bridge of 1777-80. Of at least equal importance, as the first wholly iron framed building, is Charles Bage's flax mill of 1796–7 in the Shrewsbury suburb of Ditherington. It never had any architectural graces, but a structure of five regularly fenestrated storeys nearly 200ft. long was massively and symbolically impressive. Iron framing was also used in the warehouse at Ditherington, completed by June 1805, and in the flax mill in Castlefields, Shrewsbury, built about the same time.[131] Iron was also used structurally in the columns supporting the galleries at All Saints' (1790), Wellington, commended by Bishop Cornwallis for their 'superior lightness',[132] and at new St. Chad's (1790–2), Shrewsbury, and St. Leonard's (1804–5), Malinslee. The roof of the picture gallery contrived at Attingham by Nash was also carried on iron columns, and so too was that of

the vast aisled structure of the Butter Market in Howard Street, Shrewsbury. The probably unique free-standing iron-framed staircase at Cound, was discussed above. Also unique, as far as is known, is the 'Iron House' in Hopton Wafers, a small cottage with a roof of iron plates fastened together to give a semicircular cross section.[133] More widespread examples of the use of iron are the cast-iron tracery at St. Alkmund's (1794–5), Shrewsbury, the many iron frames, lintels, and sills of windows in small houses,[134] and the iron columns of porches and shop fronts and those supporting the inserted galleries in many older churches. That such early and striking instances of the use of iron should occur in Shropshire, and especially in those parts within easy reach of the works on the Severn and the Tern, is obviously to be attributed to the precocious development of the iron industry there,[135] but, despite their interest, their effect on the architecture of the county as a whole, or even of the mid-Severn valley, is not very great; it is indeed minimal, if one compares it with the effects of the change from timber to brick in the years around 1700.

Of more importance are the indirect results of early industry, the least indirect of those being the erection of industrial buildings and houses to accommodate the works and their working population. Of the first little can be said, for little has survived from an early period and what may be gleaned from illustrations suggests that they were mainly agglomerations of *ad hoc* structures of different ages and of various kinds—historically important not for what they looked like but for what they sheltered. The larger houses that survive, and such public buildings as the Tontine Hotel and the market buildings (of the 1780s and 1790s) at Ironbridge,[136] are in themselves no different from contemporaries elsewhere, and again they are important not for what they are but for where they are. Perhaps of most significance are the terraces of small houses, the earliest known, Nailers' Row, Dale End, dating from the 1730s or earlier.[137] Such terraces, of one and a half or two storeys, with one ground-floor room or with a main room and a small service room, were not uncommon in several towns by then. In the Trinity area at Frome (Som.) and at Whitehaven (Cumb.) they survive in large numbers from the late 17th and early 18th centuries, and the earliest recorded examples in England, at Great

Yarmouth (Norf.) and of the early or mid 17th century, survived the Second World War.[138] All of these, however, were treated essentially as burgage tenements with a plot of ground of some size at the rear: about 100ft. long at Frome, and of considerable length even on the restricted site of the Rows at Great Yarmouth. It is not wholly clear what happened at Nailers' Row, though it would appear to have been built on a very narrow plot, but when Schoolhouse Row was put up in Coalbrookdale in the 1790s the houses originally had no back door, nor did some at least of those in Carpenters' Row of shortly after 1783.[139] At Newdale, a mining settlement between Wellington and Dawley, a row of back-to-back houses had been erected by 1794, and in the northern part of the coalfield, at Lilleshall and Donnington Wood for example, long lines of single-storey 'barrack houses' were put up.[140] The erection of rows of dwellings in the manner of almshouses, with no land attached, suggests that here, totally unlike the situation at Frome and elsewhere, a shelter from the elements was being provided—and nothing more; that the accommodation was intended for wage earners and not for artisans or (as perhaps at the superior Tea Kettle Row, Coalbrookdale, of the 1740s)[141] for specialist craftsmen or supervisors. Crowded into a narrow valley these terraces helped, in conjunction with the furnaces, forges, mills, and railways, to produce that unique and satanic picture that so impressed contemporaries.[142]

It was not of course lack of space which determined the amount of accommodation in these dwellings nor yet inexperience of the problems of housing industrial workers, but the need to build cheaply for men whose wages allowed nothing better. In the 1830s or 1840s Double Row, Dawley, a terrace of back-to-backs in 9-in. brick, was built for the workers of the Hinkshay furnaces. The better houses had on the ground floor a living room 13 x 12ft. and a smaller room, probably a pantry, with the stairway in it; on the first floor was a main bedroom and a landing bedroom. The majority, built to the same dimensions, were one-up-and-one-down[143] and showed no advance on the late 17th-century limestone worker's cottage identified at Church Aston.[144]

The even more indirect effects on architecture of the wealth created by the early Industrial Revolution are very difficult to estimate. One may reasonably ascribe the houses of successful ironmasters to that source, instancing the Darbys' Dale House (1715–17) and Sunniside (1750–1) in Coalbrookdale;[145] New House (later The Lawns), Broseley, built for Thomas Stephens in 1727 and remodelled for John Wilkinson in the 1760s; and Thomas Botfield's Hopton Court (remodelled for his eldest son and namesake after 1806) and Malinslee Hall (probably of the 1790s).[146] To those one may add St. Leonard's church (1805), Malinslee, and St. George's (1806), Pain's Lane (near Oakengates), for which ironmasters and their ground landlords were largely responsible.[147] It is also probable that many of the medium sized houses of the area, such as Belmont House, Ironbridge, and the Grange in Coalbrookdale, were the homes of men connected in some way with industry. But to what extent some of the most architecturally important houses of the neighbourhood are to be attributed to that source is a different matter. The Foresters (with Willey Hall by Lewis Wyatt), Isaac Hawkins Browne (with Badger Hall by James Wyatt), the Charltons (whose additions to Apley Castle were by Joseph Bromfield), the Leveson-Gowers (with Lilleshall House by Wyatville), and the Slaneys (with Hatton Grange by Pritchard) were all either investing directly in the Shropshire iron and coal industry and the associated transport undertakings, or were leasing concessions to industrialists. To that extent all were building with industrially generated wealth.[148] Yet it is unlikely that any of them then drew a major, or even a large, proportion of his income from that source, and at the same time it is difficult to see any element of their houses which distinguished their architecture from that of other men of similar status or wealth unconnected with industry. On the whole it is probable that early industry affected Shropshire architecture only slightly, creating a new kind of architectural environment in the limited area of the Severn Gorge and the east Shropshire coalfield and perhaps allowing a few grand houses in the immediate neighbourhood to be grander than they would otherwise have been.

Urban houses

From *c.*1700 enough urban dwellings have survived in Shropshire to allow something to be said about the commonest type of house. Medieval urban houses, by contrast, are so few, so altered, and so multifarious that one may do little more than list some documented, known, or surmised examples: the shop of *c*.1240—with dimensions of 14 x 6ft. and with permission to build a solar above—in Shrewsbury market place;[149] the cruck hall in Corve Street, Ludlow, mentioned in 1297;[150] in Shrewsbury the stone-built merchants' houses in Pride Hill and—perhaps contemporary with them and likewise standing behind tenements and shops fronting the street—Stury's Hall between High and Fish streets, another stone house[151] of high status;[152] the stone mansions of the Cheneys in Ludlow and of the Charltons and Vaughans in Shrewsbury;[153] the earlier-15th-century box-framed open hall (restored in 1977 to something like its original appearance) behind a three-storey early 17th-century block fronting the street as 53 Broad Street, Ludlow; the King's Head (*1403–4), Mardol, Shrewsbury, with a box-framed hall open to the roof for perhaps the first century of its existence; and the great 15th-century blocks—shops with living accommodation above, probably built as speculations—such as that (*1403-4) on the corner of King and Broad streets, Ludlow, and the Abbot's House (*1458), Butcher Row, Shrewsbury.[154] In the course of the 16th and 17th centuries most of the elements of these houses were superseded by others: stone and timber gave way to brick,[155] the open hall was eliminated,[156] and the large blocks that had no necessary connection between the occupiers of the shops and of the accommodation above were no longer built, while in their place premises for shopkeepers living 'over the shop' became standard, though in varying forms. Among the earliest recorded houses of men apparently of a lower social level were 1-4 Scotland Street, Whitchurch, now demolished; built as a terrace probably in the late 17th century, each was of 1$\frac{1}{2}$ storey, with a main ground-floor room 14 x 10ft., a smaller rear room, and corresponding rooms above. Even here there was some distinction, nos. 3-4 having slightly larger rear rooms than 1-2.[157]

An enduring element was the entry from outside into the end of a 'hall' which was the largest room in the house. In Ludlow 17 Broad Street was given just such a plan as late as 1704, as was Dinham House probably a dozen years later.[158] In their styles town houses were much the same as those in the

countryside, except that Artisan Mannerism appears occasionally in urban contexts: some in Shrewsbury and Bridgnorth have already been noticed.[159]

By the end of the 18th century the streets of most Shropshire towns were acquiring that overall 'Georgian' look which characterized southern and midland country towns until the Town and Country Planning Acts of the mid 20th century gave Development a free hand in the name of Conservation. That uniformity was brought about in part by the building of many new houses and in part by the rebuilding or re-fronting of many old ones. Often the rebuilding was a social transformation as well, a workaday street or area changing its character and its name. In Shrewsbury Swine Market Hill became St. John's Hill[160] and was developed into rows of elegant houses. Many of the developers were local tradesmen, not necessarily in the building trades. One of them who has been studied in detail was William Harrold, an immigrant from Birmingham, described at first as a cutler, later as a wool merchant. In 1740 he and another man took a 99-year building lease of a Swan Hill site occupied by two houses to be demolished; Harrold built, and lived in, what is now 2 Swan Hill. Then in 1762, having evidently prospered, he took another building lease of the site of several ruinous houses at the top of St. John's Hill on condition of erecting three substantial houses there; he moved into one of them in 1765 and sold the other two leaseholds in 1768. As usual the leases imposed strict building specifications on the developer.[161]

7 Mill Street, Ludlow

Like their medieval predecessors the individual houses varied greatly in size and splendour and catered for many classes of men or levels of wealth, and the most prominent were still those of important local landowners. Dinham House, Ludlow, the town residence successively of Richard Knight of Downton, of Thomas Johnes of Croft Castle, and of the earl of Powis, was enlarged in the course of the century to the size of a small country house,[162] and Swan Hill Court, Shrewsbury, built for the earl of Bath in 1764, was a country house brought into the town. Both of these stood rather apart from other houses. More of a truly urban dwelling was the great seven-bay house 7 Mill Street, Ludlow, readier to rub shoulders with its neighbours and built for the Baldwin family, not quite in the class of my lords

Powis and Bath. The former Judges' Lodging, 6 Belmont, Shrewsbury, built c.1701, is in a similar vein, with an imposing six-bay front, a wide entrance hall running the full depth of the building and flanked by two rooms on each side, a grand main staircase and concealed service stairs set between the front and rear rooms, and services in the basement.[163] Similar again is 12 St. John's Hill, Shrewsbury, with a pilastered front and low flanking wings but on a smaller scale and without the grand staircase and basement services of its near contemporary in Belmont.

Most houses were less grand than these, but many, especially in Ludlow, were built to a similar form with a five-bay front and a central doorway in a symmetrical elevation. One of the earliest and

54-56 Mill Street, Ludlow, with no.55 in the centre showing a four-bay plan with one of the middle bays housing the doorway

217

The Crescent, 22-25 Town Walls, Shrewsbury,
with a detail of the plaster ceiling to the ground-floor south room of no.25

The secondary staircase in no.25 The Crescent,
Town Walls, Shrewsbury,
in the two-storey kitchen

grandest is 14 The Square, Ludlow, built in 1728 for a prominent lawyer, and another, also built for a lawyer, is 41 Mill Street. Smaller than these, but yet with some pretensions, are those four-bay houses where generally the doorway is in a middle bay, entering into a staircase hall which is lit by the window at the end of the elevation, is flanked by a parlour, and leads to service rooms at the rear. An example is 55 Mill Street, Ludlow (see illustration on p.217), built in 1740, along with nos. 54 and 56, as a speculation. Shrewsbury examples are 28 St. John's Hill and 8 Swan Hill Court. A common variant had the doorway in the end bay, but the difference betweeen the four-bay variants and the five-bay houses was of degree rather than kind, as illustrated by 35, 36, and 37 Broad Street, Ludlow, built in the same style, the middle one sharing the French quoins of the others.

All of these earlier houses, including those built in twos and threes, were separate designs, for until the end of the century speculative building in Shropshire had too small a market to produce the typical Georgian terrace of several houses in a unified composition. At 38-38A Lower Street,

Cleobury Mortimer, two double-fronted houses built together achieve a striking symmetry modified only by the bow windows of no. 38, and four of the five contiguous houses at 19-23 St. John's Hill, Shrewsbury, make a symmetrical design, but the effect is lessened by the fifth. The first approach to a terrace was the Crescent (22-25 Town Walls), Shrewsbury, built by Joseph Bromfield c.1790, a block of four houses in which the two at one end mirror the two at the other end and make a whole with them. The stuccoed street front is a competent neo-classical design, and the garden elevation of six storeys with a projecting centrepiece and engaged pilasters is an imposing pile, but the Crescent is most remarkable for the internal lay-out of the houses. Each has a staircase from ground floor to third floor standing free of the side wall and top lit by the resulting gap between wall and stairway. A secondary stair runs from the lower basement through the basement to ground-floor level and, taking advantage of the steeply sloping site, the kitchen is two storeys high in the manner of some country houses and is lit from the area in a metropolitan fashion.

The outstanding Shropshire terrace, 121-4 Abbey Foregate, Shrewsbury (see illustration overleaf), is probably best seen as a neo-classical exercise and, unlike nearly every other urban house in the county of that time, has a front in the finely jointed ashlar of some great houses. In form it is like the Crescent, with the pair of houses at one end mirroring those at the other, but the raising of the roof line of the two middle houses with an attic storey turns it into a composition which might be compared with the tall central block and lower wings of some rural houses of the period. That such was not quite the intent is revealed by the distinctive character of the fenestration. The first-floor window in each end bay of the central block has its sill at a higher level than those of the other windows in the elevation, and in each wing the two first-floor windows nearest the central part are similarly differentiated.[164] As a result the division between the centre and the wings, brought about by their differing heights, is nullified by windows that link the wings to the centre and is flatly contradicted by the difference created between the inner and outer bays of each part. A 'process of dissociation and juxtaposition of parts' is a conspicuous element in

121-4 Abbey Foregate, built of finely jointed ashlar with each pair of end houses mirroring the other. The attic storey of the central two houses mirrors the tall central block and lower wings of some rural houses of the period. Notice the use of windows in unifying the design

neo-classical design and in that respect, and in the tension created between the parts, this terrace is, along with the staircase hall at Longford, the most neo-classical building in the county. That may be the result of having attempted to achieve in a small compass and within the contemporary stylistic idiom the effect of a grand terrace in a major town.

XIV   Public Buildings 1550–1800

The houses of the rich and of the comfortably-off were far and away the most prominent aspect of the architecture of the county between 1550 and 1800, followed at some distance by churches and, trailing a poor third, secular public buildings: almshouses, schools, and civic halls. The proliferation of schools and almshouses as separate institutions with their own buildings was a consequence of the decline of the Church as the main provider of education and dispenser of charity and of the necessity for laymen to play a larger, more direct, and probably more effective part in that work.[1] The majority of these buildings, and even the class as a whole, would hardly be worthy of mention in a brief survey were it not that a few of them are among the most outstanding structures of their time.

Almshouses

Almshouses have survived in greatest numbers and most of them were built to a small scale in the contemporary local idiom. Three of the same date are typical: the earl of Bradford's at High Ercall (1694), Samuel Higginson's at Whitchurch (1698), and Viscountess Dungannon's at St. Martin's (1698). They are all in red brick, of one or one and a half storey, in a single range or on a slight U plan, and with a mildly emphasized centrepiece. There are some of greater pretensions. Trinity Hospital, Clun, was built on a courtyard plan with an imposing gateway in 1618 and Kerr's Almshouses of 1724 at Calverhall were on a U plan with a pedimented centrepiece and with a large chapel occupying one of the wings.[2] Hosier's Almshouses at Ludlow, rebuilt by T.F. Pritchard in 1758–9, are similar in form to those of earlier years but on a larger scale and in the idiom of the time. In contrast, Millington's Hospital, Frankwell, completed in its original form in 1748, is a remarkably Palladian exercise by two local craftsmen.[3]

None of these, however, can stand comparison with the magnificent foundation for 12 women and 12 girls at Preston upon the Weald Moors, endowed by Lady Herbert of Chirbury and her brother Lord Torrington and built between 1716 and 1726.[4] This again is on a U plan, with a main range occupied mostly by a hall, which served also as chapel and schoolroom,[5] and with long wings terminating in originally one-storeyed arcaded quadrants.[6] The west range contained separate apartments for the women, those on the first floor being reached not by the usual separate stairways but by a single staircase and a long corridor. The east range seems to have had a large kitchen and service rooms on the ground floor and a girls' dormitory on the first floor. The walling is in red brick in Flemish bond and the ground floors of the wings are arcaded with rustic surrounds to the arches, giving the courtyard a grand and spacious air. The first-floor windows of the wings have moulded stone surrounds, with a parapet above; the hall has a stone front to the courtyard with rusticated 'Gibbs' windows, a rusticated doorway surmounted by a pediment, giant pilasters, and a balustrade over all. The south end of the courtyard is closed by a wrought-iron screen designed by Robert Bakewell of Derby.[7] Preston hospital is not surpassed in splendour by any other almshouse in the kingdom, was stylistically in advance of any great house in the county, and may well be by James Gibbs or someone in close contact with him.

Schools

It is probable that between 1550 and 1800 more schools than almshouses were founded, but many of them were accommodated in parish churches[8] or existing buildings and have therefore left little architectural evidence. Many were good but modest buildings, like those of timber at Oswestry (c.1600) and Chirbury (1675) or in brick at Cardington (c.1700), the last two containing a schoolmaster's house as well as a schoolroom. Other schools with modest buildings were Adams' grammar school at Wem, founded in 1650, and the schools at Donnington (Wroxeter) and Church Stretton illustrated in early 19th-century drawings.[9] Rather grander were Bowdler's school (1724) in Beeches Lane, Shrewsbury, and Childe's school (1735) at Cleobury Mortimer. The most imposing buildings naturally appeared in the larger towns. From 1639 the master of Bridgnorth grammar school lived in a newly built house provided by Sir William Whitmore of Apley Park. It formed the southernmost part of a long six-bay range, $2\frac{1}{2}$ storeys high, which was the second known brick structure in the town and in the same style as the fashionably up-to-date Governor's House of c.1633. Of the other two houses in the range, each with its own two-storey porch, the central one accommodated the vicar of St. Leonard's, and the northernmost became a boarding house for the school in the 1820s.[10] At the end of the 18th century the same need as at Bridgnorth to provide housing for the teachers as well as a schoolroom was reflected at Allatt's charity school in Murivance, Shrewsbury. It was built by J.H. Haycock in 1799–1800 in the form of a scaled down Palladian mansion: a tall central block, with separate accommodation for a master and mistress, linked by open arcades to lower pavilions housing the boys' and girls' schoolrooms, all in the finely jointed ashlar of the time and in a restrained classical style.

As outstanding among schools, however, as Preston hospital was among almshouses was Shrewsbury school, its original buildings housing the borough library from 1885. It was founded in 1552 and was soon educating not only the sons of leading burgesses and of local and not-so-local gentry but also those of the highest officials of the Council in the Marches of Wales: among its pupils in the 1560s were Fulke Greville and Philip Sidney. In the 1580s it had more pupils than any other school in the country, and its success was reflected in the impressive three-storey ranges built in the 1590s and 1620s.[11] At a time when almost the whole town was, or appeared to be, of timber the school proclaimed its status by the very material— Grinshill stone—in which it was built: stone associated the school with the town's churches and castle,[12] with the borough's mid 15th-century Exchequer tower[13] and market hall of 1596,[14] and with what remained of perhaps half a dozen prestigious houses.[15] When they were new the school buildings dominated the northern end of the town even more than they do now. The earlier, northern, range containing a library and chapel was altered by J.H. Haycock in 1815,[16] but both ranges, linked by a staircase tower, retain much of their original character with mullioned and transomed windows in more or less symmetrical elevations. The later range is distinguished by a central archway flanked by fluted Corinthian columns and two typically stumpy Jacobean statues representing aspiring and successful scholars.

Less grand than Shrewsbury School, but nevertheless a very fine embellishment of a small town is Adams' grammar school (founded 1656), Newport. Much altered in the early 19th century, the school remains an impressive range of buldings.[17] The outstanding quality of its buildings was owed to the immense generosity of the rich London haberdasher William Adams to his native town[18] and probably to the subsequent governance of his foundation by the city Haberdashers' Company.

Market halls

Other public buildings, such as meeting halls and business premises of one kind or another, had always been lay concerns, and the Reformation in itself made little difference to their numbers. What was more to the point was the fading power and prosperity of the guilds and the resultant increase in the building of town and market halls rather than guild halls. In form the three were often indistinguishable from one another, or from earlier examples, and many continued to be built in timber into the early 17th century: the Drapers' Hall of 1560 in Shrewsbury, and the market hall of 1619 at Church Stretton.[19] But a market hall or a town hall often combined the function of covered market and council chamber, and at Much Wenlock in 1577 and at Bridgnorth as late as 1650 the open ground floor was in stone and only the first floor in timber. The very large market hall of 1706 at Ludlow was built wholly of brick with an open ground floor; in later years and up to the mid 19th century the upper floor served as an assembly room.[20] In 1596 the market hall in Shrewsbury, commensurate with the town's unrivalled commercial standing in the county, was built wholly of stone, and later examples of the 18th century were in that material: the Butter Market at Ludlow, designed by William Baker in 1743, the town halls at Bishop's Castle and Broseley, of the 1760s and 1770s respectively, and the Court House at Clun of 1780. At its inception Shrewsbury market hall outfaced any private building in the Square, and the Butter Market at Ludlow terminated the vista up Broad Street in a satisfactorily up-to-date way, but there is little in any of the others—either in their scale or in their humdrum style—which could be seen as a manifestation of municipal pride. A very unusual work is Pritchard's 1774–6 transformation of the 14th-century aisled hall of the Palmers' guild at Ludlow into a court room. He retained the aisled form but discreetly hid the timber of the arcade posts and the magnificent roof behind contemporary panelling and plaster and clad the exterior in brick, giving it a pretty rococo 'Gothick' door case: an amusing commentary on the problems experienced by a purveyor of 'Gothick' when faced with adapting a Gothic building.

County buildings

All the buildings mentioned in the preceding paragraph were urban, not merely in the sense that they were within a town but also because they served the needs of an urban community and were but the latest stage in a long tradition of municipal building.[21] There was no such tradition of county buildings. After the Restoration the county authorities in Shropshire made use of private property (as Shrewsbury Castle had become) until, in 1712, they began to share the Shrewsbury guildhall in the Square. The Shirehall, built on the guildhall site in 1784–6, was a portent of things to come. Following the County Rate Act of 1738, and as part of the solution to the problems that a modern society was creating, a revolution in county administration began in the later 18th century. New tasks, and the more determined prosecution of old ones, would eventually require a more efficient use of resources, including the employment of professional officers and the need to accommodate them and their staffs. But locals were not quick to apprehend the new necessities, for the principal county officers— clerk, treasurer, surveyor—were part-timers, with

staff in their own offices.[22] It was an assize judge who in 1782, provoked by the makeshift courts under the market house, alfresco save for temporary partitions, laid a fine on the county to compel provision of better ones.[23] The resultant Shirehall was a pedimented structure of seven bays in a generally up-to-date style and with giant engaged Ionic columns flanking the three central doorways. In a building of two storeys and a basement, however, those doorways were extremely tall, rising from ground level to first-floor height and giving the main elevation something of an old-fashioned 'market hall' look.[24] An initially accepted design had been quickly rejected[25] in favour of one by Edward or J.H. Haycock,[26] who may not have offered the cheapest contract[27] but were well known in the town. As before, the building was to be both shirehall and borough guildhall,[28] but it did not prove sound.[29] Thomas Telford, good at getting his way with the county magistrates and bullying them into raising their aspirations,[30] had not yet arrived on the scene as county surveyor in 1783,[31] but he was there in 1832–4 to collaborate with Sir Robert Smirke, the architect of a sound and dignified new Shirehall (1833–7) worthy of the local administration that Telford himself had done so much to invigorate.[32]

*   *   *   *   *

Apart from all these there were other public buildings, new not so much in form or function as in the quantitatively greater social problems that they were meant to cope with, and in their consequent greater size. The erection, to a design by T.F. Pritchard, of a branch of the Foundling Hospital at Kingsland, Shrewsbury, in 1760–5 foreshadowed the transition to the modern world, and not less so when, some ten years after its closure c.1774, its building became the Shrewsbury house of industry.[33] Other ominous portents of the modern world were the new county gaol at Shrewsbury and the vast and stark Oswestry house of industry at Morda. The county gaol, of 1787–93, was designed by J.H. Haycock in accordance with John Howard's ideas, but modified by the new county surveyor Thomas Telford.[34] Its heavily rusticated entrance is in the manner of, but not quite so grim as, George Dance's Newgate of 1770: the bastion-like form was perhaps intended to remind contemporaries[35] of the recently demolished massive round towers of the nearby Burgess gate, above which the borough prisoners had long been confined.[36] But for the Revd. Hugh Owen, himself an amateur architect, the gaol's merits were utilitarian rather than aesthetic,[37] and the same attitude may be detected in responses to the Morda workhouse, built 1791–4: it was soon criticized for the 'ostentation and folly' of an exterior which concealed 'the abode of the indigent and wretched'.[38] It was indeed long before some of the other new institutions required by a modernizing society[39] acquired the prestige of specially designed buildings. The Salop Infirmary, a hospital in something like today's sense of that word, had opened in Shrewsbury in 1747.[40] Initial thoughts of a new building,[41] however, had soon been abandoned, and it occupied three converted houses; one, formerly Corbet Kynaston's town house, was 'plain and respectable', but its incongruous union with the other two was held to have produced a 'deformed' elevation,[42] and the Infirmary had to wait until 1827–30 for Edward Haycock's noble Doric building.[43]

XV Domestic Architecture 1830–1900: The Classes and the Masses

Despite the vast amount of church building, secular architecture in this period was at least as important as ecclesiastical. If country houses occupied architects' time proportionately less than before, there were many other buildings brought into existence, directly or indirectly, by the Industrial Revolution; and not only the more obviously industrial structures like foundries, mills, railways, and engineering workshops. There were also large and grandiose market and town halls to cope with a greater volume of trade and increasingly elaborate local administration, and to express civic pride. There were schools and other educational institutions needed by a society which could no longer be served by illiterates: large 'public' schools for the middle classes and smaller, less splendid, ones for urban and rural workers. There were all the other structures, from hospitals to pumping stations, which make a modern town viable. Above all, and in volume probably equalling all the others put together, were the innumerable new urban and suburban dwellings, not only for factory hands but also for those working in businesses and in the ever more necessary and ever expanding professions, such, for example, as that 'army of civil engineers whose ranks increased four-fold between 1841 and 1851'.[1] None of their houses was of much account by itself, but *en masse* and in the suburbs which sprang up around every town of any size they were the most conspicuous objects of all.

The country houses of the wealthy

By the 1830s a decline in the power of the landed nobility and country gentry was evident. Industry, in the sense of the owners of industrial enterprises and their often recalcitrant and always menacing work force, had now to be reckoned with. Repeal of the Corn Laws in 1846 made it clear that in a trial of strength the landed interest could be worsted by the new social forces. Nevertheless, as Engels noted 100 years ago, the industrialists never secured undivided sway, and up to the end of the century most of the great offices of state were held by noble lords or their relations.[2] Landowners thus retained some power but much more place and prestige. Those two foreigners Engels and Taine both commented on the extraordinary deference which even radical manufacturers such as W.E. Forster, for example, paid to the aristocracy.[3] In any case the aim of the new men was not to oust the old rulers but to imitate and join them.[4]

That was perhaps the easier because the distinction between landed and business interests, which had never been as sharp as the landed classes liked to pretend, was blurring rapidly. Aristocratic enterprises and speculations in 'ventures' (not always successful) had multiplied in the 16th and 17th centuries, and the 6th earl of Shrewsbury (d.1590) had been the greatest noble entrepreneur of his day. For centuries aristocrats had swapped landed blood for City money when necessary,[5] and by the middle of the 19th century many landowners were as deeply implicated as any townsman in commerce and industry and in the vast urban expansion which went with them.[6] The fabulous wealth of the marquesses of Westminster (dukes from 1874) and Bute arose far less from their rural estates than from their London and Cardiff properties,[7] and that of the duke of Sutherland and Lord Londonderry from the coalfields of the west midlands and north-east England.[8] Even in Shropshire, where things were on a more modest scale, Lords Bath, Granville, and Forester, and the Charltons (from 1858 Meyricks) of Apley Castle, for example, drew some of their income from estates that were partly urban or industrial.[9] Lord Windsor drew more than half of his from Cardiff ground rents,[10] and the chairman of the company which opened the Hotel at Church Stretton as a speculation in 1865, and later built up a chain of prestigious hotels in other towns, was Sir Charles Rouse-Boughton of Downton Hall.[11] Further, while some landed aristocrats were becoming businessmen, or dependent upon business interests, many business families were becoming aristocratic by marriage or ennoblement. As Housman, with the 'Beerage' in mind, ironically put it:

> Oh many a peer of England brews
> Livelier liquor than the Muse.

By the 1890s the amalgamation of landed, commercial, and industrial wealth, which had been developing throughout the century, was patent. In the most satirical and least appreciated of his operas, Gilbert assumed, or pretended to assume, that the directors of a limited liability company would be 'If possible, all peers and baronets'.[12] The alliance became notorious when several noble lords were embarrassed by the revelation of their unwitting involvement in Terence Hooley's swindles.[13]

In those circumstances, and once large sections of the urban population had been enfranchised (in 1868) and given the secret ballot (in 1872), the opinions and voting intentions of country squires were of less importance than formerly, and their country houses ceased to be centres of landed power with 'back rooms' for election intrigues[14] and became instead houses in the countryside, places of rural recreation for the rich of all kinds.[15] As Taine appreciated, they were 'the houses of rich people who like their comforts and know how to get them'.[16] Architects would no longer 'call the winds thro' long arcades to roar' for, in modern words: 'A magnificent classical enfilade of rooms designed as a sequence to be walked through now seemed pointless and chilly'.[17] What was needed instead was the most convenient arrangement of a number of rooms, each with its own function: hall, morning room, dining room, drawing room, and, where space was available, library, billiard room, and business room. Shropshire was less directly affected by this than some other counties, for the houses of the most important 'interests' from the 18th century

onwards—the Herberts' Oakly Park and the Clives' Walcot and Styche[18]—had been modest by national standards. The change was less one of substituting comfort for grandeur than of abandoning the formal planning of earlier years. This was all the easier because the tyranny of the symmetrical elevation had already been challenged in the 'villas' and other houses of men of little political weight or ambition, and in the admiring nostalgic descriptions by some early 19th-century novelists of old houses which had grown over the years in a rambling irregular form.[19]

As a result country houses generally, whatever their style, were free in their disposition of rooms and irregular in their elevations and sky lines. Within an architectural climate of aversion from classical norms this was the secular equivalent, conditioned by convenience, of the church building of the time, conditioned by clerical pretensions.[20] The Gothic aspect of that choice of elevation is revealed by some of those great houses which still adhered to a symmetrical front—Netley, Stanmore, and Woodcote—for that quality was matched by another: they were generally in styles less favoured at the time:[21] a heavy, somewhat Italianate, classicism at Netley, Second Empire (with a difference) at Stanmore, and a classicized Jacobean at Woodcote. All three styles depended for their effect upon symmetry, and once the style had been chosen that quality followed more or less automatically. Nevertheless, however symmetrical their elevations, the plans of these houses did not differ from the rest, for, although in one way the shackles of earlier planning had been thrown off, and a multiplicity of plan forms had appeared,[22] architects in Shropshire, whether home-grown or imported, still relied heavily on the classic double pile as the core of the house.

Where an earlier smaller house was adapted or added to, as at Tedsmore Hall[23] and Broncroft Castle,[24] the main rooms were arranged within an **L** block, with services in the re-entrant angle or tacked on the end of a wing. Generally, however, reception rooms were grouped compactly within a double pile, and the services, often exceeding the main block in extent, were in wings or blocks at the side or rear. Even when, as at Stokesay Court (1888),[25] the house was built to a Jacobethan **U** plan, the main reception rooms—hall, morning room, dining room,

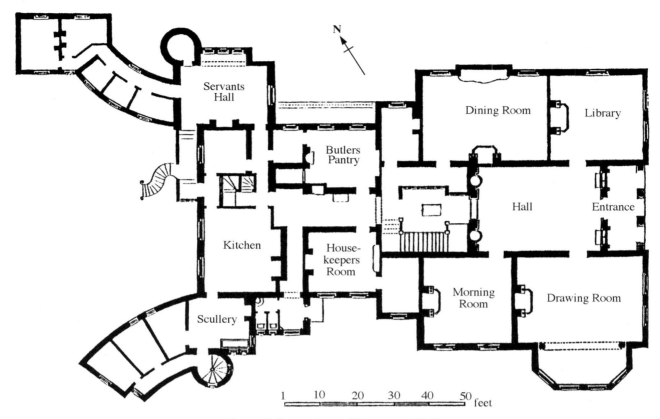

Ground-floor plan of Stanmore Hall

drawing room and anteroom, boudoir, library, and business room—were accommodated in the double-pile main range; a billiard room, card room, and what was probably a smoking room were put into the south wing and services in the north wing and its attached limbs.[26] At Boreatton Park (1854),[27] at Stanmore Hall (1870),[28] and at Bedstone Court (1884)[29] the reception rooms were within a double-pile main block; at Boreatton the services were in a courtyard range to the side, at Stanmore in what amounted to another double-pile block at the rear, and at Bedstone in a huge block at the side. On a sloping site at Cloverley in 1864 Nesfield got all the reception rooms into a comparatively small block by putting the lesser rooms—business room, morning room, and billiard room—on a lower floor, the dining room, drawing room, and library on an upper floor, and the great hall at a mezzanine level between the other two; the service rooms were at one side and in the form of a narrow double pile and an open courtyard.[30]

Thus the planners of mid-to-late 19th-century houses in Shropshire broke away from the norms of the past most clearly in the freer relationships of the rooms within the double-pile block, in the general asymmetry of the elevations, and in the asymmetrical and generally more convenient siting of the services; and on the whole they stuck more closely to the double-pile core than planners elsewhere.[31] Here again moderate size played a part, for very few Shropshire houses were built from scratch on the scale of some houses in other counties on a Jacobethan **H**, or **U**, or courtyard plan. Burwarton House was indeed huge, but it was an earlier Italianate house (1835–9) enlarged and altered in 1876–7.[32] Few designs were adventurous, and one that was, Stanmore with its one-storeyed 'butterfly' wings attached to the service block, was before its time and thereby eccentric rather than innovatory.[33]

To some extent the perpetuation of the double-pile plan was brought about by the new role of the hall. In smaller houses, like Broncroft Castle and Tedsmore Hall, the hall might still serve as an entrance hall, often with a staircase tucked away in a corner, in the manner of some 18th-century four-bayed houses in Shrewsbury. In larger houses, however, the vestibule, which had appeared earlier, had become almost standard and the hall was rarely entered directly from outside. At the same time manners were becoming less formal, and the social (and ultimately the legal) status of women, or at least of upper-class women, was improving.[34] The tendency to develop ladies' and gentlemen's areas within the house had begun earlier[35] and is clearly seen at Attingham Hall in the difference between the decoration in the rooms east and west of the hall. At Stokesay Court the south wing was almost a self-contained bachelors' unit: on the ground floor there was a billiards room, a card room, a 'parlour' probably meant as a smoking room, a set of lavatories, a separate entrance into the garden, and a separate staircase to the single bedrooms on the floor above. On the east of the main double-pile block there was a morning room for the ladies and a boudoir. The hall, more or less central in the polite part of the house, acquired a new function as neutral ground, a sitting room where all might meet.[36] Such a room, meant to be accessible from many quarters, was best accommodated in a double pile, where it could be flanked on three and sometimes four sides and could have many rooms leading off: what at Yeaton Peverey in 1890 was called 'a large living-hall'.[37] This use of the hall became so popular that in several earlier houses built around a courtyard the open space was roofed over and converted to the new type of hall: as early as 1826–9 at Aldenham Hall,[38] in the form of a circular domed top-lit hall at Downton Hall in the 1840s,[39] and at Acton Reynald Hall in the same decade.[40]

Yet to overemphasize the sitting-room nature of such halls is to miss much of their significance, for they had elements that were highly undesirable in a sitting room: they were vast, they had innumerable doorways, many of them were top-lit and lofty, and many had a grand staircase opening off them. One of the most splended is at Stokesay Court, with an arcade on all sides, a staircase at one side, and no fewer than nine openings into the room. Other two-storey halls were built at Netley Hall and Boreatton Park in the 1850s, at Ruyton Towers and Cloverley Hall in the 1860s, at Adcote, Stanmore Hall, and Woodcote Hall in the 1870s, and at Bedstone Court in 1884. And they were designed in many different styles: a mixture of Doric and Italianate at Netley, neo-Norman at Ruyton, Tudor at Boreatton,

Elizabethan with a difference at Cloverley, fake timber framing at Bedstone,[41] Jacobethan at Stokesay, 'Cotswold manor house' at Adcote, and Second Empire at Stanmore and in a design for Llwyn House,[42] Oswestry.

That these lofty rooms were meant to impress as much as to cosset is clear, and of them all probably the most impressive is Norman Shaw's hall at Adcote, with its mighty Gothic arches springing from the walls and carrying an elaborate crown-post roof, with its tall lancets in the south gable and with an eight-light window in the south-east angle. Attempts to outdo medieval master masons in their own field usually fail, but Shaw came as near success as any man could. In doing so, however, he rather gave the game away, for the hall at Adcote is in no sense at the centre of a series of rooms, but is separated from most of them by a vestibule.[43] It

The imperial staircase at Netley Hall, Longnor

Interior of the Great Hall at Adcote, Little Ness

Fireplace with extended hood in the Great Hall, Adcote

Detail of tiled foreplace surround in dining room at Adcote

exists in its own right as a great hall, and its sitting-room aspect has been tacked on to its primary function.[44] It has been said that it must have been 'unpleasant' and 'chilly',[45] but much the same may be said of other halls, and it is not easy to see how they were any less unpleasant or chilly. Their sitting-room character is only one aspect of their purpose: another is to perpetuate an age-old element of the English country house and to emphasize that, despite all the century's changes and however much the landed classes were losing political power, it was yet prestigious to belong, or to seem to belong, to them.

Nevertheless not everyone wanted, or could afford, a great hall and there was, along with the desire for feudal splendour, a need for more and smaller reception rooms as social life in country houses became less formal. Some men—especially those in post-medieval houses where the entrance hall, though large, was not lofty—were prepared to sacrifice some of this space for cosier accommodation. That happened in several 17th- and 18th-century houses, for example Hampton Hall (Worthen), Stoke House (Greete), and Whitton Hall (Westbury). The *locus classicus* is Halston Hall (*c.*1700) near Whittington, where the entrance hall originally corresponded in length with the saloon which it led into: in 1849 the new owners lopped a bay off each end of the hall to contrive two small extra rooms, part of the alterations which made the house 'more convenient'.[46]

The concentration of polite rooms in the main block and of service rooms elsewhere was usually achieved without too much trouble on the ground floor but not so easily above. That was largely because the function of the house as a place of rural recreation, at a time when the railways had made travelling easier and cheaper than before, could mean that there were unprecedented numbers of guests needing many bedrooms. The problem was well recognized, and Sir Offley Wakeman's 30 bedrooms at Yeaton Peverey in the early 1890s was the grandest of all attempts at a solution. The bedrooms of the owner and other important members of the family were invariably above the reception rooms, but others were often above service rooms. At Stanmore Hall the nursery was above the servants' hall, and there and at Bedstone there were bedrooms over the kitchen. At Stokesay Court the ladies' bedrooms were above service rooms. At Boreatton Park the architect managed to get all 13 bedrooms, together with seven dressing rooms, into the area above the reception rooms, but he did so at what was the, perhaps minor, cost of evicting the servants from their usual place on the second floor and at the major cost of putting some of his guests under the roof. The problem was often complicated by a desire to separate single men and women guests, as at Stokesay Court where the bachelors were accommodated in one wing, the ladies in the other. It was not only the quality who needed to be protected from the opposite sex—at Boreatton Park menservants and maidservants were in two separate wings, and at Bedstone the menservants' rooms on the first floor could be reached only by a separate staircase from the ground floor, so placed that it would be difficult to sneak up it unseen. Even in a comparatively small house, like, for example, the Roveries, Lydham, of 1810, separate approaches were contrived to the servants' bedrooms.[47] Separation was almost an end in itself in Victorian times, not only between sexes and classes but within those categories too. Sometimes, as at Oteley Park, the owner had a whole separate suite on the first floor, with bedroom, dressing room, and sitting room. At Yeaton Peverey the Wakemans had one entrance for the family and another for the guests. The bedrooms there were 'grouped together for the convenient accommodation of guests, the family and nurseries, the men-servants, the maid-servants, and stranger servants'.[48]

Some of these new houses—Bedstone Court,[49] Cloverley Hall,[50] Overley Hall,[51] Stokesay Court[52]—were built by businessmen moving into the countryside, but in no sense was a great hall or a great house a mark of the *nouveau riche*. Other new houses, for example Adcote[53] and Stanmore Hall,[54] were the homes of families who, while drawing wealth from business, were very far from being new in the county. Yet others—Boreatton Park,[55] Netley Hall,[56] Ruyton Park,[57] Woodcote Hall[58]—were the work of well established landowning families. So too were those like Aldenham Hall and Acton Reynald Hall, in which a courtyard was converted into a hall. And although immigrant industrialists tended to build on a large scale—Thomas Barnes, Lancashire cotton manufacturer, former M.P. for Bolton, and builder of the Quinta (*c.*1855),[59] Weston Rhyn, was a notable exception—so too did some landowners: the new Adderley Hall (1877–9)[60] and Burwarton House, as extended several times,[61] were enormous, and Yeaton Peverey (1890–2) has no fewer than 30 bedrooms. What all these owners had in common was wealth, and distinctions between old and new, whether of homes or of lineage, were less important, or at any rate were made less of, for 'age' was a quality that money could very successfully simulate or buy. Barely a decade after Stokesay Court had been built it figured in *Country Life*, and the unwary reader could have received the impression that the house had been there for centuries and was the historic replacement of Stokesay Castle.[62]

Although many of these houses were built by newcomers, such men were on the whole less likely to build a new house than to buy an old one. Examples are Eaton Mascott, bought in 1860 by a Staffordshire ironmaster;[63] Hinstock Hall, bought by a Black Country banker in 1862;[64] and Condover, bought by E.B. Fielden of the Lancashire cotton firm in 1897.[65] Moreover when the newcomers did build they had often bought as well. In 1846 and 1853 the Staffordshire ironmaster W.H. Sparrow bought Habberley Hall (to which he added a wing) and Albrighton Hall, and his son Arthur built Preen Manor (1870–2) on property which his father had bought in 1848.[66] The millionaire ship-owner J.J. Bibby bought Hardwick Grange in 1868[67] and 20 years later built Sansaw Hall for his son;[68] J.D. Allcroft bought Stokesay Castle[69] in 1869 and built Stokesay Court in 1888;[70] and in 1885 the nephew and heir of the builder of Cloverley bought Shavington,[71] perhaps the grandest house in Shropshire. But not all buyers were newly rich businessmen. Furthermore, however many houses immigrant businessmen built, they built fewer than established landowners: Bourton Cottage (1874),[72] Ferney Hall (1855–8, restored 1878),[73] and Hodnet Hall (1870)[74] may be instanced, and there were many others—Hinton Hall probably *c.*1860,[75] Culmington Manor in the 1860s,[76] Longden Manor in 1866,[77] Petton Hall (1892),[78] Leigh Manor in the 1890s.[79] Further, many local families were making large-scale additions and alterations to their houses: early examples are Sir Andrew Vincent Corbet at Acton Reynald in the 1840s,[80] C.K. Mainwaring at his new house Oteley, of 1826–30, in the 1840s and 1850s,[81] and St. John Chiverton Charlton at Apley Castle in 1856.[82] In the 1860s and 1870s William Tayleur had work done at Buntingsdale,[83] as did Sir John Dalberg-Acton at Aldenham,[84] Col. R.T. Lloyd at Aston,[85] Sir Baldwyn Leighton at Loton,[86] and M.H. Griffin at Pell Wall.[87] Work continued to be commissioned even after the onset of the agricultural depression in the later 1870s:[88] by the Corbets at Acton Reynald in the 1880s and 1890s,[89] by Stanley Leighton at Sweeney in 1884,[90] and by Col. C.J. Cotes at Pitchford in the 1880s.[91] Col. Lloyd undertook the renovation of the chapel at Aston Hall in 1887,[92] T.F. Kynnersley retored and added to Leighton Hall in 1887–8,[93] and Burlton Hall was rebuilt in 1895.[94]

In her invaluable pioneering survey Mrs. Franklin demonstrated that of 380 country houses built between 1835 and 1914 twice as many were built by businessmen as by landowners. Probably, however, there is a bias in her figure for it is mostly based, as it had to be, on national architectural publications[95] which tended to give most attention to well known architects, especially to those with a flair for publicity. Businessmen, often new arrivals in a county, were less likely than residents to

patronize a local man; more probably they would approach a London name and, as far as is known, no local architect was ever commissioned to build a country house for a newcomer to Shropshire. Local landowners there built many more houses than incoming businessmen, but London architects were employed by the latter as often as by the former. The bias in Mrs. Franklin's figures is clear, for in contrast to examples cited above, two of the five Shropshire houses which she mentions were built by industrialists,[96] a third by a banker,[97] and a fourth by a widow with an inherited business fortune of her own.[98] Of course the distinction between land and business was far from absolute, and many landed families also drew significant income from business interests.[99] Many others were descended from successful merchants and traders, connections not always easily uncovered, for their children and grandchildren were liable to forget it.[100] Despite that, however, the impact of businessmen on the rural architecture of Shropshire in the late 19th century was not in the number of new houses they built there but partly in the prominence that size and publicity gave to their houses, and mainly in the number of old houses and estates that they bought.

The last point should not be exaggerated, for even at the end of the century they were a small proportion of the whole. Land still carried social distinction, but it no longer conferred great power and was not the best investment.[101] The recent claim that 'usually the money for building or improving country houses came from agricultural rents'[102] might be difficult to substantiate, but it would seem to have most validity outside what may be called an extended home counties.[103] An analysis of the houses listed by Mrs. Franklin[104] shows that the proportion of 'business' to 'landed' builders within that area was something like five to two; elsewhere it was nearer one to one. New men whose houses were meant to shelter their leisure hours were likely to build in fashionable counties easily reached from London. Shropshire was not one of those, and most of its newcomers were drawn from a limited area: its industrialized hinterland, the west midlands, and, farther afield and to an extent, industrialized Lancashire.

It would be difficult to pretend that there was anything particularly Salopian about the houses discussed above. Very many of the known architects were London men or men of national repute. Even when a provincial man was employed he was often a 'foreigner', as the obscure Harry Percival of Rossendale at Ruyton Towers,[105] J.W. Hugall of Oxford at Stanmore Hall,[106] or the Sheffield firm of Weightman, Hadfield & Goldie at Boreatton Park.[107] Among Shropshire men the younger Edward Haycock was in charge at Netley and, to some extent, at Longden Manor;[108] Samuel Pountney Smith was responsible for Ferney Hall and Hinton Hall and for additions at Buntingsdale, Lutwyche, and Sweeney Hall;[109] and Lloyd Oswell for Astbury Hall and for additions at Leighton Hall.[110] Smith's career is perhaps illuminating. He built two country houses across the border in Wales and two in Shropshire, but his main employment on country houses was making large-scale additions or alterations. He worked at ten of the best known earlier houses in the county, including Buntingsdale, Cound, Lutwyche, and Onslow. The now demolished saloon in a Jacobethan style which he added at Lutwyche in 1851 was dismal in every way, and strictures on the 'intolerable neo-Jacobean'[111] of Ferney Hall are well deserved. On the other hand the block he added at Buntingsdale was a remarkably sensitive copy of an early 18th-century style, and some of his church restorations were equally successful. His employment at so many old houses may therefore be partly ascribed to a local appreciation of his talents in that direction, and partly, of course, to the preference among owners for employing local men on minor commissions.

Smaller houses

In smaller houses the free planning that went with the abandonment of symmetry had begun earlier, and Nash's houses at Cronkhill and Longner have already been mentioned. The change is epitomized in the history of parsonages. By the opening of the 19th century the resident rural clergy were no longer classified, as earlier they sometimes had been, along with farmers and innkeepers and offered designs in which there was no more than a kitchen, parlour, closet, and milk room on the ground floor.[112] Instead they had become members of a highly respectable and well connected profession. Many were members of landed families and, as Taine put it, were in every way 'fitted to mix with the country gentry and nobility'.[113] Their houses were typical of those of the other developing professions and of men of local importance in industry and commerce.[114] In 1804 Berrington rectory was rebuilt (for the Hon. Richard Noel Hill)[115] as a typical small country house of the time with a symmetrical five-bay front; between 1832 and 1837 Cardeston rectory was rebuilt with a near symmetrical front,[116] and c.1840 what is now Monkhopton House was built for the perpetual curate and with some attempt at symmetry.[117] Thereafter that quality was eschewed: at Melverley in 1848;[118] by the younger Edward Haycock at Weston Lullingfields in 1857 and Meole Brace[119] in 1869; by Pountney Smith at Leaton in 1859;[120] at Astley c.1861;[121] by J.P. Seddon at Holdgate in 1865;[122] by G.E. Street at Upton Magna in 1866 and Lyneal in 1875;[123] at Minsterley in 1873;[124] and at Ketley in 1881.[125] Other instances are numerous, and one may cite, for example, those at Clee St. Margaret (1875–6) and Diddlebury (c.1883).[126]

The forms of these houses varied considerably. An approximation to an **L** or **T** plan was much favoured, as at Astley, Leaton, Melverley, and Weston Lullingfields. Lyneal had a single range with a short outshut, and the much larger parsonages at Clee St. Margaret and at Diddlebury, with main ranges and wings, differed little from a minor country house like the Quinta. Such houses were smaller than the Bedstones and Stokesays, and had a more marked tendency to tuck the doorway inconspicuously away in a minor elevation, as for example at Leaton and Upton Magna vicarages. But they too had their quota of reception rooms, bedrooms, service rooms, and servants' rooms. In many of them the clergyman's study took the place of a landowner's business room. What they lacked was the lofty two-storeyed 'sitting room' that was the hallmark neither of the new nor of the old but of the rich.

Cottages and symmetry

Deliberately to avoid, or to fail to strive officiously for, a symmetrical façade was to flout the most important canon of architectural taste of the last 250 years. It was more: it was to abandon a form which clearly distinguished the houses of the élite from those of the masses, wherein irregular elevations were determined by the occupants' day-to-day bread-winning activities and not by any aesthetic theories. Throughout the 18th century, as farms were engrossed, those farmers who survived grew more prosperous and some were anxious to show that they had risen above their fellows by indulging themselves in the symmetrical façades of the upper classes. Examples were cited earlier. By the mid 19th century some farmhouses, like vicarages, were undergoing a different change. In the 1820s the Leightons of Loton rebuilt Cardeston Lower Farm in Alberbury with the same regard for symmetry which they showed at Cardeston rectory a decade later,[127] and farmhouses with symmetrical fronts continued to be built into the second half of the century. Documented examples are Berwick Grove, a farmhouse on the Burton family's estate, designed in 1844 by Edward Haycock,[128] and Stanmore Farm, built shortly after 1852,[129] and Little Mose (in Quatt), of 1868.[130] The last two were small farms, and Little Mose, with only a living room, parlour, kitchen-scullery, and dairy on the ground floor, was not much bigger than a cottage of the time. In contrast, Lower Brompton Farm, Berrington, with 1,450 acres and employing 46 men, was built in 1855 with a symmetrical main block and an attached service wing within an overall asymmetrical composition.[131] By the mid century, however, even small farms on the Loton Park estate—Ivy End (1843) and Lower Stanford (1855)—were deliberately asymmetrical designs,[132] and for those larger farmhouses which, like Lower Brompton, were comparable with gentlemen's residences asymmetry was the norm. It cannot be argued that that was a necessary consequence of their functions, for those functions were meant to be carried on in the large ranges of farm buildings associated with the houses. Rather they were asymmetrical, as their ambitious predecessors had been symmetrical, because that was the prevailing taste of polite architecture.

Many cottages, too, were built with asymmetrical fronts, for example Hawthorn Bower, Alberbury, of 1836.[133] On the Sutherland estates,

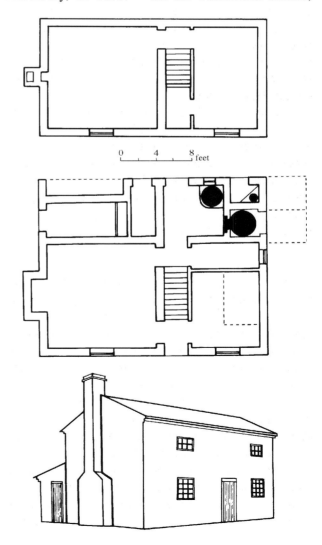

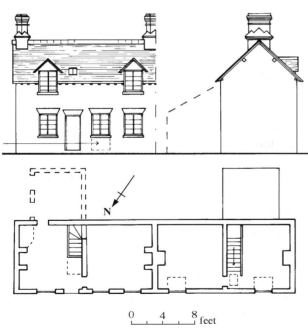

Examples of country cottages: above Sidney Cottages at Kynnersley, showing (on left) ground- and (on right) first-floor plans of a pair of semis. Right: model cottages proposed by T.N. Parker with ground- and first-floor plans

where 200 new houses were built in the 1860s and 1870s to a few standard designs,[134] asymmetry was common. The typical house there had a kitchen, a parlour, and a service room of varying functions, with three bedrooms above, and for ease of access between rooms was built to a **T** plan; and their contrast with the earlier Loton cottages, of kitchen and pantry with two bedrooms above, demonstrates the rise in the standards of 'model' accommodation. Sometimes the upright of the **T** was at the rear of the house, and the front, comprising a large kitchen and a small pantry, was almost necessarily asymmetrical. More often the accommodation was in a main range with a projecting cross wing and was asymmetrical for that reason. This latter type was the commonest on the estate, amounting to almost half of the total, but next in numbers was that in which two such asymmetrical houses were set end to end to make a pair of symmetrical semi-detached mirror-image cottages in a range between two projecting wings.[135] Other semi-detached mirror-image cottages were built by other landowners. An early example on the Leightons' Loton estate was the pair (1827) called Nag's Head Cottages,[136] and later ones were Rose Cottages (1846) and Mount Pleasant Cottages (1856).[137] There is an early pair of 1859 at Cardington; several of the 1860s at Calverhall, built by the Heywoods who were rebuilding Cloverley; a row of four such pairs in Grinshill put up by the Bibbys in 1895–6; and a symmetrically designed group of 1894 in a 'garden village' style in Quatt, put up by the squire, the Revd. F.H. Wolryche-Whitmore.[138] Terraces, in contrast, were rare and, like those of 1862 at Cleeton St. Mary, often intended as almshouses.

Thus by the mid century a curious reversal of roles had come about: the lack of symmetry which had distinguished the dwellings of the lowly for nearly three centuries had become the badge of their superiors, and that symmetry which had been *de*

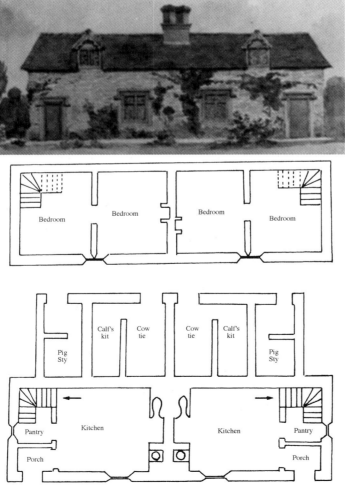

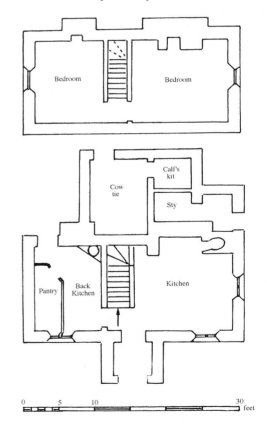

Different style cottages on the Loton Park estate.
Left: Nag's Head cottages buit in 1827.
Above: Rowton Gate cottage to same scale

rigeur among the aesthetic élite had become in the countryside the monopoly, almost, of cottagers.

The change reflected the popularity of the semi-detached house and that popularity calls for explanation. It was, of course, cheaper to build a semi-detached pair than two separate dwellings, but it was cheaper still to build a terrace rather than two or more pairs of semis. In the late 18th century rural terraces had been far from uncommon,[139] and the roadside row outside Berwick House was a very sophisticated composition in varying planes and heights. Terraces, however, were acquiring an urban and industrial aura[140] and, with the advent of the cult of the Picturesque, were being supplanted by groups of separate or semi-detached cottages, as at Blaise Hamlet (Glos.) in 1811,[141] at Ampthill (Beds.) in 1812–16,[142] and at such model villages as Edensor (Derb.) and Great Tew (Oxon.). Scattered or informally grouped cottages on an estate were the new way of expressing social relationships earlier demonstrated by formal rows outside the gates of the great house; as Archdeacon Plymley put it in 1803, 'the whole of a gentleman's estate should be his pleasure ground'.[143]

Moreover there were practical, or at any rate 'paternalist', reasons for eschewing terraces. Plymley recommended that enough land should be allotted to each cottage to allow the industrious labourer, after leaving work at six o'clock, to cultivate a plot and perhaps keep a cow;[144] and in 1813 the Oswestry Society for Bettering the Conditions and Increasing the Comforts of the Poor published plans, elevations, and specifications for a model cottage with a cow house and calf box incorporated in it.[145] If the model subjects whom Plymley envisaged had been concentrated in terraces, it would have been difficult to provide easily accessible land for them,[146] but at the same time there were also disadvantages to widely scattered cottages, for in the event of trouble or danger there might be no neighbour to lend a hand.[147] The semi-detached cottage was a happy compromise between two desirable but potentially incompatible ends.

There is, however, no law that a semi-detached pair shall be symmetrical, and asymmetrical pairs may be easily found. Nevertheless in towns or town-like streets—as 71–2 and 74–5 Abbey Foregate, Shrewsbury; a pair in Whitchurch Road, Prees;[148] and 26–28 Victoria Road, Bridgnorth—they were probably intended as a small investment, with one dwelling to be occupied by the owner and the other let to provide an income. The symmetry of the rural semi must be regarded as deliberate and not an inevitable result of the form. Very few Shropshire landowners seem to have followed Plymley's precepts[149] or availed themselves of the labours of the Oswestry Society, but Sir Baldwin Leighton appears to have meant to do so in 1827 at Rowton Gate and at Nag's Head Cottages. At each of these he planned, as part of the building, a cow house and a calf box, but to preserve the near symmetry of the first and the complete symmetry of the second he placed them at the rear of the houses.[150] In contrast the Oswestry Society, designing a workaday cottage with no aesthetic considerations in mind, allowed the cow house to be reflected architecturally in the blankness of part of the façade.[151]

The commonest semi-detached pair on the Sutherland estate, with a main range between projecting wings, was a very deliberate composition and the most striking of all the types there. It may be regarded as the ruling design, of which the commoner detached **T** plan house was an incomplete part, probably erected for a smallholder and set within his plot. The semis, to judge from their form, their small gardens, and their proximity to farmhouses, were probably meant for labourers.[152] Like the rural terrace earlier the semi-detached cottage was the mark of the humblest in the countryside[153] and contrasted with the asymmetry of the great houses and the farmhouses. Shropshire was better endowed than most counties with very rich landowners,[154] and such pairs of newly built cottages scattered thoughout his lands served to show that a proprietor who

> ... over private fields and wastes as wide
> As a Greek city for which heroes died,
> ... owned the houses and the men inside

had, at least, a paternal attitude towards the rural poor. However galling that may have been to the independently minded among the latter, it was better in most men's eyes than callous indifference; and it was an answer more convincing than any statistics or affectation of Olympian disregard, to sneers about rural slums from industrialists irked by Lord Shaftesbury's activities.[155]

It should of course be emphasized that, while these cottages were typical of those erected by landowners in the mid to late 19th century, they were not typical of rural accommodation. The number of labourers had increased disproportionately in previous years[156] and many lived in older houses of varying kinds and varying salubrity, including those of mud at Melverley and Whixall;[157] many others lived in former farmhouses converted into two or more dwellings;[158] and many walked long distances to work from overcrowded tenements in 'open' parishes, villages, and small towns.[159] It has been reckoned that estate cottages, though very prominent in the rural scene, made up about five per cent of the total national stock.[160] The figure for Shropshire may turn out to be higher than that, for rural housing there was notoriously bad[161] and stood in even more need of improvement than elsewhere: Edward Stanhope, reporting to a Commons select committee in 1868, said of cottages in Dorset that they were 'more ruinous and contain worse accommodation than those of any county I have visited except Shropshire'.[162]

It was, however, such poor houses, and the new ones erected for themselves by minor men, that gave significance to the symmetrical semi-detached and the carefully designed asymmetrical detached houses put up by landowners for their tenants and dependants. Men with more limited resources could indulge only to a slight extent in aesthetic preferences, and their homes were neither symmetrically nor asymmetrically designed, not through any aversion from contemporary educated fashion but because of the necessarily simple form of the only dwellings within their means. They had to content themselves with what had come to be regarded as the bare minimum in housing: a heated living room, a smaller service room, and a bedroom or two. Nor could everybody achieve even that. On Pontesbury Hill from c.1850 onwards many small one-storey stone cottages of two or three bays replaced the turf houses formerly in use, and such dwellings were known as well in Condover and Ford.[163] One-and-a-half-storey houses with a large chimney at one end are still common on the Clee Hills and to the west of the Stiperstones. They were built mainly for iron and lead miners, but men working on the land often occupied houses of much the same standard. On a remote site at Shirlett is a small one-and-a-half-

storey brick house with the entry into a small service room-cum-dairy, accommodating a staircase, a heated main room 12 x 13ft., and two bedrooms above. The thin floor joists are carried on a cross beam with a forked end.[164] At Acton Scott in 1810 many cottages were of timber, of two rooms, with thatched roofs, and, generally, unglazed windows.[165] All these houses are wholly unlike estate cottages in their form and appearance, and well below most of them in their level of accommodation, but it was against this dull background of rural housing that the cottages on great estates could sparkle.

Suburbs for Classes: Shrewsbury
In most accounts of late 19th-century architecture country houses figure prominently because they were conscious and conspicuous compositions, often by architects famous in their day or since; and much is known about them and their occupants. Suburban houses were often just as carefully designed, but they were smaller and there is less to be said about any particular one. What there is to say can be said about many of the others; and, apart from Shrewsbury School's boarding houses ('halls') in Kingsland, none of them in Shropshire, as far as is known, was by an architect of national repute.[166] Nevertheless, in the total amount of building and in the contribution they made to the architectural scene of most of the population, they were of greater importance.

Suburbs of a kind had been known for centuries: Abbey Foregate, Castle Foregate, Coleham, and Frankwell outside Shrewsbury, for example, and the Low Town at Bridgnorth. By the end of the 19th century all the larger Shropshire towns had suburbs in the modern sense: dormitory areas for people of all ranks who worked at a trade or profession within the town. Suburban growth is seen most clearly at Shrewsbury, which had always been the most important town in the county and by the mid 19th century was a market and administrative centre, a focus of local fashion and entertainment, a garrison town, a manufacturing town, and the hub of a railway network.

By the early 19th century there was a scatter of houses within easy walking distance of Shrewsbury, standing in their own grounds, but of medium villa-like size, such as that on the Mount where Charles Darwin was born, Ænon Cottage (see illustrations p.198) beneath the castle walls, built by John Palmer, minister of the Baptist chapel,[167] and, among others, the recently demolished Pengwern Hotel in Longden Road and the nearby Luciefelde House. These were houses outside the town rather than suburban houses, and so too, despite their relative proximity to one another, were those of the mid century beyond the Column along London and Wenlock roads. In contrast, the elegant neo-Greek terrace below the Column at the top of Abbey Foregate and the number of other houses, some of more and some of less pretensions, between it and the English Bridge show that by then that thoroughfare had become a suburb in the modern sense; and Holywell Terrace and Whitehall Street of the 1830s were extensions of it.[168] Shrewsbury's suburbs expanded steadily throughout the middle of the century, and their progress is marked by new or enlarged churches in outlying areas: St. Michael's, Ditherington, built in 1829–30, enlarged in 1873; St. George's, Frankwell, built in 1832;[169] St. Giles's, Wenlock Road, enlarged in 1860–1 and 1871–2;[170] All Saints', Castlefields, built in 1875–6;[171] and the

conversion, in 1886–7, of what had been built in 1837 as little more than a mission church into the prestigious Holy Trinity, Belle Vue.[172]

Much building occurred in other Shropshire towns, but in general it was diffuse, mostly in ones or twos, and houses of some architectural pretensions rubbed shoulders with cottages or gazed at them across a road. Occasionally an overall design was achieved. At Richmond Terrace, Station Road, Whitchurch, nos.1–8 are a terrace of no particular distinction; nos.10–17 consist of four semi-detached pairs, the outer pair identical and the inner pair identical but different from the outer pair, giving a symmetrical and almost 'terrace' appearance to the whole composition. By the end of the century homogeneous suburbs, each with its own distinctive social and architectural character, had appeared, and this was 'a process in which social aspirations and prejudices played a part as important as strictly economic factors'.[173]

It would be difficult to identify any suburb or any suburban house as typical, but a consideration of three new Shrewsbury suburbs—Kingsland,

The Poplars, 7 Butler Road, Kingsland, Shrewsbury, an example of the upper-middle-class house;
it antedated the development of Kingsland but was altered to approximate to Kingsland types

Cherry Orchard, and the area known as 'back of the Sheds' (i.e. the former railway running sheds)—may reveal their variety.

The first was the quintessential upper-middle-class retreat, brought into existence by a series of separate but connected events. As early as 1868 it had been recognized that, with a bridge over the Severn, the corporation's estate at Kingsland would be a very good site for the school and for 'houses of a better class, to accommodate families bringing their children to the Schools',[174] and the suggestion was repeated in 1872 when Kingsland was again marked down as a piece of 'land suitable for the erection of villas and other residences, the want of which has been severely felt for some time past'.[175] By 1875 Shrewsbury School, dissatisfied with its cramped and unappealing situation in the town, had

decided to move there.[176] In 1878, at the instigation of 'all right-thinking people', the Home Secretary suppressed the Shrewsbury Show, which had been held on Kingsland since the Reformation but had become a pleasure fair, where the 'lower orders' indulged in 'boisterous, sensual, tipsy jollification':[177] as Thomas Love Peacock would have put it, 'a stench in the nose of piety'. In 1883 a private company opened a toll bridge across the river,[178] replacing an inconvenient ferry and a steep slope to and from the river bank, and by then the corporation had begun to develop the land in building plots at the very high rateable values of £40 and £60.[179] The earliest residents were leading tradesmen, clergymen, and important professional men, including the town clerk and the borough medical officer of health.[180]

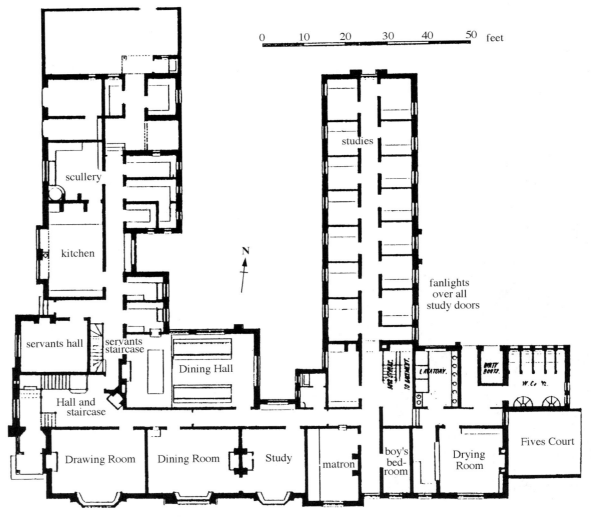

Ground-floor plan of Rigg's Hall, one of Shrewsbury's three boarding houses in Kingsland designed by William White

Most of the houses were large and detached; those that were semi-detached were little smaller.[181] Three school boarding houses—Rigg's Hall (1880), Churchill's Hall (1880), and Moser's Hall (1884)—are very large indeed; they were all designed by William White, a considerable, if somewhat eccentric, London architect.[182] Most other Kingsland houses were by such leading Shrewsbury architects as S. Pountney Smith, A.E. Lloyd Oswell,[183] and A.B. Deakin. Three houses were by architects from as far away as Chester, Liverpool, and Burnley.[184] All the detached houses, with the exception of 5 Ashton Road (Deakin, 1883) in a Queen Anne style, were determinedly asymmetrical[185] and even one pair of the mirror-image semis, 18–20 Kennedy Road (Deakin, 1885), was not quite a mirror image and managed to vary the bay windows of the two halves. As in so many smaller country dwellings, doorways in both detached and semi-detached houses were generally inconspicuously sited, often in a side elevation, and most conspicuously so, perhaps, at Rigg's Hall and Moser's Hall. Red brick in various hues, but never very staring, was almost universal and polychromy was rare and generally minimal. Its most striking use is on 3 Butler Road,[186] of yellow brick

with red brick banding and roofed with bright red tiles. It was also used, less strikingly, by White for Moser's Hall and very sparingly at 28–30 Kennedy Road (1898). Terracotta ornament from J. Parson Smith's local brick and tile works[187] was commoner and was used most notably by Owens of Liverpool at 10 Kennedy Road (1882), by the local builder Oliver Jones at the pair of semis now 9 Ashton Road (1884), by Deakin at 5 Ashton Road (1883) and 32–34 Kennedy Road (1886), and by Smith himself, working to Oswell's designs, at 13–15 Ashton Road. Projections in the form of one- or two-storeyed bays or porches were everywhere, but the turrets, so common in slightly earlier houses and conspicuous in the Victoria Road area of Oswestry, were rare. The most notable example, 1 Butler Road (Deakin, 1886), has a timber-framed upper storey from which rises a pyramidal French Renaissance roof with a dormer window. Others are 3 Butler Road and 29 Kennedy Road (1884) by Benson, a Shrewsbury architect. The style of the whole area is that variegated catch-all of the period: much simulated timber framing, sometimes on an upper storey but usually confined to dormers and gables; some Gothic tracery as at 1 Kennedy Road and Rigg's Hall, but used

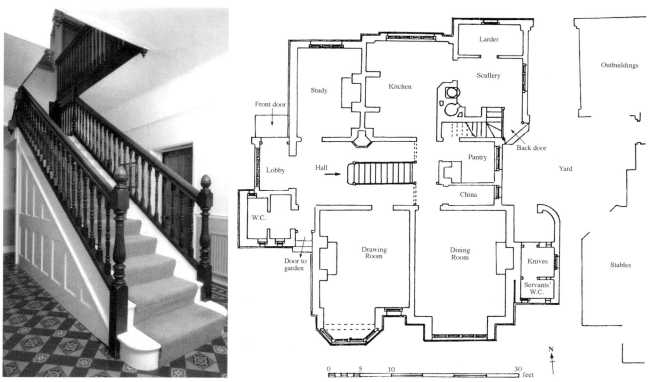

29 Kennedy Road, Kingsland, designed by Benson. Staircase hall on left, and ground floor plan on right as built for Dr. Thursfield in 1884

mainly on porches; richly moulded Gothic door-ways at Moser's Hall and 17 Ashton Road, now the headmaster's house; and some terracotta ornament, occasionally in association with hipped roofs and pedimented dormers. The overriding impression, however, is one of prominent gables above tall rectangular windows of classical derivation, with large panes, often grouped in pairs and with very plain surrounds and heads set within a red brick background. The semi-detached 28–30 Kennedy Road, by C.R. Dalgleish, of Wellington, in 1897–8, with the staircase windows of three round-headed lights rising in echelon, is a very individual piece within the general style.

In their rigorous asymmetry many of these buildings may seem to be aping country houses of the period, but then many of them were the same size as small country houses and had many of the same planning elements and amenities. No.29 Kennedy Road, for example, has a top-lit inner staircase-hall with the main rooms arranged round it, and no.33 has a long hall with a top-lit staircase at the end. Both houses have secondary stairs to the first floor and another stair, presumably to nurseries and servants' bedrooms in the attics. By the mid century it had become fashionable to include a projecting tower in an elevation and sensible to put the water tank on its top floor, to serve the house and, often, to flush a w.c. and a hand-basin below, sited away from the reception and service rooms. An early instance in Shropshire is the design for Llwyn House,[188] Oswestry, and one of the few towers in Kingsland, at 29 Kennedy Road and embellished with a pyramidal roof, has w.c.s on two floors, like a medieval garderobe block. Dr. W.N. Thursfield, the borough medical officer of health, for whom the house was built, was well known for his strong views on sanitation,[189] and the house has other 'anti-germ' devices.[190] A very similar projecting block appears to have been intended at 33 Kennedy Road, of a slightly earlier date.[191] At both these houses there were separate coach houses and stables, and, apart from lacking surrounding acres, they were little different from gentlemen's residences or new style parsonages in the countryside.

The accommodation provided in Kingsland houses ran to a pattern, with the semis slightly less commodious than the detached houses.[192] The detached houses generally had three reception rooms on the ground floor, a w.c. and cloakroom for the family, and all the usual offices, including a separate w.c. for the servants, generally outside but at 25 Kennedy Road situated in the basement which also housed the kitchen and back kitchen. The first floor would have four or five bedrooms, a bathroom and w.c., and the second floor two or three bedrooms but sometimes more. The typical semi-detached house had three reception rooms, all the usual offices, and an outside w.c. on the ground floor; on the first floor three to four bedrooms, a bathroom and w.c., and a couple of bedrooms on the second floor.

Kingsland was a local creation. Planned in Shrewsbury, designed—with a few exceptions—by Shrewsbury architects, erected by Shrewsbury builders, and paid for and occupied by Shrewsbury men. Nevertheless, although it has a very individual character, there is nothing traditionally Salopian about it. Despite the fondness for simulated timber framing only two of the houses—1 Kennedy Road (1886)[193] and 1 Butler Road (1886)—show any knowledge of the local timber-frame tradition, and another (19 Ashton Road), with its conspicuous S braces, is a reminiscence of the later framing in the town. When Gothic forms are employed they are usually Perpendicular, although that style, so common elsewhere, was least typical of late medieval Shropshire.[194] The Queen Anne motifs have no local warrant whatever. Of the three private houses known to be by 'foreign' architects, two (10 and 39 Kennedy Road) are somewhat different from the general run,[195] but on the other hand it would not be easy to point out in what way the third (33 Kennedy Road) is different; and in any case the house that is most strikingly distinguished from the rest, 3 Butler Road with its yellow brick and red banding, is by A.H. Taylor, a Shrewsbury architect. Some of the houses were built by J. Parson Smith and many used his tiles and terracotta, and to that extent they may be said to have a local tinge; but just how local is not clear, for the first house on the estate to use them was 10 Kennedy Road, by Owens of Liverpool.

What is undeniable, however, is the family likeness among the houses. None would be out of place in the superior suburbs of other towns where red brick was common, but taken together they give Kingsland a very individual character and distinguish it from Belle Vue and the area beyond the Column, despite the many grand houses within their mixtures of large and small dwellings. That is partly because nearly all of Kingsland was designed within a short time and by local men—especially Oswell and Deakin—who were able to leave their mark on a well defined and homogeneous area. The decisive factor, however, was the corporation's policy of extinguishing whatever rights the commonalty may once have had in Kingsland and then cutting it up into large and expensive plots to ensure that all the houses would be imposing and would draw their occupants exclusively from a local élite. As was stated in 1868, 'the Corporation would be able to put a veto upon the erection of any building which would be in any way objectionable'.[196] Furthermore in simultaneously co-operating with the governors to transfer the Schools there it also enhanced the architecture of the neighbourhood with large and impressive buildings, while the extensive playing fields[197] and the countryside beyond guaranteed its 'park land' character: *Rus in Urbe*, as a block plan at the Schools is labelled. It would be pleasing to think that such a pleasant suburb was brought about by a beneficent Providence, but when one traces the sequence of those covetous proposals of 1868 and 1872, the pressures that decided the school to move there in 1875,[198] the suppression of the Shrewsbury Show in 1878, the division into such enormously expensive building plots, and the provision of

access by a toll bridge, then the order of events looks less like the happy work of Providence, or of chance than a middle-class ramp: an alliance of wealthy tradesmen and leading professional men appropriating for themselves a place of recreation and a seat of education once enjoyed by large numbers of their less affluent former neighbours.[199]

At the other end of the social spectrum from Kingsland are the houses to the east of Betton Street, 'back of the Sheds'. Housing provision for the lower orders had never been a high priority for the oligarchies which controlled English towns, and Shrewsbury was no better than others.[200] By the mid century, however, housing and sanitation were matters of national concern, both for humanitarian reasons and because of the fright which disasters like the 1849 cholera epidemic had engendered.[201] By then, too, wages in some trades and in some areas were rising, and more houses were being provided at rents which some workers could afford. In Shrewsbury several streets were developed in Castlefields and to the east of Belle Vue Road in the 1860s and 1870s. Nos. 69–75 Trinity Street, a terrace of seven houses put up in 1878, are typical.[202] They are of a brownish brick, of two storeys, single-fronted, and with small front gardens. The doorways have semicircular heads and the rather narrow windows have plain lintels; doorways and windows alternate throughout the elevation. The whole is a vestigial cottage row rather than an urban terrace.

Terraces in neighbouring streets were generally similar and there is nothing comparable with the vast and uniform developments by huge industrial enterprises or philanthropic employers or large-scale speculators in the manufacturing and mining districts.[203] The town was too small and growing too slowly to allow anyone to emulate those operators, but the man who came closest to doing so was that J. Parson Smith who built 13–15 Ashton Road, Kingsland, as a speculation.[204] His earliest recorded building venture was a terrace of six houses in Belle Vue Road in 1882. Between 1883 and 1885, to the east of Betton Street (formerly Sutton Lane), he built 40 terraced houses in Rocke Street and Rea

Ground- and first-floor plans for houses at 69-75 Trinity Street, Shrewsbury, built in 1878

Street to designs by A.B. Deakin.[205] Most houses in Shrewsbury, however, were erected in small numbers by men of limited resources.

The earliest houses 'back of the Sheds' are 1–8 Rocke Street, earlier than nos. 9–23 (1883), which are built up against them, and not so tall.[206] They resemble the houses in Trinity Street more than anything in their immediate neighbourhood but are in a rather brighter brick and have wider doorways and windows. The doorways have semicircular heads with keystones and the windows plain lintels. Doors and windows alternate along the elevation and, like the Trinity Street houses, they are the last flicker of the classical tradition. They differ notably from Trinity Street, however, in having no front garden but a front door opening directly on to the street, a feature which has been the mark of working-class housing in many places.

The front door onto the street was not to be the only mark of working-class housing, for it was accompanied by attempts, some more determined than others, to impose an overall design upon a number of buildings, and by a considerable use of architectural ornament. An early example is the Belle Vue terrace of 16 houses, 5–20 Montagu Place, built by H.H. Treasure in 1878–9.[207] Again these are of two storeys and are single-fronted, but the doorways of each pair are placed side by side, giving the effect of a row of mirror-image houses.

After every fourth house the entrance to a common passage through to the rear is set between two doorways, and is emphasized with a head rising above the level of the other openings. All openings are marked with 'Tudor' drip moulds. At first-floor level a plat band of moulded brick double-nailhead ornament runs the whole length of the front and is returned along the gable wall. On the first floor of that wall is a large three-light window with a drip mould; the drip mould of the middle light is extended upwards to hold a plaque with the date 1879. The gable wall is overhung by an ornamented barge board and the roof line is punctuated by a series of four conjoined chimney shafts with moulded heads. The whole is a very deliberate composition, and its ornament can be described in the circumstances as lavish.

The attempt at overall design shown in Montagu Place, Belle Vue, was repeated in all the later terraces in Rocke Street and Rea Street 'back of the Sheds', and in a variety of ways. Hawarden Cottages, Rea Street, a terrace of eight red-brick mirror-image houses completed in 1883,[208] resembles Montagu Place in having whatever architectural unity it possesses dependent upon a moulded-brick string course running uninterruptedly above the two-centred heads of the doorways and the four-centred heads of the windows. The string course is in yellow brick and the heads of the openings have yellow and blue brick voussoirs which gave them a uniformity now destroyed by the yellow and white paint on some of them. The terrace was probably built by Smith, for the red-brick chimney stacks have courses of yellow and of over-sailing blue bricks at the tops, a feature found on all his known work in the area. Nos. 9–23 Rocke Street and 1–11 Rea Street, begun in 1883 by Smith to designs by Deakin,[209] are identical terraces, again in red brick with mirror-image houses, but unity is achieved wholly by polychrome brick banding running the whole length of the façades. There are two yellow courses with a blue course above at ground-floor lintel level, two yellow

Ground- and first-floor plans for houses at 5-20 Montagu Place built in 1878-9

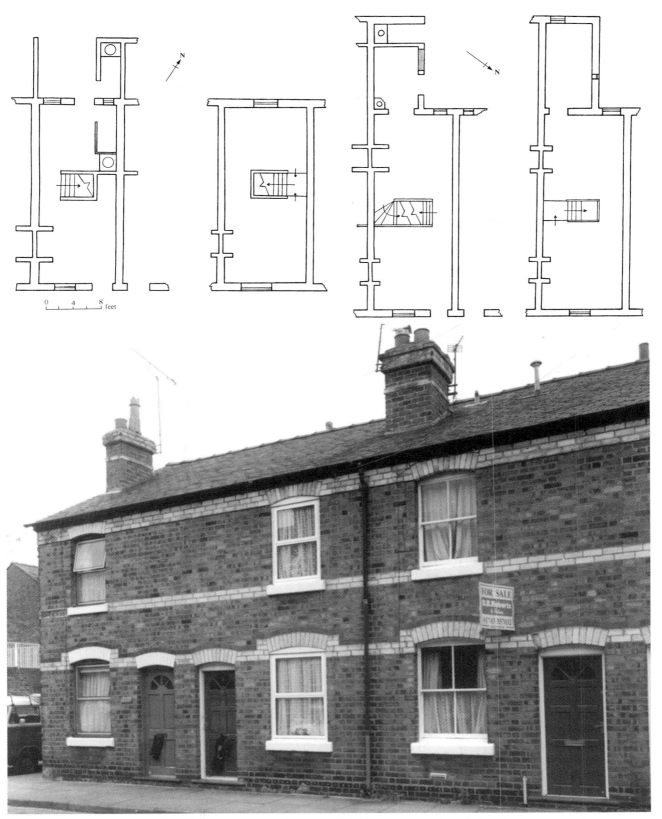

Top left: Ground- and first-floor plans of a house at 1-11 Rea Street. Top right: Ground- and first-floor plans of a house at 9-17 Rocke Street (to same scale). Bottom: 1-3 Rea Street

courses at first-floor sill level, and three yellow courses below the eaves: in all a very elaborate exercise in colour.

In these buildings one can see Deakin indulging in a last fling of polychromy, for in 1884 he designed 28–31 Rea Street, again probably with Smith as the builder.[210] There colour was eschewed, except on the chimney stacks, and instead the design was held together by a moulded red-brick string course at first-floor sill level. Each house has a gable to the street; the first-floor windows have projecting wooden frames with transoms, and the ground-floor windows two-centred and four-centred heads with stone imposts. Next year Smith and Deakin were again in partnership at 12–27 Rea Street,[211] and again polychromy was abjured except on the chimney stacks. There again the design, of mirror-image houses, was controlled with moulded red-brick string courses, one identical with that at nos. 28–31 and the other similar to it but more elaborate. The segmental-headed ground-floor openings, all at the same height, have moulded brick labels and keystones.

The level of accommodation in these houses was much the same as elsewhere, for by the last quarter of the century the example set by 'model housing', by estate cottages, and by such employers as Salt and Akroyd[212] had established an ideal, if not a norm, of a parlour or living room, a kitchen, a separate scullery, and three bedrooms.[213] If it is true, as a writer of 1860 claimed, that the poor preferred a single room—in which they cooked, ate, and sat round the fire on winter evenings—to separate rooms,[214] then they acclimatized themselves to the enforced hardships of more liberal accommodation very quickly.[215] This was the standard on the Sutherland estate, and, while there was not much housing by industrial employers in Shropshire in the later 19th century, what there was was similar—the crossing keeper's cottage[216] at Micklewood on the Shrewsbury & Hereford railway for example. Working-class housing in the county differed from that in the great industrial towns not in the form of the individual dwellings but in the more open nature of the streets, generally of some width, lined by two-storey houses, and with frequent changes of design from street to street and within a street.[217]

Nevertheless there were variations within the general formula. The Trinity Street houses and 1–11

Rea Street, of 1883, were essentially the same, each with a front door opening into a kitchen, a scullery beyond, a w.c. in the yard, and two bedrooms. In size too they were akin, with internal widths of 11ft. and lengths of about 22ft. Nos. 12–27 Rea Street, of 1885, were similar but had a bedroom in an attic lit by a skylight. Nos. 9–17 Rocke Street, however, also of 1883, broke into what was to be a very common pattern, with a parlour entered from the street, a kitchen beyond, a scullery in a narrow extension at the rear, and a w.c. in the yard. On the first floor were three bedrooms, the third one above the scullery. Again the ruling internal width was 11ft. and the length within the main block just over 27ft. Montagu Place, not 'back of the Sheds' and earlier than the houses there, was a cut above them. Most of its houses had an internal width of 14ft. and length of 28ft. The front door opened into a passage, not a room. The ground floor had a parlour, a kitchen with a one-storey scullery extension at the back, and a closet in the yard; on the first floor were three bedrooms. In all these three-bedroomed houses the third bedroom had to be reached, inconveniently, through another. That is not to be attributed to the failure of the designers to solve a not

19-20 Rea Street

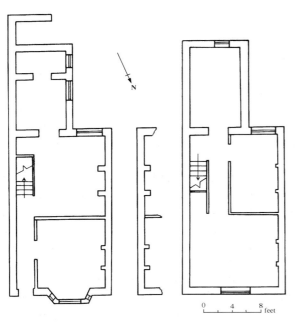

Ground- and first-floor plans of houses in Tankerville Street showing small parlours and middle bedrooms

very difficult problem, but to their understandable reluctance to lose some of their very limited space to passages and corridors. At Montagu Place, for instance, the ground-floor passage meant that the parlour was reduced to a width of less than 11ft. At two houses in Tankerville Road, Cherry Orchard, designed by E.A. Burley in 1885 with an overall internal width of 13ft., the provision of a ground-floor passage left the parlour with a width of less than 10ft. In the same design access to all three bedrooms was directly from the stair head, but at the cost of reducing the middle bedroom to just over 7ft. wide.[218]

In a few earlier terraces some dwellings had had more rooms, or larger rooms, than the rest. In them the superior houses were usually at the ends or in the centre to preserve the symmetry of the design, and the terraces were usually erected for the work force of a large enterprise, with the larger houses presumably intended for overseers or other better paid hands.[219] It is possible that one such man was being accommodated in the end house of the 1883 Rocke Street terrace, which was designed with an internal width of 16ft., in contrast with the 11ft. of the other houses. At Montagu Place the houses to the left of the common passages to the rear incorpo-

rated the space over the passage into the first floor, giving that a width of 18ft. It is certain that at 28–31 Rea Street a deliberate attempt was made to attract a superior, or better-off, class of tenant; they were entered from the side, not from the street, and had parlour, kitchen, scullery, and pantry, and three bedrooms all reached directly from the stair head. Nos.29 and 30, interlocking on the first floor over the passage between them, had similar ground-floor accommodation and no fewer than four bedrooms, none of them intercommunicating. They were designed to look like semi-detached cottages; even their chimney stacks were superior, with more blue than yellow brick courses at the heads; and with their gables they had something of the Old English style.

Such a style, however, was inappropriate to cheap housing and next year Smith and Deakin reverted to terrace-building, doubtless reckoning that the market for better housing there was limited[220]—and with good reason for the area's only advantage was its nearness to the railway Sheds. In 1896 many of the householders—guards, brakesmen, firemen, engine drivers—were clearly railway employees, and many others—fitters, mechanics, boiler makers, carpenters, painters, and labourers—may be presumed to have been.[221] In Rea Street, many of whose houses were two-up-and-two-down, there were seven firemen and only one engine driver; in Rocke Street, where the houses had separate sculleries and three bedrooms, there were three firemen and five engine drivers. The community was homogeneous, for engine drivers had been firemen and firemen would become engine drivers; yet there were differences within it, and those were reflected in a general way in the houses.[222]

The suburb that came to be known in the 1850s as Cherry Orchard was being developed in the 1830s and 1840s, and in 1851 the site of the present Bradford Street (Union Street until 1881) and of the corresponding frontage along Underdale Road was bought by the Shrewsbury Permanent Freehold Land & Building Society. Development was limited, however, and as late as 1875 there were only five houses in Union Street, and one of them had been there since 1819.[223] The rapid growth of the suburb—Bradford, Cleveland, and Tankerville streets, and Samuel Butler's Whitehall estate

245

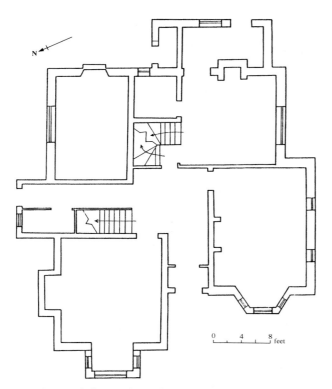

Ground-floor plan of 14 Underdale Road in Cherry Orchard, designed by A.B. Deakin

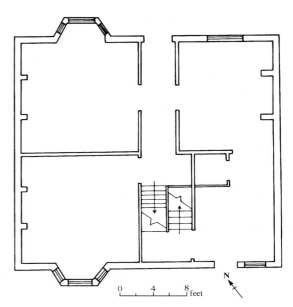

Ground-floor plan of Walden in Cherry Orchard

comprising Bishop, Canon, and Clifford streets[224]—occurred in the last two decades of the century. The neighbourhood is far less homogeneous than the other two discussed above. In Underdale Road are several large detached houses, such as no.14 designed by A.B. Deakin in 1882–3, on a scale approaching that of Kingsland houses, with three ground-floor reception rooms, four first-floor bedrooms, two internal w.c.s, a bathroom, and a servants' stair.[225] In Bradford Street, where the building society sold plots by ballot to its members, nearly all the houses were detached, such as Stoneleigh (1877) and Walden (1883),[226] or were double-fronted semi-detached, such as the pair known originally as 1 and 2 Abbeyville.[227] Not all were big. Walden was quite small, but it was remarkable for its very odd plan, with the kitchen on the street front to one side of a central passage dividing service from reception rooms. The most notable exception in the street was Brighton Terrace (1880) which consisted of five tall three-storeyed houses.[228] In contrast in Cleveland and Tankerville streets several local builders[229] were at much the same time planning terraces[230] almost identical with

69–75 Trinity Street and 1–11 Rea Street mentioned above. Despite all of these, however, the typical late 19th-century house in Cherry Orchard was one of a single-fronted mirror-image semi-detached pair.

In Cherry Orchard there was generally no difference in the accommodation provided in terraced and semi-detached houses. With few exceptions both were built to an almost standard pattern: entrance passage, front parlour and kitchen behind, scullery in a narrow extension at the rear, and three bedrooms.[231] Most were bigger than the houses 'back of the Sheds' or in Montagu Place by a foot or so in both directions, and most had a small front garden, but there was no difference in size between the types. Early in 1881 A.H. Taylor submitted two plans: for a terrace of seven houses of the standard pattern in Cleveland Street and for a semi-detached pair in the same street to the same pattern.[232] Both made a great display of bay windows and, give or take an inch or two, the rooms in the one type were the same size as those in the other.

The obvious advantage of semis over terraces was the external access to the rear, but in many terraces passages to the rear were provided between every third or fourth dwelling. In some short terraces of only four houses, for example 35–38 Cleveland Street (1881), a passage between the second and third house meant that every house in the terrace enjoyed direct external access to the rear;[233] and a similar arrangement was planned for houses in Underdale Road in 1885.[234] In even more practical matters—the provision of bathrooms and of w.c.s—there was again nothing to choose between the two types. While a large detached house like 14 Underdale Road had two internal w.c.s and a bathroom, Brighton Terrace (1880) seems to have been built without w.c.s at all.[235] After that date they were universal in the submitted plans, but for a long time only in the yard. In 1889 a pair of semis in Bishop Street, with a passage between them, were to have a w.c. in the yard and a bathroom and w.c. on the first floor,[236] but that was rare, and the houses were of two and a half storeys with six bedrooms.

What mattered at this level of accommodation was not the form of the dwelling, but its size. The general rule is clear: houses with four bedrooms or more, sometimes semi-detached but more often not, got a bathroom and internal w.c.; from a year taken at random—1893—several examples may be cited in Bradford Street, Canon Street, and Underdale Road.[237] Houses with fewer than four bedrooms had to do without, and in that same year many houses of standard small suburban plan were built in Cherry Orchard with nothing more than a w.c. in the

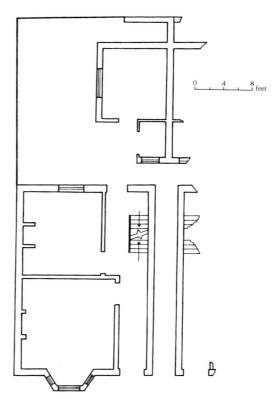

One of a pair of semis in Bishop Street showing rare provision for a w.c.—in the rear yard

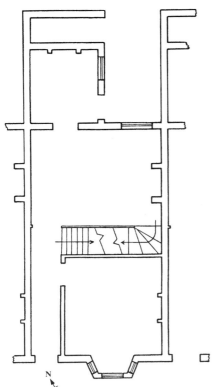

Designs by A.H. Taylor. Above: 22-23 Cleveland Street, Cherry Orchard, almost identical to a terrace of houses at 10-16 Cleveland Street (see ground-floor plan left)

yard.[238] Nevertheless changes were on the way. In that same year two three-bedroomed houses in Canon Street were built with bathrooms contrived in a space above the scullery and taken out of the third bedroom.[239] In December of that year designs that had been submitted in July for a standard semi-detached pair were amended and a bathroom contrived above the scullery.[240] Again in the same year an older pair of semis in Bradford Street (Morella Villas, now nos.1 and 2) had a bathroom installed in part of the space of a bedroom.[241]

The preference for the semi-detached house in a neighbourhood like Cherry Orchard was partly snobbish, for the terrace was increasingly coming to be associated with working-class housing and it was the occupants of suburbs such as Cherry Orchard who would feel in most danger of being regarded as working-class. Nevertheless the preference was also, it may be claimed, aesthetic, even after allowing for the influence of snobbery on taste. The semi-detached mirror-image pair with doorways in the middle and a projection, even as slight as a bay window, at the ends produced, in the town as in the countryside, a symmetrical and punctuated composition of a traditional kind. There was no great need to strive after it, for it was easily accommodated to the plan form, but it was striven after on occasion. In 1878 A.B. Deakin submitted amended plans for a pair of semis (49–51 Oakley Street, Belle Vue) with a symmetrical main range flanked by two deeply projecting wings. The original plan, which looks to have been more convenient, had the projections side by side in the middle; they gave the design an uncompleted look and were discarded.[242] Sometimes an attempt was made to produce the effect of a mirror image without the substance. In 1885 E.A. Burley designed two small detached houses for Tankerville Street, to the same plan as, and slightly smaller than, the other terraced and semi-detached houses, and he set them side by side to look like a mirror-image semi-detached pair with a passage between them,[243] exactly like some of the genuine semi-detached pairs in Canon Street.

The building of small houses in large numbers gave very limited scope to individuality in design, but one or two early semi-detached pairs achieved something of that quality, for example 22–24 Underdale Road (1880) by the local builder Oliver Jones.[244] They were no larger than the general run of

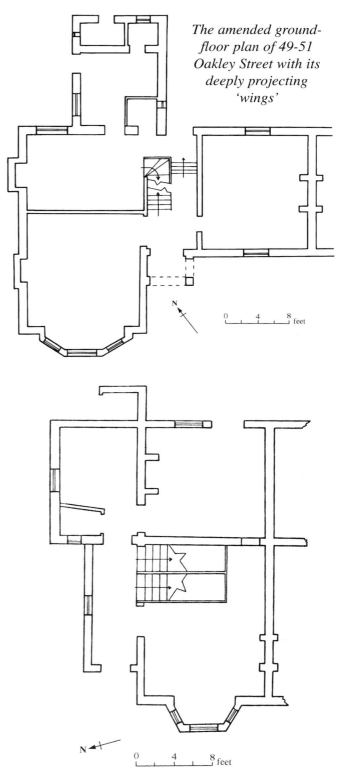

The amended ground-floor plan of 49-51 Oakley Street with its deeply projecting 'wings'

The ground-floor plan of 22-24 Underdale Road by the local builder, Oliver Jones, which shows a distinct individual design

houses in the neighbourhood and the accommodation was no more than the standard defined above, but it was arranged differently and in a way that was impossible, or very difficult, in a terrace. Kitchen and scullery, side by side at the rear, project sideways beyond the hall and parlour, and the parlour projects forward of the hall. The design is an exercise in recessed planes, and in conjunction with the two-storeyed bay windows at the front, it makes the house appear much bigger than it is. Moreover the style is different from that of most other semi-detached pairs: in a darker red brick and with a plat band of decorated terracotta panels at first-floor level. As the years passed, however, and as developments were on a larger scale, a tendency to monotony appeared in the street scene. It is most evident in rows of uniform houses in Bishop Street, and especially in the post-1900 Alfred Street, but it is also apparent in Tankerville Street, where a row of six tall identical semi-detached pairs in a hard red brick with side entrances and with gable ends to the street has something of the look of northern manufacturing towns.

The general Victorian use of derived classical forms so apparent in Kingsland was evident here as well. Even when, as at 14 Underdale Road, A.B. Deakin introduced doorways with two-centred heads, lancet windows, timber-framed gables, and bay windows with crenellated parapets, he failed to achieve anything like a Gothic effect. The clearest differences between individual houses, and between types of houses, were not in the forms but in the architectural ornament. Some larger houses, especially in Underdale Road, used a medley of motifs, mingling false timber framing with moulded-brick string courses and plat bands, some polychromy, and—at no. 27—a terracotta panel with sunflower ornament in a Queen Anne manner. But larger houses used polychromy in a minor way, and even in houses only slightly larger than most it was used with some restraint, generally in the form of yellow banding on a red-brick fabric, as at Stoneleigh (1877) and Walden (1883) in Bradford Street and, in conjunction with yellow quoins, in a terrace of three houses in Underdale Road in 1882.[245] It was used most enthusiastically on the smallest houses. Nos. 1–5 Cleveland Street, probably of 1880,[246] in red and yellow chequered brickwork were old fashioned and comparatively restrained, but the 1881 terrace

in the same street was exuberantly decorated, the red-brick fabric enlivened with bands of yellow brick, of blue brick, and of yellow and blue brick in combination. The three-storeyed Brighton Terrace (1880) was less bold but intended to impress with a façade of blue brick with yellow brick dressings. It was not unique, for the smaller 11 Underdale Road was also of blue brick with yellow brick banding. Against these the row of semis in Tankerville Street, in red brick with no other decoration than a dentil course below the gable eaves, stood out starkly in its plainness. By the next decade, however, polychromy of any kind was out of date. On the Whitehall estate it was very rare and when it appeared was subdued. The two adjoining pairs of semis in Canon Street (28–31) are alternately of red brick with yellow brick quoins and of yellow brick with red brick quoins, and there are scattered examples in Bishop Street.

Later houses, and houses of any pretensions, were more likely to use moulded brick or terracotta, as at Kingsland. Nos.22–24 Underdale Road have moulded-brick plat bands; Holly House (1893), Bradford Street,[247] has a moulded-brick string course with dentils below; 33–39 Underdale Road have egg-and-dart ornament to the string course, and 43–49 have moulded-brick labels with moulded keystones above narrow windows in a Queen Anne manner. No. 78 Bishop Street has a cornice with the dentils prolonged downwards and moulded, like very close-set machicolations: a trick also seen at the earlier Ruthwell, Bradford Street, and highly popular in Oswestry and found occasionally in Bridgnorth and Ludlow. Nos. 74–75 Bishop Street have moulded panels below the first-floor windows filled with a 'fish scale' motif. The most notable examples are on a big house (no. 6) and a small one (no. 13) in Canon Street; at the latter the first floor has a plat band with egg-and-dart below and the whole surface above covered with small panels enclosing lozenges and other motifs. Most houses, however, had only some slight decoration: a cable mould above a first-floor window or a doorway with a depressed ogee head.

Cherry Orchard was less homogeneous than Kingsland or the streets 'back of the Sheds', and Bradford Street and Underdale Road had a mixture of large and small houses, many of whose occupants were of some standing, including clergymen, businessmen, and people of independent means. Those two streets apart, it had a social character of its own, with a spread of occupations from charwomen and waiters to commercial travellers and dentists. Skilled artisans—joiners, compositors, engine drivers—were very prominent, but far and away the most numerous, almost one in three of the householders listed in street directories, were white-collar workers.[248]

By the end of the century Shrewsbury had acquired one of the architectural elements of the great manufacturing and commercial towns of the age: suburbs for classes. To some extent there had always been fashionable and less fashionable quarters of the town, and Belmont had been different from Roushill. By the 1830s Castlefields and Spring Gardens were becoming industrial areas. Physical separation, however, had until then been minimal, and rich and poor had lived more or less side by side. What was new was the appearance of separate areas each earmarked for a particular class, each with its distinctive type of house, and all widely separated from one another. To put it very briefly and schematically, the large detached houses and double-fronted semis of Kingsland were built for an oligarchy of successful professional and business men, the semi-detached pairs of Cherry Orchard for white-collar workers and better paid artisans, and the terraces 'back of the Sheds' for industrial workers. This class separation was not universal, and many quarters of the town (Belle Vue, for example) continued to be very mixed. Nevertheless the suburbs discussed above exemplify an historical process which, in its extreme forms, had a clear architectural effect.

Suburbs for Classes: Oswestry

Suburbs multiplied in all the larger Shropshire towns, but they were, like earlier ones, of mixed composition, as for example the Victoria Road area of Bridgnorth and Gravel Hill, Ludlow. It was at Oswestry, where the works and headquarters of the Cambrian Railway were sited, that the closest parallel with Shrewsbury appeared. Early to mid century building there along Leg Street and Salop Road was mostly a mixture of small two-storey terraces and imposing three-storey ones, such as Trinity Terrace (1862)[249] and the four houses (1867) numbered 15–21 in Leg Street,[250] with flanking projections and emphasized central doorways. By

the late 1860s, however, and following the building of the Assembly Rooms, Victoria Road was being developed with some small, some medium-sized, and some very grand houses. Just off Victoria Road, in Queen's Road and Queen's Park, a miniature Kingsland came into being in the 1880s and 1890s—miniature because it was much smaller and most of the houses were not quite so grand. They had all the modern conveniences of Kingsland but sometimes two rather than three reception rooms, four or five bedrooms, occasionally a separate staircase to servants' bedrooms, and, generally, smaller rooms.[251] The occupants were of similar standing—people of independent means, retired farmers, and professional and business men.[252] Like Kingsland the area had its own boys' boarding school—Salop School, a proprietary school, not in the same class as Shrewsbury School but with some architectural pretensions.[253] The physical separation from other suburbs was less than at Kingsland, but the area could be reached only from a turning off Victoria Road and was another sequestered enclave. It was even more of a local creation than Kingsland, most of the later houses being designed by a leading Oswestry architect, Edward Bremner-Smith, who may at one time have aspired to get Queen's Road renamed in his honour.[254] Not so far away, by contrast, Victoria, Edward, Weston, and Roft streets consisted mainly of long rows of terraces similar to some of those in Shrewsbury.

To some extent the countryside itself, served by a complex railway network,[255] was becoming something of a suburb. In several villages convenient to a railway station there appeared numbers of houses whose urban character distinguished them clearly from estate cottages on the one hand and from country villas on the other. Many are large detached or semi-detached houses which would not look out of place in Kingsland and they stand in plots of much the same size. Others are smaller, but again standing on small plots and similar to those in Belle Vue. Good examples are at Clive, in a favoured situation and close to Yorton station (opened 1858), and in Station Road, Baschurch (station opened 1848), and in the hamlet of Wollerton, which was no great distance from Hodnet station (opened 1867) and Tern Hill station (1899) on the Market Drayton to Wellington line, and which had its own halt between those stations from about the 1930s.

XVI   Domestic Styles 1830-1900

Mixed motifs

Victorian culture was so rich and multi-faceted that it cannot be captured in a formula, and what is true of the whole is true of one aspect of it, architecture. Sir John Summerson has commented upon the erection simultaneously and in similar circumstances of two buildings of starkly different character,[1] and Alastair Service has spoken of 'waves of fashion following each other rapidly and many cross-currents confusing the sequence of developments'.[2] In 19th-century Britain wealth and population increased at an unprecedented speed and with them the professions, the number of educated people, and the social range across which education spread. Art was no longer mainly a cult confined to the aristocracy and a small highly educated élite, and the museum and the art gallery were replacing the country house as its temple. There was a more varied clientele for architects at the very moment when architects were more numerous. Undoubtedly most of them were happy to practise what their teachers had taught them and so perpetuate a prevailing mode; equally certainly, however, some of them were ready to do anything but what they had been taught and to embark upon a wide range of new practices and new styles. They could happily do so because a heterogeneous clientele did not speak with the near-unanimity of the old aristocratic patrons and so, to a greater extent than at any time since medieval master masons had ruled the architectural roost, architects were inflicting their views upon clients rather than *vice versa*, and were determining the character of the domestic architecture of the age; within the limits, that is, of the practical requirements of house owners.[3]

Exoticism

Much of Victorian architecture was 'railway architecture', not in the sense that it was produced by or for railway companies but because the ease and cheapness of travel allowed an army of architects and architectural students to travel all over western Europe and bring back a wide assortment of styles. Styles had often been imported before but never from so many diverse sources at one time. This played some part in giving the period its variegated character, not merely because one style rapidly succeeded another but also because many coexisted at the same time, and often upon the same building.[4] Indeed complete houses, or even wings, built in a single style are rare. One example is Burwarton Hall, as remodelled in the mid century: a rambling Italianate structure with a low upper storey beneath a shallow roof with widely overhanging eaves. A more deliberate attempt at an Italian *palazzo*, albeit on a small scale and unmistakably a modest English country house in its conception, was Ashley House (*c.*1860; now the Abbey public house) in Monkmoor Road, Shrewsbury. More typical was Stanmore Hall near Bridgnorth, an 1870 amalgam of several styles, with French Renaissance roofs, Venetian Gothic windows to the upper part of the hall, ornately decorated window heads, plat bands and cornices, red and blue tiles on the roofs, and a prominent water tower with a colonnade supporting a pepperpot roof.[5] A similar use of many styles was proposed in the design of 1860 for Llwyn House, Oswestry. An approximation to a Second Empire style was a popular foreign import, and the best examples were the south-east front (1859) of Apley Castle,[6] the Hotel (1865) at Church Stretton, and the Grove,[7] Wistanstow. The four very large semi-detached houses (rivalling anything in Kingsland, Shrewsbury) which Pountney Smith erected off the west side of Belle Vue Road,[8] with mansard roofs and yet with stop-chamfered surrounds to the openings, can perhaps be best put into that pigeon-hole, if into any.[9]

The Queen Anne Llwyn and neighbouring timber-framed Careg Felin, in Queen's Park, Oswestry (see p.256)

Much commoner was the use of exotic motifs on houses of patently native derivation, and especially on those in towns and suburbs. The commonest manifestation was the use of differently coloured materials in the fabric. In the mild forms of patterning, polychromy—brickwork with headers of different colour or shade or of contrasting red brick-work with white stone dressings—had been known in England since the 16th century. What was new was the use of many more colours, of larger areas of colour, and, very often, of a violent contrast of colour. The fashion was first apparent upon churches, but within a decade had spread to secular buildings. It was not widely used in the Shropshire countryside and to a negligible extent on the larger houses there. Among smaller ones the Old Post Office at Ratlinghope, with elaborate diaper patterning in red and yellow brick, and Providence House, Ketley Bank, with alternate courses of two blue bands and one yellow one, are vivid rarities. In the towns it was used perhaps with most effect on modest terraces such as those in Rea Street and Cleveland Street, Shrewsbury. One of the earliest dated examples is 72 Oakley Street (1868),

Shrewsbury, a red brick house with a broad band of diaper patterning in blue brick. An unusual example is the semi-detached pair, with shops on the ground floor, in Scotland Street, Ellesmere, of brick in English bond and with alternate courses in pale and dark red. Some other examples in Shrewsbury suburbs have already been mentioned.[10] Polychromy was less popular by the 1880s and is not very conspicuous in Kingsland or on the later houses in Belle Vue. Nevertheless it lingered, even in houses of some standing, into the 20th century, as at Edward Terrace and Alexandra Terrace, Innage, Bridgnorth, of 1902.

It is not always possible to distinguish a taste for the exotic from a liking for Gothic, and Venetian Gothic windows—as for example upon Oswestry Cottage Hospital and the (now demolished) Raven Hotel,[11] Castle Street, Shrewsbury—satisfied both. Similarly the mansard roofs and ornate dormers of many houses in a Second Empire style were French and Renaissance at the same time. These motifs, scattered throughout a suburb or a town added yet another touch of variety to the architectural scene without ever setting their mark upon it, but satisfying that 'strange love of the age for richness and attractiveness' which Thomas Harris, the architect of Stokesay Court and Bedstone Court, commented upon.[12]

Historic styles

Foreign frills were not the major preoccupation of the domestic architecture of the time, which was far more obsessed with a yearning to relive its own past, as Harris also pointed out.[13] It did so in much the same sequence as before, and tastes for Gothic, for Tudor, for 'Jacobethan', and for 'Queen Anne' and 'Old English' succeeded ever more rapidly. These too added to the eclectic mix, but at the same time they gave it a unity and a direction. The unity was the more apparent because architects now had a common training and a national viewpoint which took little account of historic regional differences and engaged them in the search for a national style.[14] They produced generalized versions of historic styles, and as a result, and for the first time, there were national styles which, unlike earlier ones, were not confined to the mansions of the great but affected the homes of all men, down to cottagers and suburbanites. Further, as more men of no great wealth wished to build more houses of no great size in a fashionable and historic mode, that mode had to become more 'popular', and the Old English and Queen Anne styles, derived from the homes of earlier small gentry, of well-to-do farmers, and of professional men, began to oust the Gothic of feudal magnates and the grandeur of Elizabethan courtiers.

Before the 19th century the difference between secular and ecclesiastical architecture had been almost wholly one of function and form. Except in the years following the Reformation, when some churches were given a late-Gothic look, churches and houses alike had been built in the prevailing style of the time. By about 1840 a clear split had emerged as Gothic regained a total dominance in ecclesiastical architecture while in secular it was but one, and not the most favoured, among many styles. Some country houses were indeed built in a very Gothic vein, but they were negligible in number in comparison with the Gothic churches of the age. An authoritative account of the High Victorian phase mentions no more than a handful of houses and feels no need to discuss them as a class;[15] and that most

determinedly Gothic architect, William Butterfield, built only one complete country house.[16]

The revival of Gothic for church building was the outcome of an aesthetic almost blatantly controlled by ideology and was only one aspect of the revival of the Anglican church itself and its resumed proselytizing role. The choice of Gothic was perhaps not inevitable, but it was not surprising for Gothic had been the Church's style at the time of its greatest influence and power.[17] Religious practices had changed since then, but not so much that the form of a medieval church was inappropriate to the function of a 19th-century one.[18] On the other hand the function and form of houses had altered enormously, and Gothic as a domestic style had few practical advantages. Furthermore few large Gothic houses had survived the preceding centuries, during which the English house had acquired a classical character of one sort or another, and domestic Gothic had therefore little historical warrant. Moreover, while many architects might have been led by conviction to build a church in a Gothic style no matter what the difficulties, few were likely to try very hard to overcome the problems of adapting the style to modern living or to dissuade a patron whose heart was set on something else.[19] Gothic in churches had a passionate ideology behind it; in houses it was little more than an expression of a literary romanticism. Gilbert Scott expressed a view probably common among all classes when he criticized the 'manifest absurdity' of much domestic neo-Gothic and approved a 'commonsense' style that produced neither 'abbeys' nor 'castles' but 'houses'.[20] Taine said the same thing about 'comfort' in another way.[21]

There was perhaps less taste for the style in Shropshire than elsewhere. The county has nothing to rival the extravaganza of Kelham Hall (Notts.) and Eatington Park (Warws.), and the two most 'medieval' mansions were Ruyton Towers and Broncroft Castle. The latter, except for the lower of the two main towers,[22] was wholly rebuilt in the mid century and outwardly in the manner of Stokesay Castle, with an open hall lit by gabled dormers and set between flanking towers. It is as much a piece of antiquarian reconstruction as of neo-Gothic design. Ruyton Towers was built in the 1860s and early 1870s for the Walfords, a local landed family,[23] and was designed by an obscure Lancashire architect, Harry Percival of Newchurch in Rossendale.[24] The

The Quinta from the south-east

crenellated 13-bay south front, of red sandstone from a local quarry, has tiers of round-headed windows; the central bays are projected forward and have an extra storey, crenellated and machicolated, giving the impression of a keep—an impression heightened by the porch in the form of a 12th-century forebuilding. The rigid symmetry and the neo-Norman style are curiously out of date, and the massive air is in the manner of Rowton and Quatford castles of a generation earlier.

On a smaller scale, and with far less show of sham fortifications, is the Quinta at Weston Rhyn, for the same Thomas Barnes who built the Congregational chapel there.[25] It is of grey rock-faced stone with brown stone dressings and has traceried windows (some with flowing tracery), a crenellated tower, and bays and oriels irregularly disposed along the main fronts. A similar wealth of Gothic gables and windows distinguishes the additions to the medieval house at Chelmarsh.

As well as these there were a few smaller houses which made much use of the more obvious elements of the style. By 1851 the Revd. John Parker had built much of Llanyblodwel vicarage[26] with hipped roofs and two-light windows in an Early English style. Weston Lullingfields vicarage, contemporary with the church (1857),[27] has plain and trefoiled lancets and gabled dormers. Holdgate rectory (1865), by J.P. Seddon,[28] has plain and trefoiled lancets on the first floor and two-light windows in 12th-century style on the ground floor. Cwm Hall, Clunton, has some windows with trefoiled and some with **Y** tracery. Gannow Hill, in Welsh Frankton, had a slim round tower crowned by a tall pepperpot roof.[29] At Sweeney Hall, near Oswestry, a ground-floor gallery in a Gothic style was added to a neo-Greek house.

Throughout the whole period the Gothic element in houses was considerable but very thinly spread. It usually amounts to isolated motifs set within a non-

Gothic context: openings with two-centred heads, tracery, elaborate barge boards, crenellation, turrets. Most are wholly unremarkable. Two of the best doorways, richly moulded, are in Kingsland, Shrewsbury: at Moser's Hall, Greville Road, and the Headmaster's House, Ashton Road. Lyneal vicarage (c.1875)[30] has a large panel on the main wall set beneath a two-centred head with a crucifix in high relief. Window tracery was usually Perpendicular and was common in bay windows, as at Leaton vicarage (1859)[31] and the Grange, Much Wenlock. But there are exceptions. In Oswestry a pair of semi-detached houses in Queen's Road have two-light windows with trefoiled heads beneath an overall arch, and the Cottage Hospital, built in a very domestic form, has two-light windows in a Venetian-Gothic style. Crenellation was not very common in smaller houses and, when used there, was often over bay windows: 14 Underdale Road, Shrewsbury, was mentioned earlier; another example is Shelton Oak, and it was originally intended for the 'garderobe tower' at 29 Kennedy Road, Kingsland.[32] Steep gables used in profusion,

as at Pontesbury House, and highly decorated barge boards, as at Wixhill Lodge, Weston-under-Redcastle, could often give a Gothic air to very ordinary dwellings. So too could towers and turrets, especially in suburbs. Bremner-Smith's own house, 20 Victoria Road, Oswestry, had a turret with a pyramidal roof. In Shrewsbury A.B. Deakin built 1 Butler Road with a similar turret and in 1891–3 gave an up-to-date 'old world' air to Besford House by adding a turret and timber framed gables.[33] The Black Lion Hotel in Scotland Street, Ellesmere, is an extreme case of such titivation, having had a central first-floor oriel window in a Gothic style added to an unmistakably Italianate façade.

Another 'Gothic' decorative element which was not peculiar to Shropshire but was oddly popular there, especially in Oswestry, is a cornice in which the dentils are so heavily moulded and so exaggeratedly deep that they look like machicolations. There are examples in Bridgnorth, Ludlow, Shrewsbury, and a concentration in the Victoria Road area of Oswestry: the assembly rooms (1864), the Victoria works (1870), 22–24 and 32–34

The Victoria Road Assembly Rooms in Oswestry, of 1864

Victoria Road and 58–60 Roft Street. Weston House, Queen's Road, a red brick building employing these dentils and having an entrance tower surmounted by a tall pyramidal roof, flat-headed windows with simulated drip moulds and label stops in a grey stone flush with the brickwork, and with a two-light window with chamfered mullions and jambs, is an epitome of Salopian neo-Gothic.

The citing of several parsonages in the preceding paragraphs might give the impression that the clergy, from a combination of ideology and aesthetics, were more likely than the laity to go Gothic in their homes, and indeed sometimes, as at Leaton and Weston Lullingfields, a new Gothic house accompanied a new Gothic church. Most rectories and vicarages, however, were largely free of that influence. Between 1861 and 1869 the Hereford Diocesan Church Building Society gave grants towards eleven parsonages in the archdeaconry of Salop,[34] and one of them, Tugford, was built in a determinedly Gothic style. In the others the most obvious Gothic element was a taste for gabled dormers. In Haycock's vicarage (1869) at Meole Brace there is no external Gothic detail, but inside, on both floors, tall two-centred arches mark divisions between the house's different parts. What is probably the best known of all Shropshire parsonages, that at Upton Magna by G.E. Street, has a

slightly Gothic air mainly because of an attempt to give variety to the brickwork by laying it in herring-bone pattern beneath relieving arches.[35] In that respect it is typical of most and may well have influenced, if they needed influencing, some local builders and clergymen. Gothic, like other styles, could be merely cosmetic, as Bremner-Smith for one knew well: houses with identical elevations in Queen's Park, Oswestry, were thinly dressed in Gothic (Hendre Wen), Queen Anne (Llwyn), and timber-framed (Carreg Felin) styles.

Houses and the men who owned them had changed so much since the 16th century that Gothic had little practical relevance for them, however ancient the line of landed proprietors from which those owners sprang. It has been claimed that neo-Gothic was essentially the style of the established landed classes,[36] and for that reason it did not survive the post-1870 agricultural depression. Such determinedly Gothic and neo-Norman houses as Broncroft Castle and Ruyton Towers were indeed built by landowners, but so too was the Quinta, built with equal determination by an industrialist—and a nonconformist to boot. Moreover most of the landed gentry who built or enlarged their houses in the period did so in almost any style but Gothic.

The somewhat humdrum Tudor style with its large flat-headed windows, plain hood moulds, small gables, and occasional crenellation had a wide

Upton Magna Parsonage by G.E. Street

appeal by the 1820s and was used, it will be remembered, at Oteley Park, at Longner, and at Lilleshall Hall (Sheriffhales). Like its successor, neo-Elizabethan, it had practical advantages that Gothic lacked. It was, besides, both functionally and historically 'domestic' and carried an aura of romance without that 'manifest absurdity' of neo-Gothic which Scott complained of. It continued in favour throughout the 1830s and 1840s, generally in houses of moderate size, and in some town houses, for example those built for the headmaster of Shrewsbury School[37] in School Gardens. Some country houses, like Buildwas Park, Pimley Manor, Monkhopton House,[38] and Melverley vicarage were newly built; others, like Tedsmore, were older houses refronted. It appeared as well, and generally rather later, upon such small houses as the New Inn at Stanton upon Hine Heath and the house opposite it, and upon estate farmhouses and cottages such as

those on the Sutherland and Loton Hall properties. By the 1860s it was going out of fashion, and in 1869 a proposed restoration of Preen Manor in that style by W.D. Griffin of Wolverhampton was rejected in favour of Shaw's 'Old English' exercise, not without a rueful later comment that Griffin's design would not have cost a quarter of what Shaw's did.[39] On working-class housing it was used even later, and was conspicuous at Montague Terrace (1879) and, to a less extent, on Hawarden Cottages (1883), Rea Street, discussed earlier.[40]

Far and away the most popular and long-lasting of all the revivals was that 'commonsense Elizabethan' which Scott commended. It had all the practical advantages of 'Tudor' and it furnished more opportunities for ornament, for towers and projections, and for architectural virtuosity in general. Above all, at a time when Englishmen were happy to believe that they had become 'the greatest

One of the grandest houses in Shropshire in the Jacobean/Tudor style: Yeaton Pevery Hall, Bomere Heath

and most highly civilized people that ever the world saw',[41] it was associated with Good Queen Bess and Shakespeare, with the age that first glimpsed[42]

. . . the light that lit on England's way
The sundawn of her time-compelling power.

Of course the original style, like Shakespeare's drama, was more Jacobean than Elizabethan, but 'Elizabethan' was the more evocative word.

John Smalman's additions (1816, since demolished) to Stanley Hall, Astley Abbots, have been described as 'Jacobean' but were more 'Tudor' than anything else. The work of his nephew, Samuel Pountney Smith, at Lutwyche was probably the earliest example of the style in the county: he added a rear wing (1851, since demolished) and restored an Elizabethan front to a late 16th-century house that had been heavily modernized in the 18th century.[43] Boreatton Park (1854) and Pountney Smith's Ferney Hall (1856) followed soon after. The style's heyday in Shropshire was in the 1860s and 1870s, but some of its grandest effects—Stokesay Court (1888) and Yeaton Peverey (1892)—came later, and Ruckley Grange was as late as 1904. Like the original the revived style sat as happily on a vast pile like Adderley as on a smaller one like Marton House, Myddle, or on yet smaller ones like a 1½-storey house of 1893 in Aston Street, Wem, and on the doorways of an 1867 terrace in Leg Street, Oswestry. It employed brick or stone impartially, whether there were local sources of those materials or not. If it failed to capture the spirit of what it was emulating, that was not solely because it used different proportions, but because it used them in a generalized way. Shropshire houses of the late 16th and early 17th centuries had been built to a national pattern but—Condover apart—in a regional manner. Their 19th-century successors mostly copied the great prodigy houses of the earlier age and ignored the native version of the national style as seen at Wilderhope, for example, or at Lea Hall, Preston Gubbals. Even when an architect of greater talent than most broke away from the standard mould, as Shaw did at Adcote, he yet chose another generalized style and built a fashionable Cotswold manor house.

The same patriotic nostalgia that made Elizabethan so popular helped also to bring into fashion a 'black and white' style imitating traditional timber framing. There were, of course, many surviving timber buildings centuries older than the Elizabethan age, but in the late 19th century the practice was generally associated with that period. This was partly because the chronology of timber building was not well established and partly—in Shropshire at any rate—because the most conspicuous buildings could confidently be related to that period by well authenticated dates or by their easily datable Anglo-Flemish ornament.

Well before the mid century mock timber-framed buildings were appearing. At Old Hall, Wellington, a timber-framed range was extended in that style,[44] and a similar range was added at Burlton Hall, probably in 1837.[45] In those cases, and in the additions to Marrington Hall, the effect was being created more in deference to an older building than in its own right, but at Oakley Manor, Belle Vue, Shrewsbury, which Pountney Smith built for himself in the 1860s,[46] and at Shelton Oak Priory, a cottage enlarged to a gentleman's residence, the style was chosen for its own sake; and at Woolstaston rectory from 1858 onwards the original brick building and the contemporary additions were given a timber-frame cladding.[47] Nevertheless, despite such well known[48] splendid examples as Pitchford Hall[49] and Park Hall,[50] Whittington, timber was a vernacular material and not much associated with great mansions. In the late 19th century too it was rarely imitated upon the biggest houses. Thomas Harris's Bedstone Court (1884) is a notable exception, but generally, as at Yeaton Peverey, the black-and-white style was confined to a minor elevation or, as at Pitchford itself, to additions in sympathy with an earlier structure. Furthermore it was used, as Elizabethan was, in a generalized way: little attention was paid to local traditions and there was much reliance on southern practices such as the juxtaposition of exposed timber and hung tile or the setting of a timber upper part above a stone or brick ground storey. Examples are numerous. They range from Shaw's Bourton Cottage and Preen Manor of the 1870s through the Pengwern Boat Club's boathouse (J.L. Randal, 1881)[51] at Kingsland, Shrewsbury, the farmhouse of 1897 at Moreton Corbet, and Westhope Manor (1902), to the suburban examples discussed earlier. Nevertheless there were some houses in a wholly timber-framed style: the additions and refurbishings of 1880 at Black Birches,[52] Hadnall, the Home Farm at Sansaw, and the reconstruction of Bulkeley Hall,[53] Woore.

For the most part, however, timber framing, like neo-Gothic, was more a mode of decoration than a manner of building and is commonest on the gables and upper storeys of innumerable suburban houses throughout the last quarter of the 19th century and well into the 20th. Its decorative nature is vividly shown by the practice of applying thin timbers to the fabric, as at 34 High Street, Cleobury Mortimer, in 1871, or by painting timbers upon it. Sometimes, as on a house at Rodington, the effect is highly successful and one has to look twice to establish that, while one wing and the main range are of timber and of the 17th century, the other, later, wing is of brick with timbers painted upon it. Sometimes the deception—if deception were ever seriously intended—fails even from afar: presumably no one was ever deceived by Woodstile, Grinshill, where the painted 'timbers' run as truncated figures of eight from sill to wall plate—or rather from ground level to eaves. Sometimes, as at Shelvock and on the Crown Inn at Claverley, an external brick chimney has been painted to look like that near impossibility, a timber one.[54]

Genuine timber framing for anything larger than a shed was extremely rare.[55] It was used, probably early in the century, in a building put up for the rector of Acton Burnell, which comprised a coach house with accommodation for a groom above.[56] In 1866 a timber-framed school and schoolhouse was erected at Acton Scott,[57] and the mission room at Woofferton, Richard's Castle, was built of timber in 1895,[58] with posts set into sills resting on low brick walls, and Little Stretton church was built of timber in 1902. It was probably at much the same time that the timber-framed external wall at Little Stretton Manor, somewhat decayed, had another, better looking, timber-framed wall built in front of it.[59]

Among the currents of the time was a nostalgia for another happy period of English history, that of the Glorious Revolution and of the Augustan Age which was its sequel. Macaulay began his widely read *History* (published 1848–61) with the first; Thackeray turned to the second for what is arguably his best, and certainly his most deeply felt, novel, *Henry Esmond* (1852); and, later, Austin Dobson

made a literary career out of 18th-century pastiche. A liking for those eras joined very easily with a trend towards a style of architecture intended for the 'middling sort', and later suited to a wide clientele which did not want, or could not afford, the vast mansions that accommodated an Elizabethan style. Elements of the new mode were present in Shaw's Preen Manor and Bourton Cottage, combining timber framing, tile hanging, and Elizabethan windows, and again in the 1880s at Palms Hill near Wem, built in red brick with timber framing, tile hanging, and transomed windows. The so called 'Queen Anne' style used such late 17th- and early 18th-century elements as transomed windows, often with segmental heads, plat bands, deep cornices, dormer windows, hipped roofs, and white stone dressings against a red brick fabric, together with details in moulded brick and terracotta. That such an ensemble was put together for its popular quality is shown by the simultaneous rejection of the aristocratic baroque and Palladian styles that had been contemporaries, or near-contemporaries, of the original.

The earliest examples of the Queen Anne style, apart from Shaw's work, were on a large scale: Nesfield's Cloverley Hall (*c*.1864) and F.P. Cockerell's Woodcote (Sheriffhales), as rebuilt after the fire of 1874. At Cloverley Hall, which in appearance is a conventionally Elizabethan house, the new elements were minor features such as the carved panels of birds and flowers above doorways. Woodcote is a formal symmetrical design attempting to use the style in a grand manner, but it succeeds only in reproducing such Carolean creations as Swakeleys and Balls Park (both Midx.) and in reminding us that there was in the Queen Anne mode a large element of the Artisan Mannerism of which those two houses were prominent examples.

Attempts like Woodcote were almost doomed to be rarities,[60] and it was upon smaller houses, and especially on suburban ones, that the style sat most happily. Few suburban houses were built to a 17th-century form but three in Shrewsbury—7 Ashton Road (1882) and 32–34 Kennedy Road (1886), both by A.B. Deakin—are symmetrical compositions with overall hipped roofs, dormers, coved eaves, and—very much in the Artisan Mannerist mode— windows with elaborately pedimented heads in terracotta. Bremner-Smith's Llwyn (1896), Queen's

Park, Oswestry, and 55 Gravel Hill, Ludlow, on **L** plans and with windows with segmental heads and eyebrow hood moulds, have the gables of the wings outlined with, respectively, courses of moulded brick and bands of guilloche ornament in terracotta. Other examples are two adjoining houses of 1884 and 1898 in Scotland Street, Ellesmere, and a row of three shops with accommodation above (1898) in Aston Street, Wem. More in a country-house manner is Sedgeford—21 Underdale Road, Shrewsbury—with a timber-framed upper storey and a large terracotta sunflower panel on the entrance elevation. A terrace of three small houses in Oswestry, 73–77 Park Avenue, has openings with segmental heads in richly ornamented terracotta panels and keystones in the form of grotesque heads. Another terrace of four much larger houses, 43–49 Underdale Road, Shrewsbury, has tall windows with segmental heads, eyebrow hood moulds and prominent dormers outlined in moulded brick. Elements appear in many other houses, and often in very odd ways. At 5–7 Victoria Road, Oswestry, Dutch gables and pedimented windows with pedimented heads are again in an Artisan Mannerist mode. At 59–61 Gravel Hill, Ludlow, the style is almost parodied with exaggerated door and window heads in yellow dressings set against the red brick of the fabric.

The final stage in the search by architects for ever more vernacular forms for an ever wider clientele was the 'farmhouse' and 'cottage' style best known in some of the work of Lutyens and Voysey. An example is Ernest Newton's Scotsman's Field built, in what was becoming a suburb of Church Stretton,[61] on the slopes of the Long Mynd. The style was never common in the county, and what there was was nearly all 20th-century; but there had been earlier signs in large houses of an attempt at the 'common touch'. In the 1880s the hall at Acton Reynald was given an imposing fireplace with the folksy motto 'East, West, Hame's Best', and in the next decade at Shorthill, Ford, a house with a clas-

sical portico and internal doorways with eared architraves and pediments above, the dining room had that essentially northern vernacular element, an inglenook, although in a Jacobean style and with upholstered seats.

These examples also serve to show that an interior did not necessarily match the style of the exterior. It often did: at Stokesay Court the hall is in the neo-Jacobean style which one would expect from the façade, and at Yeaton Peverey the Elizabethan front is accompanied by the staircase with open-work heads to the newels and by the hall ceiling with delicate pendants. Usually, however, rooms were treated in a generalized classical manner, as at Culmington Manor where the exterior with mullioned and transomed bay windows and with many gables is at odds with ceilings with thin floral ornament and walls divided by slight pilasters. There was nothing Salopian about any of these nor yet about the William de Morgan tiles in the dining room at Adcote, but some houses made a proud display of local craftsmanship. In the vicarage at Leighton the staircase hall is lined with Jackfield tiles. George Maw, who later built the new 'Benthall' tile works in Jackfield, moved into Benthall Hall in the early 1860s and laid down in the hall there an elaborately patterned tiled floor mainly in boldly contrasting colours of dark red and yellow,[62] and in an adjoining room a more subdued floor in green and yellow.

By the end of the century all the historic styles had been exploited, and architects anxious to work within a different tradition had little choice but to trawl lower social depths and develop a cottage-style architecture adaptable to houses much bigger than cottages and needing servants to run them. In Shropshire the market for such houses was limited, and even in Church Stretton, then developing as a *rus in urbe*, little appeared until well into the next century.[63] Not until after the First World War did new suburbs, the site of the greatest building activity in the county, lose a late-Victorian air.

XVII   Commercial and Public Buildings: The 19th Century

Railway buildings

The railways' contribution to 19th-century industrial developments is a matter of dispute among economic historians.[1] What is beyond dispute is the very large contribution that their buildings made to the architectural scene—in Shropshire as elsewhere. Shrewsbury became a major railway centre after 1848,[2] and the works and head offices of the Cambrian Railways Co. were established at Oswestry in 1866;[3] there was a network of lines throughout the county,[4] and every town and many a village had its own station.[5]

Few of the stations were large, and none could rival the grandiose structures of London and of the great manufacturing towns. Despite its precocious development Shropshire had ceased to be a major industrial area by the mid century, and there was little incentive to build, for professional or business men on flying visits, those grand hotels which were adjacent to, or incorporated within, the stations of many large towns.[6] An exception—apart from the odd 'Railway Inn' or 'Station Hotel', more public house than hotel—was at Wellington, the nearest main-line junction to the east Shropshire coalfield.[7] There the Station inn, a large three-storeyed building in a red-brick Tudor style, was built next to the station as it was enlarged in the 1860s.[8] In Shrewsbury too, opposite the station, there was a large commercial Station Hotel, described as new in 1879,[9] and other hotels not far away claimed various classes of station trade.[10]

In fact most Shropshire stations were designed to look like houses, of greater or lesser pretensions according to the size of the community they served. Shropshire was the last county but one to be connected to the national network, and even then it was, as it has remained, a route to somewhere else, and its stations reflected the local nature of much of

its passenger traffic. The most obvious exceptions were at Shrewsbury and Oswestry and, to a less extent, the rebuilt joint station at Wellington.

Shrewsbury station was a joint venture by the four companies which were building or projecting lines from the town in the late 1840s;[11] it was always meant to be more than a train shed and concourse, and it housed various offices. From the moment it was built it eclipsed what until then had been the town's most architecturally prominent transport building, the large Greek Revival warehouse (1835)[12] at the Howard Street terminus of the Shrewsbury Canal, behind what became the station site. Shrewsbury station was designed by T.M. Penson, who had previously worked as a railway surveyor.[13] In its original form it was a large symmetrical building in Grinshill stone with a two-storey main block and a three-storey central tower, all in a very rich Elizabethan style with much late Gothic ornament. The interior was, in part, as ornate as the exterior and the former station master's office has a richly decorated ribbed plaster ceiling. The station looked, and was probably meant to look, like a town hall or other public building, although it could equally well have been a new range in an Oxford or Cambridge college. The symmetry, but not the general effect, was destroyed in 1854–5 when a large extension was added in the same style at the north end. In 1899 the remarkable engineering and architectural feat was begun of adding a third storey below the other two and copying the original style so carefully that it is impossible for the uninitiated, however expert in historic architecture, to guess what has happened.[14]

Oswestry station was being built some 20 years later than Shrewsbury, when railway companies were less concerned to get their presence accepted by disguising their structures as something else. It is

Shrewsbury Railway Station from a lithograph of 1849

Detail of the plasterwork ceiling of the Station Master's Office at Shrewsbury Railway Station

a symmetrical two-storeyed building with flanking pavilions and side-ranges in a modified Italianate style: with round-headed windows, a shallow roof, and overhanging eaves. It is a large station building for a town which, although it was the hub of an extensive rail network,[15] was nevertheless not on a main line.[16] In 1866, however, the offices of the newly formed Cambrian Railways Co. were moved to Oswestry, and the building looks what it was— that rarity of a prestigious office block housing a passenger station.[17]

Other Shropshire stations, even in towns, were smaller in scale and meant more to reassure than to impress. Some of the larger ones are in the form of a miniature country house: generally of two storeys, symmetrical, and with a main range set between flanking wings, as at Ellesmere and Wem; Bridgnorth has a single-storey version. In the large village of Baschurch the same formula was used, but the station had slight wings and was not wholly symmetrical. At Hodnet and Crudgington, both of one storey, the projections were no more than punctuations of the ends. Village stations generally were made to look like cottages, quite large ones at Bucknell, Knighton, and Whittington and small ones at Hadnall, Westbury, Weston Rhyn, and Yockleton. The most notable exception to this cosy English countryside manner was Gobowen station, an Italian villa with a campanile-style tower and a waiting room with an apsidal end. Nevertheless it was perhaps equally reassuring, for Cronkhill, and to a lesser extent Oxon, had domesticated the form in Shropshire a generation earlier. As a late 19th-century local commentator said of Shrewsbury station, such buildings 'might suggest to the stranger an ancient origin opposed to latter-day utility'.[18]

On the L.N.W.R.'s Crewe–Shrewsbury line, completed in 1858,[19] there was some notable standardization with 'colour coding': small stations, like Hadnall and Yorton, were of red brick with yellow dressings while large ones like Wem and Whitchurch were in black brick. Elsewhere it was lack of standardization that was most noticeable. On the Shrewsbury and Chester railway, despite all the buildings having been designed by one man, T.M. Penson,[20] Weston Rhyn station and Whittington crossing house were of stone; Rednall station and Leaton crossing house were of red brick; Baschurch, Gobowen, and Whittington stations were stuccoed; Gobowen was Italianate, Rednall Tudor; Baschurch was late 17th-century, having windows with moulded surrounds, high transoms and short hood moulds; Whittington station was given a vaguely Jacobean look with a timber-framed porch;[21] the others were mid 19th-century cottages with plain windows and prominent gables. The most prominent common features were the elaborately decorated barge boards and even those differed in design.

Buildings on other lines could be equally varied. For example Micklewood crossing house on the Shrewsbury and Hereford railway, completed as far as Ludlow in 1852,[22] is of red brick in English bond with darker red courses; Church Stretton and Craven Arms stations were both of stone, but one had hipped roofs and overhanging eaves, the other a series of differently sized gables; while Ludlow, also in stone, was in a more severe style. On the L.N.W.R. line from Craven Arms to Swansea there could hardly be a greater contrast than that between the rectangular block beneath a hipped roof that was Broome station and the stations at Bucknell and Knighton, both of 1860, with polychrome roofs, multiple gables, and elaborate barge boards.[23]

Nevertheless there was standardization of a sort. Westbury and Yockleton, neighbouring stations on the Shrewsbury–Welshpool line, opened in 1862,[24] have flat-headed openings with chamfered stone surrounds, narrow transomed windows, elaborate barge boards, and identical plans; Highley and Hampton Loade stations, of the early 1860s,[25] neighbours on the Severn Valley railway, have almost identical plans, semicircular heads to the openings, and plain barge boards; Bucknell and Knighton have already been cited; and Onibury and Craven Arms were both built of a dark stone, with broad transomed windows, patterned glazing, and plain barge boards. Such neighbourly likenesses over-rode county boundaries: the elements of Highley and Hampton Loade were repeated nearby at Bewdley in Worcestershire, and on the Shrewsbury–Birmingham railway Albrighton in Shropshire and neighbouring Codsall in Staffordshire were virtual twins.

Most early stations were built by small companies operating short lines and needing few structures and those of very varied functions. Such concerns were by their size, less attracted than larger ones to standardization and they had not the advantages which the latter enjoyed of access over their own metals to distant sources of standard materials. Furthermore the vanity of architects had to be taken into consideration, and even when one man was responsible for all the buildings along a line, as T.M. Penson was on the Shrewsbury–Chester line, the results could be very varied and in many ways. Paradoxically therefore Shropshire railway stations, apart from those on the L.N.W.R.'s Shrewsbury–Crewe line, were standardized in a very local way: local not in the sense that their likes could not have been found in other counties, but because they occur in penny packets, in groups of two or three, each group different from the others.

The styles and motifs chosen by the designers of railway stations were very varied and were often mingled on the same building. There are very few stations—apart from Shrewsbury, Gobowen, and Rednall, all by T.M. Penson—that can be seen as consistent exercises in one mode. Gothic details were mostly employed as isolated motifs upon buildings of another style or of no style at all. Good examples are the quatrefoil panels and doorways with two-centred heads at Bucknell and Knighton.

The most striking use of Gothic was for the Decorated screen of the 1860s which hid the extension of the platforms at Shrewsbury onto the Castle Foregate bridge.[26] This use of Gothic was, of course, very similar to its use on houses; on the other hand, however, timber framing, so common on houses, was almost unknown on railway stations,[27] and the element of it with most appeal was almost wholly in the form of elaborate barge boards on brick or stone gables. Italianate was used most happily on Penson's Gobowen station and on a large scale at Oswestry, but it generally appeared in the very debilitated form of the Victorian fondness for round-headed windows, as, for example, at Albrighton, Crudgington, Ellesmere, Hampton Loade, and Highley. Remarkable for its precocity was the occasional display of late 17th-century motifs. At Baschurch station narrow windows with high wooden transoms are surmounted by short unreturned hood moulds; and at Frankton (1864) on the Cambrian line the 'Dutch' gables have terracotta plaques beneath short hood moulds, and the upper parts of the segmental-headed windows of the ground floor are filled with intricate geometrical patterns in a Queen Anne manner.[28] Commonest of all, however, was a generalized Tudor–Elizabethan style. Shrewsbury was the earliest and most lavish example. Other stations were more economically

The 'Dutch' gables of Frankton Railway Station

designed, often content with not much more than stone-transomed windows and doorways with four-centred heads. Examples are—or were—at Bridgnorth, Craven Arms, Onibury, Church Stretton, Much Wenlock, Westbury, and Yockleton. Most of Penson's buildings along the Chester line, whatever their style and even including such a plain one as Leaton crossing house, included somewhere or other a doorway with a four-centred head. The popularity of the style, parallel with that in domestic architecture, is partly the result of the absence of large towns and the consequent prominence of small stations. Partly, however, it came about because the formative period of the railway network in Shropshire was from the late 1840s to the early 1860s, when 'Elizabethan' was enjoying its greatest favour nationally.

Factories

Technical progress and the amalgamation of many small concerns into a few large ones have been constant elements of modern industry, and buildings accommodating industrial processes have always been ruthlessly altered or demolished. Thus the foundries and furnaces of Coalbrookdale and the structures directly associated with them have survived, if at all, as fragmentary ruins;[29] and the once great array of chimneys and kilns at Coalport and Jackfield[30] have almost wholly vanished. They may have had little architectural character, but their loss has meant that industrial architecture in Shropshire is largely the architecture of offices, of showrooms, of warehouses, and of structures housing finishing processes. Most of these are of the mid and late 19th century; partly because earlier ones themselves were to some extent vulnerable and partly because industry was still expanding until then.[31] By then, however, modern industry had long outgrown its Salopian cradle and there was nothing erected in the county in those years as important as the Iron Bridge[32] and Bage's flax mill,[33] Ditherington, Shrewsbury, had been a century before.

The new industrialists' ambivalence towards the old society that they were transforming is now a commonplace among historians.[34] It showed itself in many ways, of which perhaps the most striking example is the well known contrast between two neighbouring London termini: Cubitt's King's Cross boldly proclaiming itself a railway station, and Scott's St. Pancras hiding an engineering achievement behind a medieval façade. In Shropshire there was no such clear division, but two different approaches were apparent. One was to erect in a well established and long-lived domestic idiom a building whose form or bulk—like that of a Pennine weavers' house with long multi-mullioned 'top-shop' windows—stated its function without emphasizing it. A late 18th-century warehouse at the Caughley China works—precursor of the Coalport works—was wholly in a small-house tradition and may indeed have been converted from that form. It was symmetrical, of three storeys of diminishing height, and with quoins at the angles, but with the centre occupied by two large semicircular headed openings, one above the other, for a waggon entrance and a hoist.[35] As enterprises expanded their buildings grew larger, but the same aesthetic approach is seen, whatever the revolutionary nature of its structure, in Bage's mill. The Great Warehouse (1838) in Coalbrookdale[36]—now the Museum of Iron—and such later buildings of the mid century as Potter's rope and leather works at Frankwell and Hudson's brush factory at Coleham were in the same vein:[37] very large four- and five-storey structures with regular tiers of plain windows interrupted, where necessary, by waggon entrances and hoists. And even the Cambrian Railway works at Oswestry

(c.1866),[38] modelled on the Shrewsbury & Hereford Railway's building in Coleham, was similar. All these, like Rodney's ships of the line, give an impression of having been built by the mile, for, as Tann has pointed out, the same type of building could serve many trades and the rectangular multi-storeyed form was the most generally satisfactory.[39]

The Long Warehouse, probably of the late 1880s,[40] at Coalbrookdale and Jones's Maltings, of 1884 and later,[41] in Belle Vue, Shrewsbury, continued the tradition of plain and identical windows, long row above long row; but they were treated in a more design-conscious fashion. At Coalbrookdale the fenestration of the two upper floors, though still plain and unvaried, is yet in a complex rhythm of broad and narrow windows on the lower floor and of broad windows and blank spaces on the upper. At the Belle Vue maltings the symmetrical three-storeyed main block and the flanking kilns and office building are unified by the fenestration and by plain giant pilasters creating a series of similar but clearly marked bays. The Long Warehouse and the Maltings were probably anticipated by the (now demolished) Circus brewery at the bottom of Bridge Street, Shrewsbury. That was a collection of mainly undistinguished structures, but one among them was very large, very plain, multi-storeyed, partly fenestrated and partly with blank walling and with a symmetrical side elevation of seven bays of very tall recessed panels in a neo-classical manner, with semicircular heads, the central bay wider than the others, having a segmental head. The business had been founded in Bridge Street in 1866 and the building was probably of a comparable date.[42] The Lilleshall Co.'s New Yard, of the 1860s, at Wrockwardine Wood, a vast one-storey structure, was in a similar vein.[43] If it is true that the industrial architect's task is 'to find architectural solutions to problems of accommodating industrial processes',[44] then the designers of these three buildings may be said,

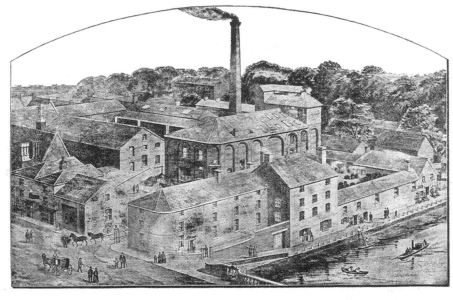

The Circus Brewery that once stood at the bottom of Bridge Street in Shrewsbury

from a late 20th-century standpoint, to have succeeded, or at any rate to have tried.

The second way of imparting architectural interest to an otherwise bald and uninspiring structure was to apply currently fashionable architectural motifs, in an attempt to suggest that the building was something other than what it was. This was necessarily a later method than the first, for it was well into the 19th century before brief fashions for historic and exotic styles became common.[45] The Coalbrookdale Co. may have been affected by it when, in 1843, they added a highly ornamental clock tower to the Great Warehouse.[46] About the same time on the bank of the Severn they built another warehouse (now the Museum Visitor Centre) linked by a plateway to the works. It was designed by their works manager, Charles Crookes,[47] and built of red brick with yellow brick dressings with a profusion of buttresses, turrets, and crenellations in a sub-Gothic style. In 1859 the company, aware of the need for technical education and actuated by a compound of enlightened self-interest and altruism, built the Coalbrookdale Literary and Scientific Institution.[48] Crookes was again the designer and the building is of blue brick with white brick dressings in a Jacobethan style with a symmetrical seven-bay front dominated, originally, by large curvilinear gables.[49] It differs very little from Ironbridge's National school (of the same date) and makes no attempt to express in form or style its different origins and function.

Until the 19th century much industry in the Severn Gorge had been small and the work places scattered: at Jackfield the pottery industry was largely carried on in kilns built on the ends of the potters' cottages.[50] As enterprises grew bigger, and as different processes were concentrated in larger complexes, the opportunity arose to hide many of them behind a screen of buildings serving ancillary functions and treated in a current architectural fashion. The Victoria Iron Works (1870)[51] at Oswestry presented a street front of red brick with yellow dressings, with the exaggerated dentil courses popular in the town and in a style similar to that of the nearby Assembly Rooms of 1864. Between 1873 and 1884 Thomas Corbett's very large Perseverance Iron Works in Shrewsbury was built, in stages,[52] with a main front to Castle Foregate: designed by Corbett's kinsman A.B. Deakin,[53] it is a very long building in red brick with blue and yellow dressings, some of the windows of two lights with cast-iron colonnettes as mullions, roughly symmetrical, punctuated by pedimented dormers along the roof line and by waggon entrances at ground level, and dominated by a central tower with a French Renaissance roof. Just to the north, in 1884 Shrewsbury Gas Light Co. erected an impressive front building with an eclectic mix of Renaissance and Italianate features (paired pilasters with ground-floor Corinthian capitals and two-storeys of round-headed windows with imposts and engraved keystones) enlivened with—*inter alia*—red and blue brickwork, friezes of moulded flowers, an eaves cornice, and elaborate ironwork along the rooftop.[54] Between 1872 and 1875 Craven Dunnill wholly rebuilt the old Thursfield works at Jackfield with a front range of greyish brick with red-brick dressings, in a style reminiscing about, rather than actually copying, Early English, with a series of ornate buttresses, pointed windows with decorative tiles in the heads, and a tower crowned originally with a spire.[55] In 1883 Maws built the new 'Benthall' works at

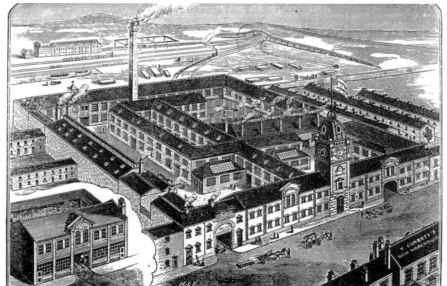

The Perseverance Iron Works in Shrewsbury in 1884

The main front to the Perseverance Iron Works in Castle Foregate, with James Guest's implement depot

Joyce Turret Clock manufacturers, Station Road, Whitchurch, showing the offices with ornamentation and the works under a plainer structure to the rear

Jackfield with the front ranges in red brick with segmental heads and with dentilled gables with round openings.[56] They make a stark contrast with the formal symmetrical frontages of similar earlier works in the Potteries.[57]

These last two were designed by Charles Lynam of Stoke-upon-Trent,[58] and, while he changed his mind about what style to work in, he continued to hide industrial aspects as far as possible and to introduce a hierarchy of architectural treatment. The great complex of buildings behind the Perseverance Iron Works had no architectural elements at all,[59] and behind the Gas Light Co.'s building of 1884 there were only the works and gasometers.[60] At Craven Dunnill's works the buildings housing the drying, firing, and decorating shops were without the pointed windows and buttresses of the offices and showrooms but were accorded more architectural status than the shops for sorting and storing the dust clay.[61] At Maws' works the long three-storey range at the rear was given some character with polychromy and string courses, but it was clearly a poor relation of the front range. Even when the building was on a small scale, like Joyce's Clock Manufactory (1904)[62] at Whitchurch, the same distinction was kept up between the offices at the front, in deep red brick and with considerable ornament including a baroque frontispiece, and the works under the same roof in pale brick and unadorned. In this respect industrial enterprises resembled contemporary country houses, where the rustic cousins of factory hands worked in vast plain ranges of service buildings discreetly tucked away behind an impressive main block.

Agricultural enterprises

Technical progress and amalgamation affected agriculture as well as industry, and by the early years of the 19th century occasionally resulted in the creation of very large and efficient farm complexes in the form of three or four one-storey or two-storey ranges around one or two fold yards.[63] The earliest known examples at Day House (1812–13), Cherrington, and Honnington Grange (1817–19), Lilleshall, were on the marquess of Stafford's estate, then being 'improved' by the 'ruthless Scot' James Loch. They were wholly up to date in lay-out and in fittings, with a steam engine at Cherrington and water-powered threshing machines at Honnington

Grange and Lilleshall Grange (c.1820). The farm buildings were accompanied by farmhouses with ample accommodation, having—apart from the usual offices—a parlour, a family room, a master's room as well at Honnington, several bedrooms, and a back stair for the servants. These ensembles of house, barns, byres, stables, granaries, etc., show their close relationship with factories of the period not only in their efficient organization of a productive process but also in the stark plainness of their elevations.[64]

Later examples at Crowleasows Farm, of 1863, in Middleton and at Stanway Manor, of 1891,[65] in Rushbury parish, were even more efficient, with covered foldyards at Stanway. At Crowleasows, on an **E** plan with the foldyards separated by a range of building, there was a 'railway' with tubs running in grooves along all the ranges and directed from one to another by turntables.[66] There were connections with industrial or commercial enterprise at both farms;[67] Crowleasows' owner Sir Charles Rouse-Boughton, of Downton Hall, was also chairman of the company which built the Hotel at Church Stretton as a speculation.[68] Unlike factories, however, which went in for some ornament in later years,[69] farm buildings continued to be very plain structures with, for example, nothing but the owner's initials and the date at Crowleasows[70] and very little decoration at Stanway. That may be because agricultural entrepreneurs did not need to build their own showrooms but could exhibit and sell at fairs and markets.

Shops

Before the mid century urban architecture, apart from the occasional public building, was essentially domestic architecture, even if many of the houses had shops on the ground floor. From the mid century onwards the town-centre scene was more diverse and increasingly dominated by public and commercial structures of a kind, and very often of a size, different from those of their predecessors. And even when not, when fulfilling old functions in a small way, shop buildings tended to proclaim their presence with a new stridency:[71]

So, friend, your shop was all your house!
Its front, astonishing the street,
Invited view ...

The Hotel (c.1865) at Church Stretton and the more or less contemporary rebuilt Raven Hotel[72] in Shrewsbury were not noticeably grander or bigger than the Talbot (1777)[73] in Shrewsbury or the slightly later Wynnstay Hotel in Oswestry; but while the last two could easily be mistaken for the town houses of local grandees,[74] the first two were clearly not. Other types of structure—town halls, markets, shops, insurance offices—were often yet more determined to attract and to serve the ever growing volume of trade.

Industrial processes were only a means to an end: to sell goods at a profit. For that showrooms and shops were needed, and at both of the Jackfield tile works there were display areas, intended for the wholesale trade, included in the front ranges. For many years past, and increasingly with the introduction of plate glass in the mid century, shop fronts had become larger and grander.[75] J. & B. Blower's cabinet maker's shop at 29–30 Pride Hill, Shrewsbury, probably of the 1870s, had three very large shop windows occupying the whole of the long ground-floor front.[76] By contrast the upper floors, of six bays in a classical façade, were designed in the age-old tradition of 'living over the shop', with the fenestration of 'shop' and 'house' markedly different. As retail trades grew in volume and variety and as enterprises grew in size the need for larger, well lit floor spaces became more pressing and could not always be solved by lateral expansion. Instead upper floors had to be used as shops, and so began that divorce between shop and house so common today. The large plate-glass windows on the first floor of Adams's ironmongery shop, 43 High Street, Shrewsbury (now the West Bromwich Building Society—and with the ground floor altered),[77] was probably inserted into an earlier front, as was the large first-floor shop window, the twin of that on the ground floor of the present wool shop in Waterloo House, Bridgnorth. In 1884 Thomas Corbett, owner of the Perseverance Iron Works, well known for its agricultural machinery,[78] put up a purpose-built two-storey warehouse opposite his works.[79] He had earlier had an interest in a warehouse opposite the railway station, an agency for 'all the leading makers' of agricultural implements. It is of three storeys, in a mixture of styles but vaguely Romanesque; very large windows on all floors have mullion-colonnettes, and originally

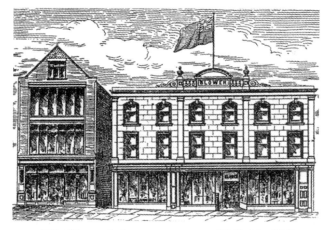

F.T. Blower's ironmongery at 28 Pride Hill

there were two ploughs mounted above the cornice.[80] F.T. Blower's three-storey ironmongery at 28 Pride Hill was in a more sober style but similar in form,[81] and so too, in a bold baroque manner, was Henry Salt's ironmonger's shop (1901) at Church Stretton.[82] Most 'astonishing' of all was Birchall's ironmongery (1904), at 40 High Street, Whitchurch,[83] with three storeys of very large windows and the whole front in a very ornate cast iron. In the small towns of Shropshire, largely serving rural communities, a main purpose of these new shops was to sell the capital goods and implements that modern agriculture needed and which modern industry supplied.

Many such shops, like earlier buildings in towns like Manchester, were a combination of showroom and warehouse and it was not ironmongers alone who could benefit from multi-storey 'display units' and large windows. Birchall's at Whitchurch used only two thirds of the impressive High Street building; the rest was occupied by an outfitters. The building was intended from the start to have more than one occupant, for the first-floor façade is in two parts: a larger one of three two-light bays and a smaller one of a single bay with three lights; at ground level there is a carriageway between the parts. In Shrewsbury 3–4 Shoplatch were built in

40-42 High Street, Whitchurch in cast iron

3-4 Shoplatch, Shrewsbury, built in 1882

1882 for Jones's Dining Rooms, with a shop on the ground floor and well lit separate ladies' and gentlemen's rooms on the floor above.[84] The two-storey auction rooms built for Hall, Wateridge & Owen in Milk Street were designed by Lloyd Oswell in 1892 with very large and prominent first-floor windows.[85] The present premises of Travelcare and Barnardo's, 17–19 Cross Street, Oswestry, have large first-floor shop windows with cast-iron colonnettes and ornament, and the Bewise shop in the same street (no.16), with the gable end-on to the road, has a huge arched window on the first floor, the enormous expanse of glass broken up by wooden glazing bars in an elaborate pattern.

The purpose-built multi-storey shop front was the mark of the future but was still an 'astonishing' intruder into the street scene, and up to the end of the century most premises retained the old 'shop and house' appearance. Nevertheless, some of those also attempted to utilize their building in the way demanded by the new commercial developments while keeping their old form, as J. & B. Blower appear to have done at 29–30 Pride Hill, where the first floor was probably used as offices.[86]

The shopping streets of country towns had developed over centuries and by the mid 19th had buildings of several different styles. Nevertheless there was an overall uniformity, for a building of any one period closely resembled its contemporaries. Furthermore most of them were built or refronted in the 18th and early 19th centuries and, despite their minor stylistic differences, were all in the same sub-classical mould. The late 19th-century buildings, however prominent, were not numerous enough wholly to alter the character of the street, and Shropshire therefore had none of the variegated and

Cross Street in Oswestry, redeveloped in 1880

overpowering late 19th-century streets found in the larger towns. There was, however, one exceptional development. In 1880 Cross Street, Oswestry, was a narrow thoroughfare lined on the north with very dilapidated buildings, and the corporation decided to widen it, totally demolishing that side.[87] Redevelopment in the 1880s produced a street of very tall buildings, with shops on the ground floor, some with the first-floor showrooms described above, and in a variety of styles, ranging from Romanesque through early Gothic, late Gothic, and timber framing to a belated Italianate. Each was impressive in itself but, for all the architects' efforts, none stood out from its rivals and the street has a uniformity of its own: 'Where everybody's somebody, Then no one's anybody'. There, given a clear field, Salopian commerce was able to produce a pure late 19th-century shopping street, similar, despite its small scale, to those of the great commercial and manufacturing towns.

Banks

Bankers were as interested as shopkeepers in impressing the world, but they did so on the whole in a genteel fashion, concerned not to dazzle their clients with catch-penny displays but to reassure them with a dignified solidity. Banks in Shropshire were generally prominent in the street scene more by their position than by anything else, often occupying a corner site or a site on a main street facing another street at right angles. None ever equalled the splendour of some of those in the great cities; their common element was their restrained but increasingly grand manner; their styles were those of the current fashions.[88]

The earliest surviving bank buildings are those of the savings banks,[89] which were established in most Shropshire towns in 1817–18[90] and which built themselves premises in the 1820s and 1830s.[91] Indeed Whitchurch savings bank, of 1823, was perhaps the first purpose-built one in England. (It was replaced in 1846 by the classical building in St. Mary's Street.)[92] Sometimes, as at Much Wenlock, they took over and converted private houses,[93] and the new bank at Oswestry, erected in 1830, looked like a private house, built of brick with plain domestic-type windows and overhanging eaves.[94] To some extent, of course, they were private houses, for all of them, whether converted or purpose built,

*Oswestry Savings Bank built in 1830
—a very domestic design*

provided living accommodation, generally above the premises—like contemporary shops.[95] The Oswestry trustees, for example, wanted a 'new Bank and residence for the Secretary'.[96] The practice continued for a long time and was not confined to savings banks. After 18 Broad Street, Ludlow, was acquired by bankers (*c.*1816) they had to mar a determinedly symmetrical front with a second doorway to the manager's quarters.[97] The incorporation of a dwelling within the building was made easier as the tyranny of symmetrical design was thrown off and separate doorways could be provided for the clients and for the manager's household without committing any architectural solecisms—as in the Salop Old Bank (now NatWest) branch built (by 1895) at 21–22 High Street, Bridgnorth,[98] where the subsidiary doorway is marked 'House' and 'no. 21'.

Not every savings bank was as domestically vernacular as those at Much Wenlock and Oswestry. The purpose built 'Bank for Savings' (1830), 7 Scotland Street, Ellesmere, now a shoe shop, was in a subdued Italianate style. That at Bridgnorth, of *c.*1837, was in a Regency style with stuccoed pilasters, and with exaggerated keystones to the ground-floor windows, those lighting the banking hall being broad and tripartite. The County Savings Bank's new building of 1838, at 1 College Hill, Shrewsbury, probably by Edward Haycock, was in a Regency style, with the banking hall differentiated externally by large windows, and with a touch of Greek Revival in the low pediment of its front to the street.[99]

Although many commercial banks began as small concerns, with a few shareholders, and were often accommodated in private houses or solicitors' offices, they were in the mainstream of economic development and, if they did not fail, were ever expanding and merging. As a result their early premises have sometimes survived as buildings but never as banks for it became necessary for a bank, as it lost its 'private' character, to have a street elevation 'arranged to show clearly the purpose for which it was built'.[100] Consequently the early premises of commercial banks are neither so prominent nor so readily identifiable as those of the savings banks. One that is, on the northern corner of the Square and High Street, Shrewsbury, was for many years occupied by the county bankers Rocke, Eyton & Co., from 1885 Eyton, Burton, Lloyd & Co. (the Salop Old Bank). It is in the same Regency style as the savings banks and originally had a banking hall lit by large windows.[101] Although in a more advantageous position, it was not noticeably grander than the savings bank in College Hill. The premises of the Shropshire Banking Co., now

Lloyds TSB,[102] in High Street, Newport, were in the same imposing but reticent style. In the late 19th century, as amalgamations were accelerating into their culminating phase in the first quarter of the next, commercial banks operated on a larger scale and needed larger and more prominent premises. At the same time architectural values had changed, and current styles, whether they expressed the architect's or the patron's predilections, had become more strident. As a result of the combination of economic advance and aesthetic change commercial banks now became, as they have remained, far more conspicuous than savings banks.

Small country banks were always vulnerable to takeovers by more widely based concerns, but one which lasted for a very long time and was responsible for several bank buildings surviving from the late 19th century and the first few years of the 20th was the Salop Old Bank. Rocke, Eyton & Co.'s former building (now the Britannia Building Society's) at the corner of the Square, Shrewsbury,

The former North & South Wales Bank (now HSBC) built at the Cross in 1890

has already been mentioned, and the Salop Old Bank and its architect, Lloyd Oswell,[103] were responsible for prominent structures in Bridgnorth and Ellesmere. The branch—mentioned above—at 21–22 High Street, Bridgnorth, is in an 'Old English' style, with a great amount of plasterwork and false timber—quite in Oswell's manner elsewhere.[104] The Old Bank's former Ellesmere branch (also now NatWest),[105] built in Scotland Street c.1900,[106] has 'Tudor' windows, a stone-fronted ground floor, a first floor with alternating bands of brown stone and red brick, and a heavy coved Queen Anne canopy over the doorway. The contrast with the 1830 savings bank next door is enormous. Carved on a small central plaque above the cornice are three leopards' heads which, like those on 21–22 High Street, Bridgnorth, proclaim the prestigious county-banking business inherited from Rocke, Eyton & Co.[107]

National or regional banks were often content to take on quite modest premises, but when they built they tended to do so on a grand scale, as the North & South Wales Bank did in 1890 at the Cross in Oswestry, a staring brick building in a 'Tudor' style.[108] Lloyds TSB branch at 16 Broad Street, Ludlow, is a tall stone building of 1879 in a style which Pevsner damned as 'pretentious mock-Tudor'.[109] Its 'Tudor', however, was not of the gimcrack variety but deliberately heavy and serious, and at a time when bank failures were not uncommon it probably inspired confidence in its depositors. The Lloyds TSB branch in Bridgnorth, probably built after Lloyds' merger with the Worcester City & County Bank in 1889,[110] has two long high frontages on High Street and Whitburn Street in a heavy version of Queen Anne with symmetrical heads to the windows and run-out roll mouldings to the jambs. What is now Barclays Bank (1886) in King Street, Ludlow, was built in an equally heavy style in red brick.[111] The quality which they all had was an assured probity.

Banks at the end of the 19th century were not reticent buildings, but they eschewed the overweening air of the plate-glass splendours of some shops, and also of the ostentation of the larger insurance companies.[112] In 1890 the Alliance Assurance Co. pulled down the old Salop Fire Office premises at 21 High Street, Shrewsbury—of three storeys in a Regency style—to erect a much taller building, with a great amount of florid Renaissance ornament, in polychrome brickwork and with a liberal display of pink Shap granite.[113] The Royal Insurance building at the corner of High Street and Mardol Head, now the Alliance & Leicester premises, emphasized the street junction and its own importance with heavy, richly decorated and boldly projecting oriels. Insurance companies and shops never had the prestige of banks and felt far more in need than they of advertising through boldly self-assertive buildings.

Civic buildings

However conspicuous other structures were, and however much they contributed as a whole to the transformation of the urban scene, it was, as it had always been, the buildings with community roles—town halls, corn exchanges, market halls—which individually were the most imposing of all. Nearly every Shropshire town built one in the second half of the century:

> The Cities are full of pride,
> Challenging each to each –

Those in the larger towns[114]—Shrewsbury, Bridgnorth, Ludlow, and Oswestry—would not have been out of place in a major city, and even the smaller towns—Ellesmere, Newport, Church Stretton, Much Wenlock, Whitchurch—made their contribution. Indeed the smaller towns were first in the field. Ellesmere (old) town hall was built in 1833, and the early 17th-century timber-framed market hall at Church Stretton was rebuilt in brick in a Jacobean style in 1838–9.[115] In 1852 Pountney Smith built, again in a Jacobean style, the Corn Market, with a reading room above, at Much Wenlock.[116] All of these were grander than most of their neighbours in the street, but with the exception of that at Ellesmere, imposing in almost any surroundings,[117] were not overwhelmingly so.

That the larger towns were belated in comparison was mainly because up to the mid century they were not ill provided, by contemporary standards, with public buildings. Shrewsbury had its market hall of 1596, a share in the Shirehall of 1784–6, and the Butter Market of 1819.[118] Ludlow had a market hall (originally of 1706) nearly as large as its successor, the Butter Market of 1743, and the medieval Palmers' Guildhall made into a Gothick court room in 1774–6.[119] Bridgnorth had the town hall of 1652.[120] In Oswestry the Cross Market, designed by Thomas Penson, opened in 1849, as did the Powis Market Hall, an enlargement of the old town hall (given to the borough by Lord Powis in 1839) used also as a new Guildhall and manor courthouse.[121] After the mid century the needs of an expanding economy and population, combined with civic pride, caused them all to rebuild. Bridgnorth, perhaps the least provided, was first, the present Market Hall, built by Robert Griffiths, opening in 1856.[122] It had an aisled market behind a rectangular main block with shops below and a large meeting hall and several smaller rooms above. It was built 'entirely of bricks in colours of red, white and blue ... in the Italian style' and it had a tall campanile-type tower rising at the angle of the two main streets. For good or ill it outshines any other building in the town centre. For some years it was the most up to date and in many ways the most

outstanding public building in Shropshire, but from 1867 it was itself surpassed by the same architect's market hall in Shrewsbury—in the same style and with as much colour, but on a larger scale and with an unusually tall tower.[123] As at Bridgnorth the new building dominated its surroundings. It did more than that, however; it demonstrated, as the Market Hall of nearly 300 years earlier had done, that the county town continued to be not only the administrative but also the commercial centre of Shropshire.

By the 1870s public buildings were in a more sober style which was part of a brief taste for Gothic, formerly eschewed in favour of almost any variety of sub-classical architecture. An early and minor example was the Cottage Hospital (1869), English Walls, Oswestry.[124] Whitchurch town hall (1872, now demolished) and the Market (1879) in Scotland Street, Ellesmere, were buildings on a small scale in a mildly Gothic manner.[125] In contrast the former Eye, Ear and Throat Hospital (1879–81), Town

Shrewsbury Market Hall, designed by Robert Griffiths, and built in 1867

Walls, Shrewsbury, is an aggressive red-brick structure with buttresses, carvings, and finials, and fenestrated in as Gothic a way as modern needs would allow.[126] In its own, then secluded, part of the town it dominated everything else, at least until the Girls' High School (1897), by Lloyd Oswell, set up on the opposite corner. Schools and hospitals were often sited on the cheaper edge of things; in contrast a public building with a commercial function, the Head Post Office (1875–7) in Shrewsbury, occupied a prominent position (the site of the Butter Market of 1819) at the corner of Pride Hill and St. Mary's Street and towered above its neighbours: resplendent with tall Gothic arcades at street level, with a tier of windows surmounted by a rose window beneath a pediment facing Pride Hill, and, facing St. Mary's Street, a corbelled chimney stack crowned by decorated shafts emphasizing the centre of the elevation.[127] It was as impressive in its surroundings as any of the earlier market halls but without their colourful bravado. It was the most conspicuous building in the Gothic style erected in any Shropshire town for four hundred years, and it was to be the last.

The three most ambitious public buildings of the end of the century were the Market Hall of 1887 in Ludlow, the Municipal Buildings of 1892–3 on the site of the old Guildhall at Bailey Head, Oswestry, and the borough police station and weights and measures office of 1893 in Swan Hill, Shrewsbury.[128] The first was a free and florid northern Renaissance design. The second, described by Pevsner as a 'free version of the Loire style',[129] was 'erected under the supervision of Messrs. Lockwood & Sons of Chester'.[130] The third is in a similar but heavier vein and with elements of Jacobethan ornament. Ludlow Market Hall was determinedly conspicuous, almost a declaration of war against everything else in the Square, but the other two were more restrained in tone and perhaps deliberately so because they were away from the busier streets. The site of the Shrewsbury building may have been fortuitous, determined by the current availability of land. At Oswestry, however, whether under the shadow of feudal lords or aristocratic landowners, the high ground of Castle Hill, overlooking the town, had always been the seat of administration, and so it remained when the town's business centre moved away in the course of the 19th century.

Schools

By the 1830s the need to provide elementary schooling on a wide scale was becoming pressing, and the government found itself involved in education: not directly but in the provision of Treasury grants to voluntary, generally religious, bodies. The Committee of Council on Education, an offshoot of the Privy Council, offered guidelines to school builders. After 1839 applications for grants had to be made to it and, since it claimed the right to inspect school buildings,[131] it had considerable influence and helped to standardize specifications, especially plans.[132] The similarities in the latter respect between the National schools at Ludlow (1855) and Ironbridge (1859) are striking, despite the differences in materials, in architectural styles, and in architects.[133] What was usually provided was a large schoolroom for the use of several classes at once, and one or two small classrooms opening off it, mostly for the older children. When there was living accommodation for one or more teachers it was often part of the main design and consisted, almost invariably, of a parlour, kitchen, scullery, and two or three bedrooms. The rooms were on much the same scale as those in Shrewsbury terraces for artisans and clerical workers.[134]

Whatever may have been the inclination to give clergymen's homes a Gothic look, it was slight[135] in comparison with the obsessive use of that style by school builders, whose work, at least up to the 1870s, bore comparison rather with church building and restoration.[136] In the 19th century all denominations agreed that education was concerned with religious indoctrination at least as much as academic or vocational instruction. As the vicar of Cleobury Mortimer inscribed on the wing which he added in 1840 to the school there, 'The Fear of the Lord is the Beginning of Wisdom'. It will be remembered that many nonconformist chapels and Roman Catholic churches had schoolrooms attached, whether for day or Sunday scholars, but most schools of the period were built by Anglicans for whom the village school was 'the nursery of the parish church'.[137] It is not surprising, therefore, that schools, with their semi-religious function, should be greatly affected, like churches, by the Gothic fashions of the mid century. In 1856–7 R. Griffiths, of Quatford and Bridgnorth, was simultaneously building the school at Morville and restoring the church.[138] As a designer of schools said in 1847, 'the styles of the Middle Ages ... are best suited for school-houses ... because the buildings themselves (like the pious and charitable institutions of olden times) partake, or ought to partake, of a semi-religious and semi-ecclesiastical character'.[139]

Nevertheless, however desirable Gothic may have been on ideological grounds, it would probably have had a less ready welcome in schools if school-rooms then had been the same height as parlours and drawing rooms. In a Victorian schoolroom, however, where several classes might be under instruction at the same time and repetition by rote in unison was a common practice, the level of noise militated against low ceilings and in favour of lofty rooms, which could accommodate both the resulting uproar and the tall windows of the Gothic style equally well. The rooms of lower height in the accompanying, and generally attached, school houses were given Gothic windows to match. Those who had to occupy them might have preferred more modern and convenient lighting, but as they were not of much social importance their views, if any, like those of labourers in picturesque cottages with low eaves and sloping roofs, did not require attention.

The very effective use of such elements which a school classroom could afford was shown by T.E. Nicholson in his National school (1855) at Ludlow. It has a profusion of Gothic doors, windows, and buttresses and of chimney stacks made to look like buttresses; and the main classroom, open to the roof, is in its elevation a copy, or at any rate a reminiscence, of the hall of Stokesay Castle, furnished with mullions, transoms, and Decorated tracery, and with three gabled dormers rising from a few feet above ground level to half way up the roof height. The Girls' school (1863) at Cleobury Mortimer, designed by Street,[140] is in the same vein, with a central schoolroom, treated like the hall at Stokesay, set between wings with three-light windows with Geometrical tracery and, in addition, with a semi-circular stair turret set in one angle and crowned with a French pepperpot roof. At Claverley in 1875[141] the central range was flanked by two ends with false gables, beneath each of which was a circular window and, below that, three lancets with Caernarvon heads.

Smaller schools, generally in villages rather than towns, were built to a less spacious plan but were similar in effect. The National school (1855) at Broseley by R. Griffiths[142] is in a dark blue, almost black, brick with yellow dressings and in an early Decorated style. The school at Morville, also by Griffiths, has cusped and trefoiled lights and a bellcot with three open trefoiled lights to the bell chamber.[143] The red brick school at Hookagate (1864)[144] has grouped lancets beneath overall depressed heads and an ornate open timber roof in the classroom. The Lilleshall Co.'s school (1871) at Priorslee[145] had a large classroom on a **T** plan, one gable having three lancets in echelon beneath a relieving arch and the other a four-light window with Decorated tracery; in addition the cloakroom was lit by an array of five windows with Caernarvon heads. In the 1870s at All Saints', Castlefields, Shrewsbury, and probably at much the same time at Dorrington, Edward Haycock put trefoils and Decorated tracery into grouped lights with two-centred heads.[146] The school (1877) at High Ercall[147] has classroom windows with trefoiled heads, and the roundel in a gable has sexfoiled cusping. Norton school (in Stockton parish) has openings with Caernarvon heads, a corbel table beneath the eaves rather than a cornice, and a bell tower with an exaggeratedly tall saddleback roof. At

Hookagate School, Bayston Hill

Norbury a very large tower has a doorway with a two-centred head, grouped lancets, and a curiously truncated broach spire. The little school at Longnor had Perpendicular tracery and a crenellated gable.[148] Even Norman Shaw, building Church Preen school in an 'Old English' manner, gave the classroom a doorway with a two-centred head and a gable window of three trefoiled lights. As late as 1893[149] an addition to the Girls' school at Cleobury Mortimer, built of yellow brick in contrast to the grey stone of the earlier structure, had tall lancets in the gable.

Most of these were National (that is Anglican) schools, but dissenters too, when they wished to impress, could play the same game very well. Madeley Wood Wesleyan School (1858) by James Wilson of Bath[150] is in a combination of yellow, pale blue, and pink brick in a more or less Early English style. It has plain and trefoiled lancets, occasional colonettes, machicolations on the gables of the schoolroom and on the belfry, which has an Early English arcade to the bell chamber and is crowned with a spire. The open roof of the schoolroom was designed—in contrast with the plain, even stark, character of most schoolrooms of the time—in the rich traditional style of the Marches, with cusping to the raking struts and the upper members of the trusses and with chamfered principals and purlins.

Like his Anglican colleagues, Wilson, an architect much patronized by nonconformist school builders,[151] was declaring that a Gothic building, and one of high status, was the best model for a modern school; and the architects of Roman Catholic schools, as at Plowden and Oswestry, seem to have thought the same. In complete contrast the builders of schools a century earlier—Bowdler's School (1724), 18 Beeches Lane, Shrewsbury, and the Lacon School (1740), Cleobury Mortimer—had been content that they should look like contemporary town houses, despite their different, or additional, functions. The difference was not merely the result of the aesthetic tyranny of mid 19th-century propagandists, for Gothic, though in some ways a shackle on design, was in others a release key. The freedom of plan, of elevation, and of sky line, referred to earlier, which allowed the outward appearance of houses to proclaim their inner reality, was of greatest effect when applied to the purpose-built structures of an industrial society, such as

workshops, railway stations, hospitals, and schools for a massively increased school population. For most of these Gothic served as well as any other style to let the elevation express the function, and the aesthetic and ideological predilections of the age and its utilitarian needs were in harmony and not at discord.

By the 1870s, however, Gothic was much less favoured in educational circles. To some extent that may be attributed to the lessening activities of religious bodies and the appearance of the new school boards as the main provider of mass education. The boards were encouraged, if not enjoined, to eschew sectarian teaching, and since Gothic was very much associated with sectarian schools the new attitude worked against it; the London School Board's offices on the Embankment were in a Renaissance style.[152] The earliest board school in Shropshire, built at Hadley in 1874 by Bidlake & Fleeming,[153] was in a hard red brick and in a style which approximated most closely to the newly fashionable 'Old English'. The school of 1875 at Bishop's Castle[154] in a softer red brick has multi-light transomed windows in a wholly 'Old English' manner. The board school of 1877 at Ketley[155] was built in a brown brick in the same style, and that at Ditherington (1882)[156] also eschewed Gothic; the latter, built tall and on top of the hill at Ditherington, vied with St. Michael's church to dominate the suburban scene to an extent unusual in Shropshire[157] but rather as contemporary schools in south-west London did.[158]

Other public bodies, the county council at Radbrook from 1896[159] and the Girls' Public Day School Trust in Shrewsbury in 1897, were supporting or building schools in styles which might be difficult to define but which were not Gothic. But it was not only public bodies that were choosing other styles.[160] The declining fortunes of that style may be seen in the contrast between Ellesmere College, projected in 1878 and designed by Carpenter & Ingelow,[161] and its earlier sister schools of Woodard inspiration.[162] Lancing (1848–57),[163] Hurstpierpoint (1850–3),[164] Bloxham (1854),[165] and Denstone (1868–73)[166] were in a Gothic style throughout and are often cited by architectural historians for that quality. At Ellesmere, however, all the domestic buildings and most of the 'communal' buildings are in a more or less Tudor style. That, it might be argued, was merely an economy measure, for Ellesmere was intended for boys of lower social standing than those of its predecessors.[167] The same, however, could not be said of Shrewsbury School's new buildings at Kingsland, where A.W. Blomfield was transforming the old Foundling Hospital in a style which contemporaries called 'Queen Anne', and in the early 1880s William White was building three boarding houses in an 'Old English' style—with a perfunctory bow to the old manner in the traceried windows of the porches.[168] In the last 20 years of the century the amount of Gothic dwindled rapidly as other styles gained ground; that happened partly because most new schools were established by statutory unsectarian bodies and partly because the growth of the school population and its concentration in larger schools, together with changes in educational practice, were eliminating the noisy multi-class schoolrooms of earlier years.

XVIII   Ecclesiastical Architecture 1550–1800

The most significant contrast between surviving medieval and post-medieval building is the markedly ecclesiastical character of the one and the even more marked secular character of the other. Nevertheless Shropshire parish churches were not neglected in the two and a half centuries that followed the Reformation. Both Cranage and Pevsner have commented on the amount of church building in the county in the period, but they have perhaps not given it the emphasis which it deserves. Cranage dealt with *c*.250 churches of medieval origin, 50 of which had been wholly or largely built or rebuilt; nearly as many had the nave, chancel, or west tower rebuilt or added; as many again had porches or aisles added, and another 20 were wholly or partly reroofed. In other words major building operations were carried on at three out of every five medieval churches. That was quite apart from internal alterations like the insertion of galleries, or external ones like the addition of a bellcot, the rebuilding of a wall, or the insertion of new windows. If those are included, then few churches received no attention in those years.[1]

This activity has been obscured by later developments. The impression of the county's parish churches today is that they are overwhelmingly Gothic in character. It has to be remembered, however, that after 1800 nearly every one suffered the attentions of ecclesiologists and restorers, who were at pains to reproduce, often on slight evidence and sometimes on none, what they considered to have been its original character. In so doing they not only put up their own creations but also pulled down those of other men, which did not happen to please them. To some degree Gothic structures too suffered from this, but very little compared with classical work. Further, when Gothic was destroyed it was replaced by Gothic of a different stamp, but when

classical work was pulled down it was invariably replaced by Gothic. More than a third of all the churches built anew in the 18th century were wholly swept away and replaced by Gothic ones in the 19th; in many other churches all the 18th-century work, whether partial rebuilding or addition, was similarly treated, and in others the 18th-century fabric was retained, but all the elements were Gothicized.

Two examples of the transformation may suffice. At Newport in the 1720s the chancel and south aisle were rebuilt in a classical style.[2] At Market Drayton the south aisle was rebuilt in 1723, and in 1784 both aisles were raised by four feet and given two tiers of windows and roofs of shallow pitch (see illustration overleaf). The building was described in 1876 as looking, from the outside, 'almost entirely modern'.[3] In the late 19th century all these works were removed and two wholly Gothic churches re-created.[4] A visitor to the county in the years around 1800 would have seen far more 17th- and 18th-century work and far less Gothic than is seen today, and he might have found it difficult to decide whether Gothic or classical forms were more typical of its churches. The modern conception of their character is largely a product of the 19th century.

Major works: new churches

Most churches built in Shropshire between 1550 and 1800 were plain structures on a simple plan, but a few were of considerable size or splendour, or both.[5] Those few had one thing in common which, as far as is known, distinguishes them from the rest: they were designed by men from outside the county who had acquired most of their experience, or at least their earliest experience, elsewhere. Minsterley church was designed in 1688 by William Taylor,[6] a London carpenter; St. Alkmund's (1712–13),

Market Drayton church after 1784 in a watercolour by Edw. Williams,
showing the north aisle with its two tiers of windows and shallow-pitched roof. (SRRC 6001/372/2.61)

Whitchurch, by John Barker of Rowsley (Derb.); All Saints' (1788–90), Wellington, and St. Chad's (1790–2), Shrewsbury, by George Steuart; and St. Mary Magdalen's (1792–4), Bridgnorth, by Thomas Telford, although by that time he had been county surveyor for two or three years. There were other churches of note: the now destroyed Welshampton (1788), Madeley (1794–7), Malinslee (1805), scaled down from Telford's Madeley design, and St. George's (1806), Pain's Lane (near Oakengates), replaced in 1861. Those, however, were of interest more for their form than for any attempt at architectural grandeur.

Minsterley, though on a simple oblong plan, is the most determinedly baroque church in the county, despite a hint of artisan mannerism in the frontispiece to its west front. With its rusticated giant pilasters and square windows with keystones it is an idiosyncratic (rather than old-fashioned) attempt by a London craftsman to cut a dash in a remote part of

the country. He succeeded better than he could have foreseen, for no other small church approaches it in decorative effect or boldness of design. It is, however, very much the odd man out among rural churches, and largely because it was erected not by the parishioners or with contributions from local gentry but at the expense of the immensely rich lord of the manor, Viscount Weymouth, of Longleat (Wilts.),[7] where Taylor had been employed earlier. It may perhaps be contrasted with the very plain chapel at Loughton paid for in 1622 by Bonham Norton, a rich London stationer with aspirations to become a landed gentleman in his family's county, high sheriff in 1611,[8] and son-in-law of the builder of Condover Hall.[9]

After the Dissolution there were no institutions that needed impressive churches in the countryside and in Shropshire few landowners who could afford to build them. Consequently all other churches in the county of any architectural pretensions were either in the towns (replacing apparently large medieval churches) or in such increasingly populous areas as the east Shropshire coalfield. Because of the nature of 17th- and 18th-century provincial towns the form and style of urban churches depended little on the individual taste of a patron or his architect but were, in varying degrees, the expression of the architectural predilections of the community. It is probably for that reason that, with the exception of St. Chad's, Shrewsbury, the more impressive churches of 18th-century Shropshire were run-of-the-mill, neither in advance of, nor behind, contemporary aesthetics.

The point is well illustrated by St. Alkmund's, Whitchurch, rebuilt after the fall of the medieval church in 1711. It remained firmly traditional in its avoidance of the use of orders and of the pedimented and steepled west fronts of up-to-date London churches. Instead it retained a tower projecting slightly from the west front and with a hint of Gothic tracery in its top stage, and it had one register of windows to the side elevations, denying the presence of galleries within. At the same time it is advanced in its motifs, in its semicircular south porch, and in the placing of the tower mostly within the body of the church, so that the nave aisles overlap it and form north and south entrance lobbies. It has, too, its little eccentricity in the aprons below the cornice spaced to correspond with those beneath the window sills, a trick the builder may have copied from the contemporary St. Philip's, Birmingham. The interior has imposing arcades of Tuscan columns and would not have seemed out of date anywhere in the country. One well travelled critic who saw it in 1735 described it as the 'prettiest and best built church I ever saw',[10] and, compared with Barker's larger St. Ann's (1709–12), Manchester, a town then at the beginning of its phenomenal expansion, it has a country-town air.

St. Alkmund's remained the only major 18th-century church in Shropshire until the early 1790s when Steuart and Telford were busy respectively at All Saints', Wellington, and St. Mary Magdalen's,

The nave and west gallery of St. Alkmund's church, Whitchurch

The apse of St. Alkmund's church, Whitchurch

favoured elongated pilasters, the other with Tuscan columns *in antis* on the west front and Ionic colonnades internally; and both had steeples with columniated or pilastered upper stages beneath cupolas. They are impressive structures: 'dignified' and 'of great gravity' in Pevsner's words, and, in the full tradition of post-Renaissance church building, striving to build a Christian church with the appearance of an antique temple. They must have pleased many and could have offended none.

In contrast, the new St. Chad's, Shrewsbury, both at its inception and for many years after, offended in one way or another nearly everybody but its architect. Steuart was called in after James Wyatt had failed to respond in any practical way to an invitation, and he at once showed the bent of his mind by persuading the committee for the new building to forsake the old churchyard for a prominent site on Town Walls. At Bridgnorth Telford sited his church, in accordance with contemporary town planning principles, to close the vista at the end of the developing and fashionable East Castle Street; at Shrewsbury Steuart placed his church more picturesquely, where it would dramatize the distant prospect from Kingsland and the nearer one from the fashionable walks laid out in 1719 between the Quarry and the curve of the Severn.[11]

Steuart's design for a circular nave found no favour with the committee; and not surprisingly, for not only was it unlike a traditional Christian church,

Bridgnorth. Both churches were well abreast of contemporary ideas, the one with neo-classical recessed arches, fine detailing, and Steuart's

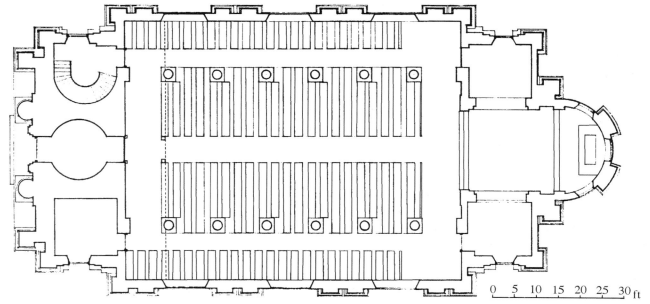

0 5 10 15 20 25 30 ft

Plan of St. Mary Magdalen's church (1792-4), Bridgnorth. The east apse was added in 1876

Looking west inside St. Mary Magdalen's church, Bridgnorth

it also bore little or no resemblance to a classical temple.[12] However, either inadvertently or deliberately, he so misled the committee, divided about everything but opposition to his preferred plan, that it was unable in the end to avoid accepting what it had at first almost unanimously rejected. He thus was able to build one of the most striking and original churches in the country. But for his lucky mistake, or not wholly reprehensible deceit, the critics would have had their own way[13] either with another good but undistinguished neo-classical church or with a forerunner of St. Alkmund's in Shrewsbury, rebuilt a couple of years later in a Gothic style.

St. Chad's is in three sections: nave, vestibule, and ritual 'west' (in fact south) tower, integrated by the plat band and balustrade linking nave and vestibule and by the rustication common to all three. The west front is so conventional, with cupola and steeple rising above a Tuscan portico,[14] that it should probably be seen as an attempt to lull the visitor's senses before springing on him the

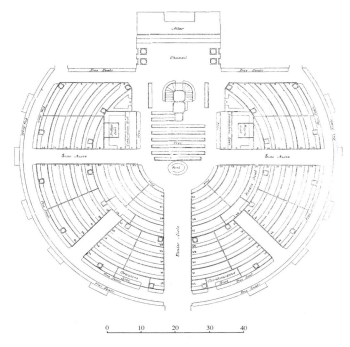

Plan of St. Chad's, Shrewsbury, by Steuart, with its circular nave

surprises of the interior. Steuart was not the first British architect to design a circular nave.[15] In the 1720s Gibbs had proposed one at St. Martin's-in-the-Fields; in 1732 William Adam had built a church at Hamilton (Lanarks.) in the form of a circle within a Greek cross; and elliptical naves had been built at All Saints', Newcastle upon Tyne, by David Stephenson and at St. Andrew's, George Street, Edinburgh, by Andrew Frazer in the 1780s.[16] What is striking in St. Chad's is the transition from the unexciting portico to an unexpected circular lobby which is itself followed by an elliptical vestibule, with elegantly curving stairs to the gallery. Finally the vestibule leads into the great circular space of the nave, where elongated cast-iron columns give height and lightness. St. Chad's is the building for which Steuart will be longest remembered, a monument to a splendid talent.

Nevertheless a building is to be judged not solely by its aesthetic merits, if that is ever possible, but also by the extent to which it fulfils its purpose. And the one criterion may be at odds with the other; indeed the more brilliantly the one aim succeeds the more clearly the failure of the other may show. Many people of moderate religious feeling, recognizing some of St. Chad's virtues, were yet uneasy about it. They tended to put their criticism into architectural terms, but the Revd. Hugh Owen diagnosed the real trouble when he said in effect that, while aesthetically the nave came as a culmination of the progress through lobby and vestibule, it was in religious terms an anticlimax.[17] His censure had, perhaps, more force then than now, for it might be argued that, whatever its faults, David Evans's highly coloured replacement in 1853 of Francis Eginton's sombre 'east' window has done something to assuage the misgivings that Owen was expressing.

It is possible to see St. Chad's as an Anglican form of the theatrical planning of some 18th-century south German churches. One early 19th-century critic allowed that St. Chad's was 'an elegant building' but blamed it for lacking a 'dignified solemnity' and for 'having too much the appearance of a place of amusement'.[18] In fact, despite its unorthodox character, it is in a native tradition of church planning and design well established by the mid century. As modes of worship changed after the Reformation there was a need for churches adapted

The lobby at St. Chad's, Shrewsbury, looking into the stairs vestibule

less to liturgical processions than to accommodating the largest possible audience within sight and sound of the pulpit. A square or circular nave best suited such a purpose, and a propensity to build to a square or slightly oblong form is evident in some of the London churches built just before or after the Great Fire, in such large town churches as All Saints' (1675–80), Northampton, in some of those put up around London under the 1710 Act for 50 new churches,[19] and in many dissenting chapels. There were also attempts to convert churches of medieval form into centralized auditoria by rearranging the seating pattern, as at old St. Julian's, Shrewsbury, focused on the middle of the nave where the pulpit and the mayoral chair faced south and north respectively.[20] Several such churches were built in Shropshire around 1800. St. Alkmund's, Shrewsbury, was built in 1793–5 with Gothick details but with the nave as a simple rectangle and the interior was described by a hostile critic as having 'much the appearance of an assembly room'.[21] Two survivors, to Telford's design, are at

The Revd. John Fletcher's chapel in Coalbrookdale (SRRC, uncatalogued)

Madeley (1794–7) and Malinslee (1805). Each has a square 'west' tower attached directly to a nave with an overall roof, octagonal on the exterior and, by the provision of vestries at the angles, slightly oblong internally.[22] Others have gone. Welshampton (1788, replaced in 1863) had an octagonal west tower in two stages, an oblong nave with the roof hipped at both ends, and slight transepts projecting by a few feet. The original St. George's (1806), Pain's Lane, pulled down shortly before 1862, was in form almost a Greek cross with a square tower giving on to an oblong vestibule which itself led into the nave, oblong in form, with a roof hipped at both ends, and set at right angles to the axis of tower and vestibule. To those one may perhaps add John Fletcher's chapel in Coalbrookdale, as extended in 1789. Its ecclesiastical standing may be in some doubt[23] but its form is unambiguous: set four-square, with a pyramidal roof, with no west tower but merely a slight projection to mark the entry.[24]

Madeley and Malinslee churches were built after 1790–2 and so too was St. George's, and it might be thought that it was St. Chad's, designed by a London architect, that introduced the centrally planned church into the county. It happens, however, that the design for Welshampton church was accepted in April 1788, before any designs had been prepared for St. Chad's (indeed the medieval church had not yet fallen), and that alone shows that provincials were well acquainted with the concept by then, for Welshampton was the first known commission of an obscure architect from Tewkesbury, Edward Edgecombe.[25] The point is important, for it helps to explain why Steuart's mistake, or manoeuvre, at St. Chad's was eventually allowed to pass. It is sometimes implied that the committee acquiesced in his design because they jibbed at the cost of alterations. But that cannot be all the story for the extra cost would have been a very small proportion of the contemplated expenditure and not enough to deter them, had there been widespread opposition in principle to his ideas. It would appear that the parishioners and their *avant garde* architect held not dissimilar views about the functions of a church, and that is probably why the trustees (successors to the committee), in attempting a last-ditch stand at the end of 1789, trumped up objections to what they were being offered on the score of lack of accommodation and poor acoustics. Unfortunately for them those criticisms were untenable, and it had to be admitted (in the words of an unfriendly critic) that, despite the church's 'theatrical air', 'by the ingenuity of the circular arrangement, all the congregation can distinctly hear and see the officiating clergyman'.[26] Having willed the widely approved ends, the trustees, like the committee before them, found it difficult to oppose the unconventional but clearly effective means, probably sensing that they would get little general support for saddling the parish with extra costs merely because they preferred their own taste to that of their freely chosen and highly admired architect. Steuart was thus able to erect a brilliantly unorthodox church because many Shropshire men were in sympathy with the concept of a centrally planned auditorium, if not necessarily of a circular one. Had he tried out his ideas 50 years earlier or later he would probably have got short shrift.

Minor works—the varying pace of building

Much building was done in parish churches between 1550 and 1800, but the amount was not evenly spread over those two and a half centuries. Most of the outstanding churches discussed above were of the late 18th century; for minor churches some early decades were more fruitful than some later ones.

At about a dozen churches, giving a few the necessary benefit of the doubt concerning their exact age, major work was carried out in the late 16th century. Langley chapel was built, or largely reconstructed, in 1564 and 1601,[27] and two wholly new buildings were erected: Aston chapel (replaced in 1742 by the present structure), near Oswestry, was completed in 1594,[28] and Melverley church is probably of the late 16th century. Halston chapel, near Whittington, was converted to its present purposes about the same time.[29] Two of the three survivors are simple rectangles with structurally undivided nave and chancel; the third, Halston, has no more than a recess for a chancel, and it is unlikely that Aston was different. Two chancels were rebuilt at this time: at Ludlow Castle chapel (1559 x 1586)[30] and at Shipton (1589). West towers were added or rebuilt at Sutton Maddock (1579),[31] and aisles or chapels were added at Ludford (c.1555)[32] and Harley,[33] and perhaps at Diddlebury.[34] Other churches had porches added, windows inserted, or walls rebuilt. Altogether the total is small, but it may be much more than was done between 1600 and 1630, for from those years one can point with certainty only to Loughton

Melverley church, probably of the late 16th century, in a watercolour of 30 June 1790 by Edw. Williams (SRRC 6001/372/2.11)

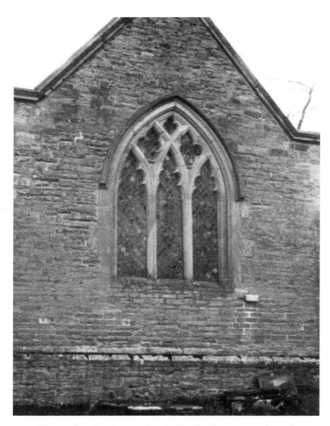

The rebuilt chancel of 1589, Shipton church

The rebuilt chancel of 1633, Astley Abbots church

chapel (in Chetton parish) built in 1622 with a small nave and separate chancel.[35]

The apparent difference in volume of building between the late 16th century and the early 17th may be the result of random documentation and survival, but it is doubtful whether the apparent upsurge in church building in the 1630s can be explained away on those grounds. From that decade seven pieces of work have survived or are recorded: an added transept at Tilstock chapel in 1630,[36] the rebuilt chancel at Astley Abbots in 1633, the west tower at Myddle in 1634, the rebuilt nave at Donington in 1635, the Shavington aisle added at Adderley in 1635–6, the west window at Church Stretton before 1639,[37] and the transept-cum-chapel at More in 1640. None is a major piece, but the amount of work done then is nearly as much as that of the last five decades of the preceding century and equals that of all but the most prolific decades of the next.

Moreover the character of the work of the 1630s is far more determinedly Gothic, almost wholly in a Decorated style, than that of the late 16th century. It

is fully in sympathy with the feelings which led Bishop Cary to pronounce that 'the old fashion of church window' was best suited to buildings of a religious character: feelings which produced the windows of Lincoln and Jesus College chapels in Oxford and of St. John's College library in Cambridge.[38] In Shropshire they may be supposed to have produced the chancel of 1633 at Astley Abbots, the aisle of 1635–6 at Adderley, the west window at Church Stretton, the windows of 1642 in the south wall at Lydham, and probably the nave of 1635 at Donington.[39] The work at More was carried out by a family that was to be firmly on Parliament's side in the Civil War,[40] and the stress on 'pure' Gothic—its coincidence with the Laudians' ascendancy in the Church notwithstanding—was not ended by Parliament's victory over Church and State: the windows inserted into the north aisle of St. Mary's, Shrewsbury, in 1651 are good copies of the 14th-century ones in the south aisle; and High Ercall church was restored in a Perpendicular style from 1657 onwards.[41] Nevertheless, and although the mechanics of the connection are not clear, it is

Timber-framed chapel at Newtown, Wem, formed from a timber range added to a two-storeyed house of c.1603, in a watercolour by Edw. Williams (SRRC 6001/372/3.67)

The interior of Llanfair Waterdine church in 1842, showing the wooden pillars of the arcade (SRRC 6021/1, p.51)

not fanciful to see the amount and nature of church building in the 1630s as the county's response to the Laudian campaign.

There was, however, another side of the coin. Much of the activity of the hundred years or so following the Reformation gives the impression of having been done as cheaply as possible: that is, in timber rather than in stone or brick. The clearest examples are the chancel of the round chapel in Ludlow Castle, Melverley church,[42] Aston chapel, the transformation at Halston of a timber building of *1437 into a chapel, and the transept of 1630 and the south aisle of 1652 at Tilstock.[43] Further, some time before 1659 a chapel was contrived at Newtown (Wem) by adding a long low timber-framed building to a two-storeyed timber-framed house of c.1600.[44]

Five churches are known to have had timber arcades. None has survived, and, while there is no positive evidence of dates, there are no indications that any was medieval. Cranage thought that the timber arcade at Harley served an Elizabethan aisle. At Llanfair Waterdine the tall wooden pillars of the arcade had capitals, marking the junction of the aisle-tie, ornamented with Renaissance scrolls and human heads, probably of the late 16th century.[45] At Loppington the aisle with a timber arcade had a 17th-century roof. In 1740 Wem church had timber arcades which presumably replaced whatever was there before the fire of 1677 gutted the interior.[46] Dudleston chapel (Ellesmere) was in existence by

1548,[47] but its earliest surviving element is a roof of 16th- or 17th-century character; it was described in 1799 as 'timber framed'[48] and 'rough cast'; after north and south aisles had been added in 1819 it had timber arcades.[49]

Timber was used as well for repairing stone structures, especially gable ends, and again more probably after the Reformation than before. The gable of the south transept at Condover is in small quatrefoil panels typical of the local 17th-century vernacular and probably part of the renovations of the 1660s. At Aston Botterell in 1799 the apex of the east gable of the south aisle was in timber with a king post and queen struts above a high collar, probably a result of the late roofing of the aisle.[50] The old church at Meole Brace, pulled down in 1799, had an east gable of timber with two tiers of queen struts and collars above the tie.[51] At Chirbury the east gable of the nave had two tiers of close studding,[52] which it seems reasonable to associate with the post-medieval abandonment of the conventual chancel.[53] The east gable of the nave at Munslow had widely spaced close studding, typical of the 16th and 17th centuries rather than of the late Middle Ages, and probably a result of the rebuilding of part of the roof in 1610.[54]

At all of these the use of timber to repair a medieval stone structure can only be inferred, and it is not possible to prove directly that the gable was not originally timber-framed and that timber has merely replaced timber, however unlikely in most cases that may seem to be. But at the now demolished Poynton chapel (High Ercall) the use of timber to repair a stone wall is beyond doubt, for in the early 19th century one of the walls with a flat-headed 'Tudor' window was timber-framed for about three quarters of its length; the other quarter was in stone with a ragged edge towards the timber framing, a clear indication that a stone wall had been largely replaced in timber.[55] It is unlikely that this use of timber, at least as a temporary measure, was wholly new in the post-Reformation era, and a timber-framed east gable of the chancel at Barrow, recorded in 1789,[56] may have been part of the repairs carried out by the prior of Wenlock in the 1520s.[57] But there is little else that can plausibly be dated earlier than that, and it must be supposed that the practice, though not unknown in the Middle Ages, became much commoner in later years.

None of these churches, except Chirbury, was an important one, and it might be thought that timber was used only upon 'vernacular' ecclesiastical buildings, but there is some evidence to the contrary. No man in the county was of higher standing than Sir Henry Sidney, or dwelt in a more prestigious house than Ludlow Castle, but when he added a chancel to the splendid round nave of the chapel there he added it in timber. Few Shropshire churches were more important than St. Mary's, Shrewsbury, which had a north porch added in timber in 1602. St. Alkmund's, Whitchurch, was a large and important church, and yet by 1684 the gable of the south porch had been rebuilt in timber and a two-storeyed structure with the upper storey in timber had been built alongside it.[58] The practice was clearly widespread and far from vulgar, and it may be seen as a mark of that less than awestruck attitude to a consecrated building which Laud so bitterly condemned.

In contrast with the richness of the 1630s the second half of the century has only 15 known works, despite the better documentation of the later period. Four are from the Interregnum, six or seven from the 1660s, and only three or four from the last 25 years. Some of the work was in response to war damage: the nave at Shrawardine of 1649,[59] the restoration of High Ercall 1658–62, the rebuilding of Benthall in 1667, and perhaps the rebuildings of nave and chancel at Stokesay in 1654 and 1664. But not all work carried out during the Interregnum and immediately after was war-damage repair: the aisle at Waters Upton built in 1658 at the charge of Ralph Humphreys of London, was almost certainly an addition to the fabric,[60] and the nave at Condover was rebuilt from 1662 onwards because it had fallen down in 1660. Indeed it is possible that the amount of war-damage repair was not so much greater before 1670 than later. Briefs for Oswestry were issued in 1657, 1675, and 1691;[61] the timber for the repair of the badly damaged church at Bishop's Castle was given by a man who did not succeed to his estate until 1687;[62] and Shrawardine chancel stood in ruins until 1722.[63] Moreover, even when war-damage repair is excluded from the reckoning, there is still as much recorded work in the 1660s as in all the three following decades. While it is likely that most of the work of this half-century was a response to man-made or natural decay, there is no reason to think that the latter was commoner in the years before 1670 than after. In any case there was work that was certainly more than large-scale repair: the nave added at Newtown (Wem) before 1659,[64] the aisle added at Sheriffhales in 1661,[65] and the new chapel at Berwick of *c*.1672.[66] All of this was well before the last quarter of the century. What perhaps distinguished the 1660s was not the amount of visible damage but the will to do something about it. That itself is probably to be related to the religious circumstances of the years following Charles II's return, for the king's restoration was also the Church's,[67] and both together gave Anglicans a new confidence, which some of them, for a short time, translated into improvements to their parish churches.

Compared with the sterility of the last quarter of the 17th century the 18th-century was extremely productive. Between 1700 and 1800 major works were begun at 70 churches, a rate of building two to three times higher than in the previous 150 years. Furthermore not only were more operations undertaken but more of them were on a large scale: half of the 70 churches were wholly or largely rebuilt, compared with about a fifth of those in earlier years. As the century wore on building work intensified, reaching a peak in the 1740s and an equally high plateau between 1780 and 1800. Doubtless that was partly because more medieval churches needed greater attention in the 18th century than in the 17th or 16th. At Chirbury, indeed, one may see the cumulative effect of time at work: in 1736 only one window of the south aisle had acquired a classical form, while by 1791 all three had been altered.[68] At Sutton Maddock the whole church was rebuilt in three separate stages: the west tower in the late 16th century, the nave in the 18th century, and the chancel at some time between 1789 and 1820.[69]

There was, too, an increasing readiness to sweep everything away, in contrast with the generally piecemeal rebuildings of earlier years. In the larger towns and the industrial areas the growing population and the challenge from nonconformity are almost sufficient in themselves to explain the great amount of total demolition and rebuilding. No such pressures, however, were then at work in rural areas. There, and to some extent in the towns as well, the new attitude is rather to be associated with aesthetic changes and the belated application of the standards of classical architecture to churches. These dictated not merely that the rebuilt parts of a medieval church should be in a classical style but militated against a mingling of styles in the same structure and encouraged total rebuilding of earlier churches. Indeed it was pointed out not long after the event that there had been no need for a total demolition of old St. Chad's at Shrewsbury, for most of the church was still structurally sound.[70] Such an all-or-nothing approach worked at first in favour of classical architecture but it could be taken up by later Gothic enthusiasts, and in the next century classical churches which had replaced medieval precursors were themselves swept away for Gothic ones, as Welshampton, completed in 1789,[71] was replaced in 1863, and Meole Brace, of 1799,[72] was replaced in 1867–70, as has been discussed earlier.

Minor works—a plain classicism

Before Telford and Steuart appeared on the scene these 18th-century churches were mostly in a plain style, generally of red brick with freestone dressings. A typical example might have a west tower of three stages, with shallow clasping buttresses at the angles, a west doorway with semicircular head with keystone and imposts, a window with a semicircular head in the middle stage, a belfry light in the top stage, and a crenellated parapet above. Sometimes, as at Petton, the doorway had a flat head and was flanked by engaged pilasters, or was rusticated as at Beckbury; sometimes there was a circular window in the middle stage, as at Cockshutt and Moreton Say, or in the top stage as at Hopton Cangeford; occasionally, as at Bolas Magna and Church Pulverbatch, the tower was surmounted by classical urns at its four corners. The nave, or nave and chancel combined, was generally of three or four bays, with freestone quoins and semicircular headed windows with keystones and imposts under overhanging eaves. Some churches of the early part of the century, like Chetwynd, had aprons beneath the windows,[73] perhaps under the influence of Whitchurch. Sometimes, as at Leighton and formerly at Withington,[74] the windows simply had plain brick voussoirs or, where the fabric was stone as in the south aisle at Chirbury, plain heads without imposts or keystone; at Coreley the imposts were carried along the wall face between the windows as

*Moreton Say church, showing the circular window in the middle stage of the tower,
in a watercolour of 28 September 1790 by Edw. Williams (SRRC 6001/372/2.69)*

a plat band. At Jackfield, and formerly at Kemberton, the windows had Gibbs surrounds.[75] Occasionally Palladian windows were introduced—in the east walls at Westbury,[76] Great Wollaston, and Wombridge, but in the south and north walls of the slight projections from the nave at Welshampton.[77] More usually, however, the east end was given a very long but otherwise standard window with a semicircular head, as at Longdon upon Tern and Moreton Say. In the middle of the century a dentilled eaves-cornice sometimes replaced overhanging eaves, as at St. Julian's, Shrewsbury, and Quatt; probably somewhat later Sutton Maddock nave was given a parapet divided into rectangular panels by short pilasters.[78] At Jackfield, the most ornate of all these, the east and west gables of the nave and the east gable of the chancel were furnished with urns on the kneelers, and there were urns at the apexes of both east gables.[79] All in all,

the typical Shropshire church of the period between *c*.1710 and *c*.1790 did not differ very much from the typical in most parts of the country.

Minor works—lingering medieval styles

It must not be thought that classicism had everything its own way, even at the height of its popularity. Up to about the Restoration all church building in the county was Gothic, positively in perpetuating late medieval elements (most obviously Decorated in the 1630s)[80] and negatively in eschewing any classical elements and instead using such 'debased' forms as straight heads to windows or uncusped lights with depressed or round-headed arches. The Foxe chapel at Ludford of *c*.1555, Langley chapel, built between 1564 and 1601, the window of the south wall at Astley, the west tower of 1579 at Sutton Maddock, the late 16th-century timber window at Easthope, and Loughton chapel of

1622 are all of a sub-Gothic 'Tudor' character. So too, as far as one may rely on the sources, are most of the other inserted windows that appear in late 18th- and early 19th-century drawings. Two identical windows in the east wall of Trinity chapel in St. Mary's, Shrewsbury, were remarkable exceptions. Replacing what was blown out in the storm of 1579 and set either side of a tall central buttress, each was set beneath a moulded ogee arch terminating in a floriated finial, and each had three tiers of three lights with two-centred heads; above the finials of the ogees was a flat-headed window of three arched lights.[81]

The idea that the 'old fashion of church window' was more religious than modern styles still lingered and is seen in the sub-Gothic form of the east window at Berwick chapel in 1672, in the east window at Minsterley of 1689, and in the provision of an east window of three lancets for the incongruous brick chancel of 1733 at Chirbury. Such Gothic as survived was—as Cranage said of the west tower at Selattyn (1703–4) with its angle-buttresses that taper on plan almost to an edge—little more than a reminiscence of earlier forms. All of it appeared on west towers and generally in the form of uncusped two-light windows in the upper stage with pointed heads and with a flat head over all. Examples occur at Aston chapel (1742)[82] in Oswestry parish, Church Pulverbatch (1773), Prees (1756 or later), and Moreton Say (1769). Even at Whitchurch the upper stage of the west tower aims at the same effect.

In the middle of the 17th century a new phenomenon had appeared: work that was neither pure Gothic nor sub-Gothic but, as far as it was anything at all, was of classical derivation. The broad round-headed windows of Stokesay and Benthall are early examples and so, in their rather different way, were the lower registers of the windows at Condover. Later examples are the flat-headed transomed windows at Berwick chapel and at Great Hanwood of 1701,[83] and the flat-headed and round-headed windows with keystones at Minsterley.

In the mid 18th century there were one or two exceptions to that very bare style. The north chapel at Acton Round, added by T. F. Pritchard in 1761–3, has a frieze with minute pointed arches, and the south door of the chancel there has an ogee head. About the same time Coton chapel (in Alveley) had

a Venetian window with an ogee head.[84] But these are rare and perhaps more rococo than Gothic. By the turn of the century, however, an appreciation of Gothic was being expressed by local antiquaries such as Owen and Blakeway, the historians of Shrewsbury. They were not alone: in 1777 Cockshutt church was given narrow pointed windows resembling lancets, and soon after 1807 Cheswardine nave seems to have had rectangular 17th-century-type windows replaced by broad pointed windows with a form of tracery in the heads.[85] The most determined attempt at a Gothic effect before the 19th-century revival was made in 1794–5 at St. Alkmund's, Shrewsbury, where the mullioned windows had cast-iron tracery in the heads and there were tapering buttresses and crenellated cornices. Even there it is little more than a style of decoration, and Joseph Bromfield, who designed plaster work for Gothic St. Alkmund's, had earlier designed it for neo-classical St. Chad's, and for many other buildings in a classical style.

West towers and west fronts

While the large churches in the more important towns and in the newly populous industrial areas eschewed not only Gothic ornament but much of the Gothic form as well, rural churches in contrast perpetuated late medieval forms. To some extent of course what was built depended on the resources available, and about half of the wholly rebuilt churches of the period had to forgo either a structurally separate chancel, or a west tower, or both. Despite that, however, the late medieval tripartite division, clad now in classical ornament, was typical of the rural post-medieval churches of the county. Just over half of the wholly rebuilt churches and nearly all the partly rebuilt churches had a structurally separate west tower. Indeed in one respect the post-Reformation era accentuated, rather than perpetuated, a medieval practice in an enhanced provision of imposing west towers. Of course many post-Reformation west towers were rebuilds, or often no more than major reconstructions, of splendid medieval ones; but not all medieval west towers were impressive, at least by later standards. Some, for example Caynham, Meole Brace, and Kinnerley, were low-built with a timber belfry stage.[86] Further, some early towers were small and in plan not much more than porches; such was that formerly at Hope Bagot and that pulled down at Welshampton in 1788.[87] In some cases the earlier west tower, if there was one, must have been narrower than the present, as at Selattyn, where the coping of the west gable of the medieval nave is cut across by the buttress of the tower of 1703–4.[88] At Sibdon Carwood the rebuilt church of 1741 was given a west tower, which its predecessor had lacked.[89] At Leebotwood the west tower is an addition of 1829.[90] At Hinstock, Hopton Cangeford, Moreton Say, Quatford, and Willey (where mid 18th-century dimensions are recorded for other parts but not for a west tower) it is reasonably certain that the present towers are additions, not replacements.[91] It is impossible to estimate how many medieval west towers have vanished without trace, but as far as the record goes it would seem that after the Reformation many more churches gained a west tower than lost one. Indeed by the end of the 18th century, as auditorium churches became common in the industrial areas, west towers played a major part in distinguishing Anglican buildings like Madeley and Malinslee churches and the first St. George's, Pain's Lane, from a meeting house like Fletcher's chapel in Coalbrookdale.[92]

It should perhaps be stressed that a boldly projecting west tower was a rural and not an urban phenomenon in 18th-century Shropshire. It will be remembered that at the rebuilding of St. Alkmund's (1712–13), Whitchurch, the west tower was allowed to project only slightly, and in that respect it was not so greatly different from the steeples of many London churches rebuilt after the Great Fire. When St. Alkmund's, Shrewsbury, was rebuilt in 1794–5 the designers, John Carline and John Tilley, gave it, unlike its namesake at Whitchurch, a Gothic dress and retained, willingly or unwillingly, the 15th-century west tower of the old church; but they wholly enveloped that tower on north and south within their new structure, so that it does not project at all from the west front. At St. Julian's, Shrewsbury, in the mid century the medieval west tower was also retained when the rest of the church was rebuilt in 1749–50. St. Julian's was 'embellished' in 1846 and 'improved' in 1883–4 and the form of its mid 18th-century west elevation is not wholly clear, but it would seem that there too the older west tower was enveloped on north and south by the body of the building.[93] Town churches gener-

ally have more restricted sites than rural ones and larger congregations to accommodate, but it cannot be claimed that exigencies of space dictated the form of any 18th-century urban church in the county. Rather it would appear that projecting west towers were eschewed by Shropshire townsmen not from any lack of space or lack of tradition, but because in earlier years and under different pressures they had been abandoned by the prestigious churches of the major towns, especially London.

Equally striking is the rarity of ornamented or emphasized west fronts among smaller churches, even though many of them suppressed the traditional south entrance in favour of a west doorway. Minsterley (1688–9) had what may be called a frontispiece, and the very plain chapel at Morton (near Llynclys) of 1744 had an east (liturgically west) end crowned with a gable, and a bellcot above, in contrast with the domestic hipped end at the west (liturgical east).[94] At the two most prestigious churches of the period—St. Chad's, Shrewsbury, and St. Mary Magdalen's, Bridgnorth—the porticoes are not merely a piece of fashionable design, but also a manifestation of civic pride, and Blomfield's slightly later church at Meole Brace is an attempt by a leading local architect to show that he could be as up to date as anyone.[95] Attention of a less assertive kind was paid to the west fronts at Welshampton, designed by Edward Edgecombe and paid for by Mrs. Mary Kynaston,[96] at Madeley, designed by Telford, at Malinslee (on the same design), and to some extent at St. George's, Pain's Lane, the last two financed partly by landowners and ironmasters.[97]

Chancels, chapels, and accommodation

The perpetuation of older forms in rural churches is seen in the treatment of the chancel. After the Reformation, and as a result of the liturgical changes which it introduced, there was a tendency either to suppress the structurally separate chancel altogether and to place the communion table within the body of the church, or else to reduce the chancel to a vestigial form, often to a short and narrow projection from the east wall of the nave, as a polygonal or semicircular apse. When the 44ft.-long chancel at Westbury was demolished in 1753 it was declared to be 'much longer than is necessary or convenient'.[98] Every one of those large churches mentioned earlier had just such a chancel originally, if it had one at all; and new urban churches like St. Julian's and St. Alkmund's at Shrewsbury had the same. In the countryside, by contrast, despite the example of Westbury, the chancel was often held in more respect and churches with a vestigial chancel or without one were far from standard. There were a few: Halston chapel with a slight rectangular projection; Chetwynd church (1721, rebuilt 1865–7) with a semicircular apse;[99] and Cockshutt chapel, built or heavily restored in 1776,[100] and Kemberton church of c.1781 (rebuilt 1889),[101] each with a polygonal chancel. At Sutton Maddock the long medieval chancel still there in 1789 was replaced by a polygonal apse before 1820.[102]

Further, in several medieval churches the space of the chancel was later encroached upon by the nave. At Culmington, Rushbury, and Tugford the string courses, which mark the extent of the 13th-century chancel added to an earlier building, finish several feet west of the present division. At Lydham

Silvington chancel arch, probably 13th-century: modernized and moved to reduce the chancel when it was refenestrated

the abutment of the distinct roofs of nave and chancel is again to the west of the junction of the two parts. Far more drastic was the encroachment at Silvington, where in the 13th century a long chancel had been added to a small 12th-century church. At some time between c.1550 and c.1700 the chancel was refenestrated and it was probably then that the chancel arch reached its present position, incorporating nearly half of the chancel into the nave.[103] At Longnor the present step cuts across the westernmost window of a group of lights in the south wall of the chancel, and the west piscina, in the south wall of the nave, which was presumably originally against a screen, is several feet west of the step. At Hughley where the top of the late medieval screen cuts across the westernmost window of the chancel, the present chancel is 16ft. long by 20ft. wide, proportions unlikely in a 14th-century church.

Often the extra space within the nave was that obtained by the removal of the rood screen, but sometimes far more was taken over, clearly intended for a growing congregation. At Chelmarsh in 1888 much of the chancel was occupied by seating and the pulpit blocked the original priest's doorway.[104] At Baschurch in 1791, when the north aisle was pulled down, some extra space was gained by throwing the western half of the chancel into the nave and reroofing that half to line up with the nave roof.[105] At old St. Julian's, Shrewsbury, in 1748 the very long chancel was almost wholly occupied by seating.[106]

To set against these examples of demotion, however, are many new or rebuilt churches with chancels as wide, or nearly as wide, as the nave and at least one bay in length. They begin with Loughton chapel of 1622 and continue through Leighton (1714) and Buildwas (1720) churches[107] to Coreley (1757–62) and Jackfield (1759) and on to Hopton Cangeford (1776) and Meole Brace (1799).[108] At Shrawardine the rebuilt chancel of 1722 is three-quarters of the length of the nave. Often, as at Bolas Magna,[109] Quatt, Stirchley, and the now demolished Withington,[110] a medieval chancel of some length was left standing when the rest of the church was rebuilt. Further, many of those churches which had no structural chancel had a large liturgical one. The arrangements of Jacobean date at Langley chapel are well known, and there the chancel occupied a quarter of the total length of the building. At Melverley the present arrangement, with a very long chancel, is probably original and, if not, goes back to a partial reconstruction c.1700. At Stokesay the mid 17th-century rebuilding clearly marked the division between nave and chancel, and the latter was a long one; and so too, in relation to the total length, was that in the nearly contemporary church at Benthall.

The presence of large 'auditorium' churches in the towns and the industrial areas may be explained—in part and within the prevailing aesthetic and religious environment[111]—by the need to accommodate large and growing congregations there; and their absence from the countryside by the lack of such a need. That, however, cannot be the whole explanation, for nonconformists were erecting meeting houses, often as small as rural churches but yet on the same auditorium principle as large urban churches. Neither size nor current liturgical practice necessitated the tripartite form of country churches. Instead, with less pressure from social change than in the towns, that form reflected the dominance of the countryside by gentry families, demanding their prestigious pews close to the pulpit and reading desk and near—or even, like their tombs, in—the chancel, as at Wroxeter where it is filled with the monuments of the Newports and their connections. The gentry did not always have everything their own way, for the clergy too might have rights to strategic pews, as at Adderley[112] and Tong.[113] Most of the pews have gone, but a splendid one survives at Stokesay; a large square pew near the pulpit dominated the scene at Langley; and there were others, appropriately decorated with armorials, at Moreton Corbet and Chirbury.[114] Sir Stephen Glynne saw a 16th-century 'covered pew' at Munslow and Jacobean ones, roofed or canopied, at Cound and Wroxeter.[115] Of course townsmen were as conscious of rank and position as countrymen, and the better sort were not ill-provided; but urban churches were mostly controlled by oligarchs rather than by single families, and the seating pattern of an auditorium or a broad nave suited that social structure very well. Indeed in town churches parts were sometimes set aside for groups rather than for families, as at St. Leonard's, Bridgnorth, where a scholars' gallery was erected 1672–3,[116] and at Oswestry which had a 'poor's chancel' and a 'scholars' chancel' in the early 18th century.[117]

Probably none of these was in the most favoured spot, but in St. Mary's, Shrewsbury, the School—impropriator of much of the parish—was entitled to use the chancel.[118]

The importance attached to accommodation in the church is illustrated as well in the building of chapels serving both as reserved sites for family monuments and as superior private pews. Where more than one well bred family worshipped in the same church the desire for precedence could bring about such unseemly wrangles as that at Adderley between the Needhams and the Corbets in the 1620s and 1630s, when adherents of the two families came to blows in the building itself.[119] Nevertheless rank-conscious families could worship in harmony in the same church, as at Claverley, where the Whitmores had the chancel and the Gatacres the chancel aisles, and at Lydbury North, where the Walcots of Walcot and their successors, the Clives, occupied the south transept and the Plowdens of Plowden (their recusancy notwithstanding) had the north.[120]

Where possible existing chapels or aisles, or screened-off parts of them, were turned into pews, as at the two churches last mentioned and at others such as Condover, where the south transept was given to the Scrivens c.1600,[121] at More where the north transept was built or largely rebuilt in 1640, and at Stoke upon Tern where a family chapel was contrived at the east end of the south aisle of the nave in 1782. Sometimes a new structure was added. An early example is that built by the *arriviste* Foxes on the north side of Ludford church in the 1550s, and later ones are the so called Cornewall chapel at Diddlebury,[122] the north aisle, with a remarkable display of Jacobean woodwork, triumphantly added by the Needhams at Adderley in 1635–7 to mark their elevation to the peerage,[123] and the 'south chancel' at Willey built by the Welds.[124] Probably of late 17th-century date is the chapel south of the south aisle at Moreton Corbet.[125] Later examples are the north chapel added by the Actons at Acton Round c.1763; the two chapels built on the north side of Bicton chapel, one for the Sandfords of the Isle in 1754 and another, provided with a fireplace, for the Wingfields of Onslow c.1833; and the north aisle added at Acton Scott in 1820 and intended for a family pew.[126] And the Adderley saga ended on a happy note when the church was largely rebuilt in 1801 and the Corbets got the new south transept for their family pew to balance the Needhams' north aisle.[127]

Porches and doorways; galleries

While it is often impossible to know the purpose of an added or rebuilt aisle or transept, the functions of a porch are clear enough: to shelter a doorway and those detained there for liturgical or other reasons.[128] More than f40 porches were added or reconstructed in the period, half of them more or less securely dated. Timber was often used throughout the 17th century and into the 18th: at St. Mary's, Shrewsbury in 1602, at Cardington in 1639, at Loppington in 1656, at Deuxhill in 1661,[129] at Atcham in 1685, and at Wistanstow as late as 1733. Brick and stone were more favoured, and early dated examples are at Cheswardine,[130] perhaps of c.1583, and Stanton upon Hine Heath (1595). Later ones were at Silvington (1662), Barrow (1705), Bettws-y-crwyn (1712),[131] and Acton Scott (1722). Most of those were on the south, but north porches are known,[132] as at Stanton upon Hine Heath and St. Mary's, Shrewsbury. Great Hanwood church (1701) had a west porch by 1790, almost certainly an addition.[133]

As religious observances changed plan forms were modified, and the traditional north and south doorways were eschewed and a west doorway became standard. By the 1720s the practice was being followed at Bolas Magna, at (now demolished) Chetwynd,[134] and at Petton. Other examples of the mid century are, or were, Preston upon the Weald Moors (1739–42), Eyton upon the Weald Moors (1743), Cardeston (1749), and Jackfield (1759); and among the latest were Kemberton some time after 1781 and Great Wollaston as rebuilt in 1789.[135] Earlier churches too were sometimes brought up to date in this way: at Whittington in 1788 and at Westbury in 1790 there was no doorway in the south wall but a classical window where a doorway might once have been, and entry for the parishioners was through the west towers added in 1747 and 1753 respectively.[136] In 1791 the south wall of the nave at Donington had four windows and no doorway, but there was evidence, in the creasing on the upper part of the wall over the second window from the west, of a demolished porch.[137] The doorway in the west tower at Condover dates from 1800.[138] By the end of the century, in audito-

The west gallery of 1634 at Moreton Say church

rium churches and in those with classical porticoes, the western entrance was standard in new buildings and was being introduced into earlier ones throughout the early years of the next century. In 1829 the south doorway at Leebotwood was blocked and a west entrance made; as late as c.1840 a west doorway was inserted at Longnor when the west gallery was extended and the north and south doorways blocked.

The west doorway would have found favour even if galleries had been unknown, but nevertheless the last example suggests that it facilitated the erection of larger west galleries and of galleries along the north and south walls—as much as north and south doorways militated against them—and thereby assisted the provision of more space for larger congregations. It is doubtful, however, whether the earliest galleries were intended, or were solely intended, for that purpose. The west gallery has always been the commonest and, to judge from dated examples, was the earliest, as at Habberley of 1575,[139] at Hopesay of 1631 (both now gone) and at Moreton Say of 1634. That last has decorated posts supporting a gallery front with tendril and jewel ornament and has symmetrically turned balusters to the staircase. Even Glynne, who disapproved of pews and galleries, found the presumably comparable gallery at Upton Magna worthy of admiration.[140]

Most galleries introduced into an earlier structure were more workaday affairs and seem to have been used at first, as some aisles were, to segregate specific groups. A scholars' gallery was erected in the south aisle of St. Lawrence's, Ludlow, in 1614,[141] another at Bridgnorth, of 1672–3, has already been mentioned, and galleries for schoolchildren were known at Berrington (by 1815), Lilleshall (by 1838), and Wistanstow.[142] Other groups also could be set apart. A gallery at Cound in 1759 was reserved for the psalm singers and one at Madeley in 1786 for the 'parish' singers;[143] that was a very common use for west galleries in particular, and music continued to be provided there throughout much of the 19th century until organs supplanted the former singers and musicians.[144] At Llanyblodwel in 1749 there were two 'private galleries', presumably family pews.[145]

In 1722 the erection of a gallery for coal and iron miners over the north aisle at Madeley was both

segregation and the provision of extra accommodation,[146] and from then on the latter was the main function of new galleries, whether as part of the design of new churches or introduced into old ones. Galleries other than at the west end had appeared before the end of the 17th century: above the west end of the north aisle at Lilleshall in 1657, in the north transept at Condover in 1665, on the south of the nave at Upton Magna in 1666,[147] and in the north transept at Ellesmere, a church which Glynne described as 'disfigured by pews and galleries'.[148] By the beginning of the 18th century north and south galleries were common both in new churches and in old ones in urban or industrial areas. In Broseley church, built c.1715, there was a west gallery from the start, a north gallery for the poor was added in 1749, and a gallery built in 1794–5 completely covered the chancel.[149] The gallery of the single-cell church at Hopton Wafers ran along the whole length of the south wall, from the west tower to the east wall of the chancel,[150] and at Market Drayton in 1846 Glynne was horrified to find a huge gallery above the west wall of the chancel;[151] a similar one in Holy Trinity, Much Wenlock, had been removed some years before his visit.[152]

In older churches the presence of a gallery generally led to the introduction into the nave of a dormer window to light the new accommodation.[153] Often the general effect, especially where medieval windows had been removed and 'debased' post-Reformation ones inserted, was to give the building a homely domesticated air, increased occasionally, as at Beckbury,[154] Great Hanwood,[155] and Whittington,[156] by external brick staircases to evidently inserted galleries. Such domestic features may have given later ecclesiologists, anxious to emphasize the sanctity of a church, yet another reason for deploring galleries. Where, as at Market Drayton, galleries were inserted into every available space of an old church, more drastic measures were necessary, and there in 1786 the side walls were in part rebuilt and in part raised and given two tiers of windows—in the manner of some purpose-built galleried churches—but that was done in a wholly different style, for the windows were given two-centred heads and Gothick tracery.[157]

In churches designed to receive them the galleries were an important element in the effect, whether engaged with magnificent Tuscan columns at St. Alkmund's, Whitchurch (see illustration p.281), or carried on elegant cast-iron ones at new St. Chad's, Shrewsbury, and All Saints', Wellington. Where, as at St. Lawrence's, Ludlow, they were inserted into a Perpendicular nave they could impair the original light and lofty effect. Whether in an old or a new church, there was the problem of lighting the gallery and the space below. At Whitchurch it was solved in a traditional way with a range of very tall windows disregarding the internal division between the aisle and the gallery above.[158] At Shrewsbury and Wellington a different method, as efficient functionally and more satisfying aesthetically, exployed two tiers of windows, emphasizing the internal arrangement.

The size of churches

It might be thought that a post-Reformation rural parish church would be smaller than its medieval predecessor, for a medieval parish church had many functions and a subsequent one had only one. The premise, however, is not wholly true: it was not uncommon for churches to house schools in the late 17th and 18th centuries, as at Lilleshall,[159] Llanyblodwel,[160] Lydbury North,[161] Shelve,[162] and Holy Cross, Shrewsbury,[163] a provision that seems second-best to school buildings in the churchyard, as at Cardington,[164] Diddlebury,[165] Oswestry,[166] and Tong.[167] That apart, there are certainly several country churches where the nave was rebuilt or partly rebuilt in the 18th century to a smaller size. When Quatford nave fell in 1714 it was reconstructed 6ft. shorter and 6ft. narrower than before.[168] In 1723 the west wall of Edstaston nave was rebuilt 11ft. east of its former position.[169] The demolition of the south aisle at Wroxeter in 1763 and the subsequent rebuilding of the south wall north of its former position decreased the floor space available to the congregation by about a third. At old St. Alkmund's, Shrewsbury, in 1792–3, when a clique of local builders was attempting to get lucrative contracts for rebuilding, part of the bait dangled before the parishioners was that the new church would need less maintenance than the old because it would be smaller.[170] And it is fairly clear that the old church at Waters Upton was much larger than the one that had replaced it by 1788.[171]

Nevertheless most rural parish churches were small anyway, and the paucity of records of demolished churches and of information from excavations, makes comparisons difficult. Where comparisons can be made they do not always bear out the claim that medieval parish churches were larger than their successors. There are many churches whose west tower and nave, or nave only, were rebuilt while the medieval chancel was left undisturbed; in nearly all the chancel is of no great size or complexity and yet is not out of proportion to the rebuilt nave. That perhaps does not prove that rebuilt naves were generally no smaller than their predecessors, but at Ryton, where the west tower was rebuilt in 1710 and the chancel in 1720, and at Donington, where the nave was probably rebuilt in 1635 between an earlier tower and chancel,[172] the present naves must be as large as the medieval ones. The church at Meole Brace pulled down in 1799 was no bigger than its successor;[173] nor was the church at Sibdon Carwood which preceded the present one of 1741.[174] If Mytton's measurements are anything like correct, then the church at Frodesley that was replaced in 1807, that at Hopton Cangeford which was demolished some time after 1733, and the one at Cardeston which was rebuilt in 1749[175] were smaller than their successors. And Preston upon the Weald Moors church was said in 1736 to be too small and was rebuilt 1739–42.[176]

Few rural churches were large and complex and it seems most likely that the common Georgian country church, with a west tower, an aisleless nave and chancel, or with nave and chancel in one, perpetuated an equally common medieval form of comparable size. Of course some of the demolished urban churches—St. Alkmund's, Whitchurch, St. Chad's and St. Alkmund's, Shrewsbury, and St. Mary Magdalen's, Bridgnorth—had been complex structures with many additions to the main body in the form of aisles, chapels, and transepts. But it is not at all certain that their total floor space was greater than that of their more compact successors. Further, nearly all of these later churches were meant from the start to incorporate galleries and could accommodate far more worshippers than predecessors of comparable overall dimensions; and they needed to, for the population in the countryside was also growing, though more slowly than that in the towns.

Influences on design—architects and clients

Up to *c.*1700 rural church building in Shropshire was abreast of that in other counties, for 'prodigy' churches[177] were virtually unknown anywhere. Although the rural churches of the county, apart from Minsterley, are usually ignored in general surveys of the period, the work of the 1630s at Adderley, Astley Abbots, and, perhaps somewhat earlier, at Church Stretton was equal to anything anywhere else; as were the hammer-beam and double hammer-beam roofs of Donington, Sheriffhales, and Shifnal; and the rebuilding and restoration of Condover and High Ercall in the years around 1660 are comparable in their way with the much-lauded church at Staunton Harold (Leics.). They were doubtless backward looking in comparison with the London churches built after the Great Fire, but not more so than small rural churches elsewhere.

For most of the 18th century, however, the rural ecclesiastical architecture of the county is wholly undistinguished, and, while often pleasant enough, is noticeable more for what it lacks than for what it has. In the country as a whole at that time urban churches were more adventurous than rural ones, but nevertheless many country churches too were important examples of new styles or of new modes of worship. Not one church in Shropshire, however, was among them. There was nothing, for example, comparable with the rococo Gothic of Hartwell (Bucks.) or Shobdon (Herefs.), and, while Pritchard's ecclesiastical Gothic in the north chapel at Acton Round is in a similar vein, it is well below the level of his secular Gothic in Ludford House, Ludlow guildhall, and, farther afield, Croft Castle (Herefs.). There is, again, nothing like the more serious Gothic of Tetbury (Glos.) and Croome D'Abitot (Worcs.). Nor on the other hand is there anything to compare with the neo-classicism of Great Packington (Warws.)[178] or the Italianate baroque of Great Witley (Worcs.). Elsewhere, as for example at Milton Abbas (Dorset), a new church might be built by a great landowner for parishioners resettled to allow him to improve the amenities of his estate; but not in Shropshire, although there was no lack there of villagers dispossessed to make way for a park.[179] And no Shropshire landowner built a great church on the scale of Aynho (Northants.) or Mistley (Essex) or, like those at Ayot St. Lawrence (Herts.), Gunton (Norfolk), and Nuneham Courtenay (Oxon.), to close a vista or embellish a view from his residence.

It was claimed earlier that because there were no great resident landowners in the county there was no Palladian phase in the history of Shropshire houses;[180] it may be suggested here that that social lack also affected church building in the countryside.[181] Much of it was carried out by the parishioners as a body, but some men and women made large financial contributions and they were almost wholly people of purely local standing. The chapel at Westhope was rebuilt, perhaps *c.*1707, by Richard Fleming, the lord of the manor;[182] the cost of the rebuilding of Petton church in 1727 was possibly borne by two local landowners, R. Wilbraham of Petton Hall[183] and Francis Chambre;[184] and Chetwynd church was rebuilt some time before 1732 by Robert Pigott of Chetwynd Park;[185] Morton

Petton church, built in 1727, from the south-east

chapel (near Llynclys) was built and endowed by a Mrs. Bridgeman in 1744.[186] In 1759 Mary Browne of Broseley Hall built a new church for Jackfield;[187] in 1788 Mrs. Mary Kynaston of Oteley rebuilt Welshampton church;[188] and in 1791 Sir Richard Hill of Hawkstone and Reginald Heber, squire, patron, and parson of Hodnet, footed most of the bill for rebuilding the chapel at Weston-under-Redcastle.

Architects of national repute, whether professionals or amateurs, were asked to design many country churches at this time, but not, so far as is known, in Shropshire. It is true that both Telford, at Madeley (1794–7), and Thomas Harrison, who built

Petton church, built in 1727, looking east

the nave at Whittington in 1805–6, were in a sense national figures, but they were not employed on that account. Telford had been county surveyor for three or four years when he was asked to undertake Madeley, and to the parishioners of Whittington in north Shropshire Harrison, of Chester, was a local man. And Edward Edgecombe, who designed Welshampton church,[189] was from Tewkesbury, but by 1798 he was living in Ellesmere. More usually architects of local repute were employed. T.F. Pritchard, who had designed St. Julian's, Shrewsbury, in 1749–50, prepared a design for Kinnerley church in 1769–70.[190] In 1799 J.H. Haycock prepared designs for a chapel of ease at Tilstock;[191] Joseph Blomfield designed a new church at Meole Brace; and in 1801 Richard Baker, son of the better known William Baker of Audlem, rebuilt Adderley church. Apart from these the only names which can be associated with country churches are those of other local men or else of men otherwise quite unknown: John Gethin who 'made' the new roof of the nave at Bromfield in 1577,[192] Thomas Twigg, carpenter, who put his name on the roof of Donington nave in 1635; John Oram who rebuilt the west tower at Condover in 1667–8;[193] Roland Richards, a mason who designed the steeple at Ryton in 1719;[194] Henry Pagett and William

Higgins, masons of Bridgnorth and Pitchford respectively, who built the west tower and nave at Quatford in 1714; John Wildigg who supervised the work at Bolas Magna 1726–9; William Cooper, a member of the company of Carpenters, Tilers, and Brickmakers at Shrewsbury and the 'ingenious architect' who built Montford church 1733–8 and rebuilt Myddle nave in 1744; and William Magley and William Griffiths who encased Moreton Say in brick in 1788.

Men such as these, less likely than known architects to leave papers or to get a mention elsewhere, were probably responsible for the design of many rural churches in Shropshire; responsible in the sense that, at the very least, they gave their own interpretation of whatever they may have gleaned from pattern books or the work of other men. What part gentlemanly amateurs played is difficult to assess. The Gothic style of the rebuilt nave at Condover may have been due to Edward Owen, who had some supervision of the work. The William Jervis whom Cranage called 'architect and builder' of the alterations to the nave at Cheswardine c.1810 may have been a local craftsman but is as likely to have been an amateur, for the Jervis monuments in the church reveal a family of some local importance since the 17th century. Some of the people noted above who paid for church rebuildings and improvements may also have had a hand in the design, but, like the craftsmen's, the papers which might have established their role have failed to survive. However the problem is perhaps an unreal one, for the evidence of the buildings themselves shows that the designers of these churches, whether amateur or professional, were hammered alike on the anvil of a common aesthetic and a common view of the purpose of church building, and they were more concerned to provide 'decent' and 'orderly' places of worship than to create architectural masterpieces.

In towns and industrial areas the problems were different. As early as 1618 a north aisle was added to Broseley church, and the church was extended in 1654, rebuilt *c.*1710–1716, and given new galleries in 1749 and 1794–5.[195] In 1722 a gallery was built over the north aisle of Madeley church for ironstone and coal miners,[196] and in 1759 Mary Browne built her church to serve the population that industrial development at Jackfield was beginning to generate.[197] By about 1800 the increasing population of the Severn Gorge and the east Shropshire coalfield generally, coupled with the urgently recognized need for the church to combat dissent and woo the indifferent, led to the direct involvement of industrialists and of landowners with industrial interests in the building of new churches at Malinslee and Pain's Lane.[198] These last are interesting examples of a radical solution to a pressing problem, but, although built at a time when improved communications had brought the provinces intellectually and aesthetically closer to the capital, they were unlikely to be exemplars of modern architecture, for they were meant primarily to accommodate as many worshippers as possible at small cost and without cutting a dash. Rather it was churches in the wealthy and fashionable parishes of the older towns that were to show the way. There too the accommodation of increasing numbers was a problem, as the trustees of St. Chad's, Shrewsbury, well appreciated when they trumped up charges against George Steuart.[199] But there a well established merchant class and a burgeoning professional class, themselves profiting from industrial changes elsewhere, had both the intellectual and aesthetic interests and the communal resources to commission London architects and to bear the costs of their

ambitious and expensive schemes. It was by their agency that urban churches in Shropshire, in parallel with domestic architecture county-wide, were again able to show work that was as good as anything in other counties: All Saints', Wellington; St. Mary Magdalen's, Bridgnorth; and above all St. Chad's, Shrewsbury.

Interior decoration

Interior decoration of a non-architectural character was rare. Some relief from the general plainness brought about by the destruction of painted glass and the obliteration of wall paintings was afforded, perhaps, by the Creed, the Decalogue,[200] or the Lord's Prayer painted upon a reredos, or, as at Stokesay, on the nave walls; or by such an oddity as the painting of 1633 upon the nave roof at old St. Chad's, Shrewbury, with emblems, scriptural texts, signs of the zodiac, and angels and animals;[201] or by an achievement of royal arms prominently displayed. Those of Elizabeth I above the entrance into the Trinity chapel in St. Mary's, Shrewsbury, were accompanied by texts extolling virtuous women, in particular Deborah, the prophetess who 'judged Israel'.[202]

Apart from royal arms, painting was generally monochrome, and what colour there might be was largely an incidental effect of the boast of heraldry

The squire's pew in the south chapel at Moreton Corbet church

The chancel ceiling at Bromfield church, painted by Thomas Francis in 1672

upon family tombs. Important families often had imposing monuments in their local churches, many of which were products, or imitations, of the Southwark marblers, with a profusion of coloured stones. Many others had conspicuous and minutely quartered achievements of arms on them, and it was an act of family piety to keep these freshly painted in their proper tinctures. Similarly, arms were sometimes painted on family pews: examples survive at Hordley, and there are records of them on the Lloyd pew at Chirbury and the Corbet pew at Moreton Corbet.[203]

The outstanding piece of interior decoration is the painted plastered ceiling of the chancel at Bromfield, signed and dated by an obscure Thomas Francis in 1672. A symbol of the Holy Trinity placed centrally in the ceiling is surrounded by cherubim holding scrolls with texts and by billowing swirling clouds. Above the altar on the east wall two angels hold an open book with texts

from Psalm LXXXV. The top two feet or so of the side walls are also painted, and the colouring, whose subject matter is now indistinguishable, is finished at the base with a cornice drawn in perspective.[204] The whole is an extension of a practice, which itself was never very common, of emphasizing an eastern altar by decorating the spaces immediately above it.[205]

Equally rare, and unhappily not surviving, was the decoration at Sibdon Carwood, where by the 1820s the walls had been 'covered with coloured paper representing Roman antiquities etc.'[206] No more detailed description of these is known to be extant, and it is to be presumed that they were either an example of the chiaroscuro wallpapers of 1750 and later, reproducing Roman statuary, or else French neo-classical designs of the early 19th century.[207]

Prominent in some interiors in the 16th and, more commonly, in the 17th century was a dazzling display of carpentry, the result of a lingering fondness for prestigious medieval elements, and appearing when advantage was taken of the need for a new roof. Magnificent roofs had not been uncommon in Shropshire, and it might be supposed that nothing more than the continuation of a tradition was at issue. The new ones, however, were nearly all of hammer-beam type, almost unknown in the county until then[208] but found in some of the grandest late medieval buildings elsewhere. The predilection may perhaps be seen as a provincial form of that at Oxford in the early 17th century for 'the showy and eccentric features of Tudor Gothic, such as the fan-vault'.[209] Hammer-beam roofs can cover a wide span, and it might be argued that was why they were used in the 1660s at St. Leonard's, Brignorth, and Condover above widths of 43 and 37ft. respectively;[210] but the majority covered very ordinary spans. Probably one of the earliest post-Reformation roofs is above the nave at Culmington, of collar-beam type with one tier of cusped wind braces; but almost as early, one may suppose, is the hammer-beam roof above the chancel at Rushbury,

with cusped wind braces in quatrefoil patterns.[211] At Shifnal, not long after 1592,[212] the double hammer beam appeared, together with Renaissance scrolls and floral ornament and three tiers of purlins with straight wind braces. At Astley Abbots in 1633 typical Jacobean decoration had come in, and at Donington in 1635 there were delicate pendants and brackets with mustachioed heads. The greatest number, all with full Jacobean decoration, appeared immediately after the Restoration at, for example, Benthall, Bridgnorth, Condover, High Ercall, and Sheriffhales.[213]

These, of course, were exceptional. Most post-Reformation roofs, for example that of 1630 above the chancel at Wistanstow, were far less splendid, or, as at Ford and Worthen were eccentric. At Ford windbraces forming quatrefoil patterns appear in the nave roof where hammer-beam and collar-and-tie-beam trusses alternate. They are probably coeval with the wooden bellcot of *c*.1600 shown in a drawing of 1790. The cusping of the wind braces is extraordinarily thin, the principals of the hammer beam are exaggeratedly stilted and almost cruck-

*The double hammer-beam roof
in the nave of Shifnal church*

*The double hammer-beam roof
in the chancel of Shifnal church*

like.[214] At Worthen the roof has alternating one-collar and two-collar trusses with thin straight members and with cusping upon the **V** struts above the collars. Despite the reference to 'the making of the church and steeple' at Worthen in 1429,[215] the roof is probably of the same time as the Jacobean pews and benches.

Prominent not only for their colour but often for their size and magnificence were the 16th- and 17th-century monuments of local families. Monuments multiplied after the Reformation and changed their character, boasting to posterity of gentility rather than beseeching its prayers, and looming over the part of the church that they were in. Shropshire had nothing to match such a mega-lomaniac structure as Sir Christopher Hatton's tomb in old St. Paul's, except perhaps the Salaboss triptych of 1588 at Burford, dominating the altar (see illustration p.89).[216]

Donington church nave, looking east: double hammer-beam roof, 1635

The nave roof (probably dating from c.1600), looking east in Ford church

The standard late medieval tomb chest with recumbent effigies remained common well into the 16th century, but with early Renaissance ornament and with figures of the deceased's children, rather than of medieval 'weepers', along the sides of the chest. At Wroxeter the tomb of Sir Thomas Bromley (d.1555), chief justice of King's Bench, is an example of the work of the early Burton alabasterers, and that of Sir John Blount (d.1531) at Kinlet is probably a local copy of their style. By the second half of the 16th century the simple tomb chest was giving way to the large two-tiered structure, often with a tester carried on classical columns—almost a building within a building—and generally with kneeling or semi-recumbent effigies. The tomb of John Botterell (d.1588) at Aston Botterell is a stage on the way, for it combines reclining effigies, the debased ornament of the later Burton school, and a great amount of heraldry within the new form. By the beginning of James I's reign the Southwark marblers were

Detail of wooden tablet to the memory of Elizabeth, Mary and Rachel Vernon, dated 1642, at Moreton Say church

Wroxeter. Equally effective in a different way is the simple, indeed simplistic, wooden wall monument erected at Moreton Say in 1642 by 'their deare sister', Jane Grosvenor, to her three sisters.[217] Occasionally an independently minded patron broke the mould and indulged an individual taste. Sir George Blount's tomb in the north transept at Kinlet is a very large two-tiered structure with late Burton-style ornament and classical columns, kneeling principals,[218] and kneeling children behind them. But it also has Gothic arches—some two-centred, some trefoiled—and a late medieval cadaver in the lower tier, a very determined exercise in the older art. Equally unusual, and more surprisingly so, for it reveals in a distant county an appreciation of the highly sophisticated likings of the cultural élite, is the tomb of Oliver Briggs (d.1596) at Shifnal. Although it falls some way below the artistic level of Sir Thomas Gresham's tomb in St. Helen's, Bishopsgate, it is in the same austere vein, eschewing the bright colours and the elaborate ornament of the age. Equally up to date for meta-

Monument to Sir George Blount (d.1581) and his wife in the north transept of Kinlet church

making their colourful mark in the county. Early and late examples are the standing wall monument of William Leighton (d.1607), chief justice of North Wales, at Cardington and that of Humphrey Coningsby (d.1624) in the south transept at Neen Sollars. The effigies are semi-recumbent, the head resting on one hand ('as though they died o' the toothache'), beneath semicircular arches and classical columns, strapwork, and female figures of the Virtues.

Much of this funerary work, and in particular the products and imitations of Burton and Southwark, was standard and conventional, but sometimes there appeared such a piece as the not very well sculptured but highly charming figure of the young Margaret Bromley upon her father's tomb at physical conceits that rival Crashaw's is the inscription upon a monument in the remote church at Milson of a woman who died of dropsy in 1639.[219] On the other hand a work by Nicholas Stone, which one might expect to be a cut above the rest, Sir Humphrey Lee's monument in the north transept at Acton Burnell, is an undistinguished Jacobean run-of-the-mill product.

Different from all those are the four wooden panels, about two feet square, now set above the spandrels of the nave arcades at Morville. They were found, probably during the restoration of 1856–7, in the west tower, and it is not unlikely that they were made for the building they are in. They were part of a larger structure, but whether a pew, a pulpit, or a chest, is uncertain.[220] The figures upon them are of the four evangelists accompanied by their symbols and seated on chairs with cable-moulded uprights. They are carved in bold relief and their style is similar to the capitals of the timber arcade of the old church at Llanfair Waterdine.[221] Such works may not have been uncommon, but Time has dealt with them as ungently as with wall paintings.

XIX   Nonconformist Architecture

Early dissent

Nonconformist buildings with architectural pretensions, such as the Congregational chapel at Frome (Som.) and Lady Huntingdon's chapel at Worcester, were rare before the end of the 18th century, and, if there ever were any in Shropshire, none has survived.[1] Such chapels as were built were unobtrusive. When the Shrewsbury Baptists moved in 1780 from their retired site in Steelyard Shut (later Golden Cross Passage) to their new chapel in Claremont Street, with its classical portico and pediment, they still hid it behind a high wall.[2] Although no longer actively persecuted, Dissenters were probably not wholly forgetful of the riots of 1715, when mobs damaged the meeting house at Oswestry and destroyed those at Shrewsbury, Wem, and Whitchurch.[3] There were wealthy Dissenter families such as the Darbys and the Reynoldses,[4] and Dissenters (especially Presbyterians) were an important element in the Whig domination of Shrewsbury affairs;[5] nevertheless Dissenters were less numerous than Anglicans, and in general they disposed individually of fewer resources. For several reasons, therefore, they built generally in a modest way and worshipped in unremarkable buildings. The most important survival from early years, the former Congregational chapel of 1778 at Market Drayton, could well be mistaken for a dwelling, and as late as 1800–14 two thirds of all premises licensed for Baptist worship were private houses.[6]

Furthermore Dissenters had an unsurprising tendency to dissent not only from the Church of England but also from one another, and even in later years, when the population had increased and their own numbers had multiplied, they usually produced several small congregations within any area. In 1851 the large and partly industrialized parish of Pontesbury had a population of c.3,500, over 800 of whom attended nonconformist worship—but did so in seven chapels belonging to four different denominations.[7] And, even though many Dissenters shared in the increase of wealth that was evident in the 19th century, they were still mostly of lower-middle-class and working-class origin.[8] Consequently it was only in large towns or conurbations that the average congregation had the resources to erect an outstanding building.

The architecture of expansion

At the end of the 17th century Dissent was probably at its strongest in the county town; elsewhere it was most prominent in north Shropshire, especially in the towns of Ellesmere, Oswestry, Wem, and Whitchurch.[9] By 1816, however, industrialization in the east and south had allowed those areas to catch up,[10] and in the course of the 19th century more chapels, and more imposing chapels at that, were built there than in the north.[11] The volume of building is impressive. Mr. Stell lists 77 chapels built between 1800 and 1850, and the full figure is probably near a hundred.[12] The heaviest concentrations were of course in the towns and industrial areas—no fewer than 11 were built or rebuilt in Shrewsbury[13] and 15 in Dawley.[14] But there was a wide scatter throughout the county. The intensive campaign of church building in the 1830s[15] was easily surpassed by that of chapel building.[16]

When so much was built in so short a time, and most of it for limited congregations, it is not surprising that very small buildings were the rule. Until later in the century all were rectangular in plan, but some had a small projection for a vestry, as at the north-west corner of the Congregational chapel of 1827 at Bomere Heath. Most had a gabled roof but sometimes a pyramidal or a half-hipped one, as at Plealey (in Pontesbury) in 1828, Myddle in 1833, and Ollerton (in Stoke upon Tern) in 1838. The smallest were three-bay structures with a doorway centrally in a side wall and flanked by two windows. Larger ones generally had the doorway set centrally in an end wall, again with a window on each side, and with a range of two or three windows in the side walls; examples are at Myddle, at Wilcott (in Great Ness) of 1834, and at Ruyton-XI-Towns of 1833. When Broseley Old Chapel of 1741 and Wistanswick chapel (in Stoke upon Tern) of *c*.1805 were enlarged in the mid century former central doorways in the side walls were blocked and new entrances made in the end walls.

The contemporary provision of a manse, or at least of one attached to the chapel, was not common, but there was one at Broseley Old Chapel, one apparently at Myddle, and one in the form of a small attached cottage at Breaden Heath (in Welshampton) of 1832. When the gentleman who had built Plealey Congregational chapel in 1828 changed his theological views in the 1830s he, as owner of the chapel, evicted those who stuck to theirs. Their defiant reply was to build themselves a new one in Pontesbury in 1839[17] and to give it a large manse as well.

Dissenters were as interested as Anglicans in educating the young, and many of their chapels, like Roman Catholic churches, had associated schools for both religious and secular teaching. Charles Darwin himself, before being entered at Shrewsbury School (1818), attended the Unitarian chapel in High Street and the school kept by its minister.[18] Among smaller congregations, like the expulsees from Plealey, the school was generally attached to the chapel, either from the beginning or, as at the Primitive Methodist chapel of 1840 in Castle Street, Oswestry, added many years later.[19] Larger congregations, and especially Methodists, often had a schoolroom and other accommodation on the ground floor or in a semi-basement and the chapel proper above. Beneath the Methodist New Connexion chapel on Town Walls, Shrewsbury, there was a schoolroom, vestry, and doorkeeper's accommodation.[20] That building was on a steeply sloping site, but others on level sites followed the same pattern: for example the Wesleyan Reformers' chapel of 1853 in Beacall's Lane, Castle Fields, Shrewsbury;[21] the Wesleyan chapel of 1871 formerly in Beatrice Street, Oswestry;[22] and the Welsh Calvinistic Methodist chapel of 1888 in Oswald Road, Oswestry, designed by the town's leading architect Edward Bremner-Smith.[23] On the other hand the very large Wesleyan chapel of 1883 in Wellington had a schoolroom above the ministers vestry.[24]

Early chapels were not only simple but also plain, rarely aspiring even to such ornament as a cornice or quoins, and nearly always with round-headed openings. Occasionally, as at Myddle, Ollerton, and Wilcott, **Y** tracery was used in windows with two-centred arched heads, and at Moreton Mill chapel of 1846, near Shawbury, the glazing bars were treated as intersecting tracery. At Ruyton, Gothic buttresses were intended to be capped with pinnacles. The use of such 'Gothick' elements continued for a long time,[25] and the Frankwell Methodist chapel of 1870 had buttresses and pointed windows with intersecting glazing bars. Brickwork was usually plain, except for an occasional red and grey or red and brown chequer pattern, as at Breaden Heath and Moreton Mill.

By the 1830s some chapels in the new urban areas were casting off the modest air so long associated with them and were asserting claims to architectural quality, at least on their entrance fronts. That their appearance reflected the increased importance and standing of the Dissenting communities is revealed not merely by their size but also by the speed with which they had often replaced earlier, but not much earlier, forerunners. The Wesleyan chapel of 1837 at Madeley Wood was the successor of John Fletcher's chapel as extended in 1821; that in Court Street, Madeley, of 1841, replaced a predecessor of 1833;[26] and the Welsh Independent chapel of 1845 in Pride Hill, Shrewsbury, was replaced in 1862 by the Tabernacle in Dogpole.[27] The large Congregational chapel of 1848 in Lion Street, Wombridge, originally with four bays of windows in the side walls, was built by a meeting that had been founded barely five years before as an offshoot from Wellington. In contrast with the low plain fronts of earlier chapels all of these have tall façades divided into three bays by pilasters and surmounted by cornices and pediments in place of the simple gable ends of earlier chapels. At Wombridge the flat-headed windows have moulded consoles to the projecting lintels, while at Madeley and Madeley Wood the two tiers of round-headed openings between the pilasters are set within recesses in a somewhat tardy neo-classical manner. At Madeley Wood the centre bay rises through the pediment to give an impression of a truncated west tower. All these were built with, or soon given, side galleries. All are of brick, and their side elevations, like those of some contemporary churches, are plain.

These advances in the newly urban areas had been anticipated, and surpassed in architectural sophistication, by two chapels in old established towns: the Congregationalists' chapel of 1832 in Wellington Road, Newport, and the Methodist New Connexion chapel of 1834 on Town Walls, Shrewsbury. The first has the three-bay pilastered façade typical of the period, but in place of a slight external porch to the doorway the centre bay is left open from ground to entablature to form a lofty recessed porch with doorways in its side walls. Further decoration is provided by aprons in the outer bays, set somewhat oddly immediately beneath the frieze. The Methodist chapel by Fallows & Hart of Birmingham,[28] who were almost simultaneously building the Howard Street warehouse at the Shrewsbury Canal terminus,[29] is a very deliberate neo-Greek design. It is of five bays with Corinthian pilasters supporting a plain entablature with a shallow central pediment and punctuated parapet above. The round-headed windows rise nearly to entablature level, and the second and fourth bays have deeply projecting porches with fluted Doric columns and entablature and parapet above. Unlike one or two of their humbler brethren neither of these chapels has any Gothic element at all. In Shropshire, as in Staffordshire, the New Connexion was 'as capable as the Wesleyans of significant architectural expression'.[30]

From the mid century onwards nonconformist architecture developed in two ways: size and prominence increased, and there was a readiness to embrace forms and elements that had earlier distinguished Anglican churches. Perhaps not surprisingly two of the earliest examples are in Dawley, where industrialization was most advanced and where religious rivalry was perhaps most intense, or at any rate where Dissent was the new orthodoxy and nonconformists far outnumbered Anglicans.[31] The Wesleyan chapel in High Street was built by Robert Griffiths of Quatford in 1860, and the Baptist chapel at Dawley Bank in the same year. Both are larger and taller than earlier chapels, with three tiers of windows to the body of the church, and each replaced a predecessor, of 1825 and 1846 respectively.[32] Furthermore, while still avoiding the Gothic favoured by Anglicans, they had abandoned the sober sub-classical style of the 1840s and 1850s for a more assertive and decorative Italianate. Chapels similar in size and style to those at Dawley were built in Shrewsbury: the Welsh Independent, Dogpole, in 1862; the Baptist, Claremont Street, in 1877; and the Wesleyan, St. John's Hill, in 1879.[33]

Those three were prominent in their settings and were in important streets, but they were wholly outdone by the Congregational chapel of 1863 in Abbey Foregate and the Presbyterian chapel of 1870 in Castle Gates. The former, in a Decorated style by George Bidlake of Wolverhampton, stands at the fork of the main roads to London and Hereford and, with the Abbey church partly obscured by the railway bridge, dominates the view for travellers out

Congregational chapel, Abbey Foregate, Shrewsbury

of town across the English bridge. The other, by R.C. Bennett of Weymouth, is a very tall neo-Norman building with four tiers of windows. Standing at the top of the steep rise of Castle Gates and giving an impression of immense height, it there challenges the visual dominance of the castle and the old buildings of Shrewsbury School, and it could fairly claim to have satisfied the congregation's demand for 'visibility'.[34] The effect of these two on contemporaries is apparent from a guide book which, encompassing all nonconformist buildings in the town in a single sentence, yet picked them out for individual mention.[35]

Architectural rapprochement with Anglican churches

The generally clear differences between Anglican churches and Dissenting chapels, which had been apparent for nearly two hundred years, began to blur in the second half of the 19th century, and many chapels acquired elements which were patently Anglican. The two Dawley chapels of 1860, mentioned earlier for their size, broke ground also in their High Victorian polychromy: both were of blue brick with yellow brick dressings, and the High Street Wesleyan chapel had yellow horizontal banding in the lower part of its walls. Polychromy was used in some smaller chapels too, as in King Street, Much Wenlock, in 1862, at Melverley in 1865, at Stanton Lacy in 1877, and by Bidlake in Abbey Foregate. Bidlake used plate tracery in his rebuilding of Swan Hill chapel and geometric tracery in Abbey Foregate. Some chapels were given west towers, and all, in true ecclesiological fashion, were asymmetrically sited. The earliest, at Griffiths's Dawley chapel, was more like a Lombardy campanile than an English west tower, but Bidlake's in Abbey Foregate was determinedly Gothic. Maesbury Marsh chapel of 1868, by W.H. Spaull of Oswestry, had a broach spire carried by dwarf columns surmounting a doorway which projected to the side of the main front, and the same architect's Christ Church, Oswestry, built for the Congregationalists in 1871, is, in Pevsner's words, 'very much a church, with its south-west broach spire'.[36]

The most determined, and very early,[37] exercise in 'Anglicanization', however, had preceded all these. It was the Quinta chapel (in St. Martin's) of

1858. The roof has polychrome banding in light grey and reddish brown slates; the heads of the two-light pointed windows have Decorated tracery; a spire carried on columns rising from the west end of the south wall forms an open belfry; a south porch has a doorway with a two-centred head; the buttresses are of Gothic form; and a structurally separate east end, intended for a vestry but looking like a chancel, has a rose window in the east wall. At first, and even at second, glance it could be taken for an Anglican parish church. In its precocious exploitation of High Victorian Gothic forms the Quinta chapel was quite exceptional, but it did no more than anticipate the changes that were to become normal within a generation.

The Quinta chapel was also exceptional in its origin. It was built and funded by a 'patron',[38] Thomas Barnes, Liberal M.P. for Bolton and recent purchaser of a local estate. He gave the chapel to the Congregationalists,[39] and they, of all nonconformist denominations, appear to have had most help from rich members who took all or most of the cost of building on themselves.[40] That had been the case even at the beginning of the 19th century, when the chapels of Dorrington, Plealey, and Wistanswick had all been provided in that way.[41] In the spurt of Congregational building stimulated by the 1862 bicentennial of the Act of Uniformity Thomas Barnes is recognizable as the Congregationalists' leading local patron: besides building and supporting the Quinta chapel he paid £50 towards the cost of Prees chapel (1862), £500 towards the cost of the Abbey Foregate chapel (1863), £295 for the chapel site at Church Stretton (1865),[42] and seems to have been involved in the rebuilding or opening of half a dozen more chapels in the 1870s and 1880s.[43] Other local Congregationalist patrons in business or the professions included Richard Maddox, the Shrewsbury draper who paid £750 for the site of the Abbey Foregate chapel,[44] Thomas Minshall, the Oswestry solicitor of an old nonconformist family, who gave the site for Whittington chapel,[45] and the Massey family, whose support for the chapel at Whixall was comparable with Barnes's at the Quinta.[46]

Congregationalists had little success proselytizing in the east Shropshire coalfield, not from lack of resources but because they appealed to strata—artisans and small tradesmen—socially and economically above most of the adherents of the New Dissent.[47] In that respect they were closer than most other denominations to the Anglicans, and their architecture may be seen as reflecting that closeness. Up to the end of the 1870s nearly all nonconformist chapels with Gothic elements in Shropshire—as in neighbouring Staffordshire[48]—were Congregational;[49] George Bidlake's Wesleyan chapel of 1864 in Shrewsbury Road, Market Drayton, is a rare exception. In the early years of the century, when most chapels were in a Georgian or classically derived style, those with **Y** tracery in pointed windows, although not unknown among other denominations (for example, the Wesleyan chapel at Caynham and the Independent chapel at Myddle), were commonest among the Congregationalists,[50] as at Great Ness and Wilcott. And the Congregationalists' determination to make some attempt at architectural effect is shown by the elegant, though now derelict, little building at Ollerton (in Stoke upon Tern), in coursed squared rubble, with a pyramidal roof, hood moulds to the pointed windows with **Y** tracery, and an external stairway to the west gallery. In the 1860s and 1870s tracery and asymmetrical west towers, sometimes in combination, appeared most commonly as features of Congregational chapels: in Abbey Foregate and Swan Hill in Shrewsbury, at Maesbury Marsh, at Christ Church, Oswestry, and at Weston Rhyn. In addition Abbey Foregate chapel and Christ Church had structural aisles, and the latter had transepts as

well. Only in the use of coloured materials did other denominations at that time depart from older practices, and the Primitive Methodists in particular took pains to enliven otherwise dull façades with polychrome dressings.

The early architectural rapprochement of Anglicans and Congregationalists was largely the result of shared prosperity. It was not because prosperity and a liking for Gothic were inseparable companions, nor yet (or at least not much) because the Congregationalists were snobbishly imitating the Anglicans.[51] The main reason was that Congregationalists, like Anglicans, were more likely than their poorer nonconformist brethren to have the cultured leisure to be aware of aesthetic developments and the means to express them in building. Anglicans were originally better placed in that respect than Congregationalists, but by the early 1860s the latter would appear to have been catching up. Their awareness of ecclesiastical fashions in architecture is perhaps shown by their criticism in 1867 of their old chapel in Swan Hill, Shrewsbury, with its plain front and pedimented doorways, as 'unsightly'.[52] It is shown as well by their frequent employment of architects like George Bidlake and W.H. Spaull, who worked impartially for Anglicans and Dissenters, and of such a leading local architect as A.B. Deakin, who in 1884 prepared the design for the refronting of the Unitarian chapel in High Street, Shrewsbury.[53] In contrast the other denominations generally turned either to local men of no note, such as the Shrewsbury borough surveyor Thomas Tisdale (Calvinistic Methodist chapel, Frankwell Quay, 1865),[54] or to those who had made their names designing nonconformist chapels: men like R.C. Bennett of Weymouth (Presbyterian chapel, Castle Street, Shrewsbury, 1870) and Richard Owens of Liverpool (Baptist chapel, Claremont Street, Shrewsbury, 1877).[55] That Congregationalists also had the resources to allow them to build in an expensive way is suggested partly by what we know of their general standing,[56] partly by the number of their chapels built wholly or partly by rich believers, and partly by the enormous contrast between the costs of their Abbey Foregate[57] and Oswestry (1871) chapels[58] and the costs of others, even such prestigious ones as those by Owens and Bennett.[59]

Congregational chapel at Ollerton,
Stoke upon Tern

By the late 1870s the increase and wider distribution of wealth, the tendency of all denominations to close ranks in face of the new enemy, secular unbelief, and the complete dominance of Gothic among leading architects had removed most obstacles to the employment of that style and were making it acceptable to many congregations. An early Wesleyan exercise in the fully fledged Anglican manner is the chapel of 1879 in St. John's Street, Whitchurch, with north-west tower, north aisle, transepts, east end, and a profusion of tracery; it is indistinguishable externally from an important, even if slightly out of date, parish church. On

Unitarian church, High Street, Shrewsbury

a less ambitious scale, but equally determined, is the Welsh Independent chapel of 1877 in Lower Brook Street, Oswestry.[60] The architecture of Dissent, as a category distinct from that of the established church, had come to an end after a history of over two hundred years, partly because the building of new chapels and of new churches was equally in decline, but partly because the struggle between the two, despite an occasional rumble from the departing storm, was becoming past history.[61]

Interior decoration

Chapel interiors were generally, indeed emphatically, plain, but sometimes richly so. The main body of the Unitarian chapel in High Street, Shrewsbury, was rebuilt in 1839, but it re-used some of the fittings of the chapel, then Presbyterian, that had been built after the riots of 1715. They included panelling—one panel with a clock face and dated 1724—and a pulpit, all with heavy bolection moulding which must have set off the Hanoverian royal arms impressively.[62] Usually there was little beyond a ceiling cornice, perhaps some plain panelling around the walls and to the front of the gallery, and whatever ornament was provided by the

capitals of the cast-iron columns supporting the gallery. In later years, however, there was a tendency towards greater ornamentation, or at least greater architectural emphasis on the site of the pulpit. It was sometimes placed in a deep recess set, like a short chancel, between side compartments accommodating a vestry or an organ, an arrangement—for communion table rather than pulpit—seen in some Anglican churches of the 1790s[63] and 1830s.[64] In the Wesleyan chapel of 1883 in Wellington and the Calvinistic Methodist chapel of 1888 in Oswestry that space was marked off from the rest of the interior with an arch, carried on enriched pilasters at the former, where there was also a circular panelled plaster ceiling to the recess, and on coupled Corinthian columns at the latter.

In many Anglican churches the splendid monuments of the mighty dead added, often theatrically, to the interest of the scene,[65] but in Dissenting chapels monuments, when present, were plain tablets, architecturally self-effacing and blending in with, rather than standing out from, the wall surface. They reinforce the feeling engendered by the plainness of the structures that these were places of worship of congregations of equals.

XX   Roman Catholic Churches

In comparison with the popular nature of protestant Dissent, Roman Catholicism in Shropshire in the l7th and l8th centuries was confined to a persecuted élite of a few landed families—together with their poorer fellow believers in the neighbourhood—able by their wealth and connections to mitigate the worst effects of the penal laws. Official returns listed 366 adult papists in the county in 1676.[1] That figure clearly understated their numbers, but a recent, admittedly generous, estimate is 'a few over a thousand' at the beginning of the 18th century,[2] and there were perhaps even fewer by c.1800.[3]

From the middle of the l8th century, as the ideas of the Enlightenment spread, the rise of British power made the old bogey of a Roman Catholic revanche carried on French bayonets ever more ludicrous; the penal laws were less rigorously enforced, and Acts of 1778 and 1791 gave some relief from the worst of their provisions.[4] There was a mass house in Madeley by 1770,[5] and in 1776–7 a chapel was built in Beeches Lane, Shrewsbury, by the prominent Shrewsbury builder Samuel Scoltock, and probably to his design.[6] The Emancipation Act of 1829 lifted most of the remaining disabilities,[7] and churches were built at Newport in 1832[8] and Wellington in 1838.[9]

Despite their new legal freedoms Roman Catholics were well aware of the ease with which traditional anti-Catholic feeling could be played upon and, like the Dissenters,[10] they erected plain inconspicuous buildings in less-frequented streets, sometimes, as at Madeley and Shrewsbury, hiding the church behind a house. Even after radical alterations in 1825-6 the latter, with its stuccoed pedimented front, probably differed little externally, except for the cross upon it, from a nonconformist chapel, and it had been built at a cost of only £549.[11] The now-demolished church in Mill Bank,

Wellington, was described in 1851 as a 'plain brick structure',[12] and the church at Newport, also of brick, is a large plain rectangular box.[13] The Actons' private chapel (1825) at Aldenham, replacing an earlier one inside the Hall, was indeed out of the ordinary—the conversion of a neo-classical garden temple of c.1780, whose Ionic portico became the new chapel's façade; but, half hidden by trees,[14] it was not easily visible to the public, even if it was more so than the usual domestic chapel indoors, sometimes in an attic storey[15]—a location by no means precluding architectural virtue, as in the case of Sir Edward Blount's chapel in Mawley Hall (c.1730), rectangular in plan and narrowed at one end by convex curves to form a deep recess for the altar.[16] By 1850, however, the Roman Catholics, like the nonconformists, had overcome their 300-year-old attitude of being thankful even to be tolerated and were setting out to challenge the pre-eminence of the established church in a fair, or more or less fair, competition. Like the nonconformists, they would thenceforth build large and conspicuous churches when they could. Unsurprisingly, in comparison with neighbouring Staffordshire, historically one of the most Catholic counties in England,[17] the change was tardy, for Holy Trinity church in Newcastle-under-Lyme had been built in a highly ornamented late-Gothic style as early as 1833–4.[18]

Landed wealth continued to be important to the church throughout the l9th century. Between 1850 and 1900 eight churches were built in Shropshire. The Actons of Aldenham gave the land, the stone, and £500 for the first Bridgnorth church (1856)[19] and much of the stone for the second one[20] built in front of it in 1895-6. Shifnal (1860) was funded by Lord Stafford,[21] Plowden (1868) by the Plowdens of Plowden,[22] Market Drayton (1886) by a recent convert from an old local family, Egerton William Harding of Old Springs, Tyrley (Staffs.),[23] and the church (1890), associated convent, and school at Oswestry by the Longuevilles of Llanforda;[24] and successive earls of Shrewsbury had largely funded the Newport church[25] and guaranteed the building costs, over £10,000, of Shrewsbury Cathedral. The cathedral site was partly provided by a scion of another landed family, the Cholmondeleys.[26] The original choice of Shrewsbury, and the later perpetuation of a see there against Bishop Brown's very reasonable wish in 1854 to transfer it to Birkenhead, far closer to the vast majority of his flock, may have been influenced by the Talbots' desire to have a cathedral in the town from which they took their title and by the understandable readiness of the hierarchy to oblige such munificent benefactors.[27] Nevertheless the 17th earl of Shrewsbury was later ready to finance the building of a pro-cathedral in Birkenhead, a scheme frustrated by his death in 1856.[28]

It was, however, industrialization and immigration which did most to spread the Old Confession in Shropshire. There had been Irish workers in Wellington since the late 18th century,[29] and there were enough in Shifnal in 1842 and 1855 to provide an excuse for anti-Irish riots.[30] Many Irish, of course, came to build the railways, but they remained in the county long after their original tasks had been done,[31] and in Shrewsbury, the county's earliest rail centre, they formed an impoverished community in which there was a great increase in pastoral work as early as 1845.[32]

Had A.W.N. Pugin lived, he would have been the architect of the new cathedral, but the task fell to his son E.W. Pugin, who was drafting specifications in 1852 and was responsible for the final design.[33] A large building was originally intended, with a tower and spire tall enough to rival those of St. Mary's and St. Alkmund's. After some £2,200 had been spent on the foundations, however, it became apparent that the soft underlying sandstone would not bear so much weight, and tower and spire were abandoned and a less ambitious church was built during the years 1853-6.[34] The site, garden land behind 11 Belmont, has not made the cathedral visually prominent in the town, and it is best seen from outside the Severn's 'adorable curve'[35] down river from Kingsland (where the Schools moved in 1882) to Coleham.

Almost simultaneously, at Madeley, in 1852–3, J.A. Hansom seems to have been contemplating a building that would challenge Telford's parish church and dwarf the nearby Methodist chapels.[36] Its aisled nave is impressive in size and height, but it stands alone. The capitals of the responds of the chancel arch, partly obscured by the blocking of the arch, show that a chancel was intended. A similar blocking of the arch at the west end suggests that a tower was too, and presumably tower and chancel were meant to be on a scale commensurate with that of the nave.

Such over-bold ventures coincided with the euphoria that frightened Lord John Russell into his outburst against 'papal aggression'[37] and was expressed in Newman's 1852 sermon on 'The Second Spring', with its specific reference to Shrewsbury.[38] It is noticeable that later 19th-century churches were more modest—not only the village church at Plowden, but also the churches in the major towns of the county: Bridgnorth, Market Drayton, Oswestry, Shifnal, and Whitchurch.

The reason for the change is perhaps not far to seek. In the mid 19th century the Roman Catholic church in England faced again the problem which she had had in Anglo-Saxon times, that of providing pastoral care over a large area with a small priesthood. She had another problem as well. A developing industrial society needed to educate not only an élite but, at least to an elementary level, the mass of the population; and mass education, such as there was, was then almost wholly in the hands of other denominations.[39] With their strictly limited resources, the parochial system which the Anglican church could afford was unattainable by Roman Catholics, and instead—perhaps much like the minsters of a thousand years before—complexes of a church, a presbytery, and, where possible, a school were built where they could best serve the greatest number of worshippers, or where, as at Plowden, a wealthy benefactor would build a church and school on his estate.

Their 'minster' rather than parochial functions, together with the celibacy of the clergy, ensured that Roman Catholic churches would look different from most Anglican ones, for they rarely stood alone but had a presbytery or school, or both, attached.[40] There was no clear pattern in the relationships between the parts. At Shifnal the presbytery is at the

Newport's Roman Catholic church in Salter's Lane

east end of the church, at Newport it is on the north side, at Market Drayton it is in a wing adjoining the east end. At Bridgnorth in 1856 Griffiths designed a dual-purpose building to serve as church and school, with a presbytery attached[41] on the south.

Other factors accentuated the differences. Since the 16th century the Roman Catholic laity had been brought physically closer to the church services,[42] and, unlike Anglican clergymen, Roman Catholic priests had lost none of their sacerdotal prestige in the last three hundred years.[43] Furthermore Roman Catholics were not to be told by schismatic Anglicans, however learned in ecclesiology, what a church should look like. In consequence Roman Catholic churches in Shropshire, apart from the cathedral and the unfinished church at Madeley, have many of the elements which Ecclesiologists deplored and few of those—notably long chancels—which they recommended.

In contrast with the large new Anglican chancels Roman Catholic churches had short ones at Market Drayton, Oswestry, Plowden, and even Shrewsbury Cathedral, while at Newport, Shifnal, and both Bridgnorth churches there was no structural chancel at all. Long chancels had the adverse effect of distancing the laity from the service, and, unlike some Anglican clergymen, yearning for the position which medieval English churchmen had held, Roman Catholic priests had no need for impressive chancels of 13th- and 14th-century type to enhance their standing with their congregations. In Roman Catholic churches large high altars and prominent reredoses usually dominated the east walls, and east windows—universal in Anglican churches—were rare. The cathedral has a great seven-light one, intended to be filled with Hardman's glass, but the only others were at Bridgnorth[44] and Whitchurch. At Whitchurch, on a cramped site, the east end has

Market Drayton's Roman Catholic church in Great Hales Street

triple lancets, but they and the lancets of the west wall were the only, and perhaps not very efficient fenestration, and a very long, and very ugly, lantern now straddles most of the ridge. The unbuilt west towers intended at Shrewsbury Cathedral and Madeley, if axial, would also have distinguished the Roman Catholics' two grandest Shropshire churches from Anglican churches built from the mid 19th century.[45] At Bridgnorth in the 1890s, however, a north-west tower was intended, more in accordance with ecclesiological preferences,[46] and at Wellington in 1885 the west front was redesigned and a small south-west turret added.[47] Even at the end of the century, however, anything approaching a west tower in appearance was as common in nonconformist chapels as in Roman Catholic churches.

With regard to aisles there seems to have been more ecclesiological conformity between Shropshire's Roman Catholic and Anglican churches. Ecclesiologists came to recognize a hierarchy of churches, with town churches ranking higher than rural ones, and they were pragmatic about aisles.[48] Thus the aisles at Shrewsbury and Madeley, and later at Oswestry, parallel the way in which accommodation was increased in some urban Anglican churches.[49]

In style the differences between Roman Catholic and Anglican churches were of emphasis rather than of kind. In contrast with the classically derived chapels in Beeches Lane, Shrewsbury, and at Aldenham, all the churches from Newport (1832) onwards were Gothic, but more commonly in the less expensive Early English manner. Decorated was used only on important buildings or in prominent positions. Lancets were usually plain, but on the lateral walls at Market Drayton coupled lancets enclosing a buttress appeared, and at Oswestry the lancets have moulded surrounds. Polychromy was sometimes used, and in 1886 Edmund Kirby, of Birkenhead, who designed many Roman Catholic churches, and some Anglican ones, in Cheshire and North Wales, used it very effectively at Market Drayton.[50] There the yellow-white brick of the fabric contrasts with the bright red Ruabon brick of the string courses, the surrounds of the lancets, and the blue-grey tiles of the roof in a composition which, in its boldness, outclasses anything which Anglicans[51] or Dissenters did.

Internally the churches, with the clear exception of the cathedral, are generally plain, and the visual interest is concentrated upon the reredos. In the church at Newport there is a plain wooden gallery at the west, a low-pitched wooden ceiling, and almost

bare walls, and the effect, lancets apart, is reminiscent of some of the Spanish mission churches—not so different in date—of southern California. The church at Market Drayton, equally plain internally, derives considerable architectural quality from its coupled lancets, from the benches, slightly bowed on plan and arranged herringbone fashion on both sides of the central aisle,[52] and from the scissor-braced roof enhancing the geometric and patterned effect. In the church at Oswestry, of 1890, the nave roof is plain, but the chancel roof has cusped queen struts and cusped principals above collar level in the traditional style of the Border counties; the north aisle, vaulted and with Decorated tracery, is later.[53]

In addition to its greater size Shrewsbury Cathedral is different from the county's other

The Roman Catholic cathedral in Shrewsbury

Roman Catholic churches, and but for its small chancel it has, or was intended to have, nearly all the attributes of a major Anglican church of the period. It is a lofty building, and its interior, with tall thin piers to the arcades, has a stretched look; but externally the height allows ample space for the spherical triangles of the six-bay clerestory, and, in contrast with their cramped forerunners at Lichfield, they dominate the side elevations. The broad west window with curvilinear tracery is as grand as the east window at St. Mary's of 1858 and does much to offset the incongruous, and originally unintended, bell turret. The general effect is rich, even ornate.

It has been said that by 1850 'there was little difference between Roman Catholic architects and those of the Church of England, except those of the highest rank'.[54] Architects designing Roman Catholic churches, however, whatever their tastes or talents or 'rank', had to do so within the limits imposed by the mode of organization of the clergy, by the liturgy, and by the funds available.[55] Shrewsbury Cathedral, for example, differs from another similarly sized Roman Catholic church by E.W. Pugin—Our Lady of Reconciliation (1859), Vauxhall Road, Liverpool. There Pugin, then lacking Lord Shrewsbury's seemingly bottomless purse, built a very large church very plainly,[56] as his father had sometimes had to do.[57] Few patrons were as rich and as pious as the 16th and 17th earls of Shrewsbury, and congregations, generally poorer than Anglican[58] and less numerous than nonconformist ones, had to eschew not only the forms but also the ornament of the Establishment. Their handful of churches in Shropshire had in consequence a very marked character of their own.

XXI   Anglican Architecture: The 19th Century

The predominance of secular over ecclesiastical architecture which had developed after the Reformation was beginning to wane by the mid 19th century. The previous hundred years had seen an unprecedented increase in the volume of industrial production, a rapid rise in population, the intellectual effects of the Enlightenment, the spread of nonconformity, and the menace of Jacobinism. To use a homely metaphor, a vast market for ideologists had been created at the moment when the established Church had lost her near monopoly of religious respectability and all was being thrown open to the bracing wind of competition. As a result ecclesiastical architecture regained some of its old importance, and in Shropshire in the 70 years after 1830 a hundred Anglican churches were built, more than a hundred nonconformist chapels, and even a handful of Roman Catholic complexes, including the only cathedral that Shropshire was ever to get.

The advent of what might be thought of as ironmasters' churches at Malinslee and Pain's Lane (St. George's) in 1805 and 1806 might have led contemporaries to believe that a campaign of church building in the east Shropshire coalfield was being initiated. But it was a false dawn.[1] As it turned out, there was to be little Anglican building in the county in the next quarter of a century. The only large-scale works were the enlarging and beautifying of Oswestry parish church in 1807;[2] the rebuilding of the ruinous nave at Wem c.1811;[3] the virtual rebuilding of Dudleston chapel in 1819;[4] the building of a new chapel of ease at Trefonen—a plain rectangular box, begun in 1821 and intended for the 'Welch inhabitants' of Oswestry parish;[5] Thomas Botfield's rebuilding of Hopton Wafers church in 1827;[6] and, architecturally the most important of all, the rebuilding of the nave at Pontesbury 1827-9.[7] Apart from those there was

nothing more than the provision of a family chapel at Acton Scott (1820),[8] of north (1821) and south (1828) transepts—the former a family chapel with 'two cozy fireplaces'—at Selattyn,[9] and of west towers, as added at Chetton (1829)[10] and Stapleton (1832).[11]

In the 1820s, however, there were portents of what was to come. In a way Hopton Wafers was one: the parish was small but was becoming industrialized with coal, iron, and limestone extraction and paper mills, and by 1820 the church was insufficient for the population; Thomas Botfield was lord of the manor and patron of the living, but only recently and thanks to an industrial fortune which also made him the employer of many of his fellow parishioners, whose church accommodation he set out to improve.[12] In 1822 an aisle as wide as the original nave was added at Little Wenlock, a parish with a mining and industrial corner and a rising population, and in 1824 galleried transepts, which increased the seating from 200 to 500, were added at Wombridge, where deep mining had begun and large new ironworks established.[13] The contrast between Selattyn's transept, built to make religion comfortable for a gentleman's family, and work intended to introduce religion to the masses, reveals the change then coming over the Church of England.

Competition of Dissent

That Methodism was instrumental in saving England from a social revolution in the years around 1800 has been long and widely, but perhaps erroneously, believed,[14] and it is a commonplace that fear of revolution stirred Parliament to pass the Church Building Act of 1818.[15] That measure allocated public funds for the erection of churches in what would today be called 'deprived' areas, and in

Pontesbury church looking east

the same year the Incorporated Church Building Society was founded to tap private wealth for similar purposes. It would appear, however, that the ruling classes in Shropshire had steadier nerves than some of their counterparts elsewhere, or thought themselves well out of the firing line, for it was more than a decade after that before anything very much was done. Church building in Shropshire got under way considerably later than in some parts of the country[16]—only in the 1830s when nearly 20 new churches were erected.[17] All but four of them were in urban and industrial areas, and most were founded as chapels of ease or new district churches and intended for an industrial population, like that at Rorrington which was built 'not far from the populous lead works of the White Grit Company'.[18]

The blatantly mission-church nature of much of the building of that decade is revealed clearly when it is compared with the rebuilding of the nave of the old rural minster at Pontesbury, begun in 1827 by a local man, John Turner of Whitchurch,[19] and given north and south aisles, a south porch, and a south-west tower. The paired lancets of the aisles have moulded mullions and jambs and continuous hood moulds, the aisle walls are punctuated by buttresses of 13th-century character, each crowned with a moulded gablet, and there is a moulded parapet above. The clerestory is similar, with a parapet above a moulded cornice. The south-west tower is of four stages and in a similar vein. Internally the nave is lofty and spacious and the piers of the arcades—which are probably copies, or at least drastic re-cuttings, of the originals—were good enough to deceive Pevsner.[20] There was no penny pinching: the work cost £5,000 and is, for its time, a remarkably successful attempt at a medieval church, a worthy companion to the imposing chancel of *c*.1300.

In contrast the new church at Coleham, Shrewsbury, completed in 1837, cost £1,800 and

West front of Coleham church.
Essentially a rectangular box, the west front
was embellished with a classical portico
with lantern above

St. George's church, Frankwell, Shrewsbury

had been built in 13 months. It was a plain rectangular box lit by round-headed windows, with a west gallery, a boarded ceiling, and open pews. Some slight external show was made by a classical portico with a lantern above.[21]

Most of the churches of the 1830s were equally plain. A distinction between the majority with structurally separate chancels and the few without would be formal rather than meaningful. The chancels are so small and plain—generally no more than a slight projection from the east wall making a recess for the communion table—that they have as little liturgical and architectural significance as their 18th-century predecessors. Furthermore some of the churches with no structural chancel had the communion table within an internal recess—as, for example, at Tilstock, where it is flanked by a vestry on the south and on the north by a 'storeroom' with an external doorway in the east wall.[22] The only attempt at distinction or emphasis is the vaulted apsidal chancel at Holy Trinity (1836), Oswestry, by the local architect Thomas Penson.[23] Apart from St. George's (1832), Frankwell, Shrewsbury, and St. Mary's (1838), Ketley, which have transepts, the naves are simple rectangles, typically with a west gallery carried on cast-iron columns. Large town churches like St. Michael's (1829), Ditherington, Shrewsbury, and Christ Church (1838), Wellington, and those in industrial areas, like St. Luke's (1835-6), Ironbridge, had galleries on three sides; even in a small church like Priorslee (1836) there were originally both west and south galleries. Half of these churches were in a broadly 'classical' or specifically Grecian style and half were Gothic, the difference lying mainly in the use of broad round-headed windows or of uncusped lancets, generally set fairly high up in the wall. Here again, however, Penson's Holy Trinity, Oswestry, was odd man out, with cusped lancets running very impressively from just above ground level to wall top. A modern comment on a

Southampton church of 1870 probably typifies the attitude of most of the men responsible for these buildings: 'uninspiring but adequate for the masses'.[24]

The fondness of 18th-century Salopians for west towers was mentioned earlier;[25] the churches of the 1830s reveal an equal, indeed an intensified, love of that feature. Throughout the early years of the 19th century west towers were occasionally added to existing naves; in the 1830s they were almost *de rigeur*, occurring in 13 of the 16 churches built then.[26] Furthermore, whatever ornament these generally very plain churches possessed was displayed at the ritual west end, and that was so whether the style was classical or Gothic and whether a tower projected from the west front or a lantern was incorporated within it. The front at Coleham was mentioned above, and two other notable examples are by Edward Haycock in Whitchurch parish: Dodington (1836), with an open second stage of twelve square columns carrying an octagonal entablature,[27] and Tilstock (1835) where the upper part of the tower has been rebuilt, giving it, as Pevsner says, the air of a campanile.[28] At the Gothic Christ Church (1838), Wellington, the west tower has three orders of mouldings to the window surrounds in contrast with the plain chamfers in the body of the church, and its upper stage is finished with a course of mock-machicolation and has crocketted turrets. Even at the remote little church of Shelve, among the mines on the western slopes of the Stiperstones and plainest of the plain,[29] the west tower has at least been given string courses, a window with **Y** tracery, and a doorway with a four-centred head.

The concentration of Anglican efforts in the 1830s on what would now be called 'deprived areas' was part of their attempt to proselytize among the growing industrial working class, and the plain preaching-box air of Anglican buildings was only an extreme example of current Anglican practice, itself brought about in part by the need in the previous century to develop an urban form of church.[30] But the preoccupation with west towers was a different matter, for a west entrance allowed the best use of space in an auditorium and a west tower to grace that entrance was the element that most clearly distinguished an Anglican church from a Dissenters' chapel.[31] The insistence upon a west tower in conjunction with the tardiness of the building programme in Shropshire—mostly after the Reform Act of 1832—suggests that Methodism as a prophylactic against Jacobinism had been found to have unwelcome side effects, partly because it was a possible threat to the hegemony of the Church of England over the population at large, and partly because it was not wholly a political soporific but had within it potentially dangerous dissident elements as well.[32] Dissent was now to be feared more than Jacobinism, and not without reason for in that decade the Dissenters are known to have erected 34 chapels, generally smaller than Anglican churches but more numerous, and the actual number may have approached 50.[33]

Rural provision

The bias of the building programme of the 1830s towards urban and industrial areas was wholly reversed in the next decade, when 19 of the 24 new churches were in the countryside and four of the other five had been completed or begun before the middle of the decade. New churches, occasionally of some splendour, were built in urbanized areas

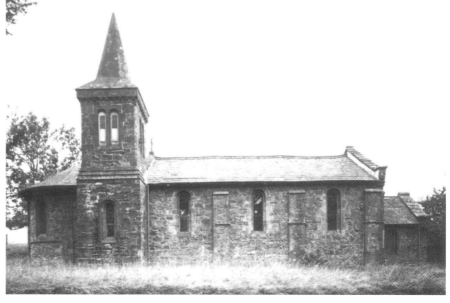

Cwm Head church with its tower on the north-east

throughout the century but never again were they more than a small proportion of the total output.

That change in the distribution of church building coincided with others. The clearest change was the abandonment of the Georgian formula of west tower, aisleless nave, and vestigial chancel. West towers, almost universal in the 1830s, were far less common in the next decade, occurring in only one in three.[34] The decline was mainly due to the absence of any towers at all, but partly—a portent of the future—to the appearance of towers sited asymmetrically: set to the north-west at Llanymynech and Little Drayton and to the north-east at Cwm Head, Wistanstow. The last, however, still had a west porch, and a west entrance was still, with few exceptions, rigidly adhered to. The aiseless nave remained the dominant form, but Broseley, Dawley, and Little Drayton churches were given north and south aisles. The medieval nave at Ellesmere never had a south aisle and its north aisle had been pulled down before the end of the 18th century, but Scott, when he rebuilt it in 1849, gave it two aisles. These four, it will be noted, were in urban areas and would doubtless have had galleries rather than aisles had they been built a few years earlier. Transepts were no more favoured than they had been earlier and occur in only three churches. Most chancels continued to be vestigial or non-structural, but a few were of some size. At Haycock's wholly undistinguished Bayston Hill church (1843) the chancel was a full bay long; Penson's neo-Norman church at Llanymynech had a chancel (c.16ft. square) of reasonably 12th-century proportions; and the little upland neo-Norman Cwm Head church (1845), has an apsidal chancel 20ft. long—over half as long as the nave and rather more than the 12th century would have asked for.

Changes in form accompanied an almost total change in idiom, in the abandonment of classical norms and the adoption of medieval styles, mostly Gothic. Two of the three churches that Edward Haycock had built in the 1830s were classical, and that, as was seen earlier, was his natural bent.[35] In

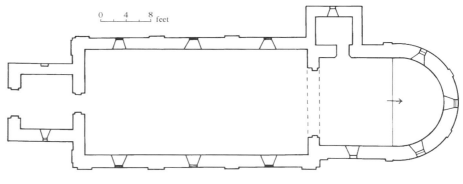

Plan of Cwm Head church

the next decade he was the most patronized of all church architects, responsible for no fewer than eight of the 24, and all in a Gothic style. He was not peculiar in that, for while half of the churches of the 1830s had been classical, none was in the 1840s. The period's Gothic, seen in 16 churches, consisted mainly of the use of lancet windows and of buttresses, string courses, and hood moulds if funds allowed. At Donnington Wood in 1843 Scott introduced plate tracery,[36] and at Harley Pountney Smith,

The chancel at Llanymynech

who was to be one of the leading local architects of the next decades, used lancets in the chancel and a mean Perpendicular in the nave. The decade's most impressive churches, but somewhat out of their time, were those in Broseley and Dawley, built by Harvey Eginton of Worcester in a 'remarkably serious' and 'very competent' Perpendicular.[37] Decorated work, not always very pure, was limited to additions and partial rebuilds; the most important examples are the north aisles at Cound (1841) and Ruyton-XI-Towns (1845), the east window of the south aisle at Hodnet (1846), the west window of the nave at Alberbury (1846), the rebuilt south aisle at Llanyblodwel (1847), the chancel at West Felton (1848), the nave at Ellesmere (1849), and the design for the east window at Astley (1849).[38]

The commonest non-lancet style was the neo-Norman, and Goodhart-Rendel has suggested why: of all non-classical forms it had the least taint of the neo-Catholic sacerdotalism, of which church builders and restorers were sometimes accused until the late 1840s.[39] At the same time an 'eclectic Romanesque' distinguished churches from Dissenting chapels, most of which—and all the prominent ones in towns and urban areas—were built in a classical style throughout the 1830s and 1840s.[40] These social and religious pressures are well reflected architecturally in John Carline's church of 1840 at Albrighton near Shrewsbury. On the one hand its neo-Norman style and its south entrance and porch distanced it from nonconformity, and on the other it remained untainted with the liturgical doctrines and sacerdotal implications of neo-Catholicism by omitting a structural chancel and setting the altar in a recess formed by two pews: that of the patron (and owner of Albrighton Hall) on the north and the smaller one of the LLoyds of Leaton Knolls on the south.[41]

Neo-Norman took several forms. Albrighton, and Carline's other church in the same vein, Grinshill (1839), have round-headed windows of classical proportions, clasping buttresses, corbel tables, and fearsomely carved human heads at the ends of the north and south walls.

Penson's Llanymynech, was a far more determined exercise in the style. The façades are covered in 12th-century motifs and even the front of the west gallery, carried on cast-iron columns with Norman capitals, has a blind arcade with intersecting round-headed arches.[42] By contrast the little church at Cwm Head, with imposts to the chancel arch and an internal string course of 12th-century profile around the chancel and apse, aimed at correctness.

The changes of the 1840s—the abandonment of classical styles, the frequent break with Georgian plan forms, the ending of the near monopoly of the lancet window in Gothic churches, and the sharp turn from urban to rural concerns—were accompanied by a great amount of building financed by incumbents. In that decade in Shropshire they built, or almost totally rebuilt, three churches,[43] drastically restored and partly rebuilt a fourth,[44] and probably played a major part in financing a fifth.[45] In addition the incumbent paid for a new north aisle at Cound[46] and rebuilt the chancel at West Felton. To the list may perhaps also be added the chapel of ease at Welsh Frankton paid for by C.A.A. Lloyd, rector of Whittington, and opened in 1835.[47] In the past clerics had sometimes contributed handsomely to the fabric of their churches, and they were to do so in the future,[48] but at that time they appear at least to have equalled the efforts of the traditional builders of rural churches, the landowners.[49]

Because of the steady rise in the status of the parish clergy during the previous hundred years[50]

The east and north façades of Llanymynech church

Looking west towards the gallery in Llanymynech church

than was necessary.[52] Thus the impulse to provide maximum preaching space at the lowest possible cost was less urgent and Penson's extravagantly ornamented church at Llanymynech, for example, increased the available seating space by only a third[53]—no more than was achieved at Ruyton-XI-Towns in 1845 by the addition of a north aisle.[54]

It was in the 1830s and 1840s, too, that the Oxford Movement, beginning in 1833,[55] was attempting to revive the militant and dogmatic spirit of the medieval church of its imagination.[56] The Movement itself had no particular views on church architecture,[57] whereas its paler blue fellow traveller the Cambridge Camden Society, founded in 1839 and renamed the Ecclesiological Society in 1846, while trying hard to avoid religious controversy[58] maintained very strong views on church architecture and its basis in historic liturgical practices.[59] The Ecclesiologists were horrified by the typical post-Reformation church, which they saw as ugly and liturgically inadequate, and they campaigned vigorously for something as different as possible from the preaching boxes they abominated: in fact for the forms and style of the early 14th century. Anglican clergymen with an interest in architecture and architects with an interest in the Church of England were among the Ecclesiological Society's members, and, since it was more than a mere aesthetic clique, it spoke for a wide range of feeling within the Church, and many who were not members came under its influence. Originally the Church at large did not wholly approve of it, but by the mid 1840s suspicions of any papist inclinations had been allayed and a considerable obstacle to the spread of its influence among Anglicans was thereby removed.[60] (Disapproval of Tractarian practices was more enduring, but in Shropshire churches built or restored on ecclesiological principles it is hard to distinguish specifically Anglo-Catholic architectural features—mostly discreet, clerically inspired sanctuary details.[61]) Moreover by the 1840s the need to erect many new churches quickly and cheaply was passing in Shropshire, and thus the Ecclesiologists began to see their aspirations carried into effect because an earlier generation had succeeded in building a great number of churches of the type they abhorred.

Not all incumbents who built churches were necessarily in sympathy with all the views of the

many early 19th-century incumbents were members, or even heads or future heads, of leading local families; they might have large resources at their command, were highly influential in their neighbourhoods, and imparted some of their standing to their less privileged colleagues.[51] By the 1840s, too, the intensive programme of building in the urban and industrialized areas was clearly well under way and the need, or desirability, of building in the countryside was attracting attention; and it was in the countryside that well connected incumbents were most likely to be found. Church builders there, however, might be motivated less by fear of Jacobinism or Methodism than by what they conceived to be their duty towards their neighbours, their tenants, and the parishioners at large. Further they and their architects, under the combined influence of piety and professional vanity, might well build more grandly

Movement or the Society. At Hengoed A.R. Lloyd, whose epitaph in the church he built (1849-50)[62] suggests that his concept of a clergyman's functions was different from theirs, provided no more than a recess for the chancel. On the other hand some of the churches with elements that the Ecclesiologists would have welcomed were built without any great financial aid from the incumbent. Nevertheless the synchronization in the 1840s of social changes within the Church, of the completion of the crash programme in the industrial and urban areas, and of the general intellectual climate were the positive factors that helped to produce the conditions in which the very varied architectural character of Shropshire churches was determined, more than ever before or after, by the parish clergy.

Local and national architects

There was also a negative element that played a part: the virtual absence of the London architect from the local scene. In earlier years most patrons had been part of a tightly knit group of aristocrats at national level or of gentry at county level, and had had an informal information service about the merits or faults of individual architects or builders. They had even had sanctions against them, of a kind, in the giving or withholding of recommendations. The success of the Smiths of Warwick, for example, had been due, in part at least, to their reputation for reliability.[63] The great increase in wealth and population in the 18th and early 19th centuries was matched by an increase in the amount of building, mostly by men of limited means. In the conditions of something like a mass market these new men, of varied origins and socially fragmented, were unable to rely on family connections to guide them through the jungle of the building trades. They needed instead a body of qualified agents, ready to put their client's lawful interest above everything except their loyalty to the ethos and standards of their profession. At the same time many practitioners of what was in danger of becoming an overcrowded calling, were anxious to break away from the socially demeaning and financially hazardous combination of architect-contractor which largely prevailed in the building industry. The Institute of British Architects was founded in 1835 as a combination of trade union and self-regulatory body, and the architect became

in effect the owner's agent, responsible not only for designing the building but also for seeing that the builder did what he had contracted to do and more or less at the price agreed. As a result a fashionable London architect could no longer pay a quick visit to the site and then send in plans and elevations for the owner to get carried out as best he could, as Wyatt did for Aston Hall in the 1790s.[64] Instead a careful supervision was now expected of the architect, with frequent inspections of the work on site. That demand gave an obvious advantage to local architects. Before 1850 all the known architects of churches in Shropshire, with the single exception of Scott at Donnington Wood in 1843 and Ellesmere in 1849, were local men: Salopians like Edward Haycock, John Carline, and George Clinton of Shrewsbury, Samuel and Thomas Smith of Madeley, Thomas Penson of Oswestry, and J. and R. Griffiths of Bridgnorth;[65] or men from neighbouring counties, such as Harvey Eginton of Worcester, George Hamilton of Stone and Wolverhampton, and James Trubshaw of Stone. Hitchcock's description of local architects as 'hack'[66] is an expression of professional snobbery masquerading as aesthetic judgement, but they were probably less abreast of the latest notions floating around the capital, and to that extent were less able, and probably less anxious, to impose their opinions on patrons in the name of taste or fashion.

By 1850, however, the advantages that local architects had long exploited were being whittled away by the development of the railway network, which allowed a London architect to 'personally supervise the erection of half-a-dozen buildings at once'.[67] That did not put local men out of business, but it forced them to share their business with others, and throughout the later 19th century the architectural responsibility for church building in Shropshire was about equally divided between local men and those from London or even farther away.[68] Nevertheless London men were likelier to be the advocates or followers of the latest architectural ideas and to have the self-assurance and prestige to press their advanced views on provincial clients; and at the same time local men were in ever closer touch with London ideas. For a generation after 1850 ecclesiastical architecture in the county was dominated by the doctrines of the Ecclesiologists as expressed by architects in the 'High Victorian' style, and it was more uniform and less local than it had been before.[69]

The inclusion of Salopian architects within a national profession and an all-pervading aesthetic climate, played an important part in the virtual elimination of the west tower, an element that had been conspicuous in Shropshire parish churches from at least the 12th century to the early 19th and in the latter part of that period was virtually a declaration in stone (or brick) of the Anglican faith. The reason for the Ecclesiologists' hostility to it is clear: a west tower was an invitation to have a west entrance instead of the liturgically proper entrance near the west end of the south wall of the nave. Its rejection by architects, however, cannot have been wholly due to Ecclesiological influence, for there was nothing to stop them from building a west tower without a west entrance and then citing good medieval precedent in their defence. Nor was it because they had been taught to eschew symmetry, for there was nothing symmetrical in the typical parochial elevation of a west tower dominating a nave which itself rose above a lower chancel; and architects were very ready, on the other hand, to design perfectly symmetrical west or east fronts. The west tower was rejected by architects because it was the unmistakeable mark of a parish church; it was something that greater Gothic churches never—well, hardly ever—descended to; and the burning ambition of most mid 19th-century architects, in Shropshire as elsewhere, was to erect a major Gothic church. Very few men achieved that aim at all, and none achieved it very often, but all could give a minor building the flavour of a great church, at least from a restricted angle, by siting a tower anywhere along the nave, except axially at the west.

If London architects had burst in numbers upon the Shropshire architectural scene in earlier years they would probably have left a very marked individual impress upon it, but the changes that brought them into the county also brought the county physi-

cally and intellectually nearer to London; and local men soon proved as well able to purvey the current fashions as anyone else. To say that is, of course, to make a value judgement, but one that is not wholly individual. In his comments on the work of London architects in Shropshire Pevsner is far from enthusiastic. Street alone gets much praise, and that mainly for St. George's; his other churches are described as 'not one of [his] masterpieces' or 'not of great interest'.[70] Of Arthur Blomfield's five churches in the county one is given a date and nothing else, two are pronounced 'of no interest', and comment on the other two is neutral at best.[71] Scott is more or less dismissed as 'smooth' and Benjamin Ferrey's work as 'large', 'lushly' carved, and 'wilful'.[72] It cannot be said that the two leading local architects, the younger Edward Haycock[73] and Samuel Pountney Smith, are treated better, but they are not treated worse; nor are such other local men as Thomas Nicholson of Hereford. Summarizing church building in the county from 1837 to (at least) 1870, Pevsner singles out four churches as worthy of mention, three of them by local men.[74] Furthermore it does not appear that London architects got the more important commissions for new churches, although the tendency of architectural historians to concentrate on the better known names might give that impression.

In the work of the younger Edward Haycock from the mid 1850s to the mid 1870s at the five churches of Weston Lullingfields (1857), Welsh

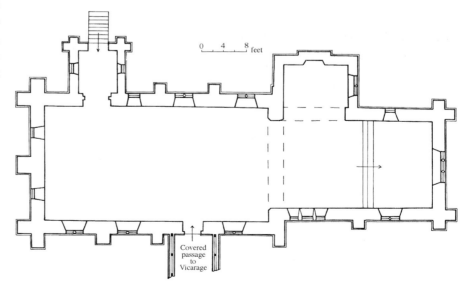

The plan of Weston Lullingfields church

Frankton (1857-63), Yockleton (1861), Meole Brace (1867-9), and All Saints' (1875-7), Castlefields, Shrewsbury, may be seen some of the elements that make up the High Victorian manner: complex planning, polychromatic effects, and an emphasis on the texture of the materials used. The simple nave-and-chancel plan of Weston Lullingfields, with its attached vicarage,[75] develops into the intricacies of Meole Brace with its square north-west tower (1870), north and south aisles to nave and chancel, south porch, north vestry, and polygonal apse to the chancel. At Welsh Frankton

Meole Brace church. Shrewsbury

there is a simple colour contrast between the red and white of the dressings. At Yockleton the dark Cardeston breccia of the walling is the background for the red and white of the dressings and the base for the banded colours of the roof. At Meole Brace white Shelvock stone is used not only for the dressings but also in horizontal bands within the fabric of red sandstone from the nearby quarry at Red Hill; and at Castlefields there is a similar use of Shelvock, Grinshill, Red Hill, and Bristol Blue Pennant stone. Stone textures as well as colours were exploited: the buff Cefn stone at Welsh Frankton, the coarse breccia at Yockleton, and the rock-faced Red Hill stone at Meole Brace and Castlefields.[76]

Other High Victorian predilections are there too. West towers are studiously avoided and instead a north-west tower appears at Meole Brace and south-west towers at Welsh Frankton and Yockleton. Clerestorys, so rare in Shropshire but so much in favour at the time, are introduced at Yockleton and Castlefields. Haycock never wholly lost a liking for lancets and for plate tracery, the latter shown most strikingly in the elaborate patterns of the west window at Yockleton; in his later churches, however, he used some geometric tracery. His interiors are unremarkable and it is unfortunate for him that the architectural qualities of the best, Meole Brace, tend to be aesthetically outshone by the glass

of Burne-Jones and Morris in the windows. At Yockleton he achieves some splendour, or at least richness, with round piers with Decorated caps to the arcade and with the orders of the chancel arch terminating on marble shafts with floriated capitals.

There is also a certain 'rogue' element in Haycock's work. The very prominent and obtrusive dormer windows of the spire at Yockleton, which Pevsner comments on,[77] may be no more than High Victorian assertiveness, but the fenestration is more than that: the heads of the nave windows can only be described as 'Moorish' and the tripartite clerestory windows with stubby lancets flanking round openings enclosing quatrefoils and trefoils are, at the least, unconventional. Similar idiosyncrasies occur at Castlefields. The west front is dominated by two very long lancets with a rose window above; the buttresses are crowned by two-bay blind arcades with quatrefoils; the main entrance from the street, though it leads into the nave by a sort of internal porch, is actually in the west end of the north aisle; and the clerestory windows alternate between cusped lancets and round openings with septfoil cusps. Finally, when he had the chance Haycock exploited the dramatic possibilities of a site. Welsh Frankton church was set upon a ridge overlooking the north Shropshire plain, and its position is emphasized by a steep flight of steps between walls with gabled parapets leading up to the entrance in the south-west tower, a romantic touch that was not lost upon contemporaries.[78] The younger Edward Haycock has never been claimed as an architect of outstanding talent, but taken as a whole his work in Shropshire is as good and interesting as the whole of anyone else's work there. At the same time there is nothing particularly Salopian about it.

Samuel Pountney Smith was more usually engaged in restoring older churches or adding to them than in building new ones,[79] and he was perhaps happiest at those tasks. He built the new church at Uffington in 1856 in an Early English style with a north aisle and a continuous nave and chancel. On the south wall he grouped lancets in pairs and linked them with an overall hood mould in the manner of the late 13th-century church at Longnor. To the west façade he gave a slightly projecting central buttress running almost to gable apex, enclosing a narrow lancet within it, and with a stone bellcot above; that was not, as one might think, a flight of Victorian fancy but a copy of the west front of the demolished church.[80] At Hope Bowdler (1863), in a somewhat earlier style and with Transitional capitals to the responds of tower and chancel arches, he built one of the very few west towers of the period, and a very heavy square-set one replacing, if not wholly reproducing, the west tower shown in a drawing of 1789.[81] Leaton (1859) was a wholly new church, but there too the slight central buttress of the west front set between two lancets was probably less a piece of High Victorianism than a memory of the old west front of Uffington.[82] He was more of an antiquarian than

Haycock and less ready to embrace the fashions of the time. Although the voussoirs of the tower arch at Hope Bowdler are of alternate red and white stones, Smith generally had little use for polychromatic effects, apart from a fondness for encaustic tiles, and he preferred to use local grey stones, often rock-faced. He had a fondness for Perpendicular too, not merely when he rebuilt Harley church in 1846 but as late as 1855, when the style was much out of date, at Shrewsbury cemetery chapel.

Another local architect, working mainly in the south of the county, was Thomas Nicholson of Hereford. He rebuilt Bishop's Castle Church in the early 1860s in very modish French Gothic with aisles, transepts, an apsidal-ended chancel, clerestorys, an Easter sepulchre, intersecting and reticulated tracery, and—for he was not a Herefordshire man for nothing—ballflower ornament on the chancel and the north porch. Much later, in 1878, he produced a very different, very simple, building at Cleeton St. Mary in an Early English style and with a west tower carrying a spire and wholly contained within the nave.[83] The main doorway is at the extreme west end of the south wall, and entrance therefore is unexpectedly and bewilderingly into something like a narthex, separated from the nave by a tall central arch and lower flanking arches. Pevsner wrote the building off as 'of no architectural interest' while Cranage, who is not usually friendly towards 19th-century churches, called it a 'very good modern church' and the west end 'rather effective and original'.[84] If surprise is an aesthetic quality, then Cleeton St. Mary is an outstanding church.

To claim that Haycock, Smith, and Nicholson were better architects than Scott, Street, Ferrey, or Blomfield might well be paradoxical, but within Shropshire their work, taken as a whole, equals that of the London men taken as a whole. Street's St. George's has been much admired for the last 50 years;[85] his quiet church at Colemere well suits its pleasant site;[86] and Blomfield's essay in stri-

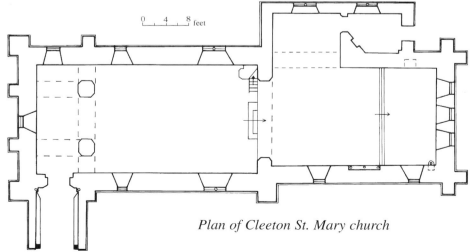

Plan of Cleeton St. Mary church

*View from the porch into the narthex at
Cleeton St. Mary church*

dent polychromy at St. Mary's, Jackfield, and Scott's zigzag patterns in green and pale blue tiles upon the roof at Welshampton were unequalled by any local man, at least upon a church. Apart from those, however, the men of note from London gave little of note to the county between 1850 and 1880, and most of what they did there appears to be run-of-the-mill, turned out in the intervals of preparing for more important tasks elsewhere. For local men, however, Shropshire was the major, or a major, field of operations and they could not afford, for their own satisfaction if not for their clients', to turn out purely routine jobs. Consequently their work, however its aesthetic value is judged, is more interesting and varied than the Londoners'.

The impact of the restorers

Between William IV's accession and Queen Victoria's death the overall character of ecclesiastical architecture in Shropshire, the product of nearly a thousand years, was rapidly and drastically transformed. In 1830 many churches were in a clas-

sical style and many in no particular style at all; many had features of a very domestic kind. The transformation had two aspects, which its initiators probably saw as one: ridding churches of their classical elements and of their secular appearance. By 1900 all were clearly consecrated buildings and all but a few were very Gothic. The building of nearly a hundred new churches in that style played a very large part in the change, but an equal effect was produced by the rebuilding, partial rebuilding, extension, and alteration of existing ones.

Over a dozen Georgian or wholly Georgianized churches were demolished and replaced by, among others, Haycock's Meole Brace, Scott's Welshampton, Street's St. George's, and Ferrey's Chetwynd.[87] Along with the total demolition of some went piecemeal rebuilding of others. At Withington and Cheswardine, for example, Street and Pearson respectively pulled down Georgian naves while retaining or restoring Gothic chancels and chapels.[88] At Beckbury Gothic aisles were added to a Georgian nave, recognizable now only by the quoins at its angles, and at Quatford in 1857 oddly tripartite Georgian windows were swept away in the building of a new south aisle.[89] At Lee Brockhurst and Buildwas Gothic chancels were added to a Georgianized church and a Georgian nave respectively.[90] Transepts and an east end in Gothic style were added at Berwick chapel to a late 17th-century building.[91] At Donington a more correct Gothic look was given to the early 17th-century nave in a Decorated style by replacing the westernmost window of the south wall by a Gothic doorway.[92] Many churches had their whole external appearance changed by a complete refenestration. At Coreley, for example, the windows of the mid 18th-century nave and chancel were altered to lancets, set within the original surrounds; at Great Hanwood in 1856 the nave was lengthened westwards and some of the original transomed windows of the building of 1701 were blocked and others replaced by openings of 13th-century character; at Cardeston (1749) and Sibdon Carwood (1741) elaborate Perpendicular windows replaced the originals.[93]

At Sibdon Carwood Gothic buttresses were added, and at Chirbury a whole range of buttresses was added to the south aisle and the Georgian openings and porch there were replaced by five two-light windows with quatrefoils in the heads.[94] Very little of the rightly admired tracery at Worfield was there in 1789, and none at all in the south elevation.[95] The unique timber-framed clerestory at Kinlet, with Perpendicular tracery in the openings, appeared in 1790 as a range of tall round-headed windows in a rendered wall.[96] The present south porch at Diddlebury replaces a classical structure with keystone to the semicircular arch and with rusticated quoins at the angles.[97] The 18th-century fashion for inserting Palladian windows into the east ends of churches was countered in the 19th by a reverse fondness for replacing Palladian windows with Gothic ones. Thus at Pitchford the east window of 1719 was replaced exactly a hundred years later by a triple lancet;[98] Palladian east and west windows at Prees were replaced, the former in 1864 and the latter probably shortly before that.[99] Among the most striking changes were those at Market Drayton, Hodnet, and Newport.[100] Market Drayton church, now a very impressive Gothic structure, looked in 1790 more like a huge Dissenting chapel, or at least like the shortly-to-be-built churches at Madeley and Malinslee, with plain untraceried windows and with the walls of the aisles raised to a height to accommodate two tiers of openings. At Hodnet the very long eight-bay south elevation of the nave, now in a 13th-century style, was wholly Georgian in 1790, apart from unmistakeably medieval buttresses, and there was a large Georgian window in the west wall. At Newport in 1791 the west tower and the clerestory, rising shyly above the very tall aisles, were the only Gothic elements in an imposing Georgian composition.

Not only classical but secular and domestic features were eliminated on a large scale. Congregations had grown bigger in the three centuries following the Reformation, and a relatively cheap way of accommodating more people was to erect one or more galleries. They needed to be lit, and the easiest solution was to introduce timber-framed dormer windows of a domestic and even homely type. By the end of the 18th century many parish churches had acquired one or more, generally at the west end of the nave: Atcham, Cardington, West Felton, and Upton Magna, may be instanced.[101] At Neen Savage there were dormers at both ends of the nave, and Hopton Wafers had a range of four, running the whole length of the

church.[102] Most examples were on a cottage scale, of one or two lights, but at Harley—where they lit nave and aisle, not a gallery—the two centrally placed opposing dormers of four mullioned and transomed lights each[103] would not have disgraced a mansion. A similar great window at Upton Magna had fashionable Elizabethan quatrefoil panels in the gable.[104] At Lilleshall there were two windows of five lights each and at Morville one of nine lights.[105] None of these has survived, but the trend was not all one way, for dormers were added in the late 19th century to two churches which previously lacked them, Llanyblodwel and St. Martin's; they were, however, of stone rather than timber.[106]

The elimination of such windows was possible because galleries were being removed from many churches. Galleries were obnoxious to Ecclesiologists not only in their own right, as unseemly usurpers of the function of aisles, but also because many, especially west galleries, accommodated a group of untrained or self-trained, singers and musicians. Ecclesiologists were as anxious to reform church music as church architecture and to introduce into the parish church the organ and surpliced choir of a cathedral or of the chapel of the Oxford or Cambridge college where they had been trained.[107] It was perhaps also more than a difference about music which inspired hostility in some clerics towards local singers and musicians. One of the founders of the Cambridge Camden Society, J.M. Neale, was very forthright—to put it charitably—about the dubious characters in west galleries with their *esprit de corps* which gave them reprehensible 'feelings of independence' and made them 'some of the worst members of the parish', 'notorious' for their 'radicalism'.[108] Neale's views must reflect feelings more general than personal, as his own experience did not extend to holding a parish living.[109] Whatever the cause, there was no longer any place for homely performers in galleries.

Galleries not only needed light for themselves, but in a Gothic church they tended to rob the space beneath them of light, and new windows had sometimes been inserted on that account. Furthermore by the early modern period many earlier windows were in need of replacement or repair, and for both of those reasons new windows were inserted in north and south walls. They were of a type that Cranage, revealing a common 19th-century attitude towards them, usually calls 'debased': plain rectangles, sometimes with equally plain rectangular-sectioned mullions and always without tracery. Again examples are numerous and one may cite at random those at Mainstone, Milson, Monkhopton, and Moreton Corbet.[110] A very rare survivor is in the south wall of the nave at Cleobury North. At Stanton upon Hine Heath restorers have impartially swept away 18th-century classical windows and an earlier rectangular one of two lights.[111] In the south transept at Stanton Lacy, where a first floor was inserted probably in the 17th century, the upper chamber so formed was lit by a long low multi-light window[112] like that of a Pennine weaver's top-shop. At Woolstaston a short south transept has replaced an opening that was a cross between a dormer and a Scottish storm window.[113]

Some churches at the beginning of the 19th century had an almost wholly secular appearance. A modern visitor transported to Bettws-y-crwyn in 1791 would wonder whether he was looking at a barn with windows inserted or a farmhouse that had lost its chimney stack.[114] At Morville, where the nave now has a clerestory with a range of three-light windows, the nine-light dormer already mentioned was set in a catslide roof as vast as that of Wenlock Abbey, and the nave itself, if isolated from west tower and chancel, could have been mistaken for a great medieval barn.[115] At Kenley the south porch and west tower, plain as they were, proclaimed the building a church, but nothing else in the south elevation did.[116] The timber-framed chapels of Tilstock, in Whitchurch parish, and Newtown, in

Wem parish, rebuilt in 1835 and 1836, were on an **L** plan and, apart from a timber bellcot that each had at the end of a wing, they had little to distinguish them from a typical 17th-century farmhouse in the area.[117] Welshampton church's south aisle was irreverently called 'the Cowshed'.[118]

There were probably few places like Clunbury in the early 19th century, where the parson put up his horse in a low structure attached to the church,[119] but much of the activity mentioned above may be regarded, like the sweeping away of the Clunbury stable, as no more than seemly tidying up. There was also, however, some smartening up of Gothic structures to make them look more authentically or richly Gothic, or, as in Aston Webb's work at Burford in the last decade of the century, more in line with Arts and Crafts predilections. For the plain merlons of the tower crenellation he substituted others in the form of traceried arcades, and he doubled the size of the windows of the top stage of the tower and filled them with tracery. He replaced the overhanging eaves of nave and chancel with a crenellated parapet and covered the merlons of the chancel parapet with blank traceried arcading. He added buttresses to the nave and gave the top stages niches with traceried heads, and replaced former tracery in the windows with some of elaborate patterning. Internally he gave the chancel a roof ornamented with angels and a great deal of heraldry.[120] At Battlefield Pountney Smith replaced an overhanging eaves with a decorated open-work parapet, added decorated crockets to the chancel buttresses, and introduced a hammer-beam roof;[121] nevertheless, although working a full generation before Webb, he behaved in a far more restrained and historically responsible manner. At Clungunford, where a north-west tower was added in 1895, trefoiled lights with quatrefoil heads were replaced by cinquefoil heads and sexfoil lights, and the original reticulated 'Wells' type tracery of the east window by a complicated design of a cusped saltire within a cusped circle above quatrefoils and trefoils.[122] At Clun in 1791 the stone-built north porch had a broad round-headed window

Bettws-y-Crywn from the south. Compare this picture to that on p.83

above the north doorway and a chimney rising above the west wall; today the chimney has gone, the window is of two narrow lancets, and the gable above it is timber-framed.[123] More usual was the kind of 'improvement' made at Neen Savage, where a two-light rectangular window was supplanted by a two-light Perpendicular one;[124] or at Hadnall where one two-light early Decorated window was introduced into blank walling and another displaced a Perpendicular one.[125]

It was not only Gothic features that were restored or gratuitously inserted. In his restoration work in the Norman nave of Shrewsbury Abbey in 1860–1 Pountney Smith inserted colonnettes into the triforium openings.[126] At Bedstone, a small church of 12th-century origin, a south doorway and porch, probably of later date, were destroyed in order to insert a large Norman window of ingenious design, with seven lights externally, three of them blocked, and four internally; at the same time a 14th-century

The four windows in the south wall of the nave at Bedstone church

window was removed from the chancel to make way for a round-headed lancet, and a 12th-century-style doorway, perhaps a copy of the original south doorway, was put into the west wall.[127] A similar change occurred at the now ruinous Burwarton church between 1791 and 1844, where a south porch was removed, a south doorway blocked up, and a new doorway made for, or the old south one inserted in, the west wall beneath a new Norman window of two round-headed lights under an overall arch. The west end of the nave was rebuilt;[128] it was reported to be in a very bad state in 1793 but aroused no comment in 1829, and the work is probably between those dates.[129] At Aston Eyre a two-light rectangular window in the south wall of the chancel has given way to two lancets, and the 14th-century east window to one with three round-headed lancets which have a continuous hood mould externally and, internally, nook-shafts and elaborately decorated heads:[130] apparently an attempt to make the chancel worthy of the famous 12th-century tympanum of the south doorway.

The elimination of Perpendicular elements in order to insert Early English or Decorated work, so common in the country at large, was rare in Shropshire, probably because there was not much to eliminate,[131] and the best example is Street's restoration of the early 14th-century chancel at Edgmond. There he got rid of a low-pitched roof and a crenellated parapet and returned the building to what was probably its original form with a high-pitched roof and overhanging eaves.[132] Commoner than such large-scale alteration, but still rare, was the replacement of an inserted Perpendicular

Bedstone church from the south-west

East wall of the chancel at Aston Eyre showing the reredos and altar

window by one that may reasonably be supposed to resemble the original, as, for instance, the lancet now at the west end of the south wall of Rushbury chancel, which replaces a two-light traceried window beneath a flat head.[133]

Foreshadowing the 20th century

By about 1880 the surge of church building had receded. Only ten new ones were built in the last two decades of the century, and only two of those were by London men. Many of the churches of the time were large and expensive-looking, as, for example, that at Kemberton (1881) by Joseph Farmer of Newport and the very grand red-brick proprietary and memorial church at Lea Cross (1888) by J.L. Randal of Shrewsbury.[134] Even St. Anne's (1882–3), Weston Cotton, intended mainly for the inmates of the huge Oswestry workhouse, Morda House, was built with some show of splendour (at the Hon. Mrs. Stapleton-Cotton's expense), with north and south transepts, apsidal chancel, and west narthex.[135]

None of those could be mistaken for anything but a Victorian church, but men who saw Norman Shaw's All Saints', Batchcott, Richard's Castle, a hundred years ago might then have wondered whether they were looking at a church at all. The fabric of light-brown rock-faced stones, small in size, with Grinshill stone for the dressings,[136] is set off by the vast red expanse of the nave's catslide roof and the smaller roofs of the south-west tower and chancel. Seen from beyond the green pasture below it and against a blue sky it is a pastel composition in broad Impressionistic patches of colour wholly different from the vivid detailing in horizontal bands and around openings of mid-century polychromy. Like Welsh Frankton it is set upon a ridge and the main entrance is approached up a slope; here, however, there is no sense of drama or awe but instead the expectation of a pleasant welcome at the very wide entrance arch in the tower, above which is a small asymmetrically sited four-light window in a domestic style. The lower floor of the tower is occupied by a broad flight of shallow steps leading not into the church itself but into a linking passage that might be the entrance vestibule of a country house. Inside an air of sweetness and light is produced by the high roof and large clear windows, their black cames forming tendril and leaf patterns that follow the lines of the window heads' tracery and partly complement it.[137] The nave could be the assembly hall of a progressive school or the lecture hall of a learned society. Batchcott, built in 1891–2, is Shropshire's first 20th-century church, prophetic of those changes in the stance of the Church of England which are so apparent today.

References
&
Index

References

Abbreviations used

A.-S., *A.-S.*	Anglo-Saxon, *Anglo-Saxon*
Alum. Oxon.	J. Foster, *Alumni Oxonienses* (1887–92)
Ang.-Norm. Text Soc.	Anglo-Norman Text Society
Antiq. Jnl.	*Antiquaries Journal*
Arch. Camb.	*Archaeologia Cambrensis*
Arch. Cant.	*Archaeologia Cantiana*
Arch. Jnl.	*Archaeological Journal*
B.L.	British Library, London
Bodl.	Bodleian Library, Oxford
Brit. Arch. Assn.	British Archaeological Association
C.S.	Cantilupe Society
Cal. Chart. R.	*Calendar of the Charter Rolls* (H.M.S.O. 1903–27)
Cal. Close	*Calendar of the Close Rolls* (H.M.S.O. 18921963)
Cal. Inq. p.m.	*Calendar of Inquisitions post mortem* (H.M.S.O. 1904–in progress)
Cal. Pat.	*Calendar of Patent Rolls* (H.M.S.O. 1891-in progress)
Camd.	Camden Series, Royal Historical Society
Camd. Soc.	Camden Society
Close R.	*Close Rolls of the Reign of Henry III* (H.M.S.O. 1902–75)
Cranage	D.H.S. Cranage, *An Architectural Account of the Churches of Shropshire* (Wellington; 2 vols. 1901 and 1912, published in 10 parts 1894–1912). Cited by part number
D.N.B.	*Dictionary of Nationa Biography* (1885–in progress)
Econ. Hist. Rev.	*Economic History Review*
Eyton	R.W. Eyton, *Antiquities of Shropshire* (12 vols. 1854–60)
Harl. Soc.	Harleian Society
L. & P. Hen. VIII	*Letters & Papers, Foreign and Domestic, of the Reign of Henry VIII* (H.M.S.O. 1864–1932)
Leighton, 'Sketches', ivii	S.R.R. 6805/17
Leland, *Itin.* ed. Toulmin Smith	*Itinerary of John Leland*, ed. L. Toulmin Smith (190–68)
Med. Arch.	*Medieval Archaeology*
Mont. Coll.	*Montgomeryshire Collections: Journal of the Powysland Club*
Mytton Papers	Birmingham University Library, Special Collections, MSS./ii/1–7
N.L.W.	National Library of Wales, Aberystwyth
N.M.R.	National Monuments Record Centre (English Heritage), Swindon
O.S.	Ordnance Survey
Orders of Q. Sess.	*Abstract of the Orders made by the Court of Quarter Sessions*, ed. R. Ll. Kenyon and Sir Offley Wakeman (Shropshire County Records nos. 2-5, 7, 9, 1117 [Shrewsbury, 1901–16])
P.R.O.	Public Record Office (in 2003 joined with the Historical MSS. Commission to form the National Archives), Kew
Pat. R.	*Patent Rolls* 1216–32 (H.M.S.O. 1901–3)
Pevsner, Salop.	N. Pevsner, Shropshire (The Buildings of England, 1958)
R.C.H.M.E.	Royal Commission on the Historical Monuments of England (merged with English Heritage from 1999)
R.I.B.A.	Royal Institute of British Architects
R.O.	Record Office
Rec. Com.	Record Commission
Rot. Litt. Claus.	*Rotuli Litterarum Clausarum in Turri Londinensi asservati*, ed. T.D. Hardy (Rec. Com. 1833–44)
S.A.	prefix to primary record no. in Shropshire Sites and Monuments Record, Shropshire County Council Community and Environment Services Department
S.A.B.C.	Shrewsbury and Atcham Borough Council
S.C.C.	Shropshire (formerly Salop) County Council
S.H.C.	*Collections for a History of Staffordshire* (Staffordshire Record Society, formerly the William Salt Archaeological Society)
S.P.R.	*Shropshire Parish Registers* (Shropshire Parish Register Society, merged in the Shropshire Archaeological and Historical Society). Cited by diocese series and volume and part numbers.
S.R.R.	Shropshire Records and Research Centre (Shropshire Archives from 2003), Shrewsbury
S.R.S.	*Shropshire Record Series* (Centre for Local History, University of Keele)
Salop. N. & Q.	*Shropshire Notes & Queries* (1884–1942)
Soc. of Antiq.	Society of Antiquaries of London
Suss. Rec. Soc.	Sussex Record Society
T.S.A.S.	*Transactions of the Shropshire Archaeological and Historical Society*
Tax. Eccl.	*Taxatio Ecclesiastica Angliae et Walliae auctoritate P. Nicholai IV,* circa *A.D. 1291*, ed.T. Astle, S. Ayscough and J. Caley (Rec. Com. 1802)
Trinder, *Ind. Rev. Salop.*	B. Trinder, *The Industrial Revolution in Shropshire* (1981)
V.A.	*Vernacular Architecture*
V.A.G.	Vernacular Architecture Group
V.C.H.	*Victoria History of the Counties of England*
Valor Eccl.	Valor Ecclesiasticus, temp.Henrici VIII, auctoritate regia institutus, ed. J. Caley and J. Hunter (Rec.Com. 1810–34)
W.S.L.	William Salt Library, Stafford
Woolhope Trans.	*Transactions of theWoolhope Naturalists' Field Club*

Chapter I

1. *V.C.H. Salop.* i, figs. 12a and 12b facing p.228.
2. For Quatt see *T.S.A.S.* lxvi. 1519. The Ang.-Saxon date proposed for the S. aisle wall at H. Trin., M. Wenlock (*Jnl. Brit. Arch. Assoc.* 3rd ser. xxviii. 16-38), is untenable: D.C. Cox and M.D. Watson, 'H. Trin. Ch., M. Wenlock: a re-assessment', *ibid.* cxl. 76-87.
3. Cranage, iii. 176. G.E. Street created the chamfers during a restoration of *c.*1851: *V.C.H. Salop.* x. 232.
4. *V.C.H. Salop.* i. 315-16, 318, 321, 347. Diddlebury appears as the ch. of Corfham man.
5. *Eccl. Hist. of Ordericus Vitalis*, ed. M. Chibnall, iii (1972), 6-7.
6. H.M. and J. Taylor, *A.-S. Archit.* i (1965), 31-2; ii (1965), 694-5.
7. *Eng. Medieval Industries*, ed. J. Blair and N. Ramsey (1991), 13-14.
8. Cranage (vii. 556) would not concede that Atcham was Ang.-Saxon at all, and the nave as a whole is probably not, for it is much larger than any other supposed Saxon nave in Salop.
9. E. Fernie, *Archit. of Ang.-Saxons* (1983), 149, 163, suggests that Diddlebury is 11th-cent. and Stanton Lacy *c.*1100.
10. The chancel E. wall was depicted in 1789 (S.R.R. 6001/372/1, p.113) with a late medieval or early modern timber-framed gable. It was twice rebuilt in the 19th cent.: *V.C.H. Salop.* x. 232.
11. *Jnl. Brit. Arch. Assoc.* cxl. 76-87. A.W. Clapham (*Archaeologia*, lxxii. 108), Rose Graham (*Jnl. Brit. Arch. Assoc.* 3rd ser. iv. 119 sqq.), Fletcher and Jackson (*ibid.* 3rd ser. xxviii. 18), and the Taylors (*A.-S. Archit.* i. 45-34) argued a Saxon date. Baldwin Brown (*Arts in Early Eng.* (1925), ii. 472) was noncommital, and E. Fernie (*Archit. of Ang.-Saxons,* 64, 72) ruled out, partly by implication, Saxon work. Cranage was the only advocate of a Norman date; he has now been vindicated, in a way.
12. *T.S.A.S.* 2nd ser. vi. 358-71.
13. E.A. Fisher, *Greater A.-S. Churches* (1962), 237-8.
14. Cranage, iv. 36-56; Pevsner, *Salop.* 297-8; Taylor, *A.-S. Archit.* ii. 580.
15. Cranage (iv. 365) suggested a deer and a net.
16. The stone is now cracked across the middle.
17. But (to do it justice) it is not much below the level of the carving on the tympanum at Beckford (Worcs.).
18. Fisher, *Greater A.-S. Chs.* 289-90.
19. Taylor, *A.-S. Archit.* i. 231-3.
20. *Ibid.* 122-6.
21. For claims on behalf of part of Quatt's chancel see above.
22. *Jnl. Brit. Arch. Assoc.* 3rd ser. xxix. 53-60.
23. Taylor, *A.-S. Archit.* i. 50.
24. *Jnl. Brit. Arch. Assoc.* 3rd ser. xxix. 57.
25. *Ibid.* 60; Cranage, iii. 177; Taylor, *A.-S. Archit.* i. 50; *V.C.H. Salop.* x. 232.
26. Taylor, *A.-S. Archit.* ii. 570.

27. P. Klein (*St. Peters Ch., Stanton Lacy* (Leominster, 1983), 4) based a similar suggestion on a difference between the pilaster strips of the nave and those of the transept. One of Sir Steph. Glynne's rare structural observations was that the N. wall had been rebuilt: *S.R.S.* i. 100.

28. Taylor, *A.-S. Archit.* i. 211 sqq., discusses it at some length.

29. M.T. Clanchy, *Eng. and its Rulers 1066-1272* (1983), 41, quoting the *Gesta Regum* (Rolls Ser.), 306.

30. Pevsner, *Salop.* 289.

31. Recording 59 chs. in Salop. and its Welsh territories (including Holdgate and St. Mic.'s in Shrews. Castle, both founded since 1066); Leintwardine and Llanarmon-yn-Iâl ('Yale'), not recorded in Salop. after 1086, are here ignored. The pars. of 3 chs. in Staffs. in 1086 (Alveley, Sheriffhales, and Worfield) were soon afterwards transferred (partly so in the case of Sheriffhales, whose ch. remained in Staffs. until 1895) to Salop., where they remain.

32. Unmentioned in Dom. Bk., Alberbury, Atcham, and Barrow chs. were almost certainly pre-Conquest. Idsall (*i.e.* Shifnal) and Pontesbury chs., also unmentioned but later known to have been portionary, were probably pre-Conquest too—but cf. below, n.38; p.19.

33. Fernie, *A.-S. Archit.* 163, 178.

34. *V.C.H. Salop.* x. 8.

35. The likenesses between Stanton Lacy and St. Mary-in-Castro, Dover, in form, scale, and amount of survival were mentioned above, p.3. Their histories are similar too. St. Mary's, which had been a superior ch. in the late-Saxon hill-top burh, was superseded after 1070 by the new St. Martin's-le-Grand in the town, where most of the canons probably moved to: *Minsters and Par. Chs.: The Local Ch. in Transition 950-1200*, ed. J. Blair (1988), 106-10. St. Mary's has outlasted St. Martin's.

36. It is notorious that over the country at large Dom. Bk. is inconsistent in its recording of churches (*Dom. Bk.: A Reassessment*, ed. P. Sawyer (1986), 106 sqq.), but there are reasons for believing that in Salop it is fairly reliable, apart from the odd mistake or omission inevitable in all compilations: *T.S.A.S.* forthcoming.

37. Holdgate and Prees, later recorded with more than one portioner (*V.C.H. Salop.* x. 143 sqq.; Eyton, ix. 225-6, 256), might thus claim 'superiority'.

38. Holdgate and Quatford (*V.C.H. Salop.* ii. 123-4; x. 143) show that portionary chs. may be post-Conquest foundations.

39. Lydham is counted here as a superior ch. Lydham was Rog. of Montgomery's only manor in Rinlau hund. He made a habit of keeping all the manors with hund. *capita* he could, and it is likely that Lydham, rather than the bp. of Hereford's manor of Lydbury North (apart from Lydham the only other manor in Rinlau hund. to have a ch.), was the hund. *caput*.

40. There were 15 Salop. hunds. in 1086, but Shrews. hund., not having a *caput* like the others, is here ignored. Corfham, *caput* of Culvestan, had become *caput* of Patton hund. also, superseding Patton.

41. And yet there almost certainly was a minster ch. at Alberbury in 1086: *V.C.H. Salop.* viii. 213.

42. Below, cap. II.

43. Four at Wroxeter, 2 at Baschurch, 2 at Ellesmere.

44. Twelve at Bromfield, 2 at Burford, 8 at Morville, 2 at Stanton Lacy. The church of Wenlock might deserve treatment as a former minster, but no clergy nos. are available; in any case they would leave the present argument unaffected and, even (by swelling the southern figures) reinforced. In Shrews. there were 28, but how they fit into the pastoral organization is not clear to me.

45. *T.S.A.S.* forthcoming.

46. Siward, one of the two richest thegns in pre-Conquest Salop., was a grandson of King Edw.'s half-sis. Edith: A. Williams, *The English and the Norman Conquest* (1995), pp.[xiv], 89, 91-6.

47. 1 hide at Boreton (in Condover) and 1 hide at the Lowe (in Stottesdon): *ibid.* 94; *V.C.H. Salop.* i. 312, 34-5; viii. 40.

48. Williams, *op. cit.* 94; *Cart. Shrews. Abbey*, ed. U. Rees (1975), i, p.33.

49. *Eccl. Hist. of Orderic Vitalis*, ed. Chibnall, iii. 142-3.

50. Z.N. Brooke, *The Eng. Church and the Papacy from the Conquest to the Reign of John* (1952), 1345; C. Morris, *The Papal Monarchy: The Western Church from 1050 to 1250* (1991), 145-6.

51. Baschurch, Hodnet, and Wrockwardine. Shrews. and Leintwardine hunds. are omitted from what follows. The nos. of manors in each hund. are most conveniently set out in *Dom. Bk.: Salop.* ed. F. and C. Thorn (1986), maps and map keys.

52. Alnodestreu, Condetret, Condover, Culvestan, Overs, and Patton.

53. Mersete, Rinlau, Ruesset, and Whittery.

Chapter II

1. R.K. Morris, 'The Ch. in the Countryside: two lines of Inquiry', *Medieval Villages: a review of current work*, ed. D. Hooke (1985), 51-3.

2. For St. Peter's, in what was to become the Abbey Foregate, Shrews., see above, cap. I.

3. H.M. Taylor, 'St. Giles' Ch., Barrow', *Arch. Jnl.* cxxvii. 211-12.

4. *T.S.A.S.* lxiv. 17-24.

5. The return of the earlier W. wall is visible on the internal face of the N. wall and marked out on the ground. Cranage, vii. 656, attributes the W. extension to the 13th cent. and is followed by C.A. Ralegh Radford in *Arch. Jnl.* cxiii. 209-10.

6. At Diddlebury, Rushbury, and Tugford the E. extensions of the late 12th and early 13th cents. encompass not only the chancels but also the E. ends of the present naves. Cranage (ii. 150) thought Rushbury's nave might have encroached on the chancel when the present roofs were erected in the 16th cent., and it is argued below that that happened (not necessarily in the 16th cent.) at several chs. But at Diddlebury the nave's early extension E. is clear from the difference in build between the E. end of the nave and the chancel.

7. Improvement began *c*.1000 but was probably not having much effect before the later 11th cent.: H.H. Lamb, *Eng. Climate* (1964), 162; *idem, Changing Climate* (1966), 174; F. Barlow, *Edw. the Confessor* (1970), 139.

8. *De Gestis Regum* (Rolls Ser.), ii. 306 (cited by M.T. Clanchy, *Eng. and its Rulers 1066-1272* (1983), 41, 44); cf. A. Gransden, *Historical Writing in Eng. c.550 to c.1307* (1974), 173-5, 205.

9. What is at issue is not great men acquiring vast estates (cf. D. Hooke, 'Aspects of A.-S. Staffs.' *Staffs. Studies*, ed. P. Morgan (Keele, 1987), 35-6), but minor Norman lords holding larger and more consolidated estates than lesser English thegns.

10. Eyton, vi. 268-9, 285; *V.C.H. Salop.* viii. 115, 117, 119, 122-3.

11. In this section bldgs. are referred to as 'parish churches' or 'chapels' when their (12th-cent.) ecclesiatical status is at issue, otherwise normally just as 'churches'.

12. Cranage, i. 30.

13. *T.S.A.S.* lxxii. 106.

14. *Ibid.* viii. 450-3.

15. Excavation has revealed three such cases in Yorks.: *Wharram Percy: The Church of St. Martin*, ed. J.G. Hurst and P. Rahtz (1987), 76.

16. A.W. Clapham, *Eng. Romanesque Archit.* ii (1934), 102, 104.

17. Nearly 70 Salop. churches have evidence of 12th-cent. fabric and *c*.100 have 12th-cent. elements, *e.g.* fonts, re-used doorways. There is necessarily a subjective element in these figures. Other enumerators might obtain slightly different results, but the argument of this para. would not be affected thereby.

18. *Minsters and Par. Chs.: The Local Church in Transition 950-1200*, ed. J. Blair (1988), 141; *R.C.H.M.E. Chs. of S.E. Wilts.* 13; *R.C.H.M.E. Northants.* vi, p. lxxvi; *Trans. Lichfield & S. Staffs. Arch. & Hist. Soc.* iv. 12.

19. Pevsner, *Salop.* 147.

20. Its probable length before it was extended W.

21. Ruyton, however, stands out from the other chapels as a castle chapel of the Stranges: see below.

22. Lee Brockhurst has a structurally separate chancel, but in 1791 it had not and the bldg. was more or less the length of the present nave: S.R.R. 6001/372/1, p. 87.

23. Moreton Say's form and proportions made it easy for late 18th-cent. improvers to give it a modern appearance by cladding it in brick.

24. For the tendency and the disappointments see *V.C.H. Salop.* ii. 19. Liturgical changes must also have played a part: C.F. Davidson, 'Written in Stone: Archit., Liturgy and the Laity in Eng. Par. Chs. *c*.1125-*c*.1250' (Lond. Univ. Ph.D. thesis, 1998).

25. Personal communication from Prof. Peter Kidson. For the golden section see P. Kidson, 'A Metrological Investigation', *Jnl. Warburg and Courtauld Institutes*, liii. 71-97, esp. 76-7, 86-8, 94-7.

26. T. Rowley, *Salop. Landscape* (1972), 162 sqq.

27. The words are from R. Gem's lucid summary of the essentials of Romanesque archit.: *Camb. Guide to Arts in Brit.* ed. B. Ford, i (1988), 227.

28. Edstaston is now 49ft. long, but before part of the W. end fell in 1723 it was *c*.60 ft.: Mytton Papers, ii. 441. The bldg. may be older than its late 12th-cent. decoration for there are signs that the E. end has been rebuilt or extended.

29. At Middleton (in Bitterley) too little of the original settlement remains to suggest an explanation. At Clive the ground falls sharply to the S. but there is nevertheless a S. doorway, although it is less splendid than that on the N.

30. Cranage, x. 1050, listing W. doorways but surprisingly omitting Wistanstow, where earlier (iii. 171) he had argued for one.

31. Clapham, *Eng. Romanesque Archit.* ii. 108; N. Pevsner, *Worcs.* (Bldgs. of Eng. 1968), 15, 45.

32. Morville had an early 12th-cent. chancel, but the doorway is in the late 12th-cent. extension.

33. R.C.H.M.E. *Northants.* v. 242-3; vi, pl.lxxx. Heath chapel, Morville, Ruyton-XI-Towns, and Upton Magna are examples.

34. Cranage, x. 1045.

35. Almost by definition, but not quite, if timber is taken into account.

36. The window's richly decorated internal surround, with two orders of zigzags enclosing a third order of linked chains, may not be *in situ*. The form is more that of a doorway, the ornament stopping abruptly against the sill, as though cut to fit the opening. In 1789 the window looked externally like a 17th-cent. 2-light rectangular one (S.R.R. 6001/372/1, p.106), but inside it was what we see today: cf. S.R.R. 6001/6865, p.146; B.L. Add. MS. 21237, f. 291, cited in *V.C.H. Salop.* x. 363-4.

37. As the ld. of Hordley discovered in 1232 when he attempted to free his fairly new chap. from dependency on Baschurch: Eyton, x. 123-4.

38. Cranage, v. 436, argues for transepts at Clun, but that is difficult to prove or disprove for a contemporary report of the restoration of 1877 stated that it had been found 'necessary to rebuild the whole of the columns and arches': *Salopian Shreds & Patches*, ii. 233.

39. S.R.R. 6001/372/3, p. 23.

40. Above, p.15.

41. *V.C.H. Salop.* x. 436, 439.

42. *Ibid.* 191 n. 53; xi. 127; Eyton, ii. 265-6, 330-1. First mention of Idsall (*i.e.* Shifnal) ch. may be in 1121 as a gift to Shrews. Abbey by Rob. fitz Tetbald (fl.1086 and apparently after 1108): cf. *ibid.* 266-7; *Cartulary of Shrews. Abbey*, ed. U. Rees (1975), i, p.34. *Pace* Rees (*ibid.* p.39; ii, p.261), *Cal. Docs. preserved in France*, ed. J.H. Round (1899), no. 655, is not absolute proof that Rob. d.1087, though *ibid.* no. 656, if authentic, would be and would imply Idsall ch.'s existence by 1087. Portioners there 1108 x 1128 (Rees, *Cart. Shrews.* ii, p.256) may imply a pre-Conquest ch.—but see above, cap. I, nn. 32, 38.

43. *V.C.H. Salop.* iii. 11.

44. Eyton, xi. 194, 196. It had been served by more than one priest in 1086.

45. *V.C.H. Salop.* ii. 119.

46. Eyton, xi. 178-9.

47. *V.C.H. Salop.* iii. 8.

48. Full acct. and descr. in *T.S.A.S.* lxvi. 20-9.

49. *Jnl. Brit. Arch. Assn.* cxli. 124-58.

50. See below, p.48.

51. S.R.R. 6001/372/1, pp. 65-6.

52. *Ibid.* pp.28, 49-50; /3, p.98.

53. He also refounded Wenlock as a Cluniac priory and founded a collegiate ch. at Quatford and a chap. in Shrews. Castle: *V.C.H. Salop.* ii. 18, 22, 30-1, 38-40, 123-4.

54. Brit. Arch. Assn. *Conference Trans.* i. 17.

55. The latest acct. of the bldgs. is *Shrews. Abbey: Studies in the arch. and hist. of an urban abbey*, ed. N. Baker (Salop. Arch. and Hist. Soc. monograph ser. ii). Dr. Baker's 1985-8 excavations were on precinct sites SW. of the abbey ch.

56. The colonnettes were added by S. Pountney Smith in 1860-1; there were none in 1821. For early 19th-cent. views and descr. of the nave see B.L. Add. MS. 36378, ff. 80-1; S.R.R. 6001/198, f. 451; S.R.S. i. 97.

57. Brit. Arch. Assn. *Conf. Trans.* vii. 16-29. Tewkesbury was consecr. in 1123.

58. *Eccl. Hist. of Orderic Vitalis*, ed. M. Chibnall, iii (1972), 148; *Cart. Shrews.* ed. Rees, i, p.32. The W. doorway, set in a slight projection, suggests that the W. end was not completed until well into the 12th cent. As late as the mid cent. grants of tithes were being made to the 'building' of the abbey: *ibid.* ii, pp.296, 301-2.

59. *V.C.H. Salop.* ii. 50-1; J. Bilson, 'Archit. of Cistercians', *Arch. Jnl.* 2nd ser. xvi. 199.

60. It is claimed that some work had started earlier (P. Fergusson, *Archit. of Solitude—Cistercian Abbeys in 12th Cent. Eng.* (1984), 92 n. 4), but it is far from certain that the room beneath the N. end of the N. transept was a crypt.

61. J. Potter, *Remains of Ancient Monastic Archit. in Eng.* (1847), includes a comprehensive survey of the bldgs. *c.*1844.

62. R. Stalley, *Cistercian Monasteries of Ireland* (1987), 141, so explains the apparent flouting by several Eng. Cistercian chs. of their statute of 1157 which forbade the erection of stone bell towers. P. Fergusson, however, argues (*Jnl. Soc. of Archit. Historians*, xxix. 211-21) that the statute meant no more than to forbid 'extravagant' towers. Either way Buildwas would seem to have been in the clear. A.W. Clapham attributed Cistercian crossing towers quite simply to a native Eng. tradition (*Eng.*

63. *Romanesque Archit.* ii. 79); aided, presumably, by a master mason's ability to get his own way with technical arguments far above the head of the most learned abbot.

64. The screen betw. nave and N. aisle, separating ordained monks from lay bros., was of stone in contrast with the general Cistercian use of timber. The use is commented on by C. Brooke (in *Cistercian Art and Archit.* ed. C. Norton and D. Oark (1986), 17) and by Stalley (*op. cit.* 136).

64. Fergusson, *Archit. of Solitude*, 94.

65. *Ibid.* 91-4.

66. Below, p.27.

67. *V.C.H. Salop.* ii. 62-3.

68. *Arch. Jnl.* lxvi. 285-6; cxxxviii. 29-31, 47.

69. *V.C.H. Salop.* ii, pl. facing p.78.

70. *Ibid.* 70-1.

71. *Ibid.* pl. facing p.79.

72. S. Rigold, *Lilleshall Abbey* (Dept. of Environment guide, 3rd impr. 1980), dates the nave to the 13th cent. without attempting to explain the presence of these capitals. Pevsner, *Salop.* 167, sees the westernmost bay as 'Transitional' but comments that the vaulting shafts look 'decidedly later than the rest'. The assumption of deliberate archaism is made by Rigold (*op. cit.* 4, 10), by *V.C.H. Salop.* ii. 79, and by L. Butler and C. Given-Wilson, *Medieval Monasteries of Gt. Brit.* (1979), 281.

73. For the occurrence of w. doorways with a four-centred or other flattened arch beneath a very large window (and thus in similar contexts), see J.H. Harvey, 'Som. Perpendicular: The Dating Evidence', *Trans. Anct. Monuments Soc.* N.S. xxvii.50.

74. Below, p.55.

75. C. Wilson in Brit. Arch. Assn. *Conf. Trans.* i. 80-1.

76. *Arch. Jnl.* cxxxviii. 29-31.

77. *Ibid.* 47.

78. The nunnery is first mentioned in a charter of 1186 or earlier; the community was well established by 1189, and most of its property came as 'small gifts from local fams. of modest wealth': *V.C.H. Salop.* ii. 83.

79. Pevsner proposed a date of *c.*1150-80 (*Salop.* 209), but the striking difference in character betw. the ornament of the chapter ho. and the sculpture on the lavatorium of late 12th-cent. appearance would suggest that the former is closer to 1150 than to 1180. J.F. King ('W. Country Influences upon Archit. in Normandy', *Jnl. Brit. Arch. Assn.* cxxix. 29, 32, 37 n. 37) contemplates a date before the mid 12th cent., but the evidence is perhaps tenuous and seems to imply that the lintel above the S. doorway of the chapter ho. is integral with the decoration of the wall face, which it is not (below, pp.32-3).

80. *V.C.H. Salop.* ii, pl. facing p.79.

81. Ruyton was part of the large fief which John le Strange held from the FitzAlans in 1166; in the late 12th cent. his son John was one of the most powerful men in Salop, a loyal servant of the FitzAlans and of the king. Ruyton Castle was apparently destroyed by the Welsh in 1202 and the Stranges did not rebuild it. See H. le Strange, *Le Strange Records* (1916), 32-33, 67, 69.

82. *Archaeologia*, lxi. 271-5 and pl. xxxvi (facing p.258).

83. It presumably acquired a private character in the later 16th cent. when Sir Hen. Sidney put in a floor, fenestrated the ground floor, built a wooden gallery from his lodging to a first-floor opening, and rebuilt the chancel in timber: *ibid.* 275-6.

84. Shrews. Abbey eventually overtook it: *V.C.H. Salop.* ii. 33, 44.

85. *Ibid.* x. 409.

86. *Ibid.* ii, pl. facing p.45.

87. *Ibid.* pl. facing p.78; and see next note.

88. The standing figures were inserted in the surrounds of the openings of the chapter ho. and of the processional doorway in the 14th cent.

89. *Ibid.* pl. facing p.79.

90. *Ibid.* pl. facing p.58.

91. The origins of Ludlow Castle, both its builder and its date, are matters of contention; its importance by the mid 12th cent. is not.

92. *Salop.* 251.

93. *V.C.H. Salop.* ii. 27.

94. Eyton, iv. 235; vi. 224.

95. In 1085 Edstaston, along with Wem, was part of Wm. Pantulf's large est.; it was later part of the man. of Wem: Eyton, ix. 179.

96. It is also found at faraway St. David's Cath., where it is probably of the last 20 yrs. of the 12th cent.

97. Pevsner, *Salop.* 88; G. Webb, *Archit. in Brit.—The Middle Ages* (1956), 45; Clapham, *Eng. Romanesque Archit.* ii. 77; Stalley, *Cistercian Monasteries of Irel.* 183; Fergusson, *Archit. of Solitude*, 93.

98. The Sidbury font is a copy of that which was destroyed in a fire following the restoration of 1878-81. There is a faded photo. of the original in the vestry.

99. G. Zarnecki, *Later Eng. Romanesque Sculpture* (1958), 14.

100. A recent analysis of the iconography of the Kilpeck carvings ignores these motifs and their reappearance upside down at Shobdon and Stottesdon, M. Thurlby, *The Herefs. Sch. of Romanesque Sculpture* (1999).

101. Appropriate enough in the county where the great editor's fam. can be traced back many centuries: S.R.R. 6001/4077, p.120.

102. Above, p.2.

103. The stone is a friable conglomerate with large pebbles, geol. provenance uncertain.

104. It obliterates the lower parts of two colonnettes which belong to the scheme of decoration of the wall face, and, despite the pellets, is in a wholly different vein.

105. *Artibus et Historiae*, xxii (1990), 189; J. Hunt and M.A. Stokes, 'Sculpture and Patronage on a Salop. Manor: a Group of 12th-Cent. Sculptures from Alveley', *Jnl. Brit. Arch. Assn.* cl. 27-47, pls. ix-xi. The first known ref. to the sculptures is in the Salop. Hist. Antiquities Assoc. min. bk. (S.R.R. 4584/1) 28 Feb. 1920. The first known published ref. is in *Bridgnorth Jnl.* 28 Mar. 1980.

106. The obvious assumption is that the stones come from Alveley church just across the way, but see next note.

107. Mr. James Lawson has proposed (pers. communication 1998) that they could be from St. Giles's chap., Romsley, arguing that Alveley's building hist. (Cranage, iv. 259-67) does not suggest post-medieval availability of 12th-cent. sculptures for incorporation in the Bell inn (probably 17th-cent.: Dept. of Environment, *List of Bldgs. of Special Archit. or Historic Interest: R.D. of Bridgnorth* (1974), 7). But at St. Giles's, 2-3 miles S., there were evidently sculptures—a zodiacal Leo and Sagittarius and a bird possibly from a pier capital—which survive nearby at Lower Ho. Fm. and a neighbouring cottage (Eyton, iii. 203-4; *W. Midlands Arch. News Sheet*, xviii. 70-1; xix. 59); they and the Old Bell Ho. stones may thus be bits of a wide scatter from a demolition of St. Giles's 1524 x 1790 (*Reg. Bothe* (C.S.), 360; S.R.R. 6001/372/2, p. 30v.).

108. *Jnl. Brit. Arch. Assn.* cl. 30.

109. It is tempting to associate them with the grant of Alveley man. in 1154-5 to the important Guy le Strange, sheriff in 1160 and later. The benefice was perh. a perquisite for kinsmen, for the first known incumbent (by 1189) was Wm. le Strange: Eyton, i. 120; iii. 122, 126-8.

110. The Poers could have built St. Giles's. Their name has lost its resonance, for they subinfeudated many manors, sometimes perh. to cadets taking other names. But in the 12th cent. they may have been the Stranges' equals: they held large Worcs. and Glos. estates of the bp. of Worc. and Pershore and Westminster abbeys, and in Salop. Romsley and an est. in Badger of the baron of Ric.'s Castle, the first of whom, by 1086, was a fellow tenant of Wal. Ponther (the first Poer) under the bp. See *e.g. V.C.H. Worcs.* i. 260; iii. 515-16; iv. 140, 181-2, 186-7, 378; *V.C.H. Glos.* vi. 252; viii. 39; *V.C.H. Salop.* x. 215; Eyton, iii. 197 sqq.; J.H. Round, *Feudal Eng.* (1964), 145, 244.

111. The claim (Pevsner, *Salop.* 64; *Arch. Jnl.* cxxxviii. 14-15) rests on a misinterpretation of Prof. Zarnecki's 'Aston' (*Later Eng. Romanesque Sculpture*, 14) as Aston Eyre (Salop.) instead of Aston (Herefs.). Prof. Zarnecki assures me very firmly that he does not regard Aston Eyre as Herefs. work.

112. Rob. fitz Aer gave land and tithes to the ch. and graveyard at Aston in 1138-9 (Eyton, i. 140, 207-8), but that does not necessarily date the present structure.

113. Pevsner, *Salop.* 64. R. Halsey (*Arch. Jnl.* cxxxviii. 15) thought that that would have been very difficult, but he was assuming that the sculpture had always been where it is now.

114. Zarnecki, *Later Eng. Romanesque Sculpture*, 47 and figs. 113-14.

115. *Arch. Jnl.* cxxxviii. 15.

116. *Jnl. Brit. Arch. Assn.* cxl. 66.

117. To all the influences, near and far, upon the origins and development of the 'Herefordshire' sch. has now been added that of Romano-Brit. survivals in the Glouc. area: *ibid.* cl. 223.

118. It is not certain that the 'Tree of Life' is intended, for its fruits, to be eaten by the Righteous, are absent. E. Gethyn-Jones, *Dymock Sch. of Sculpture* (1979), pl. 19a, sees High Ercall as a far-flung work of the Dymock 'school', but the attempt is not convincing.

119. E.S. Prior, *A Hist. of Gothic Art in Eng.* (1900), 35.

Chapter III

1. All trace of Wigmore Abbey's cell at Ratlinghope disappeared long ago: *V.C.H. Salop.* ii. 80. Wenlock Priory's 12th-cent. cell at Preen (*ibid.* 38; *T.S.A.S.* lxx. 194-6) had a parochial nave and is discussed below with the par. chs.

2. *V.C.H. Salop.* ii. 47; *T.S.A.S.* 4th ser. xi. 257, 260; Eyton, vii. 92.

3. *T.S.A.S.* 4th ser. xi. 296-303.

4. *V.C.H. Salop.* ii. 59-61.

5. Excavated remains of the *c.*1200 cloister arcade are described and illustr. in *Medieval Arch.* xxiv. 210-13.

6. Above, pp.24-6.

7. R. Graham, 'Hist. of Alien Priory of Wenlock', *Jnl. Brit. Arch. Assn.* 3rd ser. iv. 128-9.

8. A similar but not wholly comparable arrangement occurs at Peterborough Abbey: noted in *V.C.H. Salop.* x. 409 n. 43.

9. View stated or implied by Cranage in *Archaeologia*, lxxii. 109; G.F. Webb, *Archit. in Brit. in Middle Ages* (1956), 95; P. Brieger, *Eng. Art 1216-1307* (1957), 64; Pevsner, *Salop.* 209; M.M. Chibnall in *V.C.H. Salop.* ii. 45.

10. B. Morley, *Wenlock Priory* (Hist. Bldgs. and Monuments Com. for Eng.), 5.

11. Eyton, xi. 235-42, dating the appropriation 1219 x 1224.

12. *Hereford 1079-1234*, ed. J. Barrow (Eng. Episcopal Acta, vii), pp. 289-90, redating it 1230 x 1234; *V.C.H. Salop.* x. 197 (not noting the revised date) and source cited *ibid.* n. 65.

13. Monastic cathedrals are excl. from the reckoning; their inclusion would make the proportion of monastic chs. building in the 13th cent. much higher.

14. By 1262 the priory was seriously in debt, but for exactly how much and why is not clear: *V.C.H. Salop.* ii. 41-2.

15. Franciscans at Bridgnorth and Shrews., Dominicans at Shrews., and Augustinians at Ludlow, Shrews., and Woodhouse nr. Cleobury Mortimer: *V.C.H. Salop.* ii. 89-93, 95-8.

16. Some early 16th-cent. remains of the Shrews. Franciscans still stand, and more did so until the late 1960s.

17. *Archaeologia*, xxxix. 173-88.

18. *V.C.H. Salop.* ii. 91-3.

19. Full acct. in *T.S.A.S.* lxxi. 33-82.

20. *Ibid.* 76.

21. Cranage (i. 55; v. 436) suggested, and Pevsner (*Salop.* 108, 324) was inclined to agree, that there were 12th-cent. transepts at Clun and Worfield. Both were important chs. then, but the evidence for transepts is slight. The now destroyed collegiate St. Chad's and St. Alkmund's, Shrews., had full transepts by the end of the 12th cent. See Cranage, x. 894, 899; S.R.R. 6001/372/1, pp.49-50, 128; /3, p.98.

22. Cf. D. Miles, 'An Archaic Roof at Wistanstow', *V.A.* xxviii. 105-6.

23. Cranage, ix. 749.

24. S.R.R. 6001/372/1, p.46.

25. Ellesmere, Shifnal: Eyton, ii. 265-6, 330; x. 232, 246-7.

26. Lydbury North, Ch. Stretton, Wistanstow (probably represented by the priest at Woolston): *V.C.H. Salop.* i. 311, 317, 336, 348; *Salop. Domesday* [Intro. and Translation], ed. A. Williams and R.W.H. Erskine (1990), p.24.

27. Condover, Wrockwardine.

28. The much earlier and probably cruciform ch. of Stanton Lacy was of similar importance as the ch. of a very large manor, having 2 priests in 1086, and holding 1½ hide.

29. At both the walling above the arcade is considerably thinner than that of the outer walls.

30. S.R.R. 6001/372/1, p.46. That pier now appears to be the easternmost respond of the former arcade, but the former easternmost bay has been filled by the N.W. pier and buttress of the crossing tower.

31. Chelmarsh was largely rebuilt in the mid 14th cent., but the N. aisle is earlier than that. There is no clear support for Cranage's claim (iv. 282) of Norman masonry but the width (6½ft.) and the blocked late Norman doorway, not *in situ*, in the N. wall make a date of *c.*1200 probable.

32. Cranage (ix. 769-70) argued that the aisle at Gt. Ness had never been built, and Pevsner (*Salop.* 134) seemed to agree. Arguments for the contrary view are set out in S.R.R. 7069.

33. The nave and N. aisle at Pontesbury, pulled down in 1825, are shown in drawings of 1788 (S.R.R. 6001/372/1, p.69) and 1824 (*Gent. Mag.* xcvii (1), pl. i facing p.297). The N. aisle was descr. as having had 'semicircular arches, supported by clustered columns' (*ibid.* 297).

34. For practical and ritual explanations see G H. Cook, *The Eng. Mediaeval Parish Church* (1954), 96-7; R.H. Morris, *Churches in the Landscape* (1988), 292-3.

35. *Jnl. Brit. Arch. Assn.* cxiii. 195.

36. For Shifnal and Stottesdon see above, p.19. At Shawbury Dom. Bk. records a priest; he probably served the mother ch. of a large Saxon par.: Eyton, vii. 146-9. High Ercall ch. may be the successor to ones at Rodington and Rowton in 1086 (cf. Eyton, ix. 107-8; *T.S.A.S.* lxii. 4-5); by *c.*1228 it served a large par. and was staffed by a rector and a vicar (Eyton, ix. 109).

37. It exceeds those of the naves of Shrews., Buildwas, and Lilleshall abbeys and the rebuilt Wenlock Priory.

38. Below, pp.288-9.
39. S.R.R. 6001/372/2, p 6.
40. *T.S.A.S.* i. 214.
41. Drawings of the S. elevation of Ellesmere (in the vestry and in S.R.R.) before restoration show no S. aisle, and Scott's specifications for the rebuilding (in the vicar's possession) refer to the remains of an arcade on the N. but not on the S.
42. *V.C.H. Salop.* x. 317.
43. *i.e.* multiplication of saints' days and other feasts and of votive and private masses, altars, processions, and religious fraternities: T. Klauser, *Short Hist. of the Western Liturgy* (1979), 95-7, 101 sqq.; A. Hamilton Thompson, *The Ground Plan of the Eng. Par. Ch.* (1911), 66-8.
44. The N. aisle survives. A 1790 drawing (S.R.R. 6001/372/2, p.12) could be interpreted as showing a blocked S. arcade.
45. *Cartulary of Haughmond Abbey*, ed. U. Rees (1985), pp.139-41.
46. Above, pp.27-8.
47. The original chancel, whether added or not, was probably nearly square. An internal plinth runs E. from a point 14ft. E. of the nave-chancel junction for *c.*14ft. to the E. wall: perhaps evidence of a later 13th-cent. extension of the chancel to the present 2:1 proportions.
48. The present windows, renewals, are close copies of the originals: S.R.R. 6001/372/2, p.55.
49. Cranage (vii. 598) and Pevsner (*Salop.* 165) thought that the windows with reticulated tracery at the E. end of the chancel at St. Mic.'s, Lilleshall, were evidence of a 14th-cent. extension rather than 14th-cent. insertions. There is no break of masonry between the E. and W. ends of the chancel; the S. window in the E. end is a modern replacement (S.R.R. 6001/372/1, p.40) and the others may be too; and the earlier chancel, if the present form is the result of a later extension, would have been remarkably short for its time.
50. Rushbury and Culmington naves have encroached on their chancels since the 13th cent., altering their relative lengths.
51. Eyton, v. 83-4; *V.C.H. Herefs.* i. 324; *Charters and Rec. of Heref. Cath.* (C.S.), 127; D.W.B. Baron, *St. Mary Magdalene's, Ashford Carbonel: a Guide to the Ch.* (1985), 13-15.
52. *V.C.H. Salop.* x. 182, 184-5.
53. Recently discovered paintings on the N. wall at Leebotwood suggest a date of *c.*1200.
54. P. Kidson in Brit. Arch. Assn. *Conference Transactions*, viii. 32.
55. Much the same ratio is true of W. towers: below, p.49.
56. Cranage (iii. 204) and Pevsner (*Salop.* 168) see Linley ch. as all of one date. But (i) there is some difference in date between the ornament of the tympana of the N. and S. doorways of the nave and that upon the tower arch; (ii) the S. doorway has been moved west so that its W. jamb abuts the tower; and (iii) there is evidence that the W. wall of the nave has been thickened on its W. face to take the tower's extra weight. A thickening of the W. wall of the nave when a W. tower was added seems to have occurred also at Milson.
57. Gt. Ness chancel was enlarged in the 13th cent., but evidence of an earlier chancel, probably coeval with the nave, survives on the N. wall.
58. Above, pp.17-18.
59. Bromfield, originally collegiate, became a Benedictine cell in the 12th cent. The nave was used as a par. ch.: *V.C.H. Salop.* ii. 27.
60. S.R.R. 6001/372/1, p.69; /3, p.102.
61. *V.C.H. Salop.* xi. 63.
62. Cranage, x. 1047.
63. The truncated-pyramid roofs of the last three may be seen across the border at Kerry and Llanidloes.
64. P. Curnow, 'The Tower Ho. at Hopton Castle', *Studies in Medieval Hist.* ed. C. Harper-Bill *et al.* (1989), 96.
65. Above, p.24.
66. Above, p.26.
68. Pevsner (*Salop.* 121) says that all the arches are pointed, but Cranage (v. 192) gets it right.
69. The present windows copy those there in 1789: S.R.R. 6001/372/1, p.110.
70. The present openings copy those revealed in the 1882-3 restoration: *Jnl. Brit. Arch. Assn.* xxxix. 223-30.
71. S.R.R. 6001/372/3, p.54. A similar window, but with pierced spandrels, formerly in the destroyed St. Maurice's, York, is illustr. in J. H. Parker, *Intro. to Gothic Archit.* (11th edn. 1895), 64, dating it *c.*1180.
72. S.R.R. 6001/372/1, p. 128; /3, p.98.
73. Many ch. windows were restored or replaced in the 19th cent. The only examples cited here are those known from early drawings or documents.
74. Soc. of Antiq. MS. 477, p.103; S.R.R. 6001/372/1, p.58; /2, p.45; /3, pp.27, 93.
75. S.R.R. 6001/372/1, p. 130; /3, p. 35. Both chs. belonged to great abbeys:

Bromfield to Glouc. from 1155 (*V.C.H. Salop.* ii. 27), Caynham to Wigmore probably from the late 12th cent. (Eyton, iv. 361, 363).
76. For the massed lancets in the chancel at Acton Burnell see below.
77. S.R.R. 6001/372/1, pp.3, 14, 35, 126, 142; /2, p.45; /3, p.48.
78. *Ibid.* /1, pp.49-50.
79. *Ibid.* pp.26, 110; /2, pp.45, 51.
80. *Salop.* 49.
81. S.R.R. 6001/372/2, p.30.
82. *Ibid.* /3, p.102.
83. *Ibid.* p.51; /2, p.48.
84. *Ibid.* /1, p.37.
85. *Ibid.* /1, p.40.
86. *Ibid.* /3, p.35. Caynham was almost wholly rebuilt in 1885. Central doorways are rare in par. ch. naves and so too are long lancets, and it could be that the medieval S. wall had been remodelled by an 18th-cent. antiquary; but the timber porch shown in the drawing appears to be 15th- or 16th-cent. Glynne recorded in 1870 that the S. wall of the nave had 'a small Norman window and three simple lancets which have the heads slightly ogeed, an unusual form': *S.R.S.* i. 19. That is not easily reconciled with the 1791 drawing.
87. S.R.R. 6001/372/2, p.5.
88. Built after Mytton's visit *c.*1734: Soc. of Antiq. MS. 477, p.407.
89. Eyton, xi. 254.
90. Eyton, x. 28; H. le Strange, *Le Strange Records* (1916), 35-6.
91. *V.C.H. Salop.* viii. 264, 283.
92. *Ibid.* ii. 72, 78; Eyton, viii. 227.
93. Eyton, iv. 321, 331.
94. Brit. Arch. Assn. *Conf. Trans.* i. 85.
95. The stops at Lilleshall are sadly defaced; their general character can be made out from the Bucks' engraving of 1731.
96. Brit. Arch. Assn. *Conf. Trans.* i. 83.
97. *Arch. Jnl.* cxxxviii. 40.
98. *The Eng. Decorated Style: Gothic archit. transformed 1250-1350* (1979), 14.
99. 'Dying Mouldings ... in 13th-Cent. Archit.' *Jnl. Brit. Arch. Assn.* cxxxv. 52.
100. Or at least with the N. transept's N. window: S.R.R. 6001/372/1, p.15.
101. It is noticeable that Longnor has none of Acton Burnell's richness. It was probably built by Rog. Sprenchose, lord of the manor and, for a remarkably long period (1278-86), sheriff: Eyton, vi. 57; *V.C.H. Salop.* iii. 17.

Chapter IV
1. *V.C.H. Salop.* ii. 90, 93, 95; *Archaeologia*, xxxix. 182-3; P. Klein and A. Roe, *Carmelite Friary, Ludlow* (Ludlow Hist. Research Paper, vi [1988]), 5-7.
2. D. Lloyd, *Par. Ch. of St. Laurence* (Ludlow, 1980), 7.
3. G.A. Holmes, *Estates of Higher Nobility in 14th-Cent. Eng.* (1957), 35-8.
4. *Complete Peerage*, xii (2), 251.
5. Eyton, iii. 46.
6. Cranage (iv. 279-85) argued for a single build (S. of the N. aisle), but on that basis dated everything to shortly before 1345.
7. J. Bony, *The Eng. Decorated Style* (1979), 12-13.
8. S.R.R. 6001/372/3, p.16
9. *e.g.* Bony (*op. cit.* 26) for Shifnal and Pevsner (*Salop.* 213) for Munslow.
10. R.K. Morris, 'Late Decorated Archit. in N. Herefs.' *Woolhope Trans.* xliv. 55.
11. P. Draper in Brit. Arch. Assn. *Conf. Trans.* iv. 20-2.
12. *V.C.H. Salop.* ii. 128-9.
13. A drawing of 1790 (S.R.R. 6001/372/2, p.65) dispels any notion that the windows at Battlefield may be written off as 19th-cent. inventions. The usage at Ludlow may be found elsewhere, *e.g.* in the W. Country and Norf. (R.K. Morris in Brit. Arch. Assn. *Conf. Trans.* vii. 116; J. Evans, *Eng. Art 1307-1461* [1949], 367); that at Battlefield may be unique.
14. Bony, *Eng. Decorated Style*, 28.
15. R.K. Morris's conclusions about work at Ric.'s Castle and Ludlow (*Woolhope Trans.* xliv. 41-50) can probably be applied to Salop as a whole.
16. Brit. Arch. Assn. *Conf. Trans.* vi. 97.
17. But see below, p.60, for a possible date of *c.*1330 for Nash.
18. Cranage, iii. 251.
19. Pevsner, *Salop.* 110.
20. Cranage, v. 389-94.
21. S.R.R. 6001/372/3, p.16. Many of the windows at Clungunford were replaced with more elaborate forms in 1895, but the present difference in style between the windows probably perpetuates an earlier one.
22. The plinth of the N. wall, different from and earlier than that of the other walls, runs from the 14th-cent. NW. buttress to *c.*10ft. short of the E. wall, where a modern boiler house obscures it.

23. Eyton, iv. 333.
24. *Ibid*. 294, 296-7.
25. *Ibid*. xi. 301-2
26. *Ibid*. x. 230; *V.C.H. Salop*. ii. 81.
27. *V.C.H. Staffs*. iii. 143; Eyton, ix. 256-9.
28. *V.C.H. Salop*. x. 194, 196, 340, 344-5.
29. Prees is not quite a rectangle for the N. aisle stops a few ft. short of the E. wall of the chancel.
30. See above, pp.10 sqq.
31. Despite restoration Stottesdon's external appearance has survived unaltered: S.R.R. 6001/372/3, p.42.
32. As happened about the same time at Stanton Lacy, when the S. aisle was extended E. into the former S. transept: Cranage, ii. 155-60.
33. S.R.R. 6001/372/1, p.38. Edgmond chancel was heavily restored by Street in 1877-8: the side walls were lowered, the battlements removed, the roof raised and given a steeper pitch, and the present windows inserted.
34. S.R.R. 6001/372/1, p.122.
35. In 1815 there was a large Georgian window in the E. wall: B.L. Add. MS. 21181, f.4.
36. A caption to the 1815 drawing mentions a 'large pointed [chancel] arch with circular pilasters and grotesque capitals'.
37. Pevsner's descr. (*Salop*. 103) is as adequate as any: 'a trefoil arrangement of radially placed straight-sided arches filled each with two small arches and a trefoil over'.
38. B.L. Add. MS. 21013, f.41.
39. *Ibid*. 21181, f. 41.
40. In Mr. Peter Klein's possession. The paper has a watermark of 1805, but the drawing may be considerably later than that. It is, however, earlier than 1827, for it shows the W. tower with the low steeple that was replaced by the battlements shown in the view of 9 July 1827. The window itself was replaced in 1828-9 (S.R.R. 3800/V/1, 10 Dec. 1828), its successor in 1869.
41. B.L. Add. MS. 21011, f.141.
42. The present chancel is a rebuild of 1864 but must be much the same length as its predecessor: S.R.R. 6001/372/3, p.77.
43. The flowing tracery of the W. window is shown in a drawing of 1786: *ibid*. /1, p.15.
44. Cf. V.C.H. Salop. x. 346. For other examples of this practice see below, p.294. If that shift did occur, it was probably in the first half of the 17th cent. The Jacobean pulpit in the NE. angle of the present nave is reached from the chancel through an opening contrived in the screen by eliminating cross members and a panel; a 19th-cent. removal would have shown more respect for such a fine screen, as when the screen's bottom panels were preserved after an 1842 repewing: *V.C.H. Salop*. x. 347.
45. Cranage, x. 908-10, 923-4.
46. Cranage (vii. 598) admits that there is no evidence for lengthening in the masonry itself and relies on the character of a window in the N. wall. Pevsner (*Salop*. 165) cites the E. window, but that is modern according to Cranage; and the N. window looks very suspect. Even if both were original, they would not prove a lengthening for they could be insertions into a 13th-cent. structure.
47. Cranage, iv. 314; Pevsner, *Salop*. 160.
48. The plinth at that point does return, but all the plinths appear to have been rebuilt in the late 19th-cent. restoration.
49. *V.C.H. Salop*. x. 1923, 24-5.
50. Which, however, failed to secure a title to the advowson of the vicarage: *ibid*. viii. 214.
51. *Ibid*. 283; Eyton, i. 109; ii. 158-9, 181; iii. 117; iv. 154; ix. 126.
52. See below, n.88.
53. B.L. Add. MS. 21180, ff.32, 34.
54. S.R.R. 6001/372/2, p.30.
55. Rog. (restored as earl of March 1354) was perh. born in 1327 and died in 1360: *D.N.B.*
56. B.L. Add. MS. 21015, f.50.
57. A 12th-cent. origin has been argued from two low broad projections on the S. wall, claimed as cut-down clasping buttresses to the original chancel (demoted to a chancel aisle after 1199), and an early piscina in the S. wall: Cranage, ii. 106-7; Pevsner, *Salop*. 177; *Arch. Jnl*. cxiii. 195. As clasping buttresses are very broad indeed and, as the plinth of the 15th-cent. S. aisle runs around, and is incorporated in, them, of very dubious 12th-cent. date. The piscina may not be *in situ*: J.T. Irvine in *Handbk. to Ludlow* (3rd edn., John Evans, Ludlow, 1865), 37.
58. Cranage (iv. 370-3) thought that the chancel S. aisle at Upton Cressett was 13th-cent. while Pevsner (*Salop*. 306) assigned it to the 19th. In the 1730s it was called the 'new south chancel' (Mytton Papers, vii. 1499) and appears with plain flat-headed openings in a drawing of 1789 (S.R.R. 6001/372/1, p 107).

59. Cranage, v. 392.
60. Above, p.54.
61. The piers are the two easternmost, which, however, Cranage (x. 942-3) considered to be late Decorated–early Perpendicular, coeval with the rebuilding of Trinity chap.
62. C. Daniell, *Death and Burial in Medieval Eng*. (1997), 96-8, 186-7.
63. That of Thos. Forster (d.1520), vicar; he was also prior of Wombridge and a former warden of Battlefield Coll.
64. A 1790 drawing of Stanton Lacy might suggest that those on the chancel were not there then (S.R.R. 6001/372/2, p.55), but the one at the E. end of the S. wall at Tugford certainly was (*ibid*. p.35).
65. Pevsner, *Salop*. 23. Examples are Cleobury Mortimer, Coreley, Ditton Priors, Neen Savage, and Neen Sollars.
66. *Ibid*. 178; Bony, *Eng. Decorated Style*, 38.
67. Bony, *op. cit*. 83 n. 16.
68. The third is at Chipping Norton (Oxon.).
69. The tracery seems to be mainly original. Unfortunately a drawing of 1815 (B.L. Add MS. 21181, f.4) is not clear enough to confirm or deny its authenticity.
70. In association with cusped intersecting tracery.
71. Pevsner's descr. is perhaps as good as any: a spherical triangle, convex sided, enclosing a concave-sided triangle, with the remaining spaces filled with three cusped arch-heads pointing inwards: *Salop*. 54.
72. On a visit to Moreton Corbet (Sept. 1988) by the Soc. of Archit. Historians of Gt. Brit.
73. *V.C.H. Salop*. viii. 197-9; Eyton, x. 183.
74. Cf. Eyton, x. 183, 189-91; *V.C.H. Salop*. viii. 197.
75. A drawing in S.R.R. of the window at Moreton Corbet dated '29-X-11' is, despite the date '1811' pencilled on it, almost certainly of 1911. Nevertheless the windows were at Alberbury by 1858 and Moreton Corbet by 1860: Eyton, vii. 56; x. 192.
76. The first shows a central hub with six radiating cuspless 'petals'; the 1827 drawing is less clear, but seems to be showing the same or a similar arrangement.
77. S.R.R. 6001/6862, f.85v.
78. Rob. Corbet held the man. 1310-75, but, as he was only 6 yrs. old when he inherited, both windows would have to be after *c*.1325 to be attributed to him personally.
79. Shown in J. Buckler's 1815 engraving of the ch. (copy in S.R.R., H.W. Adnitt, 'Shrews. Illustr.' v) and to be presumed medieval. It escaped destruction in the storm of 1579 (*T.S.A.S*. iii. 283) and survived, partly restored in St. Mary's Victorian restoration.
80. There was a trefoil within the triangle. Buckler shows both spheric triangles blocked in 1815, and that in the Trinity gable did not then open into any interior space as that part of the gable was above the chap. roof.
81. Cranage, x. 939, dates it as late as *c*.1360 and compares it with the N. window of the chap., which combines reticulated and early Perpendicular tracery; but the N. window may well be an insertion.
82. *Trans. Bristol and Glos. Arch. Soc*. xv. 65.
83. Cranage, iv. 255-7; S.R.R. 6001/372/3, p.41.
84. It may have been used more richly on the sedilia of the Austin friars' ch. at Ludlow: *Archaeologia*, xxxix. 182-3. No institution seems ever to have used ballflower twice: R.K. Morris in Brit. Arch. Assn. *Conf. Trans*. vii. 112.
85. Above, p.69.
86. Pevsner, *Salop*. 22.
87. There is a striking similarity between the plan of Prees, with a double pier in the arcade at the junction of nave and choir, and that of the W. part of the Austin friars' ch. at Ludlow as revealed by excavation: *Archaeologia*, xxxix. 182 and pl. XII. The intersecting tracery at the one and ballflower ornament at the other, suggest contemporaneity.
88. Arguments for the plan of the original ch. and the date of the added aisle are set out in S.R.R. 7069.
89. D.C. Cox and M.D. Watson, 'H. Trin. Ch., M. Wenlock: a Reassessment', *Jnl. Brit. Arch. Assn*. cxl. 83.
90. *V.C.H. Salop*. ii. 89-93, 96.
91. *Ibid*. iv. 73-5.

Chapter V

1. A. Hamilton Thompson, *Eng. Clergy and their Organization in Later Middle Ages* (1947), 128; J.H. Harvey, *The Perpendicular Style 1330–1485* (1978), 18.
2. Below, p.79.
3. Below, pp.81-2 and n.24.
4. Founded as the Cambridge Camden Soc. 1839, renamed 1846.
5. S.R.R. 6001/372/1, pp.49–50, 128; /3, p.391; Bodl. MS. Top. Salop. c.2, f.521.

6. Cranage, x. 941–2; S.R.R. 6001/372/1, p.128; P.R.O., PROB 11/10, 27 Vox (Hugh Hosier); PROB 11/11, 4 Moore (Wm. Moyne). I am grateful to Mr. W.A. Champion for the last two refs.

7. *V.C.H. Salop.* ii. 129.

8. The nave roof had wholly gone by 1790 (S.R.R. 6001/372/2, p.65). The present parapets of nave and chancel are of the 1860s.

9. *V.C.H. Salop.* ii. 131.

10. *Ibid.* 129.

11. *Ibid.* 131.

12. The present hammer-beam trusses date from the mid 19th-cent. restoration, but the roof's lofty pitch is original.

13. Harvey, *Perpendicular Style*, 155.

14. A faculty for rebldg. the 'choir' was issued in 1433: D. Lloyd, *Par. Ch. of St. Laurence: Hist. and Guide* (Ludlow, 1980), 3. The tower was being roofed as late as 1469–70: *T.S.A.S.* 2nd ser. i. 239.

15. S.R.R. 6001/372/2, p.18; /3, pp.77, 81.

16. Cranage, x. 941–4.

17. Lds. of Man. from 1406: *Cal. Pat.* 1405–8, 201–2.

18. J. Peake, *Ellesmere* (Shrews. 1889), 14; *V.C.H. Salop.* iv. 78, 133.

19. Below, p.88.

20. Below, p.82.

21. *T.S.A.S.* 3rd ser. ii. 296.

22. Below, p.79.

23. R. Gough, *Antiquities & Memoirs of Par. of Myddle* (Shrews. 1875), 12.

24. Some of the W. towers ascribed to the 15th and early 16th cent. may be a result of late 16th-cent. changes in campanology: A. Woodger, 'Post-Reformation Mixed Gothic in Hunts. Ch. Towers and its Campanological Assocs.' *Arch. Jnl.* cxli. 269–308.

25. The remodelled Halston chap. is a very early example, perh. of the 1560s (below, cap. XVIII n.29).

26. S.R.R. 6001/372/3, p.75.

27. Cranage, viii. 697; Pevsner, *Salop.* 155.

28. Probably built by the 3rd earl of Shrews.: Cranage, viii. 672; cf. *Complete Peerage*, xi. 706.

29. For a similar conclusion about quatrefoil friezes elsewhere see J.H. Harvey, 'Somerset Perpendicular: the dating evidence', *Trans. Anct. Monuments Soc.* N.S. xxvii. 56.

30. The arms of Ric. le Strange (d.1449) impaling those of his 2nd wife Eliz. *née* Cobham (marr.1439: *Complete Peerage*, xii (1), 355–6) date the completion of the work. I am grateful to Mrs. E.D. Parker of Ellesmere for the identification.

31. C. Coulson, 'Hierarchism in Conventual Crenellation', *Med. Arch.* xxvi. 69–100.

32. S.R.R. 6001/372/1, p.45; /2, p.65; /3, p.4.

33. *Ibid.* /1, p.38. The present high-pitched chancel roof is Street's work (1877–8), presumably intended to restore the chancel to its supposed original form.

34. *Ibid.* /3, p.81.

35. F.W. Bond, *Gothic Archit. in Eng.* (1905), 504; J.M. Maddison, 'Master Masons of the Dioc. of Lichfield: a Study in 14th-Cent. Archit. at the time of the Black Death', *Trans. Lancs. & Ches. Antiq. Soc.* lxxxv. 126–30, 141.

36. *Trans. Anct. Monuments Soc.* N.S. xxvii. 53, 55, 57.

37. The Palmers' Guild was buying planks for the stalls that yr.: Lloyd, *Ch. of St. Laurence*, 11.

38. S.R.R. 6001/372/3, p.75.

39. *Ibid.* p.128.

40. Above, cap. IV (pp. [11, 21]).

41. Brit. Arch. Assn. *Conference Trans.* i. 133–4.

42. *Trans. Lancs. & Ches. Antiq. Soc.* lxxxv. 131–4.

43. J.W. Nankivell, *St. Mary the Virgin, Ellesmere* (1973), 3, 15 (copy in S.R.R., G 97 v.f.).

44. *Robson's Com. Dir.* (1840), ii, Salop. p.52.

45. The most important examples are Burford and Highley W. towers and the upper stages of towers at Harley, Munslow, and Stoke St. Milborough.

46. Drawing (watermarked 1805) of Ludford ch., in possession of Mr. Peter Klein (reproduced above, p.62).

47. S.R.R. 6001/372/2, p.74.

48. The two-tiered upper stages of the towers at Clun, Hopesay, and More may be late. Some belfries with timber broach spires, as formerly at Greete and Monkhopton, may have been early: S.R.R. 6001/372/1, p.106; /3, p.48. The broach spire formerly at Melverley was on a bldg. probably of the 16th cent.: Bodl. MS. Top. Salop. c.2, f.521.

49. Bodl. MS. Top. Salop. c.2, f.388.

50. *V.C.H. Salop.* iv. 28, 31, 74.

51. Illustr. in T. Dingley, *Hist. from Marble* (Camd. Soc. xciv and xcvii, 1867–8); T.C. Duggan, *Hist. of Whitchurch* (Whitchurch, 1935), pl. facing p.56.

52. I am grateful to Mr. Bob Meeson for much inf. about Staffs. examples.

53. J.L. Bolton, *Med. Eng. Econ. 1150–1500* (1985), 190; *V.C.H. Salop.* iv. 73, 75.

54. Bolton, *op. cit.* 228; G.W. Bernard, *The Power of the Early Tudor Nobility: A Study of the 4th and 5th Earls of Shrews.* (Brighton, 1984), 140, 144.

55. *V.C.H. Salop.* ii. 128–9.

56. *Ibid.* ii. 131; iii. 235. A Wellington burgage (*ibid.* xi. 215) may have been acquired late.

57. *Ibid.* ii. 136, 138.

58. S.R.R. 6001/4079, pp. 1126–7. Sir Wm. Mainwaring had served long in Guienne under the Black Prince and John of Gaunt (P. Morgan, *War and Society in Medieval Ches.* (Chetham Soc. 3rd ser. xxxiv), 21, 155–6, 158–9, 165, 167–9, 198), and his half bros. ('good' Wm.'s uncle and father) were courtiers before and after 1399; Perp. work in Acton and Over Peover chaps. attest the fam. piety and prosperity: *ibid.* 176, 214; G. Ormerod, *Hist. Co. Palatine of Chester* (1882), i. 477, 480–1, 485; iii. 349–50; *Trans. Lancs. & Ches. Antiq. Soc.* lxxxv. 129, 134-9, 144, 148, 165, 169.

59. By marr. to Margaret (*Cal. Pat.* 1436–41, 349) *née* Warren (d.1474).

60. Commemorated in brass and glass: *T.S.A.S.* 2nd ser. vii. 406–7; Sir W. Dugdale, *Chartularium Mainwaringianum*, f.16). I am grateful to Dr. P. Morgan for the inf. contained in the latter source, which remains in private hands.

61. *T.S.A.S.* 3rd ser. x. 325.

62. W. Cathrall, *Hist. of Oswestry* (Oswestry, 1855), 35–7, 47; *V.C.H. Salop.* iv. 76–7 (where 'Donnington ... Shrewsbury,' should read 'Down, near Lydbury North,').

63. *V.C.H. Salop.* iv. 77.

64. Notably in Suss.: *ibid.* 78.

65. *Ibid.* 103.

66. *Ibid.* 77.

67. *Ibid.* 107.

68. *Ibid.* 98.

69. T.C. Mendenhall, *Shrews. Drapers and Welsh Wool Trade in 16th and 17th Cents.* (1953), 2–3, 28–9; S.R.R. 6001/6855, pp.21–9.

70. E. Mercer, *Furniture 700–1700* (1969), 86–7.

71. Some may have been destroyed as late as the early 19th cent. At Ightfield until 1801 a screen 'of handsome oak carving' secluded the chancel, but in the manner of that time the altar site was occupied by Hall Fm. pew (W.S.L., S. MS. 350/2/40), evidently private behind the screen.

72. But a date of c.1500 has been suggested (*Arch. Camb.* cxi. 61, 67, 85) because of the resemblance of some elements of the Hughley screen to screens in Wales.

73. P. Klein, *Misericords and Choir Stalls of Ludlow Par. Ch.*

74. S.R.R. 6001/372/3, p. 24.

75. Cranage, x. 1060–1.

76. *S.R.S.* i. 50.

77. The nave and transepts of Wenlock Priory ch. may have had wooden vaulting ribs (*Jnl. Brit. Arch. Assn.* cl. 53), but they would have been very different from the roofs discussed here. Crown-post roofs were common in secular bldgs. but not in churches.

78. Below, p.303.

79. Much of the nave roof was destroyed when the spire fell in 1894, but it was restored; an engraving by E.H. Buckler shows it as it was before the 1864 restoration.

80. *V.C.H. Salop.* iii. 44, 54, 80; x. 323–4, 332; Eyton, iv. 266–8; *Cal. Pat.* 1452–61, 542; *L. & P. Hen. VIII*, xx (2), p.449.

81. Mercer, *Furniture*, 120.

82. E. Mercer, *Eng. Art 1553–1625* (1962), 149–50, 217–18.

83. *T.S.A.S.* 3rd ser iii. pp. i–ii.

84. In 1789 the roof of the porch at Acton Round was carried by a box-framed truss, probably 17th-cent.: S.R.R. 6001/372/1, p.105. It is now carried by a re-used cruck couple which, as Cranage suggested (iv. 258), may have come from the old roof of the nave, presumably an upper cruck above a tie or a collar.

85. W.C. Leedy, *Fan Vaulting: A Study of Form, Technology and Meaning* (1980).

86. J.C. Wedgwood and A.D. Holt, *Hist. Parl.: Biogs. Commons 1439–1509* (1936), 907–8.

87. *T.S.A.S.* 3rd ser. viii. 222–3.

88. *Ibid.* 172 sqq., 180–1; *Visit. Salop. 1623*, ii (Harl. Soc. xxix), 469–74.

89. From Hen. III's bro. Ric., earl of Cornwall and king of the Romans: *Visit. Salop. 1623*, i (Harl. Soc. xxviii), 146.

90. *Ibid.*; *T.S.A.S.* 4th ser. xi. 6–7; S.R.R. 6001/2791, pp.351, 365–6; *Complete Peerage*, v. 253–4; *V.C.H. Beds.* iii. 270, 272.

91. S.R.R. 6001/19295. The paintings were visible in 1846 but very faint: *ibid.* pocket at end, letter T.F. Dukes to C.R. Smith 17 Aug. 1846. Dukes

reported them briefly in 1846: *Jnl. Brit. Arch. Assn.* ii. 308. Glynne visited the ch. in 1856 but made no mention of them: *S.R.S.* i. 40–1. John Steward said that they had been obliterated: S.R.R. 6001/19295, pocket at end, letter to T.J. Pettigrew 25 May 1860. C.F. Keyser (*Bldgs. with Mural Decorations* (1883), 94), Cranage (viii. 684), and E.W. Tristram (*Eng. Wall-Paintings of 14th Cent.* (1955), 167) all described paintings at Edstaston, but it is doubtful whether they could have distinguished much. Keyser reported a 'Virgin and Child' on the W. wall, which, however, had fallen down and been rebuilt 11ft. farther E. in 1723 (Mytton Papers, ii. 441).

92. G.L. Wasey, *Our Ancient Parishes, or a Lecture on 'Quatford, Morville and Aston Eyre 800 yrs. ago'* (Bridgnorth, 1859), 35–6 (copy in S.R.R., O 64).

93. In view of the proven ability of the stained-glass maker David Evans to copy old glass, e.g. that in Winchester Coll. chap. (J.D. Le Couteur, *Ancient Glass in Winchester* (1920), 69 sqq.; Lloyd, *Ch. of St. Laurence*, 12–13), many pieces may be replacements; that immediately beneath the Crucified Christ in the Jesse window's topmost quatrefoil is inscribed 'D. Evans, Wyle Cop, Shrewsbury, restored the whole of this window 1859'. I am grateful to Mr. David Shepherd for showing me his photo. of it, taken when the window was recently dismantled.

94. E.W. Ganderton and J. Lafond, *Ludlow Stained and Painted Glass* (Ludlow, 1961), 12.

95. Given 1332 x 1353 by Ld. Charlton of Powis, but to which ch? The suggestion that it was originally in the Franciscan ch. has been doubted, and the Charltons long had close connexions with Shrews. Abbey. Cf. H. Owen and J.B. Blakeway, *Hist. Shrews.* (1825), ii. 318–19; *V.C.H. Salop.* ii. 35, 90.

96. Its heraldry establishes its origin.

97. Ganderton and Lafond, *Ludlow Glass*, 61–2.

98. Mainly of the FitzAlans and Staffords and their connections: Owen and Blakeway, *op. cit.* ii. 77–80.

99. The FitzAlans, Stranges, and Husseys figure prominently: *T.S.A.S.* 3rd ser. iii. 19. Drawings (in S.R.R. 6189; probably by Edw. Williams) of glass formerly in the ch. include many armorial designs, depictions of saints (with invocations of their prayers), a memorial of the first master of the coll., and the story of St. John the Baptist's martyrdom filling a great 3-light window.

100. Pembridges, Vernons, Lingens, etc.: Eyton, ii. 256–7.

101. T. Dineley, *Acct. of Progress ... of 1st Duke of Beaufort through Wales, 1684*, ed. R.W. Banks (1883), p. xxiv.

102. *Ibid.* 1.

103. Perh. donated by John Parys (d.1449), a leading burgess: S.R.R. 356, box 520, will pr. 10 Dec. 1449.

104. Ganderton and Lafond, *Ludlow Glass*, 56.

105. *T.S.A.S.* lxxii. 31. The window is described at length *ibid.* 26–37.

Chapter VI

1. Ludlow, as a residence of the prince of Wales from 1473 and soon the seat of the Council in the Marches of Wales, was maintained and even modernized over the next 200 yrs.: *V.C.H. Salop.* iii. 80; M. Faraday, *Ludlow 1085–1660: A Social, Economic and Political Hist.* (Chichester, 1991), 96.

2. The classic acct. is W.H. St. John Hope, 'The Castle of Ludlow', *Archaeologia*, lxi. 257–328. D. Renn has modified some details of Hope's conclusions: *Castles in Wales and the Marches*, ed. J.R. Kenyon and R. Avent (1987), 55–73. *Ludlow Castle: Its Hist. & Bldgs.* ed. R. Shoesmith and A. Johnson (2000), gives a richly documented acct. and a meticulous description of the castle throughout its hist.

3. In 1101 Bridgnorth had been fortified by Rob. of Bellême (confounded with his father as 'Roger de Belehealme' in *Fouke le Fitz Waryn*), widely renowned for his military engineering skill (and equally infamous for his cruelty, shocking even to a cruel age: *Studies in Medieval Hist.* ed. C. Harper-Bill *et al.* (1989), 194). Provoked to open rebellion and beaten by Hen. I, however, he lost his Eng. possessions in 1102. Bridgnorth and its castle developed under royal auspices after Hen. II retook it in 1155. Cf. J. F. A. Mason, *Hist. of Bridgnorth 1157–1957* (Bridgnorth, 1957), 6-8, 14; below, n.35.

4. They held over 70 Herefs. manors in chief, and two thirds of the value of their Salop. manors came from those held in chief: *Domesday Bk.: Herefs.* ed. F. and C. Thorn (1983); *Domesday Bk.: Salop.* ed. F. and C. Thorn (1986).

5. D.J. Cathcart King, *The Castle in Eng. and Wales* (1988), 11. Mr. King was sceptical of the 'strategic' intent of most castles.

6. *V.C.H. Herefs.* i. 306.

7. The romance *Fouke le Fitz Waryn* led some to think that Earl Rog. 'began' Ludlow ('Dynan') castle: T. Wright, *Hist. of Ludlow* (1852), 34. The

possibility was suggested again in 1987 (Kenyon and Avent, *Castles*, 56–8) without fresh evidence but reviving Eyton's interpretation of a Domesday ref. to Lyde (Herefs.) as one to Ludlow (cf. *ibid.* 55–6; Eyton, v. 235–8), an interpretation convincingly demolished by Round in 1908 (*V.C.H. Herefs.* i. 305–6). *Fouke* is a 14th-cent. prose reworking of a 13th-cent. poem, and in the opinions of Eyton (v. 234–5, 243–4; vii. 72) and of one of its modern editors (Ang.-Norm. Text Soc. xxvi-xxviii), Prof. A.D. Wilshere (personal communication), it is not a reliable source for events to c.1100, when the Lacys had Ludlow (*T.S.A.S.* lxx. 175, 182 n. 44; Faraday, *Ludlow*, 3–5). If *Fouke* contains a germ of the truth, it may be that Rog. de Lacy fortified Ludlow encouraged by Earl Rog. during his 1088 rebellion against Wm. II: Eyton, v. 236–7.

8. For a very heavy concentration in the upper reaches of the Rea brook, in the Camlad valley, and in the vale of Montgomery see *T.S.A.S.* liii. 83–90; D.J. Cathcart King and C.J. Spurgeon, 'Mottes in Vale of Montgomery', *Arch. Camb.* cxiv. 69–86.

9. W.L. Warren, *Hen. II* (1973), 167–9, 202.

10. Eyton, vii. 75; *Rot. Litt. Claus.* (Rec. Com.), i. 460a.

11. Eyton, vii. 15; x. 97; xi. 29; Sir J.E. Lloyd, *Hist. of Wales* (1954), ii. 643, 661, 679–80. For a useful synopsis of Welsh incursions into Salop. 1065–1296 see F.C. Suppe, *Military Institutions on the Welsh Marches: Salop. 1066–1300* (1994), 154–61, and refs. *passim*.

12. Perh. few castles were then in a ready state of defence, if Shrews. was typical. Its bailey seems to have been in multiple ownership by the early 12th cent. In the 1120s and 1230s e.g. Shrews. Abbey bought a ho. and land there—not from the Crown—and was given a rent from a piece of land lying next to other private property; *Cart. Shrews Abbey*, ed. U. Rees (1975), i, pp.2–3, 42, 147–8, 199–200.

13. Evidence for the dates of most of these is provided by their remains. For Bryn Amlwg see L. Alcock *et al.* 'Excavations at Castell Bryn Amlwg', *Mont. Coll.* lx. 8–27.

14. Hubert de Burgh's work there in the 1220s may have led to the final abandonment of the former royal castle at Ch. Stretton: cf. Suppe, *Military Institutions*, 20–1, 106 sqq., 137–8; *V.C.H. Salop.* x. 76.

15. *V.C.H. Salop.* viii. 308.

16. Moreton Corbet (below, p.96) and Redcastle at Weston were built at that time, but it is difficult to see either of them, 14–15 miles E. of Knockin and Whittington, as part of a strategic line of defence. A castle at Moreton existed by 1215, and Hen. de Audley was licensed to fortify (*firmare*) Redcastle in 1227: Eyton, x. 184–5, 327; xi. 130; *Pat. R.* 1225–32, 138.

17. The Corbets at Callow, Caus, Lee, Pontesbury, Sibdon Carwood, and Wattlesborough, the FitzAlans at Clun, Bryn Amlwg, Oswestry, and Shrawardine.

18. Depending on the amount of batter given to a wall 9ft. thick at, or perhaps just below, the original ground level.

19. *V.C.H. Salop.* viii. 308–9.

20. P.R.O., C 139/98, no. 28. I owe this and other P.R.O. and S.R.R. refs. to Clun to the kindness of Dr. Henry Summerson.

21. Above, pp.27–8.

22. R.K. Morriss, *Clun Castle* (City of Heref. Arch. Unit, 1993). The publication is not paginated but divided into sections, some very long. Sections 2 and 4 are the most relevant.

23. *Ibid.* section 2.

24. Possibly structural, not military, safety was the prime concern of the builders, unsure whether the top of the motte could bear a large multi-storey stone bldg.: J.R. Kenyon, *Medieval Fortifications* (1990), 39. Any earlier bldg. on the top was presumably of timber.

25. P. Brieger, *Eng. Art 1216–1307* (1957), 185; R.C.H.M.E. *St. Alban's Cath.* (1982 edn.), 25.

26. Wattlesborough is called a 'conscious anachronism', dated to the late 13th cent., and seen as influenced by Clun *inter alia*: *Arch. Jnl.* cxxxviii. 34.

27. Probably by Hen. III: *Hist. King's Wks.* ed. H.M. Colvin, ii (1963), 836.

28. Faraday, *Ludlow*, 7.

29. What follows differs in detail from, but (apart from the dates) is in general agreement with, the views of R.K. Morriss and M. Thompson in *Ludlow Castle: Hist. & Bldgs.* ed. Shoesmith and Johnson, 155–74.

30. *V.C.H. Salop.* viii. 197.

31. E. Blore, 'Wattlesborough Tower', *Arch. Jnl.* xxv. 97–102.

32. Later and on a lower social level the bastles along the Scottish border had a similar form and purpose: H.G. Ramm *et al. Shielings and Bastles* (R.C.H.M.E. Occasional Paper, 1970), 61–95.

33. *Arch. Jnl.* cxxxviii. 33–4; P. Curnow, 'The Tower Ho. at Hopton Castle and its Affinities', *Studies in Medieval Hist.* ed. Harper-Bill, 97–8. Mr. Curnow has since revised his views on Wattlesborough and the argument of this para. is derived from a visit there in his company.

34. Attributed to Fulk Fitz Warin (III), ld. of Alberbury *c.*1200–*c.*1250: *V.C.H. Salop.* viii. 195-6.

35. Probably 1165 x 1173: Colvin, *Hist. King's Wks.* ii. 576; cf. above, n.3.

36. M*edieval Military Archit. in Eng.* (1884), 273–8.

37. Eyton, iv. 5–6; *V.C.H. Salop.* i. 485; iv. 45.

38. The nail-head ornament on the capitals of the moulded jambs of the window in the N. wall is generally of *c.*1200 and the window itself is retarded in comparison with those at Acton Burnell and Longnor chs. of the 1260s and 1270s, but it may be contemporary with them. For his early 14th-cent. date Pevsner relies on the doorway (*Salop.* 200), but that is inserted (see next note).

39. The fullest accts. are by M. E. Wood and J. Salmon (*Arch. Jnl.* cv, Supplement, 70–2; *T.S.A.S.* liii. 61–7) and M. Moran and D. James (*The Forester's Lodge, Upper Millichope* (Ludlow [1986]); cf. *V.C.H. Salop.* x. 328. The present floor joists of *c.**1633 probably date the rebldg. of the N. wall. The doorway there is an insertion of *c.*1633 or later, possibly brought from Millichope chap., mentioned in 1331 (Eyton, iii. 314).

40. R.B. Pugh, *Imprisonment in Medieval Eng.* (1968), 5, 14, 20–1, 130–2, 137, 198–9, 356.

41. The inmates would not have been undergoing punishment but awaiting trial, generally for days or weeks rather than months or yrs. Medieval prisons were often in what now seem inappropriate places—at Caus Castle beneath the chap.: *S.R.R.* 279/131.

42. He acquired Stokesay in or before 1281 and was licensed to crenellate in 1291: Eyton v. 36–7; *Cal. Pat.* 1281–92, 450.

43. J.F.A. Mason, *Stokesay Castle* (Derby, c.1986), pp.[2–3].

44. It abuts the S. end of a low extension from the solar block but in practice is free standing, for the entry into the chambers is at first-floor level by an external stair.

45. Below, p.111.

46. Access from the hall to the solar block was by an external doorway at the N. (dais) end of the hall into a short covered way leading to a doorway cut through the S.wall of the projection of the solar beyond the E. wall of the hall. Immediately inside was a stone stair, squeezed into the corner between the S. and E. walls of the solar and giving access to the first-floor chamber.

47. Gifts of timber from the royal forests of Lythwood and Shirlett were made 1283–6 and crenellation was licensed in 1284: *V.C.H. Salop.* iv. 47; viii. 7–8.

48. The latest accts. of Acton Burnell are in *Collectanea Historica*, ed. A. Detsicas (1981), 86–92; *Arch. Jnl.* cxxxviii. 31–2.

49. The view that the N.E. turret housed a chap. (*Studies in Bldg. Hist.* ed. E.M. Jope (1961), 97; *Arch. Jnl.* cxiii. 201) now seems untenable.

50. Below, p.113.

51. *S.R.R.* 6001/372/1, p. 10. The bldg. was converted to a barn, perh. soon after 1731: *V.C.H. Salop.* viii. 8.

52. Morriss, *Clun Castle*, section 4.4.

53. It may also have been due in later yrs. to the Eng. fondness for low-pitched roofs: L.F. Salzman, *Bldg. in Eng.* (1952), 262 n. 7.

54. Colvin, *Hist. King's Wks.* i (1963), 124.

55. *Antiq. Jnl.* lxxv. 165.

56. Curnow in *Studies in Medieval Hist.* ed. Harper-Bill, 89, 102; *V.C.H. Salop.* iii. 16–17.

Chapter VII

1. *Bede's Eccl. Hist. of Eng. People*, ed. B. Colgrave and R.A.B. Mynors (1969), 182–5.

2. M. Thompson, *The Medieval Hall 600–1600 A.D.* (Aldershot, 1995), 11–14.

3. *Vita Wulfstani* (Camd. 3rd ser. xl), 52. The *Vita* is Wm. of Malmesbury's Latin translation of a lost Eng. text by Coleman, a monk of Worc., so the sentiment may have been Coleman's.

4. M. Carver, 'Kingship and material culture in early Ang.-Sax. East Anglia', *The Origins of A.-S. Kingdoms*, ed. S. Bassett (1989), 156–8.

5. F.M. Stenton, *First Cent. of Eng. Feudalism 1066–1166* (1932), 42 and nn.

6. Vestiges of the landlord–tenant bond may be traced into modern times: *V.C.H. Salop.* iv. 216–18, 254.

7. C.R.J. Currie, 'Larger Medieval Hos. in Vale of White Horse', *Oxoniensia*, lvii. 87; J. Blair, 'Hall and Chamber: Eng. Domestic Planning 1000–1250', *Manorial Domestic Bldgs. in Eng. and N. France*, ed. G. Meirion-Jones and M. Jones (1993), 1–21.

8. Eyton, iii. 38 sqq., 44.

9. Below, p.111.

10. Sir Thos. Botterell, appointed constable of Clun Castle by Rog. Mortimer, was a man of considerable local importance in the late 13th cent.: Eyton, i. 224–8; x. 50, 54, 62, 83, 116, 144; xi. 199. The evidence of the ho. is ambiguous; the stone range has been truncated.

11. Below, p.110.

12. T.H. Turner and J.H. Parker, *Some Acct. of Domestic Archit. in Eng.* i (1851), 3–6.

13. The claim that excavation had established a timber hall abutting the stone block at Wharram Percy (M. Beresford and J. Hurst, *Wharram Percy, Deserted Medieval Village* (1990), pl. 9, p.126) always had difficulties and has now been dropped: inf. from Dr. P. A. Stamper, deputy dir. of excavation. The stone block may have been self-sufficient after all.

14. Above, pp.99–100.

15. His word is *vestibulum*.

16. *V.C.H. Salop.* x. 410 (fig. 42); below, pp.113–5.

17. Son-in-law of the great Wm. Marshal, earl of Pembroke; his dau. Joan was Hen. III's sis.-in-law, and his younger son Wm. (*D.N.B.* s.v. Munchensi) was a prominent baronial reformer.

18. Blair, 'Hall and Chamber 1000–1250', 7, 11; S. Pearson, *Medieval Hos. of Kent: An Historical Analysis* (1994), 23.

19. S. Rigold, *Lilleshall Abbey* (H.M.S.O. 1969); 7; S.R.R. 6001/198, p. 459; /199, p. 12. In the 'Abbot's Lodging' at Buildwas, now occupied by Eastern Merchant Generation Ltd., a stone bldg. of two 2-storeyed ranges at right angles has a late 12th-cent. external doorway on the 1st floor and a now vanished timber hall: Brit. Arch. Assn. *Collectanea Archaeologica*, i (1862), pl. viii; F. Stackhouse Acton, *Garrisons of Salop. during the Civil War 1642–8* (1867), 39.

20. Blair, 'Hall and Chamber 1000–1250', 14.

21. *Ibid.* 17 n. 4.

22. *T.S.A.S.* lxviii. 57.

23. *Ibid.* 9–18.

24. S.R.R. 6001/200, pp. 281-306. The drawings differ in detail but a 14th-cent. 1st-floor hall seems clear. The roof, burnt in 1917, was probably late 15th-cent. The Vaughans seem to have been successful merchants who by the end of the 14th cent. had attained knightly status. See H. Owen and J.B. Blakeway, *Hist. Shrews.* (1825); i. 524–5; *T.S.A.S.* 3rd ser. i. 331–2.

25. S.R.R. 6001/200, pp. 361–4; H. Owen, *Some Acct. of the Ancient and Present State of Shrews.* (Shrews. 1808), 524–5.

26. *D.N.B.* s.v. Charlton, John (d.1353).

27. *Cal. Pat.* 1324–7, 178.

28. Cf. Owen, *Ancient and Present State of Shrews.* 481–2; B.L. Add. MSS. 21016, ff. 19–20; 36378, ff. 146–7, 170; S.R.R. 6001/200, p.279; /5326, ff. 9–10; H.W. Adnitt, 'Old Prints: Shrews.' (accession 5245, class qD 66), ff. 75–7.

29. e.g. the Charltons and Vaughans, the Sturys at Stury's Hall, and the Ludlows at Bennett's Hall: D. Cromarty, *Everyday Life in Medieval Shrews.* (1991), 18; S.R.R. 6000/3943; inf. from Mr. W.A. Champion.

30. For Ludlow see Ludlow Research Papers ii–iv: D. Lloyd and M. Moran, *The Corner Shop* [1978], 23–8; D. Lloyd, *Broad St. through eight centuries* (1979), 43–7; M.E. Speight, *The Gt. Ho. 1270–1980* (1980). Whether the upper floors of another large corner property, the Abbot's Ho., Butcher Row, Shrews., with shops on the ground floor, were intended for multiple occupation is not yet clear.

31. Pearson, *Medieval Hos. of Kent*, 12.

32. *V.C.H. Salop.* x. 407–9. The bp. of Heref. almost certainly had a tower at Bp.'s Castle, but he was acting there as a very secular magnate: M. Thompson, *Medieval Bps,' Hos. in Eng. and Wales* (Aldershot, 1998), 103. The prior of Wenlock, also a secular magnate, had a tower at Madeley Ct. in 1498: *V.C.H. Salop.* xi. 37. Nothing like a tower survives. Nor has extensive excavation definitely revealed one, though masonry (possibly 12th-cent. and probably the earliest on the site) to the east of the 13th–cent. hall will at least bear interpretation as the remains of a 'detached first-floor chamber block': C. Moffett, 'Madeley Ct.: from monastic grange to country ho.' [rep. of excavations by R.A. Meeson in 1978–9 and C. Moffett in 1987]. I am grateful to Bob Meeson and Cameron Moffett for access to their work in advance of its publication by Salop. Arch. and Hist. Soc.

33. Despite its administrative functions the chapter ho. was treated architecturally as part of the church.

34. The late 12th-cent. sculptured panels appear to have been added to an earlier structure.

35. *Med. Arch.* xxiv. 210–13.

36. Other sites have been proposed for the infirmary at Wenlock, but none is more convincing that this, for which no other plausible function has been suggested.

37. Pearson, *Medieval Hos. of Kent*, 24–26; C. Giles, *Rural Hos. of W. Yorks. 1400–1830* (1986), 27–36.

38. *Arch. Jnl.* cxv. 169. The bldg. has been variously called the Refectory and the Infirmary, but Abbot's Hall seems a likelier identification: see sources cited below, n.84.

39. Above, p.104.

40. Pearson, *Medieval Hos. of Kent*, 26.

41. Madeley had belonged to the ch. of Wenlock since the 8th cent., Gt. Oxenbold was acquired in 1244: *V.C.H. Salop*. x. 198, 358; xi. 35.

42. The present opening is later in date or type than the doorway to the upper compartment, and originally the undercroft could have been reached only by the stairway from the 'hall'.

43. Above, p.105.

44. *Close R*. 1247–51, 567; *Cal. Chart. R*. 1226–57, 369; *V.C.H. Salop*. xi. 41. Madeley pk. was restocked with deer of the king's gift in the 1290s: *Cal. Close* 1288–96, 184, 364.

45. *Salop. News Letter*, xxvi. 1; Moffett, 'Madeley Ct.' For the only possible pre-13th-cent. remains see above, n.32.

46. N.M.R. Archives, 'Madeley Ct.' (1977);] Moffett, *op.cit*.

47. At Gt. Oxenbold the lower narrow bldg. to the E., abutting the 'hall', was once a chap. for it has a piscina, apparently *in situ*, in the S. wall. But the piscina is at a level incompatible with the present floor, which is itself compatible with the 13th-cent. doorway at the W. end of the N. wall. In its present form the bldg. is mid to late 13th-cent. with a range of lancets in the upper part of the N. wall beneath a corbel table. Masonry differences betw. the upper and lower parts of the wall may suggest that there was an earlier bldg. on the site, since largely rebuilt. A rough sketch of 1857 (Northants. R.O., Hartshorne album xx, f. 33) shows a bldg. of uncertain date there; and windows with flat heads and central stone mullions in the 'hall'.

48. Lead roofs were not uncommon in 13th-cent. great hos.: L.F. Salzman, *Bldg. in Eng. down to 1540: a Documentary Hist*. (1952), 216, 262.

49. For a fuller acct. of Gt. Oxenbold see *T.S.A.S.* lxxii. 9–25. The interpretation there is interesting but fails to explain (i) why the doorway from the staircase into the upper floor, and the claimed original window in the E. wall, lack the quoins of all the certainly original openings; (ii) why the staircase from ground floor to basement—the only original communication betw. them—is partly blocked by the staircase from ground to upper floor; and (iii) why the original window in the S. wall is placed centrally betw. the E. wall and the suggested fireplace canopy at the W. end of that wall and would have been awkwardly sited in a solar.

50. In the North there was generally a timber-and-plaster firehood against an end wall of the hall; a fireplace in a lateral wall became common in great hos. in later yrs., as e.g. at Ludlow Castle.

51. P.R.O., C 139/98, no. 28; S.R.R. 279/131 (acct. of receiver of Caus 1399–1400).

52. Holdgate Castle (from which only a corner tower, encapsulated in the later Hall Fm., survives: *V.C.H. Salop*. x, pl. 10) may have been another early ground-floor-hall ho. but was probably later than Stokesay. Rob. Burnell bought the site *c*.1284 but died (1292) leaving only a capital messuage worth ½ mark p.a. and an 'old castle' worth nothing: *ibid*. 138–9; Eyton, iv. 68–9.

53. To these may perh. be added the Old Grammar Sch., Mill St., Ludlow, former town ho. of the Cheneys: D. Lloyd and P. Klein, *Ludlow: Historic Town in Words and Pictures* (1984), 87.

54. From a careful survey by the City of Heref. Arch. Unit: *Apley Castle, Salop.: Interim Rep*. (1989).

55. Pevsner, *Salop*. 215; R. Gough, *Antiquities & Memoirs of Par. of Myddle* (Shrews. 1875), 27–8. Substantial remains of the castle disappeared in the mid or later 17th cent. Gough (writing *c*.1700) remembered them, and the bldg. he took to be the hall (where the ct. leet had been held) was entered on the ground floor.

56. Above, p.106.

57. See illustration p.116.

58. T.H. Lloyd, *Eng. Wool Trade in Middle Ages* (1977), 76. Lawrence's father Nic., a Shrews. burgess (*Cal. Chart. R*. 1257–1300, 54), was a 'king's merchant' in 1278 (*Cal. Pat*. 1272–81, 256). Some of Lawrence's dealings with, and for, the Crown and magnates may be traced in the patent and close rolls 1279–94.

59. *T.S.A.S.* 4th ser. ix. 46–7.

60. Eyton, iv. 345; ix. 333.

61. *Cal. Inq. p.m*. v, pp. 124–5; vi, pp. 97–8.

62. At Wrickton and Walkerslow (in Stottesdon) and Ashfield (in Ditton Priors); the last, however, was illicitly alienated to a dau. *c*.1225: Eyton, ii. 65, 72; iv. 163 sqq.; *V.C.H. Salop*. x. 307.

63. Broseley (with members W. Bradeley and Arlescott) and Shushions and pt. of Ashley: *T.S.A.S.* i. 285-6; *V.C.H. Salop*. x. 224, 266, 268, 421; *V.C.H. Staffs*. iv. 97. All but Ashley (see next note) were held of Wenlock Priory.

64. Of whom Ashley (Staffs.) was held in 1263: *S.H.C*. N.S. xii. 251, 260–1.

65. Besides those mentioned in the preceding notes Billingsley and Silvington (Eyton, i. 65–6; iv. 381) and Water Eaton,

66. e.g. three days' ceremonial attendance on the prior of Wenlock at Christmas: *V.C.H. Salop*. x. 266, and sources cited.

67. To Alice Burnell, niece of Bp. Burnell (Eyton, ii. 134), builder of Acton Burnell Castle.

68. *Ibid*. iv. 167.

69. Whole background in *T.S.A.S.* lxxiii. 13–19.

70. For involvement in the Shrews. goings-on John le Strange of Knockin (presumably the future 2nd Ld.) suffered a huge £100 fine: *ibid*. 18. There is no reason to think his career would have been blighted, had he lived to have one.

71. Wal.'s grandson marr. a Mortimer of Chelmarsh; they were childless, and the est. passed to a Beysin marr. to Sir Rog. de Charlton: Eyton, iv. 168–71.

72. More of Ashley was bought *c*.1317. By 1344 the fam. also had Upper Millichope and land in Little Poston and Thonglands; there seems to be little in the suggestion that those estates came with Alice Burnell, so they too may have been bought, perh. from the de la Mares: cf. *T.S.A.S.* i. 295; *V.C.H. Salop*. x. 160, 168, 328.

73. *Cal. Pat*. 1327–30, 145.

74. *D.N.B.*; *T.S.A.S.* liii. 263.

75. Eyton, ix. 56.

76. *T.S.A.S.* liii. 263.

77. Neglecting appropriated rectories and gross values of collegiate or portionary chs., it was, at £12 p.a., among the best benefices in 1291, and at £48 p.a. was second only to Whitchurch by 1535: *Tax. Eccl*. (Rec. Com.), 248; *Valor Eccl*. (Rec. Com.), iii. 187.

78. Eyton, ix. 128; above, cap. v n.95. The rector of the 1320s was succ. by a Charlton (*ibid*. 129), and Charlton, where Ld. Charlton had been licensed to crenellate his ho. in 1316, was held of the abbey and was in a par. where the abbey's patronage could make a living available for a Charlton (*V.C.H. Salop*. xi. 312–13, 318).

79. *Cal. Pat*. 1307–13, 62.

80. Eyton, x. 68.

81. H. le Strange, *Le Strange Records* (1916), 308. 'Yeoman' would be the rank of his post in the king's household. John, the future Ld. Charlton of Powis, began his life at court as a yeoman in the household of the future Edw. II, eventually rising to become chamberlain of that king's house-hold: T.F. Tout, *Chapters in the Admin. Hist. of Medieval Eng*. ii (1937), 172, 198, 224–5; *Complete Peerage*, iii. 160.

82. The apparent entry into the bldg. is towards the centre rather than towards one end of a lateral wall, but the same happens at Barnard Castle (co. Dur.), where the original hall was rebuilt in the 14th cent. on an equally restricted site. It is, however, not certain that a single- rather than a two-storey bldg. is at issue at Whittington, for a short stretch of the internal masonry with blind arcading could be interpreted as that of an under-croft.

83. Eyton, xi. 39–41.

84. Usual identification corrected in *Trans. Hist. Soc. Lancs. and Ches*. cxxviii. 109, 111 (nn. 60–1); *Arch. Jnl*. cxxxviii. 47.

85. I use the term 'mere' knights in the sense in which H.R. Trevor-Roper used that of 'mere' gentry: *The Gentry 1540–1640* (Econ. Hist. Rev. Suppl. i, 1953), 22, 26 sqq.

86. *V.C.H. Salop*. iii. 1, 54.

87. See M.T. Clanchy, *From Memory to Written Record: Eng. 1066–1307* (1979), esp. 29–59; *Profit, Piety and the Professions in Late-Medieval Eng*. ed. M. Hicks (1990), 91–102.

88. Above, p.104.

89. Eyton, i. 205; ix. 313-14.

90. *Ibid*. i. 206; *T.S.A.S.* lxxi. 25; *V.C.H. Salop*. iii. 28.

91. Eyton, ix. 314-20.

92. *Cal. Pat*. 1327–30, 145.

93. Eyton, i. 224–9.

94. *Ibid*. xi. 42; *V.C.H. Salop*. xi. 262–3, 313.

95. B. Ross, 'Accts. of Talbot Household at Blakemere 1394–1425' (Australian Nat. Univ., Canberra, M.A. thesis, 1970), ii. 21 (copy in S.R.R. 2683).

96. P.R.O., C 139/98, no. 28; S.R.R. 279/131 (acct. of receiver of Caus 1399–1400).

97. *V.C.H. Salop*. iii. 235; viii. 108.

98. C. Richmond, 'Religion and the 15th Cent. Gentleman', *The Church, Politics and Patronage in the 15th Cent*. ed. R.B. Dobson (Glouc. 1984), 198–9.

99. Hen. III maintained at least 50 chaps. in his various hos.: *Hist. King's Wks*. ed. H.M. Colvin, i (1963), 124.

100. For Gt. Oxenbold see above, p.109 and n.47, for Madeley Ct. *V.C.H.*

Salop. xi. 37; Moffett, 'Madeley Ct.'

101. S.E. of the present ch. (E.A. Paddock, *Meole Brace through the Centuries* (1935), p. [4]), the medieval ch. (demolished 1799) was a stone's throw from the castle (in Meole Brace Hall grounds: SA 70) whose tower and other 'very poor' bldgs. belonged to the nobleman Geo. de Cantelou in 1273: *Cal. Inq. p.m.* ii, p. 19. In the 11th and 12th cents. the Mortimers of Wigmore had held the man. in chief: Eyton, vi. 350–1.

102. J.F.A. Mason, *The Boro. of Bridgnorth 1157–1957* (Bridgnorth, 1957), 47.

103. S.R.R. 6001/372/1, pp.16, 82.

104. Above, p.56 and n.101, for the connection between the Sprenchoses and Longnor ch.

105. S.R.R. 6001/200, p.11. So little of the Franciscan friary remains that identification is more of a guess than usual. Owen considered that this was probably the refectory: *Ancient and Present State of Shrews*. 304.

106. It long stood isolated from the ch. by Telford's Holyhead road, forlorn amid squalid surroundings.

107. S.R.R. 6001/198, p.459; *V.C.H. Salop.* ii, frontispiece.

108. Bps. too were building and improving their residences on a vast scale at that time: *Wealth and Power in Tudor Eng.* ed. E.W. Ives (1978), 152 sqq.

109. It is not certain that this was the prior's hall or that the infirmary occupied the rooms N. of it, but these long established names remain the handiest labels.

110. That the present wooden post on the ground floor below the site of the hearth is not a copy of an original post but a symbolic substitute for a stone pillar is shown by the positions of the splices in the beams carrying the 1st floor. The practice was widespread, occurring e.g. in Bolton Castle, Wensleydale, and several smaller hos. in Kent: E.W. Parkin, 'Lake Ho., Eastwell', *Arch. Cant.* lxxxiii. 151–61; idem, 'The Old Rectory of St. Alphege, Cant.' *ibid.* lxxxiv. 201–12.

111. They are in principle similar to the famous staircase at Chambord (Loir-et-Cher) but of course very much less spacious. Interlocking staircases had been known since the early 14th cent.: *Eng. Archit. Public and Private*, ed. J. Bold and E. Chaney (1993), 1–9.

112. The upper gallery is now reached from the ground floor by a vice in the N. and E. ranges. The original entry may have been from the S. range through the doorway at the S. end of the gallery, where the elaborate fenestration of the W. front of the E. range is prolonged beyond the return of the S. wall of the range. A modern staircase occupies the site.

113. Above, p.80.

114. External galleries were common enough in inns and in ranges of lodgings but never given so elaborate an architectural mask.

115. Inf. from Arrol & Snell, architects in charge of the fabric.

116. Above, n.111.

117. The artist who drew Aston Eyre Hall in 1789 called it a 'priory': Bodl. MS. Top. Salop. c. 2, f. 73.

118. *Itin.* ed. Toulmin Smith, v. 15.

119. *Cal. Pat.* 1381–5, 31; 1391–6, 500.

120. A floor was inserted 1534 x 1568. The hall is near the ch. and may have been a court ho.: *V.A.* xxvii. 105–6.

121. S.R.R. 552/1/1201; P.R.O., C 139/98, no. 28.

122. At Acton Burnell, Apley, Aston Botterell, Aston Eyre, Chelmarsh, Edgmond, Holdgate, Madeley, Gt. Oxenbold, Silvington, Stokesay, and Whitton.

123. At Charlton, Dawley, Myddle, and Gt. Wytheford. Licences to crenellate issued in 1308, 1316, and 1327: *V.C.H. Salop.* xi. 113, 313; above, pp.110–1.

124. Above, p.111.

125. S.R.R., QE/5/2/2, 12 Aug. 1806.

126. At Apley Castle: *V.C.H. Salop.* xi. 216–7.

127. As seems to have happened, in somewhat similar circumstances, at Stokesay Castle: above, pp.97–9.

128. *V.C.H. Salop.* iii. 62–3, 235–6. The Burleys had prospered in royal service since the early 14th cent.: *T.S.A.S.* lvi. 264.

129. *V.C.H. Salop.* iii. 235.

130. His licence to crenellate (1 Sept. 1394) was perh. a reward for going to Irel. on the king's service: *Cal. Pat.* 1391–6, 481.

Chapter VIII

1. Much of this cap. is based on inf. from, and discussions with, Mrs. M. Moran, and I am more than grateful for her ever ready help. She is not, of course, to be held responsible for all the opinions expressed here.

2. i.e. the areas covered in *V.C.H. Salop.* viii, x–xi: see *ibid.* x, p.xvi.

3. *Ibid.* viii. 171–4, 304, 306.

4. S.R.R. 6000/2796.

5. The dendrochronological date of a bldg. is not certainly correct but is statistically very probably so.

6. M. Wood, *The Eng. Medieval Ho.* (1968), 35–6.

7. Above, pp.104-5, 107

8. S. Pearson, *Medieval Hos. of Kent: An Historical Analysis* (1994), 151; C. Giles, *Rural Hos. of W. Yorks. 1400–1830* (1986), 31.

9. A view thoughtlessly adopted in E. Mercer, *Eng. Vernacular Hos.: a study of traditional farmhos. and cottages* (1975), 100.

10. The notion subconsciously buttressed by the odd use of the term 'quasi-aisled' for a bldg. without aisles: see e.g. *ibid.* 10.

11. *Arch. Jnl.* cxxvi. 176, 187–8; *V.A.* xii. 39; xiv. 62.

12. 'In aula sint postes debitis intersticiis distincti' (*De Utensilibus*); cf. above, pp.104-5.

13. Above, pp.94, 96.

14. J. Blair, 'Hall and Chamber: Eng. Domestic Planning 1000–1250', *Manorial Domestic Bldgs. in Eng. and N. France*, ed. G. Meirion-Jones and M. Jones (1993), 14.

15. *V.A.* xx. 41.

16. Wood, *Eng. Medieval Ho.* 139.

17. Below, p.133.

18. *T.S.A.S.* lxvii. 79–92.

19. *Timber Bldg. in Brit.* (1985), 95, 120, 122.

20. *T.S.A.S.* lvi. 155–6; lxv. 41–4.

21. *V.A.* i. 7–11; Pearson, *Medieval Hos. of Kent,* 25–6, 151.

22. *V.A.* xxv. 31.

23. Pearson, *op. cit.* 63–4.

24. Eyton, xi. 220. Wm. of Plowden, probably Phil.'s uncle, was second on the jury list.

25. *Ibid.* i. 155–6.

26. *Ibid.* iv. 119.

27. *Ibid.* ix. 268.

28. *Ibid.* i. 140–4; *V.C.H. Salop.* iii. 81; S.R.R. 6001/2791, pp. 446, 450; J. B. Blakeway, *Sheriffs of Salop.* (Shrews. 1831), 15, 69. The fam.'s officially recorded lineage began with Hugh's shrievalty: *Visit. Salop. 1623* i (Harl. Soc. xxviii), 157.

29. *Visit. Salop. 1623*, i. 64, 277.

30. *V.A.* i. 7–11.

31. P. Smith, *Hos. of the Welsh Countryside: a study in historical geography* (1988), 401.

32. R.R. Davies, *Lordship and Society in Marches of Wales* (1978), 203–4.

33. e.g. Upper Ho., Llanbedr Painscastle, built probably after 1410 and possibly for the steward of the earls of Warwick: V.A.G. *Spring Conf.: 1996 Radnors.* 13.

34. Pearson, *Medieval Hos. of Kent*, 33.

35. *Arch. Jnl.* clxii. 352.

36. M.E. Speight, *The Gt. Ho. 1270–1980* (Ludlow Research Paper iv, 1980). Mr. Alan Snell also suggests the bldg. (part of Berrington Ho.) betw. 2–3 St. Alkmund's Sq. and 13–15 St. Mary's St., Shrews.

37. The painting has been dated 1450 x 1520: letter from D. Park (Courtauld Inst.) to Arrol & Snell, architects. For a similar example in Suff. see Mercer, *Eng. Vernacular Hos.* 203, pl. 13.

38. Brewho., oven, malt kiln and mill: sources in next note. This is also Mr. Snell's view.

39. *T.S.A.S.* 2nd ser. xii. 196–7; lxxv. 60–2, 66. The 2nd-floor bays in Hen. Tudor Ho. were, and one is, open to the roof (inf. from Arrol & Snell, architects of the 1977–8 restoration; J.T. Smith, 'Shrews.: Topog. and Domestic Archit. to middle 17th cent.' (Birm. Univ. M.A. thesis, 1953), 281), and the principal rm. on the floor below has been seen as a 1st-floor hall (Smith, *op. cit.* 280–3; but cf. above,p.105). On the W. side of Barrack Passage the Clements also had, or acquired, a ground-floor open hall—reserved for Nic.'s widow in 1455; 18th-cent. bricking (*T.S.A.S.* lxxv. 60, 69) obscures its original wall structure, but Mr. Snell has found evidence to suggest box-framing, put up after Hen. Tudor Ho.

40. D. Lloyd and M. Moran, *The Corner Shop* (Ludlow Research Paper ii [1978]).

41. Mrs. Sylvia Coleman's survey of Bury St. Edmunds, together with documentary research by D. P. Dymond, shows that from the 1460s many hos. there were built without open halls: letter from Mrs. Coleman 25 July 1994; *Antiquaries Jnl.* lxxviii. 267–87.

42. And the yard betw. 15 Dogpole and 15 St. Mary's St. probably represents part of the courtyard of Berrington Ho.: H.E. Forrest, *Old Hos. of Shrews.* (Shrews. 1935), 74.

43. *V.C.H. Salop.* iii. 235; viii. 108–9.

44. *Ibid.* iii. 63–4. Thos. Horde may have built the very large and much altered Hoards Pk., Astley Abbots.

45. *Ibid.* x. 59; *Visit. Salop. 1623*, ii (Harl. Soc. xxix), 323; J.B. Blakeway, *Sheriffs of Salop.* (Shrews. 1832), 75.

46. *V.C.H. Salop.* viii. 43, 132, 135, 277. Jennings of Walleybourne is in *Visit. Salop. 1623*, i. 277–8.

47. S.R.R. 6001/7522, m. 2.
48. *T.S.A.S.* 2nd ser. iv. 308.
49. Eyton, iv. 56.
50. *Ibid*. 180–2.
51. It is noticeable how few claimants, even successful ones, could prove their ancestry before the 15th cent. See e.g. above, n.28.
52. B.L. Eg. MS. 3712, f. 54v.; S.R.R. 6000/1796.
53. The cruck couple at 3 Upton Magna (*1269) is either re-used or in a rebuilt structure. It antedates the earliest known base cruck in the county by a generation and all other surviving crucks there by more than 100 yrs. It is perh. to be seen as a relic of that stage in gentry housing which preceded base crucks.
54. *T.S.A.S.* lxv. 46, 48.
55. Mercer, *Eng. Vernacular Hos*. 196.
56. V.A.G. *Salop. 1982* [conf. programme 14–16 Apr.], 4, 19.
57. *Ibid*. 24.
58. *T.S.A.S.* lvi. 149–57.
59. *Ibid*. lxiii. 45–9.
60. V.A.G. *Salop. 1982*, 3. The bldg. was formerly known as the Small Ho. to distinguish it from the big ho.—Condover Hall.
61. *Ibid*. 28.
62. S.R.R. 3763/78/4/11.
63. Mercer, *Eng. Vernacular Hos*. 196.
64. *V.C.H. Salop*. viii. 304.
65. *T.S.A.S.* lxiii. 16.
66. At Spoad Fm., Newcastle, the cruck wing is of inferior construction and may have housed animals.
67. Mercer, *Eng. Vernacular Hos*. 7, 174 (mon. 209), 178 (mon. 230), 209–10 (mons. 411, 418), 213 (mon. 434).
68. Below, pp.135-7, 151, 153-4.
69. *Arch. Jnl*. cxlii. 342–3.
70. Smith, *Hos. of Welsh Countryside*, 107.
71. S.R.R. 6000/2796.
72. S.R.R., LB/5/2/551.
73. *V.C.H. Salop*. viii. 33.
74. B.L. Eg. MS. 3712, f. 54v.
75. *V.C.H. Salop*. viii. 33, 37, 48, 67.
76. *Ibid*. 36, 44, 46.
77. *Ibid*. 206, 304.
78. *Ibid*. 171, 174.
79. S.R.R. 6000/1796.
80. *V.C.H. Salop*. iv. 34.
81. *Ibid*. 108.
82. Davies, *Lordship and Society*, 395.
83. V.A.G. *Spring Conf. 5–9 Apr. 1994: Bucks*. 32.
84. M.T. Clanchy, *From Memory to Written Record: Eng. 1066–1307* (1979), 34–5, 259; *V.C.H. Salop*. IV. 108; x. 368, 371, 376; Dept. of Environment, *List of Bldgs. of Special Archit. or Hist. Interest: R.D. of Bridgnorth* (1974), 212-15, 218-20. I am grateful to Mr. Edward Roberts (whose study of Hants hos. 1250–1700 illuminates these matters) for his observations on the complexities of peasant holdings and the sparse documentation of their hos. He also points to the problems of defining peasants and how Prof. Dyer's definition of them (as those, distinct from rentiers, who earned a living working rented land) complicates the 15th-cent. Hants scene. Not only the Hants scene. The obscure John Broadstone may have lorded it in his wife's Hall in Larden, but a mile away at Brockton, where he rented demesne, how distinct was he from upper peasants?
85. V.A.G. *Spring Conf. 1994: Bucks*. 32–3.
86. C. Dyer, *Standards of Living in Middle Ages* (1989), 167.
87. *V.C.H. Salop*. iv. 112.
88. S.R.R. 552/1/39. *Domus*, in the phrase *longa domus*, did not mean 'house' (*V.A*. iii. 9–10), but *domus* by itself can hardly mean anything else.
89. In 1301 all 15 Bicton tenants had been bondmen, 10 of them holding a messuage and 1/2 virgate each, each of the others a messuage and 5–8 a. One 1/2-virgater owed 2s. rent, but the rest paid between 4s. and 4s. 5d.: *Two Est. Surveys of the Fitzalan Earls of Arundel* (Suss. Rec. Soc. lxvii), 59. By 1411 some consolidation of holdings (cf. *V.C.H. Salop*. iv. 109) into whole virgates may be presumed, while rent probably did not increase (so is here assumed to have approached 10s. a virgate *c*.1411). Indeed, although a generation of landlords had enjoyed some recovery of prosperity in the late 14th cent., that may have been vitiated on the Border by Glyn Dwr's war (*ibid*. 76–7), and between 1301 and 1404 (probably after 1350) the lord's revenues from Clun appear to have fallen, perh. by 10 per cent or more: cf. *Two Est. Surveys*, 65; S.R.R. 552/1/1164–5; the latter sources (fragile, but kindly made available by

Mr. A.J. Davidson) show the trend in the lordship as a whole, though they are less detailed than the former, and probable bailiwick changes prevent local comparisons. Erratically fluctuating 14th-cent. prices, settling into a steadier rise from the 1390s (E.H. Phelps Brown and S.V. Hopkins, 'Seven Cents. of Prices', *Economica*, N.S. xxiii. 311), may also have reduced tenants' ability to pay more rent.
90. If the men of 1411 held no more than the men of 1301, their hos. must have been even cheaper than is here suggested.
91. If rent stability (cf. *V.C.H. Salop*. iv. 110–11) is conceded, any assumption that the 1411 Bicton rebates covered bldg. costs of £2–£3 for 3-bay hos. would seem to imply both a much greater consolidation of peasant holdings than is warranted by known examples (*ibid*. 107, 109) and also many more virgates at Bicton in 1411 than had existed in 1301.
92. *T.S.A.S.* 3rd ser. x. 69–70. In contrast, in 1552–3 2s. 6d. was paid for felling and squaring 70 trees for a hunting lodge in Oakly Pk.: P.R.O., E 101/47, no. 24.
93. N. Mayhew, *Sterling: The Hist. of a Currency* (2000), 39 sqq., 281.
94. Dyer, *Standards of Living*, 166.
95. *Cart. of Haughmond Abbey*, ed. U. Rees (1985), nos. 161, 182, 185–6, 300, 488, 581, 594, 783, 830–1, 1134, 1176, 1307.
96. Dr. N.W. Alcock's invaluable indexes of all dendrochronological dates (*V.A*. xviii; xxix), and subsequent lists in vols. xxx–xxxi, allow the relevant inf. to be found easily and quickly.
97. See e.g. J. Grenville, *Medieval Housing* (1997), 123–34.
98. R. Leach, 'The symbolic hall: Historical Context and Merchant Culture in the early modern City', *V.A*. xxxi. 1–10 (esp. pp.3–7).
99. Pearson, *Medieval Hos. of Kent*, 63–4.
100. The impression given in Grenville, *op.cit*. 130, that the holding was a peasant yardland, is misleading. It was a freehold and was held at all relevant times by men holding other properties also. An earlier owner, and a possible builder, may have been a sgt., and a later owner was a king's sgt. at arms: *V.A*. xvii. 51.
101. That static concept of a changeless Middle Ages is all too common. Grenville, *op.cit*. 124–33, e.g. claims peasant origins for several 13th- and 14th-cent. bldgs. because they have cruck trusses of those dates. It is like arguing that motor cars were owned by ordinary men in 1900 because ordinary men owned them in 2000.
102. I am grateful to Mr. J.W. Tonkin and Miss Sarah Pearson for this inf.
103. C.R.J. Currie, 'Larger Medieval Hos. in Vale of White Horse', *Oxoniensia*, lvii. 95.
104. *V.C.H. Salop*. iii. 54, 234–6; iv. 78–9, 103, 129.
105. *Arch. Jnl*. cxlii. 276–9.
106. *Wealth and Power in Tudor Eng*. ed. E.W. Ives *et al*. (1978), 148–50. The bp. of Heref.'s residence at Lydbury North (*Woolhope Trans*. xlii. 64) was almost certainly Bp.'s Castle. In the mid 15th cent. the bp. of Coventry and Lichfield, claiming poverty, was demolishing his residences in outlying parts of his dioc., including Prees, where a cruck farmho. of *1553–4 occupies the site: *V.C.H. Staffs*. iii. 22–3; *V.A*. xxvi. 71. The bp. of St. Asaph's residence in St. Martin's par., said to have been burnt down (1400 x 1410) by Glyn Dwr, was rebuilt later that cent. as a cruck farmho. and doubtless let: W. Cathrall, *Hist. of Oswestry* (1855), 273; [A. Menuge], *Er'w'r Esgob* (R.C.H.M.E. Historic Bldg. Rep., Swindon, 1995), 1–2, 5.
107. M. Thompson, *Medieval Bps.' Hos. in Eng. and Wales* (1998), 103, 118, 120, 173–4, 177–8, 186–7.
108. *V.C.H. Salop*. iii. 39.
109. *Ibid*. 54.
110. Davies, *Lordship and Society*, 191–3.
111. *Arch. Jnl*. cxlii. 276–9.
112. A. Emery, *Greater Medieval Hos. of Eng. and Wales*, i (1996), 179.
113. H. Ramm *et al.*, *Shielings and Bastles* (R.C.H.M.E. 1970), 61–95.

Chapter IX

1. In Scotland, and perhaps in N. England, old traditions may have endured longer. In 'Troilus and Creseide', written at the end of the 15th cent., Creseide is summoned from a chamber to the hall for 'supper': *Poems and Fables of Rob. Henryson*, ed. H.H. Wood (1958), 117.
2. *V.A*. xxiii. 58–9.
3. *Ibid*. xxvi. 69, 71. The modern 'WL 1593' over the doorway is not known to replace an earlier inscription there: *T.S.A.S.* viii. 197. In the 1730s a bedhead at Habberley was inscribed 'WL 1593': Mytton Papers, iv. 698. The date has probably been transferred from bed to doorway by folk memory or proprietorial pride.
4. For a comparable example at Hundon (Suff.) see E. Mercer, *Eng. Vernacular. Hos.: a study of traditional farmhos. and cottages* (1975), 203, pl. 7.
5. *V.A*. xxv. 31.
6. Above, p.106.

7. Above, cap. VIII n.41.
8. It was introduced into some hos. built originally with a one-storey hall, e.g. Oakwell Hall, Gomersal, and Ham Ho. (Surr.): C. Giles, *Rural Hos. of W. Yorks. 1400–1830* (1986), 197; *Ham Ho.* (H.M.S.O. 1976), 10.
9. S.R.R. 279/131 (receiver's acct. 1399–1400).
10. M. Johnson, *Housing Culture* (1993), caps. 6, 10. Whether a rise in the status of women played much part, except in upper-class circles, is doubtful; among those who had to work for their living it had long been recognized that the grey mare was often the better horse.
11. Following Maine: Sir F. Pollock and F.W. Maitland, *Hist. Eng. Law* (2nd edn.), ii. 232–3.
12. *Econ. Hist. Rev.* xlvi. 658–78.
13. By the early 16th cent. husbandry leases for terms of yrs. had full legal protection and some of the distinction between copyhold and freehold had been eroded: J.H. Baker, *Intro. to Eng. Legal Hist.* (3rd edn.), 339–41, 349–50. From the 14th cent. Haughmond abbey was granting leases for life and for 20, 60, 80, and 91 yrs.: *Cart. of Haughmond Abbey*, ed. U. Rees (1975), nos. 161, 182, 185–6, 594, 783, 830–1, 1176. Shrews. Abbey, Wenlock Priory, and the FitzAlans were also leasing demesnes: *V.C.H. Salop.* iv. 32.
14. The medieval recognition of the obligations of ownership towards the 'family' is discussed in *Family and Inheritance*, ed. J. Goody *et al.* (1976), 328–60.
15. R.W. Hoyle, 'Taxation and the Mid-Tudor Crisis', *Econ. Hist. Rev.* li. 649–75.
16. S.T. Bindoff, *Tudor Eng.* (1955), 114–21; N. Mayhew, *Sterling: The Hist. of a Currency* (2000), cap. 2 (esp. p.47).
17. And, to survive, even established landlords 'hacked their way through to solvency' by putting their affairs on a 'strictly commercial basis': Bindoff, *op.cit.* 121.
18. The present internal flight of steps from the hall to the basement is an alteration.
19. e.g. J.R. Lander, *Wars of the Roses* (1990), 19–20.
20. G. Goodman, *Ct. of Jas. I*, ed. J. Brewer (1839), i. 174.
21. 'On Building' first appeared in the 1625 edn. of Bacon's *Essays* and was probably written not long before.
22. Hardy was as good a witness to rustic sentiment in Victorian Dorset as anyone could be.
23. *V.C.H. Salop.* iv. 254.
24. *Reliquiae Wottonianae* (1651), 261. Bacon, more pragmatic, allowed it in some circumstances.
25. *T.S.A.S.* lxvi. 90–6.
26. F. Stackhouse Acton, *Castles and Old Mansions of Salop.* (Shrews. 1868) 31; *Country Life*, 26 May 1917. Plaish may not have been unique in its day for there is some evidence for an open hall of similar date at Morville: S.R.R. 7069, Morville.
27. *V.C.H. Salop.* x. 60.
28. The present doorway is an insertion in the original partition.
29. Below, p.158 and cap. XI n.5.
30. And probably at Little Wenlock Manor: H.E. Forrest, *The Old Hos. of Wenlock and Wenlock Edge* (Shrews. 1915), facing p.112.
31. H.E. Forrest, *Some Old Salop. Hos. and their Owners* (Shrews. 1924), 61–2; S.R.R. 7069, Larden.
32. *T.S.A.S.* lxv. 56–63.
33. For them see *T.S.A.S.* 2nd ser. vii. 361–80; Leland, *Itin.* ed. Toulmin Smith, iii. 66.
34. The ho. has been much altered (S. Leighton, *Salop. Houses* (1901), 3), but the stages in the development of the courtyard front are clear.
35. *Country Life*, 30 May (pp.1426–31), 6 June (pp.1510–13) 1968.
36. *T.S.A.S.* 4th ser. iii, p. xv; Soc. of Archit. Historians of Gt. Brit. *Conf. Programme 1988*, 23–5. The date of the ho. is less clear than the Corbet connection.
37. R.K. Morriss and R. Shoesmith, *Apley Castle* (City of Heref. Arch. Unit, 1989).
38. The evidence for a late 16th-cent. rebuild is the painting of 1756 in the ho.: cf. *Country Life*, 23 June 1977, p.1736.
39. The entrance tower at the hall's lower end was to an extent balanced by a 2-storey bay window at the upper end, and by the 1730s a central door (replacing the side entrance via the tower porch) enhanced the hall range's symmetry. Later, perh. *c.*1769, the bay window was removed (the masonry there is in smaller more regular pieces than elsewhere), leaving the central doorway as focus of symmetry. By 1834 the tower-porch entrance was restored (S.R.R. 6001/201, f.68) and the central door had evidently gone. This modifies the acct. in *V.C.H. Salop.* x. 370–1, which fails to notice that the 'undated' drawing in S.R.R. 6001/3065 (no.32) is the source of the '*c.*1730' sketch (reproduced as fig.37 in *V.C.H. loc. cit.*) in Mytton Papers, v.1187; the sketch ought to

40. N.M.R. archives, Whixall.
41. The date, with the Corfields' initials, is on panelling in the hall. The ho. is of several builds and '1659' probably refers to the bldg., or rebldg., in stone of the hall and parlour.
42. *V.C.H. Salop.* xi. 188.
43. Its length is less than 50ft. and the bays less than 6ft. wide internally.
44. *V.C.H. Salop.* x. 32.
45. R. Gough, *Antiquities and Memoirs of the Par. of Myddle* (Shrews. 1875), 101.
46. *V.C.H. Salop.* viii. 41–2.
47. Now demolished. Illustr. in Forrest, *Old Salop. Hos.* 17; cf. Loton Hall MSS., mid 19th-cent. plan.
48. N.M.R. archives.
49. At Lutwyche the side wall of a projection at the rear retains a slit window.
50. There are remains of a 16th-cent. ho. in the cellars.
51. Stackhouse Acton, *Castles and Old Mansions*, 58.
52. The top floor at Whitehall, Shrews., was originally divided into two rooms running the whole length of the ho., one of which may have been used as a gallery.
53. *T.S.A.S.* lxv. 67.
54. *Ibid.* 3rd ser. iv, p.xix.
55. 'Double-pile' structures of two ranges built side by side were of course nothing new in the 16th cent.: apart from urban examples, Middleham Castle (Yorks. N.R.) assumed that form in the 13th cent. and Acton Burnell (above, pp.99-101) was built in the late 13th. Here, however, the term is used in the sense given in the text and with reference to a limited period.
56. Bachegraig (Flints.) of 1567, built around a central chimney stack, was more an attempt at a Palladian villa than a double-pile plan and was an import from the Netherlands by Gresham's agent in Antwerp. Its form, but not its style, found several imitations in Wales (P. Smith, *Houses of the Welsh Countryside* (1988), 228, 240–1) and in Oswestry at the Hayes, which is probably earlier than the 1651 date upon an over mantel; a description and plan of the house is in *T.S.A.S.* lvi. 295–307.
57. Prince's career is set out in Bill Champion, *Everyday Life in Tudor Shrews.* (Shrews. 1994), 66–7, 96–7.
58. Penkridge is dated 1590 (on the gable), Whitley 1667 (on the staircase).
59. West Coppice (now gone), Buildwas, probably of *c.*1600, seems to have been another example.
60. *The Archit. of Sir Rog. Pratt*, ed. R. T. Gunter (1928), 24–33; T. Fuller, *The Holy State* (Cambridge, 1648), bk. iii, cap. 7, maxim 7.
61. *Country Life*, 13 (pp.328–31) and 20 (pp.392–6) Feb. 1964.
62. Leighton, 'Sketches', ii. The hall is now divided by a transverse wall.
63. Soc. of Archit. Historians of Gt. Brit. *Conf. Programme 1988*, 46–7; S.R.R. 7069.
64. O. Hill and J. Lees-Milne, *Eng. Country Hos.: Baroque* (1970), 270.
65. *Country Life*, 3 (pp.92–8) and 10 (pp.112–17) Aug. 1918.
66. Below, p.180.
67. The staircase at Halston is a remarkably good copy, made in the 1920s, of a late 17th-cent. one: craftsman's accts. in owner's possession. The hall has been reduced in size, probably in 1849: W. Cathrall, *Hist. of Oswestry* (Oswestry, 1855), 253.
68. G.E. Mingay, *Eng. Landed Society in the 18th Cent.* (1963), 84–5.

Chapter X

1. *T.S.A.S.* lxiii. 15.
2. *V.A.* xxiv. 58.
3. *Ibid.* 59.
4. *Ibid.* xxv. 33.
5. Dates on the bldgs.
6. In Yorks., by contrast, lobby-entrance hos. on a large scale were sometimes built by gentry fams.: C. Giles, *Rural Hos. of W. Yorks. 1400–1830* (1986), 67 (fig.28), 72 (fig.31), 80, 192 (no.30), 196 (no.51), 201 (no.93).
7. An exception is Tyr-y-Coed, Melverley.
8. For this and the next para, the evidence of bldgs. themselves can sometimes be supplemented from N.M.R. archives.
9. Above, p.105.
10. For inf. and discussion about Westbury I am indebted to Miss Carole Ryan.
11. P. Smith, *Hos. of the Welsh Countryside: a study in historical geography* (1988), 162.
12. R.C.H.M.E. *Monuments Threatened or Destroyed* (1963), 54.
13. E. Mercer, *Eng. Vernacular Hos.: a study of traditional farmhos. and cottages* (1975), 195; *T.S.A.S.* lxiv. 75.

14. Inf. (1983) from the occupier since 1967.
15. *V.C.H. Salop.* viii. 253.
16. D.C.G. Davies, 'Historic Farmstead and Farmho. Types in the Salop. Region' (Manchester Univ. M.A. thesis, 1952), cap. 6 and App. 5a.
17. For Fulway Cottage and Golding Hall see *V.A.* xxv. 33.
18. *Ibid.*; V.A.G. *Shropshire 1982* [conf. programme 14–16 Apr.], 11.
19. *V.A.* xxv. 33.
20. Date on dormer window inserted into former hall.
21. Exceptions are Eye Fm., Leighton, of 2¹/₂ storeys in one range, and nos. 29–30 Kempton, of 2 storeys on a **T** plan.
22. *V.C.H. Salop.* iv. 150–2.
23. Descr. of the ho., by the then occupiers, as it was *c.*1970. I am grateful to Mrs. P. Woodward for this inf.
24. Some of them were the homes of local clergy. Cardeston rectory was a 3-bay 1¹/₂-storey lobby-entrance ho. (Loton Hall, Lady Leighton's album, nos. 24–5, 27, 32); that at Preston upon the Weald Moors was a baffle-entry ho. (*V.C.H. Salop.* xi. 181).
25. The development into a fully capitalist agric. was not inevitable. It did not e.g. occur in New Eng. or some other northern states of the U.S.A.: T.J. Byres, *Capitalism from Above and Capitalism from Below: an essay in comparative political economy* (1996), 342–436.
26. *T.S.A.S.* lii. 59; *V.C.H. Salop.* viii. 18, 90, 112, 166.
27. *V.C.H. Salop.* viii. 62, 64–5.
28. *Ibid.* 262, 276.
29. Date on parlour range.
30. *Salop. N. & Q.* 2nd ser. iii. 47.
31. At Sambrook, at Cross Ho., Longden, and at High Ercall a central entrance in the front wall and a corridor from front to back has been contrived out of one of the parlours.
32. The eccentricity of a chimney stack at each corner of the ho. had occurred earlier at Wharton Ct.: R.C.H.M.E. *Inv. of Historical Monuments in Herefs.* iii (1934), 127–8.
33. M. Wheat, *A story about Sambrook Par.* (Newport, 1955), 9–11.
34. *V.A.* xxv. 33; date plaque on brick wing.

Chapter XI
1. Above, p.140 and n.39.
2. *T.S.A.S.* lxv. 56–63.
3. A similar trick was played at Chastleton (Oxon.) and Burton Agnes (Yorks. E.R.). At Ludstone it was later found intolerable, and some time after *c.*1840, probably in the early 1870s, a central entrance was contrived on the original site of the bow window; the original arrangement was reverted to 1892 x 1952, perh. after 1910: cf. S.R.R., uncat. drawing (1807); *T.S.A.S.* 2nd ser. i, p.xv; Leach, *Co. Seats of Salop.* (Shrews. 1891), pl. facing p.175; Leighton, 'Sketches', ii; *Country Life*, 11 (pp.92 (figs.1–2), 95) and 18 (p.155) Jan. 1952.
4. Camden, *Britannia*, ed. P. Holland (1610), 594.
5. *Arch. Jnl.* cxxxviii. 46. But 'after the Italian model' came into Camden's text only in 1610 with the publication of Holland's transl.: *T.S.A.S.* lxx. 187.
6. In 1791 the severely classical entrance front of Aldenham Hall had a doorway flanked by Ionic columns and with two heraldic lions upon a pediment: *Country Life*, 23 June 1977, p.1735.
7. *T.S.A.S.* 4th ser. iv. 210. *V.C.H. Salop.* viii. 309, interprets the 'walke' as a bldg. below the castle. The earliest known occurrence is the brick chimney stack at the King's Head, Mardol, Shrews., with an early 15th-cent. painting upon it.
8. *T.S.A.S.* lxvi. 90–6.
9. There were similar shafts at the now demolished Wootton (in Onibury): F. Stackhouse Acton, *Castles & Old Mansions of Salop.* (Shrews. 1868), facing p.55. The brick chimney stacks, not shafts, on the school and school ho. at Moreton Say, of 1871, match any of these—with bold diamond patterning recessed into the brickwork from the ground to the gable apex.
10. S.R.R. 6001/372/2, pp. 14, 14b.
11. These may be due to the Dutch brickmakers brought to nearby Kyre Pk. (Worcs.) in the early or mid 17th cent.: *T.S.A.S.* xliv. 86–91.
12. There is a rural example just over the county boundary at Bleathwood (in Little Heref.).
13. For the last two see Bodl. MS. Blakeway 16, notes betw. pp.6-7; R.K. Morriss and R. Little, *The Park Inn: 37–38 Abbey Foregate, Shrews.* (Mercian Heritage ser. ci; Bromlow, 2000). I am grateful to Mr. W. A. Champion for the first source and for the identification of the two hos. being built in 1665 at 'St. Christopher's Corner'.
14. S.R.R. 1671/1.
15. *Arch. Jnl.* cxxxviii. 20.
16. That may be connected with the failure of Salopians to get themselves lucrative offices by royal favour: G.E. Aylmer, *The King's Servants*

1625–42 (1974), 268.
17. The date is above the entrance to the former hall. The present ho. incorporates an earlier bldg. The suggestion that an original **H** plan ho. had the space between the wings filled in (*Country Life*, 18 Oct. 1946, p.716) appears to be incompatible with the siting of the chimney stacks and the disposition of the walling.
18. *Arch. Jnl.* cxxxviii. 356; S.R.R. 6001/3066, no. 37. The present 'Dutch gable' effect is of the mid 19th cent.
19. The oft cited date of 1694 rests upon a MS. acct. of 1821 (W. Cathrall, *Hist. of Oswestry* (1855), 250), which probably misinterprets a statement of 1770. The pediment may be a later addition.
20. The cornice at Aldenham, probably late 17th-cent., is noticeably unskilful.
21. *T.S.A.S.* lv. 56–63; lxiv. 119–20.
22. H.E. Forrest, *Old Hos. of Shrews.: their hist. and associations* (Shrews. 1912), 80–1; S.R.R., drawings of Gibbon's Mansion by A.W. Ward 1944 (D71.4 v.f.).
23. Acton, *Castles & Old Mansions*, 35; *Country Life*, 4 Mar. 1905, pp.306–7, 310, 312.
24. The date is on the porch, but that appears to be more or less contemporary with the main range.
25. *T.S.A.S.* lxv. 62.
26. The date is on the W. gable.
27. Acton, *Castles & Old Mansions*, 29.
28. The Feathers has been much altered and restored. The present street front is as it was in 1886 (*Brit. Architect*, 25 Feb. 1887), but in 1846 it was without the balconies and in 1822 the doorway was at the left end of the elevation (D. Lloyd and P. Klein, *Ludlow: Historic Town in Words and Pictures* (Chichester, 1984), 91).
29. Much illustr.: e.g. Wm. Twopenny's drawing (1837) in B.L. Add. MS. 36378, Hen. Blunt's lithograph (1838), photo. in S.R.R. Cf. Forrest, *Old Hos. of Shrews.* 33.
30. Owen's Mansion was restored and more or less gutted by S. Pountney Smith in 1877, but the front was preserved in something like its original state: *Salopian Shreds & Patches*, ii. 223.
31. The bold patterning at Habberley is upon wings added to the bldg. of 1555, probably in the early 17th cent.
32. The date appears upon the remarkable free-standing stone sundial, once in the Hall garden and now in the garden of the cottage at the end of the drive. It does not date the front elevation of the ho., which is almost wholly of the 19th cent.
33. The date is painted on the gable and has no known authority.
34. The '1604' in plaster on the street front does not date the bldg., which is a long 15th-cent. range truncated in the late 19th cent.: Leighton, 'Sketches', iv; I. Ferris and S. Litherland, *Survey of Llwyd Mansion, Oswestry* (Birm. Univ. Field Arch. Unit [1988]).
35. The date is on the gable of the wing but is part of a modern restoration.
36. Acton, *Castles and Old Mansions*, 32.
37. N.M.R. archives, Berrington.
38. *Ibid.* Astley Abbots.
39. Relatively speaking, and despite such hos. as Dial Cottage (1667), Wem, and the 1682 additions to Reynalds Mansion, M. Wenlock.
40. By the early 17th cent. the fashionable were beginning to follow the French manner of putting a picture, generally the best piece in the room, above the fireplace. The mode was slow to take on in Eng., where, up to the mid century, the Long Gallery was the place for pictures. Whitton may be seen as a provincial move towards the fashion: not substituting a picture for the overmantel but painting a picture on it.
41. P. Smith, *Hos. of the Welsh Countryside* (1988), 285a.
42. H.E. Forrest, *Some Old Salop. Hos. and their Owners* (Shrews. 1924), 19, 38–9.
43. Over 80 examples have been found. I am grateful to Mrs. Madge Moran for help and inf. and to Dr. Kathryn Baird for what follows.
44. One, now demolished, was in Dowles Manor—in Salop. until its transfer to Worcs. in 1895.
45. By Buckler (1828). Cf. *V.C.H. Salop.* x. 410 (fig.42, where the scheme is discernible in its setting).
46. Removed by the owner when the property was let: inf. from Dr. Baird.

Chapter XII
1. See A. Gomme, *Smith of Warwick: Fra. Smith, Architect and Master-Builder* (Stamford, 2000), 1-25, for a full discussion of the craftsman-architect. I am grateful to Prof. Gomme for allowing me to see the text of his book before publication, and for much help and advice.
2. Gomme, *Smith*, 142.
3. Date stone.
4. Date stone.
5. Date stone.

6. These two hos. are not examples of provincial backwardness, for as late as *c.*1722 Hawksmoor designed Colby Hall, Kensington, with a similar entrance hall; and perhaps as late as 1740 Jas. Gibbs prepared a similar plan for Catton Hall (Derb.): *The Country Seat*, ed. H. Colvin and J. Harris (1970), 94-5, 157-163.

7. There are rare exceptions, e.g. the early 18th-cent. range at the Old Rectory, Eaton-under-Heywood, with the doorway off-centre in a 4-bay elevation. The form was common in towns: there are examples in Swan Hill, Shrews.

8. The type is well known elsewhere: M. Barley in *Arch. Jnl.* cxxxvi. 259. Other Salop. examples are Madeley Hall and Garmston Ho.

9. A point I owe to Prof. Gomme.

10. Built by a farmer with an armigerous wife who brought him a modest fortune: *V.C.H. Salop.* x. 28. The ho.'s origins seem to be reflected in the contrast between the fashionable front, with its achievement of arms, and the homely character of the rear elevation and most of the interior.

11. Felhampton Ct. is now more or less double-pile, but its original **L** plan is clear.

12. Garmston Ho., beginning as a timber-framed bldg. *c.*1600, was remodelled and extended in brick in the early 18th cent.

13. The price paid at Ford Ho. for a large entrance hall was similar to, but on a smaller scale than, that paid earlier at Longnor: above, p.149.

14. The hall at Dinthill is unusual in having a fireplace (in the wall opposite the entry), but it is an extremely shallow projection and appears to be later.

15. At Catton (above, n.6) Gibbs prepared an alternative plan with a smaller central hall.

16. In Salop. early one-bay halls and centrally recessed rear elevations tend to be associated, perhaps because both are responses to limited resources.

17. The stairs at Garmston are now in the front of the hall, but their earlier position at the rear is established by the form of the attic and the roof.

18. Described as 'new built' in 1771; probably built by Edw. Hall, of a local fam. who bought in 1760: inf. from deeds in possession of the owner, Mr. P.D. McLean.

19. N.M.R. archives.

20. The secondary staircase recently removed from Withington Hall was a 19th-cent. contrivance.

21. Bodl. MS. Gough Salop. 11, f.11v. The saloon is in fact labelled 'Smoking Room'.

22. Ford Ho. and Broseley Hall are hos. of some pretensions but with restricted 'prospects' to the front, and the siting of the kitchens is perh. to be seen as an early, somewhat unavoidable, down-grading of the rooms along the entrance front in favour of those along the garden front.

23. Built by the Grove, Betton, and Griffiths fams. respectively. Whatever their origins, all were gentle by the early 18th cent.: *T.S.A.S.* 2nd ser. v, p. xii; ix. 203; 3rd ser. viii. 68; 4th ser. iv, pp. x-xi; viii. 87-91.

24. R. Donaldson-Hudson, *Par. of Cheswardine* (Shrews. 1939), 155-8; *V.C.H. Salop.* viii. 36, 47, 226, 260; x. 28; *T.S.A.S.* 4th ser. vi. 288–92.

25. Above, p.155.

26. J.H. Baker, *The Legal Profession and the Common Law* (1986), 129-135. I have to thank Mr. W.A. Champion for drawing my attention to this.

27. *Law, Economy and Society 1750–1914*, ed. G.R. Rubin and D. Sugerman (1984), 475-9.

28. For Prince's career see Bill Champion, *Everyday Life in Tudor Shrews.* (Shrews. 1994), 66-7.

29. G.E. Mingay, *Eng. Landed Society in the 18th Cent.* (1963), 85–6.

30. *Country Life*, 2 Mar. 1978, pp.523-4.

31. *Ibid.* 27 July 1952, p.18.

32. Gomme, *Smith*, 188-9, 538.

33. *Country Life*, 15 June 1918, p.554. The date 1705-13 given there for Hardwick is far from firm.

34. G.H. Thompson, *The King's Ley: The Story of Alveley* (Shrews. 1951), pp.x, 10.

35. *Country Life*, 21 Sept. 1989, pp.209-10.

36. *T.S.A.S.* 4th ser. viii. 75-8.

37. *Ibid.* xlviii. 202-3.

38. Hawkstone is richly documented: A. Gomme, 'The Bldg. of Hawkstone Hall: a Reconsideration of the Evidence', *Arch. Jnl.* cxli. 309-25.

39. S. Leighton, *Salop. Hos. Past and Present* (1901), 8.

40. *T.S.A.S.* xlix. 58-9.

41. The John Prince who surveyed the Harleys' Marylebone est., etc., is presumed to be the John Prince who designed Cound. There seems to be no reason to call him, as Pevsner (*Salop.* 114) did, 'of Shrews.' See H. Colvin, *Biog. Dict. Brit. Architects* (1978), 661-2; Gomme, *Smith*, 195-6.

42. *V.C.H. Salop.* viii, pl. facing p.82.

43. Gomme, *Smith*, 191-6.

44. Brogyntyn was remodelled in 1814–15 and, as a drawing in Mr. Peter Reid's possession shows, had been considerably altered well before that. Nevertheless its form, as revealed in the drawing, and its known association with Fra. Smith, suggest that it was in the same vein as those cited above.

45. *Arch. Jnl.* cxli. 314, 316.

46. Badger Hall was remodelled internally and added to by Jas. Wyatt, but illustrations and a sketch plan (N.M.R. archives) show that he retained largely unaltered the E. front of the earlier bldg.

47. *Arch. Jnl.* cxli. 319.

48. The date is on the parapets of the S. and E. fronts.

49. Cound may of course have had vanished rivals or forerunners. A survey of Lancelot Lee's est. in Alveley, completed before 1730, has a drawing of Coton Hall with a main front with a central astylar range of 5 bays and 3 storeys, a balustraded parapet, and French quoins, all flanked by two lower wings in the same vein and with hipped roofs masking earlier ranges: Thompson, *King's Ley*, pp.x, 10. The bldg. is a smaller version of Umberslade (1695–1700): Gomme, *Smith*, 94–7.

50. Colvin, *Biog. Dict.* 748.

51. Above, p.175.

52. *Jnl. R. Soc. of Arts*, 1959, p.540.

53. Bodl. MS. Gough Salop. 11, f.11v.

54. A feature it shares with Erddig (nr. Wrexham), built 1684–7 by Thos. Webb, a Middlewich mason.

55. Above, p.141. The doorway had been moved back to its present (and original) position by 1834: S.R.R. 6001/201, f 1. At Ludstone a similar to-and-fro treatment of the doorway seems to have occurred, but later—probably in the early 1870s and earlier 20th cent.: above, n.3.

56. Pevsner's date of *c.*1700 seems too early. On the other hand the fact that the arms on the pediment were granted only in 1737 need not mean that the ho. was not built before then: the Davisons had in fact used the arms for many years before the grant: *T.S.A.S.* lix. 577.

57. The ceiling of the room to the N. of the hall, now of three bays, has been raised by *c.*2ft., presumably to give it decent proportions after lengthening it southwards by one bay.

58. The inconvenience of that arrangement is shown by the additions, intended to end it, at the rear of, *inter alia*, Ludstone, Lutwyche, and Shipton Halls, and at Aston Hall, Munslow.

59. For a general discussion of bedrooms as public rooms and of beds as 'chairs of estate' see E. Mercer, *Furniture 700–1700* (1969), 62-3.

60. S.R.R. 112/9/2169. The plan is roughly drawn and not to scale, but it must relate to an existing bldg., not a proposed one, for the dimensions of every room are given down to inches (e.g. '7 ft. 2 in.') and even half inches (e.g. '19 ft. 2½ in.'), and nobody ever designed a bldg. to such tolerances. By 1718 the staircase had already lost some of its splendour, for a bedchamber anteroom had been contrived, partly by enlarging the S.W. wing and partly by encroaching on the staircase hall.

61. For the alterations to Hawkstone from 1719 see *Arch. Jnl.* cxli. 309–25.

62. The moulded plinths of the formerly external E. and W. walls (now in the basement) were roughly cut through to give access to the basements of the added bays.

63. *Country Life*, 21 Sept. 1989, pp. 209–10.

64. The porticoes and their corresponding pilasters appear on the 1718 plan, but as additions even more roughly drawn than the plan itself and without dimensions for their size and positions. They seem to be an attempt to bring the plan up to date at an early stage of the remodelling.

65. Gomme, *Smith*, 325.

66. The treatment in the saloon at Davenport Ho. is exceptional.

67. Inf. from the owner, Mr. B.J. Treasure.

Chapter XIII

1. *Country Life*, 7 Sept. 1961, p.503.

2. A. Gomme, 'The Building of Hawkstone Hall: a Reconsideration of the Evidence', *Arch. Jnl.* cxli. 321–2.

3. K. Downes, *Hawksmoor* (1969), 152–5.

4. Jos. Bromfield drastically remodelled Styche Hall 1796–8 (S.R.R. 552/10/901, pp.10–14; /12/407, 776), but there is little to suggest eliminated Palladian elements other than a now blocked Venetian window. Walcot too has been altered, but again with no sign that Palladian elements have gone.

5. J. Burke, *Eng. Art 1714-1800* (1976), 7.

6. S.R.R. 6002/241; *Salop. News Letter*, xlii. 10.

7. Wm. and John Haycock greatly altered the bldg. in 1785–6. To judge from the original design, they inserted roundels in the pediments, added a portico to, and a cupola above, the main block, replaced the eaves of the linking ranges with parapets and the pediments of the pavilions with parapets and urns, and added quoins to the main block and pavilions.

They also stripped off whatever rendering there may have been. Cf. E.V.N. Lloyd, *Hist. of Millington's Hosp.* [1982], esp. 9, 32.

8. Public bldgs. of the 1740s–1750s are Wm. Baker's Butter Cross and T.F. Pritchard's rebldg. of Hosier's Alsmhos., both in Ludlow. In 1745 too Baker prepared an estimate for Bp.'s Cas. town hall, with a design not significantly different from the present bldg., and (with Hen. Flitcroft: *Arch. Jn*l. cxli. 321-2) an unexecuted design for the Salop Infirmary, Shrews.

9. *T.S.A.S.* lvi. 39-40. In 1800 the Revd. Jas. Matthews, with obvious ref. to Sir Ric. Hill, declared that 'the consolidation of small farms is the grand cause of the present distress': *ibid.* lv. 29.

10. J. Plymley, *Gen. View of Agric. of Salop.* (1803), 120 sqq.; *V.C.H. Salop.* iv. 213; *Atlas of Rural Protest in Brit. 1548-1900*, ed. A. Charlesworth (1983), 27-8.

11. J. Loch, *Acct. of Improvements on Est. of Marquess of Stafford* (1820); *V.C.H. Salop.* xi. 160.

12. M. Guppy, 'The Duke of Sutherland's Cottages' (Birm. Sch. of Archit. dissertation, 1984).

13. Above, p.173.

14. S. Blutman, 'Bks. of Designs for Country Hos. 1780-1815', *Archit. Hist.* xi. 25-33.

15. Loton Hall, Lady Leighton's album, f.32.

16. In 1793 it was considered 'sufficient for a rector of Cardeston who had not other preferment': S.R.R. 6001/6863, p.25. The living then had a clear yearly value of £41.

17. Presented by his uncle Sir Baldwin in 1828: *S.P.R. Heref.* v (7), pp iii, v; *T.S.A.S.* lix. 139.

18. The chamber floor had 5 bedrooms, a dressing room, a nursery, a day nursery, and a servant's bedroom: Loton Hall, Lady Leighton's album, ff. 24, 25.

19. *V.C.H. Salop.* viii. 25, 220.

20. *Ibid.* 176.

21. *Ibid.* xi. 62, 169, 183; *T.S.A.S.* lxxi. 135.

22. *V.C.H. Salop.* viii. 131, 136.

23. *Ibid.* 192.

24. Possibly, as in other counties, something like a through passage was contrived by placing furniture, generally long high-backed settles, to screen the space between the opposing doorways from the rest of the room.

25. There are plausible date stones on all these.

26. *V.C.H. Salop.* x. 271.

27. N.M.R. archives. The ho. has been demolished.

28. Loton Hall, Lady Leighton's album, ff.41-2.

29. Above, pp.153, 154-5.

30. Other gentry builders were the Cornewalls at Delbury, the Harries fam. at Cruckton, the Lloyds at Aston Hall, Oswestry, and the Parkers at Sweeney Hall.

31. Bldg. accts., etc., in the possession of Mr. Patrick Wrigley, Delbury Hall (copies in S.R.R. 4454).

32. Shrews. School Libr., Haycock's original proposals (copies in N.M.R.).

33. See below, pp.196 sqq.

34. In the 19th cent. the large halls of several 17th- and early 18th-cent. hos. were much reduced in size: Halston Hall, Hampton Hall, Peplow Hall, Stoke Ct., and Whitton Hall.

35. *Country Life*, 14 Sept. 1961, p.560.

36. G. Griffiths, Hist. of Tong (*c*.1815), 90; *Hist. Parl., Commons*, 1754-90, ii. 371-2.

37. C. Hussey (*Country Life*, 27 Sept. 1946, p.581) attributed the design of the ho. to Brown, but D. Stroud (*Capability Brown* 1975, p.148), qualifies this, raising the possibility that Durant's own ideas may have been realized by Brown but claimed as his own by a builder Theophilus Shelton. J. Harris (*Archit. Hist.* ii. 18) has suggested the Shrews. archit. T.F. Pritchard, for whose work see below, p.195.

38. S.R.R. 6001/3167 (sale cat. 1855).

39. It seems likely that Bromfield's remodelling of Styche Hall 1796-8 (above, n.4) replaced a large entrance hall with the present small one.

40. Contemporaries used 'hall' and 'vestibule' interchangeably, but the difference is real, necessitating the distinction made here. The Tong sale cat. of 1855 (above, n.38) calls what is clearly the hall the 'vestibule' but makes up for that by calling the staircase hall, to one side of it, the 'Grand hall and staircase'.

41. *Jnl. Soc. of Archit. Historians of Gt. Brit.* xxxiii. 75–82.

42. S.R.R. 3719/2/6.

43. The date of the later alterations at Hopton Ct. is uncertain. J.C. Loudon's design, later published in his *Treatise on Farming, Improving and Managing Country Residences* (1806), was rejected, and probably soon afterwards 'another by Mr. Nash in the Italian style was preferred': B.

Botfield, *Stemmata Botevilliana* (Westminster, 1858), pp. ccxxi–ccxxii.

44. Photos. in S.R.R., PH/L/3. The ho. was demolished in 1955.

45. An arrangement suppressed in the 1970s: *V.C.H. Salop.* x. 159.

46. Loudon was generalizing from hos. of this type when he recommended to builders of lesser ones that a small hall, vaulted and gloomy, would make other apartments seem larger: *Encyclopaedia of Cottage, Farm, and Villa Archit. and Furniture* (1833).

47. See e.g. W. and J. Halfpenny, R. Morris, and T. Lightoler, *The Modern Builder's Assistant* (1757).

48. R. Morris, *Rural Archit.* (1750), preface.

49. Source cited above, n.32.

50. J. Harris, *Georgian Country Hos.* (R.I.B.A. Drawings Ser. 1968), pl.24.

51. A 1792 drawing by Moses Griffiths (S.R.R. 4187/14) shows Lythwood Hall in its pristine state.

52. A notable exception, if an early 19th-cent. drawing can be trusted, was Whitton Hall, Westbury, where nearly all openings had keystones and rustication: S.R.R. 6001/3066, f.41.

53. N.M.R. archives.

54. For John Prince (archit. of Cound and Buntingsdale) and the Smiths see above, cap. XII.

55. It was not a wholly professional blindness. In all his visits to country hos. Horace Walpole never went to one in Salop.: P. Toynbee, 'Horace Walpole's Visits to Country Seats, &c.' *Walpole Soc.* xvi. 9–80.

56. Mainly on the strength of visits recorded in his diary (ed. 1955: A.E. Richardson, *Rob. Mylne, Archit. and Engineer, 1733 to 1811*) Mylne's name is connected with several Salop. hos., but there is little that can confidently be attributed to him, and some work that has been is now known not to be his (cf. refs. in Pevsner, *Salop.*; *T.S.A.S.* lix. 187), e.g. the saloon at Halston or at any rate the Adam-style decoration there (below, p.209). At Woodhouse, which encapsulates a timber-framed bldg., most of the interior decoration is early 19th-cent., and the entrance front's columns *in antis* and the garden front's great bow window, may also be of that date. Mylne's diary may in fact record no more than a not-too-successful 'fishing expedition'. Some of what he may have done here and there (*T.S.A.S.* lxvi. 104) may have been swept away in later alterations.

57. All are in H. Colvin, *Biog. Dict. of Brit. Architects* (1978), with lists of their wks.

58. S.R.R. 6001/2737, pp.267, 270; *T.S.A.S.* lxvi. 103–4.

59. J. Ionides, *Thos. Farnolls Pritchard of Shrews.* (Ludlow, 1999), esp. 205–18.

60. Pritchard's 1759 work at Tern Hall seems to have consisted of extending, and adding a new front to, a ho. of 1701: *T.S.A.S.* lxvi. 97, 99, 102-4.

61. Rockingham's death (1782) marks it as much as any one event could do: see e.g. R. Pares, *King Geo. III and the Politicians* (1953), 57-60, 117–18, 120-1; C. Hobhouse, *Fox* (1964), 13–16, 116, 125–6.

62. *Letters of Horace Walpole*, ed. C.B. Lucas (1904), 9 (to Ric. West 1739).

63. Bonomi so reduced the depth of frieze and architrave at Longford as almost to eliminate the distinction between them.

64. J. Mordaunt Crook, *The Greek Revival: Neo-Classical Attitudes in Brit. Archit. 1760-1870* (1972), 102.

65. Knight may have been his own architect, but it is uncertain how much help he had at Downton from T.F. Pritchard and later from John Nash: A. Rowan, 'Downton Castle', *The Country Seat*, ed. H.M. Colvin and J. Harris (1970), 170–3.

66. *Letters*, ed. Lucas, 562 (to the Revd. W. Cole 15 Aug. 1774).

67. J.B. Lawson in *Nat. Trust Yr. Bk. 1975-6*, 10.

68. J. Peake, *Ellesmere, Salop.* (Shrews. 1889), 18-19.

69. Of hills—the Lawley and Caer Caradoc—that were not only picturesque but also Corbett's own (as ld. of Lydley and Cardington). See S.R.R. 7069; *V.C.H. Salop.* viii. 110; x. 24, 27, 34, 74.

70. *Country Life*, 10 Feb. 1977, p.310.

71. B. Jones, *Follies and Grottoes* (1953), 169, 379. *V.C.H. Salop.* viii. 5; inf. (1984) from Mr. R.B. Hewlings (Eng. Heritage), citing bldg. accts. for Sham Castle.

72. A 1786 drawing (S.R.R. 6001/372/1, p.10) shows the S. front with over hanging eaves.

73. *Corresp. of Thos. Percy & Wm. Shenstone*, ed. C. Brooks (1977), 64. The board was soon blown down. Weaver improved another prospect by having an ash tree painted white 'leaves and all', with unhappy results.

74. *Orders of Q. Sess.* ii. 245, 249.

75. As the original Citadel at Hawkstone was at first the residence of Hill's steward: cf. *V.C.H. Salop.* iv. 207; *Country Life*, 21 Aug. 1958, pp. 368–9.

76. Cronkhill was probably part of the improvements made to Ld. Berwick's est. by Nash and Repton from 1797 onwards: *Arch. Jnl.* cxxxviii. 46–7.

77. E. Hyams, *Capability Brown and Humphry Repton* (1971), 177.

78. S.R.R. 5245/1 ('Old Prints, Shrews.'; qD 66), p.26.

79. J. Summerson, *Archit. in Brit. 1530 to 1830* (1963), 290.

80. *Salop. N. & Q.* 5 Aug. 1892, 7; S.R.R. 6001/3055, pp.7–8; Birm. Univ. Libr., MS. 14, p.68. See p.198.

81. It was occasionally used in the country at large on landowners' cottages. Those (1811) at Blaise Castle are well known: Summerson, *op.cit.* 291. Others (1812–16) are at Ampthill on the Woburn est.: E. Mercer, *Eng. Vernacular Hos.: a study of traditional farmhos. and cottages* (1975), 137, pl.87.

82. It may be that the Whig oligarchy used mid 18th-cent. Gothic to give historical colour to their pose as defenders of ancient liberty (M. Baridon in *Fashioning and Functioning of the Brit. Country House*, ed. G. Jackson-Stops *et al.* (Washington D.C. 1989), 373-92) or as a national manifesto (M. McCarthy, *Origins of the Gothic Revival* (1987), 27-30).

83. *Wks. of Ld. Macaulay* (Albany edn.), viii (1898), 314. Or as Walpole, anticipating his critic, said of himself 'eager about trifles, and indifferent to everything serious': *Letters*, ed. Lucas, 564 (to H.S. Conway 18 Aug. 1774).

84. McCarthy, *op.cit.* 12-13.

85. Above, pp.191-2.

86. Griffiths, *Tong*, 90.

87. Its detail is much the same as that of Kent's Esher Place (1730s). J. Harris calls it one of the 'children of Esher': Jackson-Stops, *Brit. Country Ho.* 252.

88. *Agric. of Salop.* (1803), 109–10.

89. *V.C.H. Salop.* x.236. Caughley Hall, rebuilt *c.*1790 and pulled down in 1833, was in the very plain style of the late 18th cent.

90. S.R.R. 783, box 25, 'Proposals to Alter and Repair two parlours, a staircase, &c. 21 Aug. 1761'.

91. Colvin, *Biog. Dict.* 662; J. Harris, 'Pritchard Redivivus', *Archit. Hist.* ii. 17-24, figs. 1–8.

92. N. Cossons and B. Trinder, *The Iron Bridge* (1979), 25–6, give Pritchard more credit for the concept and design of the bridge than did J. Randall, *Hist. of Madeley* (Madeley, 1880), 336-8, and A. Raistrick, *Dynasty of Iron Founders: the Darbys and Coalbrookdale* (1953), cap. 11. Julia Ionides makes a strong case for Pritchard's involvement in every aspect of its construction: *Pritchard*, 261–5.

93. T.J. Howell, *Stranger in Shrews.* (1816), 177.

94. Photos. in S.R.R., PH/O/6; Peake, *Ellesmere*, 18–19.

95. At the Woodlands, Glazeley, e.g. the openings have two-centred heads, but the proportions are those of contemporary sashed windows.

96. He had a good medieval exemplar. In the prior's lodging of *c.*1425 at M. Wenlock the windows of the gallery and of the 1st-floor reception rooms were highly decorated, while those of the ground-floor service rooms were not.

97. Though he made alterations, partly Gothic, partly 'Roman classical', at Stanage Pk. (Radnors.), where his father seems to have worked earlier: cf. R. Haslam, *Powys* (Bldgs. of Wales, 1979), 59, 276; W.A. Hanbury-Tenison, 'Edw. Haycock, Archit., and the Salop. Tradition' (Camb. Univ. undergraduate dissertation, 1984), 52–3 (copy in S.R.R., qBH 41).

98. See above, n.65; below, n.113.

99. Crook, *Greek Revival*, 100.

100. H. Honour, *Neo-Classicism* (1977 edn.), 113.

101. C. Hussey, *Eng. Country Hos.: Late Georgian 1800–1840* (1958), 151–60.

102. Leighton, 'Sketches', iv.

103. The patron Thos. Eyton obviously co-operated with his son, the new vicar: *V.C.H. Salop.* xi. 239-40.

104. S.C.C. Planning Dept. file D/H/Scheme 7, Wellington U.D.C.

105. Summerson, *Archit. in Brit.* 246, seems to go further and suggest that J.-A. Gabriel's work in France was to some extent influenced by 'the pull exercised by English architecture towards simplicity and restraint'.

106. Crook, *Greek Revival*, 102; and see below, pp.219-20.

107. Strictly speaking, the rejected design for Onslow Hall later used at Lythwood.

108. Date stone.

109. Ludstone Hall was designed in the early 17th cent. with a central bow window rising to the full height of the S. (entrance) front (above, cap.XI, n.3), but the wings on either side make it a less dominant feature than those at Buntingsdale and Woodhouse (above, n.56).

110. The fullest acct. of Haycock's work is Gareth Williams, 'Edw. Haycock and the Picturesque—the country Ho. Practice of a Border Archit.' (Manchester Univ. thesis, 1992). I am grateful to Mr. Williams for a copy.

111. This is the reverse side of a point made by Colvin, *Biog. Dict.* 39-40, about the effect of rlys. on archit. practice.

112. Wyatt's elevations were adhered to, but a comparison of his original plan with the present one shows that the plan was altered, apparently without

113. In 1836 it was claimed that the owner J.A. LLoyd designed Leaton Knolls (Colvin, *Biog. Dict.* 407), but its colonnade motif is repeated at Clytha Ct. (Mon.) by Haycock, who was working at Leaton Knolls in 1824 (N.L.W., Aston Hall 3316). So it seems likely that Haycock had, at the least, an important role in designing the ho. and that its remodelling began in the mid 1820s.

113. his involvement: N.L.W., Aston Hall 5234–5. In 1804 J.H. Haycock was doing minor work at Aston (*ibid*. 3307); he had supplied a door and a window earlier and may have been the builder in the 1790s. On the other hand John Carline was supplying chimney pieces then (*ibid*. 4689) and may have been doing more.

114. Below, p.224.

115. *V.C.H. Salop.* x. 159.

116. R.K. Morriss *et al.*, *The Music Hall, Shrews.* (Mercian Heritage Ser. civ; Bromlow, 2000), 31-4, 72–88.

117. A comparable design (*c.*1785) for the Swedish naval base at Karlskrona was never carried out: Honour, *Neo-Classicism* (1968 edn.), 126-7.

118. Re-use of wainscot is a notorious trap, even when there was no intention to deceive. In 1761 T.F. Pritchard was to 'take down and make good the old wainscot and fix up do. in the best manner round the rooms' in Ludford Ho.: S.R.R. 783, box 25, 'Proposals, &c.'

119. *T.S.A.S.* lxvi. 93–5.

120. Inf. from Maj. and Mrs. J.L. Harvey, of Halston Hall, and Mr. R.B. Hewlings.

121. In both halls there are discordant elements. At Shipton the doorways, surmounted by broken pediments, may belong to an earlier modification of the ho. than Pritchard's in the mid cent.; at Lutwyche the ceiling ornament is 19th-cent., but its main divisions are determined by the disposition of the beams of the original hall.

122. Hussey, *Eng. Country Hos.: Late Georgian*, 153.

123. Much of the rest of the interior decoration at Woodhouse appears to be of the second quarter of the 19th cent.

124. At Aston and Styche John Carline (Carline & Linnell) supplied the chimney pieces: N.L.W., Aston Hall 4689; S.R.R. 552/10/901, p.11.

125. Top-lit staircases unsupported by load-bearing walls also occur slightly later in the Crescent (22-25 Town Walls), Shrews.; of timber and in a restricted space they are meant to solve problems of access between front and rear rooms.

126. Gomme, *Smith of Warwick*, 311, 315 n.92, 323.

127. G. Beard, *Craftsmen and Interior Decoration in Eng. 1660–1820* (1981), 242-3, 253, 259, 288-9, 291; *Arch. Jnl.* cxli. 322.

128. Halston Hall saloon is also oval in plan, but the decoration is of the 1920s (above, p.209) and the form may be too.

129. *V.C.H. Salop.* xi. 217.

130. I am grateful to Miss Jean Hamilton, of the Victoria and Albert Mus., for identifying these papers and for inf. about them.

131. M. Macleod, B. Trinder, and M. Worthington, *Ditherington Flax Mill* (Ironbridge Inst. Research Paper xxx, 1988), 8-9. The Castlefields mill (mostly demolished by 1837) was built when Bage and the Benyons ceased to be partners in the Ditherington business in 1804: B. Trinder, *Ind. Arch. Salop.* (Chichester, 1996), 146-7.

132. Cranage, x. 1012.

133. P.B. Hewitt in *Bull. Assoc. for Ind. Arch.* xvii (3), 2. The now demolished stables at Ditherington flax mill are said to have had an iron roof (*Nat. Trust Yr. Bk. 1975–6*, 49), but they had no more than iron trusses to the roof: Macleod *et al. op.cit.* 39.

134. See e.g. *V.C.H. Salop.* xi. 28.

135. Nevertheless in 1796 the iron-framed windows for Telford's new ch. at Madeley were bought in Birm.: *ibid.* 64.

136. W.G. Muter, *The Bldgs. of an Ind. Community: Coalbrookdale and Ironbridge* (1979), 15, 17. J.H. Haycock designed the Tontine: Cossons and Trinder, *Iron Bridge*, 41.

137. Muter, *op.cit.* 36. It is possible that they had been preceded by 'cottages' erected by an ironmaster at Tern Hall *c.*1713: *T.S.A.S.* lxvi. 99–100.

138. R. Leech, *Early Ind. Housing: the Trinity Area of Frome* (R.C.H.M.E. 1981); S. Collier, *Whitehaven* (R.C.H.M.E. 1991), 85–6; B.H. St.J. O'Neil in *Archaeologia*, xcv. 141–80.

139. Muter, *op.cit.* 38–9, figs. 21–2.

140. Trinder, *Ind. Rev. Salop.* 192–4; *V.C.H. Salop.* xi. 149–51, 277.

141. Muter, *op.cit.* 36, fig.19.

142. F.D. Klingender, *Art and the Industrial Revolution*, ed. A. Elton (St. Albans, 1975), cap. 5; S. Smith, *A View from the Iron Bridge* (1979), 3–11.

143. *Salop. News Letter*, xxxiii. 1–6.

144. *Ibid.* xlv. 15.

145. E. Thomas, *Coalbrookdale and the Darby Fam.* (York, 1999), 18–19, 43; *V.C.H. Salop.* xi. 39.

146. *V.C.H. Salop.* x. 261; xi. 114; above, p.192.
147. Trinder, *Ind. Rev. Salop.* 118, 174–5; cf. below, p.319 and n.1.
148. For the involvement of these fams. in local projects at the time see Trinder, *Ind. Rev. Salop.* passim; *V.C.H. Salop.* xi passim.
149. *Cart. Shrews. Abbey,* ed. U. Rees (1975), i, p.190.
150. Above, p.128.
151. Above, pp.105-6. What remained of Stury's Hall in 1880 is described (and misinterpreted) in *T.S.A.S.* vi. 257, 261, 268-70. See also *ibid.* 3rd ser. vii. 322; lxviii. 54-59 (but cf. *ibid.* lxi. 43, 45 n.16, 109); S.R.R. 6000/3493; D. Cromarty, *Everyday Life in Medieval Shrews.* (1991), 18–19. I have to thank Mr. W.A. Champion for drawing my attention to Stury's Hall. Dr. N.J. Baker's forthcoming study of the archaeology of Shrews. will throw much more light on the town's fabric.
152. By 1300 the Sturys were among the oldest and richest merchant dynasties of Shrews.: Cromarty, op. cit. 17-21; D. and R. Cromarty, *The Wealth of Shrews. in the Early 14th Cent.* (Salop. Arch. and Hist. Soc. 1993), 53–5.
153. Above, pp.105, 110 and n.53.
154. Above, pp123-4; D. Lloyd, *Broad St. through eight cents.* (Ludlow Research Paper iii, 1979), 37-8, 43, 45–8, 53, 67.
155. In Shrews. Rowley's Mansion (1618) was the first prestigious brick ho. (below, cap. XIV, n.15), just a few yrs. after a last fling in stone—the 'Great Stone House' built c.1610 for Humph. Lee (*T.S.A.S.* 3rd ser. ix 251–2; liii. 240), of Langley, cr. Salop.'s first bt. 1620. Stone Ho. was demolished to make way for the Nurses' Home (1908–10), now Watergate Mansions.
156. Above, pp.135-7, 151, 153.
157. Nos. 1-3 have each a small room, 4ft. wide, taken out of them and given its own window: SA 12612.
158. Lloyd, *Broad St.* 53, 55–6; idem, *Dinham Ho. & its Grounds: A Short Hist.* (Ludlow, 1982), 3-5, 8; S.R.R. 2705/14.
159. Above, pp.159-60.
160. J.L. Hobbs, *Shrews. Street-Names* (Shrews. 1954), 95-6.
161. Bldg. leases, etc., in S.R.R. 261/74; 717/1–2; D3651/B/10/1/68/2. These sources were used after reading Mrs. Helen Salmon's unpublished art. on Harrold, from which some other details are taken. I am very grateful to Mrs. Salmon for a sight of her art. and to Mrs. Marion Roberts for bringing it to my attention.
162. Mr. David Lloyd kindly provided inf. about Ludlow bldgs. not otherwise documented.
163. H.E. Forrest, *Old Hos. of Shrews.* (Shrews. 1935), 44–5; *V.C.H. Salop.* iii. 133; inf. from Salop. County Council. The ho. was built by Jonathan Scott (b.1677), of a very successful merchant dynasty, purchasing the est. of Betton Strange outside Shrews. The county bought it for a Judges' Lodging in 1821 and sold it in 1996.
164. Four of the windows with raised sills are above doorways, but that is not the reason for their eccentricity for the two windows that are crucial to the effect—in each wing the one immediately next to the main block—are not above doorways.

Chapter XIV
1. W.K. Jordan, *Philanthropy in Eng. 1480–1660* (1959), 240 sqq.; idem, *The Charities of Rural Eng. 1480–1660* (1961), 21-2. Some of Jordan's statistics may need refining (e.g. in light of Phelps Brown and Hopkins, *op.cit.* above, cap.VIII n.89; cf. Jordan, *Philanthropy,* 34-5), but careful comment on e.g. his Yorks. data (W.E. Tate, *A.F. Leach as a Historian of Yorks. Educ.* (St. Anthony's Hall Publn. xxiii, 1963), 37–40) sustains the basic soundness of his work.
2. Its appearance before Nesfield's alterations of the 1870s is shown in a drawing of 1791: S.R.R. 6001/372/3, p.76.
3. Above, p.187.
4. *Country Life,* 16 Apr. 1964, pp.902–5; *V.C.H. Salop.* xi. 183.
5. Combinations of almshos. and sch. occur as well as Adams' grammar sch. (founded 1656), Newport, and Millington's Hosp. (founded 1737–49): E.V.N. Lloyd, *Hist. of Millington's Hosp., Shrews.* (Caradoc and Severn Valley Field Club [1982]), 4, 7, 9-10, 15 sqq.; *V.C.H. Salop.* ii. 150.
6. J.H. Haycock raised the quadrants to two storeys c.1826–7. He worked sympathetically: his rainwater heads dated 1826 are careful copies of those dated 1726, and his brickwork can be distinguished from the original only by his use of light-coloured headers.
7. *Country Life,* 11 Mar. 1982, p.673.
8. As at Worfield, where in 1551 St. Mary's chap. was 'now our school house' (*T.S.A.S.* 3rd ser. ix. 117, 124 n.2), or at Holdgate (Cranage, ii. 99) and Llanyblodwel (Mytton Papers, iv. 825; S.R.S. i. 60). Cf. next note; p.298.
9. *V.C.H. Salop.* ii. 144, 158; S.R.R. 6001/3065, nos. 312, 317. Sch. had been taught in Stretton ch. as late as 1693: *V.C.H. Salop.* x. 118.
10. *V.C.H. Salop.* ii. 142–3; *T.S.A.S.* ix. 200; S.R.R., BB/C/1/1/1, ff. 9, 22v.;

J.F.A. Mason, 'Bridgnorth Grammar Sch.' (TS. 1968; copy in S.R.O. 3763/11/3), p.5.
11. *V.C.H. Salop.* ii. 154-5, 157 and facing plate.
12. Modest stone towers (only one surviving today) formerly punctuated the town walls.
13. Adjoining the boro. guildhall: M.C. Hill, *Hist. of Shropshire's Many Shirehalls* (Shrews. 1963), 1; *V.C.H. Salop.* iii, pl. facing p.97.
14. The Shearmen's Hall (perh. 14th-cent.) too was of stone (photo. in S.R.R., PH/S/13/H/3), though in 1560 the more powerful Drapers built in timber: below.
15. H.E. Forrest, *The Old Hos. of Shrews.: their hist. and associations* (Shrews. 1935), 8-10; H. Owen, *Some Acct. of the Ancient and Present State of Shrews.* (1808), 480-527. Today the most substantial remains (apart from suburban Whitehall) are those of Vaughan's Mansion. Rowley's Mansion (1618) introduced brick to the town as a prestige bldg. material.
16. His alterations included the present parapets.
17. Fra. Perry's mid 18th-cent. drawing (Bodl. Gough Maps 28, p.241) shows the original bldgs. Repairs in 1802 probably left it as depicted in I.W. Archer, *Hist. of Haberdashers' Co.* (1991), 118 (pl 28). Since the alterations of 1821–3 (*ibid.* 185; S.R.R. 6001/6742, p.23) it has looked much as it is today. I am grateful to David and Ruth Taylor for bringing these drawings to my attention; their forthcoming hist. of the sch. will elucidate its building hist.
18. W.K. Jordan, *The Charities of London 1480–1660* (1960), 160, 171, 246-7, 364-5, 369, 397.
19. Built in the early 17th cent. by a rich London stationer, replaced c.1837: *V.C.H. Salop.* x. 93, 101, pl.39; *Salopian Shreds & Patches,* ii. 140; Bodl. MS. Top. Salop. c.2, f.458a.
20. D. Lloyd and P. Klein, *Ludlow: Historic Town in Words and Pictures* (Chichester, 1984), 79.
21. See e.g. R. Tittler, *Archit. and Power: the town hall and the Eng. urban community* c.*1500–1640* (1991).
22. *V.C.H. Salop.* iii. 97, 115, 120-2, 127-8, 146.
23. Hill, *Shropshire's Shirehalls,* 2; *Orders of Q. Sess.* ii. 258; iii, pp.xxi, 3; Owen, *Ancient and Present Shrews.* 439 n.; *V.C.H. Salop.* iii. 128.
24. Illustr. in *Shropshire Mag.* Feb. 1960, 17. Exigencies of space may have precluded the more conventional flight of external steps from street to ground floor.
25. The rejected design has been supposed Geo. Steuart's: *Salop. News Letter,* xliv. 18. But the source cited (S.R.R., QA/11/1/8) is amplified by others suggesting rather that Steuart (then at Tern) was asked to help to judge the designs ('A'–'G') submitted, to be surveyor, and to prepare working drawings for the winner, 'G' (perh. by Mr. Croft, of Nottingham): QA/11/1/3/18–23, 45, 53 (esp. 19, recording a meeting not minuted in QA/11/1/8).
26. Plans initialled 'E.H.' (QA/11/2/5–6) were evidently part of design 'F', attributed to J.H. Haycock, the 1784 contractor, who was to prepare his own working drawings: QA/11/1/3/44-5, 48, 53. E.H. must have been his bro. Edw.: *Shropshire Mag.* Feb. 1960, p. 17. The other extant design is Jas. Smith's 'C': cf. QA/11/1/3/45; QA/11/2/1/1–4.
27. Haycock's contract was for £4,924: QA/11/1/3/48; QA/11/1/8, f. 13. Jas. Smith (Shifnal) and Wm. Turner (Whitchurch) would have cost under £5,000 and under £4,000 respectively, John Standbridge (Warwick) couldn't 'speak to expense': QA/11/1/3/15. The Shirehall cost £10,345: QA/11/1/6/1–2. Cf. the Foundling Hosp. (over £12,000) and co. gaol (c.£30,000): Owen, *Ancient and Present Shrews.* 334, 430.
28. As was so until 1915: *V.C.H. Salop.* iii. 222; QA/11/1/23.
29. *Orders of Q. Sess.* iii, p. xxi.
30. *V.C.H. Salop.* iii. 127.
31. He began with work on the co. gaol in 1788: *ibid.* 126; below. The surveyor's wk. was the oversight of co. bldgs. which, before 1821 (when the Judges' Lodgings were added), consisted of the Shirehall, co. gaol, lock-ups, and co. bridges. The bridges, though not dealt with here, added much to the architectural scene as well as to the amenities of travel. See *ibid.* 126-8, 147-8.
32. *Ibid.* 128; *Orders of Q. Sess.* iii. 293, 304; S.R.R., QA/11/1/15-24, 27-31; QA/11/2/4, 7–11.
33. Owen, *Ancient and Present Shrews.* 339–41; Tony Carr, *Shrews.: A Pictorial Hist.* (Chichester, 1994), no.6.
34. *V.C.H. Salop.* iii. 124–6; below, cap.XVIII n.22.
35. The W. bastion had a practical use too. After the gaol opened and while executions were public (1793–1868) 61 felons were hanged there 1795–1863 before the public and assembled prisoners: S.R.R. 1904/91; Owen, *op.cit.* 432.
36. The boro. prisoners were sent to the new county gaol when it opened. See Owen, *op.cit.* 76–7, 436; S.R.R. 6001/198, p.283; /5326, ff.31, 39–40.

37. Owen, *op.cit.* 431.

38. *Border Counties Adv.* 15 Sept. 1976, p.4; W. Cathrall, *Hist. of Oswestry* (1855), 120. Morda Ho. was burnt and demolished in 1982.

39. For hospitals see M.D. George, *Eng. in Transition* (1953), 69-70; *Eng. Hospitals 1660–1948: a survey of their archit. and design*, ed. M. Richardson (R.C.H.M.E. 1998).

40. M. Keeling-Roberts, *In Retrospect: Short Hist. of Royal Salop Infirmary* (Wem, 1981), 9-13, pls.iii-vi. xiv.

41. Wm. Baker had submitted plans in 1745: H. Colvin, *Biog. Dict. Brit. Architects 1600–1840* (1978), 83.

42. Owen, *Ancient and Present Shrews.*, 332.

43. Keeling-Roberts, *In Retrospect*, 25-7, pl.xiii.

Chapter XV

1. T.R. Gourvish, *Rlys. and the Brit. Economy 1830–1914* (1980), 21.

2. F. Engels, *Socialism, Utopian and Scientific*, transl. E. Aveling (1892), pp. xxxii–xxxiv. Recent historians have come afresh to similar conclusions: D. Cannadine, *Decline and Fall of Brit. Aristocracy* (1990).

3. Engels, *op. cit.* pp. xxxii–xxxiv; *Taine's Notes on Eng.* transl. E. Hyams (1957), 155. For Forster cf. *D.N.B.*; R.C.K. Ensor, *Eng. 1870–1914* (1936), 19, 33, 66–7.

4. That more landowners than industrialists were among the richest men in Brit. until *c.*1890 (W.D. Rubinstein, 'Brit. Millionaires, 1809–1949', *Bull. Inst. Hist. Research*, xlvii. 204) does not show that they were the dominant class but how many of them had been able, individually, to profit from the industrial development of their estates.

5. Other active entrepreneurs were the Egertons, Lowthers, Sidneys, and Willoughbys. See L. Stone, *Crisis of the Aristocracy 1558–1641* (1965), cap. 7 (esp. pp.348, 351, 375–6) and pp.627–32. In Salop. itself the Corbets were exploiting lead mines at Shelve *c.*1220: *Cart. Shrews. Abbey*, ed. U. Rees (1975), ii, pp.273–4.

6. F.M.L. Thompson, *Eng. Landed Soc. in the 19th Cent.* (1980), 256–68.

7. And Bute's from his Rhondda and N.E. Eng. coalfields also: J. Bateman, *Gt. Landowners of Gt. Brit. and Irel.* (1883), 69, 472; *The Grosvenor Est. in Mayfair, Pt. I* (Survey of Lond. xxxix), 1, 34; M.J. Daunton, *Coal Metropolis: Cardiff 1870–1914* (1977), 5, 18, 22, 30, 73–82.

8. R. Church, *Hist. Brit. Coal Ind.* iii: *1830–1913: Victorian Pre-eminence* (1986), 38, 67–8, 122–3, 130; *V.C.H. Salop.* xi. 162–4, 270–1, 326.

9. *V.C.H. Salop.* iii. 343; viii. 178, 308, 311, 322–4; x. 238, 276, 427; xi. 86–7, 215, 232, 292–3, 326, 329; Thompson, *op. cit.* 174, 266; cf. (for Granville) Church, *op. cit.* 123; *V.C.H. Staffs.* ii. 83, 99, 131–2, 257, 309; viii. 143–5, 147, 152, 163, 169–71, 185.

10. J. Franklin, *The Gentleman's Country Ho. and its plan 1835–1914* (1981), 30; Daunton, *Coal Metropolis*, 49, 51, 75–9, 82; Bateman, *Gt. Landowners*, 484.

11. *P.O. Dir. Salop.* (1870), 36; *V.C.H. Salop.* x. 85, 105; *Shrews. Chron.* 16 Aug. 1901, suppl.

12. *Utopia Limited, or The Flowers of Progress*, first publicly performed in 1893.

13. G.R. Searle, *Corruption in Brit. Politics 1895–1930* (1987), 10–11.

14. The last such Salop. intrigue, conducted without 'reticence' in 1876, was nullified by the ballot: *T.S.A.S.* lix. 170–80; *V.C.H. Salop.* iii. 322–4.

15. M. Girouard, *Life in Eng. Country Ho.* (1978), and Franklin, *Gent.'s Country Ho.*, have established this point.

16. *Taine's Notes on Eng.* 148.

17. Franklin, *op. cit.* 42.

18. *V.C.H. Salop.* iii. 254–6.

19. *Fashioning and Functioning of Brit. Country Ho.* ed. G. Jackson-Stops *et al.* (Washington, 1989), 395–415.

20. Below, cap. XXI.

21. Stokesay Ct. and Ferney Hall, symmetrical and in a popular Jacobean style, are exceptions.

22. Franklin, *Gent.'s Country Ho.* 129–239, distinguishes over 20 types and sub-types.

23. Built after 1764 by Ric. Bulkeley Hatchett, added to by his heirs in the 1860s and 1870s: *T.S.A.S.* 3rd ser. ii. 405–6; F.D. How, *The Revd. T.M.B. Bulkeley-Owen: A Memoir* (1914), 113–14.

24. S.R.R., SC/30/24.

25. For the most recent authoritative acct. see J. M. Robinson, 'Stokesay Ct. and the Allcroft Fam.' *Contents of Stokesay Ct.* (Sotheby's, 1994), i. 12–26; cf. Franklin, *Gent.'s Country Ho.* 196–7 (plan, orientation reversed).

26. *Contents of Stokesay Ct.* i. 15.

27. Y. Brown, *Boreatton Pk.* (Ruyton-XI-Towns, 1989), 22–3.

28. *The Builder,* 1 Oct. 1870, pp.784–7.

29. *Ibid.* 20 Dec. 1884, p.839.

30. Franklin, *Gent.'s Country Ho.* 211–14.

31. In the country at large the proportion of double-pile plans to others was about equal: *ibid.* 238.

32. *Country Life*, 17 Mar. 1960, p.582; source cited below, n.61.

33. Pevsner called the architect, J.W. Hugall, 'one of the naughtier High Victorians': *Herefs.* (Bldgs. of Eng. 1963), 237.

34. J. Lewis, *Women in Eng. 1870–1950: Sexual Divisions and Social Change* (1984), esp. pp.75, 78. Middle-class women were in some important ways less independent than their working-class and aristocratic sisters.

35. A comparison with king's and queen's apartments in earlier royal residences is not wholly valid for they had separate households, and relations between couples at a high social level were usually extremely formal.

36. *Contents of Stokesay Ct.* i. 15.

37. *The Builder*, 31 May 1890, p.936. The bell panel in the servants' corridor calls it the 'living hall'.

38. *Country Life*, 7 July 1977, pp.18–21.

39. *Ibid.* 31 July 1917, pp.60–66.

40. By G.H. Birch: Pevsner, *Salop.* 51; below, p.231.

41. '... to which has been added a Jacobean feeling': *The Builder*, 20 Dec. 1884, p.839.

42. *The Bldg. News*, 23 March 1860. Its top-lit hall was perh. meant for no more than an entrance hall. There is no local record, and the ho. was prob. never built.

43. A critic complained that it was 'inconvenient to the normal service arrangements of a modern house': *Country Life*, 25 Dec. 1909, p.917.

44. Franklin, *Gent.'s Country Ho.* 68, makes a very similar point.

45. 'One cannot visualize anyone ever sitting in it with pleasure; its presence must have cast a certain chill on the house': M. Girouard, *Victorian Country Ho.* (1979), 363. The present occupants find that it is the siting of the main doorway to face the prevailing S.W. winds which casts the chill.

46. W. Cathrall, *Hist. of Oswestry* (1855), 253.

47. S.R.R. 3719/2/8.

48. *The Builder*, 31 May 1890, p.296

49. Franklin, *Gent.'s Country Ho.* 257.

50. For a millionaire banker: *ibid.* 258; cf. *V.C.H. Salop.* iii. 322; iv. 211.

51. *V.C.H. Salop.* iv. 212; xi. 309.

52. *Ibid.* iv. 211.

53. The Darbys had ceased to be 'new men' *c.*50 yrs. before Adcote was built.

54. John Pritchard who built Stanmore in the 1870s was a banker in Broseley (J. Randall, *Worfield and its Townships* (Madeley, 1887), 113–14) but was important enough locally to be M.P. for Bridgnorth 1853–68: *V.C.H. Salop.* iii. 334–5; iv. 211–12 (corr. *ibid.* x. 510); x. 271.

55. Rowland Hunt's ho.: Brown, *Boreatton Pk.* 9–14.

56. T.H. Hope-Edwardes's ho.: *V.C.H. Salop.* viii. 163, 165.

57. The Revd. T.H. Hunt's ho.: Y. Brown, *Ruyton XI Towns* (Studley, 1988), 106–7.

58. Seat of the Cotes fam., local but with wide connections: D. Hudson, *Munby, Man of Two Worlds* (1972), 14.

59. *P.O. Dir. Salop.* (1856), 109. The earlier bldg. on the site had been descr. shortly before as 'a handsome castellated residence': S. Bagshaw, *Dir. Salop.* (1851), 161.

60. By Geo. Devey for H.R. Corbet: S.R.R. 327/9/1/186/19.

61. Burwarton was built, in part at least, with money from coal mining: J. Allibone, *Ant. Salvin: Pioneer of Gothic Revival Archit.* (1987), 69, 90, 160, 196.

62. *Country Life*, 2 Mar. 1901, pp.272–7.

63. *V.C.H. Salop.* iv. 211; viii. 18, 21.

64. *Ibid.* iv. 212.

65. *Ibid.* viii. 39. Other hos. and their buyers are Halston Hall (a well connected Manchester man, 1847: Cathrall, *Oswestry*, 253; W. Hughes, *Sheriffs of Salop. 1831–86* (Shrews. 1886), 51; Burke, *Peerage* (1949), 1407), Apley Pk. (a Black Country ironmaster, 1867: *ibid.* 208; S.R.R. 5886/2/2/15–16), Peplow Hall (a N. Staffs. ironmaster, 1873: *V.C.H. Salop.* iv. 210–11), Ludstone Hall (a Sedgeley fire-brick manufacturer, 1874: W. Mate & Sons Ltd. *Shropshire: Historical, Descriptive, Biographical* (1906), pt. i, pp.220–1; pt. ii, p.120), and Berwick Ho. (a Birm. businessman, 1875: *V.C.H. Salop.* iii. 352).

66. *V.C.H. Salop.* iv. 211; viii. 125–6, 240; *T.S.A.S.* 2nd ser. i. 101; A. Saint, *Ric. Norman Shaw* (1977), 408.

67. From Ld. Hill: S.R.R. 731/2/2569; *Bull. Inst. Hist. Res.* xlvii. 210.

68. On property bought from the Gardners: Mate, *Shropshire*, pt. 1, p.165; *T.S.A.S.* 2nd ser. ii. 350; Burke, *Peerage* (1967), 243; *Kelly's Dir. Salop.* (1891), 297; rainwater heads dated 1888.

69. From Ld. Craven: *V.C.H. Salop.* iv. 203.

70. *Country Life*, 2 Mar. 1901, pp.272–7.

71. From Ld. Kilmorey: *V.C.H. Salop.* iv. 209.

72. For Ld. Wenlock: *ibid.* x. 421; Saint, *Shaw*, 409.

73. For the Sitwells: F. Leach, *County Seats of Salop.* (Shrews. 1891), 125–7; Burke, *Land. Gent.* (1937), 2058–9.
74. For A.C. Heber-Percy: Mate, *Shropshire*, pt. 1, pp.175–7; pt. 2, p.40; Pevsner, *Salop.* 151.
75. For R.P. Ethelston: Mate, *op. cit.* pt. 1, pp.173–4; pt. 2, p.36; cf. *P.O. Dir. Salop.* (1856), 58; (1863), 694; G. Ormerod, *Hist. Co. Palatine of Chester* (1882), iii. 460–1; Burke, *Land. Gent.* (18th edn.), iii (1972), 293.
76. For Edw. Wood, whose father (alive when the ho. was built) had bought the property: S.R.R. 6001/4418, f. 15; cf. *P.O. Dir. Salop.* (1863), 679; (1870), 46.
77. For H. de G. Warter: *V.C.H. Salop.* iv. 211; viii. 263.
78. For Mrs. E.B. Cunliffe, the Sparlings' heiress: Mate, *op. cit.* pt. 1, pp.56, 160; pt. 2, p.33; Pevsner, *Salop.* 227.
79. For W.C. Bridgeman: Mate, *op.cit.* pt. 1, pp.60, 282; pt. 2, p.20; *The Modernisation of Conservative Politics: Diaries and Letters of Wm. Bridgeman 1904–35*, ed. P. Williamson (1988), 3, 5.
80. Date stones show alterations and extensions in the 1840s, 1880s, and 1890s.
81. Pevsner, *Salop.* 226; cf. Loton Hall MSS., Sir Baldwin Leighton's diary 19 Nov. 1850.
82. *V.C.H. Salop.* xi. 217.
83. By S. Pountney Smith of Shrews.: S. Leighton, *Salop. Hos.* (1901), 30; *Shrews. Jnl.* 7 Nov. 1883, p.5.
84. About 1865. See *Country Life*, 23 June (p.17–34) and 7 July (p.21) 1977; Leighton, *Salop. Hos.* 37.
85. By John Douglas of Chester: N.L.W., Aston Hall 4529.
86. The most important element was a ballrm.: *V.C.H. Salop.* viii. 199–200.
87. Griffin was grand-neph. of the original builder: Burke, *Land. Gent.* (1937), 981; *ibid.* (18th edn.), ii (1969), 561; *S.H.C.* 1945–6, 258. Pell Wall was in Staffs. until 1965: *V.C.H. Salop.* ii. 204.
88. *V.C.H. Salop.* iv. 232 sqq.
89. Above, n.80. The folksy motto over the fireplace, 'East, West, Hame's Best', is dated 1881.
90. *Shrews. Jnl.* 7 Nov. 1883, p.5; S.R.R. 2868/234–5, 241–3.
91. Using Geo. Devey: *V.C.H. Salop.* viii. 119–20.
92. N.L.W., Aston Hall 4368, 4519; Leighton, *Salop. Hos.* 24.
93. Leach, *County Seats*, 201.
94. Mate, *Shropshire*, pt. 2, p.60; M. Jones, *Burlton Village* (1989), 17.
95. Franklin, *Gent.'s Country Ho.* 25 (fig. 1, resuming the inf. on pp.24–34); cf. *ibid.* 254.
96. Sir H.W. Ripley (Bedstone Ct.) and J.D. Allcroft (Stokesay Ct.): Franklin, *op.cit.* 257, 268.
97. J.P. Heywood (Cloverley Hall): *ibid.* 258.
98. Rebecca Darby née Christy (Adcote): *ibid.* 255; Burke, *Land. Gent.* (1937), 411; F. Boase, *Modern Eng. Biog.* i (1892), 618. The 5th ho. mentioned (Franklin, *op. cit.* 255) is Adderley Hall.
99. Above, pp.225-6.
100. Sometimes with good reason: the Bensons of Lutwyche descended from a Liverpool slave trader, and the Sparlings of Petton had had 18th-cent. W. Indies connections: *V.C.H. Salop.* iv. 211, and sources there cited.
101. *Ibid.* 188.
102. Allibone, *Salvin*, 69.
103. i.e., in addition to Essex, Kent, Mdx., and Surr., Berks., Bucks., Hants, Herts., and Suss.
104. *Gent.'s Country Ho.* 254–69; cf. *ibid.* 24–38.
105. *The Builder*, 15 Oct. 1870, p.836. Probably to be explained by John Walford's marr. (1862) to Mary Slaney of Rossendale: Brown, *Ruyton XI Towns*, 110.
106. *The Builder*, 1 Oct. 1870, pp.784–7.
107. Brown, *Boreatton Pk.* 22–3.
108. *V.C.H. Salop.* viii. 163, 263; Leach, *County Seats*, 179.
109. Obit. in *Shrews. Jnl.* 7 Nov. 1883, p.5.
110. *Kelly's Dir. Salop.* (1891), 285; Leach, *County Seats*, 201.
111. Pevsner, *Salop.* 130.
112. e.g. W. Halfpenny, *Useful Archit. ... for erecting Parsonage-Hos., Farm-Hos. and Inns* (1752).
113. *Taine's Notes on Eng.* 159.
114. The change is seen clearly in the contrast betw. Cardeston old and new (1833) rectories: Loton Hall, Lady Leighton's album of watercolours, ff.24, 25, 27, 32.
115. *V.C.H. Salop.* viii. 16.
116. Loton Hall, Lady Leighton's album, ff.24, 27.
117. *V.C.H. Salop.* x. 363. The curate's uncle, the patron, built it, and it remained private property.
118. See next para.
119. The plans, deposited in Heref. Dioc. Regy. (reg. 1869–83, pp.22–3, 25, 102), cannot now be found, but ch. and vicarage were rebuilt in one

campaign 1867–70 (E.A. Paddock, *Meole Brace through the Centuries* (1994), 15–17, 34), Haycock presumably remaining in charge.
120. *The Builder*, 12 Nov. 1859, p.751.
121. *S.R.S.* v. 14.
122. *V.C.H. Salop.* x. 145.
123. See next para.
124. *The Builder*, 25 Jan. 1873, p.62.
125. *V.C.H. Salop.* xi. 274.
126. S.R.R. 1704/15, 44–6; 4367/Pge/1–3.
127. Loton Hall, Lady Leighton's album of watercolours, ff.24–7, 30.
128. Longner Hall archives.
129. J.J. Lake, 'Survey of Fm. Bldgs. on Dudmaston Est.' (1982), p.1 (TS. in possession of Nat. Trust, Attingham).
130. *Ibid.* p.56.
131. J.J. Lake, 'Survey of Attingham Est.' (1982; TS. in possession of Nat. Trust, Attingham).
132. Lady Leighton's album, ff.69–70, 75.
133. *Ibid.* f.62.
134. This section depends largely on M. Guppy, 'The Duke of Sutherland's Cottages' (Birm. Polytechnic Sch. of Archit. M.A. dissertation, 1984). I am grateful to Mr. Guppy for allowing me an early view of it.
135. *Ibid.* 17.
136. Lady Leighton's album, ff.49, 50.
137. *Ibid.* ff. 71, 81.
138. The dates, and often the owner's crest or initials, are on all these bldgs. Dr. J.F.A. Mason kindly provided inf. on Wolryche-Whitmore.
139. e.g. at Wimbledon (Surr.) of 1770, at E. Malling (Kent) of c.1780, at Elstow (Beds.) of 1798, and at Gt. Barford (Beds.) of c.1800: E. Mercer, *Eng. Vernacular Hos.: A study of traditional farmhos. and cottages* (1975), 137, 173, 209.
140. Not merely from those 18th-cent. terraces at Coalbrookdale referred to earlier, but from such later developments as the miners' cottages c.1800 at New England (G. Nair, *Highley* (1988), 241), the Barracks of c.1810 or earlier at Donnington Wood (*V.C.H. Salop.* xi. 149, 151), and the row of back-to-backs of c.1811–33 at Hinkshay, Dawley (*ibid.* 109, pl.41).
141. J. Summerson, *Archit. in Brit. 1530–1830* (1963), 294.
142. Mercer, *Eng. Vernacular Hos.* 137.
143. J. Plymley, *Agric. of Salop.* (1803), 110.
144. *Ibid.* 114–16.
145. T.N. Parker, *Plans, Specifications, Estimates and Remarks on Cottages* (Oswestry, 1813).
146. He recommended 3–6 a.
147. Plymley, *Agric. of Salop.* 110. But on the whole Plymley favoured separate dwellings.
148. See M. Moran, *Vernacular Bldgs. of Whitchurch & Area* (Logaston, 1999), 243.
149. Farmers seem to have been increasingly opposed to letting land to labourers: *V.C.H. Salop.* iv. 226–9.
150. Loton Hall, Lady Leighton's album of watercolours, ff. 47–50.
151. Parker, *Remarks on Cottages*. Had it been wanted, a symmetrical elevation could have been achieved easily, as it had been in Cornw. many yrs. earlier, with a false window in the byre: V.M. and F.J. Chesher, *The Cornishman's Ho.* (Truro, 1968), frontispiece and p.89.
152. Guppy, 'Duke of Sutherland's Cottages', 41.
153. As late as 1919, when smallholdings were provided at Emstrey, the co. council designed detached hos. for the larger holdings and semis for the smallest: *V.C.H. Salop.* iv. 264.
154. *Ibid.* 250–1.
155. J.L. and B. Hammond, *Ld. Shaftesbury* (Harmondsworth, 1939), 88 sqq., 162 sqq.
156. *The Victorian Countryside*, ed. G.E. Mingay (1981), ii. 493.
157. *V.C.H. Salop.* iv. 230.
158. The conversions can be seen easily enough in many former farmhos.—or could be before so many were converted back to 'country cottages'. A documented example is Lr. Stanford, Alberbury: Lady Leighton's album, f. 74.
159. *V.C.H. Salop.* iv. 230. Contemporaries were well aware that the neatness and order of 'closed' estate pars. depended on the squalor and disorder of 'open' ones: J. Burnett, *Social Hist. of Housing* (1978), 128–9.
160. Mingay, *Victorian Countryside*, ii. 470–1.
161. *V.C.H. Salop.* iv. 221, 230–1.
162. K.D.M. Snell, *Annals of the Labouring Poor* (1985), 381.
163. *V.C.H. Salop.* viii *passim*. On Pontesford Hill there were mud huts and a 'clod cottage' in 1858: *ibid.* 254.
164. Such a timber-saving device is common in ill-wooded areas; its use in Salop. plainly declares straitened means.

165. *V.C.H. Salop.* x. 11.
166. In 1901 the not very famous firm of Nicholson & Colsette, New Sq., Lincoln's Inn, submitted plans for 7 Kennedy Rd.: S.A.B.C. bldg.-control plans, Kingsland files (for which see below, n.192).
167. *Victorian Shrews.* ed. B. Trinder (Shrews. 1984), 106; *T.S.A.S.* lxxii. 64; above, p.199.
168. Trinder, *op.cit.* 115–16.
169. Pevsner, *Salop.* 262, 264.
170. S.R.R. 4078/Ch/17, 20; *Eddowes's Shrews. Jnl.* 13 Mar. 1861, p.6; 3 [p.4] and 10 [p.6] Apr. 1872 (refs. kindly provided by Dr. D.C. Cox).
171. Pevsner, *Salop.* 257.
172. Belle Vue is comprehensively dealt with in *Belle Vue Conservation Area* (S.A.B.C. [1992]); for the ch. see below, cap. XXI.
173. J.R. Kellett, *Impact of Rlys. on Victorian Cities* (1969), 419.
174. *Shrews. Chron.* 3 Apr. 1868, p.7; S.R.R., Watton press cuttings, xvi. 34.
175. Trinder, *Victorian Shrews.* 146. *The Salopian*, 21 Sept. 1872, reported Ald. Peele in the same sense: S.R.R., Watton press cuttings, xvi. 117.
176. J.B. Oldham, *Hist. Shrews. Sch.* (1952), 130–5; J.B. Lawson in *Salopian Newsletter*, xc (May 1982), n.p.
177. Trinder, *op. cit.* 145–7, 152.
178. The date 1881 is on the bridge, which had been mooted as early as 1868: cf. sources cited above, n.174; *V.C.H. Salop.* iii. 329.
179. *Eddowes's Jnl.* 31 Dec. 1884, p.5.
180. *Ibid.* Others included the supt. of the Shrews. & Heref. Rly., boro. councillors like Jas. Cock, businessmen like W.W. Naunton, solicitors like E.G.S. Corser, etc.: *Wilding's Dir. Shrews.* (1896), 19, 85, 144. Many of them had moved from hos. in the town: cf. *Crocker's Shrews. Dir.* (1880–1); *P.O. Shrews. Dir.* (1882–3).
181. Unless otherwise stated, dates and identifications will be found in S.A.B.C. regs. of bldg.-control plans (extant from 1894), in the plans themselves (from 1877) or in n.192), or in *Eddowes's Jnl.* 31 Dec. 1884, p.5. I have to thank Mr. Gordon Stringfellow, Mr. Graham Cook, and Ruth Jones, of S.A.B.C., for their help, and Mr. J.B. Lawson for identifying the present street nos. of the original plots.
182. S. Muthesius, *High Victorian Movement in Archit. 1850–1870* (1972), 42–4, 72–3, 76–82.
183. Towards the end of Smith's career he and Oswell were partners, and plans for Kingsland and elsewhere were being registered by 'Smith & Oswell' throughout the 1880s; but Smith had died in 1883 (obit. in *Salopian Shreds & Patches*, v. 209–10) and everything commissioned after that was by Oswell.
184. Nos. 10, 33, and 39 Kennedy Rd. by Ric. Owens of Liverpool, Rawncliffe of Burnley, and Lockwood of Chester respectively.
185. The symmetry of 5 Ashton Rd. was later destroyed by an addition at the N. end.
186. By A.H. Taylor of Shrews. There is a date of 1881 on the bldg. In 1884 N. Taylor of Dogpole submitted plans for the same site, perh. for an extension.
187. For Smith's activities elsewhere see below. His tiles had been used in 1877 on Berrington ch. and were then called 'patent pressed Ridge Hill tiles': *Salopian Shreds & Patches*, ii. 185.
188. *The Bldg. News*, 23 March 1860, p.283.
189. *Eddowes's Jnl.* 31 Dec. 1884, p. 5; *V.C.H. Salop.* iii. 207–8. He had a national reputation and gave evidence to the R. Com. on Labour of 1892–4: P. Horn, *Labouring Life in the Victorian Countryside* (1987), 195. He recommended, with as much common sense as technical expertise, that every rural sch. should have clothes-drying facilities.
190. e.g. sanitary bricks in the scullery, and skirting boards flush with the wall face.
191. The S.A.B.C. bldg.-control plan shows a bathroom and w.c. on the 1st floor; on the ground floor 'w.c.' has been deleted and 'Butler's Parlour' inserted.
192. S.A.B.C. bldg.-control plans are arranged by yr. and serial no. Those for Kingsland have been removed to two files labelled 'Kingsland'; they are in no discernible order and many have lost the accompanying applicn. and serial no. Among those used for this para. are those for 17 Ashton Rd., 3 Butler Rd., 6–8, 25, 28–30, 29, 32–4, and 33 Kennedy Rd.
193. It is tempting to suggest Deakin as the designer of 1 Kennedy Rd.
194. Above, cap. V.
195. No. 39 (Cyngfeld), very large, in extensive grounds, and at the out-of-town end of Kingsland, was built for E.C. Peele, 'lord high everything else' (*V.C.H. Salop.* iii. 147, 188, 227–8, pl. facing p.177).
196. Sources cited above, n.174.
197. An important reason for the sch.'s move was to allow it to compete with the 'playing fields of Rugby and Marlborough' (*Salopian Newsletter*, xc), more especially as, in the 1860s, it was felt to be on the 'boundary

line' betw. the country's public schs. and other endowed schs. (C. Leach, *A Sch. at Shrews.* (1990), 44–9).
198. *Salopian Newsletter*, xc.
199. These points evoked adverse comment at the time: *Shrews. Chron.* 1 Aug. 1873, p.8; S.R.R., Watton press cuttings, xvi. 128–9.
200. Trinder, *Victorian Shrews.* caps. 5–6. The best gen. surveys of industrial housing are E. Gauldie, *Cruel Habitations—A Hist. of Working-Class Housing 1780–1918* (1974), and Burnett, *Social Hist. of Housing.*
201. As late as 1870 the low standard of the miners' cottages at Snailbeach was held responsible for 'most frequent' epidemics of typhoid and scarlet fever: *V.C.H. Salop.* viii. 308. Cf. *ibid.* xi. 58, 126.
202. S.A.B.C. bldg.-control plan 1878/20 (builder John Rowlands).
203. L. Caffyn, *Workers' Housing in W. Yorks. 1750–1920* (1986), gives many examples. Nor was there anything similar in the E. Salop. coalfield, where settlements were small and scattered and most late 19th-cent. bldg. was of short terraces: Trinder, *Ind. Rev. Salop.* 325. That was, of course, in some contrast with the long terraces, of a low standard of accommodation, which industrialists were building for employees in the early yrs. of the cent.
204. Above, p.239. Smith appears in *P.O. Dir. Salop.* (1870), 143, as a coal, lime and salt merchant in Castle Foregate; *Kelly's Dir. Salop.* (1885), 959, adds brick to the list. *Eddowes's Jnl.* 31 Dec. 1884, p.5, referred to his 'celebrated tiles of very ornamental and pleasing tint' and to his 'pressed (roofing) tiles'. He is probably the J.P. Smith who, apparently early in his career, built Cressage new ch. to Edw. Haycock's design: S.R.R., Watton press cuttings, iv. 64.
205. S.A.B.C. bldg.-control plans 1882/50 and 60 (repeating 50 with minor changes); 1883/40; 1884/88; 1885/30.
206. Gordon Stringfellow's unpublished TS. 'The building of "The Back of the Sheds"' has been of great help with what follows.
207. *Ibid.* 1878/88; date stone.
208. Date stone.
209. S.A.B.C. bldg.-control plan 1883/40.
210. *Ibid.* 1884/88.
211. *Ibid.* 1885/30.
212. G. Darley, *Villages of Vision* (1978), 131–5; Caffyn, *Workers' Housing in W. Yorks.* 58–63, 66, 78, 85, 88, 90, 99–100.
213. To judge from the examples cited by Caffyn, *op. cit.*; S. Muthesius, *Eng. Terraced Ho.* (1982); and J. Lowe, *Welsh Industrial Workers' Housing 1775–1875* (1977). Some reformers were especially appalled by the 'indecency' of parents and children and of children of both sexes sharing bedrms. (cf. *V.C.H. Salop.* iv. 230); and three rms. were needed to avoid that. Some designs specified the parents', boys', and girls' rms.: Caffyn, *op. cit.* 85, 95. Boys seem to have come off worst.
214. *Quarterly Rev.* 1860, quoted in P.R. Thompson, *Wm. Butterfield* (1971), 358.
215. The evid. in Trinder, *Ind. Rev. Salop.* 322–5, suggests that generally one living rm. was what they got, whether they liked it or not.
216. It controls the lane to Netley Old Hall from the Shrews.–Ludlow rd.
217. There was nothing unusual about the development of working-class housing in Shrews., but it occurred somewhat later than in (e.g.) the Potteries, industrialized earlier and more intensively: *V.C.H. Staffs.* viii. 85–6, 113–19.
218. S.A.B.C. bldg.-control plan 1885/4. Burley was not local but came originally from Birm.: Trinder, *Victorian Shrews.* 119.
219. e.g. Dumb Clock Row, E. Malling (Kent), Stone Rows, Moira (Leics.), and the range now 10–17 (with no.18 demolished *c.*1977) Severn St., Shrews.: Mercer, *Eng. Vernacular Hos.* 173, 185–6; N.M.R. archive.
220. Smith probably built 28–31 Rea St., but not as one of his speculations for the notification of intent to build was submitted by A.B. Deakin for Thos. Deakin and not, as elsewhere, for J.P. Smith.
221. *Wilding's Dir. Shrews.* (1896), 105–6.
222. The 1851 census reveals a similar broad correlation between type of ho. and grade of employee at Hinkshay Rows, Dawley: *Salop. News Letter*, xliv. 23–4.
223. Trinder, *Victorian Shrews.* 114–29.
224. Butler named Bishop and Canon streets after his grandfather and father (more, one must suspect of the author of *The Way of All Flesh*, from impishness than filial piety) and Clifford St. after his lodging in Clifford's Inn. Alfred St., named after his clk., and probably King St. were parts of the same development but built after 1900. See H. Festing Jones, *Sam. Butler* (1919), ii. 344.
225. S.A.B.C. bldg.-control plan 1883/16; date stone of 1882.
236. S.A.B.C. bldg.-control plans 1877/28; 1883/8.
227. Trinder, *Victorian Shrews.* 120–1.
228. The date stone's off-centre position and the imbalance of the façade show that 6 hos. were originally intended.

229. Rob. Everall, who was building in Belle Vue and Kingsland in the 1870s and 1880s; John Cross (a boro. councillor), also building in Kingsland as well as Cherry Orchard; and E.A. Burley, of Birm. (S.A.B.C. bldg.-control plan 1882/32), later of Cherry Orchard.
230. *Ibid.* 1877/20; 1880/50; 1882/107.
231. And before long hos. of the older two-up-and-two-down type were having sculleries added at the rear and w.c.s installed in the yard, as e.g., in a terrace of six in Belle Vue Rd.: *ibid.* 1893/24.
232. *Ibid.* 1881/25 and 41.
233. *Ibid.* 1881/82.
234. *Ibid.* 1885/46.
235. But in 1882 five w.c.s were installed there: *ibid.* 1882/31.
236. *Ibid.* 1889/15.
237. *Ibid.* 1893/16, 23, 39.
238. *Ibid.* 1893/9, 20, 27, 47–8. Many of them were still called 'cottages'. Shrews. lagged behind London: as early as 1881 bathrooms were becoming *de rigeur* in many terrace hos. in Battersea: *The Park Town Est. and the Battersea Tangle* (Lond. Topographical Soc. cxxi), 45, 57 n.13.
239. S.A.B.C. bldg.-control plans 1893/52–3.
240. *Ibid.* 1893/49.
241. *Ibid.* 1893/4.
242. *Ibid.* 1877/18; 1878/21.
243. *Ibid.* 1885/4.
244. *Ibid.* 1880/66.
245. *Ibid.* 1882/57 (by A.B. Deakin).
246. *Ibid.* 1880/50 appears to refer to these hos. (only 5 of the 6 applied for having been built).
247. *Ibid.* 1893/39.
248. The dirs. do not give every householder's occupation. Everyone 'back of the Sheds' had his or her occupation listed, not many in Bradford St. and Underdale Rd., and very few in Kingsland. Thus, broadly speaking, a street's social cachet was directly proportional to the no. of house holders without listed occupation.
249. I. Watkin, *Oswestry* (1920), 250.
250. Date stone.
251. Examples are Croftside (1880), 3 hos. of similar plan (1889) in Queen's Pk., Glenwood (1894), and Sherwood (1894): S.R.R., DA 4/710/64, 310, 366, 371. The plans were not always carried out in every detail.
252. P.R.O., RG 12/2117, ff. 128–129v.
253. *Ibid.* f. 129 (no. 210); *Kelly's Dir. Salop.* (1895), 914–15, 1087; (1885), 164, 167, 382. It was purpose-built, with classrms. and a headmaster's ho.
254. On the official form accompanying the plan of Glenwood, which Smith's office submitted to the council, Queen's Rd. was labelled 'Bremner Street'. But perh. Smith was joking. Watkin, *Oswestry*, 194, has a brief biog. of him.
255. *T.S.A.S.* lxiv. 89–105.

Chapter XVI
1. *Victorian Archit.* (1970), 47–75.
2. *Edwardian Archit. and its Origins*, ed. A. Service (1975), 3.
3. The development may of course be seen from another angle. 'Without the protection of a noble patron the architect was at the mercy of the open market': J. Mordaunt Crook in *Archit. Hist.* xii. 66. Authors had faced the same dilemma a hundred yrs. or so before architects. It is the fashion to play down the significance of Johnson's letter to Ld. Chesterfield, but whatever earlier examples there may be of authors independent of patronage but dependent on their own work—and nearly all of them were in Grub St.—Johnson's letter was the profession's Declaration of Independence.
4. Bedstone, in a timber framed style, was described as having 'a Jacobean feeling' (*The Builder*, 20 Dec. 1884, p.839), and Stokesay Ct. has recently been called 'Jacobethan—softened by Arts and Crafts ideas' (J.M. Robinson in *Contents of Stokesay Ct.* (Sotheby's, 1994), i. 16).
5. Photo. in S.R.R., PH/W/33.
6. Photos. *ibid.* PH/A/16; cf. F. Leach, *Co. Seats of Salop.* (Shrews. 1891), 55 and facing pl.
7. Photos. in S.R.R., PH/C/42/3.
8. In what has recently been named Pountney Gdns.
9. Referred to in *Eddowes's Shrews. Jnl.* 19 July, 23 Aug. 1876.
10. Above, pp.239, 242, 244, 248-9.
11. Photos. in S.R.R., PH/S/13/C/10.
12. H.A.N. Brockman, *The Brit. Architect in Industry 1841–1940* (1974), 44, 55.
13. *Ibid.* 72–3. But he also noted that even foreign historic styles were eagerly copied.

14. The terms of the competition for the new Hos. of Parliament reveal a desire to develop a national style.
15. S. Muthesius, *High Victorian Movement in Archit. 1850–70* (1972).
16. P. R. Thompson, *Wm. Butterfield* (1971), 407.
17. The late 18th-cent. Salop. flowering of Georgian ch. archit. (*T.S.A.S.* lxxi. 83–134; below, p.279) did not obliterate a feeling that Gothic—even if it was no more than a Gothic dress, as at St. Alkmund's, Shrews.—was proper to chs. (*T.S.A.S.* lxxi. 110–26, esp. 118); and in the early yrs. of the 19th cent. proto-ecclesiological developments in S. Eng. (N. Yates, *Anglican Ritualism in Victorian Brit. 1830–1910* (1999), 49–50) were marking the turn of the tide which was to bring in the Gothic flood.
18. Yates, *op.cit.* caps. I–II.
19. Roderick Gradidge's forcibly expressed view, that 'Most architects suffer from megalomania, forcing onto their clients their ideas' (*Dream Hos.: the Edwardian Ideal* (1980), 49), is perh. exaggerated. At Adderley in 1877–9 Geo. Devey's plans and elevations were strongly criticized and ruthlessly altered by the owner (or his wife): S.R.R. 327/9/1/186/19.
20. G.G. Scott, *Remarks on Secular and Domestic Archit.* (1858). He did not always follow his own precepts, but, as Muthesius has noted (*High Victorian Movement*, 141), some of his colleagues didn't either.
21. Above, p.226.
22. Above, p.116.
23. Y. Brown, *Ruyton XI Towns* (1988), 106–7.
24. *The Builder*, 15 Oct. 1870, 836. The main block and one wing had then been completed.
25. Below, p.310; *P.O. Dir. Salop.* (1856), 109. The previous bldg. on the site had been descr. earlier as a 'handsome castellated residence': S. Bagshaw, *Dir. Salop.* (1851), 161.
26. S. Bagshaw, *Dir. Salop.* (1851), 154.
27. Above, cap. XXI (p. [22]).
28. *V.C.H. Salop.* x. 145.
29. D. Pratt, *A Pictorial Hist. of Ellesmere and Dist. 1790–1950* (1983), 58.
30. Descr. in *Lich. Dioc. Ch. Cal.* (1875), as 'very picturesque'.
31. *The Builder*, 12 Dec. 1859, p.751.
32. S.A.B.C., bldg.-control plans, Kingsland file.
33. *Ibid.*; S.A.B.C., bldg.-control plans 1891/43, 1893/17.
34. Heref. Dioc. Ch. Bldg. Soc. Rep. (Ludlow, 1870), 17–19.
35. G. Stamp and A. Goulancourt, *The Eng. House 1860–1914* (1986), 58–9.
36. S. Tyack in *Archit. Hist.* xxii. 44, 86.
37. They bear the initials of Dr. Sam. Butler, who bought the properties in 1814 and 1825; the sch. bought his hos. in 1862: *V.C.H. Salop.* ii. 156.
38. *Ibid.* x. 356, 363.
39. S.R.R. 6001/6740, ff. 4–5.
40. Above, p.242.
41. A remark by Macaulay quoted in Thompson, *Butterfield*, 372.
42. Swinburne was eulogizing Cromwell, but his republicanism was biasing his historical judgement.
43. *V.C.H. Salop.* x. 64–5.
44. *Ibid.* xi. 221.
45. M. Jones, *Burlton Village* (1989), 17–18.
46. He bought the land in 1862: B. Philpott, *Oakley Manor, Shrews.* (1982), 5 (copy in S.R.R.).
47. *V.C.H. Salop.* viii. 171, 176.
48. The very splendid early 17th-cent. framing of Beslow Fm. (in Wroxeter) was probably unknown, concealed by external rendering, as it was until its demolition: *T.S.A.S.* lxv. 56–63.
49. *V.C.H. Salop.* viii. 119–20 and pl. facing p.132.
50. *Burke's and Savills Guide to Country Hos.* ii (1980), 106–8.
51. S.R.R., Pengwern Boat Club Cttee. Rep. 30 Jan. 1882.
52. Date stone.
53. J.A. Bradley, *Woore Bazaar Souvenir: Hist. of the Church and Village* (1904), 25–7 (copy in S.R.R.).
54. There were of course many timber and plaster fire hoods, but they were internal and set against a brick or stone reredos at ground level.
55. The use of Baltic timber of slight scantling, common in south and east Eng., was virtually unknown in Salop.
56. Inf. from Mrs. M. Moran.
57. *V.C.H. Salop.* x. 21.
58. *Kelly's Dir. Salop.* (1895), 180.
59. Genuine timber framing had a last and very grand fling in the impressive Wistanstow village hall (1925).
60. M. Girouard, *Sweetness and Light: the 'Queen Anne' Movement 1860–1900* (1977), 129.
61. *V.C.H. Salop.* x. 81.
62. In 1918 it was covered and protected by a hardwood floor: inf. from Mr. Jas. Benthall.
63. *V.C.H. Salop.* x. 80–1.

Chapter XVII

1. See e.g. T.R. Gourvish, *Rlys. and the Brit. Economy 1830–1914* (1980).
2. Within 20 yrs. lines radiated to Birm., Chester, Crewe, Heref., Llanymynech, Stafford (over Shrews.–Birm. metals to Wellington), Welshpool, and Worc. (via Bewdley and Hartlebury Junc.): R.K. Morriss, *Rlys. of Salop.: A brief hist.* (Shrews. 1991); *T.S.A.S.* lxiv. 89–105.
3. After the 1864 amalgamation which created the co.: C.P. Gascoigne, *The Story of the Cambrian* (1922), 108.
4. *T.S.A.S.* lxiv. 91.
5. Unusually Whittington had two (*ibid.* 104), one on the Cambrian, one on the G.W.R.
6. The early rly. cos.' neglect of the county in general and of the E. Salop. industrial area in particular has been remarked upon by a leading rly. historian: J. Simmons, *The Victorian Rly.* (1991), 357–9.
7. *V.C.H. Salop.* xi. 202.
8. G. Evans, *Wellington and The Wrekin in old picture postcards* (Zaltbommel, 1987), pls. 22–3; *P.O. Dir. Salop.* (1870), 255; *T.S.A.S.* lxiv. 103.
9. In Castle Gates, its site now occupied by the Gala bingo club, opened as the Granada cinema and theatre in 1934: *P.O. Dir. Salop.* (1879), co. advts. p.86; O.S. Map 1/500, Salop. XXXIV.11.1 (1882 edn.); *Shrews. Chron.* 9 Nov. 1934.
10. The grand old-established Raven, Castle St., reconstructed in the 1860s as the 'Raven and Railway Hotel' (L.C. Lloyd, *The Inns of Shrews.* (Shrews. 1942), 47), was nevertheless not exclusively a stn. hotel. Opposite the stn. the tall, singular, red-brick Cleveland Temperance Hotel (1891), Castle Foregate, served a distinctive clientele: M. Owen, 'The Surridge Dawson bldgs.' (TS. in S.R.R., D 71.6 v.f.). Later the rebuilt Crown claimed to be 3 mins. from the stn. (H.E. Forrest, *Old Hos. of Shrews.* (1935 edn.), advt. at end), though, in St. Mary's St., it was farther away than the Raven.
11. For this para. see D. Jenkins, 'Shrews. General Rly. Stn.' (Keele Univ. M.A. thesis, 1991).
12. Above, p.208.
13. For an attempt to clear up the confusion that has surrounded the Penson archit. dynasty see D. Jenkins, 'Misc. Material from Ches. R.O.' (TS. in S.R.R., BP 41 v.f.).
14. A.M. Carr, *Shrews. as it was* (Nelson, 1978), pl. 37.
15. R. Christiansen and R.W. Miller, *The Cambrian Railways* (1967), i. 138; ii. 10.
16. In 1872 the boro., making an astonishingly weak argument for a large capital investment, petitioned the G.W.R. to bring the main line to the town because elderly people found it inconvenient to change at Gobowen: P.R.O., RAIL 256/9. Ref. owed to the late Prof. J. Simmons.
17. M. Bennett, *Oswestry in old picture postcards* (Zaltbommel, 1983), pls. 35–6.
18. Wm. Macdonald & Co. Ltd. *An Illustr. Guide to Shrews. and its Surroundings* [*c*.1900] (copy in S.R.R., qF66).
19. Morriss, *Rlys. of Salop.*, 27.
20. Jenkins, 'Shrews. Rly. Stn.' *T.S.A.S.* lxiv. 95, 102, attributes Gobowen and Shrews. stns. to T.K. Penson—a slip for T.M.
21. *T.S.A.S.* lxiv. 98; J. Betjeman, 'The Seeing Eye: or How to Like Everything', *Archit. Rev.* lxxxvi (no. 516, Nov. 1939), 201–2.
22. *V.C.H. Salop.* x. 78.
23. Date plaques; J. Piper and J. Betjeman, *Salop.: A Shell Guide* (1951), 18.
24. *T.S.A.S.* lxiv. 104.
25. *Ibid.* 95–6.
26. Carr, *Shrews. as it was*, pl. 36.
27. T.M. Penson pioneered the 'black and white' revival in Chester in the 1850s but generally eschewed the style on his rly. stns. He used it fancifully on the (now removed) turret at Baschurch: G. Biddle and J. Spence, *The Brit. Rly. Stn.* (1977), 57.
28. Date plaque.
29. The Lower furnace (1715), Coalbrookdale, was described in 1801 as 'a considerable pile of buildings' (J. Tann, *Development of the Factory* (1970), 11; cf. *T.S.A.S.* lviii. 253); and the remains of the mid 17th-cent. Upper furnace (rebuilt in the 18th cent.) stood in 'shockingly sordid' surroundings in 1956 (Pevsner, *Salop.* 156), a state of affairs remedied from 1959.
30. *V.C.H. Salop.* x. 279 (fig. 27), pls. 32, 34; xi, pl. 12.
31. For the Salop. iron trade the mid cent. was a period of 'uneasy stability', the last three decades one of 'precipitate decline' (B. Trinder, *Ind. Rev. Salop.* (1981), 239), but other inds., e.g. tile making, still prospered.
32. B. Trinder, *Ind. Arch. Salop.* (Chichester, 1996), 130–1.
33. *Ibid.* 140 sqq.
34. Above, pp.225-6.
35. Ironbridge Gorge Museum Trust, *Coalport China Wks. Mus.* (1978), 8.
36. I.G.M.T. *Handbk.* (rev. edn. 1986), 5.
37. *Descr. Acct. of Shrews. Illustr.* (Robinson, Son & Pike [*c*.1895]), 28, 33.

38. It is not clear whether the designer was Benj. Piercey of Welshpool who, *inter alia*, participated in promoting and surveying the Whitchurch–Oswestry line from 1860 and in 1864 was asked to prepare plans for the wks. at Oswestry (S.R.R. 6008/R138, R142; P.E. Baughan, *Regional Hist. of Rlys. of Gt. Brit.: N. and Mid Wales* (1980), 52–3) or John Robinson of Manchester who supervised most of the work (R. Christiansen and R.W. Miller, *The Cambrian Rlys. 1852–1888* (1967), 138).
39. Tann, *Development of Factory*, 151.
40. The date is uncertain: O.S. maps show it there in 1902 but not in 1883.
41. The office bldg. has a date stone of 1884, and a wing at the far end has one of 1895; the maltings themselves are of 1888: *Illustr. Guide to Shrews. and Surroundings* [*c*.1900].
42. *Acct. of Shrews. Illustr.* [*c*.1895], 32.
43. *V.C.H. Salop.* xi, pl. 10.
44. I have to thank Dr. Barrie Trinder for this formulation, but he is not to be held accountable for my use of it.
45. In W. Yorks. not before 1825 (C. Giles and I. Goodall, *Yorks. Textile Mills 1770–1830* (1992), 23) and in the country at large not before 1835 (E. Jones, *Industrial Archit. in Brit. 1750–1939* (1985), 75–6).
46. Date stone.
47. I.G.M.T. *Handbk.* 5. It was there by 1849: W.G. Muter, *Bldgs. of an Ind. Community: Coalbrookdale and Ironbridge* (1979), 17.
48. Trinder, *Ind. Rev. Salop.* 199. Printed *Rules* (1859; copy in S.R.R., M 35.8 v.f.) show that the aims of the Institution, of which Crookes was vice-president, were more liberal and less purely vocational than those of the earlier Ironbridge Mechanics' Inst. (*ibid. Rules*, 1844).
49. Muter, *Coalbrookdale and Ironbridge*, 21.
50. *V.C.H. Salop.* x. 279. Some are shown on est. maps of Jackfield: S.R.R. 6001/2365, f. 22.
51. Date stone.
52. Date stones. The enterprise had been founded in the mid 1860s: *Acct. of Shrews. Illustr.* [*c*.1895], 25; *Illustr. Guide to Shrews. and Surroundings* [*c*.1900]. Cf. Trinder, *Ind. Arch. Salop.* 60–1.
53. Trinder, *Ind. Arch. Salop.* 61.
54. Photos. in S.R.R., PH/S/13/C/3; date on bldg., which, apart from the ground-floor façade, was demolished in the 1970s.
55. *V.C.H. Salop.* x. 279 (fig. 27).
56. J. Randall, *Clay Industries ... on the Banks of the Severn* (Madeley, 1877), 29; A. Mugridge, *Brick and Roofing Tile Manufactories in the Severn Gorge* (Jackfield, 1987), 13, 16; *V.C.H. Salop.* x. 278, 279 (fig. 27).
57. See e.g. *V.C.H. Staffs.* viii. 134–8.
58. *V.C.H. Salop.* x. 278. Lynam was something of a 'tile-factory expert', capable of designing in many styles and fond of polychromy: G. Kay, 'Chas. Lynam—An Archit. of Tile Factories', *Jnl. of Tiles and Archit. Ceramics Soc.* iv. 21–28.
59. *Acct. of Shrews. Illustr.* [*c*.1895], 25.
60. O.S. Map 1/2,500, Salop. XXXIV.7 (1902 edn.).
61. Randall, *Clay Indust.* 29–30; *Jnl. Tiles and Archit. Ceramics Soc.* iv. 12–28.
62. D.J. Elliott, *Salop. Clock and Watchmakers* (1979), 147.
63. There is what appears to be an earlier complex at Eardiston Ho., Ruyton-XI-Towns. In conjunction with the ho. three ranges of farm bldgs. nearly enclose a very large farmyard *c*.80ft. by over 100ft. internally. All the ranges are of red sandstone to half-height and of timber above. The timber is of slight scantling in rectangular panels, with many re-used timbers of heavier scantling in the N. range. The complex was probably built, perh. in stages, *c*.1700, and that may be the date of the earlier part of the ho.
64. J. Loch, *Acct. of Improvements on Estates of Marquess of Stafford* (1820), App. IX, pp. 80 sqq.; *V.C.H. Salop.* iv. 185–7, 193, 204; xi. 160.
65. *Building News*, 18 Dec. 1891.
66. There were remains of a rly. at the Hay, Madeley, perhaps of 18th-cent. date, and one has been preserved at Honnington Grange, Lilleshall: local inf.
67. Stanway Manor was built in 1863 for a retired Black Country colliery owner and archit. and by the early 1890s was occupied by an eminent rly. engineer: *V.C.H. Salop.* x. 55, 62.
68. Above, pp.225-6.
69. Above, pp.265-7.
70. *V.C.H. Salop.* iv, pl. facing p.173.
71. Browning (1876) was less intent on describing contemporary shop fronts than on commenting, half-pityingly, on an empty life.
72. Demolished 1960: cf. *Changing Face of Shrews.* (Salop. Co. Libr. and Shrews. Chron. 1977), 26; D. Trumper, *Lost Shrews.* (Thrupp, 1997), 99. In 1918 it (or perh. its 1860s façade at least) was believed to be Ruskin's design: *Letters of Edwin Lutyens to his wife Lady Emily*, ed. C. Percy and J. Ridley (1985), 360.

73. Photos. in S.R.R.., PH/S/13/M/9; date 1777 on rainwater heads (Forrest, *Old Hos. of Shrews.* 50)—not invariably an accurate dating record: cf. that of 1710 on the bldg. which replaced the timber 46 Pride Hill after its demolition in the 1880s (above, p.162).

74. And indeed the Talbot was the former Ottley ho. until the fam. left trade (Forrest, *op. cit.* 50), buying Pitchford in 1473 and rebldg. the Hall there *c*.1550 (*V.C.H. Salop.* viii. 119).

75. The process may have been accelerated earlier by town regs. of the 1820s which ordered bow windows projecting beyond the bldg. line to be replaced by flat ones: *Victorian Shrews.* 59.

76. *Illustr. Guide to Shrews. and Surroundings* [*c*.1900].

77. Photos. in S.R.R., PH/S/13/H/3.

78. *V.C.H. Salop.* iv. 193–4.

79. Date stone.

80. *Acct. of Shrews. Illustr.* [*c*.1895], 34. The premises have been united with Cleveland Ho. (above, n.10) as a furniture shop.

81. *Illustr. Guide to Shrews. and Surroundings* [*c*.1900].

82. Date stone; D. Bilbey, *Ch. Stretton: A Salop. Town and its People* (1985), pl. 74.

83. The former site of Joyce's manufactory, vacated in 1904. The architect was Wm. Webb of Bargates, Whitchurch; the cast-iron front was supplied by McFarlane of Glasgow: Whitchurch Area Arch. Group, *Whitchurch Remembered* (Shrews. 1980), 14.

84. Date stone; *Acct. of Shrews. Illustr.* [*c*.1895], 52.

85. S.A.B.C. bldg.-control plans 1892/46. The ground floor has been remodelled. The street doorway originally had a date stone of 1895 over it. It is likely that here Oswell was influenced by the form of Halls' existing premises on the site, the old Shearmen's Hall: its stone gable, end-on to the street, had three large tall windows above a low ground floor: cf. Carr, *Shrews. as it wa*s, pl.18; above, p.222 and n.14).

86. *Illustr. Guide to Shrews. and Surroundings* [*c*.1900].

87. I. Watkin, *Oswestry* (1920), 219.

88. And the big banks sometimes built in sympathy with local styles (J. Booker, *Temples of Mammon: the archit. of banking* (Edinburgh, 1990), 188–9, 221, 241, 327), as did Lloyds in Shrews. in the 1870s and the N. & S. Wales Bank in Ludlow in 1907.

89. For reasons not entirely clear purpose built savings banks were primarily a North of Eng. phenomenon: *ibid.* 104 sqq.

90. Following the Savings Banks Act, 1817, 57 Geo. III, c. 130.

91. Booker, *op. cit.* App. I (pp. 300–11), lists 7—at Bridgnorth, Mkt. Drayton, Ellesmere, Oswestry, Shrews., M. Wenlock, and Whitchurch.

92. *Ibid.* 97–8, 106, 310.

93. The ho. has a date plaque of 1829 (the yr. it was leased to the Savings Bank: *V.C.H. Salop.* x. 431) beneath a window sill inscribed 'Savings Bank'.

94. A. Harrison, *W. Midland Trustee Savings Bank 1816–1966* (Shrews. 1966), 74.

95. Sometimes, surprisingly, they were let to non-banking tenants (as e.g. at Bridgnorth): Booker, *Temples of Mammon*, 108.

96. Harrison, *op. cit.* 74.

97. D. Lloyd, *Broad St.: its hos. and residents through eight cents.* (Ludlow Research Paper iii, 1979), 20, 27, 41, 53, 55.

98. *Kelly's Dir. Salop.* (1895), 307.

99. Harrison, *W. Midland Trustee Savings Bank*, 12, 43, 52; Booker, T*emples of Mammon*, 113, 309.

100. *Seven Victorian Architects*, ed. J. Fawcett (1976), 42, quoting *The Builder*, 12 Oct. 1864, pp.758–9. The example cited looks in fact less certainly like a bank than several Salop. examples of comparable date.

101. Photo. in S.R.R., PH/S/13/S/32; cf. *V.C.H. Salop.* iii. 147.

102. Cf. Booker, *Temples of Mammon*, 51; R.S. Sayers, *Lloyds Bank in the Hist. of Eng. Banking* (1957), 277.

103. Lloyds took him on when they took over the bank: cf. Booker, *op. cit.* 202; below, n.107.

104. e.g. Shrews. Girls' High Sch. (see below).

105. The Old Bank's Bridgnorth and Ellesmere branches, redundant for Lloyds business and eventually acquired by the Nat. Provincial Bank (below, n.107; *Kelly's Dir. Salop.* (1926), 379; (1934), 394), duly became NatWest.

106. The Old Bank moved from the Square to Scotland St. 1900 x 1905: *Kelly's Dir. Salop.* (1900), 327; (1905), 340.

107. In 1907, a yr. after it lost the county banking contract, the Old Bank (Eyton, Burton, Lloyd & Co.) was absorbed by the Capital & Counties Bank, amalgamated with Lloyds in 1918: *V.C.H. Salop.* iii. 188; Sayers, *Lloyds Bank*, 265, 287.

108. Now an HSBC (former Midland Bank) branch. The date is on the bldg. The architects were Grayson & Ould, of Liverpool: Watkin, *Oswestry*, 132. Its 'N. & S.' Welsh origins are apparent from the arms on it: 1st

and 4th quarters seem to be those of Llewelyn ap Griffith (d.1282), the Gwynedd ruler who became prince of Wales (quarterly 4 lions passant gardant: J. and J.B. Burke, *Gen. Armory* (1842), s.vv.), while 2nd and 3rd quarters approximate to those which some authorities attribute to Rhys ap Tewdwr Mawr (d.1093), prince of Deheubarth and ruler of S. Wales (3 lions coward passant regardant: *Arch. Camb.* 6th ser. xi. 407).

109. Lloyd and Klein, *Ludlow*, 69, 109; Pevsner, *Salop.* 187.

110. Sayers, Lloyds Bank, 279; *Kelly's Dir. Salop.* (1885), 1036; (1891), 512.

111. It opened as a bank in 1886 (plaque). The bldg. is probably no older than that for there is no sign of alteration, and its large ground-floor windows, very different from shop windows, are typical of a banking hall. Directories do not refer to a bank in King St. before 1891 when there was a branch of the Birm. Dist. & Counties Bank, successor of the Birm., Dudley & Dist. Bank's Corve St. branch: *Kelly's Dir. Salop.* (1885), 882, 1025; (1891), 349, 512. It was part of the United Counties Bank by 1913 and of Barclays by 1917: *ibid.* (1913), 358; (1917), 341.

112. Cf. Dickens's Anglo-Bengalee insurance co.: 'staring the city out of countenance after office-hours on working days, and all day long on Sundays; and looking bolder than the Bank': *Martin Chuzzlewit,* cap. XXVII (1843).

113. Now the Halifax premises. See S.A.B.C. bldg.-control plans 1890/46; *Acct. of Shrews. Illustr.* [*c*.1895], 54.

114. Kipling was thinking of cities of worldwide fame like Bombay, but his words apply equally well to Salop.

115. Cf. *V.C.H. Salop.* x. 101; *The Strettons: Scenes From the Past* (Salop. Librs. 1979), pl. 10 (inaccurate caption); Bilbey, *Ch. Stretton*, pl. 50.

116. *The Builder*, 8 May 1852, p.299; *V.C.H. Salop.* x. 415, 428, and pl. 22.

117. Here, recalling such similarly striking bldgs. as St. Cath.'s, Dodington (in Whitchurch: Cranage, viii. 674), and Ellesmere savings bank (erected on a 99-yr. Bridgwater est. bldg. lease: Booker, *Temples of Mammon*, 304), one may suspect the influence of the dowager ctss. of Bridgwater or the managers of the Bridgwater est. in the 1830s (cf. *V.C.H. Salop.* iv. 204).

118. Above, pp.222-3; *T.S.A.S.* liv. 130.

119. Above, pp.222-3.

120. J.F.A. Mason, *Boro. of Bridgnorth 1157–1957* (Bridgnorth, 1957), 26–7; above, p.222.

121. See W. Cathrall, *Hist. of Oswestry* (1855), frontispiece, 102–4; Watkin, *Oswestry*, 312–13; V. Palmer, *Oswestry and Dist.: A Portrait in Old Picture Postcards* (Loggerheads, 1989), 28–9. The Powis Mkt. Hall was demolished in 1963 and replaced by a new bldg.

122. S.R.R., Watton's news cuttings, ix. 243–4; *The Builder*, 28 Feb. 1857.

123. *The Builder*, 2 Feb. 1867, p.77.

124. Watkin, *Oswestry*, 150. The foundation stone was laid in 1869.

125. *Kelly's Dir. Salop.* (1895), 84, 987; the date of the Ellesmere mkt. is on the bldg.

126. *The Builder*, 20 Sept. 1879, p.1050; inscr. on bldg. (which became Kingsland Bridge Mansions in 2001).

127. *The Telepost*, vol. 4 (1875), no. 2, p. 16; *T.S.A.S.* liv. 130; photos. in S.R.R., PH/S/13/P/5.

128. *Kelly's Dir. Salop.* (1891), 346; (1895), 160. Ludlow Mkt. Hall was pulled down in 1986. The Swan Hill bldg. was also intended to accommodate the chief const. and two police inspectors: *ibid.* (1900), 203; date stone.

129. Pevsner, *Salop.* 224. Called the Guildhall in *An Illustr. Guide to Oswestry and the Cambrian Rly.* [*c*.1900], intro. by J. Parry Jones, p. [3], it replaced the old Guildhall, whose plainness had been relieved only by the decoration within a large pediment (Cathrall, *Oswestry*, pl. facing p.103).

130. *Kelly's Dir. Salop.* (1895), 160. It is strikingly different from Ludlow Mkt. Hall and yet apparently by the same archit., H.A. Cheers of Twickenham. It is not clear what part he, and what part the Lockwoods, played in its design.

131. For much of this para. see M. Seaborne, *The Eng. Sch. 1370–1870* (1971), 199–211.

132. Because the 'provision of the plan fully [met] their views' the Cttee. contributed £900 towards the £2,400 needed at Ludlow: *The Builder*, 15 Sept. 1855, 438–9.

133. *Ibid.*; Muter, *Coalbrookdale and Ironbridge*, 19.

134. Above, pp.246-8.

135. Above, p.256.

136. Many non-Gothic churches were rebuilt in, or converted to, a Gothic style in the 19th cent.: above, pp.253, 323 sqq.

137. Nearly four fifths of all state grants went to Anglican schs. 1833–9; but that fig. exaggerates the no. of such schs., for distribution was biased towards Anglican foundations and towards large schs.: F. Smith, *Hist. of Eng. Elem. Educ. 1760–1902* (1931), 140.

138. S.R.R., Watton newscuttings, ix. 230–1; *The Builder*, 3 Jan. 1857, p.9.

139. Seaborne, *Eng. Sch.* 212. There were exceptions. In 1848 Whitchurch grammar sch. was rebuilt in an Elizabethan style, in red brick with diaper patterning.
140. F.C. Childe, *Sketch of Par. of Cleobury Mortimer* (Shrews. 1874), 39.
141. W.H. Dawkes, *Hist. of Claverley* (Willenhall, *c.*1971), 35–6.
142. S.R.R. 1564/45-6.
143. *Ibid.*, /224-7.
144. Date on bldg.
145. *The Builder*, 16 Mar. 1872, p. 206; *V.C.H. Salop.* xi. 305. The archit. was Jos. Fogerty of Shifnal, perh. the Jos. Fogerty who was resident engineer to the Alb. Edw. Bridge nr. Coalbrookdale: *Eddowes's Jnl.* 16 Nov. 1864, p.5.
146. Haycock was building All Saints' ch. in the 1870s, and the sch. there is so similar to the ch. that it must be more or less contemporary. Dorrington sch. is similar to All Saints' sch. and wholly different from Dorrington ch. and is also probably of the 1870s.
147. Date on bldg.
148. S.R.R. 6001/3066, no. 22 (engraving).
149. Date on bldg.
150. S.R.R. 1564/203–10.
151. Seaborne, *Eng. Sch.*, 243–5.
152. Illustr. in J.S. Curl, *Victorian Archit.* (Newton Abbot, 1990), 133.
153. *V.C.H. Salop.* xi. 265; *The Builder*, 20 Sept. 1879, p.1065.
154. Date on bldg.
155. *V.C.H. Salop.* xi. 282.
156. By the Shrews. archit. J.L. Randal: S.A.B.C. bldg.-control plans 1882/117.
157. A county of comparatively few sch. bds.—and therefore few bd. schs.: *V.C.H. Salop.* iii. 175.
158. Where Conan Doyle, speaking through Sherlock Holmes in 'The Adventure of the Naval Treaty' (1893), singled them out: 'big, isolated clumps of building rising up above the slates, like brick islands in a lead-coloured sea ... Lighthouses, ... Beacons of the future!' J. Carey, *The Intellectuals and The Masses* (1992), 16, makes the same point with a different purpose.
159. By C.R. Dalgleish: Pevsner, *Salop.* 268. Salop. Tech. Sch. for Girls, founded and endowed from funds of Preston upon the Weald Moors hosp. (Char. Com. Scheme 21 Nov. 1895; *Shrews. Chron.* 11 July 1952), received some county-council support (*V.C.H. Salop.* iii. 198).
160. Wellington Coll., built as a national monument to the Iron Duke and so necessarily unsectarian, was begun, in a style which is a precursor to the 'Queen Anne' style, as early as 1859: Seaborne, *Eng. Sch.* 255.
161. *The Builder*, 28 Sept. 1878, p.1026.
162. Nat. Woodard advocated, and to a degree succeeded in providing, an education based upon sound religious principles and catering, at varying charges, for all sections of the middle classes, as well as for prosperous artisans, clerks, etc. See L. and W. Cowie, *That One Idea: Nat. Woodard and his Schs.* (1991), 7–8.
163. Seaborne, *Eng. Sch.* 253. Lancing's chapel (1868–1978) was the country's last-finished big Gothic bldg.: *The Times*, 13 May 1978, p.3.
164. Seaborne, *op.cit.* 253.
165. S. Muthesius, *High Victorian Movement in Archit. 1850–1870* (1972), 50.
166. N. Pevsner, *Staffs.* (Bldgs. of Eng. 1974), 114–15.
167. Its proposed ann. fees in 1880 were 20 gns. compared with Denstone's 34 (*The Builder*, 8 May 1880, p.570); they had dropped to 18 gns. by 1884 (*ibid.* 27 Dec. 1884, p.856). In 1878 Ellesmere was intended for 'middle-class boys', in 1879 for 'lower middle-class boys', and by 1884 for 'the sons of the lower middle-classes and upper artisan class': *The Builder*, 5 May 1878, p.1047; 6 Sept. 1879, p.994; 27 Dec. 1884, p.856. Cf. *V.C.H. Salop.* ii. 162.
168. S.A.B.C. bldg.-control plans, Kingsland file; above, p.239.

Chapter XVIII
1. In this cap. H. Colvin, *Biog. Dict. Brit. Architects 1600–1840* (1978), and Cranage are not cited for statements easily verifiable from them but only when there is reason to disagree with, or supplement, them.
2. S.R.R. 6001/372/3, p.82.
3. In the architects' rep.: S.R.R. 3916/1/8, loose enclosure. They claimed to have found the date 1723 in the fabric.
4. Below, p.331.
5. For detailed and intensely documented accts. of the greater chs. see T. Friedman, 'The Golden Age of Ch. Archit. in Salop.' *T.S.A.S.* lxxi. 83–134.
6. Most of Taylor's work was in S. Eng., but he had been employed in Salop. as early as 1674: Hugh Pagan Ltd. *Archit. Catalogue* no. 19, pp. 62–4.
7. *V.C.H. Salop.* viii. 329 and pl. facing p. 253; *Mytton Papers*, iv. 881.
8. *V.C.H. Salop.* x. 76, 79, 93; J. B. Blakeway, *Sheriffs of Salop.* (Shrews. 1831), 102.

9. Thos. Owen: *V.C.H. Salop.* iii. 238, 241; viii. 38–9; *Hist. Parl., Commons, 1558–1603*, iii. 163–4.
10. *Salopian Shreds & Patches*, ix. 36, quoting B.L. Add. MS. 5842.
11. By 1735 said to surpass those in St. Jas.'s Pk. See H. Owen and J. B. Blakeway, *Hist. Shrews.* (1825), i. 581; *Salopian Shreds & Patches*, ix. 36; M. Girouard, *The Eng. Town* (1990), 147, 153–4, 268–9.
12. For the importance of this point see T. Friedman, *Jas. Gibbs* (1984), 56–7.
13. Accts. of negotiations betw. Steuart and the par. are in Owen and Blakeway, *Hist. Shrews.* ii. 248–50; P.F. Norton and M. Hill, *New St. Chad's and its Architect* (1974); *T.S.A.S.* lxxi. 93–101.
14. And it would still be conventional had Steuart been allowed the spire he wanted.
15. Nor was St. Chad's the first in Salop.: see next para. but two.
16. J. Summerson, *Archit. in Brit.* (1977), 350–3; J.G. Dunbar, *Historic Archit. of Scot.* (1966), 166. Circular and elliptical forms seem to have had much appeal for 18th-cent. Scottish architects.
17. Owen's MS. notes (for a new edn.) on pp.186–7 of his copy (Shrews. Sch. Libr., S XII 67) of *Some Acct. of Ancient and Present State of Shrews.* (Shrews. 1808).
18. B.L. Add. MS. 21015, f. 87.
19. 9 Anne, c. 22.
20. S.R.R. 6001/299, f. 263.
21. Owen's MS. notes in his *Ancient and Present State of Shrews.* (Shrews. Sch. Libr., S XII 67), p. 286.
22. *V.C.H. Salop.* xi. 64, 129–30. The county gaol chap., Shrews., octagonal externally and circular internally, may have been Telford's idea rather than J.H. Haycock's, the commissioned archit., for in 1788 Telford claimed to have made a 'thorough reformation' and 'remodelling' of Haycock's design: cf. J.B. Lawson, 'Thos. Telford in Shrews.' *Thos. Telford, Engineer*, ed. A. Penfold (1980), 3; *V.C.H. Salop.* iii. 124–6.
23. Perh. initially more a proprietary or par. chap. (cf. B.F.L. Clarke, *The Bldg. of the 18th-Cent. Ch.* (1963), cap. 14) than a dissenting one: Fletcher, as vicar, projected it, and for yrs. after his death (1785) his Methodists did not separate from the Ch. of Eng.: *V.C.H. Salop.* xi. 62, 68–9.
24. It was devised as a small, nearly square bldg. Not until 1789 was it enlarged to the form shown in an early 19th-cent. drawing: R.F. Skinner, *Nonconformity in Salop.* (Shrews. 1964), 94 n. 2; S.R.R., uncat. drawing. I have to thank my former colleague Mr. Christopher Stell for guidance about the chapel.
25. *T.S.A.S.* lxxi. 89–92.
26. S. Bagshaw, *Dir. Salop.* (1851), 48.
27. *V.C.H. Salop.* viii. 145 and pl. facing p. 144. There was said to have been, at the end of the 17th cent., an outside stone inscribed 'RL FL 1564': *Mytton Papers*, iv. 806; Cranage, x. 995. The 'F' was probably a worn 'E': Ric. Langley owned the chap. 1561–91 and was marr. to Eleanor *née* Wrottesley: S.R.R. 1514/140; 6001/4078, p. 1020; *V.C.H. Salop.* viii. 143 (corr. *ibid.* x. 513).
28. Leighton, 'Sketches', iv.
29. The structure at Halston is of *1437 but its transformation into a ch. was probably 1552 x *c.*1570. In one spandrel a double-headed eagle (from the Myttons' arms: F.W. Kittermaster, *Salop. Arms and Lineages* (1869), 47) is carved, and in another the famous Beauchamp bear and ragged staff, later used by the Grevilles. Two sons of Ric. Mytton (d.1591) marr. Greville ladies: the eldest son, marr. 1552, was dead by 1567, and both ladies (one remarried) died in 1572: *T.S.A.S.* xlvii. 203.
30. *Archaeologia*, lxi. 259, 274–5.
31. Cranage, vii. 601–2, gives good reasons for a post-Dissolution rebldg. of the upper part.
32. The earliest monument in the chap. is to Wm. Foxe (d.1554).
33. *Gent. Mag.* N.S. xxxix. 50–1.
34. The Cornewall chap. there is late 16th- or early 17th-cent.
35. But the fine 'Decorated' W. window at Ch. Stretton may be of 1619: below, n.37.
36. S.R.R. 6001/372/3, p. 73.
37. Jane Norton built the W. window at Ch. Stretton before 1639 (*T.S.A.S.* 3rd ser. i. 356), perh. in 1619 (date over window). It differs from the windows in the transepts in having a fillet on the mullions and slightly looser cusping beneath slightly broader heads. The E. window, called mid 17th-cent. by Pevsner (*Salop.* 101), is probably the rector's work *c.*1819: *V.C.H. Salop.* x. 115.
38. R.C.H.M.E. *City of Camb.* ii. 188, 196–7, pl. 235; *City of Oxf.* 60, 67–8, pls. 121–5.
39. The Donington roof is dated 1635, and it is probable, as Cranage suggests, that the nave was rebuilt then.
40. *D.N.B.* s.vv. More, Ric. (d.1643) and Sam.
41. Cranage (vii. 579 sqq.) makes a good case for more medieval work surviving than Pevsner (*Salop.* 148) will allow.

42. At Melverley the plainness of the roof, the cusping of the wind braces (identical with those in the Old Mkt. Ho. (1596), Shrews.), and the form of the windows all suggest a late 16th-cent. date. Cranage (ix. 804–5) was ready to accept a 15th- or even late 14th-cent. origin because of the heavy scantling and because he attributed the form of the windows to the restoration of 1878; but in 1790 the windows had the same form as now: S.R.R. 6001/372/2, p.11. The E. wall is modern and does not follow the original design.
43. S.R.R. 6001/372/3, p.73.
44. *Ibid.* p.67. The chap. was not consecr. until 1666 because the endowment was insufficient: S. Garbet, *Hist. of Wem* (1818), 314–15 (written in the 1740s).
45. *T.S.A.S.* 4th ser. vi, figs. 5 and 8 betw. pp.96 and 97.
46. Garbet, *Wem*, 232.
47. *T.S.A.S.* 3rd ser. x. 278, 347, 379.
48. S.R.R. 3916/1/1, f. 92.
49. A 1789 drawing shows an aisleless bldg., with quoins (S.R.R. 6001/372/1, p.94) presumably painted on the rough cast. The 'wooden columns' supporting the arcades of 1819 may have been former external timber walls pierced for aisles. In 1799 the timbers were 'good, very substantial, and well compacted'. In 1850 Glynne noted 'very poor arcades of plain flat arches with octagonal piers without capitals' (*S.R.S.* i. 38), which might imply openings cut through a timber-framed wall.
50. S.R.R. 6001/372/3, p.10.
51. *Ibid.* /1, p. 32.
52. *Ibid.* /3, p. 60; above, p.38.
53. *V.C.H. Salop.* ii. 61.
54. S.R.R. 6001/201, f. 68.
55. *Ibid.* /372/3, p. 78.
56. *Ibid.* /1, p. 113.
57. *V.C.H. Salop.* x. 232.
58. Bodl. MS. Top. Salop. c. 2, f. 521 (early 19th-cent. copy of earlier drawing).
59. *T.S.A.S.* 2nd ser. vii. 142.
60. Mytton Papers, vii. 1504.
61. J. Pryce-Jones, *Oswestry Par. Ch.: its early hist.* (1992), 25. Medieval work at the W. end of the nave arcade may have survived until 1873–4, but it is impossible to say whether the rest of the very plain arcades and the chancel arch are late 17th-cent. or of 1807: cf. *ibid.* 25–7; below, cap. XXI, n.2.
62. *T.S.A.S.* 2nd ser. x. 52.
63. *Ibid.* vii. 146.
64. Above, p.288.
65. Date on easternmost truss of the roof.
66. The chap. must be coeval with the associated almshos. (date stone 1672).
67. Symbolized locally by the dedication of Newtown chap. (at its consecr. in 1666) to King Chas. the Martyr, a commemoration of whose death had been added to the Prayer Bk. in 1662.
68. Mytton Papers, ii. 276; S.R.R. 6001/372/3, p.60.
69. S.R.R. 6001/372/1, p.126; Bodl. MS. Top. Salop. c.2, ff.459–60.
70. Owen and Blakeway, *Hist. Shrews.* ii. 248.
71. S.R.R. 6001/372/3, p. 68.
72. *Ibid.* /1, p.32; 6001/6863, f.103; Bodl. MS. Top. Salop. c 2, f.383.
73. S.R.R. 6001/372/3, p.5.
74. *Ibid.* /2, p.79.
75. *Ibid.* /3, pp.1, 64.
76. Bodl. MS. Top. Salop. c. 2, f. 527; *V.C.H. Salop.* viii. 328.
77. S.R.R. 6001/372/2, pp.15, 75; /3, p.68.
78. *Ibid.* /1, p.126.
79. *Ibid.* /3, p.64.
80. Above, p.287.
81. Characteristically Cranage (x. 930, 945, 962) calls the windows 'poor' and the much larger E. window in the chancel (all shown in J. Buckler's 1815 *View of St. Mary's*, H.W. Adnitt, 'Shrews. Illustr.' v) 'debased Elizabethan'. In the apex of Trinity chap. gable the trefoil within a spheric triangle is medieval (cf. above, p.71), though partly restored.
82. S.R.R. 6001/372/2, p.81.
83. Leighton, 'Sketches', iv.
84. S.R.R. 6001/372/2, p.30b.
85. A 1791 drawing (*ibid.* /3, p.7) shows 17th-cent.-type windows in the S. wall of the nave; one of 1823 (S.R.R. 6001/5582, f.60) shows broad pointed windows in the N. wall of the nave. The nave was wholly rebuilt 1886–9.
86. S.R.R. 6001/372/1, pp.17, 32; /3, p.35.
87. Mytton Papers, iv. 728.
88. The tower arch might have indicated whether or not the tower was an addition, but it was rebuilt or refashioned in the 1891–2 restoration.
89. Soc. of Antiquaries MS. 477, p.354; S.R.R. 6001/5582, 26.
90. *V.C.H. Salop.* viii. 106; S.R.R. 3916/1/2, no.28.
91. Mytton Papers, iv. 763, 768, 899; v. 1072, 1075; vii. 1577.
92. The distinction was perh. clearer then than earlier, for the Presbyterian chap. at Leeds of *c.*1700 had a W. tower and the chap. at Frenchay nr. Bristol, of *c.*1720, had a tower above the W. entry: inf. from Mr. Stell. For Coalbrookdale chap. see above, p.285 and nn.23–24.
93. A 1748 drawing of the proposed new ch. shows the W. tower standing free, but pencilled additions seem to show the outline of a structure overlapping it (S.R.R. 6001/299, f.258). A 1789 drawing shows the overlapping beyond doubt and in the same style as the rest of the ch.: *ibid.* /372/1, p.127.
94. W. Price, *Hist. of Oswestry* (1815), 158; S.R.R. 6001/372/2, p.73.
95. Inf. from Mr. James Lawson; B.L. Add. MS. 21010, f.39.
96. S.R.R. 6001/372/3, p.68.
97. Below, cap. XXI n.1.
98. *V.C.H. Salop.* viii. 328. The utility of long chancels (as distinct from an ideological preference for them) returned with mid 19th-cent. reform of choirs: below, cap. XXI n.106.
99. S.R.R. 6001/5582, 50; Mytton Papers, ii. 262.
100. S.R.R. 6001/372/3, p.69.
101. *Ibid.* p.1.
102. *Ibid.* /1, p.126; Bodl. MS. Top. Salop. c.2, ff.459–60.
103. S.R.R. 6001/372/3, p.57. The encroachment is clear, but it may be that (a) the N. and S. walls of the chancel were rebuilt rather than refenestrated, and (b) the chancel arch is a copy of the original rather than much restored.
104. Herefs. R.O., draft of bp.'s reg., faculty to restore 31 Mar. 1888.
105. S.R.R., P 22/B/2/5–6.
106. S.R.R. 6001/299, f.263.
107. *Ibid.* /372/2, p.23.
108. Bodl. MS. Top. Salop. c.2, f.383.
109. The chancel was possibly built, rather than merely restored, in the late 17th cent. If so, that strengthens the point made in this para.
110. S.R.R. 6001/372/2, p.79.
111. In 1862, when the whole cultural environment had changed, the classical auditorium ch. of St. Geo.'s, Pain's La., was replaced by a ch. 'gothic in both form and style'.
112. Below, n.119.
113. Mytton Papers, vii.1491.
114. *Ibid.* ii. 278; iv.888.
115. *S.R.S.* i. 36, 73, 118.
116. S.R.R. 4001/I/5/3, p.875. There may have been a similar one before the 1646 fire: J.F.A. Mason, 'Bridgnorth Grammar Sch.' (TS. 1968; copy in S.R.R. 3763/11/3), p.1 n.1.
117. Mytton Papers, v. 986.
118. Owen, *Ancient and Present State of Shrews.* 350–l.
119. Harrod, *Shavington*, 32–9, 44–64. The rector's pew contributed to the trouble: it and the Corbets' monopolized the chancel and edged the Needhams out into the cold.
120. Mytton Papers, ii. 280; iv. 810.
121. *V.C.H. Salop.* viii. 54.
122. The chap. was used as a Cornewall fam. pew but is not known to have been built for that purpose.
123. Harrod, *Shavington*, 57–61.
124. Mytton Papers, vii. 1577; *V.C.H. Salop.* x. 459.
125. Cranage, viii. 704, suggests that the present chap. is of *c.*1778. If so, it replaces the 'little chancel' on the same site and of much the same size in 1736: Mytton Papers, iv. 888. Drawings of *c.*1700 and 1788 (Shrews. Sch. Libr., S IX 100; S.R.R. 6001/372/1, p.62) show a chap. similar in site and size to the present one but with a rectangular S. window of three transomed lights and E. and W. walls several ft. lower than now.
126. *V.C.H. Salop.* x. 21.
127. Harrod, *Shavington*, 117.
128. E.A. Greening Lamborn, *The Par. Ch.: its Archit. and Antiquities* (1936), 95 sqq.
129. *V.C.H. Salop.* x. 299.
130. The porch was of stone in 1791: S.R.R. 6001/372/3, p.7.
131. Now gone: *ibid.* p.24.
132. A small N. porch at Madeley (*ibid.* /1, p.80) was of unknown date. The nearest access from street or road was on the N. at Madeley, Stanton, and St. Mary's, Shrews.
133. Below, n.155.
134. The ch.'s rebldg. has been dated to the 1750s (S.R.R. 6001/5582, f.58; Cranage, v. 565), but a 1791 drawing, endorsed in a contemporary hand 'Rebuilt 1721' (S.R.R. 6001/372/3, p.5), is nearer the truth, for it was descr. in 1732 as 'lately built' (Mytton Papers, ii. 262).

135. S.R.R. 6001/372/2, p.15.
136. *Ibid.* /1, p.55; /2, p.5.
137. *Ibid.* /3, p.3.
138. *V.C.H. Salop.* viii. 54.
139. *S.R.S.* i. 44.
140. *Ibid.* 111.
141. D. Lloyd, *The Par. Ch. of St. Laurence's, Ludlow* (1980), 5.
142. *V.C.H. Salop.* viii. 26; xi. 169; Cranage, iii. 169.
143. *V.C.H. Salop.* viii. 54; xi. 64.
144. Glynne (*S.R.S.* i) notes many W. galleries with organs. The *locus classicus* of the change is Mellstock in Wessex.
145. D.R. Thomas, *Hist. Dioc. St. Asaph*, iii (1913), 27–8.
146. *V.C.H. Salop.* xi. 22, 64.
147. *Ibid.* viii. 54; xi. 169; *S.R.S.* i. 111.
148. S.R.R. 6001/372/1, p. 46; *S.R.S.* i. 42.
149. *V.C.H. Salop.* x. 287.
150. S.R.R. 6001/372/3, p.44.
151. *S.R.S.* i. 65.
152. *Ibid.* 69–70; *V.C.H. Salop.* x. 440–1.
153. Not every dormer lit a gallery. Harley had no recorded gallery (*Gent. Mag.* N.S. xxxix. 50–1; *T.S.A.S.* iv. 329–30), but two central four-light mullioned and transomed dormers lit the nave (from the S.) and N. aisle: S.R.R. 6001/372/1, p. 60; /3, p.103.
154. *V.C.H. Salop.* x. 246.
155. At the N. end of the W. front: Bodl. MS. Top. Salop, c.2, f.301. A porch occupied most of the W. front; a 1790 drawing shows its S. side elevation: S.R.R. 6001/372/2, p.81.
156. It led to a modern doorway high up in the S. wall at the E. of the nave: S.R.R. 6001/372/1, p.55.
157. S.R.R. 6001/372/2, p.61; T.R. Marshall, *Hist. Mkt. Drayton Par. Ch.* (1884), 34–5.
158. The single tier of windows there seems to have been a deliberate local choice, for in 1712 it had been agreed that there could be two tiers if desired: S.R.R. 212/1. The designer John Barker had just completed the very similar St. Ann's, Manchester, with two tiers. The N. and S. galleries were removed in the early 1970s: inf. from the Revd. R.D. Jenkins.
159. End of N. aisle: Mytton Papers, iv. 815. Within 20 yrs. it was replaced by a sch. ho.: *V.C.H. Salop.* xi. 174.
160. End of N. aisle: Mytton Papers, iv. 825.
161. Room above S. transept: Cranage, v. 412.
162. Chancel, warmed in 1797 by a fireplace with a timber and plaster flue: S.R.R. 6001/6863, f.147.
163. Above N. porch: Cranage, x. 889.
164. *V.C.H. Salop.* x. 43.
165. Mytton Papers, ii. 380.
166. *V.C.H. Salop.* ii. 152, pl. facing p.156.
167. With bedchamber: Mytton Papers, vii. 1491. Demolished *c*.1815, the bldg. was resurrected by Dickens in 1840: *The Old Curiosity Shop*, caps. 46, 52; *T.S.A.S.* 3rd ser. viii. 175–6.
168. Mytton Papers, v. 1075.
169. *Ibid.* ii. 441; Garbet, *Wem*, 276.
170. Owen and Blakeway, *Hist. Shrews.* ii. 298.
171. Mytton Papers, vii. 1504; S.R.R. 6001/372/1, p.72.
172. The windows, of early 17th-cent. character, are good evidence but not conclusive. See S.R.R. 6001/372/3, p.3.
173. Bodl. MS. Top. Salop. c.2, f.383.
174. Soc. of Antiquaries MS. 477, p.354; Mytton Papers, v. 1194.
175. Mytton Papers, ii. 251, 468; iv. 763.
176. *V.C.H. Salop.* xi. 182–3, but mainly because of the larger congregation after the bldg. of Preston hosp.
177. A rare example is that built by Eliz. I's favourite, Leicester, at Denbigh: L. Butler in *Jnl. Brit. Arch. Assn.* 3rd ser. xxxviii. 40–62.
178. Perh. the nearest approach is Thos. Harrison's nave at Whittington, now much altered.
179. T. Rowley, *Salop. Landscape* (1972), 128–34.
180. Above, pp.185-7.
181. As in the Perpendicular period: above, cap. v..
182. Mytton papers, ii. 380; Cranage, x. 1014.
183. A tablet put up in 1727 to commemorate the rebldg. implies only that Wilbraham (and Fra. Chambre) were laudably active in the matter (Mytton Papers, v. 1012), perh. like the Stokesay wardens whose 'pious oversight' of the 1654 rebldg. there is recorded on a plaque (*S.P.R. Heref.* xvii (3), p.vii).
184. Claimed on his monument, put up after 1734: Cranage, x. 1004.
185. Mytton Papers, ii. 262.
186. W. Price, *Hist. of Oswestry* (1815), 158. The founder was probably Sir
187. John Bridgeman's dau. Judith (1702–55), who erected a monument to him in 1752: S.R.R. 6001/2794, vii, ff.350, 353; /4645, f.30.
187. Replaced 1863, demolished *c*.1961: *V.C.H. Salop.* x. 288.
188. S.R.R. 6001/372/3, p.68; S.R.R. P294/E/6/1, pp.7-9.
189. *T.S.A.S.* lxxi. 89–92.
190. He is also said to have designed Jackfield ch. (S.R.R. 6000/18498), but contemporary authority is lacking, despite record of his other work in Broseley: *V.C.H. Salop.* x. 261, 271.
191. *T.S.A.S.* lxxi. 89–90.
192. Cf. Cranage, ii. 73; *Salopian Shreds & Patches*, ix. 145.
193. *V.C.H. Salop.* viii. 54.
194. For Richards see Colvin, *Biog. Dict. Brit. Archit.* 606.
195. *V.C.H. Salop.* x. 287.
196. *Ibid.* xi. 64.
197. *Ibid.* x. 288. It is an unhappy commentary on the power of social conditions to nullify philanthropic motives that, although Jackfield was meant to benefit the poor of Broseley par., there were in fact proportionally no more free seats there than in the par. ch.: Trinder, *Ind. Rev. Salop.* 174.
198. Above, p.293.
199. Above, pp.285-6.
200. Commanded 'by authority', as the Worfield wardens noted *c*.1576: *T.S.A.S.* 3rd ser. v. 64. See *T.S.A.S.* lxxiii. 25, for an illustr. of a 1561 Decalogue in St. Lawrence's, Ludlow.
201. Owen, *Ancient and Present State of Shrews.* 164.
202. *Ibid.* 248.
203. Mytton Papers, ii. 276; iv. 888.
204. Cranage (ii. 72–3) says that the whole chancel was originally painted in the same fashion. But the painted cornice at the base of the colouring suggests that the lower part of the wall was always meant to be distinguished from the upper.
205. G.W.O. Addleshaw and F. Etchells, *Archit. Setting of Anglican Worship* (1948), 155–6.
206. S.R.R. 6001/5582, 26.
207. I am grateful to Miss Jean Hamilton of the Victoria and Albert Mus. for inf. about these wallpapers.
208. Above, pp.85, 88.
209. R.C.H.M.E. *City of Oxf.* p.xx.
210. The Condover roof has been much rebuilt, partly using original timbers: *V.C.H. Salop.* viii. 54; *Salopian Shreds & Patches*, ii. 206.
211. Rushbury chancel roof is probably coeval with the finely carved early 17th-cent. pews (Cranage, ii. 150) beneath it, and hammer-beam roofs in Salop. chs. seem mostly to be post-Reformation (see next note).
212. The dates of these roofs are derived either from known rebuilds of the fabric beneath them or from inscriptions on the timbers.
213. In 1661 (the date on the roof) Sheriffhales ch., with the E. half of the par., was in Staffs., but the roof is part of the local ensemble.
214. *V.C.H. Salop.* viii, pl. facing p. 217; S.R.R. 6001/372/2, p.3. The western most bay of the roof is plain, presumably because it was the site of the bellcot.
215. Will of Wm. Bromshill of Aston Rogers 1 July 1429: *T.S.A.S.* i. 214.
216. Cf. Pevsner, *Salop.* 91–2.
217. A very early instance of a monument signed by the carver (W. Pue).
218. Detail illustr. in *V.C.H. Salop.* iii, pl. facing p.176.
219. It impressed Mytton 100 yrs. later: Mytton Papers, v. 942.
220. Each panel has had a rectangular piece—all of differing dimensions—cut from the top of the centre, perh. for the locks of a chest.
221. Above, p.288.

Chapter XIX

1. In this cap. statements based on C.F. Stell, *Inv. of Nonconf. Chaps. and Meeting Hos. in Central Eng.* (R.C.H.M.E. 1986), 191–206, will not invariably be separately footnoted. I have to thank my former colleague Mr. Christopher Stell for guidance about nonconf. chaps. in general, and also Mrs. J.V. Cox for much help and advice and for allowing me to see her paper on Shrews. nonconf. meeting hos. and chaps. before its publication in *T.S.A.S.* lxxii. 52-97.
2. *T.S.A.S.* lxxii. 65.
3. P.R.O., E 178/6907. Ref. kindly provided by Mrs. Cox.
4. See e.g. the refs. to the two fams. in *V.C.H. Salop.* xi.
5. *Ibid.* iii. 268; *Gent. Mag.* iv. 217; H. Owen and J.B. Blakeway, *Hist. Shrews.* (1825), ii. 476–87.
6. R.F. Skinner, *Nonconf. in Salop. 1662-1816* (Shrews. 1964), 28.
7. *V.C.H. Salop.* viii. 251, 291.
8. *Ibid.* 291, for a mid 19th-cent. analysis of the standing of Anglicans and Dissenters in Pontesbury par.
9. Skinner, *Nonconf. in Salop.* 13-23, pl. ix.

10. *Ibid*. pl. xv. J. W. Fletcher's long, if interrupted, ministry (1760–85) may well have played a large part in the spread of Methodism from Madeley (*V.C.H. Salop*. xi. 61), but only in conjunction with other forces.

11. Stell's figures (*Nonconf. Chaps.*) are incomplete, for his main concern is with survivors, but there is no reason to think that N. Salop. has suffered worse than S. Salop. from later destruction.

12. Cf. Stell's figures (mainly of survivals) with foundations recorded in *V.C.H. Salop*. viii, xxi.

13. *T.S.A.S.* lxxii. 57.

14. *V.C.H. Salop*. xi. 131-3.

15. Below, cap. XXI.

16. Again the 34 listed by Stell are not the full number, which may have approached 50.

17. *V.C.H. Salop*. viii. 255, 292.

18. *Chas. Darwin: His Life in an Autobiographical Chapter,* ed. F. Darwin (1902), 5–8.

19. I. Watkin, *Oswestry* (Oswestry, 1920), 165.

20. *T.S.A.S.* lxxii. 76.

21. *Ibid*. 83-4. Cf. *V.C.H. Salop*. ii. 16.

22. Watkin, *Oswestry*, 328.

23. S.R.R., DA 4/710/283.

24. J.H. Lenton, *Methodism in Wellington* (1982), 17.

25. There was always a tendency in larger nonconf. chaps. to indulge in some ornament and in Gothic: C. Stell, 'Nonconf. Archit. and the Camb. Camden Soc.' in *'A Church as it Should be': The Cambridge Camden Soc. and its influence*, ed. C. Webster and J. Elliott (Stamford, 2000), 317–19.

26. *V.C.H. Salop*. xi. 69.

27. *T.S.A.S.* lxxii. 79.

28. *Ibid*. 76.

29. Above, pp.208, 261.

30. C. Wakeling, 'Methodist Archit. in N. Staffs.: The First Seventy-Five Yrs.' *Staffs. Studies*, ed. P. Morgan (Keele, 1987), 165.

31. *V.C.H. Salop*. xi. 131.

32. *Ibid*. 131-2, pl. 39.

33. *T.S.A.S.* lxxii. 65, 68, 79.

34. *Ibid*. 89.

35. *Illustr. Guide to Shrews*. [*c*.1896–7]; cf. *P.O. Dir. Salop*. (1870), 130.

36. *Salop*. 225.

37. But for the Bridgnorth Catholic Apostolic ch. see below, cap. XXI.

38. Of course 'patron' in a sense different from the Anglican meaning of the word. See C. Stell, *Architects of dissent: some nonconf. patrons and their architects* (1976).

39. *Hist. of Congregationalism in Salop*. ed. E. Elliot (Oswestry, *c*.1898), 280-8. A similar instance of a determinedly Gothic chap. built by a 'patron' for Congregationalists had occurred at Armitage (Staffs.) a generation earlier (1820): Stell, *Nonconf. Chaps*. 208–9.

40. But the earliest 'patron' traced is John Appleton of Roushill, Shrews., who built the Methodist chap. (1781), Hill's Lane, at his own cost: *T.S.A.S.* lxxii. 68.

41. *V.C.H. Salop*. viii. 56, 292; Elliot, *op. cit*. 177.

42. Elliot, *op. cit*. 152, 289, 294.

43. Perh. as the Salop. Assn. treasurer (below, n.56), his involvement commemorated by the laying of foundation stones, etc.: *ibid*. 49, 129, 158, 199, 224, 308.

44. B.M. Philpott, *A Name, A Man, A House: Oakley Manor, Belle Vue, Shrews.* (priv. print. Shrews. 1983), 6 (copy in S.R.R., D 71.4 v.f.).

45. Elliot, *op. cit*. 57–8; *Bye-Gones* 1889-90, 357-9; 1911-12, 8-9.

46. Elliot, *op. cit*. 134-6.

47. B. Trinder, *Ind. Rev. Salop*. (1981), 176–8.

48. For the Congregationalists' Gothic bias in Staffs., e.g. at Armitage (1820), Burton-upon-Trent (1842), Cheadle (1850), Newcastle-under-Lyme (1859), and Leek (1860), see Stell, *Nonconf. Chaps*. 208–15.

49. Surveying the wider scene, Mr. Stell notes that Unitarians were as likely to build a church-like chapel as were Congregationalists, and perhaps even more precociously: Webster and Elliott, *'A Church as it Should be'*, 323–5.

50. See e.g. illustrns. in Elliot, *Congregationalism*, 51, 184, 189, 229, 241, 245, and perh. 172, 175 (pointed windows, tracery indistinct).

51. Some socially ambitious Dissenters, e.g. Abraham Darby (IV) and his relatives and Jos. Reynolds, joined the established ch. (E. Thomas, *Coalbrookdale and the Darby Fam*. (1999), 149, 152; S.R.R., P47/A/2/1, p.46 no. 368), but they were probably not representative of their fellows.

52. *T.S.A.S.* lxxii. 68.

53. A copy of the 1884 design for the elevation, dated 1884, is preserved in the chap.

54. *T.S.A.S.* lxxii. 84.

55. *Ibid*. 65, 89.

56. The Salop. Assn. treasurers 1820-87 were Sir John Bickerton Williams (*D.N.B.*), J. B. Grierson, the Bridgnorth carpet manufacturer, etc. (J.F.A. Mason, *Boro. of Bridgnorth 1157-1957* (Bridgnorth, 1957), 42; S. Bagshaw, *Dir. Salop*. (1851), 617, 632, 634; Harrison, Harrod & Co. *Dir. Staffs. & Salop*. (1861), 593, and Thos. Barnes (Elliot, *Congregationalism*, 11).

57. £5-6,000: *T.S.A.S.* lxxii. 86.

58. About £5,000: Elliot, *op. cit*. 45.

59. About £2,500 and £3,500 (incl. £1,500 for the site) respectively: *T.S.A.S.* lxxii. 65, 89. The Independent chap. (1845), Castle Gates, cost £3,000, the Welsh Independent Tabernacle (1862), Dogpole, nearly £2,000: *ibid*. 79, 81. Except for the Wesleyan chap., St. John's Hill (over £2,000: *ibid*. 68), all the other chaps. cost much less.

60. Watkin, *Oswestry*, 28.

61. The 1902 Education Act for instance was received much more calmly in Salop. than it was in (e.g.) Wales and Stafford: cf. *V.C.H. Salop*. iii. 199; P. Murcott, 'Passive Resisters in Stafford', *Trans. Stafford Hist. and Civic Soc.* 1965–7, 36–45.

62. An early 20th-cent. photo. in the chap. shows the arms stored in a room, but presumably they were originally in their present position above the pulpit.

63. e.g. in St. Mary Magdalen's (1792–6), Bridgnorth, where Telford contrived a small chancel between entrance lobbies: A. Webb, *Brief Hist. of Par. Ch. of St. Mary Magdalene, Bridgnorth* (Bridgnorth, 2001), 7. A similar arrangement was made in another of Telford's chs.—Madeley (1794–7): *V.C.H. Salop*. xi. 64.

64. Tilstock ch. (1835): below, p.321.

65. The role played in Rom. Cath. chs. by saints' statues.

Chapter XX

1. *Compton Census*, ed. Whiteman, 255-60, 441-3, 448, 507–8; *T.S.A.S.* 2nd ser. i. 76-7. The census omitted 44 Salop. pars. and chapelries.

2. P. Phillips, 'A Catholic Community: Shrews.' *Recusant Hist*. xx. 239.

3. As at Madeley: *V.C.H. Salop*. ii. 9; xi. 66–7.

4. Papists Relief Acts 1778, 18 Geo. III, c. 60, and 1791, 31 Geo. III, c. 32.

5. *V.C.H. Salop*. xi. 67. Cf. B. Little, *Catholic Churches since 1623* (1966), 28.

6. *Recusant Hist*. xx. 244; J. Hall, *A Sacrament in Stone: Shrews. Cathedral* (Stoke-on-Trent, *c*.1984), 12-13.

7. Relief Act, 1829, 10 Geo. IV, c. 7.

8. *Kelly's Dir. Salop*. (1917), 156; E. Abbott, H*ist. of Dioc. of Shrews. 1850-1986* (Bolton, *c*.1987), 82.

9. *V.C.H. Salop*. xi. 242.

10. Little, *Catholic Churches*, 27, 36-8.

11. Hall, *Shrews. Cath*. l3; illustr. in 'Monasteries Shrews.' (in S.R.R., qD 97) opposite p. 476 of a portion of H. Owen and J.B. Blakeway, *Hist. Shrews*. (1825), ii. Cf. *Recusant Hist*. xx. 251-2; H. Pidgeon, *Memorials of Shrews*. (1837), 98.

12. S. Bagshaw, *Dir. Salop*. (1851), 423.

13. The ch.'s original plainness is disguised on the W. front, whose Decorated window is said to date from 1920: R. Prentice, *Hist. of Newport* (1986), 76.

14. *Country Life*, 7 July 1977, p.21.

15. Linley Hall had an 18th-cent. attic chap., and one in Middleton Lodge in 1851 (*V.C.H. Salop*. x. 319, 354) may have been as old.

16. A. Gomme, *Smith of Warwick: Fra. Smith, Archit. and Master-Builder* (Stamford, 2000), 327-8, pl. 204. Blount may have dictated the design, perh. inspired by taking in S. Carlo alle Quattro Fontane, Rome, on his grand tour.

17. J. Bossy, *The Eng. Catholic Community 1570-1850* (1975), 410; *The Eng. Catholics 1850-1950*, ed. G.A. Beck (1950), 49.

18. *V.C.H. Staffs*. viii. 54–5 and pl. facing p.55; N. Pevsner, *Staffs*. (Bldgs. of Eng. 1974), 209.

19. Abbott, *Hist. Dioc. Shrews*. 47.

20. C. Magner, *St. John the Evangelist, Bridgnorth: Portrait of a Par. 1855 to 2000* (priv. print. 2000), 23 (copy in S.R.R., qO 96).

21. *Kelly's Dir. Salop*. (19l7), 196.

22. *Ibid*. 133. A schoolroom was provided there in 1874 and enlarged in 1896: *ibid*. 134; Abbott, *op. cit*. 86; 1896 date plaque.

23. Abbott, *op. cit*. 76; *Shrews. Dioc. Yr. Bk*. (1988), 125. Ch. and presbytery cost, £1,825.

24. Abbott, *op. cit*. 84.

25. *Ibid*. 81; Prentice, *Newport*, 76.

26. Hall, *Shrews. Cath*. 17, 20; Abbott, *Hist. Dioc. Shrews*. 82; S.R.R., Watton's newscuttings, ix, p.125; *Recusant Hist*. xx. 383-4; *Shrews. Chron.* 29 Jan. 1897, p.6 (Canon Chas. Cholmondeley's obit.); cf. Burke, *Land. Gent.* (1898), i. 274; *Alum. Oxon.* 1715-1886, i. 249.

27. Hall, *op.cit.* 20-3; *Recusant Hist.* xx. 259, 387–8. Brown (d.1881), initially reluctant to live in Shrews., did not do so until 1868, and some of his successors lived in Birkenhead: *ibid.* 382–3, 392; *V.C.H. Ches.* iii. 95-6.

28. Little, *Catholic Churches*, 101; *Recusant Hist.* xx. 387–8.

29. *V.C.H. Salop.* xi. 242.

30. Abbott, *Hist. Dioc. Shrews.* 94; *Bye-Gones* N.S. xii. 165, 188–9.

31. Hall, *Shrews. Cath.* 17.

32. *Recusant Hist.* xx. 256–8.

33. Hall, *op.cit.* 20–3; Little, *Catholic Churches*, 101.

34. Hall, *op.cit.* 20–5; *Recusant Hist.* xx. 385–9.

35. Ronald Knox's phrase; the cathedral is in the view from the Schools, where, in 1915–16, he meditated his spiritual future: E. Waugh, *Ronald Knox: A Biog.* (1959), 143-50; Hall, *op.cit.* 29.

36. *V.C.H. Salop.* xi. 67.

37. Sir Ll. Woodward, *The Age of Reform 1815–70* (1979), 522.

38. Hall, *Shrews. Cath.* 23.

39. Rom. Cath. schs., legalized in 1778, had existed earlier, but only in the few places (e.g. Madeley in the late 17th cent.: *V.C.H. Salop.* xi. 67) where there were enough Catholics to make one practicable.

40. Anglican celibates too had clergy hos. attached to chs., in e.g. Lond. and on the S. Coast: see A. Savidge, *The Parsonage in Eng.: its Hist and Archit.* (1964). Some (e.g. at St. Barnabas, Hove) are much bigger than Rom. Cath. presbyteries; they might equally suit clergy living in common or a philoprogenitive married incumbent.

41. Magner, *St. John, Bridgnorth*, 14-16, 66.

42. T. Klauser, *Short Hist. of Western Liturgy* (1979), 139, 149–50.

43. Point well made by Lytton Strachey, *Eminent Victorians* (Harmondsworth, 1948), 63.

44. Lunn's Gothic ch. of 1895-6 has a pair of E. lancets (Magner, *St. John, Bridgnorth*, frontispiece and pl. facing p.27) enclosing a buttress.

45. Below, p.327.

46. Below, pp.323, 327; Bridgnorth presbytery, archit. drawing of ch. 'when complete' (Wm. Lunn, Gt. Malvern)—reproduced on cover of Magner, *op. cit.* Ground conditions prevented construction (*ibid.* 23), as at Shrews.

47. Abbott, *Hist. Dioc. Shrews.* 103. The bldg. was deconsecrated in 1906. For the 1885 W. front with a rose window and S.W. tower, as it was in 1911, see F. Brown, *Silver Screen Memories* (Shrews. 1984), 19.

48. S. Muthesius, *High Victorian Movement in Archit. 1850-1870* (1972), 8, 160-1.

49. Below, p.323.

50. *Shrews. Dioc. Yr. Bk.* (1988), 125; N. Pevsner and E. Hubbard, *Ches.* (Bldgs. of Eng. 1971); E. Hubbard, *Clwyd* (Bldgs. of Wales, 1986).

51. Apart from Norman Shaw's ch. at Batchcott (below, p.334), in a very different vein.

52. It is a practical arrangement of seats in an auditorium and had appeared in a design of 1811 for a Wesleyan chap. in Stafford: C. Wakeling, 'Methodist Archit. in N. Staffs.: The First Seventy-Five Yrs.' *Staffs. Studies*, ed. P. Morgan (Keele, l987), 156-8.

53. Another Longueville gift (1926, by Adrian Gilb. Scott): *Kelly's Dir. Salop.* (1941), 180.

54. Muthesius, *High Victorian Movement in Archit.* 150.

55. In Irel. Rom. Cath. and Church of Irel. chs. can be distinguished more by dedication, size, and site than by style or form: *Victorian Church*, ed. C. Brooks and A. Saint (1995), 148-9.

56. Muthesius, *op.cit.* 150-1.

57. Cf. the contrasting Rom. Cath. St. Chad's cath. (1839–41), Birm., and St. Giles's (1840–6), Cheadle (Staffs.). A need for economy partly explains the former's plainness; the latter was lavishly funded by the 16th earl of Shrews.: P. Stanton, *Pugin* (1971), 60, 104, 108.

58. See e.g. Magner, *St. John, Bridgnorth*, 18-19. At Mkt. Drayton in 1884 'most of the Catholics were poor and many of Irish ancestry': *Shrews. Dioc. Yr. Bk.* (1988), 125.

Chapter XXI

1. Perh. owing much to the charitable trustees of Isaac Hawkins, owner and worker of the Malinslee mines 100 yrs. before. They probably paid most, or even all, of the cost of Malinslee ch., and their big contribution to St. Geo.'s may have been the stimulus necessary to get the area's rich men (landlords, industrialists, revd. pluralist) to stump up. See *V.C.H. Salop.* xi. 114, 119, 129–30, 170; S. Shaw, *Hist. Staffs.* i (1798), 10–11.

2. D.R. Thomas, *Hist. of Dioc. of St. Asaph*, iii (1913), 53. It is difficult to say whether the very plain arcades and chancel arch present before the restoration of 1873-4 (*ibid.* 54–7) are of this date or earlier.

3. S.R.R., P295/B/5/1/1.

4. Cranage, ix. 783-4; above, p.289.

5. Cranage, ix. 834; Pigot, *Nat. Com. Dir.* (1835), 367.

6. Pevsner, *Salop.* 154.

7. *Gent. Mag.* xcvii (1), 297; below. The nave had been demolished in 1825 because of its 'dangerous condition' after the fall of the N. tower.

8. *V.C.H. Salop.* x. 21.

9. Thomas, *Dioc. of St. Asaph*, iii. 77.

10. Cranage, iv. 286.

11. *V.C.H. Salop.* viii. 169.

12. Botfield's marble monument in the chancel (so well descr. by Pevsner, *Salop.* 154) suggests that that was not his sole motive for rebuilding. And see S.R.R. 6001/6860, ff.86, 87v., 88-9, 90v.-91; *T.S.A.S.* xlix. 128-30, 134, 145-6, 160-4; liii. 147-8, 152, 158; B. Botfield, *Stemmata Botevilliana* (1858), pp.87-8, ccxlvii-ccxlviii.

13. *V.C.H. Salop.* xi. 78, 86-7, 90-1, 292-3, 299.

14. E.P. Thompson, *Making of Eng. Working Class* (1963), 178, denies E. Halévy's claim (in *Hist. of Eng. People in 19th Cent.* i 1949).

15. H.R. Hitchcock, *Early Victorian Archit. in Brit.* (1954), 56-7; H.S. Goodhart-Rendel, *Eng. Archit. since the Regency* (1953), 50.

16. Comparison with neighbouring Eng. counties is instructive. In highly industrialized Staffs. there was a great amount of bldg. in the 1820s and 1830s. In Ches. and Worcs., which like Salop. had industrialized areas on their fringes, the Salop pattern recurs: the 1820s were lean, the 1830s fat. In almost wholly rural Herefs. there was virtually nothing in either decade.

17. Sixteen are known: those which have survived in whole or in part and those for which there is known documentation. The exact no. will not emerge until the topographical vols. of the *V.C.H.* have covered the county. The 1835 chap. of ease at Welsh Frankton was demolished in 1863 (S.R.R. 4288/Par/1), and Geo. Clinton's H. Trin. (1836–7), Coleham, was replaced piecemeal (new chancel 1862, new nave 1886–7) by a larger bldg. (S.R.R. 3598/Ch/5-10, 13-16, 18, 20-6).

18. S.R.R., Watton's newscuttings, iv, p.36.

19. For this para. see *V.C.H. Salop.* viii. 288-9. Turner died before the wk. was finished and was succ. by Sam. Smith of Madeley.

20. He was partly influenced by the shortness of the piers, standing on very tall bases, though he himself pointed out that the bases were useful for accommodating box pews: *Salop.* 230.

21. H. Pidgeon, *Memorials of Shrews.* (1851), 135-7.

22. For a similar arrangement in Albrighton ch. see below, p.324. For no obvious reason Tilstock is orientated N.-S.; ritual E. is geographical N.

23. Source cited above, cap. XVII (n.13), is essential for distinguishing various Pensons and their wks.

24. D. Cole, *Wk. of Sir Gilb. Scott* (1980), 142.

25. Above, pp.292-3.

26. One of the few exceptions is Penson's H. Trin., Oswestry, whose W. tower was added in the 1890s.

27. Oriented to the W. for easy access from the street.

28. *Salop.* 301. The style and brickwork of the upper part is markedly different from the lower.

29. The S. wall lancets have dressed surrounds, the N. wall ones only dressed sills. Shelve elicited Cranage's contempt: 'the dullest and dreariest style' displaying 'the greatest debasement of the Gothic revival' (vii. 552). Pevsner (*Salop.* 242) called it 'a sweet little rubble church'.

30. Above, pp.280–6, 293, 301.

31. Summerson noted that the designers of Commissioners' chs. in the metropolis were very concerned to make 'a great show at the west end', whatever happened elsewhere: *Archit. in Brit. 1530–1830* (1963), 316.

32. For the many-sided nature of Methodist ideology see Thompson, *Making of Eng. Working Class*, esp. 389-400.

33. Above, p.307 and cap. XIX n.16. Throughout the cent. Dissenters built or rebuilt more places of worship than the Anglicans, but the latter carried out more 'restorations': *Victorian Church*, ed. C. Brooks and A. Saint (1995), 9–12.

34. In the three following decades, 1850-79, they occurred in less than a tenth of all chs. built.

35. Above, pp.202, 207–8.

36. He had joined the Cambridge Camden Soc. the yr. before: Cole, *Sir G. Scott*, 22–3.

37. Pevsner, *Salop.* 86, 119.

38. With intersecting cusped tracery and diagonal buttresses, by Ric. Dodson, builder, of Shrews.: Shrews. Sch. Libr., bailiff's bks. iii. 1; S. Bagshaw, *Dir. Salop.* (1851), 118.

39. *Eng. Archit. since the Regency*, 79, 90.

40. C.F. Stell, *Inv. of Nonconf. Chaps. and Meeting Hos. in Central Eng.* (R.C.H.M.E. 1986), 191–206.

41. Shrews. Sch. Libr., bailiff's box A/8, plan dated Nov. 1839. The cost was mainly defrayed by contributions from tenants and occupiers of fms. in the par.: trustees' min. bk. 5 July 1839.

42. Pevsner called Llanymynech 'crazy'. He and Cranage were scathing about some of its details.
43. Hengoed, Middleton Scriven, More.
44. Llanymynech.
45. At Broseley the Hon. O.W.W. Weld-Forester, rector and later 4th Ld. Forester, was instrumental in having the ch. built of stone rather than the brick the parishioners wanted: Cranage, iii. 188. Presumably his strongest argument was a large contribution to the cost.
46. Strictly, his mother, whom he succ. as ld. of the man., paid for it: *V.C.H. Salop.* viii. 64, 70–1.
47. S.R.R. 4288/Par/1; cf. S.R.R., Watton's newscuttings, ix, pp.90b, 134. It was superseded by the younger Edw. Haycock's ch. of 1857–8 (tower and spire completed in 1863 after Haycock had 'studied spires more fully').
48. e.g. the rector of Pontesbury 2nd portion, who built the very grand ch. at Lea Cross in 1888: *V.C.H. Salop.* viii. 290.
49. The latter were of course building chs. then, and were to intensify their activities later. One may cite from the second quarter of the cent. Hopton Wafers (1827, Thos. Botfield), Doddington (1849, his widow), Tilstock and Dodington (1835 and 1836, earl and ctss. of Bridgwater), Ketley and Donnington Wood (1838 and 1843, duke of Sutherland), and Dorrington (1845, J.T. Hope of Netley). In addition Lady Bridgwater paid over three-fifths of the cost of rebldg. the nave at Ellesmere: J.W. Nankivell, *Chaps. from Hist. of Ellesmere* (1983), 50.
50. Above, pp.173, 188.
51. Jane Austen shows the development at a late, but not wholly completed, stage. Two clergymen she wanted us to like, Hen. Tilney and Edm. Bertram, were sons of county fams. destined for a fam. living, while Collins and Elton, whom she clearly despised, were not. Edw. Ferrers, third of the approved clerics, was a new phenomenon: heir, originally, to a large fortune but with a mission for the Church. An incarnation of the last type is the founder of All Saint's, Castlefields; he was unusual in being not only a 'country gentleman' in holy orders but also the founder of a town ch.: F.D. How,*The Revd. Thos. Mainwaring Bulkeley Bulkeley-Owen: A Memoir* (1914), cap. v (esp. p.107).
52. In S.E. Devon the amount of ch. bldg. in squires' pars. was greater than in 'squireless' ones, and there was no close connexion betw. bldg. and pop. increase: Brooks and Saint, *Victorian Ch.* 56.
53. According to the contemporary plaque on the W. wall.
54. *T.S.A.S.* 2nd ser. viii. 361–2.
55. With Keble's Oxf. assize sermon on 'National Apostasy': J.H. Newman, *Hist. of My Religious Opinions* (1865), 35.
56. By renewed emphasis on patristic studies and in accordance with 'High Church' ideals of earlier cents. N. Yates, *Bldgs., Faith and Worship: the liturgical arrangement of Anglican Chs. 1600–1900* (2000), carefully distinguishes the Tractarian and Ecclesiological strands of Anglicanism.
57. Newman e.g. was by no means biased towards Gothic: P. Stanton, *Pugin* (1971), 108.
58. S. Muthesius, *The High Victorian Movement in Archit. 1850-1870* (1972), 6-7.
59. G.W.O. Addleshaw and F. Etchells, *Archit. Setting of Anglican Worship* (1948), cap. 7. *A Few Words to Ch. Builders* (1841), by one of the Soc.'s founders, J.M.Neale, was clearly aimed at incumbents contemplating bldg. *'A Church as it Should be': The Cambridge Camden Soc. and its influence*, ed. C. Webster and J. Elliott (Stamford, 2000), provides detailed accounts of many aspects of the Ecclesiological movement, but wholly divorced from the historical and ideological background.
60. Hitchcock, *Early Victorian Archit.* 132.
61. Not perh. before the 1860s: seven steps up to the predella at Welshampton (1863: perh. Salop.'s first new-built Ang.-Cath. ch.) and Colemere (1870), where there is also an additional door from sacristy to chancel; a similar flight at All Saints' (1875–7), Castlefields; a crowned head of Bl. Virgin Mary on a Welshampton capital; and chancel stalls at Stoke upon Tern for R.W. Corbet's regular clergy (C. Milner, '19th-Cent. Post-Tractarian Clergy in Archd. of Salop' (Univ. of Leeds M.Phil. thesis, 1972, cap. 5). I am grateful to Mr. Christopher Jobson for these insights.
62. *T.S.A.S.* 2nd ser. ix. 67–8. Lloyd's cos. was ld. of the man. of Whittington and patron of Whittington and Selattyn, from which pars. Hengoed eccl. dist. was formed; his fr., C.A.A. Lloyd, had held both livings: cf. *S.P.R. St. Asaph*, i (2), p. iv; ii (1), p. v.
63. H. Colvin, *Biog. Dict. Brit. Architects 1600-1840* (1978), 748.
64. See above, p.207. A man who executed nearly 200 commissions throughout the Brit. Isles (J.M. Robinson, *The Wyatts: an archit. dynasty* (1979), 239–46) must have treated many quite cursorily.
65. There was a tendency in the mid cent. to move out of the county: Clinton to Cardiff, the Pensons to Chester, and the Griffithses to Wolverhampton.

66. *Early Victorian Archit.* 99.
67. Colvin, *Dict. Brit. Architects 1600–1840*, 39.
68. e.g. Hadley (1856) by T.E. Owen of Southsea.
69. Colvin, *op. cit.* 40, refers with illuminating exaggeration to Gilb. Scott's being able to 'rebuild half the parish churches of England in accordance with his own conception of Gothic architecture'.
70. Salop. 99, 108, 192, 223, 239, 307-8, 318, 321. Street was highly regarded by mid and late 20th-cent. writers, and this coolness is remarkable.
71. *Ibid.* 132, 158, 181, 216, 268.
72. *Ibid.* 97-8, 122, 127, 130, 240, 309.
73. Edw. Haycock snr. lived until 1870, but the marked change in style between Haycock chs. of the 1840s and those from the 1850s suggests that the younger Haycock had more or less taken over by the mid cent. A change in style as the son came into the practice was probably common in fam. firms in the provinces; for an instance in Leics. see Brooks and Saint, *Victorian Ch.* 184–7.
74. *Salop.* 44. He made the same point directly elsewhere: in Port Sunlight Londoners' bldgs. 'do not stand out as being superior to those by local men': N. Pevsner and E. Hubbard, *Ches.* (Bldgs. of Eng. 1971), 306.
75. Ch. and vicarage were designed as one: the timber-framed passage connecting them rests on a stone plinth, the return of the plinth of the nave S. wall. In Salop. this is the nearest Anglican approach to the Rom. Cath. formula of ch. and attached presbytery (above, pp.314–5). But the resemblance is not close, and Ang.-Cath. influence at Weston is not known: Milner, 'Post-Tractarian Clergy in Salop', App. III, pp. 7-8.
76. Stones identified by M.A. Scard, *Bldg. Stones of Salop.* Shrews. 1990), 30-1, 65, 81.
77. *Salop.* 331.
78. S.R.R., Watton's newscuttings, ix, p.90b.
79. His wks. are listed in *Shrews. Jnl.* 7 Nov. 1883, p.5 (obit.); cf. below, n.135.
80. S.R.R. 6001/372/1, pp. 65-66. The first known Salop. occurrence of this oddity is on the W. front of the Heath chap.; it occurs on the 1887 rebuild of Mainstone ch. and may there, as at Uffington, reproduce an original feature.
81. *Ibid.* p.93.
82. At Leaton *c*.10 ft. above ground level the slight projection turns into a flying buttress, terminating on a mass of masonry projecting from the main wall; it seems to be a version of that at Uffington old church where, *c*.5 ft. above ground level, the pilaster-like buttress became one of deep projection.
83. Geo. Pardoe of Nash Ct. paid for it and for the adjoining sch., almshos., and vicarage: *Salopian Shreds & Patches*, vii. 10.
84. Pevsner, *Salop.* 105; Cranage, iv. 288.
85. Cranage (vii. 620), needless to say, showed no sign of being impressed.
86. The ch. is in an Early Decorated style, but the W. front has a band of incised diaper ornament and the S. doorway is set in a slight thickening of the wall, a practice very common locally in the 12th cent.
87. B.L. Add. MS. 21010, p.39; S.R.R. 6001/372/3, pp.5, 68, 104.
88. S.R.R. 6001/372/2, p.79; /3, p.7.
89. *Ibid.* /1, p.124; /2, p.32.
90. *Ibid.* /1, p.87; /2, p.23.
91. *Ibid.* /1, p.44.
92. *Ibid.* /3, p.3.
93. *Ibid.* /2, pp.16, 81; /3, pp.36, 46.
94. *Ibid.* /3, p.60; Mytton Papers, ii. 276.
95. S.R.R. 6001/372/1, p.122.
96. *Ibid.* /2, p.28.
97. *Ibid.* p.58; Soc. of Antiquaries of Lond. MS. 477, p.121.
98. *V.C.H. Salop.* viii. 123.
99. S.R.R. 6001/372/1, p.83; /3, p.77; M. Preston, *Hist. of Prees* (Rudgeway, 1996), 78.
100. S.R.R. 6001/372/2, pp.61-2; /3, p.82.
101. *Ibid.* /1, pp.8, 12, 36; /2, p.70.
102. *Ibid.* /3, pp.44-5.
103. *Ibid.* /1, p.60; /3, p.103; cf. above, cap. XVIII, n.153.
104. S.R.R. 6001/372/1, p. 8, 60; /3, p. 103.
105. *Ibid.* /1, pp. 40, 110.
106. *Ibid.* p. 96; /2, p. 71.
107. B. Rainbow, *The Choral Revival in the Anglican Ch. 1839-1872* (1972). And the Ecclesiologists' revival of the chancel had posed the problem of what to do with it; now it could accommodate a reformed choir: Muthesius, *High Victorian Movement in Archit.* 78.
108. Rainbow, *op. cit.* 320. It is difficult to recognize the best known of all evicted choirs—at Mellstock in Wessex—from that description. But what might, to a Victorian cleric, seem to be independence, pride, and radicalism was perhaps no more than the innate dignity of self-respecting men and women.

109. *D.N.B.*
110. S.R.R. 6001/372/1, pp.62, 106; /3, pp.23, 54.
111. *Ibid.* /1, p.86.
112. *Ibid.* /2, p.55.
113. *Ibid.* /1, p.42.
114. *Ibid.* /3, p.24.
115. *Ibid.* /1, p.110.
116. *Ibid.* p.7.
117. *Ibid.* /3, pp.67, 78.
118. Local tradition reported by Mr. Jobson.
119. Probably the bldg. at the E. end of the chancel in 1791: S.R.R. 6001/372/3, p.21. In Cwm Head chapelyard there is pony stabling and a coach ho. (for a trap) in a bldg. contemporary with the ch. and nr. its E. end.
120. *Ibid.* p.50; Soc. of Antiquaries MS. 477, p.48.
121. S.R.R. 6001/372/2, p.65.
122. *Ibid.* /3, p.16.
123. An odd reversal of the commoner practice of replacing a timber-framed gable with a stone one. For the 1791 view see *ibid.* p.27.
124. *Ibid.* /3, p.45.
125. *Ibid.* /1, p.28.
126. S.R.R., P250/B/27/2/1, 23 Nov. 1860; above, cap. II n.56.
127. S.R.R. 6001/372/3, p.17.
128. *Ibid.* p. 8; S.R.R. 6009/40; *T.S.A.S.* lxvi. 44, 46.
129. S.R.R. 6001/6864, p.26. It was probably at the same time that a rectangular window in the nave was replaced by a Georgian one and a dormer removed.
130. S.R.R. 6001/372/1, p.108.
131. Above, cap. V.
132. S.R.R. 6001/372/1, p.38.
133. *Ibid.* p.91.
134. *V.C.H. Salop.* viii. 290.
135. Demolished 1990. Designed by Pountney Smith (S.R.R. 122/7, pp. 640-1, 653–4, 660; *Shrews. Jnl.* 31 Oct. 1883, p.7), though not listed in his obit. (*ibid.* 7 Nov. 1883, p.5).
136. Scard, *Bldg. Stones of Salop.* 80.
137. This use of cames appears in the side windows of Doddington ch. (1849) and in Frith's painting (1862) of Paddington stn. (opened 1854). Shaw seems to have intended stained glass (*Woolhope Trans.* xliv. 23, 28), but in view of his criticisms of the state of the art in his time (A. Saint, *Ric. Norman Shaw* (1977), 302-3) he may not have been wholehearted about it.

Index

The index uses certain categories of entry, notably: Architectural Elements, Architectural Styles, Gardens and Parklands, Houses, Ornamentation, Plan Types, Public Buildings, Timber Construction

Abbey Dore (Herefs) 37, 55
Abcott Manor, Clungunford 159, 162, 166
Acts of Parliament
    Act of Uniformity,
        1862 bicentennial of 310
    Church Building Act 1818 319
    Corn Laws, Repeal of 1846 225
    County Rate Act 1738 223
    Emancipation Act 1829 313
    Reform Act 1832 322
    Town & Country Planning Acts,
        mid 20th century 216
Acton, family 139, 295
    Edward de 124
    Thomas 124
Acton Burnell, Castle 94, 99, *100*, 101,
        104, 105, 112, 113, 132, 198
    Castle, Parliament barn 105
    Church *40*, 41, 53, 53, 54, 55, 56,
        68, 71, 112, 113, 306
    Hall 203, 205
    Park 197
    Rector of 259
Acton Reynald, Mansion 147, 210, 228,
    231, 231, 260
Acton Round, Church 292, 295, 299
    Hall 169, 173, 175, 176, 179, 183
Acton Scott, Church 295, 296
        family chapel 319
    cottages at 236
    Hall 147, *148*, *149*
    timber-framed school 259
Acton, Edward de 112
Actons of Aldenham 145, 313
Adam, Robert 169
    William 284
Adams, William 222
Adcote, mansion, Little Ness 228, *229*,
    258, 260
Adderley, Church 287, 295, 295, 299,
    300
    Hall 206, 230, 258
Admaston, Spa 205
Agricultural Enterprises 267-68
Alberbury, Abbey 37, 51, 65, 69, 70, *70*,
    71, 72, 84, 85
    Loton Chapel 44, 66, *67*, 69
    Cardeston Lower Farm 233
    Castle 91, 96
    Church 324
    Hawthorn Bower 233
    Manor 7

Red Abbey 190, *190*
    White Abbey 37, 159
Albright Hussey 163
    Rector of 82
Albrighton, Church 17, 61, *61*, 62, *62*,
        63, 324
    Hall 159, 231
    Station 263, 264
Aldenham Hall 139, 161, 213, 228, 230,
    231
    Acton's private chapel 313, 316
Alenham, Court of Hill 150, 160
Alken, Sefferin 211
Alkington Hall 159
All Saints', Newcastle-upon-Tyne 284
All Saints', Northampton 284
All Stretton, Manor 162
Allcroft, J.D. 231
Alliance & Leicester Building Society
    273
Almshouses 221
Alveley, Church 41, 43, 49, 51, 54, 66,
    77
    old Bell House 33, *33*
    Coton Chapel 292
    Coton Hall 173, 176, 180
    manor 54
    Pool Hall 169, 170, 172
Ampthill (Beds.), cottages at 235
Anglican Architecture 319-332
    architects, local and national 326,
        327, 328, 329, 330
    competiton of Dissent 319-22
    Decorated style 324, 330, 333
    Early English style 329, *329*, 333
    Ecclesioligical influence 327
    French Gothic 329
    galleries 319, 321, 331
        Georgian 324, 330, 331
    Gothic 322-24, 327, 330-33
    High Victorian manner 328, 329
    Perpendicular 324, 330, 331, 333
    polychromy 330, 334
    restorers, impact of 330, 331, 332,
        333, 334
    rural provision 322, 323, 324, 325,
        326
    Tractarian practices 325
    transepts 319, 323
    'Well' type tracery 332
Anglican Church 253, 314
    village school, the 275
Anglicans 307, 311, 311, 315, 325

associated schools 308
Apley, Castle 110, 112, 139, 140, 141,
        205, 213, 215, 231, 251
    Park 111, 201, 202
Architectural Elements
    aisles 41, 43-44
        added 286-7, 288
    apse 294
    butresses 17, 38, 62, 69, 79, 266,
        290, 293, 308, 316
        flying 61
    capitals 50
    chancel 44-48, 286, 289, 294, 315
        arches 55
        sizes 46-8, 63, 64
    clerestory 37, 38, 52, 70, 72, 73,
        77, 80, 86, 88, 318
    corbel tables 50
    fan-vault 303
    fonts 30-32
    gallery 312, 317
    hood mould 53, 54, 77
    lavatorium 34, 35
    pews 295, 302
    piscina 44
    pulpit 312
    reredos 317
    rood 84
    roofs 84-87, 118, 121, 123, 125
        hammer-beam 85, 88, 299,
            303
        pyramidal 78, 81, 239
    screens 87
    Shafts 50
    spire 72
        broach 69
    tower 17
    tympanum 32-34
    towers (churches) 17, 48-50, 286
        and west fronts 292, 293
    transept 17, 39-41
    triforium(ia) 37, 38, 94
    tympana 32-34, 50
    window, curvilinear 77
        coupled lancets 316
        cusp headed mullions /
            transoms 80
        cusped lancets 54
        fan vault 88
        'Gibbs' 221
        herringbone masonry (*see*
            under Architectural
            Styles, Anglo-Saxon)

hood mould 53, 54, 80
lancets 53, 54, 56, 316, 317
reticulated 77
'Wyatt' 213
Architectural Styles
Anglo-Saxon 1-8, 50
herringbone masonry 1, 4,
5, *5*, 8, 52
Classical 249, 279, 290, 291
neo-classical 202-04, 299
Decorated 276
Early English 50-4, 73, 277, 316
Elizabethan 85, 143, 158, 160,
181, 228, 257-60,
261, 264, 288
neo-Elizabethan 257
Georgian
neo-Georgian 186
Gothic 38, 50, 51, 55, 73, 94, 96,
194, 196, 199, 202,
226, 240, 249, 252-
57, 264, 271, 274,
275, 277-79, 283,
287, 290-93, 299,
300, 308-11, 316
Batty Langley type 201
High Victorian 253, 310
late-Gothic style 313
neo-Gothic 253, 256, 259
Pritchard's ecclesiastical
299
Strawberry Hill 101
Tudor 77, 188, 202, 303
Venetian 251, 252, 255
West of England school 72
Gothick 199-202, 223
Greek 196
Revival 194, 199, 202, 206,
207, 208, 209, 261,
271
neo-Greek design 309
Italianate 186, 228, 251, 266, 271
baroque 299
Jacobean 85, 143, 144, 155, 158,
160, 181, 226, 227,
253, 258, 260, 266,
273, 295
neo-Jacobean 205, 232, 260
Laudian campaign 287, 288
Old English 253, 273, 277
Palladian 174, 182, 185-88, 195,
196, 199, 202, 221,
291, 299
neo-Palladian 201
proto-Palladianism 183
Perpenidcular 41, 59, 73-90, 133,
202, 240, 255, 277,
297, 298
increase in ornament 83-90

Picturesque, the 196, 197, 198,
199
Queen Anne 253, 256, 259, 264,
273
Regency 271, 272, 273
Renaissance 266, 275
French Renaissance 239,
251, 266
Romanesque 9-36, 50, 51, 94, 96,
107, 268, 271
neo-Romanesque 228
Second Empire 251, 252
Stuart 85
Tudor 202, 228, 242, 253, 257-58,
261, 264, 289, 292
mock 273
Vernacular 196, 289
elimiantion of 188, 189, 190
Arleston Manor, Wellington 151, 153
Artari, Giuseppe 211
Arthur, Prince of Wales 88
Ash, Hall 170, 171, *171*, 173, 181, 182,
191
Ash Parva, Elms, the 191
Ashby Cottage, Westbere (Kent) 131
Ashford Bowdler, Hall 172, 180, 191
Ashford Carbonell, Church 14, 46, 47, 52
mansion 206
Astbury, Hall 232
Astley, Church 291
House 206
Astley Abbots, Church 287, *287*, 299,
303
Colemere Farm 123
Great Binnal 123
The Nine Worthies 167, *168*
Stanley Hall 201, 202, 258
Aston, Chapel 288
Aston Abbots, Church 287
Aston Botterell, Church 11, 41, 111, 289,
304
mansion 111, 165
The Bold *119*, 120, 121
Aston Eyre, Castle 99, 104, 104, 110,
111, 112, 116, 132
Church 15, *34*, 35, 333, *334*
Aston Hall, Church Aston 204, 206, 231
chapel at 231
Aston Hall, Oswestry 192, 195, 203-07,
210, 211, 213
Aston Munslow Hall 141, 143, 145, 147
Aston, Hall 203, 206, 326
Atcham, Church 1, 6, 9, 48, 50, 296, 331
Attingham 137, 191, 194, 195, 198, 203,
205, 209, 210, 211, 212, 214, 228
Audley End, mansion 138
Augustan Age 259
Aynho (Northants.) 299
Ayot St. Lawrence (Herts.) 299

Bacon, Francis 138
Badger Hall 172, 173, 175, 177, 195, 215
Baker, Richard of Audlem 300
William 200, 223
William of Audlem 195
Baldwin, family 217
Balls Park (Midx.) 259
Banks 271-73
Barker, John of Rowsley (Derb.) 280
Barnes, Thomas, Liberal MP for Bolton
254, 310
Barrow, Church 3, *3*, 6, 7, 9, 12, 15, 17,
48, 81, 289, 296
Barton Seagrave, Church 70
Baschurch, Church 19, 20, 44, 49, 52,
294
Station 262, 263, 264
Station Road 250
Batemans, of Shobdon Court (Herefs.)
195
Bath, Lords 225
Battlefield, Church 71, 76, *76*, 79-81, 90,
332
College 73, 75, 82
Bayston Hill, Church 323
Beambridge, 'Smithy', the so-called 201
Beaufort, family 82, 116
Beckbury, Church 61, 63, 65, 290, 297,
330
Beckford, Church (Glos.) 35
Bede, the Venerable 103
Bedstone, Court 227, 230, 253, 258
Manor 125, *125*, *126*, *127*, 128,
128, 129
Bedstone Church 333, *333*
Bellstone Hall 106
Belsay (Northumb.) 193
Belswardine Hall 144, 163, 166, 182,
184, 214
Bennett, R.C., of Weymouth 310, 311
Bennett's, Hall 106
Benson 239
Benthall, Church 289, 292, 295, 303
Hall 140, 141, 143, 145, 158, 165-
67, *165*, *166*
Berrington, Church 32, *32*, 35, 39, 43,
43, 44, 68, 77, 297
Donkey House 152
Hall 211
Hall, the present 188
Lower Brompton Farm 233
Manor 144, 151, 153, 163
Rectory 232
Berwick, Chapel 292, 330
House 173, 175, 180
House, row outside 235
new Chapel 290
Berwick, Lord 137, 191, 195, 198
Berwick Maviston, mansion 145

Besford, Grange 191
        House 255
Beslow, Farm (prev Beslow Hall) 158
        Hall 139, 161, 162
Bettws-y-Crwyn, Church *83*, 84, *84*, 296,
        332, *332*
Beverley, Abbey 79
Beysin, Thomas de 110
        Walter de 110
Bibby, family 234
        J.J. 231
Bicton, Chapel 295
        hamlet 130
Bidlake, George 309, 310, 311
Bidlake & Fleeming 277
Billingsley, Church 15
Birkenhead, prospective RC pro cathedral
        314
Bishop's Castle 122
        Castle Hotel 169
        Church 50, 289, 329
        episcopal residence 133
        Town Hall (1760s) 223
Bitterley, Church 10, *10*, 13, 46, 49
        Crowleasows Farm 159-60, *159*
        Henley Hall 174, 182
Blaise Hamlet (Glos.), cottages at 235
Blakemere, mansion 112
Blakeway, family, of Berrington 154
        Joshua 191
        historian of Shrewsbury 292
Blenheim Palace 174
Blomfield, A.W. 278
        Joseph 300
Blount, family 173
        Sir Edward 313
        Sir George 305
        Sir John 304
Bloxham 277
Boarhunt Church (Hants.) 2
Bolas Magna, Church 290, 294, 296, 300
Bold, The, Acton Botterell *119*, 120, 121
Bold, Adam of 122
Bolton Castle, Wensleydale 93, 105, 136
Bomere Heath, Congregational Chapel
        (1827) 307
        Yeaton Pevery Hall 228, 230, *257*,
        258, 260
Bonomi, Joseph 192, 195, 212
Bony, Jean 56, 69
Border-Right tenancy 134
Boreatton, Park 227, 228, 230, 232
Borfield, Thomas 319
Bostock Hall *141*, 143
Botfield, Thomas 215
Botterell, family 111
        John 304
        Sir Thomas 111
Bourton Cottage 258, 259
        Grange 231

Bowdler, family 123, 128, 129
Boyton Church (Wilts) 71
Braggington Hall 142, 143, 156, 165
Bremner-Smith, Edward 250, 255, 256,
        259, 308
Brick 157-61, 266, 308, 310
        English bond 169, 263
        Flemish bond 169, 221
        Ruabon 317
        Tudor style 261
Brickhouse Farm, Greete 155, *155*, 169,
        170, 172, 173
Bridgeman, Mrs. 300
Bridgnorth 160, 216, 249, 255, 273
        a house in Mill Street 160
        Alexandra Terrace, Innage 252
        Castle 91, 96, 97, 111, 112
                St Mary Magdalen Chapel
                65
        Church 297, 303
        Edward Terrace, Innage 252
        Friary 39
        Grammar School 222
                Governor's House 222
        Lloyds TSB, High Street /
                Whitburn Street 273
        Low Town 236
        Market and Council Chamber
                (1650) 222
        Market Hall (present) 274
        RC church (1856) 313, 314, 315,
                316
        Salop Old Bank (now Nat West),
                21-22 High Street 271, 273
        St. Leonard's Church 295, 303
        St. Mary Magdalen Church 280-82
                282, *283*, 293, 298, 301
        Stanmore Hall 251
        Station 262, 264
        Town Hall (1652) 274
        Victoria Road area 250
                26-28 Victoria Road 235
        Wool shop, Waterloo House 268
Briggs, Oliver 305
Bristol 72
        St Augustine's Abbey, Berkeley
                Chapel 71
Britannia Building Society 272
Brockton, the Miller of 128, 129
Bromfield, Church 300, 302, *302*
        Priory 26, 50, 52, *52*, 77, 81
                Halford chapel 30
Bromfield, Joseph 188, 197, 207, 213,
        215, 219, 292, 293
        Joseph, the elder 195
Bromley, Margaret 305
        Sir Thomas, Chief Justice of King's
                Bench 304, 305
Broncroft, Castle 101, 116, 226, 256
Brongyntyn, mansion 173, 175

Brookgate Farm, Pontesbury 121, *121*,
        122, 124, 125, 127-29, 135, 151
Broome, Station 263
Broseley, Church 297, 301, 323, 324
        Hall 170, 173, 191, 197, 201
        Manse 308
        National School 276
        Old Chapel 308
        the Lawns 182, 183
        Town Hall (1770s) 223
Broseley family, Fitz Warin cadets 110
Brown, Bishop 314
Browne, Isaac Hawkins 215
        Mary of Broseley 300, 301
Brunskill, Dr. 120
Bryn Amlwg, Castle 92
Bryndraenog near Beguildy 123
Bucknell, Station 262, 263
Buildwas, Abbey 22, *22*, *23*, 26, 27, 30,
        37, 55
        Abbot's Lodging 166
        Chapter House 51
        Church 294, 330
        Park 257
Buntingsdale, mansion 173, 175, 176,
        182, 184, 194, 195, 206, 231, 232
Burford, Church 54, 60, *88*, 89, *89*, 304,
        332
        House 170, 173, 182, 183, 184
Burgess Gate 224
Burghley, Lord 137
Burley, E.A. 248
        John 116
        William, of Broncroft 124
Burlington, Lord 185
Burlton, Hall 231, 258
Burnell, Robert, Chanc. of England & Bp.
        of Bath & Wells 41, 53, 56, 99,
                100, 101
Burnell family 99
Burwarton, Church 333
        House 227, 230, 251
Bury St. Edmunds 135
Butler, Samuel 245
Butterfield, William 253
Byland (Yorks. N.R.), Abbey 22, 24
Bywell St. Peter, Church (Northumb.) 3

Calverhall, Kerr's Almshouses 221
Calverhill, cottages at 234
Cambrian Railway 250, 261, 262, 264
Cambridge Camden Society, (sub
        Ecclesiological Society) 325, 331
Campbell, Colen 185
Campion, family 128, 129
Capability Brown 187, 192, 196, 197
Cardeston, Church 296, 330
        Lower Farm 205
        Manor 188
        Rectory 155, 188, *189*, 201-02, 232

Cardington 221
    Barracks, the 123
    Chatwall Farm 139
    Chatwall Hall 141
    Church 13, 46, 49, 296, 298, 305
    cottages at 234
    Holt Farm 142, 145
    Hope Farm *141*
    School 170
    Shootrough 125, 166
Carline, John 195, 207, 293, 324, 326
Carlisle Cathedral 81
Carlyle, Thomas 136
Carpenter & Ingelow 277
Carpentry, Ludlow 162
Cary, Bishop 287
Castel Caereinion, Montgomeryshire, Ty-Mawr 128
Castle Howard 174
Castle Pulverbach, White Horse Inn 127
Castles 92-95
    licence to crenellate 101
    ornament for domestic comfort 93
    Solar Towers 95-99
Catherton Cottage, Hopton Wafers 125, 128
Caughley, China Works, w'house at 265
    Hall 201
Caus, Castle 92, 110, 112, 159
Caynham, Church 15, 49, *49*, 52, 54, 292
    Wesleyan chapel 311
Chambers, William 187, 195, 211
Chambre, Francis 299
Chantry chapels 88, 89
Charles II, King 290
Charlton, Castle 112
    Hill House 143
Charlton, family 54, 112, 116, 139, 215, 216
    (from 1858 Meyricks), of Apley Castle 225
    Sir Alan 110, 111
    Lord, of Powis 111
    St John Chiverton 231
    Thomas, Bishop of Hereford 111
Chatford House, Condover 173, 191, 194
Chelmarsh, Church 41, 57, 58, 58, 59, *59*, 60, 67, 69, 294
    Hall 104, 107, 111, 160
    Medieval House 254
Cheney family 216
Cherrington, Day House 267
    steam engine at 267
    Manor 154, 155, 162
Chester Cathedral 56
Chester railway line 264
Cheswardine, Church 53, 54, 66, 79, 79, 81, 296, 300, 330
    mansion 54

Chetton, Church 54, 319
    Loughton Chapel 286, 287, 291, 294
    Grange 204
Chetwynd, Church 290, 294, 296, 299, 330
    Sambrook Manor 155, 169, 170, 173
Cheyne, Sir Hugh 116
Child's Ercall, Church 41, 43
    Lea Gates, Hungry Hatton 151
Childe, family 173
Chirbury 221
    Abbey 37, 38, *38*, 51
    Church 289, 290, 295, 302, 330
    Lord Herbert of 160
Cholmondeley, family, a scion of 314
Church Aston, Aston Hall 204, 206, 231
    limestone worker's cottage 215
Church of England 307, 325, 334
Church Preen, Church 39, 46, 52
    School 277
Church Pulverbach 82
    Church 290, 292
    Lower House Farm 189, *189*, 190
    Walleybourne 123, 124
Church Stretton 260, 273
    Buck's Head, the 123
    Church 15, 17, 35, 41, 47, 85, 287, 299
    Congregational Chapel (1865) 310
    Henry Salt's inronmonger's shop 269
    Hotel, the 226, 251, 268
    Market Hall (1619) 222
    Market Hall (1838-9) 273
    Old Rectory 197
    school at 222
    Scotsman's Field 260
    Station 263, 264
Civic Buildings 273-75
Civil War, the 129, 146, 149, 150, 162, 287
Clare, Elizabeth de, (m) Theobald de Verdun 57
Claremont, near Esher 187
Claverley,
    3-4 Aston 152
    Church 31, 41, 44, 50, 58, 62, 63, 65, 69, 71, 73, 77, 79, 80, 84, 295
    High Grosvenor 120, 121, 135, 139, 151, 165
    Nevin's House 170
    School 276
Clee Hills, Kenley, stone cottages 152
    one and a half storey houses common on 236
Clee St. Maragret, Church 1, 4, 5, 9, 12, 46, 51

parsonage house at 232
Cleeton St. Mary, Church 329, *329, 330*
Cleeton Court 120, 121
    terraces at 234
Clement, Nicholas 124
Cleobury Mortimer,
    2 Church Street 170
    Childe's School 222
    Church 41, *42*, 45, 45, 49, 50, 52, 55, 65, 66, 69, 72, 81, 85
    Girls' School 276, 277
    34 High Street 259
    Lacon School 277
    38-38A Lower Street 219
    School 275
    St. Nicholas Chapel 66
    Vicar of 275
Cleobury North, Church 332
Clerley, Crown Inn 259
Clinton, Old Farm 151
Clinton, George of Shrewsbury 326
    Roger de, Bishop of Chester 22
Clive 250
    Church 14, 73
Clive, family 226, 295
    of India 186, 187, 191, 192, 197
Cloverley, Hall 227, 228, 230, 231, 234, 259
Clun 82, 130
    Castle 91, 92, 93, *93*, 94, 96, 99, 105, 110, 111, 112, 116, 136
    Church 17, 19, 41, 43, 50, 51, 52, 68, 84
    Court House (1780) 223
    Farm 127
    lordship of 130
    Lower Spoad Farm 164
    Trinity Hospital 221
    Vicarage 169, 170
Clunbury, Church 11, 49, 332
Clungunford, Abcott Manor 159, 162, 166
    Broadwood House 201
    Church 58, 59, 60, 66, 332
    Hall 203
Coalbrookdale 214
    Carpenters' Row 215
    Darby's Dale House 215
    furnaces of 264
    Grange, the 215
    Great Warehouse (now Museum of Iron) 265
    58-9 Hodgebower 152
    Iron Bridge, the 201, 214
    John Fletcher's Chapel 285, *285*, 293
    Library and Scientific Inst. 266
    Long Warehouse 265
    one-cell cottages at 152
    Schoolhouse Row 215

Sunniside 215
Tea Kettle Row 215
Coalbrookdale Co, Great Warehouse (now Museum Visitor Centre) 266
Coalport, kilns 264
    works 265
Cobin, William 128, 129
Cockerell, C.R. 192, 207, 208, 209, 212, 213
    F.P. 259
Cockshutt 164
    Chapel 290, 294
Codsall Station (Staffs.) 263
Colchester, Castle 91, 132
Coleham, Shrewsbury & Hereford Railway's Building 265
Colemere, Lower Harcourt Cottages (poss prev Harcourt Manor Farm) 124
Coleshill (Berks.) 149, 179
Collins, Thomas 211
Commercial 261-78
    Stations 261-6
Committee of Council on Education 275
Commonwealth the 149
Condover 117, 129, 130
    Chatford House 173, 191, 194
    Church 17, 41, 51, 289, 295, 296, 297, 299, 300, 303, 303
    Church House 128, 131
    Court 125, 127, 128, 131, 139, 144, 145, 147, 157, 157, 158, 160, 164, 230, 258
    Old School House 125, 128, 131
    Wheathall 125, 131, 151, 172, 173, 184, 190, 191
Congregational Chapel Frome (Som.) 307
Coningsby, Humphrey 305
Copthorne House 203, 204
Corbet, family 44, 70, 92, 112, 139, 146, 231, 295
    of Moreton Corbet and Acton Reynald 145
    of Wattleborough 118
    Lords of Caus 54
    Sir Andrew Vincent 231
    Panton 197
    Richard 67
    Robert 158
    Thomas 266, 268
    Sir Vincent 142
Corbett, family 149
Coreley, Church 290, 294, 330
Corfham, Royal Manor 6
Cornewall, family 89
    Sir John of Ampthill (Beds) 89
Cornwallis, Bishop 214
Cotes, Col. C.J. 231
Cottages and symmetry 232-36
Council in the Marches of Wales 222
Cound, Church 43, 52, 295, 297, 324

Hall 173, 174, 174, 175, 179, 183, 194, 195, 211, 214, 232
Fulway Cottage 152
Golding Hall 153
Country houses 225-32
Cranage 41, 59, 64, 71, 73, 79, 80, 279, 288, 292, 300, 329, 331
Cranford St. Andrew Church (Northants.) 70
Craven Arms, Station 263, 264
Craven Dunnill 266, 267
Cressett, family 123, 173
    of Upton Cressett 145
Croft Castle (Herefs.) 201
Cromwell, Ralph, Lord, Treasurer of England 133
Cronkhill, mansion 197, 198, 199, 211, 213, 232
Crookes, Charles 266
Croome D'Abitot (Worcs.) 299
Cross House, Longden 153, 154, 155, 191
Cross, family 154
Crowleasows Farm, Bitterley 159-60, 159
Crowther's House, Easthope 127
Cruckton, Hall 177, 191
Crudgington, Station 262
Cubitt, architect 264
Culmington, Church 1, 4-6, 12, 13, 17, 46, 68, 72, 81, 84, 294, 303
    Manor 231, 260
Cwm Head, Church 323, 323, 324

Dalberg-Acton, Sir John 231
Darby family 307
Darwin, Charles 236, 308
Dating Problems 57, 58, 59
Davenport, House 173, 175, 178, 179, 179, 182, 183, 183
Dawley 307
    Church 323, 324
    Double Row 215
    Wesleyan Chapel (1860) High Street 309, 310
Dawley Bank, Baptist Chapel (1860) 309, 310
Deakin, A.B. 239, 241, 242, 244, 245, 248, 249, 255, 259, 266, 311
Decker Hill 204, 204, 206
Decorated Period 57-72, 84
    Accomodation of the laity 65-68
Defensive Houses 91-102
    fortified manor houses 99
Delbury Hall 191, 194, 197, 201
dendrochronology 128, 130, 153
    roof dating 115
Denstone 277
Deuxhill, Church 296

Hall Farm 163
Diddlebury, Church 1-6, 5, 9, 13, 41, 46, 48, 68, 81, 286, 298, 331
    Cornewall Chapel 295
    Glebe Farm 155
    parsonage house at 232
    Sutton Court, Little Sutton 166
Dinthill, Hall 172, 173
Dissenters 307, 311, 313
Dissolution the 136, 280
Ditchley 181
Ditton Priors, Church 39, 44, 51, 52, 53, 77
Dobson, Austin 259
Dodington, Church 322
Domesday Book 5, 6, 7, 9, 41, 81, 91
Donington, Church 61, 63, 65, 82, 287, 296, 298, 299, 300, 303, 304, 330
Donnington Wood, 'barrack houses' 215
    Church 323, 326
Dorrington 276
    Chapel 310
    Congregational Chapel 310
Down 82
Downton (Herefs.) 196
Downton Hall 228
Dudleston, Chapel 288-89, 319
    Church 44
    Pentre Morgan 145, 165, 172
    Shelbrook Hill 199, 204
Dudmaston Hall 150, 169, 176, 179
Dunval, mansion 140, 158, 163
Durant, George 192, 199

Eardington Grange 191
    Grange Farm 189, 190, 191
    Manor 203
Earnwood, Birch Farm 144
Easthope, Church 291
    Cottage 121, 122
    Cottage Farm 120
    Crowther's House 127
    Manor 123, 166
Easton Mascott, Hall 173
Eatington Park (Warwks.) 253
Eaton Constantine, Baxter's House 151
Eaton Mascott 230
    Hall 142, 177, 182, 186
Eaton-under-Heywood, Church 11, 13, 46, 50, 68, 85, 85
    Forester's Lodge 97, 97
    New Hall 135, 167
    Wolverton Hall 120, 120, 121, 151
Ecclesiological Society (prev Cambridge Camden Society) 73, 325, 331
Ecclesiologists the 326, 331
Edensor (Derb.), model village 235
Edgecombe, Edward 293
Edward, from Tewkesbury 285, 300
Edgmond, Abbey 111, 112

Provost's House (former Refectory) 104, *104*
Refectory 110
Church 31, 41, 61, 63, 65, 73, *74*, 79, 81, 333
Edstaston, Church 14, 15, 18, 28, 30, 55, 77, 89, 298
Eginton, Harvey of Worcester 324, 326
Elizabeth I, Queen 301
Ellesmere 273, 278, 307
 'Bank for Savings', 7 Scotland St. 271
 Black Lion Hotel, Scotland St. 255
 Church 41, 44, 67, 73, 77, 79, 80, 81, 82, 86, 297, 323, 324, 326
 College 277, 278
 Dudleston Chapel 288-89, 319
 house in Scotland St. 260
 Lee Old Hall 164
 Lyth 199
 Market (1879), Scotland St. 274
 Old Town Hall (1833) 273
 Salop Old Bank (now NatWest) Scotland St. 273
 Scotland St. 252
 St. John's Chapel 80
 Station 262, 264
Ely, Bishop of, London House (St. Etheldreda's, Ely Place) 58
 Cathedral 79
Enlightenment the 313, 319
Evans, David 284
Evelith Manor, Shifnal 197, 203, 206
Exeter, Cathedral 58
 Lady Chapel 58
Eykyn, Roger 211
Eyton 65, 97
Eyton Burton Lloyd & Co, (Salop Old Bank) 272
Eyton upon the Weald Moors, Church 296

Factories 264-67
Fallows & Hart of Birmingham 208, 309
Farmer, Joseph, of Newport 334
Felhampton, Court 171, 172, 190, 191
Felton, Church 10
Ferney Hall 231, 232, 258
Ferrey, Benjamin 327, 329, 330
Fetcham Park (Surrey) 149
Fielden, E.B. 230
Fitz Osbern, Barony 54
Fitz Warin family 92, 111, 112
 (III), Fulk 37, 92, 93
FitzAer, family 111
 Hugh 111
 Sir John 111
 Margery, (m) Alan Charlton 111
FitzAlan, family 36, 54, 60, 92, 94, 116, 123

Earls of Arundel 83, 133
Fleming, Richard 299
Flitcroft 209
 Henry 186
Ford, Church 12, 47, 303, *304*
 House 117, 170, 172, 173, 184, 197, 210
 Mansion 191, 194
 Shorthill 260
Forester, Lord 225
Forester's Lodge, Eaton-under-Heywood 97, *97*
Foresters, The, mansion 215
Forster, W.E. 225
Francis, Thomas 302
Franklin, Mrs. 231
Frankton, Station 264, *264*
Frazer, Andrew 284
Frodesley, Church 298
 Lodge 147, 190
Frome (Som.), Trinity area 214, 215
Fuller 149
Fulway Cottage, Cound 152

Garbot, Goodwife 130
Gardens and Parklands,
 Gothic Style 197
 Greek Revival 197
 grottoes 197, 198
 landscapes, copied from Claude Lorrain & Poussin 199
 'natural/ landscapes' 196, 197
 neo-classicism 197
 picturesque landscape 197
 'Sham Castle' 198
 'Shell House' 197
 temples 197
 Versailles, formal gardens of 196
Garmston House 171, 172
Gatacre, family 295
Gaunt, John of 89
Genneville, family 95
 Geoffrey de 95
Gentleman's Residence 1550-1700 135-50
George Dance's Newgate (1770) 223
Gethin, John 300
Gibbon, Edward 188
Gibbons, family, of Shrewsbury 142
Gibbs, James 221, 284
Girls Public Day School Trust, Shrewsbury 277
Glastonbury Abbey (Som.) 37
Glenyrafon, Llanblodwell 203, 205, 213
Glorious Revolution, the 259
Glyn Dwr, Owain 82, 110, 133
Glynne, Sir Stephen 295, 297
Gobowen, Station 263, 264
Golding Hall, Cound 153
Gomme, Professor 186, 211

Goodhart-Rendel 324
Goodman, Bishop 137
Gosnell family 128, 129
Grange, the, Northington (Hants.) 179
Granville, Lord 225
Great Binnal 123
 Nine Worthies 167, *168*
Great Chalfield (Wilts.) 157
Great Fire, the 299
Great Hanwood, Church 292, 296, 297, 330
Great Lyth, mansion 142, 143, 156, 188
Great Ness, Church 41, 44, 46, 49, 64, 73, 85
 Congregational Chapel 311
 Wilcot Chapel (1834) 308
Great Oxenbold, mansion 107, 108, *108*, 109, 112
Great Packington (Worcs.) 299
Great Tew (Oxon.), model village 235
Great Witley (Worcs.) 299
Great Wollaston, Church 291, 296
Great Wytheford, mansion 111
Great Yarmouth (Norf.) 214, 215
Greete, Brickhouse Farm 155, *155*, 169, 170, 172, 173
 Church 52
 Court 144
 Stoke Court 169, 177
 Stoke House 144, 158, 170, 229
Greville, Fulk 222
Griffin, M.H. 231
 W.D. of Wolverhampton 257
Griffiths, J & R of Bridgnorth 326
 R. of Quatford & Bridgnorth 275, 276
 Robert 274
 Robert of Quatford 309, 310, 315
 William 300
Grindley Brook, Lock House 199
Grinshill, Church 324
 cottages at 234
 Woodstile 259
Grove (Beds.), royal manor house at 105
Guilds, Palmer's 76, 82, 117
 Shearman's 90
 Shrewsbury Drapers 77
Gunton (Norf.) 299
Gwernfyrda, (Montgom.) 164
Gwynn, John 199

Habberley, Church 297
 Hall 135, *135*, 139, 162, 231
Hadley, Board School 277
 Manor House 112
Hadnall, Black Birches 259
 Church 12, 14
 Station 263
Hagley (Worcs.) 211
Halston, Chapel 84, 286, 288, 294

Hall *149*, 150, 160, 176, 209
Hamilton, George of Stone and
    Wolverhampton 326
Hampton, Hall 147, 156, 160
Hampton Loade, Station 263, 264
Hanbury Hall (Worcs.) 149
Hanson, J.A. 314
Harding, Egerton William of Tyrley
    (Staffs) 314
Hardwick, Grange 173, 175, 177, 179,
    201, 202, 231
    Hall 180, 184
Harley, Church 44, 286, 288, 323, 331
    No 3 152
Harris, Thomas 253, 258
Harrison, of Chester 300
    Thomas 300
    Thomas of Chester 206
Harrold, William 216
Hartwell (Bucks.) 299
Harvey, family 139
Harwell (Berks.) 117, 120
Hatfield 138
Hatton, Sir Christopher, tomb in old St
    Paul's 304
Hatton Grange 191, 194, 195, 209, 211,
    212, 215
Haughmond, Abbey 23, *23*, 24, 25, 26,
    28, *29*, 30, 37, 44, 71, 111, 130
        Abbot's Lodging 113
        Refectory 113
Havering, Castle 101
Hawkstone Hall 174-76, 178, 181, *181*,
    184, 186, 188, 202, 211
    Citadel at 198, 201, 213
Haycock, Edward 192, 193, 202, 206,
    208, 213, 223, 224, 233,
    271, 276, 322, 323, 326
    Edward (the Younger) 232, 232,
        256, 327, 329, 328, 330
    John Hiram 192, 194, 195, 197,
        205, 210, 212, 222, 300
    T.H. 223
Heath, Chapel 11, *11*, 17, 19, 21
Heber, Reginald 202, 300
Hengoed, Church 326
Henley Hall, Bitterley 174, 182
Henry II, King 92, 96
Henry III, King 92
Henry III, King 101
Henry IV, King 82
Herbert, family 226
    Lady, of Chirbury 221
Hereford Cathedral 47
    Bishop Losinga's Chapel 28
Hereford Diocesan Church Building
    Society 256
Herefordshire School of Romanesque
    Sculpture 31, 33, *33*, 35
Herstmonceux (Sussex) 115, 202

Heywood, family 234
Higgins, William, mason of Pitchford 300
High Ercall, Church 35, 43, 51, 287, 289,
    299, 303
    Earl of Bradford's Almshouses
        221
    Old Vicarage 155
    Poynton Chapel 289
    School 276
    Sir Francis Newport's great house
        160
High Grosvenor, Claverley 120, 121,
    135, 139, 151, 165
Highley, Church 77, 84, 86, *86*
    Manor 86
    Station 263, 264
Hill, family 146
    of Court of Hill 149
    of Hawkstone 209
    Noel 195
    Richard 188
    Richard Noel 188
    Hon. Richard Noel 232
    Sir Richard of Hawkstone 300
    Thomas 195
Hinkshay, furnaces 215
Hinstock, a house in 204
    Church 293
    Hall 230
Hinton Hall 231, 232
Hiorns of Warwick 195
Hodnet, Church 65, *65*, 67, *68*, 69, 71,
    72, 324, 331
    19-21 Drayton Road 125
    22 Drayton Road 151, 152
    Hall 231
    Rectory 201, 202
    1 Shrewsbury Road 151, 152,
        153
    Station 262
Holdgate, Church 15, 21, 34, 45, 46, 112
    Parsonage House 232
    Rectory 254
Holkam 181
Holland, Henry 187
Holt Preen, manor 142
Hookgate, School 276
    Welbatch 191
Hope, Court 205
Hope Bagot, Church 10, *10*, 11, 12, 14,
    46, 51, 293
Hope Bowdler, Church 81, 84, 329
Hopesay, Church 12, 46, 50, 54, 55, 84,
    297
Hopton, Castle 91, 99, 101, *101*, *102*,
    104, 105
    Court 192, *193*, 197, 211, 213, 215
Hopton, Walter of 101
Hopton Cangeford, Church 290, 293,
    294, 298

Hopton Wafers, Catherton Cottage 125,
    128
    Church 297, 319, 331
    'Iron House' 214
Horde, Thomas 124
Hordley, Church 12, *12*, 14, 15
Houghton 174, 181
House construction 151-160
    (1700-40) 169-84
    (1740-1830) 185-220
        'Cound' style 173-80, 182
        greater houses 174
        lesser houses 174, 177
        Gentlemen's houses 171-73
    axial chimney 153
    baffle entry 152, 153
    Cotswold manor house 228
    cottages, asymmetrical 235
        symmetrical 235
    Court style 174
    crogloft 152
    double-pile 146-50, 171, 172, 191
    entrance hall 137
    first floor halls 105
    fortified manor house 110
    gentry houses 173, 188
    great chamber 139, 143-46
    gound floor halls 105, 107
    lobby entrance 151, 153
    medieval 132-34, 253
    model housing 244
    open hall 135-38, 151, 152
    Picturesque 235
    pleasaunce 147, 153
    reception hall 142
    screens passage 145
    servants' hall 137
    solar 95-99, 105
    stair turret 144
    stairways 138, 143-46
    tenants' parlour 137
    terraces 235
    two storey hall 135
    urban 215-20
Howard, John 223
Hugall, J.W. of Oxford 232
Hughley, Church 59, 60, 63, *63*, 84, 294
    Old Hall 166
    the demesne at 130
Hull, Holy Trinity Church 79
Humbert, Prior of Wenlock 108, 109
Humphreys, Ralph, of London 289
Hurstpierpoint 277

Ightfield, Church 73, 77, 79, 80, 81, 82
    Old Rectory 206
Incorporated Church Building Society
    320
Industrial Revolution, the 201, 211
Institute of British Architects 326

Iron Bridge, the 264
Iron, use of 214, 302, 312
Ironbridge, Belmont House 215
    market buildings 214
    National School 266, 275
    small house terraces, Nailers' Row,
        Dale End 214, 215
    St. Luke's Church 321

Jackfield, 'Benthall' Works 260, 266-67,
    268
    Church 291, 294, 300, 301, 330
    kilns 264
    Pottery House 266
    Thursfield Works 266, 267
Jacobinism 319, 322, 325
James I, King 147, 163, 304
Jansen, Virginia 56
Jaundrell, family 189
Jenks, family of Wolverton 123
Jennings, Thomas 124
Jervis, William 300
Jesus College Chapel, Oxford 287
John, King 92
Johnes, Thomas, of Croft Castle 217
Jones, Thomas of Chester 197, 202
Joynes, Henry 186, 195

Kelham Hall (Notts.) 253
Kemberton, Church 291, 294, 296, 334
Kempton, No 25 152
    Nos 26-7 151
Kenley, Church 85, 332
    Mapps Cottage 152
    stone cottages at 152
Kent, architect 209
Kent's Horse Guards 187
Ketley, Board School 277
    parsonage house at 232
Ketley Bank, Providence House 252
Kilmorey, Viscounts 161
Kilpeck Church (Herefs) 31, 32, 35
King's Cross, London 264, 265
Kinlet, Birch Farm 143
    Church 11, *16*, 17, 41, *42*, 43, 50,
        55, 58, 64, *64*, 66, 69, 77,
        87, 88, 304-5, *305*, 331
    Earnwood 158
    Hall 170, 173, 175, 177, *177*, 179,
        183
Kinnerley, Castle 92
    Church 300
    Llwyn-y-Go 125, 127
    Tir-y-Coed 120
Kirby, Edmund, of Birkenhead 317
Kirby Muxloe (Leics) 202
Kirkstall, Abbey (Yorks W.R.) 22
Knight, Richard Payne 196
    Richard, of Downton 217
Knighton, Station 262, 263

Knockin, Castle 44, 92
    Church 17, 39, 44, 112
Knole 163
Kynaston, family 173
    of Oteley 145
    Mrs. Mary 293, 300
Kynnersley, Sidney Cottages at 233
Kynnersley, T.F. 231

L.N.W.R. Shrewsbury - Swansea railway
    line 263
L.N.W.R., Crewe – Shrewsbury railway
    line 263
Lacy, family 6, 91
Lady Huntingdon's Chapel, Worcester
    307
Lancing (Sussex) 277
Langley, Chapel 291, 294
    Church 295
    Gatehouse 162
Langley, family, of Golding 156
    George 154
Larden, Hall 139, 144
Laud, Archbishop 289
Lea Hall, Preston Gubbals 158, 164, 258
Lea Cross, Memorial Church 334
Leaton 256
    crossing house 263
    Parsonage House 232
Leaton Knolls, mansion 193, 206, 208
Lee, Old Hall 162
Lee, family 60
    Sir Humphrey 306
Lee Brockhurst, Church 12, 330
Leebotwood, Church 12, 39, 47, 293, 297
    No 1 151, 152
Leeke, Ralph 192
Lees, family, of Alveley 173
Leigh Manor 231
Leighton, Church 290, 294
    Hall 186, 231, 232
    Vicarage 260
Leighton, family 124, 139, 174, 180
    of Loton 145, 149, 233
    of Paish 142, 146
    Sir Baldwi(y)n 231, 235
    Frances 188
    Stanley 231
    William, Chief Justice of North
        Wales 305
Leland 57, 116
Leveson-Gower family 188, 215
Lichfield, Cathedral 58, 60, 70, 72, 94,
    318
    Dean & Chapter 65
Lilleshall 189
    'barrack houses' 215
    Abbey 23-28, *24*, *25*, 30, 37, 38,
        46, 51, 54, 55, 65, 104, 107,
        112

Church 15, 54, 55, 297, 298, 331
Honnington Grange 188, 267
House (sub Hall) 202, 215
St. Michaels Church 31, 54, 64
Lime Tree House, Harwell (Berks) 132
Lincoln Cathedral, St. Hugh's Choir 47
Lincoln College Chapel, Oxford 287
Linley, Church 14, 15, 17, *17*, 30, *30*, 31-
    33, *32*, *33*, 35, 48, 81
    Hall (More) 180, 185, *185*, 186,
        187, 191, 195, 206, 208, 211
Little Dawley, Ivy Farm 157
Little Drayton, Church 323
Little Hanwood, Moat Hall 164, 165
Little Ness, Adcote mansion 228, *229*,
    258, 260
    Church 12, 14, 15, 77
Little Stretton, Church 259
    Manor 139, 259
Little Wenlock, Church 14, 319
Llanfair Waterdine, Church 44, 288, 306
Llanyblodwel, Church 77, 297, 298, 324,
    331
    Glenyrafon 203, 205, 213
    Vicarage 254
Llanymynech, Church 323-25, *323*, *324*,
    325
Lloyd, A.R. 326
    Revd C.A.A. Rector of Whittington
        324
    J.R., Rector of Whittington and
        Selattyn 192
    Col. R.T. 231
Lloyds, of Leaton Knolls 324
Llwyn-y-Go, Kinnerley 125, 127
Llwynmelyn (Montgomery) 164
Llynclys, Morton Chapel 299, 300
Loch, James 267
Lockwood & Sons of Chester 275
London School Board's Offices 277
Londonderry, Lord 225
Long Crendon (Bucks.) 129
Longden, Cross House 153, 154, 155,
    191
    Manor 231
Longdon upon Tern, Church 291
Longford Hall 159, 192, 203, 205, 206,
    211, 212, *212*, 213, *213*, 220
Longnor, Church 53, *53*, 54, 56, 112,
    113, 294, 297, 329
    Hall 112, 149, 150, 160, 165-66,
        165, *167*, 175, 198, 202,
        212, 232
    little school at 277
    Micklewood Farm 142, 143, 156,
        160
    Moat House, the 123, *124*, 125,
        133
    Netley Hall 226, 228, *228*, 230,
        232

Oratory 124
Oteley Park 197, 212, 231, 257
Longuevilles, of Llanforda 314
Loppington, Church 59, 60, 73, 77, 79,
 81, 296
 Church Farm 151, 153
 Hatchett's Farm 152
 Holly Cottage 125
 Laburnum Cottage 152
 Nook, the 142
 Old Farm House 153
 Old House Farm 125
Lord Charlton of Powis 106
Loton Park 150, 174, 175, 176, 180, 180,
 181, 231
 Bretchell Farm 191
 Ivy End Farm 233
 Nag's Head Cottages 234, *234*,
  235
 Pleasant Cottages 234
 Rose Cottages 234
 Rowtion Gate Cottage *234*, 235
 properties 257
Lower House Farm, Church Pulverbatch
 189, *189*, 190
Lower Spoad Farm, Clun 164
Ludford, Church 62, 62, 63, 70, 71, 72,
 286, 295
 Foxe Chapel 291
 House 166, 201
Ludlow 106, 216, 217, 249, 255, 263,
 273
 Abbey, Austin Friars 39
 Barclays Bank, King Street 273
 Bodenham's, King/Broad Sts. 124,
  135
 3-4 Broad Street 123
 17 Broad Street 216
 18 Broad Street 271
 35, 36 & 37 Broad Street 219
 39 Broad Street 186
 53 Broad Street 124, 216
 Butter Market (1743) 273
 Castle 91, 92, 94, 95, 99, 104, 105,
  110, 112, 133, 289
  Great Tower 132
  round chapel 10, 27, *27*, 28,
   44, 93, 286, 288
 Corve Street 128
  cruck hall 216
  112 Corve Street 124
 Dinham House 216, 217
 Feathers Inn 162, *162*
 Gravel Hill 250
  55 Gravel Hill 260
  59-61 Gravel Hill 260
 Guildhall 84, 85, 117, *118*
 Hosier's Almshouses 221
 Lloyds TSB, 16 Broad Street 273
 Market Hall (1706) 222, 273

Market Hall (1887) 275
 7 Mill Street *216*, 217
 41 Mill Street 219
 54-56 Mill Street *217*, 219
 National School (1855) 275, 276
 Palmer's Guild College 123
 Palmers' Guildhall 223, 273
 Rectory, the, College Street 123
 shops with living accom,
  King/Broad Sts. 216
 St. Lawrence's Church 43, 57, 59,
  60, 66, *66*, 69, 71, 72,
  73, 76-86, *78*, 88,
  112, 117, 297, 298
  Lady Chapel 90
  Palmers' Guild Chapel 77, 87
 Station 263
 14 The Square 219
Ludlow, John the Moneyer of 110
 family, of Stokesay 124
  Lawrence of 97, 98, 110,
   113, 133, 188
Ludstone Hall 140, 141, 144, 147, 158,
 160, 163, 164, 165, 178
Lulworth Castle (Dorset) 181
Lutwyche Hall 143, 144, 182, 201, 209,
 211, 232, 258
Lutyens, Sir Edwin 260
Lydbury North 82
 Church 11, 17, 19, *40*, 41, 47, 81,
  295, 298
 episcopal (Hereford) manor 106
 Plowden Hall 119-22
 Red House 142, 144
Lydham, Church 12, 39, 47, 287, 294
 Roveries, the 192, 230
Lynam, Charles, of Stoke-upon-Trent 267
Lyneal, parsonage house at 232
 Vicarage 255
Lythwood Hall 191, 194, 195, 203, 206

Macauley 259
Mackworth, family 173
Maddox, Richard 310
Madeley 189
 Church 50, 280, 285, 293, 297,
  300, 301, 331
 Court 107, 108, 109, 167
 Mass House 313
 prospective RC church 314, 315
 Vicarage 170, 172, 173
 Wesleyan John Fletcher's chapel,
  Court Street 308
 Wesleyan School 277
Madeley Wood, Wesleyan Chapel (1837)
 308, 309
Maesbury Marsh, Chapel (1868) 310
 Congregational Chapel 311
Magley, William 300
Mainstone, Church 18, *19*, 332

Mainwaring, C.K. 231
 Charles 197
 'good' William 82
Maitland 136
Malinslee, Chapel 83
 Church 214, 215, 280, 285, 293,
  301, 319, 331
 Hall 204, 215
Malmesbury, William of 103
March, earldom of 86
Market Drayton 279
 Church 67, 69, *280*, 297, 331
 Clotton's House, (57 Shropshire
  Street) 167, *168*
 Congregational Chapel 307
 Holly Grove 191, 194
 Pell Wall 192, 204, 206, 231
 RC Church (1886) 313, 314, 315,
  316, *316*, 317
 Wesleyan Chapel (1864)
  Shrewsbury Road 311
Market Drayton to Wellington line 250
Market Halls 222-23
Marrington Hall 154, 155, 163, 258
Marshe, Manor 163
Marx, Karl 136
Massey, family 310
 Edward 187
Maw 260, 266, 267
Mawley Hall 169, 170, 173, 175, 177,
 182-84, 211
 Chapel 313
Meeson Hall 158
Melverley, 25 Kempton, Tyr-y-Coed 125
 Chapel (1862) 310
 Church 286, *286*, 288, 295
 houses of mud at 236
 parsonage house at 232
 Vicarage 257
Meole Brace, Church 112, 290, 292, 293,
 294, 300, 328, *328*, 330
 Old Church 289, 298
Merton College Chapel 58
Micklewood, crossing house 263
 crossing keeper's cottage 244
Middleham Castle (Yorks N.R.) 100
Middleton, Church 14
 Crowleasows Farm 268
Millichope Hall/Park 140, 147, 162, 193,
 193, 197, 206, 208, 213
Millington's Hospital, Frankwell 187,
 187, 221
Milson, Church 12, 14, 19, 51, *51*, 52,
 306, 332
Milton Abbas (Dorset) 299
Mingay, Professor 150
Minshall, Thomas of Oswestry 310
Minsterley, Church 279, 280, 292, 293,
 299
 parsonage house at 232

Toll House 200
Mistley (Essex) 299
Moat House, Little Hanwood 164, 165
Moat House, Longnor 123, *124*, 125, 133
Monastic Buildings 21-28, 37-39, 106, 107
  diminution in building 82
Monastic Orders, Arrouaisian 37
  Augustinian 23, 72
  Austin Friars 57
  Carmelites 57
  Cistercian 22, 36
  Franciscans 57
  Grandmontine 37
  Savigniac 22
Monkhampton, Church 332
  House 257
Monkhopton, Church 15
  House, (formerly Curate's House) 232
Montford, Church 300
  Toll House 205
Montgomery, Castle 92, 111
Montgomery, Roger, Earl of 21
Moor Park 173, 175, 176, 180
Morda, Workhouse 211
More, Church 50, 287
More, Robert, MP for Bishop's Castle and sub Shrewsbury 185
Moreton Corbet, Castle 91, 96, 194, 212
  Church 66, 70, 71, 71, 72, 78, 79, 81, 295, *301*, 302, 332
  farmhouse, the 258
  mansion 139, 158, *158*, 160, 186, 191
Moreton Mill, Chapel (1846) 308
Moreton Say, Church 12, 12, 44, 47, 55, 290-93, *291*, *296*, 297, 300, 305
  Oldfields Farm 121
Morris, Robert 194
Mortimer, family 92, 133
  Cadet branch of 104, 107
  of Wigmore 60, 94
  Hugh de 57, 60
  Maude de, (m.) Theobald de Verdun 57
  Roger 95
  Roger de 66
Morton (near Llynclys), Chapel 293
Morville, Church 6, 11, 15, 17-18, 30-35, 41, 46, 49, 51, 52, 53, 89, 275, 306, 331, 332
  Hall 183, 194, 198, 210
  School 276
Much Wenlock 123, 271, 273
  23 Barrow Street 120, 121
  Castle 99
  Chapel (1862), King Street 310
  Grange 255

15 High Street 120
Holy Trinity Church 11, 17-20, 28, 41, 46, 49, 58, 60, 66, 67, 72, 77, 297
15 Hope Street 121
Market and Council Chamber (1577) 222
Market/Reading Room (1852) 273
Priory 6, 26, 32, 34, 35, 38, 39, 55, 60, 66, 86, 104, 105, 107, 109, 111, 332
  Chapter House 28, *28*, *29*
  Church 1, 10, 37, 51
  Lavatorium 28, 107
  Prior of 65, 112
  Prior's House 80, 113-15, *114*, *115*, 133, 167
3 & 5 St. Mary's Lane 200, 201
St Owen's Well House 125
Station 264
Munslow, Church 17, 30, 41, 44, 49, 58, 65, 84, 289, 295
  Home Farm 205
  Hungerford Farm 186
  Munslow Farm 168
Myddle, Castle 101, 110, 111
  Chapel (1833) 307, 308, 311
  Church 77, 78, 287, 300
  Manse 308
  Marton House 258
Mylne, Robert 195, 209, 210
Myttons, of Halston 149

Nantwich, Church 79
Nash, Church 54, 59, 60, 63
Nash, John 202, 204, 212, 214, 232
Neale, J.M. 331
Neath, the, Church 46
Neckham, Alexander 104, 117
Needham, family 295
  of Shavington 149
Neen Savage, Church 12, 14, 15, 17, 30, 39, 47, *48*, 49, 73, 331, 333
Neen Sollars, Church 59, 60, *60*, 305
Neenton, Church Farm 167
Nesfield 227, 259
Netley Hall, Longnor 226, 228, *228*, 230, 232
Nether Larden, Lord of 129
Newcastle, Lower Spoad House 127
Newcastle-under-Lyme, Holy Trinity 313
Newdale, (a mining settlement between Wellington & Dawley) 215
Newman, Cardinal 314
Newport 279
  Adams' Grammar School 222
  Church 331
  Congregational Chapel (1832), Wellington Road 309
  Guildhall 123

Lloyds TSB, College Hill 272
Trent House, Chetwynd End 205, *205*
RC church (1832) 313, 314, 315, *315*, 316, 317
Newport, family 146
  of High Ercall and of Eyton on Severn 145
  Sir Francis 160
Newton, Ernest 260
Nicholson, T.E. 276
  Thomas of Hereford 327, 329
Nonconformism, Congregational 311
  Early dissent 307
  Methodism 308, 319, 325
  New dissent 311
Nonconformist Architecture 307-12
Nonconformist Chapels, schoolrooms attached 275
Nonconformity, challenge from 290
Norbury, School 277
Northam (Northumb.), Castle 100
Norton, Bonham 280
Norton-in-Hales, Betton House 206
  Brand Hall 178, 182, 186
Nottingham alabasterers 88
Nuneham Courtney (Oxon.) 299

Oakly, Park 192, 206, 207, 208, 209, 212, 213, 226
Oldefields, William 123
Oldfields, Richard 123
  Thomas 123
Oldfields farm, Moreton Say 121
Onibury, Church 11, 15, 46
  Padmore 123-25, 128
  Station 263, 264
Onslow Hall 192, 194, 205, 207, 208, 211, 213, 232
Ordericus Vitalis 1
Orleton Hall, Wrockwardine 194
Ornamentation 15, 28, 29, 30, 83-90, 162-68, 182, 209-14, 301-06, 312
  Adamesque 209
  amphisbaena 164
  Anglo-Flemish 164, 258
  arcading, blind 91, 162
    round headed 162
  Artisan Mannerism 160-61
  ballflower 57, 64, 67, 71, 329
  barley-sugar columns 161, 162
  baroque 166, 186
  battlementing 78, 79, 101
  Biblical stories 164
  billet mould 164
  black and white 'antique' work 166
  bobbin motif 164
  bolection moulding 183, 312

boss 77
Burton alabasterers 304
Carolean 144, 162, 259
carvings 41, 79, 145, 161, 164, 273
    Herefordshire School of Romanesque 31, 33, *33*, 35
    Norman 50
ceiling 163, 165, 302
chamfer 71
chancel screen adornment 83, 84
chimney stacks 159
chinoiserie 196
cinquefoils 57
circels 56
cloths 168
Corinthian 309, 312
crenellation 73, 79, 81, 101, 266
cusping 71, 79, 121, 123, 304
diaper patterning 159
dog-tooth motif 50
Doric 164, 228, 309
egg and dart motif 249
figure sculpture 32
fillets 50, 71
fireplaces 163, 164
foliage 37, 41, 50, 164
Gothic 186, 261, 281, 284, 292, 297
    rococo Gothic 299
Jackfield tiles 260
Jacobean 160, 162, 303
joinery 183
lioncels 79
lozenges 85, 161, 162, 249
merlons 79
Moorish 199
mouldings 50
Nine Worthies, the 167
painted decoration 166-168
Palladianism 160
panelling 77, 82, 162, 183, 306, 312
parquetry 183
pilasters 183
polychromy 310, 317
pomegranate 166
Pratt and Talman style 161
quatrefoils 57, 62, 77, 79, 82, 84, 86, 263
    degenerate 161, 162
    sunk 161, 162
Queen Anne 249
Renaissance 273, 288
rococo 183, 186, 196
roofs 84-88
saltires 82
scallop motifs 41, 91
sexfoils 57, 69, 71

Southwark marblers 304, 305
staircase 164, 165, 184
stiff leaf motif 41, 50
tracery 58, 59, 60, 61, 66, 69, 70-72, 77-80, 310
    curvilinear 59
    cusped 57, 60, 61
    Decorated 317
    Gothic 239
    rayonnant 71
    reticulated 59, 61, 62, 66, 71, 75, 80
    Y tracery 78, 202, 254, 308, 311
trefoils 84-86, 254, 276, 277
triptych 89
Tuscan columns 281, 283, 298
vine scroll 161
wall paintings 301
wave mould 71
William de Morgan tiles 260
'Wyatt window' 213
zigzag pattern 159
Oswell, A.E. Lloyd 232, 239, 270, 273, 275
Oswestry 82, 221, 249, 261, 262, 271, 273, 307
    Assembly Rooms, Victoria Road 250, 255, *255*, 266
    Aston Chapel 286, 292
    Aston Hall 192, 195, 203-07, 210, 211, 213
    Calvinistic Methodist Chapel (1888) 312
    Cambrian Railway Works 265
    Carreg Felin, Queen's Park *252*, 256
    Castle 92
    Castle Hill, high ground of 275
    Church 50, 295, 298, 319
    Congregational Christ Church 310, 311
    Cottage Hospital 252, 255, 274
    Cross Market (1849) 274
    Cross Street *270*, 271
        16 Cross Street 270
        17-19 Cross Street 270
    Edward Street 250
    Hendre Wen, houses in 256
    Holy Trinity Church 321
    Leg Street, 250
        15-21 Leg Street 250
        Terrace (1867) 258
    Llwyd Manor 163
    Llwyn House 228, 240, 251
    Llwyn, Queen's Park *252*, 256, 259, 260
    Meeting House 307
    model cottages at *233*
    Municipal Buildings (1892-3),

    Bailey Head 275
    North & South Wales Bank, the Cross 273
    Old Guildhall, Bailey Head 275
    Oswestry Savings Bank *271*
    73-77 Park Avenue 260
    Powis Market Hall 274
    Primitive Methodist Chapel (1840), Castle Street 308
    Queen's Park 250
    Queen's Road 250, 255
    RC church 314, 315, 316, 317
    RC School 277
    Roft Street 250
        58-60 Roft Street 256
    Salop Road 250
        Trinity Terrace 250
    St. Oswald's Church 83
    Station 261, 264
    Sweeney Hall 205, 231, 232, 254
    Victoria Works 255, 266
    Victoria Road area 239
        5-7 Victoria Road 260
        20 Victoria Road 255
        22-24 Victoria Road 255
        32-34 Victoria Road 255, 256
    Victoria Street 250
    Welsh Calvinists Methodist Chapel (1888), Oswald Road 308
    Welsh Independent Chapel (1877) Lower Brook Street 312
    Wesleyan Chapel (1871) Beatrice Street 308
    Weston Street 250
    Weston House, Queen's Road 256
    Workhouse (Morda House) 223, 224, 334
    Wynnstay Hotel 268
Oswestry Society for Bettering the Conditions and Increasing the Comforts of the Poor 235
Oteley Park, Longnor 197, 212, 231, 257
Ottley, family 139
    of Pitchford 145
Overley Hall 230
Owen, family 173, 174
    of Condover 145
    of Liverpool 239, 240
    Edward 300
    historian of Shrewsbury 292
    Revd. Hugh 224, 284
    William 188
Owens, Richard, of Liverpool 311
Oxford Movement, the 325

Padmore, Onibury 123-25, 128
Pagett, Henry, mason of Bridgnorth 300
Pains Lane, Church 215, 280, 285, 293, 301, 319

Palladio 187
    designs by 158
Palmer, John 199, 237
Park, Hall 164
Parker, Revd. John 254
Patton, Manor 7
Pearson 330
Pell Wall, Market Drayton 192, 204, 206, 231
Pembridge, Sir Fulk (de) 82, 116
    Isabel de 75, 89
Pengwerm Boat Club's boathouse 258
Penkridge Hall 147, 162
Penson, T.M. 261, 263, 264
    Thomas 274, 321, 323, 324
    Thomas of Oswestry 326
Pentre Morgan, Dudleston, mansion 145, 165, 172
Peplow Hall 171, 175, *175*, *176*, 181, 182, *184*
Percival, Harry, of Rossendale 232
    Hugh of Newchurch, Rossendale 253
Pershore Abbey (Worcs.) 37-38
Petsey, mansion 144
Petton, Church 290, 296, 299, *300*
    Hall 231
Pevensey (Sussex), Roman Fort 91
Pevsner 53, 64, 69, 79, 273, 275, 279, 282, 310, 320, 322, 327, 328, 329
Pigott, Robert, of Chetwynd Park 299
Pitchford, Church 1, 4, 5, 9, 46, 52, 331
    Hall 139, 140, 143, 145, 158, 161, *161*, 162, 258
Plaish, Hall 116, 138, 139, 140, 143, 158, *159*, 164, 167, 209
    Hope Farm 143
Plan Development 190-94
Plan Types
    E plan 268
    H 141, 142, 143, 145, 147, 149, 156-60, 179, 227
    L plan 143, 145, 171, 172, 189, 191, 226
    T 91, 143, 153-56, 234, 235, 276
    U 141, 142, 145, 147, 157, 158, 160, 180, 182, 221, 226, 227, 221
Plealey, Congregational Chapel (1828) 307, 310
    Manse 308
    School 308
Plimley, Manor 257
Plowden Hall, Lydbury North 119-22
Plowden, RC church (1868) 313-15
    Roman Catholic School 277
Plowdens, of Plowden 295, 313
    Philip of 122
Plymley, Archdeacon 70, 200, 235
Pontesbury 124, 152

Birch Row 125
Brookgate Farm 121, *121*, *122*, 124, 125, 127-29, 135, 151
    Church 41, 50, 54, 58, 61, *61*, 63, 65, 66, 69, 84, 85, 319, 320, *320*
    Earlsdale 201
    House 255
    Newnham 170, 173
    Parish of 307
    Sibberscott 127
Pontesbury Hill, small one-storey cottages on 236
Pool Hall 173
Popes at Woolstaston 149
Pountney Smith, Samuel 232, 239, 251, 258, 273, 323, 327, 329, 332, 333
Powells, of Hampton Hall, Worthen 149
Powis, Castle 196
Powis, earl of 217
    Lord 274
Powys, family, branch of 174
    Thomas 173
Pratt, Sir Roger 149, 161, 169
Preen, Manor 231, 258, 259
Prees, Church 59, 60, 63, 67, 72, 77, 292, 331
    Congregational Chapel (1862) 310
    Cross End Cottages 125
    2 Shrewsbury 152
    Whitchurch Road, pair of cottages in 235
Preeshenlle, Old Hall (near Gobowen) 155
Preston Brockhurst, Hall 142, 143, 145, 158, 183
    No 39 151
Preston Gubbals, Lea Hall 158, 164, 258
Preston Montford, mansion 184
Preston upon the Weald Moors 189
    Church 296, 298
    Foundation 221, 222
    Primitive Methodists 311
Prince, John 174, 175, 176, 195
    Richard 146, 173
Priorslee, Church 321
    Hall 175
    Lilleshall Co's School (1871) 276
Pritchard, T.F. 195, 196, 201, 206, 207, 210, 212, 215, 221, 223, 292, 300
Private Chapels 112
Public Buildings 221-24, 275-78
    County buildings 223
    Market Halls 222-23
    Schools 221-22, 275-78
Pugin, A.W. 314
    E.W. 314, 318

Quatford, Church 15, 293, 298, 300, 330
    Castle 201, 254

Quatt, Church 1, 67, 73, 291, 294
    cottages at in a 'garden style' 234
    Dower House 169, 170
    Little Mose 233

Radbrook, County Coucil School 277
Ragley (Warwks) 181
Railway buildings 261-64
Rambouillet, Mme. de 178
Randal, J.L. 258, 334
Ratlinghope, Old Post Office, the 252
Reaside, Manor 145, 166
Red Abbey, Alberbury 190, *190*
Red House, Lydbury North 142, 144
Rednall, Station 263
Reformation, the 73, 81, 87-88, 136, 238, 253, 279, 284, 288-89, 293, 303-04, 319, 331
Rennaisance 137-41, 197
Repton, Humphry 196, 197, 198
Restoration, the 145, 146, 160, 163, 223, 290, 291
Reynolds, family 307
Richard I, King 92
Richard's Castle, All Saints' Church, Batchott 334
    Rectory 186
    Woofferton 259
Richards, Roland, mason 300
Richardson, George 195
Richmond (Yorks N.R.), Castle 91
Roche Abbey (Yorks W.R.) 22, 24
Rocke, Eyton & Co 272, 273
Rodlington, a house at 259
Roman Catholic Church in England 314
Roman Catholic, Churches 313, 314-18
    Schools attached 275, 308
    Oswestry 314
Ronbridge, Tontine Hotel 214
Rous Lench Church (Worcs.) 35
Rouse-Boughton, Sir Charles, 226, 268
Roveries, the, Lydham 192, 230
Rowton, Castle 202, 254
Ruckley, Grange 258
Rudge, Hall 186, 202
Ruperra (Glam.) 181
Rushbury, Church 1, 9, 46, *47*, 49, 52, 73, 294, 303
    Coats Farm 123, 124
    Stanway Manor 268
    Stonehouse Farm 169
Russell, John 181
    Lord John 314
Ruyton Park 230
Ruyton Towers 228, 232, 253, 256
Ruyton Towers-XI-Towns,
    Congregational Chapel (1833) 308
    Church 12, 14, 18, 27, 30, 64, 65, 81, 85, 112, 324, 325
    Cottage, the 191

Ryton, Church 298, 300

St. Alban's Abbey 94
St. Andrew's, George Street, Edinburgh
        284
St. Ann's, Church, Manchester 281
St. Helen's, Bishopsgate, tomb of Sir
        Thomas Gresham at 305
St. John's College Library, Cambridge
        287
St. Leonard's, Vicar of 222
St. Martin's, Church 73, 78, 85, 331
        Quinta Chapel 310
        Viscountess Dungannon's
                Almshouses 221
St. Martin-in-the-Fields. Lonodon 284
St. Mary Redcliffe, Church, Bristol 69,
        71
St. Mary-in-Castro, Church, Dover 3
St. Pancras, London 265
St. Philip's, Birmingham 281
Salaboss, Melchior 89
Salisbury, Lord 138
Salop Fire Office 273
Salop School, Oswestry 250
Salt & Ackroyd 244
Sambrook, family 156
Sansaw, Hall 231
        Home Farm 259
Sawey, family 173
Schools 221-22, 275-78
Scoltock, Richard 187
        Samuel 313
Scoltocks of Shrewsbury 195
Scott, Gilbert 253, 257, 265, 323, 326,
        329, 330
Scriven, family 295
Scrope, family 136
Seddon, J.P. 232, 254
Selattyn, Church 292, 293, 319
Serena, Francesco 211
Service, Alastair 251
Severn Gorge 214, 215, 266, 301
Severn Valley Railway 263
Shadeoak 157, 164
Shaftesbury, Lord 235
Shavington 231
        Church 287
        Hall 149, 160, 165, 166
Shaw, Norman 228, 258, 259, 277, 334
Shawbury,
        2-3 Muckleton 153
        Church 15, *15*, *16*, 17, 41, *42*, 43,
                45-46, 73, 77, 80
        Wytheford Grange 153
Sheinton Manor 203, 204
Shelbrook Hill, Dudleston, mansion 199,
        204
Shelton Oak 255
        Priory 258

Shelve, Church 298, 322
Sheriffhales, Church 290, 299, 303
        Lilleshall Hall 257
Shevlock 259
Shifnal 189
        Church 10, 15, 17, 19, *19, 40*, 41,
                43, 51, 58, 67-69, 71, 77,
                299, 303, *303*, 305
        Evelith Manor 197, 203, 206
        Idsall House 170
        RC church (1860) 313-15
Shipton, Church 286, *287*
        Hall 140-41, 143-44, 147, 158,
                163, 178, 201, 209-10, *210*
        Thatched Cottage, the 152
        Parish, Brockton 129
                Larden 129
Shirlett, small brick house at 236
Shobdon (Herefs.) 299
Shootrough, Cardington 125, 126
Shops 106, 268-71
Shrawardine, Castle 92
        Church 289, *289*, 294
        Steps Cottage 152
Shrewsbury 162, 188, 249, 268, 309,
                160, 216, 227, 255, 273,
                278, 307
        Abbey 10, 21-23, *21*, 37, 38, 47,
                65, 71, 73, 76, 79-81, 90,
                113, 333
        Abbey Foregate 236, 237
                35-6 Abbey Foregate 160
                71-2 Abbey Foregate 235
                121-4 Abbey Foregate 203,
                        219, *220*
        Abbey Foregate Church (prev St.
                Mary) 7
        Abbot's House, Butcher Row 124,
                216
        Ænon Cottage *198*, 199, 236
        Alfred Street 249
        All Saints, Castlefields 237, 276,
                328
        Allatt's School 204
        Ashley House (now Abbey Pub),
                Monkmore Road 251
        Ashton Road
                5 Ashton Road 239
                9 Ashton Road 239
                7 Ashton Road 259
                13-15 Ashton Road 239,
                        241
                17 Ashton Road 240
                19 Ashton Road 240
                Headmaster's House 255,
                        257
        'back of the sheds' 238, 244, 246,
                249
        Bage's Flax Mill, Ditherington
                214, 264

Baptist Chapel (1877), Claremont
        Street 307, 309, 311
Baptist Chapel, Steelyard (sub
        Golden Cross Passage) 307
Barrack Passage, box-framed
        range, east side 124
Battle of, 1403 82
Belle Vue 241, 250, 251, 252
Belmont 250
        6 Belmont 217
        11 Belmont 314
Betton St., (prev Sutton Lane) 241
Bishop Street 246, *247*, 249
        74-75 Bishop Street 249
        78 Bishop Street 249
Borough Police Station & Weights
        & Measures Office (1893),
        Swan Hill 275
Bowdler's School, Beeches
        Lane 222, 277
Bradford St. (prev Union St.) 245
        1 & 2 (prev Morella Villas)
                248
        1 & 2 Abbeyville 246
        Brighton Terrace 246, *247*,
                249
        Ruthwell 249
        Stoneleigh 246, 249
        Walden 246, *246*, 249
1 Butler Road 239, 240, 255
3 Butler Road 239, 240
The Poplars, 7 Butler Road *237*
Butter Market (1819) 273, 275
Butter Market, Howard Street 208,
        208, 209, 214
Calvinistic Methodist Chapel,
        Frankwell Quay 311
Canon Street 246, 247, 248, 249
        6 Canon Street 249
        13 Canon Street 249
Castle 92, 94, 97, 104, 105, 223
        Laura's Tower 201
Castle Foregate 236
        Bridge 264, *264*
25 Castle Street 204
Castlefields 241, 250
Cathedral, R.C. 314, 315, 316,
        317, *317*, 318
Charity School, Murivance 222
Charlton Hall 110
Cherry Orchard 238, 246-50
        Church 322
1 Church Street 160
Churchill's Hall, Kingsland 239
Circus Brewery, Bridge St. 265, *265*
1-8 Claremont Bank 206, *207*
Cleveland Street 245, 246, 252
        1-5 Cleveland Street 249
        10–16 Cleveland Street *247*
        22-23 Cleveland Street *247*

Clifford Street 246
Coleham 236, 314
    Church 320, *321*
College Hill House 204
Congregational Chapel (1863),
    Abbey Foregate 309, *309*,
        310, 311
Congregational chapel, Swan Hill
    311
County Gaol 223
Ditherington, St. Michael's Church
    277
14-15 & 20 (the Old House),
    Dogpole 124, *163*, 164, *164*
Dominican Friary 39
Drapers' Hall 162, 222
Eye, Ear and Throat Hospital
    (1879-81), Town Walls 274
Exchequer tower 222
Flax Mill, Castlefields 214
Foundling Hospital, Kingsland 223
Frankwell 236
    92 Frankwell 128
Gas Light Co 266, 267
Gatehouse to Council of the
    Marches 162
Gibbon's Mansion, Wyle Cop 161
Girls' High School 275
Grey Friar's 'refectory' 113
Guildhall, the Square 223
Hall, Wateridge & Owen, auction
    rooms, Owen Street 270
Head Post Office (1875-7) 275
Henry Tudor House, Wyle Cop
    124
21 High Street 273
43 High Street 268
Holly House, Bradford Street 249
Holy Cross Church 298
Holy Trinity, Belle Vue 237
Holywell Terrace 237
House of Industry 223
Hudson's Brush Factory, Coleham
    265
Ireland's Mansion 162
Jones's Maltings, Belle Vue 265
Jones's Mansion, St. Mary's Street
    165
1 Kennedy Road 239, 240
10 Kennedy Road 239, 240
18-20 Kennedy Road 239
25 Kennedy Road 240
28-30 Kennedy Road 239, 240
29 Kennedy Road *239*, 240, 255
32-34 Kennedy Road 239, 259
39 Kennedy Road 240
King's Head, Mardol 124, 135,
    216
Kingsland 236-38, 240-41, 246,
    249-52, *249*, *250*, 258, 314

Luciefelde House 237
Market Hall (1596) 222-23, 273
Market Hall (1867) 274, *274*
Meeting House 307
Meole Brace Vicarage 232, 256
Methodist Chapel, Frankwell 308
Methodist New Connexion Chapel
    (1834), Town Walls 308, 309
Millington's Hospital 187, *187*
Montagu Place 244, 245, 246
    5-20 Montagu Place 242,
        242
Montagu Terrace 257
Moser's Hall, Kingsland 239, 240,
    255
Mount, the 236
Music Hall, the 208
Mytton's Mansion, Wyle Cop 124
Nag's Head, the, Wyle Cop 123,
    124
Newport House (from *c.*1920
    Guildhall) 170
North & South Wales Bank (now
    the HSBC) *272*
Oakeley Manor, Belle Vue 258
49-51 Oakley Street 248, *248*
72 Oakley Street 252
old Foundling Hospital 278
Old House, the, 11 Dogpole 124,
    163, 164, *164*
Oxon Hall 199
Pengwern Hotel, Longden Rd. 237
Perseverance Iron Works 266-68,
    266, *267*
Potter's Rope and Leather Works,
    Frankwell 265
Presbyterian Chapel (1870), Castle
    Gates 309, 311
Pride Hill 106, 216
    28 Pride Hill 269, *269*
    29-30 Pride Hill 268, 270
    46 Pride Hill (demolished in
        the 1880s) 162
Raven Hotel, Castle St. 252, 268
RC chapel (1776-7), Beeches Lane
    313, 316
Rea Street, Belle Vue 241-45, 252
    1-3 Rea Street *243*
    1-11 Rea Street 242, *243*,
        246
    12-27 Rea Street 244
    23-31 Rea Street 244
    28-31 Rea Street 244, 245
    29-30 Rea Street 245
    Hawarden Cottages,
        Rea Street 257
Rigg's Hall, Kingsland *238*, 239
Rocke Street 241-45
    1-23 Rocke Street 242
    9-23 Rocke Street 242, *243*

Roushill 250
Royal Insurance Building,
    High St. / Mardol Head 273
St. Alkmund's Church 6, 21, 52,
    73, 77, 79-81, *79*, 214, 283-
    84, 292-94, 298, 314
St. Chad's Church 21, 52, 63-64,
    73, 77, 214, 280-85, 290,
    292-93, 298, *298*, 301
St. George's Church, Frankwell
    237, 321, *321*, 327, 329, 330
St. Giles's, Wenlock Road 237
    St. Julian's Church 66, 81-
        82, 284, 291, 293-94
        294, 300
St. John's Hill 172
    12 St. John's Hill 217
    19-23 St. John's Hill 219
St. Margaret's Church 5
St. Mary Church (sub Abbey
    Foregate) 7
St. Mary's Church 2, 10, 15, 17,
    17, 19, *20*, 21, 26, 27,
    30, 39, 41, *41*, 43, 45,
    46, 48, 50-52, 55, 63,
    67, 73, 77, 79, 80, 81,
    86, 88, 90, 287, 289,
    295, 296, 314
    St. Catherine's Chapel 71
    Trinity Chapel 71, 77, 292,
        301
15 St. Mary's Street 145
St. Michael's, Ditherington 237
Salop Infirmary, the 208, 224
School 222, 238, 239, 250, 278,
    308, 310
    boarding houses
        ('halls') 236
School Gardens, Headmaster's
    House 202
Scott's Mansion, Claremont Hill
    160
Shirehall(s) 204, 208, 223, 273
3-4 Shoplatch 269, *269*, 270
Show 238, 241
Spring Gardens 250
Station 261, *262*, 263, 263
Station Hotel 261
Stury's Hall, between High & Fish
    Streets 216
2 Swan Hill 216
Swan Hill Chapel 310
Swan Hill Court 194, 195
Swan Hill House 213
Swine Market Hill (sub St, John's
    Hill) 216
Tabernacle, Dogpole 308
Talbot Hotel 268
Tankerville Street *245*, 246, 248,
    249

The County Savings Bank, 1 College Hill 271
The Crescent, 22-25 Town Walls *218*, 219, *219*
7 The Square 201
Trinity Street, Belle Vue 241, 242, 244
67-75 Trinity Street, Belle Vue 241, *241*, 246
16-20 Town Wall, Crescent Place 206
Underdale Road 245-49
  14 Underdale Road *246*, 247, 249, 255
  22-24 Underdale Road 248-49, *248*
  33-39 Underdale Road 249
  43-49 Underdale Road 249, 260
  Sedgefield 260
Unitarian Chapel (1884), High Street 308, 311, 312, *312*
Vaughan's Mansion 106, *106*
Ware House, Ditherington 214
Welsh Independent Chapel (1845) Pride Hill 308
Welsh Independent Chapel (1862) Dogpole 309
Wesleyan Chapel (1879) St. John's Hill 309
Wesleyan Reformers Chapel (1853) Beacalls Lane 308
Whitehall 146, *146*, 147, 157
Whitehall estate, Cherry Orchard 245
Windsor House, off Castle Street 165
Wyle Cop 195
Shrewsbury, earls of 314
  6th Earl of 225
  16th & 17th Earls of 318
  17th Earl of 314
Shrewsbury – Birmingham Railway 263
Shrewsbury – Welshpool railway line 263
Shrewsbury and Chester Railway 263
Shrewsbury and Hereford Railway 244, 263
Shropshire Banking Co. 272
Sibberscot, Pontesbury 127
Sibdon Carwood 200, 201, 210, 211
  Church 293, 298, 302, 330
Sidbury, Church 1, 4, 5, 11, 12, 14, 31, *31*, 34, 35, 71
Sidney, Sir Henry 289
  Philip 222
Silvington, Church 17, 294, *294*, 296
  Manor House 110, 112
Slaney, family 215
  Plowden 191

Smalman, Francis 138
  John 201, 202, 258
Smirke, Robert 204, 208, 223
Smith, Francis 169, 176, 211
  J. Parson 239, 240, 241, 242, 244, 245
  Samuel & Thomas of Madeley 326
Smith, Francis and William, of Warwick 176, 195, 326
Smiths of Shifnal 195
Soane, Sir John 192, 204, 206
Solar Towers 95-99
Soulton Hall 146, 147
South Elmham St. Cross Church (Suff.) 2
South Wingfield (Derb.), mansion 115, 133
South Wraxall (Wilts.) 157
Southrop, Church (Glos.) 35
Sparrow, Arthur 231
  W.H. 230
Spaull, W.H., of Oswestry 310, 311
Sprenchose, family 53
  of Longnor 54
  Roger, of Longnor 113
Stafford, Lord 313
  Marquess of, estate 267
Stanhope, Edward 236
Stanley Hall, Astley Abbots 201, 202, 258
Stanleys, boss with badge of 77
Stanmore, Farm 233
  Hall 226, 227, *227*, 230, 232
Stanton Fitzwarren, Church (Wilts.) 35
Stanton Lacy, Chapel (1877) 310
  Church 1-6, *4*, 9, 17, 45-46, *45*, 65, 68, 69, 71, 72, 332
  Lodge, the 201
  Manor 91
Stanton Long, Church 68
Stanton upon Hine Heath, Church 1, 4-5, 14, 44, 49, 81, 296
  New Inn 257
Stanwardine, Hall 144, 164
Stanwardine in the Wood, mansion 139, 143
Stapleton, Church 12, 39, 52, 319
  Moat Farm 164
Staunton Harold (Leics.) 299
Stell, Mr. 307
Stephen, Thomas 215
Stephenson, David 284
Steuart, George 194-95, 197, 203, 205, 208, 212, 280-82, 28-85, 290, 301
Steventon Manor 140, *140*, 143, 144, 158, 164
Stiperstones, houses on 236
Stirchley, Church 9, 15, 294
  Hall 141
Stockton, Rectory 173
Stockton Parish, National School 276

Stoke Court, mansion 182
Stoke St. Milborough, Church 11
Stoke upon Tern, Church 295
  Congregational Chapel (1838), Ollerton 308, 311, *311*
  Petsey 166
  Woodhouse Farm 200, 201, *201*, 203, 204, 212, 213
Stokesay, Castle 91, 96-97, *97*, *98*, 104, 110, 112-13, 116, 132, 136, 164, 188, 231, 253, 276
  Church 289, 292, 295, 301
  Court 226, 228, 230, 253, 258, 260
Stone Buildings 103-116, 157-61
  Halls, ground-floor 109, 110
  Halls, first floor 104-06
Stone Types
  Bristol Blue Pennant stone 328
  Cefn stone 328
  Cardeston breccia 328
  Grinshill stone 222, 261, 328, 334
  Red Hill stone 328
  Shelvock stone 328
Stone, Nicholas 306
Stoney Stanton, Manor Farm 127
Stoney Stretton, Manor Farm 128, 129
Stottesdon, Chorley Hall 213
  Church 1-2, *2*, 6, 9, 17, *18*, 19, 30-32, *31*, 41, 43, 58, 60, 61, 65, 67, 69, *69*, 72
  Hall Farm 116
  Lower Harcourt Cottages 123
Strange, family 30, 36, 44, 53, 54, 66, 67, 92
  John le 111
  Lord, of Knockin 111
  Ralph le 44
Street, G.E. 232, 256, 329, 330, 333
  Stoke Court, Greete 169, 177
Stoke House, Greete 144, 158, 170, 229
Stretton Sugwas Church (Herefs.) 34
Styche Hall near Market Drayton 186, 191, 195, 206, 211, 226
Suburbs, development of 237-50
Suffolk, Lord 138
Summerson, John 251
Sundorne Castle 201, 212
Sutherland, Duke of 225
  estates 233, 244, 257
Sutton Maddock, Brockton House 204
  Church 52, 77, 286, 290, 291, 294
  Parish 128
Sutton Scarsdale (Derby) 211
Sutton upon Tern, Colehurst Manor 142
Swakeleys (Midx.) 259

Taine 253
Talbot, family 88, 112, 116, 124, 314
  earls of Shrewsbury 133
  of Longford 145

Tann 265
Tayleur, William 231
Taylor, A.H. 240, 246
    William, a London carpenter 279, 280
Tedsmore, Hall 226, 257
Telford, Thomas 201, 223, 280, 281, 284, 290, 293, 300
Tern Hall 191, 195, 198
Tern Hill 206
    Station 250
Tetbury (Glos.) 299
Tewkesbury Abbey (Glos.) 21
Thackeray 259
Theobalds, mansion 137
Thonglands, mansion 162
Thornbury Castle (Glos.) 196
Thornton Hall 205
Thorpe Hall 149
Thursfield, Dr. W.N. 240
Tilstock, Chapel 287, 288, 300, 321, 332
Timber Construction 104, 117-35, 141, 143, 144, 152, 162, 222, 271, 273, 288
    Box-framed 123-25, 128
    cruck construction 88, 117-23, 125-32, 135, 151, 153
    halls, aisled 117-23
        unaisled 118, 123
    peasant houses 131
    roofs 118, 121, 123, 125
    spere truss 121, 122, 124, 125, 135
Tintern Abbey (Mon) 24
Tir-y-Coed, Kinnerely 120
Tisdale, Thomas 311
Tissington 163
Tistock, Chapel 322
Tombs 67, 68, 71
Tong, Abbey 77
    Castle 116, 192, 194, 199, *200*, 201
    Church 71, 75, 79, 84, 90, 295, 298
        Golden Chapel 77, 88, *88*
    College 73, 75, 82
    Talbots' house at 159
Torrington, Lord 221
Towneley Hall, Burnley (Lancs.) 211
Treflack, Hall 144, *145*, 178
Trefonen, near Oswestry, Pentre Farm 160
Trubshaw, James of Stone 326
Tugford, Church 13, *13*, 14, 21, 46, 47, 49, 55, *67*, 68, 294
Tunstall Hall 176, 186
Turner, John of Whitchurch 320
Twigg, Thomas, carpenter 300

Uffington, Church 329
Umberslade (Warwks.), mansion 176

Upper Berwick, mansion 170-73, 184
Upper Millichope, in Eaton-under-Heywood, Forester's Lodge 97, *97*
Uppington, Church 15, 32
Upton, family 123
Upton Cressett, Church 11, 14, 15, 19, 31, 34, 35, 46, 66
    Gatehouse 166
    Hall 120, 121, 122, 123, 144, 159
Upton Magna 128
    Church 14, 81, 297, 331
    Downton Farm 162
    No 3 125
    No 8 151, 152
    Old Shop, the, at Somerwood 152
    Parsonage 232, 256, *256*

Vanbrugh, Sir John 169, 186
Vassali, Francesco 211
Vaughan, family 216
Vauxhall Glassworks, proprietor of 173
Verdun, Theobald de 57
Vernon, family 77, 82, 88, 89, 116
    Sir Henry 88
Victoria, Queen 201, 330
Viroconium 1
Voysey 260

Wakeman, family 230
    Sir Offley 230
Walcot Hall near Bishop's Castle 186, 187, 191, 194, 195, 206, 209, 211, 226
Walcots, of Walcot 295
Walford family 253
Walleybourne, Church Pulverbatch 123, 124
Walpole, Horace 189, 196, 199
Wanstead 174
Waters Upton, Church 289, 298
Wattlesborough Hall 91, 94, 95-96, *95*, *96*, 98, 101
Waverley Abbey (Surrey) 24
Weaver, Arthur 198
Webb, Aston 332
    John, of Armitage (Staffs.) 202
Weightman, Hadfield & Goldie 232
Welbatch, houses at 203
Weld family 295
Wellington 308, 314
    All Saints' Church 73, 214, 280, 281, 298, 301
    Arleston Manor (prev. Arleston House) 151, 153
    Christ Church 321, 322
    Old Hall 258
    RC church, Mill Bank 313
    Priory, The (house) 203, 204, 206, 213

    RC church (1838) 313, 316
    Station 261
    Station Inn 261
    Wesleyan Chapel (1883) 308, 312
Wells Cathedral 37, 55
    Lady Chapel 58, 59
    Bishop's Palace 58
Welsh Frankton, Church 324, 327, 328, 334
    Gannow Hill 254
Welsh wool trade 83
Welshampton, Church 280, 285, 290, 291, 293, 300, 330, *330*, 332
    Manse, Breaden Heath 308
Wem 307
    Adams' Grammar School 222
    Aston Street 258, 260
    Church 288, 319
    91 High Street 204
    Meeting House 307
    Newtown Chapel 288, 288, 290, 332
    Palms Hill 259
    Station 262, 263
    Well House, Drawwell Lane 153, *153*
    Wolverley Farm 143
    Wolverley Hall 158
Wenlock Priory (*see under* Much Wenlock)
West Bromwich Manor House (Staffs.) 119, 120
West Felton, Church 14, 17, 41, 44, 84, 324, 331
Westbury, Brooke Cottage 152
    Church 41, 54, 291, 293, 294, 296
    Lower Wigmore, Marsh 152
    Parish 124, 152
    Station 263, 264
    Upper Lake Farm 128, 129
Whitton Hall 142, *143*, 229
Westhope, Chapel 299
    Manor 258
Westley, Middle Farm 151, 152
Westminster Abbey 70, 72, 76
Westminster, Marquess (Duke from 1874) of 225
Weston Cotton, St. Anne's Church 334
Weston Lullingfields, Church 327, *327*, 328
    Vicarage 232, 254, 256
Weston Rhyn, Congregational Chapel 254, 311
    Moreton Hall 142, *142*, 143
    Quinta, the 254, *254*, 256
    Station 263
Weston-under-Redcastle, Church 300
Wixhill Lodge 255
Weymouth, Viscount, of Longleat (Wilts.) 280

Wheathall, Condover 125, 131, 151, 172, 173, 184, 190, 191
Whitchurch 82, 273, 307
 Ashwood 153
 Downton Hall 169
 40-42 High Street 269, *269*
 Joyce's Clock Manufactury 267, *267*
 Meeting House 307
 RC Church 314, 315
 10-17 Richmond Terrace 237
 1-4 Scotland Street 216
 1-8 Richmond Terrace 237
 St. Alkmund's Church 73, 81, 82, 279, 280, 281, *281*, 282, 289, 293, 298, *298*, 322
 Samuel Hugginson's Almshouses 221
 Savings Bank 271
 Town Hall (1872) 274
 Weslesyan Chapel (1879) St. John's Street 312
White, William 239, 278
White Ladies Priory 26
White Tower, London 91, 132
Whitehaven (Cumbria) 214
Whitington, Station 262
Whitley, Grange 145, 147, *147*, 165, 188
Whitmore, family 173, 295
Whittingham, crossing 263
Whittington, Castle 92, 111, 112
 Church 296, 297, 300
 Halston Hall 229, 230
 Park Hall 140, 158, 161, 166, 258
 Farm 160
Whitton, Court 110, 112, 139, 140, 143, 158, 164, 166, 167, 182, 184
Whixall, Bostock Hall 140, 141
 Congregational Chapel 310
 Gandersbank 152
 houses of mud at 236
Wigmore, Abbey 86
 Castle 111
Wilbraham, R., of Petton Hall 299
Wilcott, Congregational Chapel 311
Wilderhope Manor 138, *138*, *139*, 143, 144, *144*, 158, 164, *164*, 166, *166*, 258

Wildigg, John 300
Wilkinson, John 215
Willey, Church 293, 295
 Hall 192, 197, 203, 206, 213, 215
William I, King 91
William IV, King 330
Willstone near Cardington, Lower Farm 169, 170, *170*, 172, 173
Wilson, James, of Bath 277
Wilton, William 211
Winchester, bishop of 132
Winchester Cathedral 79
Windsor, Lord 226
Wingfield, a Mr. of Shrewsbury 142
Wingfields of Onslow 295
Winkelmann 203
Winnington, Green Farm 164
Wistanstow, Church 14, 17, 39, 41, 47, 51, 53, 84, 296, 297, 303, *322*, 323
 Grove, the 251
 Parish, Arngrove Manor 129
Wistanswick, Congregational Chapel 310
Withington, Church 290, 294
 Hall 170, 172
 Old Hall 184
Wollaston, Plas-y-Court 165
Wollerton 250
Wolryches at Dudmaston 149
Wolryche-Whitmore, Revd. F.H. 234
Wolverley Hall, Wem 158
Wolverton Hall, Eaton-under-Heywood 120, *120*, 121, 151
Wolvesey Manor (Hants.) 105
Wombridge, Abbey 60
 Church 291, 319
 Congregational Chapel (1848), Lion Street 308
 Farm 205
Wood, Margaret 119
Woodard, inspiration of 277
Woodcote, Church 77, 79
 Hall 226, 230, 259
Woodhouse Farm, Stoke upon Tern 200, 201, *201*, 203, 204, 212, 213
Woodhouse Friary 39
Woodstock, Castle 101
Woolstaston, Church 39, 52, 332

 Nos 29-30 123
 Nos 38-9 125, 128
 Rectory 189, 258
Woore, Bulkeley Hall 259
Worcester, Abbey 37, 38
 Cathedral 52, 55, 80
Worcester City & County Bank 273
Worfield, Ackleton House 203
 Church 50, 61, 65, 69, 71, 71, 72, 331
 churchwardens of 130
Worth, Church (Sussex) 3
Worthen, Binweston Farm 127
 Church 44, 50, 81, 303, 304
 Hampton Hall 229
Wotton, Sir Henry 138
Wren, Sir Christopher 169
Wrockwardine, Church 41, 77, 81
 Orleton Hall 194
Wrockwardine Wood, The Lilleshall Co's New Yard 265
Wroxeter, Charlton Hill House 144, 160, 164, 165
 Church 1, 6, 9, 13, 46, 49, 53, 54, 77, 80, 82, 198, 295, *295*, 298, 304, 305
 Donnington, school at 222
Wulfstan, Bishop of Worcester 103
Wyatt, George 202
 James 173, 192, 195, 215, 282, 326
 Jeffry 192, 207
 Lewis 181, 192, 203, 215
Wyatville 215
 Sir Jeffry 202

Yeaton Pevery Hall, Bomere Heath 228, 230, *257*, 258, 260
Yockleton, Brook Farm 152
 Church 328
 Station 263, 264
Yorton, Station 250, 263

Zouche, Lord 111

Vernacular Buildings of Shropshire
by Madge Moran

Just under 600 pages with over 1,500 drawings and photographs; paperback: £25
ISBN: 1 873827 93 8

Over a period spanning thirty years, Madge Moran has visited, decyphered and recorded many of Shropshire's vernacular buildings that owe their origins to the period commencing *c.*1200. This book brings together that work, with the exception of the area around Whitchurch which has been covered in the earlier publication *Vernacular Buildings of Whitchurch and Area and their occupants.*

Initial chapters track the changes from buildings designed with defence in mind to first-floor halls of both stone and timber-framing and thence to ground-floor halls. Cruck buildings are given their own chapter, as are box-framed and jettied houses. Roof construction, with its various forms across Shropshire, is also accorded its own section. The changes from the fully developed three-part plan medieval house with its clearly defined solar and service ends or wings, screens passage and open hall to what may be called the 'early modern' house, fully floored, with a central entrance and displaying symmetry to a greater or lesser degree, are covered in a chapter on the Transitional House. Other chapters cover wallpaintings and dendrochronology—the latter an important aspect of Madge Moran's work and which provides much of the dating information in this book.

With a concentration of buildings in Ludlow, Shrewsbury and Much Wenlock that have both survived and provided an opportunity for inspection, these towns are given a series of their own chapters which develop themes specific to each town. The wealth of information relating to other properties spread across Shropshire is recorded in a gazetteer which is organised on a parish basis.

This book provides a series of very readable chapters that tell the story of Shropshire's vernacular buildings, as well as providing an invaluable reference work.

Tewkesbury Abbey: History, Art & Architecture
edited by Richard K. Morris & Ron Shoesmith

364 pages, over 200 black and white and 25 colour photographs, drawings and plans
Hardback £25 ISBN: 1 904396 02 X Paperback £17.50 ISBN: 1 904396 03 8

Tewkesbury Abbey is an internationally famous example of a Benedictine monastic church, outstanding for its medieval architecture and stained glass, and with a collection of aristocratic tombs and chantries second only to Westminster Abbey. The completeness of its survival is due to the purchase of the church by the town in 1543, and thereafter follows an eventful history of the abbey as parish church. Thankfully it escaped the excesses of Victorian restoration, even though the modest activities there of Sir George Gilbert Scott from 1875 caused William Morris to found the Society for the Protection of Ancient Buildings. During the 20th century, the abbey established a reputation for fine liturgy and music which continues today. It is the second largest parish church in the country and larger than 16 of the English cathedrals: an object of pride to all Tewkesburians and greatly admired by its many thousands of visitors.

This is the first major book to appear on the abbey for over a century and the most comprehensive ever to be written on the subject. It is designed to be accessible and attractive to anyone with an interest in the abbey and its history, but also presents new research in sufficient depth to be of interest to specialists in church architecture and archaeology. This wide-ranging book covers the history, art and architecture of the abbey and its site from pre-Norman beginnings to the year 2002, the 900th anniversary of the arrival of Benedictine monks from Cranborne. It brings together 18 authors, all of them acknowledged experts in their respective fields and in their acquaintance with the abbey.